I0796363

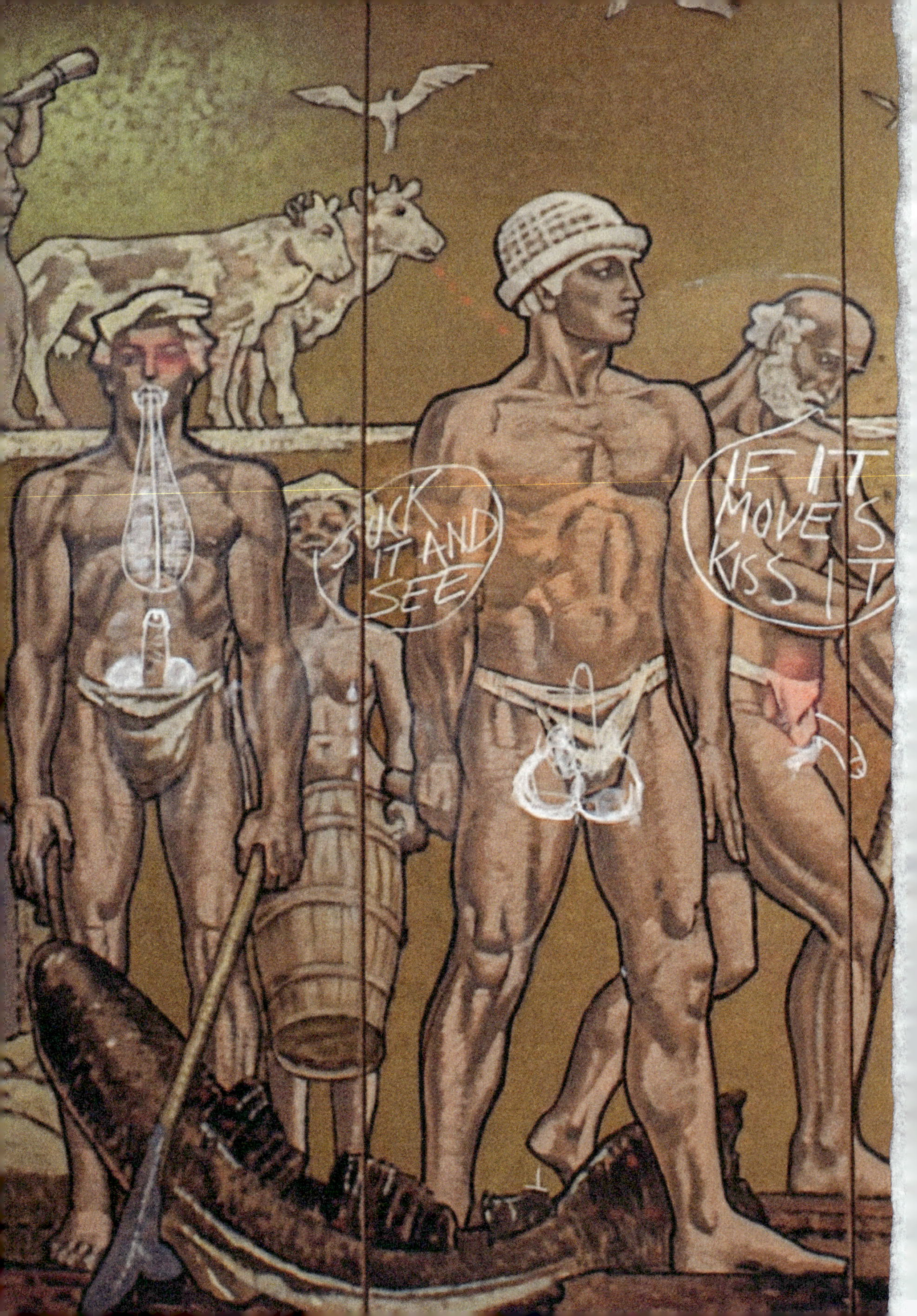
SUCK IT AND SEE
IF IT MOVES KISS IT

100 MOVIES OF THE 1970s

ED. JÜRGEN MÜLLER

100 MOVIES OF THE 1970s

IN COLLABORATION WITH DEFD AND CINEMA, HAMBURG
BRITISH FILM INSTITUTE, LONDON

TASCHEN

1971

Straw Dogs SAM PECKINPAH 32

Klute ALAN J. PAKULA 40

Dirty Harry DON SIEGEL 48

Silent Running DOUGLAS TRUMBULL 56

Shaft GORDON PARKS 64

A Clockwork Orange STANLEY KUBRICK 70

The French Connection WILLIAM FRIEDKIN 78

Fellini's Roma FEDERICO FELLINI 86

Harold and Maude HAL ASHBY 94

The Last Picture Show PETER BOGDANOVICH 100

Get Carter MIKE HODGES 108

Deliverance JOHN BOORMAN 116

Cabaret BOB FOSSE 124

The Godfather FRANCIS FORD COPPOLA 132

The Discreet Charm of the Bourgeoisie LUIS BUÑUEL 144

Solaris ANDREI TARKOVSKY 152

Last Tango in Paris BERNARDO BERTOLUCCI 158

What's Up, Doc? PETER BOGDANOVICH 166

Super Fly GORDON PARKS JR. 172

1973

Badlands TERRENCE MALICK 180

Enter the Dragon ROBERT CLOUSE 188

Day for Night FRANÇOIS TRUFFAUT 196

Westworld MICHAEL CRICHTON 204

Andy Warhol's Frankenstein 210
PAUL MORRISSEY, ANTONIO MARGHERITI

Pat Garrett and Billy the Kid 220
SAM PECKINPAH

The Exorcist WILLIAM FRIEDKIN 228

Don't Look Now NICOLAS ROEG 234

The Sting GEORGE ROY HILL 242

My Name is Nobody 250
TONINO VALERII

The Legend of Paul and Paula 258
HEINER CAROW

Soylent Green RICHARD FLEISCHER 266

Papillon FRANKLIN J. SCHAFFNER 274

American Graffiti GEORGE LUCAS 282

1974

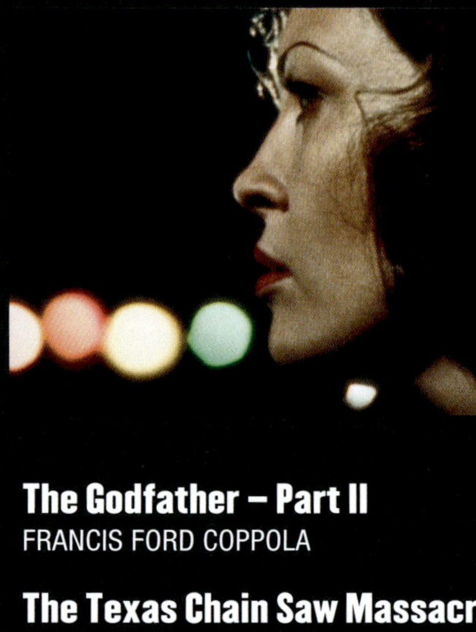

The Godfather – Part II
FRANCIS FORD COPPOLA

The Texas Chain Saw Massacre
TOBE HOOPER

A Woman Under the Influence
JOHN CASSAVETES

The Passenger
MICHELANGELO ANTONIONI

Chinatown ROMAN POLANSKI

Young Frankenstein MEL BROOKS

The Great Gatsby JACK CLAYTON

The Yakuza SYDNEY POLLACK

1975

1976

Jaws STEVEN SPIELBERG 348

One Flew Over the Cuckoo's Nest MILOŠ FORMAN 356

The Lost Honor of Katharina Blum VOLKER SCHLÖNDORFF, MARGARETHE VON TROTTA 364

Supervixens RUSS MEYER 372

Taxi Driver MARTIN SCORSESE 380

Barry Lyndon STANLEY KUBRICK 388

Dog Day Afternoon SIDNEY LUMET 396

Three Days of the Condor SYDNEY POLLACK 402

The Rocky Horror Picture Show JIM SHARMAN 410

1900 BERNARDO BERTOLUCCI 418

Carrie BRIAN DE PALMA 432

Marathon Man JOHN SCHLESINGER 440

The Pink Panther Strikes Again BLAKE EDWARDS 448

All the President's Men ALAN J. PAKULA 456

Rocky JOHN G. AVILDSEN 464

Network SIDNEY LUMET 472

In the Realm of the Senses NAGISA OSHIMA 480

The Wing or the Thigh CLAUDE ZIDI 486

Fellini's Casanova FEDERICO FELLINI 494

Assault on Precinct 13 JOHN CARPENTER 502

1977

The American Friend WIM WENDERS 508

That Obscure Object of Desire LUIS BUÑUEL 514

Star Wars GEORGE LUCAS 522

Eraserhead DAVID LYNCH 532

Saturday Night Fever JOHN BADHAM 540

Close Encounters of the Third Kind STEVEN SPIELBERG 548

Annie Hall WOODY ALLEN 556

Padre Padrone PAOLO TAVIANI, VITTORIO TAVIANI 562

1978

Coming Home HAL ASHBY 568

Nosferatu WERNER HERZOG 574

The Deer Hunter MICHAEL CIMINO 584

Birds of a Feather ÉDOUARD MOLINARO 594

Days of Heaven TERRENCE MALICK 602

The Marriage of Maria Braun RAINER WERNER FASSBINDER 610

Halloween JOHN CARPENTER 618

Autumn Sonata INGMAR BERGMAN 626

Dawn of the Dead GEORGE A. ROMERO 632

Midnight Express ALAN PARKER 638

1979

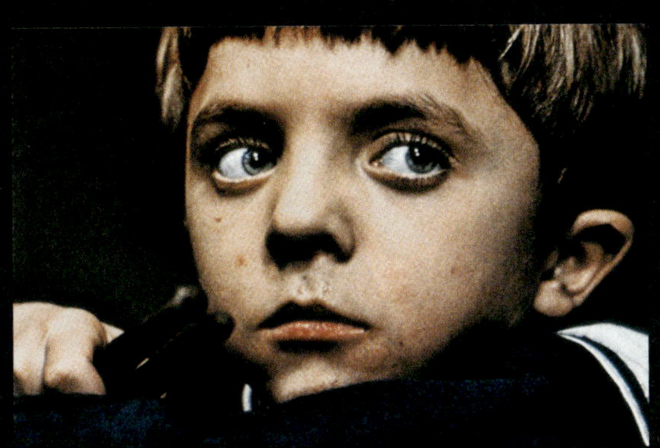

Manhattan WOODY ALLEN 646

Alien RIDLEY SCOTT 654

The Tin Drum VOLKER SCHLÖNDORFF 662

Kramer vs. Kramer ROBERT BENTON 670

Mad Max GEORGE MILLER 678

Monty Python's Life of Brian TERRY JONES 684

Apocalypse Now FRANCIS FORD COPPOLA 690

Being There HAL ASHBY 698

The China Syndrome JAMES BRIDGES 706

1980

The Elephant Man DAVID LYNCH 714

The Last Metro FRANÇOIS TRUFFAUT 722

Dressed to Kill BRIAN DE PALMA 730

Gloria JOHN CASSAVETES 738

Raging Bull MARTIN SCORSESE 744

The Blues Brothers JOHN LANDIS 752

Kagemusha AKIRA KUROSAWA 758

Atlantic City LOUIS MALLE 764

Diva JEAN-JACQUES BEINEIX 770

The Shining STANLEY KUBRICK 778

Heaven's Gate MICHAEL CIMINO 786

Star Wars: Episode V – The Empire Strikes Back IRVIN KERSHNER 796

Academy Awards 807

Index 812

About the Authors 822

Credits 823

Imprint 824

THE SKEPTICAL EYE
Notes on the Cinema of the 70s

"Municipal Flatblock 18a, Linear North. This was where I lived with my dadda and mum," says Alex (Malcolm McDowell), as he strolls home whistling between the houses of a suburban housing development somewhere in the middle of nowhere. The place is like a labyrinth. Lights burn in a few windows, weakly illuminating the protagonist's path. There's something strangely static about the camera that accompanies him through these streets in a single parallel tracking shot. The dramatic impression is not created by Hollywood's standard techniques—shot/reverse shot—but by a camera that glides like a ghost through dilapidated flowerbeds full of discarded junk.

In this dismal environment, the film's young hero is the only sign of life, and he's just enjoyed a good night out. Alex and his droogs have tolchocked an old tramp and a writer, raped a devotchka, stolen a car, and forced a respectable number of fellow drivers into the roadside ditch. Horror show.

Alex is in a splendid mood. Accompanying him homewards, we become highly aware of the camera's presence. We're waiting for a cut, but the camera does not blink, staring persistently at Alex as it slides along at his side. What we see here is more than a happily whistling hoodlum; we're seeing the fact that we see him.

Stanley Kubrick's *A Clockwork Orange* (1971, p. 70) is one of the key cult movies of the 70s, and certainly the most controversial. It might be described as the hinge that links the 60s with the 70s, for Kubrick's film may well be seen as a skeptical critique of the ideals formulated by the 60s student movement. Yet although the movie makes constant allusions to the progressive optimism of

that decade, its purview includes the entire century and the inhuman ideologies that marked it out.

It's hard to think of another film that assigns us the role of voyeur so effectively. In a shocking way, *A Clockwork Orange* makes all of us share responsibility for the things it shows. Thus the eloquent off-screen narrator who tells us his story never doubts for a second that he has our sympathy—and our consent. Again and again, he addresses us as "brothers." Still, the risk remains that we might have to see things from another perspective; and once, indeed, we find ourselves in the role of the victim—with Alex insisting we take a *veddy* good look… In this respect, Kubrick plays with the viewer's expectations. The film insists on breaking the bounds of fiction and assigning a series of different roles to us, the spectators. It's as if the director wanted to demonstrate his awareness of the pleasure we take in voyeurism, while also demanding that we see the world through Alex's eyes.

But Kubrick takes possession of us to an even greater extent than this, using all cinematic means available to give an authentic representation of Alex's world. We don't just see through Alex's eyes; we hear through his ears; and the music that accompanies his atrocities "allows" us to share his visceral pleasure in cruelty. As we watch a vicious brawl in a disused cinema, we hear Rossini's *La gazza ladra*; but this doesn't mean that Kubrick is trivializing violence.

On the contrary; the fighters' fun is simply being made plain to us. Kubrick is attempting to show—to make us *feel*—what violence looks like from the inside. Here, violence is presented as a creative principle. It signifies

lust, intoxication, as described by Nietzsche in *The Birth of Tragedy.* The film sketches a theory of ecstasy as the true fulfillment experienced by any human being who escapes the limits of his individuality. One scene shows this with particular vividness: like a satyr of the ancient world, Alex embraces a stone phallus—life petrified into art—and reawakens it in a grotesque balletic dance.

As we accompany Alex back to the flat, we get so close to him that we almost enter his Holy of Holies—home itself, with dadda and mum. In the entrance hall of his apartment block, the camera blinks; and now we're gliding along in front of a mural. Once again, the director has flouted our expectations. Naturally, we interpret this tracking shot as if we see what we're seeing through Alex's eyes, or as if we had just escorted him into the foyer; yet now, to our surprise, we see him enter the frame from the opposite direction. And while we wait for him to arrive, there's time to examine the heaps of garbage, the parched and trampled lawns. With the passage of time, this once impressive stairwell, with its murals and its potted plants, has adapted itself to the forbidding and inhospitable concrete jungle that surrounds it. The tenants' rage is directed at the "beautifications"—and especially at the mural, which is now disfigured by paint smears and obscene graffiti. The building's inhabitants, waiting in vain for the broken-down elevator, can only have taken pleasure in this fresco for a very short period. For they've "improved" it by adding enormous male sex organs, along with some helpful advice: "Suck it and see," says a boy bearing a narrow barrel, as he gazes down on his beholders from the painting on the wall.

Yet even without the obscenities, these heroic images of the working class don't really fit into their grim concrete environs. We see men and women of all ages united in their praise of skilled labor, agriculture and industry, an assurance of the happy future awaiting mankind. Here, careful planning and conscientious work are two sides of the same coin. Thinkers and doers, young and old, farmers, laborers and craftsmen, all striving together in the service of a better life, a new world forged by a vigorous humanity. At the center of the painting stands a man whose physique and headgear mark him out as a leader; brave and strong, he gazes heroically towards the future.

The fresco in the foyer of Alex's parents' apartment block seems very familiar—as if we had encountered it all over Europe in course of the 20th century. We know this kind of agitprop art; we've seen it in Berlin and Rome, in Bucharest and Moscow. It's as if Kubrick wished to comment, in passing, on a century marked by totalitarian systems. But this director doesn't make it easy for the audience; he's set us a trap by asking us to sympathize with this apparently peaceful world, now defiled by vandalism. But who are the vandals? The kids who've desecrated the artwork with filthy graffiti? Or the state technocrats who think they know the fate of humanity, and who paint a rosy future to conceal the inhumanity of the present?

Alex and his droogs counter moralists of all colors with the growled refrain, "If it moves, kiss it," while attaching outsized phalli to the heroes of classical antiquity. The droogs are shamelessly, indeed proudly, evil, and they're clearly convinced that work is for jerks.

Commentators who have written about this film have so far failed to notice that the mural in question is based on designs by Fritz Erler, a German painter and Hitler portraitist who readily adopted the themes of National Socialist art. Kubrick confronts us with two separate examples of state-ordained schemes to improve the world—modern urban architecture and the painted image of a utopian society—before letting loose their anarchistic adversaries. For the patently starry-eyed idealism debunks itself, leading inexorably as it does to a world in which the only choices left are between violence or boredom, hurting or being hurt; a world inhabited solely by brainless conformists and evil geniuses.

"VIDDY WELL"

Alex, the hoodlum, is pure literature. His language is a bizarre patois invented by Anthony Burgess, a potpourri of adolescent slang, onomatopoeia and Russian. In Kubrick's apocalyptic vision, Alex mutates into a creature of cinema whose "Gulliver" is haunted by the dreams and nightmares of 60s movies, from Warhol's *Vinyl* (1965) via Hammer's *Dracula* (1958, 1960, 1965; further productions of the same subject were realized by the Hammer Studios in 1968, 1970, 1972 and 1974) to Antonioni's *Zabriskie Point* (1969). We all have the freedom to worship our own personal graven images; and in Alex's

case, these happen to be Beethoven, manslaughter, rape, and the products of the Deutsche Grammophon record label.

The paradoxical truth of Kubrick's film consists in the assessment that there can be no morality as long as human beings are not free to flout it—even if the upshot is the collapse of civilization while Free Will stands by and applauds. *A Clockwork Orange* aestheticizes violence in order to express the autonomy of creativity; indeed, this is one of the film's central theses. Implicitly, the American director Kubrick is narrating the Fall of Man in the 20th century. He is showing us how the dictators—Hitler first and foremost—became conscious of the power of film and realized that the medium could do much more than merely tell stories and deliver snapshots of reality. In the 20th century, the camera became a perpetrator of violence. What's more, the camera is the viewers' ally, and it presupposes they will acquiescence—and relish the experience—when it shows them images of brutality. "Viddy well, little brother. Viddy well," says Alex, getting ready to rape, as he stares into the camera and makes

In *A Clockwork Orange*, the camera does not move enquiringly through cinematic space: instead, the camera's large-scale movements constitute and confirm this space's right to exist. It forms the stage on which the camera operates with icy precision, putting the beloved protagonist through his paces; first with pathos, later with pity, the camera follows its hero, bending the cinematic space to its will, so that Alex may bestride it like a king. When he struts through the record store, it's his spatial environment that seems to adjust to his trajectory, rather than vice-versa.

The few scenes we have described are enough to make it clear that *seeing* constitutes one of the major themes of *A Clockwork Orange*. The film sketches seeing as a sensual pleasure, if not an instinctual drive, and shows us as no more than its agents: cheerful voyeurs and accomplices, gourmets of the violence displayed with such narcissistic vanity. Thus it's no surprise that we even continue watching as Alex pisses blissfully in the toilet bowl.

Only a few films in the history of cinema have

Kael, for example, was one film critic who despised this movie, and it inspired her to pen a veritable tirade: *A Clockwork Orange*, said Kael, "might be the work of a strict and exacting German professor who set out to make a porno-violent sci-fi comedy." Well, Alex would probably be delighted by this judgment; but why, one wonders, a "German" professor…?

In any case, the peasants and proletarians in the foyer mosaic do seem to be German; and this grandiloquent glorification of social upheaval is lost in the midst of an urban landscape that has now buried Utopia in a concrete crypt. Though Anthony Burgess tells us that the story takes place "somewhere in Europe," the location could as easily be anywhere else in the world.

Yet there's even more German in Kubrick's film: the uniforms sported by Billy Boy's gang, for instance; and of course the music of Ludwig van Beethoven, which fills Alex's head with magnificent dreams of death and destruction. (In this respect at least, he may well resemble some German professors before him…) In the conglomerate of qualities regarded as "typically Teutonic," Kubrick finds a paradigmatic relationship between genius and madness, high art and barbarism, the creative powers of genius and the horror of mass murder.

A Clockwork Orange is also, and not least, a film about the power of music. Though the book describes a lover of classical music in general, Kubrick makes him a fanatical fan of Beethoven in particular. Alex describes his auditory experiences with his usual inimitable eloquence: "Oh bliss! Bliss and heaven! Oh, it was gorgeousness and gorgeousity made flesh. It was like a bird of rarest-spun heaven metal or like silvery wine flowing in a spaceship, gravity all nonsense now. As I slooshied, I knew such lovely pictures!"

The second movement of Beethoven's Ninth Symphony (*Molto vivace*) is accompanied by a wild carnival of images; this associative montage does not balk at mocking Jesus as a naked, quadrupled, porcelain Messiah, flinging his arms around to the strains of the glorious Ninth. In this world, there is no inconsistency between the outer limits of blasphemy and the adulation of the Most Sacred—though in this case, of course, the latter is represented by Beethoven. Kubrick is attempting nothing less than to show, without losing his ironic

distance, the ecstasy of a human being whose individuality dissolves in the experience of music. Alex loses himself deliberately in order to find refuge in the sublime. Images of Beethoven's portrait and Alex's face are repeatedly intercut. For Alex, the German composer is a kind of *Übermensch*, an ideal representation of creative genius; and above all, he's the source of inspiration for Alex's explosions of violence.

This is one of the most absurd sequences in film history: the prostrate Pop Art goddess, the Jesus can-can, the designer nightmare of the parental apartment... These images overwhelm us and capture our sympathies for these slick-talking sadists. The pictures we see are indistinguishable from Alex's narcissistic view of himself: Alex *is* the camera, and he has his eye on us, his "brothers and only friends." Anyone who observes participates; and why should we of all people, the audience in the cinema, not be seduced by the pleasures of violence and sly blasphemy?

PAVLOV'S DOG

Seeing is always a deliberate act, as Kubrick makes clear in a variety of ways. Most clearly perhaps, when he decorates Alex's cufflinks with a set of artificial eyeballs; every criminal act committed by his hands is witnessed by these symbolic onlookers. There's a similarly suggestive connection between the eye and the phallus in the sequence where Alex kills "Cat Woman" (Miriam Karlin). First of all, we see this elderly woman performing her gymnastic exercises. She is presented in a vulgar and somewhat indecent manner, which already places any male viewer in the position of a Peeping Tom. At the climax of the struggle between her and Alex, he beats her to death with an outsized sculpture of a penis. The killing itself creates a parallel between the camera and the phallus, so that seeing itself becomes an act of homicide. For as Alex raises his arms to work up the momentum for the fatal blow, we find we are watching from the viewpoint of the phallus. The camera must be located at its tip. Kubrick makes much of this scene, showing us twice in quick succession how Alex hoists the statue aloft.

Seeing as a starting-point for profound manipulations: this is a theme examined by the director in other sequences too, as when Alex is committed to the care of Dr. Brodsky (Carl Duering) and forced to sample his

methods of treatment. "The ineluctable modality of the visible" (James Joyce) is misused in the interest of the state: Alex, his head immobilized and his eyes prised open, is forced to watch images of the Second World War while the "therapists" play the works of his beloved "Ludwig Van."

Dr. Brodsky's methods are reminiscent of the experiments of Ivan Pavlov, the famous Russian behavioral scientist who conducted experiments on dogs at the beginning of the 20th century. He succeeded in conditioning his animals to salivate at the mere sound of a bell. The tests carried out on Alex after his therapy demonstrate Dr. Brodsky's success: for Alex, the very thought of violence has become equivalent to the violent act itself. The image has replaced the deed.

A Clockwork Orange conveys a significant and pervasive mood in the cinema of the 70s. With this film, an American director expresses his skepticism about the emancipatory potential of technology, science and morality. Kubrick doubts whether any of these can ever lead humanity, driven as it is by fears and instincts, onto the right path—whatever that may be. At the same time, the director is providing a commentary on the 20th century, which began with unparalleled aspirations to improve the world, and soon led to the most dreadful catastrophes. In the 20th century, the cinema became an important artistic medium; and at the same time, it turned out to be the most effective method of manipulation (as with the propaganda of the totalitarian systems). But Kubrick is not content to leave it at that. For it's significant that two of Alex's droogs have become policemen in the second half of the movie. Although his former friends have now changed sides, they haven't had to give up their passion for brutality. Humankind, whatever it does, is always stuck with violence.

THE WUNDERKINDER

Even today, the films of the 70s have an astonishing potency. This applies not least to the American cinema of the decade, which experienced an unprecedented renewal that few would have considered possible. It was a time of unparalleled freedoms, and many felt they were living through a kind of revolution.

By exploiting the possibilities of commercial cinema with a new vigor, and by examining the myths as

critically as the social realities, cinematography achieved a new truthfulness, which emancipated it once more from the pre-eminence of TV. Though the monumental Cinemascope epics of the 60s may have paraded the silver screen's superiority to the box, the cinema only realized its true strength when it began to fill that screen with new subject matter. In America, there were particularly good reasons to do so, for the USA was a deeply traumatized and divided nation. The war in Vietnam continued to drag on unbearably, consuming more and more victims; and the political justification for the military intervention was in any case more than questionable. What little trust was left in the political administration was destroyed by the Watergate scandal. America had lost its credibility as a moral instance, and U.S. cinema traced the causes and effects of this trauma in a series of memorable films. The basic skepticism of 70s cinema is balanced by the filmmakers' huge enthusiasm for their medium. Their curiosity, creative will and refusal to compromise now seem more fascinating than ever, for we live in an age in which Hollywood seems ever more rationalized

At the end of the 60s, a period described by Hans C. Blumenberg as "the most dismal and boring decade" in American cinema history, Hollywood was on the ropes, both economically and artistically. In the face of the prevalent societal crisis, the cinema had lost its power to form identity; and for anyone after mere distraction, the TV was clearly the simpler and cheaper alternative. As the movies declined in importance, the old studio system was doomed to collapse, for it had been showing signs of sickness since the early 1950s. The last of the old-style Hollywood moguls stepped down, and a younger generation took over the management of the studios, which were now almost all owned by major corporations. By this time, the studios were barely developing a single project themselves.

Such was the situation as the 60s drew to a close; until a few small movies, most of them produced independently, turned out to be surprise hits—simply by encapsulating the rebellious spirit of the age. In *Bonnie and Clyde* (1967), for example, Warren Beatty and Faye Dunaway blaze an anarchic trail through the South and Midwest,

love and a gesture of defiant revolt. In *Easy Rider* (1969), Peter Fonda and Dennis Hopper transverse the vastness of America, ostensibly to sell drugs, but in fact quite simply for the hell of it—to be on the road, to be free. These new heroes were not just excitingly beautiful and cool; they also embodied a truth irreconcilable with the truth of their elders. And this is what the young wanted to see at the movies: actors who gave a face to their yearnings.

These films gave a decisive impulse to the New Hollywood. From now on, the studios would give young filmmakers a chance. And they knew how to use it; with Francis Ford Coppola, Brian De Palma, George Lucas, Steven Spielberg, Peter Bogdanovich, William Friedkin, Paul Schrader and Martin Scorsese, the 70s produced a generation of "child prodigies," who defined a new kind of Hollywood cinema. These young movie-maniacs helped the American film industry to make an unexpected and lasting commercial comeback. For their films included some of the biggest box-office hits of the decade—*The Godfather* (1972, p. 132; Part II, 1974, p. 288), *The Exorcist* (1973, p. 228), *Jaws* (1975, p. 348), *Close Encounters of the Third Kind* (1977, p. 548) and *Star Wars* (1977, p. 522).

Naturally, one has to be careful when comparing the *Wunderkinder* with European *auteurs* in the tradition of the *Nouvelle Vague*, but the influence of the latter on the New Hollywood is readily apparent. In the 70s, American directors enjoyed a stronger position than any of their predecessors since the days of Griffith—and this in a film industry characterized by specialization. The decade marked a highpoint of directorial independence. Having begun with the death of the old Dream Factory, it ended with the invention of the blockbuster: an "event-movie" swaddled in a tailor-made marketing strategy, with which today's Hollywood continues to rule the commercial cinema practically worldwide.

THE BACK DOORS OF POWER

The most important American director of the decade is Francis Ford Coppola. He is also the one who most radically upheld his position as a "film author." As the first director of the New Hollywood, he scored a major triumph. *The Godfather* was an artistic and commercial success,

and he even managed to top this with the second part. Marlon Brando, the one-time embodiment of rebellious youth, was an indubitable sensation as Don Vito Corleone, the massive patriarch with the rasping voice. There were, however, other reasons for the film's enormous popularity.

The epic tale of the Corleone Mafia clan marked the first cinematic treatment of a non-WASP American family history. Until this film appeared, the white Anglo-Saxon protestant majority had enjoyed uncontested cultural dominance. *The Godfather* shows how the Corleones succeed in transplanting their Sicilian ideas of family and business onto American soil, where they take root and flourish.

Thus, *The Godfather* corrects the traditional and long-established Hollywood image of the birth of modern America. Its methods include the positively Mediterranean flair of the opulent wedding scene at the start of the film, an effective contrast to the gloomy rooms where the men settle their business matters. What's more, the sedate, almost operatic tempo of Coppola's film stands in stark contrast to the feverish dynamics of the American gangster movie, which celebrates the apparently boundless power and freedom of the individual. In *The Godfather*, events proceed with fatal inevitability, while brilliant editing emphasizes how strongly each figure is bound to the family system. Thus there seems no way for the sensitive Michael Corleone (Al Pacino) to avoid being transformed into the unscrupulous Don. The law of the Family insists on it.

Coppola's film revealed the existence of a parallel world alongside "official" America. The average decent citizen, however, knew no more of it than he read in the newspaper. Coppola showed us insulated centers of power, impervious to external influence. In the terrifying final scene of Part I, Kay (Diane Keaton) realizes that her husband Michael is the new Godfather. The door is ajar, and she sees him greeting his accomplices; as a sign of deference, they kiss his hands. Then the door closes before Kay's eyes, and the picture fades to black. This film's pessimism captured the mood of an entire nation.

GOD'S LONELY MAN

Martin Scorsese was the second great Italian-American director to make a breakthrough. In contrast

to Coppola,the son of established middle-class parents, Scorsese came from a poor family of Sicilian immigrants to New York. He grew up in Little Italy and had first-hand experience of life on the mean streets: the claustrophobic narrowness, the co-existence of the Catholic Church and the Mafia, the open and repressed aggression. All of this can be seen clearly in Scorsese's films. *Mean Streets* (1973) and *Raging Bull* (1980, p. 744) convey the atmosphere of Little Italy with such intensity that they permit no doubt of the therapeutic function of film-making. This personal aspect was an excitingly new development in the commercial American cinema. Scorsese filmed the sexual frustrations, the eruptions of violence, with a brutal directness that was quite unprecedented in the history of film—and in Robert De Niro, he found an ideal partner. Like Scorsese, De Niro immersed himself in the film-making process with an almost fanatical intensity; and he, too, wanted to explore the depths of his own psyche.

The most spectacular film Scorsese made in the 70s was *Taxi Driver* (1975, p. 380). As the flipped-out Vietnam vet Travis Bickle, De Niro gave definitive, threatening form to the existential nausea, frustration and blocked-up aggression of the lonely city dweller. It was all the more disturbing because the film allowed us the opportunity to identify with Bickle. The scene in which De Niro, armed to the teeth, poses in front of the mirror must be one of the most frequently quoted in film history.

Taxi Driver shows New York through the eyes of its psychotic protagonist. Night after night, he drives his yellow cab through a sick city that infects its inhabitants, a monstrous metropolis that mirrors the decadence of society. The film's atmosphere is dark and the use of color is disturbing, a typical example of how even non-political films gave expression to distrust of the American political system and showed the growing brutality of a society undergoing cataclysmic change. Certainly, the corruption of the political classes was directly addressed in various political dramas, such as Alan J. Pakula's Watergate thriller *All the President's Men* (1976, p. 456) or Sydney Pollack's *Three Days of the Condor* (1975, p. 402). But in the American cinema of the 70s, a general loss of confidence is perceptible almost everywhere—in disaster movies such as *The Towering Inferno* (1974) and in countless paranoia thrillers. In such a situation,

the return of the horror film is no surprise—and George A. Romero, Tobe Hooper, Wes Craven and John Carpenter created some real classics, though William Friedkin's *The Exorcist* is probably the most notable example of the genre.

Towards the end of the 70s, the U.S. cinema began dealing explicitly with the Vietnam War. Here, too, Coppola was the pioneer. In *Apocalypse Now* (1979, p. 690), he attempted to grasp the nature of war. The film depicts a regression to an anti-humanist world in which good and evil have become indistinguishable. Here, Coppola made a radical break with the alleged realism of the war-film genre, by combining the greatest possible degree of authenticity—the film was made on location in the jungle —with a lurid, expressive artificiality.

Apocalypse Now is one of the most daring projects in cinematic history. It stands as proof of a passionate filmmaker's unbroken faith in himself, for Coppola was prepared to risk both his livelihood and his health in order to realize his vision. In retrospect, however, the project's very radicalism seems to presage the end of large-scale "authorial cinema" in the New Hollywood era. Soon after Michael Cimino's box-office disaster *Heaven's Gate* (1980, p. 786) supplied the death certificate.

It took so long to complete *Apocalypse Now*—while the media speculated avidly about the project's impending collapse—that other Vietnam films reached the theaters sooner. Hal Ashby scored a considerable success with his melodrama *Coming Home* (1978, p. 568), the story of a soldier's wife (Jane Fonda) who falls in love with an invalid war veteran (Jon Voight). This was a relatively conventional tale, told in the best liberal Hollywood manner.

By contrast, Cimino's *The Deer Hunter* (1978, p. 584) was the source of considerable controversy, with the negative representation of the Vietcong arousing particular criticism. If truth be told, the film is completely uninterested in a balanced representation of events, and less interested in the conflict itself than in what the American film scholar Robin Wood called "the invasion of America by Vietnam"—the war's penetration of the American psyche. In Wood's reading of the film, Cimino is examining the myth of an ideal America at the moment of its dissolution. Vietnam initiated a process

of increasing awareness, a terrible dawning. At the end of the film, the survivors join together in singing "God Bless America," and the song is heavy with grief. These people are in mourning, not just for their dead friend, but for a lost ideal.

THE COMEBACK OF THE CLASSICS

Following the lead of the French auteurs, young American cineasts discovered the great classics of U.S. cinema. For not a few of these new directors, the older movies were their declared models, and they paid tribute to them in their own films. Peter Bogdanovich began his career as a film journalist, interviewing Hollywood legends such as Orson Welles and John Ford. When he himself took up directing, most of his films were homages to the Hollywood movies of the past. With *What's Up, Doc?* (1972, p. 166), he attempted to create a screwball comedy *à la* Howard Hawks. "Reclaiming" such classic genres was typical of the *Wunderkinder.* In this case, the result was a splendidly exuberant film-buff's jamboree, packed full of movie quotations and amusing nods to past classics. Nonetheless, the film worked even for those who were less in the know, partly thanks to the comic talent of Barbra Streisand, one of the top female stars of the 70s.

New York, New York (1977) was Martin Scorsese's extravagant attempt to revive interest in the musical. To evoke the Golden Age of the genre, he placed all his bets on the glamour and star quality of a Broadway icon: Liza Minnelli. Although the daughter of Vincente Minnelli and Judy Garland had received a lot of attention for her lead role in Bob Fosse's *Cabaret* (1972, p. 124), *New York, New York* failed to attract a big audience. Instead, moviegoers flocked to pop musicals like *Hair* (1978) and the tongue-in-cheek *The Rocky Horror Picture Show* (1975, p. 410). These were two films that achieved remarkable cult status—yet ultimately, they too were isolated, one-off hits.

Of course, Neo-Noirs such as *Taxi Driver* were also modeled on classic films of the past; yet they reveal much more than the cinematic preferences of their creators. In the pessimistic perspective of *Film Noir*, it's obvious that these filmmakers saw clear parallels to their own take on American reality. And so they didn't merely adopt the dark visual style of 40s and 50s thrillers; they also facilitated

the comeback of a genre with a supremely skeptical outlook on social mechanisms: the detective film.

Roman Polanski's *Chinatown* (1974, p. 318) is a masterpiece of the genre, and one of the best films of the decade. The Polish-born director created a magnificent portrait of universal corruption and violence, while also managing to conjure up the glory that was Hollywood. Nonetheless, his film was much more than a mere hommage, thanks not least to some fabulous actors. Faye Dunaway perfectly embodied the mysterious erotic allure of a 30s film vamp, without ever seeming like a mere ghost from movies past. Jack Nicholson's private detective was also far more than yet another Bogart clone: J. J. Gittes is an authentic figure, a tough little gumshoe made of flesh and blood, who maintains his credibility even with a plaster on his nose. For a moralist like Gittes, a sliced nostril is just another hazard that goes with the job.

The U.S. cinema of the 70s took a skeptical and pessimistic attitude to the myths of the nation, and this had its effect on the most American film genre of them all—the Western. John Ford, Howard Hawks and John Wayne all died within a few years, and these were the personalities who had stamped the genre for decades. Ever since the late 50s, a process of demystification had been at work; and now the *content* of the Western was also taken to its logical conclusion.

The classical Western had always taken an optimistic attitude to history and progress. Sam Peckinpah's *Pat Garrett and Billy the Kid* (1973, p. 220) is a sorrowful elegy for the old Western, and a complete reversal of its basic worldview. As the film sees it, the growing influence of capital on social relationships meant the end of the utopia of freedom. Individuals can only succumb and conform to a corrupt society, or else they are doomed to perish, like Billy the Kid. Kris Kristofferson gave Billy the aura of a hippie idol—and with the outlaw's demise, the film also buried the hopes and ideals of the Woodstock generation.

It was clear that Western heroes would no longer serve as the icons of reactionary America. Their successors were "urban cowboys" like the protagonist of Don Siegel's controversial *Dirty Harry* (1971, p. 48): Clint Eastwood plays a cynical cop who takes the law into his own hands—because the legal system only serves

crooks—and who makes no bones about despising the democratic legitimation of power. When Dirty Harry Callahan has completed his mission by killing the psychopath, he gazes down on the floating corpse—and throws his police badge in the water.

The primordial American yearning for freedom and the open road were now better expressed in road movies such as *Easy Rider* (1969), Monte Hellman's *Two-Lane Blacktop* (1971) or even star vehicles like *Smokey and the Bandit* (1977), featuring Burt Reynolds. But as demonstrated by Steven Spielberg's feature-film debut *Duel* (1971), even the endless highway offered no refuge from the paranoid nightmares of the 70s.

THE TRIUMPH OF THE "JEDI KNIGHTS"

During the 1970s, Vietnam and Watergate cast their dark shadows across the cinema screens. The divisions in the national psyche came to expression in horror and paranoia movies as well as pessimistic thrillers, war films and do-it-yourself-justice potboilers. In the midst of the crisis, many people wanted one thing and one thing only from the cinema: a short vacation from real life. Hollywood was more than happy to cater for their needs. At the end of the decade, the science fiction genre boldly went where no films had gone before. The sensational success of George Lucas' *Star Wars* and Steven Spielberg's *Close Encounters of the Third Kind* laid the foundations for the blockbuster movies of the decades to come.

One reason for this triumph of these films was their sheer technical perfection, which made a substantial contribution to the credibility of their plots. In addition, Lucas and Spielberg succeeded in bringing together so many different elements of popular film so convincingly that these movies, however fantastic their premises, offered a huge potential for identification. *Close Encounters* and *Star Wars* are also remarkable for their overwhelming visual power. These were cinematic adventures that even adults could enjoy with childlike pleasure, and millions were happy to do so. The escapism of these films anticipated the cinema of the 80s.

THE RETURN OF GERMAN FILM

The enlivening influence of the French *Nouvelle Vague* was felt not only in America. "New Waves" arose

everywhere, including West Germany. Artistically, the 70s were the most interesting decade in German cinema since the Golden Age of the 20s and early 30s. Film authors such as Werner Herzog, Rainer Werner Fassbinder, Wim Wenders and Volker Schlöndorff drew the world's attention to the New German Cinema.

Many of these young filmmakers forged conscious links to the traditions of classic German cinema, seeing themselves as the legitimate heirs to a body of work supplanted by Nazism and forgotten ever since. In this respect, Werner Herzog's *Nosferatu* (*Nosferatu – Phantom der Nacht*, 1978, p. 574) seems almost programmatic, for it is a spectacular remake of a famous silent film by Friedrich Wilhelm Murnau.

Like most of Herzog's films, *Nosferatu* bears witness to the director's sympathy for outcasts, for lonely and eccentric personalities. Klaus Kinski provided the ideal embodiment of such figures, in this and in five other Herzog films. Artistically at least, the two men complemented each other perfectly: an obsessive director with a touch of genius, and a wildly eccentric actor who endowed each of his roles with all the strangeness and seemingly unrestrained intensity of his personality. In their jungle projects *Aguirre, Wrath of God* (*Aguirre, der Zorn Gottes*, 1972) and *Fitzcarraldo* (1978–81), this was a constellation that almost led to catastrophe; but the final results were two utterly original film creations. As was *Nosferatu*, in which Kinski added a tragic dimension to the vampire's existential loneliness—an astonishing achievement when we consider the grotesque horror of the vampire's appearance. In a world of bourgeois businessmen, Kinski's Nosferatu is a creature crucified by despairing love.

The tragedy of an individual life is also the focus of each of the films made by the most productive German director of the time. In a tempo that can only be described as feverish, Rainer Werner Fassbinder made more than 40 films in the 13 years before his early death (in 1982). These included genre films, literary adaptations, melodramas, radically "committed" films, intimate character studies, and even movies with popular appeal, such as *The Marriage of Maria Braun* (*Die Ehe der Maria Braun*, 1978, p. 610). Both in form and content, Fassbinder's films are uncompromising studies

of society's brutality and emotional coldness. At the same time, they are also reflections on his work as a filmmaker and his personal demons. Fassbinder's fame is also founded on his genius as an actor-director; and the female members of his "film family"—first and foremost, Hanna Schygulla—stamped the image of the New German Cinema.

Volker Schlöndorff, by contrast, made his name by adapting works of literature. *The Tin Drum* (*Die Blechtrommel*, 1979, p. 662), brought him the Oscar for Best Foreign Film, and he is the first German director to have won this award. (The second German is Caroline Link who won an Oscar for *Nirgendwo in Afrika*, 2001.) In the role of the little drummer boy Oskar Matzerath, David Bennent played a large part in assisting the New German Cinema to its greatest triumph. Only a few years later, however, Fassbinder's death marked the almost complete collapse of the German *Autorenfilm.* The sole director to preserve his status was Wim Wenders, whose films displayed a fascination for the American cinema. At that time, however, his enthrallment was also tempered by critical reflection.

AN "AUTHORS' CINEMA," IN SPITE OF EVERYTHING

By the time the 60s ended, most people in France regarded the *Nouvelle Vague* as essentially over. Not least under the impact of the student revolts of May 1968, the movement's former protagonists—Jean-Luc Godard, François Truffaut, Claude Chabrol, Eric Rohmer, and Jacques Rivette—moved apart, or began to pursue their own ideas more assertively.

Since the mid-60s, Godard, the most important force for change in European cinema, had increasingly seen the film medium as an instrument of political dissent. Post-'68, he turned his back completely on the commercial cinema, devoting his time to experimental, political film-projects. The one exception was *Everything's Fine* (*Tout va bien/Crepa padrone, tutto va bene*, 1972). Only in 1980 did Godard return to the mainstream cinema with his "second first film:" *Every Man for Himself* aka *Slow Motion* (*Sauve qui peut [la vie]*) was a resigned, allegorical commentary on the state of cinema and society.

While Godard chose radical opposition to commerce, the 70s saw François Truffaut, Claude Chabrol and other French *auteurs* become increasingly established as

popular filmmakers. With *Day for Night* (*La Nuit américaine*, 1973, p. 196), Truffaut achieved a considerable feat: this intelligent and entertaining movie tells the story of how a film is made, and managed to appeal both to cineasts and a broad movie-going public. In 1974, Truffaut's wonderful homage to filmmaking earned him the Oscar for the Best Foreign Film.

The Last Metro (*Le Dernier Métro*, 1980, p. 722) even succeeded in reconciling the art-cinema of the French *auteurs* with the perennial appeal of the stars. It tells the tale of a love triangle during the German occupation of Paris, and brought Truffaut an exceptional box-office success. As the woman beside Gérard Depardieu and Heinz Bennent, Catherine Deneuve gave a performance that established her reputation as the *grande dame* of French cinema. Some critics, though, were less than complimentary; to them, the film's classical brilliance exemplified the kind of sterile, workmanlike cinema that Truffaut had so doggedly opposed in his days as a film journalist. Despite his detractors' polemics, however, Truffaut remained one of the leading theorists and practitioners of the French cinema until his death in 1984. His influence on the European cinema can be felt even today.

For Britain's film industry, the 70s were a difficult decade and the continuing success of the James Bond films could do nothing to alter this fact. The problematic situation had much to do the industry's traditional economic dependency on foreign (especially American) film productions made in British studios. Though there had been many such productions in the past, their numbers were now in decline. In addition, the Free Cinema directors had by now lost their clout. Though they had initiated a renewal of the style and subject matter of British film from the late 50s onwards, the time of the Angry Young Men had clearly been and gone. The number of films produced in Britain sank rapidly, and even more English filmmakers than previously now felt forced to seek work in America. Many of them, indeed, remained on the other side of the Atlantic.

Nonetheless, pronounced individualists such as Nicolas Roeg continued to work frequently in Britain. Roeg's extravagant thriller *Don't Look Now* (1973, p. 234) was a British production that included a wonderfully

sensuous love scene between Julie Christie and Donald Sutherland, a sequence unrivaled in any other U.S. production of the time.

The American Stanley Kubrick was another director who valued the freer production conditions outside Hollywood. He had emigrated to England in the 60s. With *Barry Lyndon* (1975, p. 388) he made an outstandingly beautiful costume drama that seemed gloriously indifferent to any kind of commercial consideration. Kubrick did return temporarily to the States to make his Stephen King adaptation *The Shining* (1980, p. 778), but he shot the interiors of the Overlook Hotel in the time-honored Elstree Studios near London.

SCEPTICS IN THE EMPIRE OF THE SENSES

In Italy, the situation looked very different. At the beginning of the decade, many commercially successful films were being made. Spaghetti Westerns were still selling well abroad, but the genre had long since passed its artistic zenith, with Sergio Leone's *Once Upon a Time in the West* (*C'era una volta il West*, 1969). Directors such as Luchino Visconti, Michelangelo Antonioni and Federico Fellini, many of whom had their roots in the neorealism of the 40s and early 50s, sustained the Italian cinema's international reputation.

But it was another director, one of the leading members of the intellectual avant-garde, who was responsible for the most ambitious Italian project of the decade: Bernardo Bertolucci's *1900* (Part I and II) (*Novecento,* 1975/76, p. 418) was a monumental two-part epic featuring a cast of international stars. It traced the history of Italy in the 20th century by following the lives of a few people from a single country estate—and might well have been entitled "Once Upon A Time In Italy."

Three years previously, Bernardo Bertolucci had caused a different kind of hullabaloo. His *Last Tango in Paris* (*Ultimo Tango a Parigi/Le dernier Tango à Paris,* 1972, p. 158) examined the self-destructive sexual relationship between a cynical, ageing American in Paris (Marlon Brando) and a young Frenchwoman (Maria Schneider). The film's representation of sexuality was extreme for its time, and provoked a storm of protest. Attempts to ban screenings of the movie led to an avalanche of court cases in Italy.

The sexual revolution continued in the cinema. Particularly in European films, there was more and more sex on the screen. Nevertheless—or rather, for that very reason—the 70s were also a decade of "scandal films." Bertolucci's *Last Tango* was by no means an isolated exception. Many moviegoers were also outraged by Pier Paolo Pasolini's *Salo, or The 120 Days of Sodom* (*Salò o le 120 giornate di Sodoma*, 1975). A deeply pessimistic film that transferred the plot of a De Sade novel to the Italy of the Fascist era, it depicted the sadistic fantasies of a decadent *grande bourgeoisie* in images of icy perversion that are hard to watch even today. In many countries, the film was censored. Another movie to hit the headlines was Nagisa Oshima's Japanese-French co-production *In the Realm of the Senses* (*Ai no corrida/L'Empire des sens,* 1976, p. 480). A ballad of sexual dependency, the film tells the story of an *amour fou* that ends in physical mutilation. During Berlin's International Film Festival in 1977, the German authorities temporarily confiscated the film, suspecting it of contravening pornography laws. Isolated actions such as these, however, did little to hinder the general tendency towards liberalization. Naturally, this was not entirely unconnected to the fact that sex sells.

Looking back at the movies of the 70s, it seems that the freedoms brought by the influence of the film authors are reflected in a highly heterogeneous range of visual styles. Quite clearly, the director's personality determined the look of a film much more strongly than in previous decades. There was certainly a trend towards stylization apparent in many Neo-Noirs, SF and horror films. Yet the realistic elements and faith in a good storyline were just as new, and more significant. Movies shot on location increasingly supplanted those made on studio sets. In the 70s, films were made in real streets, real backyards, and real apartments.

The recording technology too developed an unprecedented, dynamic mobility. Nervous hand cameras were soon practically standard, and opened up new frontiers, even for the commercial movie business. The Steadycam made it possible to film smooth pans and tracking shots without laying down cumbersome tracks; and for the simulation of amateur film sequences in *Mean Streets* and *Raging Bull*, Martin Scorsese even used an 8mm camera.

Clearly, many 1970s directors were looking for something closer to real life—which doesn't mean they were trying to slavishly reproduce the world around them. Though Coppola set up his cameras in the primeval jungle, what he produced was a war film that looked liked an acid trip: "This is not a movie about Vietnam. It is Vietnam."

In the 70s, it became clear at last that the old myths would no longer suffice. Vietnam and Watergate were only the most blatant symptoms justifying the terrible diagnosis of the decade's filmmakers: the Enlightenment had failed, and reports of humanity's progress had been premature. The American cinema of the period cast a strong light on the murky depths of American society. This was a country that felt recklessly secure in its possession of democracy and free speech. And the filmmakers were as skeptical about personal relationships as they were about politics. Predictions of sexual liberation, apparently as much of a myth as the Enlightenment itself, remained stubbornly unfulfilled.

If we turn our thoughts once again to Kubrick's *A Clockwork Orange*, the prophetic quality of the film becomes clear. For the American director is questioning nothing less than the idea of a world without violence. By postulating a future in which there is nothing but oppression, revolt and opportunism, he is rejecting the utopia of a conflict-free society. In Kubrick's film, sadism and ignorance are more than merely "lapses" by an individual, a group, or an institution.

The film takes its leave of the idea that humanity is perfectible. If the cinema nonetheless remains an instrument of enlightenment, then the main reason is this: it forces us to undergo a paradoxical experience. For film can only retain its integrity by refusing to shield us from the irrational nature of the world. But it's not only the filmmakers' findings that undermine rationality. Our simple desire to *look* sometimes makes the movies seem more real us to us than our own lives. As Alex remarks during the therapy inflicted on him by Dr. Brodsky: "It's funny how the colors of the real world only seem really real when you viddy them on a screen."

Jürgen Müller / Jörn Hetebrügge

STRAW DOGS

1971 – GREAT BRITAIN / USA – 118 MIN.

GENRE

THRILLER

DIRECTOR

SAM PECKINPAH

SCREENPLAY

DAVID ZELAG GOODMAN, SAM PECKINPAH,
based on the novel *THE SIEGE OF TRENCHER'S FARM*
by GORDON WILLIAMS

DIRECTOR OF PHOTOGRAPHY

JOHN COQUILLON

EDITING

PAUL DAVIES, TONY LAWSON, ROGER SPOTTISWOODE

MUSIC

JERRY FIELDING

PRODUCTION

DANIEL MELNICK for ABC PICTURES CORPORATION,
AMERBROCO, TALENT ASSOCIATES LTD.

STARRING

DUSTIN HOFFMAN (David Sumner), SUSAN GEORGE (Amy Sumner),
PETER VAUGHAN (Tom Hedden), T. P. MCKENNA (Major John Scott),
DEL HENNEY (Charlie Venner), JIM NORTON (Chris Cawsey),
DONALD WEBSTER (Riddaway), KEN HUTCHISON (Norman Scutt),
LEN JONES (Bobby Hedden), SALLY THOMSETT (Janice Hedden),
ROBERT KEEGAN (Harry Ware), PETER ARNE (John Niles),
DAVID WARNER (Henry Niles), CHERINA SCHAER (Louise Hood),
COLIN WELLAND (Reverend)

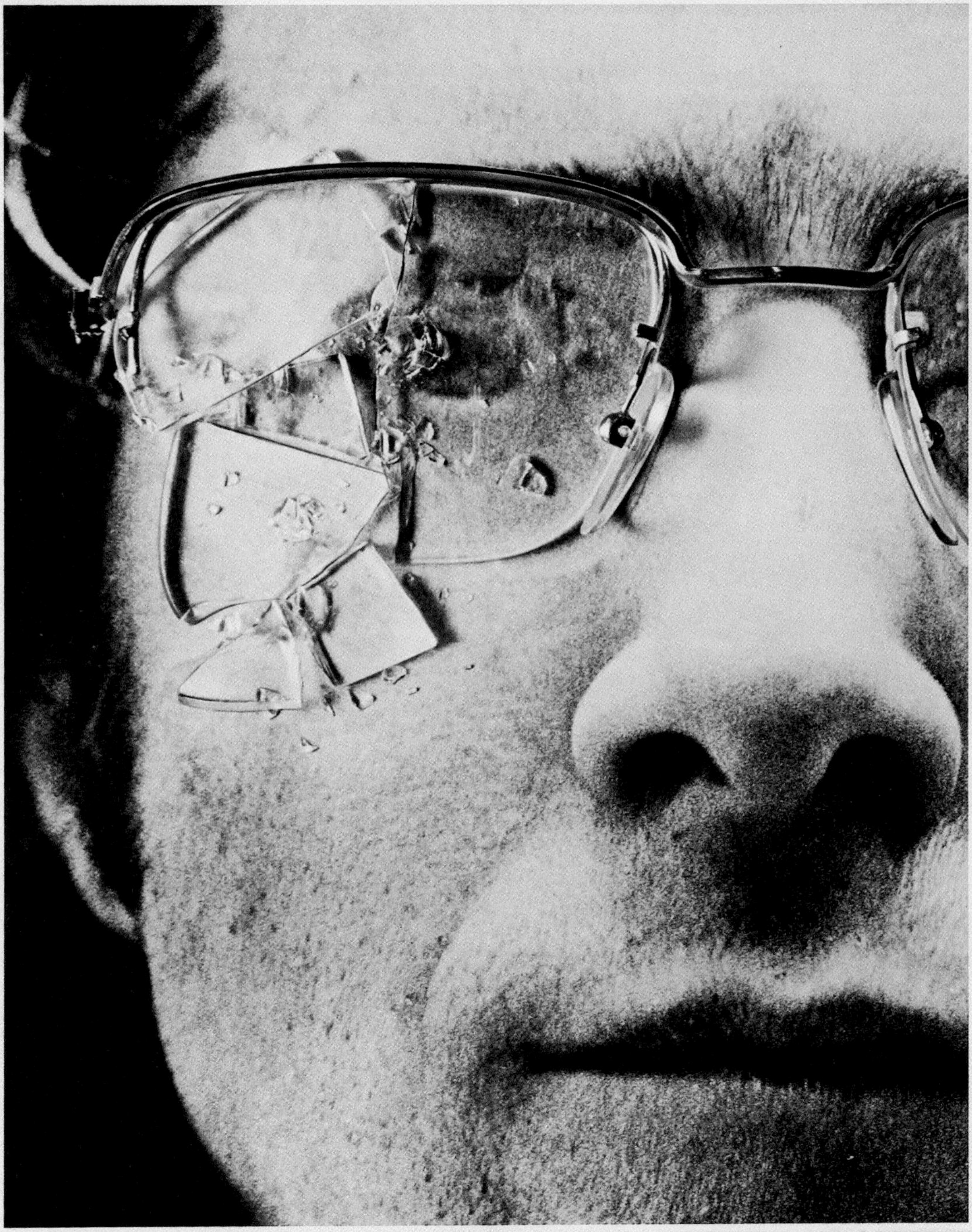

ABC PICTURES CORP. presents

DUSTIN HOFFMAN

in SAM PECKINPAH'S

"STRAW DOGS"

A DANIEL MELNICK Production

Starring SUSAN GEORGE as Amy

Music by JERRY FIELDING Screenplay by DAVID ZELAG GOODMAN and SAM PECKINPAH

Produced by DANIEL MELNICK Directed by SAM PECKINPAH

A SUBSIDIARY OF THE AMERICAN BROADCASTING COMPANIES, INC. | COLOR | DISTRIBUTED BY CINERAMA RELEASING

R RESTRICTED Under 17 requires accompanying Parent or Adult Guardian

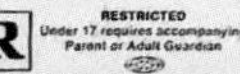

1

Young American mathematician David Sumner (Dustin Hoffman) has taken up residence with his wife Amy (Susan George) on an old farm in Cornwall, England. It is the house of Amy's parents, and David hopes to find peace and quiet for his work. But the opposite proves to be true. In the nearby village, the newcomers are greeted with suspicion. And the men whom David has hired to repair the garage roof of the farmhouse show their disdain for him with increasing audacity. David, who feels intellectually superior, tries to ignore this, as well as the growing dissatisfaction of his sensually lascivious wife, who is bored and feels bothered by the workers. But the tension gradually intensifies and ultimately the situation escalates.

After the frustrating bickering over *The Wild Bunch* (1969)—Warner Brothers released a heavily edited version—*Straw Dogs* presented Sam Peckinpah the welcome opportunity to shoot in Europe for the first time and more importantly, independence from the big Hollywood Studios. *Straw Dogs*, shot on location in the English countryside and in London's Twickenham Studios, was Peckinpah's first film outside of the Western genre. And perhaps it is this missing genre context that was one of the reasons

SAM PECKINPAH His rough manner was just as notorious as the violence in his films: Sam Peckinpah (born February 21, 1925 in Fresno, California, died December 28, 1984 in Inglewood, California) doubtless belongs to the most legendary Hollywood outsiders. After taking some acting courses, he began his career toward the beginning of the 1950s as a stage hand for television. Within a few years he rose to become the assistant for action specialist Don Siegel, and before long he was writing and dramatizing Western series for TV. And when the second-class script for the Western *The Deadly Companions* (1961) came across his desk, he took his chance without hesitation. His second feature film, *Ride the High Country* (1962), like most of his films a swan song to the old West, thrust him into the international limelight. But shortly thereafter, with his next project, the epic army Western *Major Dundee* (1964/65), Peckinpah's famed recurring problems with his producers began: the film was released in a heavily edited version. This fate also befell his subsequent film, *The Wild Bunch* (1969), considered his masterpiece, as well as his melancholic Western *Pat Garrett and Billy the Kid* (1973). After *The Wild Bunch* Peckinpah was repeatedly criticized for his extreme portrayal of violence, not least for *Straw Dogs* (1971), his first foray outside the Western format, which the critics blasted for its fascist undertones. Cynicism and pessimism aside, the fact that Sam Peckinpah was often able to reveal a tender depiction of the characters in his films—most notably in *The Ballad of Cable Hogue* (1970) and *Junior Bonner* (1972)—is seldom praised. Peckinpah is regarded as a brilliant stylist, though from the mid-70s onwards his films seldom achieved the same quality as his earlier works.

2

1 How low can we go? In Sam Peckinpah's films, civilization is a thin sheet of ice over an abyss of brutality.

2 It's a man's world: One of the few significant women in Peckinpah's films is Amy (Susan George), whose naive sensuality provokes an escalation of violence.

3 The odd couple. The marriage of David (Dustin Hoffman), a mathematician, and his sensual wife Amy is increasingly dogged by frustration.

"The film is a provocation and a diagnosis. It takes the hysterical debate about the portrayal of violence in the media to new heights, thus questioning its own right to exist. Withdrawal treatments of this kind are vitally necessary." *DIE ZEIT*

why the violent scenes in *Straw Dogs* caused such unusually heavy indignation. Two scenes in particular provoked repugnance: Amy's rape by two villagers, which she seems to enjoy, and during which she is depicted anything but innocently. The second, more controversial still, was the bloody finale. David, Amy and the feeble-minded Henry Niles (David Warner) barricade themselves from a fanatical mob in the farmhouse and kill off one besieger after another with shocking brutality. This showdown inspired several polemical attacks by critics who accused Peckinpah of propagating fascist violence.

Straw Dogs is doubtless a highly provocative and upsetting film. From the beginning, an atmosphere of oppressive violence looms over the bucolic setting, and the

4

“I can think of no other film which screws violence up into so tight a knot of terror that one begins to feel that civilization is crumbling before one’s eyes.”

Tom Milne

5

apparent archaic simplicity of the villagers undeniably recalls the notorious scenery of the Peckinpah Western. David, the rational man, seems to be the diametric opposite of the locals, though he is in no way a sympathetic figure. Hoffman’s character is a far cry from the endearing helplessness of his Benjamin Braddock in *The Graduate* (1967). Contrary to Amy, David seems unable to decode the behavioral language of the locals and attempts to cover up his insecurity with cowardly servility. His frustration that he is unable to implement his intellectual superiority against the aggressive physicality of the villagers is expressed instead in his degrading condescension toward Amy. The deep-seated violence that lies beneath this cultivated form of cruelty comes to the surface when David finally throws his habitual reservation overboard and allows his shocking aggression to burst forth, which is all the more effective for spectators as this is what they expect from the locals. Here Peckinpah expresses the same deeply pessimistic view of civilization that is evident in his Westerns: every man, the film posits, is capable of bestial atrocities when he finds himself in the relevant situation. The observation by some critics that this commentary represents emancipation for David Sumner, placing his eruption in a positive light, seems questionable at best. In the end, David drives through the night with Niles, the supposedly harmless village idiot. "I don't know my way home," says Niles. "That's okay," responds David, "I don't either."

JH

4 Trouble brewing: The village pub in *Straw Dogs* is strikingly reminiscent of the Western saloons in other Peckinpah films.

5 Scandal. The brutal rape scene met with particular outrage—and for Peckinpah, a full-scale offensive from the censors.

6 Home sweet home: David and Amy's lifestyle contrasts strongly with that of the rough and ready villagers.

1971 – USA – 114 MIN.

GENRE

THRILLER

DIRECTOR

ALAN J. PAKULA

SCREENPLAY

ANDY LEWIS, DAVE LEWIS

DIRECTOR OF PHOTOGRAPHY

GORDON WILLIS

EDITING

CARL LERNER

MUSIC

MICHAEL SMALL

PRODUCTION

ALAN J. PAKULA for WARNER BROS.,
GUS PRODUCTIONS

STARRING

JANE FONDA (Bree Daniels), DONALD SUTHERLAND (John Klute),
CHARLES CIOFFI (Peter Cable), ROY SCHEIDER (Frank Ligourin),
DOROTHY TRISTAN (Arlyn Page), RITA GAM (Trina), VIVIAN NATHAN (Psychiatrist),
NATHAN GEORGE (Trask), MORRIS STRASSBERG (Mr. Goldfarb),
BARRY SNIDER (Berger), ROBERT MILLI (Tom Gruneman)

ACADEMY AWARDS 1972

OSCAR for BEST ACTRESS (Jane Fonda)

One man is missing. Two girls lie dead.

jane fonda · donald sutherland

you'd never take her for a call girl

you'd never take him for a cop

in an alan j. pakula production klute

an alan j. pakula production starring jane fonda · donald sutherland in "klute" co-starring charles cioffi · nathan george · dorothy tristan
roy r. scheider · rita gam · music by michael small · written by andy and dave lewis · co-produced by david lange
produced and directed by alan j. pakula · panavision® technicolor® from warner bros., a kinney leisure service

R RESTRICTED Under 17 requires accompanying Parent or Adult Guardian

original soundtrack available on warner bros. records

1

"Tell me, Klute. Did we get you a little? Huh? Just a little bit? Us city folk? The sin, the glitter, the wickedness?"

A man has disappeared without trace... All efforts to pinpoint the whereabouts of upstanding Pennsylvania family man Tom Gruneman (Robert Milli) have led nowhere. When the police declare the investigation closed, private detective and family friend John Klute (Donald Sutherland) takes on the case.

He follows a lead to New York, as evidence suggests that Gruneman wrote obscene letters to call girl Bree Daniels (Jane Fonda) before he vanished. Klute tries to question the woman, but doesn't get very far. Highly suspicious of the snoop, Bree tells him to stick it to himself. Only after Klute taps her phone line and uses snippets of the conversations to pressure her does Bree agree to cooperate. Although she claims to have no recollection of Gruneman, she confides in Klute, telling him about an experience with a violent john—a dumper as she puts it—who might have something to do with a string of anonymous phone calls she has been receiving. Bree admits to being afraid, but finds her anxiety ridiculous. Klute, however, senses that Bree is truly in danger. His hunch is confirmed when one night he notices from inside Bree's apartment that the two of them are being watched.

Paranoia thrillers reached their zenith in the USA of the 70s. Vietnam and Watergate devastated the nation. The malignant state of emergency and the American people's growing distrust of the Nixon administration were magnified in films like Francis Ford Coppola's *The Conversation* (1974), Sydney Pollack's *Three Days of the Condor* (1975) along with Alan J. Pakula's so-called paranoia trilogy, which included *Klute* (1971). *The Parallax View* (1974) and *All the President's Men* (1976).

In *Klute,* Pakula paints a portrait of a relentless, invisible menace. Even during the picture's prolog, the seed of anxiety begins to take root, as the camera reveals a

JANE FONDA Prior to her 1960 screen debut in Joshua Logan's *Tall Story*, Jane Fonda (born December 21, 1937 in New York), daughter of Hollywood legend Henry Fonda, had already worked as a fashion model and theatre actress. She completed her studies at the Lee Strasberg Actor's Studio prior to her film career. Initially, Jane Fonda appeared in a number of romantic comedies. In the mid-60s, the young ingénue went to France—to "discover herself"—where she met her husband Roger Vadim, starring in several of his pictures, most notably *Barbarella: Queen of the Galaxy* (1968). Following her return to the U.S., she garnered her first Academy Award nomination for her performance in Sydney Pollack's *They Shoot Horses, Don't They?* (1969). In 1972, Jane Fonda was recognized with the Best Actress Oscar for her stunning portrayal of a Manhattan call girl in Alan J. Pakula's thriller *Klute* (1971). In the years that followed, she used her fame to support human rights and to get politically involved, for example, against the Vietnam War. Only towards the end of the 1970s did Jane Fonda begin to focus on her film career again, winning her second Best Actress Oscar for her role as a woman who volunteers at the local veterans' hospital in Hal Ashby's *Coming Home* (1978). Ms. Fonda's career took yet another surprising turn in the 1980s, when she started her decade-long reign as the nation's most prominent fitness guru thanks to her best-selling series of workout videos. In 1989, she took a leave of absence from film and married media mogul Ted Turner two years later (they divorced in 2001). Since then, she has appeared in several comedies and TV shows, such as *Grace and Frankie* (2015), and received numerous awards for her lifetime achievement.

2

"Jane Fonda dominates the film from her first to her last appearance. In a brilliant performance that almost bursts the confines of the character she plays, she combines subtle expressiveness with intelligence and feminine self-assurance. Yet she also shows the suffering and uncertainty of a lonely human being." *Stuttgarter Zeitung*

tape recorder picking up the conversation at a serene holiday dinner at the Grunemans. The oppressive atmosphere gains momentum, eventually engulfing the entire film. Surveillance equipment seems to be planted in every crevice, in a private sphere wholly unprotected from unknown predators. The piece's shadowy images, lacking both depth and sharpness, seem to come from a hidden camera. The tinny audio track has a bugged-sounding quality to it, giving us the impression that even life's most intimate moments do not go unobserved. Pakula thus forces his audience into the role of a conscious voyeur, an impression accentuated by frequent switches back and forth between the maniac's diabolical mousetrap and Bree's suffocating frenzy. The audience is left squirming in their seats, gasping as terror encroaches upon them. Pakula's direction suggests that the imminent danger he depicts is more than just a story, but a universal threat that extends far beyond the confines of his film.

1 Fond of Jane: In the early 70s, Jane Fonda was the premier personality among America's female movie stars. She was awarded her first Oscar for her role as call girl Bree Daniels in *Klute*.

2 Not just film partners: Jane Fonda and Donald Sutherland made the most of their fame and worked together to oppose America's military intervention in Vietnam.

3 Getting past their inhibitions (Jane Fonda and Donald Sutherland): *Klute* made a clean break with the clichés of the genre.

3

4 All talk? Bree mistrusts the world around her—and she doesn't find it easy to open up to Klute.

5 A girl about town: The title "Klute" is misleading: Jane Fonda is clearly the central focus of the film. Her performance made Alan J. Pakula's thriller one of the most gripping and sensitive portraits of a woman in 70s cinema.

"This film belongs to Jane Fonda. She portrays a prostitute who is both the classic victim and the captain of her fate." *James Monaco, in: American Film Now*

Klute is, nonetheless, much more than just an example of a masterfully executed, claustrophobic thriller. Pakula's film is also a complex portrait of a woman. Contrary to what one might assume from both the film's title and premise, it is not the investigator who serves as this film's centerpiece but Bree Daniels. This can be attributed, without question, to Jane Fonda's incomparable, Oscar-winning performance. She portrays Bree as a prostitute but avoids the clichés. Neither the moral wreck, nor the hooker with a heart of gold, she is a young woman shielding herself behind a harsh and cynical suit of armor. Alone in the world, she has no illusions about the fickleness and egocentrism of human nature. The wary Bree is a woman full of contradictions, who attempts to assert herself in a hostile, male-dominated society. Her greatest aspiration is to become an actress, claiming that her performance as a call girl already proves that that she ranks among the world's greatest. At the time, in the early days of the so-called New Hollywood, this assertion was no gentle poke at the chauvinist female images dominating the contemporary American cinema. It was nothing less than a slap in the face. JH

5

DIRTY HARRY

1971 – USA – 102 MIN.

GENRE

THRILLER

DIRECTOR

DON SIEGEL

SCREENPLAY

HARRY JULIAN FINK, RITA M. FINK,
DEAN RIESNER

DIRECTOR OF PHOTOGRAPHY

BRUCE SURTEES

EDITING

CARL PINGITORE

MUSIC

LALO SCHIFRIN

PRODUCTION

DON SIEGEL for THE MALPASO COMPANY,
WARNER BROS.

STARRING

CLINT EASTWOOD (“Dirty” Harry Callahan), HARRY GUARDINO (Bressler),
RENI SANTONI (Chico Gonzalez), JOHN VERNON (Mayor),
ANDREW ROBINSON (Scorpio, the Killer), JOHN LARCH (Chief),
JOHN MITCHUM (Frank DiGiorgio), MAE MERCER (Mrs. Russell),
LYN EDGINGTON (Norma), JOSEF SOMMER (Rothko)

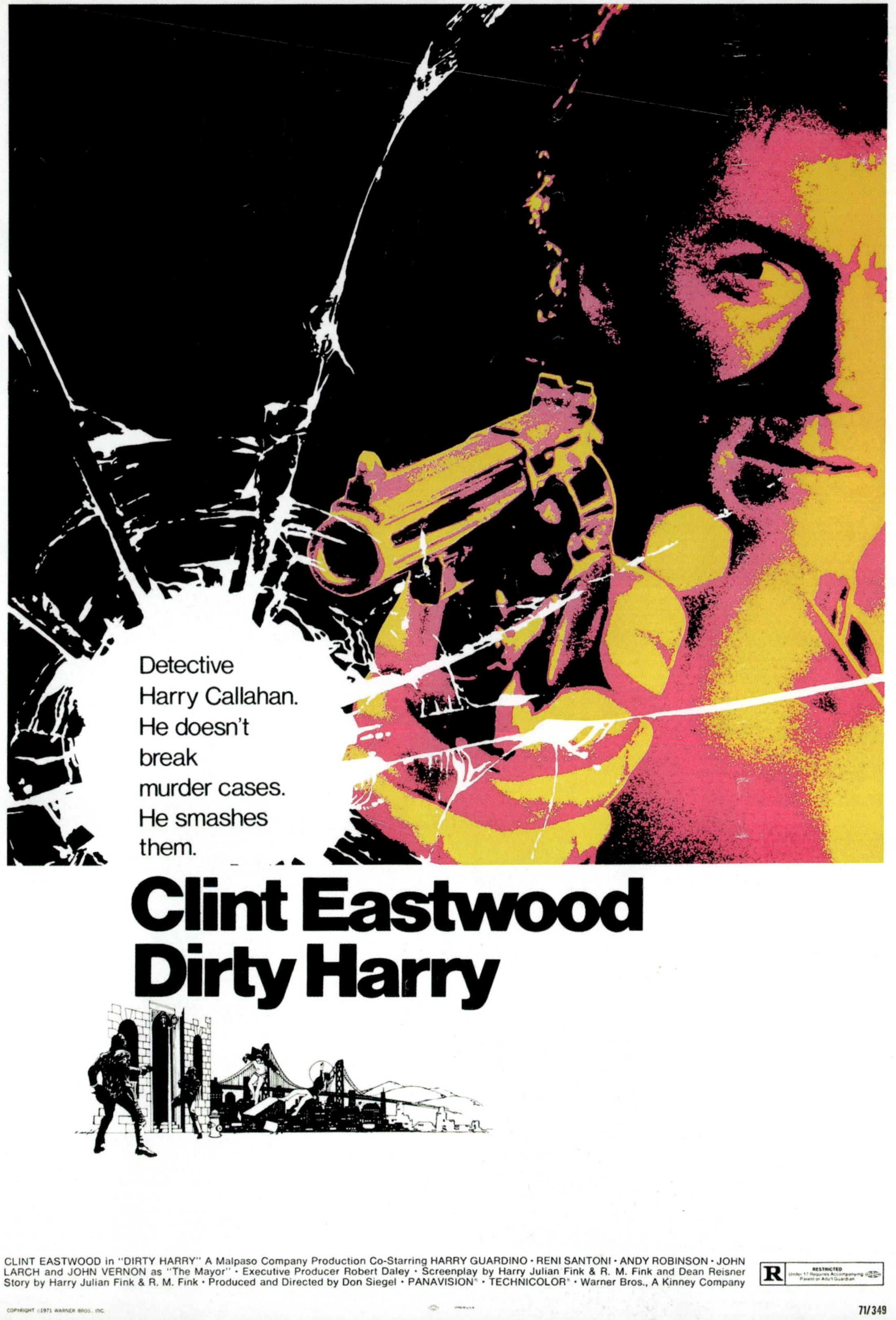

Detective
Harry Callahan.
He doesn't
break
murder cases.
He smashes
them.

Clint Eastwood
Dirty Harry

CLINT EASTWOOD in "DIRTY HARRY" A Malpaso Company Production Co-Starring HARRY GUARDINO · RENI SANTONI · ANDY ROBINSON · JOHN LARCH and JOHN VERNON as "The Mayor" · Executive Producer Robert Daley · Screenplay by Harry Julian Fink & R. M. Fink and Dean Reisner Story by Harry Julian Fink & R. M. Fink · Produced and Directed by Don Siegel · PANAVISION® · TECHNICOLOR® · Warner Bros., A Kinney Company

COPYRIGHT ©1971 WARNER BROS., INC.

71/349

1
ONE WAY

A killer lurks on the rooftops of San Francisco. A young woman becomes his first victim. Sensuously following her movements through his telescopic lens, he watches her rise from her lounge chair on the top of a high-rise across the way and dive elegantly into a pool. The killer lets her swim a few laps, and then squeezes the trigger. The clear water in the light-blue pool turns dark red and the girl momentarily flails about, and then dies in a thick cloud of her own blood.

Some time later, police inspector Harry Callahan (Clint Eastwood) scrutinizes the crime scene from the killer's perspective—clearly a voyeuristic spot. But it is all too apparent that what had once been a pleasure in watching has now become a pleasure in killing. And the killer has just one objective: at the scene of the crime, Callahan finds a note from the mysterious man, who calls himself Scorpio (Andrew Robinson). If he does not receive $100,000 he will continue to kill one person a day—anyone from a "Catholic priest," to a "Nigger." The mayor (John Vernon) wants to agree to the demands. Callahan's advice, however, is to investigate and search for the suspect without further delay. Experience tells him that Scorpio will most definitely kill again—for the sheer fun of it. Callahan's prophecy turns out to be correct. Intensified surveillance of the high-rise buildings, including helicopter sorties, does not stop Scorpio pursuing his murder spree. Soon, Callahan sets a trap for the killer and Scorpio is just a few steps away. But he eludes capture by shooting indiscriminately and killing a police officer.

Scorpio then changes his tactics. He kidnaps a 14-year-old girl, demanding $200,000 in ransom. Callahan takes control of the hand-over and begins a battle

LALO SCHIFRIN Composer and director Lalo Schifrin, born in Buenos Aires in 1932, fundamentally shaped the sound of the 60s and 70s. His themes are immediately recognizable and consistently contemporary. The recognizable melody from *Bullitt* (1968) was used again decades later in a commercial, and the robust title music from the TV series *Mission: Impossible* (1966–1973) was rerecorded and used in 1988 for the new episodes of the series, as well as for the subsequent movie versions with Tom Cruise (1996, 2000). Schifrin's name is closely associated with Clint Eastwood's movies, which made him a regular composer for Don Siegel's police films such as *Coogan's Bluff* (1968) and the *Dirty Harry* series (1971, 1973, 1983, 1988), with the exception of *Dirty Harry III – The Enforcer* (1976). A further classic is Schifrin's musical contribution to the Bruce Lee film *Enter the Dragon* (1973), its gentle grooves and symphonic jazz enriched by influences from the Far East.
Lalo Schifrin is a classically trained conductor. In Buenos Aires he studied with Enrique Barenboim, in Paris with Olivier Messiaen. But the gifted musical scholar fell out of favor with Messiaen because of his nightly appearances in Paris jazz clubs. He did this not only to earn money for his studies, but out of his passion for the music of Thelonious Monk and Art Tatum.
He studied both classical music and jazz simultaneously, and this mixture heavily influenced his later work for the cinema, which in addition to the typical Schifrin sound, also includes chamber music soundtracks like the one from Mark Rydell's D. H. Lawrence adaptation *The Fox* (1967). In 2018, he was awarded an honorary Oscar for his lifetime achievement.

2

against the clock—the girl only has a limited supply of air to breathe. Callahan is able to confront Scorpio in an empty football stadium. The camera pulls back, ascending and allowing the action in the stadium to disappear behind a thick mist. What the audience can only suspect in this dramatic moment is proved true when the district attorney is seen harshly admonishing Callahan. Callahan tortured the suspect in order to find out where the girl was stashed and save her. But he failed: the girl is found dead. And because of Callahan's illegal methods, Scorpio is set free.

Upon his release, Scorpio devises a perfidious strategy to get rid of his stubborn adversary once and for all. He has not yet given up his original plan to blackmail the city for $200,000. This time he seizes a school bus. And Callahan, despite strict orders to the contrary, confronts Scorpio once again.

Dirty Harry was the fourth collaboration between director Don Siegel and Clint Eastwood. In their first project, *Coogan's Bluff* (1968), the two skillfully relocated Eastwood's successful Western image to the modern city. With *Dirty Harry*—a project originally conceived for Frank Sinatra—they elaborated upon the idea. The Eastwood character has since become a man with a history: he was married and lost his wife in an accident. Years of police work hardened him and made him reckless toward both his partners and himself. When he inadvertently stumbles into the middle of a bank robbery, he marches toward the armed culprits with his pistol drawn, the thought of taking

3

1 "The most powerful handgun in the world:" Harry Callahan (Clint Eastwood) in action.

2 Moments later: Dirty Harry trashes the bank robbers' car.

3 Enemy of the people: "Scorpio" (Andrew Robinson) hijacks a school bus and takes passengers hostage.

4 Chico (Reni Santoni) and the man: Harry's new Mexican partner finds that the tight-lipped cop can be one tough nut to crack.

"As suspense craftsmanship, the picture is trim, brutal, and exciting; it was directed in the sleekest style by the veteran urban-action director Don Siegel, and Lalo Schifrin's pulsating, jazzy electronic trickery drives the picture forward." *The New Yorker*

cover not even crossing his mind. Behavior that might seem heroic on Main Street in a Western here indicates a latent suicidal tendency.

Again and again, Siegel allows the ambivalence of the character to come to the fore, revealing a basic similarity with the rampant killer Scorpio: both indulge in voyeurism. Harry can't turn his eyes away when he observes a couple playing around amorously. His duty offers him a clandestine view: from above the high rises, from the helicopter, and from the police car that crawls the city streets. This underlying similarity to the killer allows him to get closer and closer to the criminal, but scares him deeply. When he throws away his badge in the end, we could put it down to frustration with bureaucracy. But perhaps it's also a rousing moment of self-perception.

HK

SILENT RUNNING

1971 – USA – 89 MIN.

GENRE

SCIENCE FICTION

DIRECTOR

DOUGLAS TRUMBULL

SCREENPLAY

DERIC WASHBURN, MICHAEL CIMINO,
STEVEN BOCHCO

DIRECTOR OF PHOTOGRAPHY

CHARLES F. WHEELER

EDITING

AARON STELL

MUSIC

PETER SCHICKELE, JOAN BAEZ (Songs)

PRODUCTION

MICHAEL GRUSKOFF, DOUGLAS TRUMBULL for
MICHAEL GRUSKOFF PRODUCTIONS, UNIVERSAL PICTURES

STARRING

BRUCE DERN (Freeman Lowell), CLIFF POTTS (John Keenan),
RON RIFKIN (Marty Barker), JESSE VINT (Andy Wolf),
CHERYL SPARKS (Drone 1 / Dewey),
MARK PERSONS (Drone 2 / Huey), STEVE BROWN (Drone)

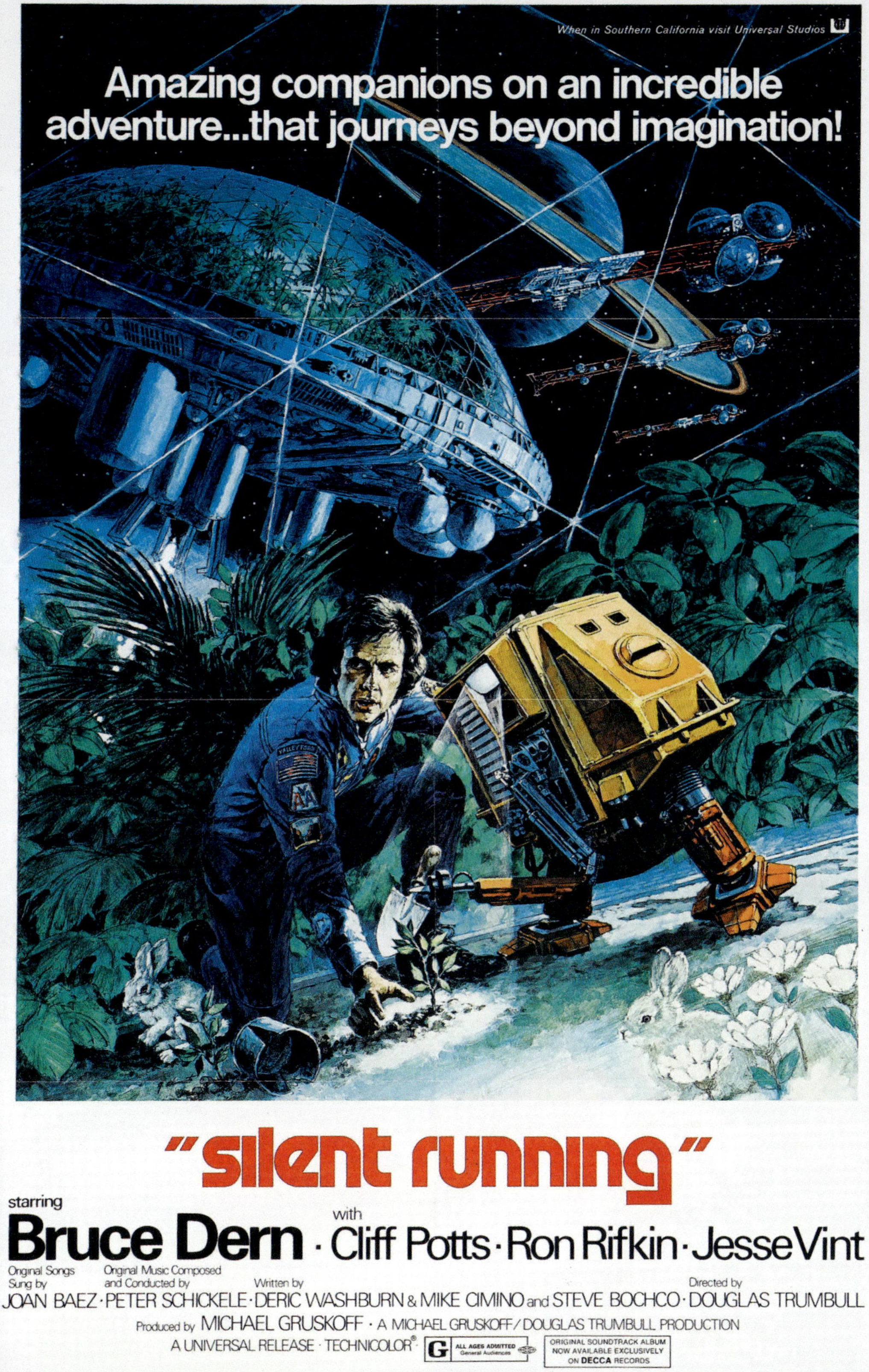

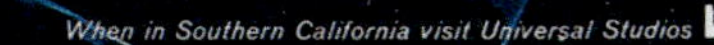

When in Southern California visit Universal Studios
Amazing companions on an incredible adventure...that journeys beyond imagination!
"silent running"
starring
Bruce Dern
with
Cliff Potts · Ron Rifkin · Jesse Vint
Original Songs Sung by JOAN BAEZ
Original Music Composed and Conducted by PETER SCHICKELE
Written by DERIC WASHBURN & MIKE CIMINO and STEVE BOCHCO
Directed by DOUGLAS TRUMBULL
Produced by MICHAEL GRUSKOFF · A MICHAEL GRUSKOFF / DOUGLAS TRUMBULL PRODUCTION
A UNIVERSAL RELEASE · TECHNICOLOR®
G ALL AGES ADMITTED General Audiences
ORIGINAL SOUNDTRACK ALBUM NOW AVAILABLE EXCLUSIVELY ON DECCA RECORDS

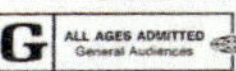

1

In March, 2001, in Cornwall, England, the "Eden Project" came into being: eight greenhouses standing in the middle of a stony landscape almost destroyed by mining. Combined, they are as big as 35 football fields and look like giant golf balls. Thousands of exotic plants grow underneath a skin of air cushions that are stretched into a steel construction. It is no coincidence that the futuristic aesthetic of these hot houses recalls a cult film of the 1970s. Architect Nicholas Grimshaw based his design on the contrast between nature and technology that is the subject of Douglas Trumbull's *Silent Running*.

Trumbull's film is set in 2008. After a nuclear catastrophe, the Earth is devoid of plants and animals. All that could be saved was shot into space and is on its way to the planet Saturn. The "Valley Forge" floats in space like a kind of Noah's Ark. It is one of numerous spaceships that serve as greenhouses—a literal Garden of Eden with lush plants and cascading waterfalls in which deer, rabbits,

BRUCE DERN American actor Bruce Dern was born on June 4, 1936 in Chicago, Illinois. Dern, who comes from a family of politicians and wealthy businessmen, dropped out of the University of Pennsylvania, to the displeasure of his parents, to study at Lee Strasberg's Actors Studio in New York. During his acting debut on Broadway in 1960, he was discovered by Elia Kazan and given a role in *Wild River* (1960). After playing a psychopath in an episode of Alfred Hitchcock's television series *The Alfred Hitchcock Hour* (1962–65), he was typecast as a villain for years to come, in films like *Marnie* (1964) and *The Wild Angels* (1966).

Only in the 70s was Dern able to establish himself as a character actor. Many of the films Bruce Dern appeared in over the course of his 40-plus years in the business are considered classics today. The long list includes *They Shoot Horses, Don't They?* (1969, Director: Sydney Pollack), *The Great Gatsby* (1974, Director: Jack Clayton), *Black Sunday* (1977, Director: John Frankenheimer), and *Coming Home* (1978, Director: Hal Ashby). Dern is married to Andrea Beckett, his third marriage. His daughter, Laura Dern, was born of his second marriage (1960–69) to the actress Diane Ladd. Even at over 80 years old, he continues to appear in film and TV productions.

1 Hug a tree: Galactic botanist Freeman Lowell's (Bruce Dern) love for nature can be smothering to humans …

2 Space, the final frontier: The model of the Valley Forge space cruiser included everything but actual jet propulsion. Compiled of wood, steel and plastic, the "compact" ship measured in at 60 feet.

3 Many hands make light work: Trumball kept production costs down by "employing" student interns to work on the special effects.

4 All heart: The robots prove to be Lowell's most cherished playmates and able guardians of the natural world.

"Lowell is an old-fashioned, unreconstructed plant-freak, an organic food loon who keeps The Conservationist's Pledge pasted next to his bunk." *The New York Times*

turtles, and frogs can live without worry. Astro-botanist Freeman Lowell (Bruce Dern) and his crew colleagues make sure that the flora and fauna are well maintained and preserved until a time when suitable living conditions prevail once more on planet Earth.

Freeman Lowell longs for the news that the "Valley Forge" can finally return to Earth. But an unexpected order comes: the experiment is to be terminated, the artificial biospheres are to be destroyed and the man-made paradise abandoned. When ordered to destroy his beloved forests, Freeman goes mad. He kills his colleagues and attempts to flee in the spaceship.

Silent Running was Douglas Trumbull's directorial debut. He made his entrance into film a few years earlier with Stanley Kubrick's *2001: A Space Odyssey* (1968), to whose special effects he made a fundamental contribution. It is no coincidence that *Silent Running* seems like a direct descendant of Kubrick's *2001*. It takes place seven years later and, as in *2001*, the protagonist finds himself alone on a spaceship without humans, surrounded by machines. But in contrast to the cool, collected Bowman of *2001*, Lowell is fragile and fallible, just like the small robots, Huey, Dewey, and Louie, who are more reminiscent of a Disney film than of Kubrick's super-computer Hal. After Freeman reprograms them, they become almost human: not only can they play poker, they are also able to look after the Garden Eden entirely by themselves. All they lack is the ability to feel.

Michael Cimino and Steven Bochco joined Deric Washburn in producing the film's screenplay. The three authors concentrated entirely on their protagonist and the other characters remain mere sketches, with just enough contours to help emphasize Lowell's humanity.

Trumbull used the science fiction genre to call attention to contemporary ecological and social problems. This connects him with other films from the same period like Richard Fleischer's *Soylent Green* (1973) and Michael Campus' *ZPG – Zero Population Growth* (1972). But in contrast to these films, the "spaceship Earth" from *Silent Running* has stood the test of time—not only in the hearts of its fans, but also as an ecological theme park in a man-made crater on the coast of Cornwall. APO

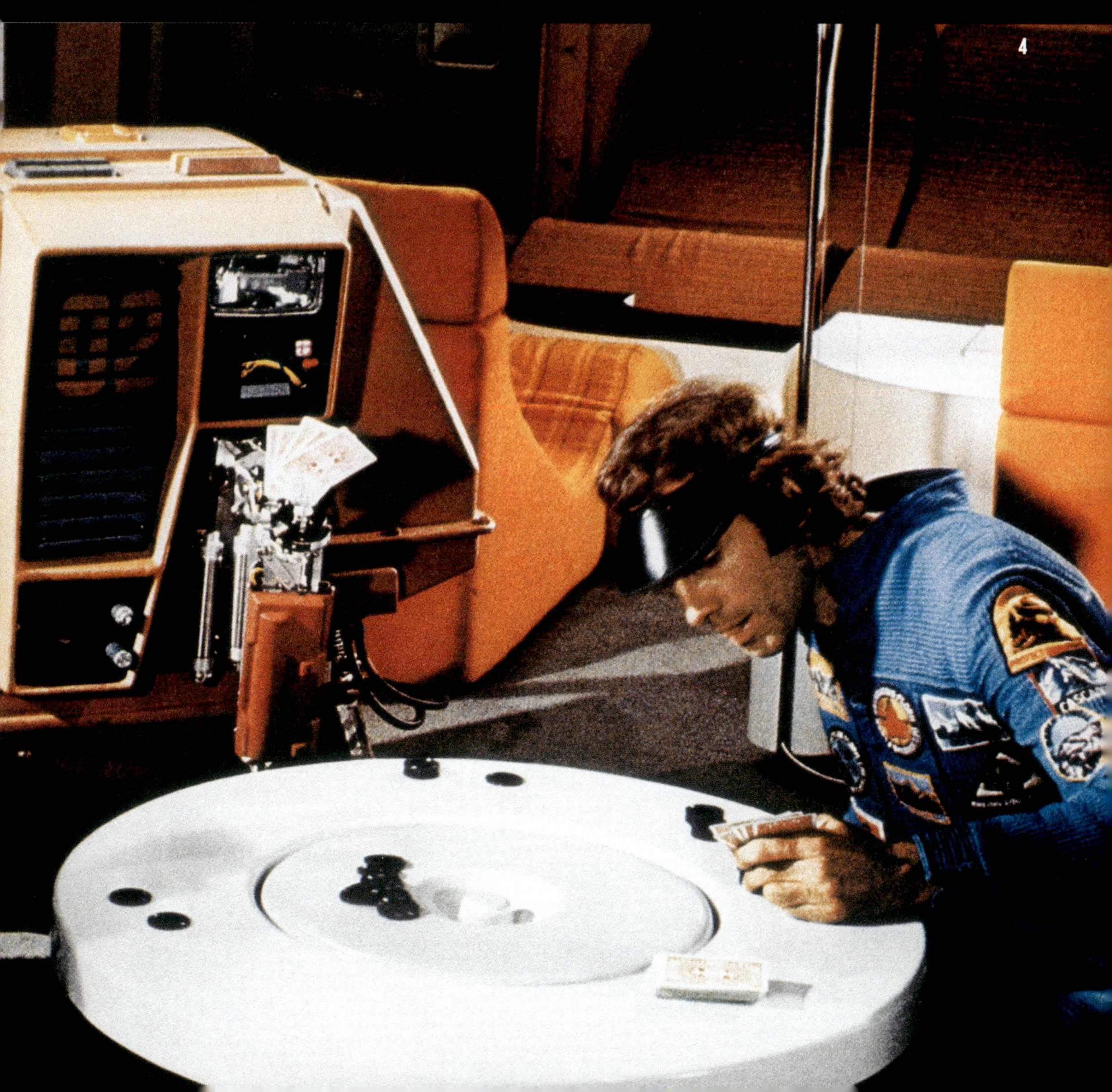

SHAFT

1971 – USA – 100 MIN.

GENRE

DETECTIVE FILM, THRILLER

DIRECTOR

GORDON PARKS

SCREENPLAY

ERNEST TIDYMAN, JOHN D. F. BLACK,
based on the novel of the same name by ERNEST TIDYMAN

DIRECTOR OF PHOTOGRAPHY

URS FURRER

EDITING

HUGH A. ROBERTSON

MUSIC

ISAAC HAYES

PRODUCTION

JOEL FREEMAN for SHAFT PRODUCTIONS LTD., MGM

STARRING

RICHARD ROUNDTREE (John Shaft), MOSES GUNN (Bumpy Jonas),
CHARLES CIOFFI (Vic Androzzi), CHRISTOPHER ST. JOHN (Ben Buford),
GWENN MITCHELL (Ellie Moore), LAWRENCE PRESSMAN (Sergeant Tom Hannon),
VICTOR ARNOLD (Charlie), SHERRI BREWER (Marcy), REX ROBBINS (Rollie),
CAMILLE YARBROUGH (Diana Greene)

ACADEMY AWARDS 1972

OSCAR for BEST SONG: “THEME FROM SHAFT” (Isaac Hayes)

The mob wanted
Harlem back.
They got Shaft...
up to here.
SHAFT
SHAFT's his name. SHAFT's his game.
METRO-GOLDWYN-MAYER Presents "SHAFT" Starring RICHARD ROUNDTREE · Co-Starring MOSES GUNN
Screenplay by ERNEST TIDYMAN and JOHN D. F. BLACK · Based upon the novel by ERNEST TIDYMAN
Music by ISAAC HAYES · Produced by JOEL FREEMAN · Directed by GORDON PARKS · METROCOLOR
R
RESTRICTED
MGM

1

"He's a complicated man, no one understands him but his woman."

Now and again, a film comes along that strikes the nerve of its age with instinctive certainty. *Shaft*, developed as a technically simple, low-budget project with neither expensive stars nor a renowned director, became the surprise hit of 1971 and saved MGM Studios from looming bankruptcy. With *Shaft*, the multi-talented Gordon Parks Sr., a photographer, novelist, composer, and director, eveloped a unique language of images still referred to in the iconography of today's rap videos. And John Shaft (Richard Roundtree) became the embodiment of black selfconfidence—at least for black males.

The first images of the film, underscored by Isaac Hayes' explosively sizzling title theme, immediately signal a character who follows his own rules. The camera aptly captures John Shaft as he emerges from a subway station—the depths of the underworld in more ways than one—and enters the lively scenery in and around New York's Times Square. He weaves through the traffic, lean, black, and self-confident. The themes of the opening sequence are sustained—protagonist John Shaft does not knuckle under to anyone, whether white cops or black drug gangsters. He sympathizes with a militant black organization and refuses to tolerate demands made on him. He cannot be assigned to any form of male organization, instead enjoying the adulation of women, a privilege he savors to its fullest extent. But his sensually charged relationships have no master-slave dimension to them.

Even Bumpy Jonas (Moses Gunn), the black underworld boss who controls Harlem, must accept that Shaft is a truly independent character; one of Bumpy's handymen who is sent out with an associate to escort Shaft back to his boss doesn't survive the incursion. But Bumpy wants to avoid a quarrel at all costs, as he is pursuing a personal matter. Accordingly, he makes an exception to the norm, visiting Shaft in his office. He even sheds a few crocodile tears when he reveals that his daughter Marcy (Sherri Brewer) has been kidnapped. Shaft is to bring her back safely—and money is no object.

ISAAC HAYES The suspense-filled title track, perfectly fitting John Shaft's first appearance in the film (*Shaft*, 1971), immediately caught audiences in its spell. It was the work of Isaac Hayes, one of the most reliable hit makers of the preceding decade. In collaboration with songwriter David Porter, the autodidact wrote and produced a handful of successful songs for the Memphis-based Stax-Volt label, including "Soul Man," "Hold On, I'm Coming," "B-A-B-Y," and many more. Most of the tunes were performed by the soul duo Sam & Dave.

Only in 1967 did Hayes (1942–2008) try his luck as a solo artist, and he soon created his own brand of symphonic soul, with a grand orchestra and an eccentric stage show. This was the determining sound of the double album *Shaft* soundtrack. His enigmatic, physically driven appearances destined Hayes for a film career. Initially he appeared in *Shaft*-inspired "Blaxploitation" films like Duccio Tessari's *Three Tough Guys* (*Uomini duri*, 1973), and Jonathan Kaplan's *Truck Turner* (1974), naturally composing the music for the soundtracks as well. In later years, he appeared in films like John Carpenter's *Escape from New York* (1981) and Keenan Ivory Wayans' "Blaxploitation" parody, *I'm Gonna Git You Sucka* (1988), among several others. He made a guest appearance in the television series *The Rockford Files* (1974–1980) in 1977 with his occasional musical partner, Dionne Warwick.

Shaft is the first picture to show a black man who leads a life free of racial torment. He is black and proud of it, but not obsessed with it ...”

ESSENCE magazine

1 Neighborhood watch: Ben Buford (Christopher St. John), leader of a black gang, supports Shaft in his investigations.

2 Movin’ in on his turf: Bumpy Jonas (Moses Gunn) is king of the Harlem underworld—and white gangsters want what he’s got.

3 Solid as a rock: John Shaft (Richard Roundtree) is his own man, and he won't knuckle under to the cops or the gangsters.

4 Outsourcing: The syndicate has flown in killers from elsewhere—and they take their work seriously.

Shaft's investigations take him all through Harlem, through the milieu of hobos, pickpockets, and small-time crooks. He is searching for Ben Buford (Christopher St. John), an earlier companion who is now the leader of a militant civil rights group. Shaft eventually meets him at a conspiratorial gathering. But their conversation is interrupted by an arson attack in which most of Ben's men are killed. Shaft pulls Buford from the danger zone and brings him to safety at a friend's house. It soon becomes clear that the Mafia is behind the attack, as well as the kidnapping, which was carried out in an attempt to force Bumpy from his territory. Shaft demands financial retribution from Bumpy for the death of Ben's men, since he withheld the genuine background to the kidnapping from him. Bumpy pays up and Ben agrees to aid Shaft in the liberation mission.

Marcy is holed up in a small hotel guarded by numerous thugs. Shaft comes up with a spectacular rescue plan: while Ben's men act as hotel personnel and neutralize the guards, he will let himself down from the roof with a rope and jump through the closed window, directly into the gangsters' room.

Shaft is driven by the visual talents of long-time *Life* photographer, Gordon Parks, whose son Gordon Parks Jr. also delivered a black cinema sensation with *Super Fly* (1972) before dying in 1979 in a plane crash. With cool images from wintry New York, specifically the sequences of Harlem at night, Parks Sr. gave the film an almost documentary-like veneer. This partially harsh realism is intensified by Isaac Hayes' soundtrack, which ranges from rebellious funk to atmospheric ballads. Just like the film, the theme song also had a sequel: Isaac Hayes' band, the Bar-Kays recorded the piece "The Son of Shaft," which was used in the concert film *Wattstax* (1972).

HK

A CLOCKWORK ORANGE

1971 – GREAT BRITAIN – 137 MIN.

GENRE

LITERARY ADAPTATION, THRILLER

DIRECTOR

STANLEY KUBRICK

SCREENPLAY

STANLEY KUBRICK, based on the novel of the same name by ANTHONY BURGESS

DIRECTOR OF PHOTOGRAPHY

JOHN ALCOTT

EDITING

BILL BUTLER

MUSIC

WALTER CARLOS

PRODUCTION

STANLEY KUBRICK for POLARIS PRODUCTIONS, HAWK FILMS LTD., WARNER BROS.

STARRING

MALCOLM MCDOWELL (Alex), PATRICK MAGEE (Frank Alexander), MICHAEL BATES (Chief Guard Barnes), WARREN CLARKE (Dim), JOHN CLIVE (Stage Actor), PAUL FARRELL (Tramp), ADRIENNE CORRI (Mrs. Alexander), CARL DUERING (Doktor Brodsky), CLIVE FRANCIS (Joe), MICHAEL GOVER (Prison Governor), MIRIAM KARLIN (Miss Weatherly)

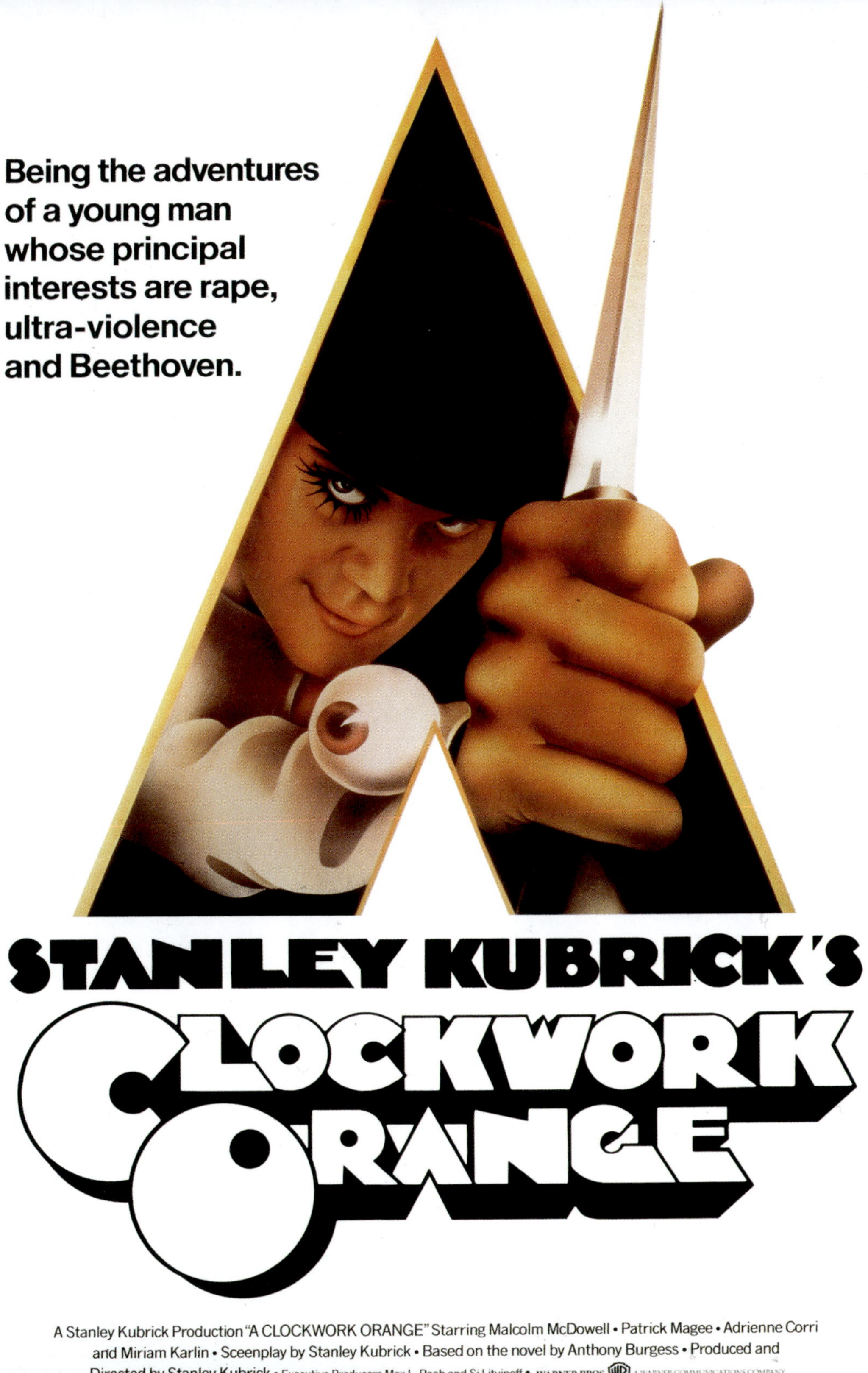

Being the adventures
of a young man
whose principal
interests are rape,
ultra-violence
and Beethoven.

STANLEY KUBRICK'S

A Stanley Kubrick Production "A CLOCKWORK ORANGE" Starring Malcolm McDowell • Patrick Magee • Adrienne Corri and Miriam Karlin • Sceenplay by Stanley Kubrick • Based on the novel by Anthony Burgess • Produced and Directed by Stanley Kubrick • Executive Producers Max L. Raab and Si Litvinoff • WARNER BROS WB A WARNER COMMUNICATIONS COMPANY

1

"Viddy well, little brother, viddy well."

A Clockwork Orange was banned in England until Stanley Kubrick's death in 1999. The director himself had withdrawn it in 1974, and the motivation for his self-censorship remains obscure. Perhaps he had simply grown tired of being blamed for glorifying violence, but it's possible he had actually been threatened. This is not as outlandish a suggestion as it may seem, for the film had occasioned a great deal of heated debate. No film before *A Clockwork Orange* had depicted violence in such an aestheticized manner, and with such a laconic refusal to justify itself. The critics accused Kubrick not merely of fomenting an appetite for extreme brutality, but of failing to challenge or even question that appetite. The violence on screen, they felt, was crying out to be imitated in real life. But Kubrick is no moralist, and no psychologist either; he doesn't explain what he shows. The audience is forced to decide for itself what it wants to see in his film, and the price we pay for this freedom includes accepting the risk that Nazi skinheads will love it.

Black bowler and bovver boots, white shirt and pants, tastefully topped off with an eyecatching, fortified codpiece: this is the uniform of Alex (Malcolm McDowell) and his Droogs, a teenage gang in constant search of some real "horrorshow" action. On a particularly enjoyable night out, they start off with a few drinks in the Korova Milkbar before going on to kick a drunken bum to pulp, indulge in a

MALCOLM MCDOWELL *A Clockwork Orange* (1971) would not have been made without him. For Stanley Kubrick, Alex simply had to be Malcolm McDowell. At that time, the 27-year-old had almost nothing to show for himself. He had just made his very first major film, the impressive *If...* (1968), set in an English boarding school and directed by Lindsay Anderson. But Kubrick was convinced of the qualities of the young, unknown actor, for he saw in him the human being in a natural state. And so Malcolm McDowell became a star. His instant success was also a kind a curse, for his face came to stand for everything evil, incalculable and dangerous, and he has rarely been permitted to play anything but the villain.
Born in Leeds in 1943, McDowell worked as a coffee salesman before going to drama school in London. Later, he acted with the Royal Shakespeare Company. After *A Clockwork Orange*, he went on to make two more films with Lindsay Anderson, both of them intelligent satires: *O Lucky Man!* (1973) and *Britannia Hospital* (1982). In 1979, he caused another stir, this time as the notorious dictator in Tinto Brass' controversial *Caligula*. He then disappeared from view, showing up almost only in B-movies, although he did have some interesting supporting roles in movies such as Paul Schrader's *Cat People* (1982). In the 90s, however, MacDowell was a very busy man, making around 50 appearances in movies or TV series, for example in *Star Trek: Generations* (1994), where he faced off Captains Kirk and Picard, and in Paul McGuigan's *Gangster No.1* (2000).

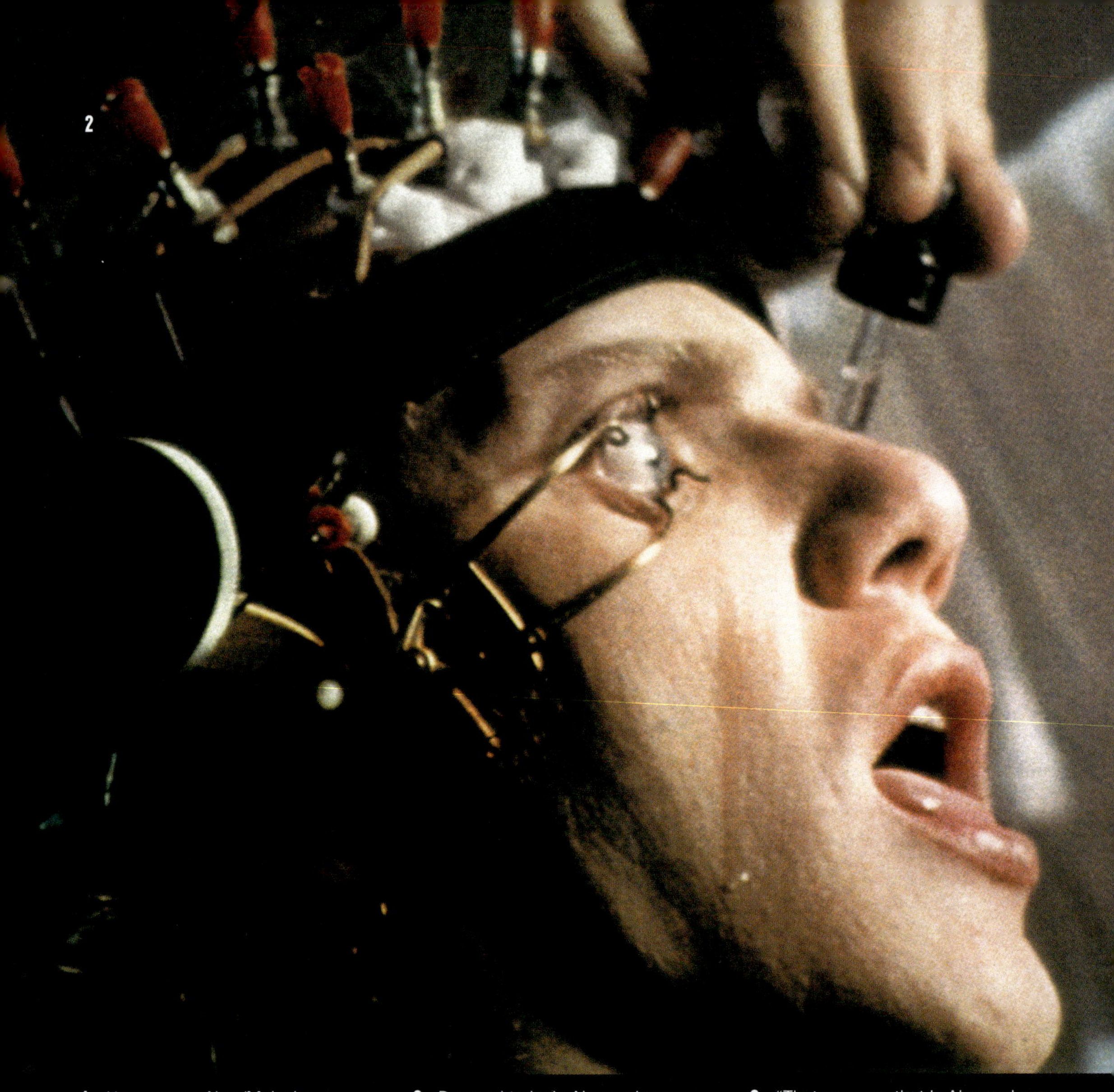

2

1 Here comes Alex (Malcolm McDowell)—the personification of brutality.

2 Doomed to look: Alex undergoes the Ludovico therapy.

3 "That was me, that is Alex and my three droogs, that is Pete, Georgie and Dim. And we sat in the Korova Milkbar, trying to make up our razudoks what to do with the evening."

"In my opinion, Kubrick has made a movie that exploits only the mystery and variety of human conduct. And because it refuses to use the emotions conventionally, demanding instead that we keep a constant, intellectual grip on things, it's a most unusual—and disorienting—movie experience." *The New York Times* rumble with a rival gang, and play "road hogs" in a stolen car. Having warmed up, they proceed to break into the country house of a successful author and take turns at raping his wife, making very sure that the elderly writer—bound and gagged—gets a first-class view of her lengthy ordeal. Back at the bar, "feeling a bit shagged and fagged and fashed," they chill out with a "moloko plus" (milk with a little something added) before heading "bedways."

It's not so much the brutality that makes *A Clockwork Orange* such a haunting experience: it's the choreography. Alex above all, adoring fan of Ludwig Van, celebrates and savors his own "appearances" like works of performance art. In the writer's villa, he parodies Gene Kelly in "Singin' In The Rain," keeping time to the music with a series of kicks to his victim's guts. In contrast to his three mates, who expect to pick up some booty on their raids, he has little interest in money. To show them who's "Master and Leader," he beats them up. This will turn out to be a fateful difference of opinion. For later, when Alex inadvertently kills a woman with an *objet d'art* (a giant phallus), his disgruntled and mutinous droogs smash a bottle in his face and leave him to be found by the police. He is sentenced to 14 years in jail, but thanks to a new resocialization program and a revolutionary therapeutic technique, he is granted an early release. From now on, Alex will be violently sick whenever he's tempted to indulge in "a bit of the old ultra-violence." But though he can't hurt a fly, his past is inescapable: the world is full of people who suffered under his rule, and who will now exact revenge on their helpless ex-tormentor.

A Clockwork Orange is a complex discourse on the connections between violence, aesthetics and the media. The film gives no answers, it merely asks questions, and it calls some assumptions into doubt: for example, that violence in the cinema will inevitably lead to violence in the world. Alex's therapy consists of forced viewings of brutal films. The longer he's bound to his seat with his eyes propped open, the worse he feels—an effect reinforced by the drug he's been given. Alex the Doer is transformed into Alex the Watcher. For the former hoodlum, it's a terrible torture; for the average moviegoer, it's a regular delight: to become a mere seeing eye, with no obligation to act; to watch, entranced, happily "glued to the seat." Kubrick almost literally pulls the audience into

4 "A truly Satanic cinematic satire, made with almost unimaginable perfection," said *Der Spiegel*. In this scene, Kubrick himself operated the hand-held camera.

5 The writer Alexander (Patrick Magee) is a victim of Alex and his droogs. But he'll wreak his revenge.

6 Pop art: Alex batters a woman to death with a giant phallus.

the film. Alex often looks straight into the camera, apparently addressing the spectators. Before he rapes the writer's wife, he kneels down before her on the floor: "Viddy well," he says to the captive woman, and to the captivated audience in the argot of the droogs: "take a good look." The real scandal of *A Clockwork Orange* is that we catch ourselves looking forward with excitement to whatever is going to come next. It's not what Kubrick shows us that shocks, but how we react as spectators, fascinated by a masterly and unforgettable film.

NM

"Objectively, it has to be said that there has seldom been a film of such assured technical brilliance" *Der Tagesspiegel*

6

THE FRENCH CONNECTION

1971 – USA – 104 MIN.

GENRE

POLICE FILM

DIRECTOR

WILLIAM FRIEDKIN

SCREENPLAY

ERNEST TIDYMAN,
based on a work of non-fiction by ROBIN MOORE

DIRECTOR OF PHOTOGRAPHY

OWEN ROIZMAN

EDITING

GERALD B. GREENBERG

MUSIC

DON ELLIS

PRODUCTION

PHILIP D'ANTONI for D'ANTONI PRODUCTIONS,
20TH CENTURY FOX FILM CORPORATION

STARRING

GENE HACKMAN (Detective Jimmy "Popeye" Doyle),
ROY SCHEIDER (Detective Buddy "Cloudy" Russo), FERNANDO REY (Alain Charnier),
TONY LO BIANCO (Sal Boca), MARCEL BOZZUFFI (Pierre Nicoli),
FRÉDÉRIC DE PASQUALE (Henri Devereaux), BILL HICKMAN (Bill Mulderig),
ANN REBBOT (Mrs. Marie Charnier), HAROLD GARY (Joel Weinstock),
ARLENE FARBER (Angie Boca), EDDIE EGAN (Commander Walt Simonson),
SONNY GROSSO (Bill Klein)

ACADEMY AWARDS 1972

OSCARS for BEST PICTURE (Philip D'Antoni),
BEST DIRECTOR (William Friedkin),
BEST ACTOR (Gene Hackman),
BEST ADAPTED SCREENPLAY (Ernest Tidyman),
and BEST FILM EDITING (Gerald B. Greenberg)

A $32,000,000 CHASE TURNS INTO THE AMERICAN THRILLER OF THE YEAR!

THE FRENCH CONNECTION

20TH CENTURY-FOX PRESENTS "THE FRENCH CONNECTION" A PHILIP D'ANTONI PRODUCTION STARRING GENE HACKMAN
FERNANDO REY ROY SCHEIDER TONY LO BIANCO MARCEL BOZZUFFI DIRECTED BY WILLIAM FRIEDKIN
PRODUCED BY PHILIP D'ANTONI ASSOCIATE PRODUCER KENNETH UTT EXECUTIVE PRODUCER G.DAVID SCHINE SCREENPLAY BY ERNEST TIDYMAN
MUSIC COMPOSED AND CONDUCTED BY DON ELLIS COLOR BY DE LUXE®

1

It's like a desert full of junkies out there!

"Today's world will brand him a racist," said director William Friedkin of *The French Connection's* singleminded protagonist, Jimmy "Popeye" Doyle (Gene Hackman). As it turned out, the Academy of Motion Picture Arts and Sciences was not only impressed with the then unknown Hackman, honoring his performance with an Oscar, but with the provocative Friedkin himself (*The Exorcist,* 1973). *The French Connection* swept the major categories of that year's award ceremonies, taking a total of five accolades, and making the then 32-year-old Friedkin the youngest person in Academy Award history to receive the Best Director Oscar, a distinction he still holds.

Even without a female lead in its cast, everything magically clicked into place for this picture. As the posters rightly said of its hero, "Doyle is bad news but a good cop." The role itself was based on New York police officer Eddie Egan, a detective in the narcotics bureau, whom the film promotes to Division Commander. In 1962, Egan and his partner Sonny Grosso (the Buddy Russo character played by Roy Scheider) stumbled onto the trail of an astounding 112-pound heroin sale and busted the deal after weeks of fieldwork. With this landmark victory in law enforcement *The French Connection's* story was born.

Hanging out at an Eastside bar after work, "Popeye" and "Cloudy" notice suspiciously large sums of money being flashed by crooked playboy Sal Boca (Tony Lo Bianco) and on a long shot decide to tail him through the icy winter night. At about 7 o'clock in the morning, they witness a drug drop at a corner store that soon puts them in hot pursuit of French drug boss Alain Charnier (Fernando Rey). With the help of French actor Henri Devereaux (Frédéric de Pasquale), Charnier intends to flood the practically bone dry New York drug market—a plan Doyle and Russo will stop at nothing to foil.

No one is willing to believe the allegations of the two cops and with good reason. Not only does the fanatic Doyle have a reputation that precedes him among the city's scum, but his dubious crime-fighting methods have also

RUNNING ON EMPTY—THE BIG SCREEN CHASE Movies are movement by definition. It is therefore only fitting that the so-called "chase" is one of the most beloved silver screen phenomena. Several films throughout cinematic history from *M* (1931), *The Sugarland Express* (1974) to *The Fugitive* (1993) and beyond are basically tributes to this device. The chase can be born out of escape, as in the case of *Vanishing Point* (1970), and quickly take the guise of a road movie. They seldom take place without the enlistment of a motor vehicle and often serve as the climax of thrillers and detective capers like *Bullitt* (1968), *The French Connection* (1971) and *To Live and Die in L. A.* (1985). Walter Hill's 1978 movie *The Driver* is in fact a non-stop car chase from start to finish.

Over time, the four-wheel hunt eventually proved most suitable for TV crime series *à la Starsky & Hutch* (1975–79) or *Miami Vice* (1984–89). It did, however, continue to thrive in science-fiction films and space odysseys. One need only be vaguely familiar with the *Star Wars* pictures (1977, 1980, 1983, 1999, 2002, 2005, 2015, 2016) to realize that they often consist of car chases transplanted into the outer reaches of the universe. Also worthy of mention are variations on the traditional chase like plane vs. pedestrian as in *North by Northwest* (1959), or pedestrian vs. motor scooter as in *Diva* (1980), or even pedestrian and planes vs. locomotives as in *Silver Streak* (1976). Irrespective of the means of transport, the characters involved are often only loosely linked to the chase venue as far as the plot is concerned. It also seems to be less significant whether the quarry is caught than how well one can negotiate and command the terrain itself. Who is better at dealing with the given physical elements and recognizing the means of narrow escape? One rule almost always holds true, irrespective of plot detail: those who are chased are usually the chasers themselves.

2

tarnished his name among fellow officers and superiors. This, however, all proves of no consequence when the two detectives locate Devereaux's car, which seems to be peculiarly overweight ...

Despite or because of his do-or-die work ethic, the Popeye Doyle character presents a striking alternative to the orthodox police officer. He is cynical, brutal and utterly impetuous. In his fervor, he has been known to wage personal wars against corruption, even sacrificing the life of a fellow cop in the process.

In the spirit of Egan and Grosso's round the clock shadowing, director Friedkin relentlessly accompanied these two great policemen on their beat for several weeks. The dialog of the two leading actors stems in part from genuine cop conversations and slang. Even the legendary line, "Did you ever pick your feet in Poughkeepsie?" were the words the real-life Egan uttered during his interrogation to get the suspect to give himself away.

Such fastidious details made for one of the bleakest, most deliciously pessimistic police capers of all time. The shoot took place on location during the harsh New York winter, forcing both cast and crew to battle against often subzero temperatures. Much of the energy that sparks the film to life is the result of brilliant improvisation. Cinematographer Owen Roizman went to great lengths to ensure that the film would look 100% realistic and have an almost

3

4

1 Gene Hackman's Popeye Doyle is a bull on a rampage, whose ruthless and unconventional methods aggravate cops and underworld kings alike.

2 Tough as nails: with a bit of persistence and sheer luck, the two cops pick up on the trail of the drugs ring.

3 Doyle's partner Buddy Russo (Roy Scheider) is his last loyal ally. Both characters were based on real-life policemen.

4 No thinking cap, no dice: Popeye Doyle seems naked without his pork-pie hat.

5 The law is down and dirty, while evil smells like a rose.

"If you start counting 'movie moments' in *The French Connection*, you'll have to stop by about number eight—it's simply impossible to keep up."

steadycam

5

6

documentary feel. Actors and camera crew regularly rehearsed separately from one another to give the visuals an added sense of naturalism. The result is that the camera often seems to have been in the right place at the right time by pure coincidence.

To make the sequence underneath the tracks of the elevated train as convincing as possible (a scene many still consider the greatest cinematic car chase of all time), Friedkin and his team decided to violate traffic laws rather than prearrange to have the street blocked off. Thus the 90-mph visuals caught on film were actually shot in

"Many things I experienced close up as a child went into *The French Connection*. I knew how policemen deal with one another." *William Friedkin*

7

6 The gangster (Fernando Rey) and his henchman (Marcel Bozzuffi) check out the lie of the land.

7 Stopped short: After the obligatory showdown, director William Friedkin surprises his audience with an abrupt ending.

8 Huffing and puffing: One of the most spectacular chases in film history leaves Doyle *a bout de souffle*. The words on the steps show Friedkin's instinct for irony.

the middle of usual city traffic. Friedkin's ballsy bit of gambling certainly paid off, undeniably one-upping the classic chase scene in *Bullitt* (1968) with Steve McQueen, which had held the "all time best" title before *The French Connection* hit the screen. While the film can still pride itself on the effectiveness of its intentionally raw look—the result of painstaking efforts to wipe all traces of artistry from the visuals—the piece surprisingly ends with an almost surreal sequence. We watch as a forlorn Doyle stumbles aimlessly into the darkness, until he disappears completely. A lone shot is suddenly heard, but we are left with no answers as to who plugged whom or why. It is an intriguingly obscure conclusion that even goes unexplained in the 1975 John Frankenheimer sequel *The French Connection II*, a piece that would prove to be yet another undisputed milestone in police drama. SH

ROMA

FELLINI'S ROMA

1971 – ITALY / FRANCE – 128 MIN.

GENRE

GROTESQUE

DIRECTOR

FEDERICO FELLINI

SCREENPLAY

FEDERICO FELLINI, BERNARDINO ZAPPONI

DIRECTOR OF PHOTOGRAPHY

GIUSEPPE ROTUNNO

EDITING

RUGGERO MASTROIANNI

MUSIC

NINO ROTA

PRODUCTION

TURI VASILE for ULTRA FILM, LES PRODUCTIONS ARTISTES ASSOCIÉS, PRODUZIONI EUROPEE ASSOCIATI

STARRING

PETER GONZALES (Fellini as an 18-year-old), FIONA FLORENCE (Young Prostitute), PIA DE DOSES (Princess Domitilla), MARNE MAITLAND (Engineer) RENATO GIOVANNOLI (Cardinal Ottaviani), STEFANO MAYORE (Fellini as a Child), ELISA MAINARDI (Pharmacist's Wife), GALLIANO SBARRA (Compère), ANNA MAGNANI (Herself) GORE VIDAL (Himself)

una co-produzione italo-francese Ultra Film · Roma Les Productions Artistes Associés S.A. · Parigi
federico
fellini
roma
Soggetto e sceneggiatura di
FEDERICO FELLINI e BERNARDINO ZAPPONI
EASTMANCOLOR
ROTOPRESS - ROMA

1

"It's the stench of the ages!"

"The unusual, the mysterious, is right there before us. You only have to look closely to find the terror and beauty in everyday life." Thus spake Federico Fellini after completing his film *La dolce vita* (1959/60). The implication was clear: sedentary and immobile, he had no need to travel to distant countries in order to create exotic films. Ten years later, he furnished the proof: *Fellini's Roma* is an affectionate portrait of a city that's populated by the strangest of people—at least in Fellini's eyes. He sees Rome as a baroque construction where history, culture, religion and voluptuous life meet and mix unceasingly.

Fellini's Roma needs no dramatic storyline and has only one protagonist: Fellini himself. In a series of episodes, he tells how he dreamt as a child of the alluring city, and how he arrived there as a young man in 1939. He tells of his first evening in the metropolis, stepping off the train at Roma Termini, finding a seat in a crowded trattoria, standing in line at a shabby bordello. Fellini jumps to and fro between past and present, battles his way through the packed streets with a camera team in tow, visits a cacophonous wartime theater, hangs out with the hippies on the Spanish Steps, sits in an air-raid shelter and meets a German girl.

In Fellini's vision, Rome is an organic entity. At a dinner party, someone quotes a Roman proverb: "As you eat, so will you shit." The people are vulgar, obstreperous, argumentative, noisy. They smoke, they sweat, their children piss on the floor of the theater, and they only ever appear

THE CITY IN FILM As the modern city was undergoing radical change, thanks to electricity, tramlines and the separation of life and work, film was discovering its language: montage. The cut from one shot to another, the change of viewpoint and camera-angle—these resemble a streetcar journey through the city, with ever-changing views of narrow streets, tall buildings, strange faces, shop windows swooping past, and sudden, spacious squares. City and film are interdependent. In the early days of the medium, no one could understand an edited film unless he had experienced the city.
In the earliest films, the city was not merely a backdrop to the story; it was the story itself. The Berlin films made by the Brothers Skladanowsky in 1896 record the street life on Alexanderplatz or on the boulevard Unter den Linden. Since then, the image of the city in film has gone through several transformations. It has been shown as a brutal counterpart to the idyllic natural world, as in Friedrich Wilhelm Murnau's *City Girl* (1929/30), as a place of historical memory, as in Wim Wenders' *Wings of Desire* (*Der Himmel über Berlin/Les Ailes du désir*, 1987) or as a configuration of neon lights and shopping malls, as in *Fallen Angels* (*Duo luo tian shi*, 1995) by Wong Kar-wai. And—at regular intervals—there have been declarations of love to one city or another, as in *Manhattan* (1979) by Woody Allen or *Fellini's Roma* (*Roma*, 1971).

2

en masse: in the young Fellini's apartment house, there are an incredible number of subtenants; people push for room at the dinner table, gobbling snails and tripe. The hippies, playing love games, practically tie themselves in knots. There's no such thing as privacy, everyone takes part in everyone else's life. The streets of Rome, says the narrator, are like corridors, and the public squares are living rooms.

The Rome we see here is so idealized that Fellini could find it only in the studio. Thus, he had an entire stretch of the Via Albalonga rebuilt in Cinecittà, including the trams.

"As Rome to Fellini, so Dublin to Joyce, Cologne to Heinrich Böll and Turin to Pavese... but it's hard to think of another film director as close to a city, a country, an ever-present locus of lived experience, as Fellini is to Rome."
Frankfurter Rundschau

1 Basking in the cinema: Country boy Fellini first discovered Rome at the movies.

2 Lining up for a rendezvous with the wife of the provincial pharmacist. "She's worse than Messalina," say the local men.

3 Puppy love: Young people on the Spanish Steps cast Fellini's mind back to the days when love was something shameful and furtive banished to brothels or public toilets.

4

4 Fellini's assembly of the weird and the wonderful. He had originally planned several more city scenes, including a soccer match between Lazio and AS Roma.

5 Running wild: Fellini said Rome was an ideal breeding ground for the imagination. Rome is the perfect mother, indifferent, "with too many children to waste time on you personally."

The real Rome appears only occasionally, above all at the end, as the camera accompanies a horde of bikers on their night journey through the city.

In one scene, the camera goes underground to film the building of the subway. Like a monstrous worm, the drill bores through the entrails of the city. The engineer explains that Rome was built in eight layers, and that a burial chamber has just been discovered in the fifth layer. Suddenly, they're up against another hollow space; the drill breaks through the wall to reveal an ancient Roman villa—there are mosaics in the untouched baths, and stunningly beautiful frescos. Abruptly, the paintings on the walls begin to fade and crumble to dust; they cannot survive contact with the air of the outside world. What fascinates Fellini is the clash of opposites in Rome: antiquity and modernity, the old and the new; how the past permeates the present, and how partial destruction is sometimes necessary to ensure the survival of the total organism called Rome.

Fellini cuts into the body of the city and takes a look beneath its surface; but he cannot grasp Rome as a whole. It never stops changing, said Fellini after filming: "This city is like a woman. You think you've had her, undressed her, heard her moan… but then you see her again a week later, and you see that she's nothing like the woman you thought you had possessed. In short, I still have the desire to make a film, another film, about Rome." Things turned out differently, though. In his next film, *Amarcord* (1973), Fellini revisited the scene of his childhood: Rimini.

NM

HAROLD AND MAUDE

1971 – USA – 91 MIN.

GENRE

TRAGICOMEDY, SATIRE

DIRECTOR

HAL ASHBY

SCREENPLAY

COLIN HIGGINS,
based on his novel of the same name

DIRECTOR OF PHOTOGRAPHY

JOHN A. ALONZO

EDITING

WILLIAM A. SAWYER, EDWARD WARSCHILKA

MUSIC

CAT STEVENS

PRODUCTION

CHARLES MULVEHILL, COLIN HIGGINS,
MILDRED LEWIS for PARAMOUNT PICTURES

STARRING

BUD CORT (Harold Chasen), RUTH GORDON (Maude),
VIVIAN PICKLES (Mrs. Chasen), CYRIL CUSACK (Glaucus),
CHARLES TYNER (Uncle Victor), ELLEN GEER (Sunshine Doré),
ERIC CHRISTMAS (Priest), G. WOOD (Psychiatrist),
JUDY ENGLES (Candy Gulf), SHARI SUMMERS (Edith Phern)

This is Harold
Fully equipped to deal with life.

Paramount Pictures Presents

Harold and Maude

Starring
Ruth Gordon Bud Cort

Co-starring
VIVIAN PICKLES CYRIL CUSACK CHARLES TYNER ELLEN GEER
Produced by COLIN HIGGINS and CHARLES B. MULVEHILL
Executive Producer MILDRED LEWIS Written by COLIN HIGGINS
Directed by HAL ASHBY Songs by CAT STEVENS
Colour by TECHNICOLOR®

Paramount
A G+W Company
A Paramount Picture Distributed by Cinema International Corporation

Printed in England by Lonsdale & Bartholomew Ltd

1

"What kind of flower would you like to be?"

When *Harold and Maude* hit American theaters in 1971, the off-beat love story about a stoic sixteen-year-old boy and an eighty-year-old woman flopped at the box office. It was not until 1979, when the picture was re-released, that it triumphed with audiences. Looking back, it makes perfect sense. How could a nation who had elected the staunchly conservative Nixon as its president embrace a tender, anarchic comedy, in which figures of authority like police officers, soldiers and members of the church get the proverbial "pie in the face," and where material wealth is not depicted as the pot of gold at the end of the rainbow. As Harold's home life shows us, money is arguably the root of spiritual barrenness. All the more reason why the movie spoke to so many people worldwide, capturing the hearts of younger audiences in particular, who felt boxed in by the social conventions of the era. As Cat Stevens' ballad inspiringly echoes throughout the film, "You can do what you want," and "If you want to be free, be free."

Yet *Harold and Maude* is much more than a love story. At heart, the film is also a social satire, a coming-of-age movie and a black comedy. Director Hal Ashby suavely negotiates the tightrope between the private and political arena, comedy and sentimentality, between the grotesque and the banal.

The story starts off macabre. Harold Chasen (Bud Cort), a young man from a wealthy family, turns on the phonograph, lights a candle, steps up onto a chair—and hangs himself. Moments later, his mother (Vivian Pickles) enters the room and seems completely unaffected by the event. She cancels an appointment at the hairdresser's and exits the room after informing Harold that dinner will be served promptly at eight.

Harold's staged "suicides" (there will be more of them to come as the film progresses) function as a sort of ritual, an utterly twisted and failed attempt at communicating with his mother. For the scenes between Harold and Mrs.

RUTH GORDON When Ruth Gordon won an Oscar at the age of 72 for her delightfully sinister supporting performance in *Rosemary's Baby* (1968), her amusing remark "I can't tell you how encouraging a thing like this is" nicely summed up the energy and optimism she displayed over a then 50-year career, which had begun with a 1915 stage debut as Peter Pan. The legendary actress soon landed bit parts in silent movies, but remained true to the stage for the next 25 years. Reaching the upper echelons of Broadway fame, she first made her way to Hollywood in the early 40s. Tinseltown readily supplied Gordon with character and supporting roles in films like *Dr. Ehrlich's Magic Bullet/The Story of Dr. Ehrlich's Magic Bullet* (1939/40) and the celebrated wartime drama *Action in the North Atlantic* (1943).
Her career quickly took a new turn after she entered into her second marriage in 1942 with actor/director Garson Kanin. Together with Kanin, she wrote screenplays, many of which were filmed by George Cukor. These included the Katharine Hepburn/Spencer Tracy comedies *Adam's Rib* (1949) and *Pat and Mike* (1952), as well as the Judy Holliday films *The Marrying Kind* (1952) and *It Should Happen to You* (1954). Gordon's script for *The Actress* (1953) was based on her autobiographical stage play *Years Ago* and deals with her years as an adolescent when she decided to work in the theater despite her father's vehement disapproval. Her career experienced a miraculous renaissance in the mid-60s when she won the above-mentioned Oscar. She became a cult icon with *Harold and Maude* (1971) and proceeded to work in film and television right up to the end of her life. In 1985, the world said goodbye to the great Ruth Gordon.

***Harold and Maude* is a poeticized slice of American life, in which automobile graveyards, garbage dumps, slums and junkyards are all awakened to new life. The film is a ballad, an allegory of life and death—in which life is ultimately triumphant.”** *Frankfurter Allgemeine Zeitung*

1 80 years old and still going strong: Maude (Ruth Gordon) is ready for anything.

2 Crying bloody murder: Harold’s (Bud Cort) form of protest against his ice mama throws even house guests for a fatal loop.

3 A shared hobby: Visiting the funerals of strangers. Maude approaches Harold.

Chasen all follow the same pattern. She throws an endless barrage of nonsense at Harold while he says stands there silently. When he does respond to her on occasion, it's simply water off a duck's back.

The Chasens live on a lavish estate, which director Hal Ashby plays up with long shots to accentuate its larger-than-life quality. Its rooms, on the other hand, are dark and oppressive and cage Harold in just as much as his wardrobe, exclusively made up of pressed suits and ties. Harold's body language is stiff and clumsy and his facial expressions appear to be frozen from ear to ear.

Harold is the polar opposite of Maude (Ruth Gordon). The two of them meet one day while partaking in their shared hobby. Both routinely attend the funerals of people they don't know. Brassy to the core and a fireball of energy, the eighty-year-old Maude is always on the move. She likes getting around by car, stealing one right after another and recklessly zooming around the bends.

Maude's youthfulness is so convincing (she puts the moves on Harold during a funeral service) that their putative misalliance never seems awkward. Indeed, the ones we want to shake our heads at are those who are so vehemently opposed to their relationship.

Harold awakens to life when Maude literally shoves him into motion. She encourages him to sing and dance, gives him a banjo and implores him to somersault whenever the spirit so moves him. After all, there's something new to be tried every day, she insists.

Another saying Maude lives by is that you should never stop moving. Never commit to anything too long because you just might get stuck in a rut. In the end, it is the living world that she no longer wants to commit to and resolutely brings her own life to a close on her eightieth birthday. Harold is left, yet again, without someone to share his thoughts with, but he has learned from Maude's example. Ashby revisits the suicide theme one last time in the film's closing sequence as we watch Harold's Jaguar, which he has converted into a hearse, race along the coast and plummet off a cliff. With an upward swoop of the camera we see Harold still atop the hill, exuding life and playing that banjo Maude gave him.

LP

THE LAST PICTURE SHOW

1971 – USA – 118 MIN.

GENRE

DRAMA

DIRECTOR

PETER BOGDANOVICH

SCREENPLAY

LARRY MCMURTRY, PETER BOGDANOVICH,
based on the novel of the same name by LARRY MCMURTRY

DIRECTOR OF PHOTOGRAPHY

ROBERT SURTEES

EDITING

DONN CAMBERN

MUSIC

Songs by EDDIE ARNOLD, HANK WILLIAMS, TONY BENNETT,
FRANKIE LAINE, JOHNNY RAY, HAY STARR

PRODUCTION

STEPHEN J. FRIEDMAN for BBS PRODUCTIONS,
COLUMBIA PICTURES CORPORATION

STARRING

TIMOTHY BOTTOMS (Sonny Crawford), JEFF BRIDGES (Duane Jackson),
CYBILL SHEPHERD (Jacy Farrow), BEN JOHNSON (Sam the Lion),
CLORIS LEACHMAN (Ruth Popper), ELLEN BURSTYN (Lois Farrow),
EILEEN BRENNAN (Genevieve), SAM BOTTOMS (Billy),
JOHN HILLERMAN (School Teacher), RANDY QUAID (Lester Marlow)

ACADEMY AWARDS 1972

OSCARS for BEST SUPPORTING ACTRESS (Cloris Leachman),
and BEST SUPPORTING ACTOR (Ben Johnson)

Anarene, Texas, 1951.

Nothing much has changed...

COLUMBIA PICTURES Presents A BBS PRODUCTION

THE LAST PICTURE SHOW

A Film By
PETER BOGDANOVICH

starring
TIMOTHY BOTTOMS / JEFF BRIDGES / ELLEN BURSTYN / BEN JOHNSON / CLORIS LEACHMAN

and introducing CYBILL SHEPHERD as Jacy / Directed by PETER BOGDANOVICH / Screenplay by LARRY McMURTRY and PETER BOGDANOVICH Based on the novel by LARRY McMURTRY Executive Producer BERT SCHNEIDER / Produced by STEPHEN J. FRIEDMAN

Original Soundtrack Album on MGM Records.

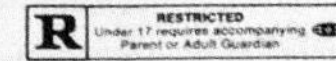

1

"Sam the Lion is dead!"

Anarene, Texas 1951. A Podunk dust-bowl where nothing's changed much in years, and there isn't a whole lot to discover. The "Royal," an old movie house, stands at the end of Main Street, just a few feet from Sam's pool hall. The place boasts two game tables, an adjoining diner run by Genevieve and a fully functioning jukebox in the corner. That pretty much sums up the town sights. If the pick-ups didn't have radios, people might inadvertently forget that time really does march onward.

Not exactly the most exciting spot on the map if you're young and have your whole life ahead of you. Disenchanted dreamer Sonny (Timothy Bottoms), local star athlete Duane (Jeff Bridges) and transparently manipulative village beauty Jacy (Cybill Shepherd) are all feeling the burn of small town life. They're each about to graduate from high school, but that doesn't mean a heck of a lot in Anarene. The only thing the local adult population really cares about in terms of high school is whether or not the football team wins the title. In fact, the grown-ups treat the teenage boys like dirt when their last game of the season ends in defeat. The nickelodeon offers the local teens their only solace and taste of intimacy. They nestle in the comfort of the back row, where they can be with each other for a few stolen moments. In these shadows, the kids seek oblivion from the world around them.

The Last Picture Show (1971) was Peter Bogdanovich's first major critical and box-office sensation. His next two projects (*What's Up Doc?*, 1972 and *Paper Moon*, 1973),

JEFF BRIDGES Son of actor Lloyd Bridges (1913–1998), Jeff Bridges (born 1949 in Los Angeles) made his screen debut when he was still sucking at his pacifier. A baby was needed for *The Company She Keeps* (1950), and father Lloyd was willing to supply his six-month-old son. For years Jeff Bridges wanted to be a musician and never saw himself as an actor. At the age of eight, he appeared in various TV series with his brother Beau. Jeff Bridges' breakthrough came in 1971 with *The Last Picture Show*, which earned him an Oscar nod. Bridges quickly put his musical ambitions on hold, although he was able to live them out years later in *The Fabulous Baker Boys* (1989). Initially, he gravitated toward doomed heroes, whom audiences loved because they could see their inevitable end from miles away. He was a class act as the hobbling car thief in Michael Cimino's *Thunderbolt and Lightfoot* (1974). Who would have guessed that behind a winning smile and bum leg lay a slick professional felon? Many parts, such as in *Fearless* (1993), *The Big Lebowski* (1998), *Tron* (1982) and *Heaven's Gate* (1980), were hailed by only select audiences. Bridges also starred in *Texasville* (1990), the sequel to *The Last Picture Show*, featuring Duane as a middle-aged oil baron and married father of four, who still holds a candle for Jacy. In 2002, *Premiere* magazine elected Bridges America's most underrated actor. Praiseworthy not only as a fine actor capable of achieving the presidency in front of the camera in *The Contender* (2000), but also as the true humanitarian who co-founded the "Hunger Network." After several nominations, Bridges finally won a Best Actor Oscar for his role in *Crazy Heart* (2009).

“With his second feature, Director Bogdanovich, 31, has achieved a tactile sense of time and place. More, he has performed that most difficult of all cinematic feats: he has made ennui fascinating. Together, that is enough to herald him as the most exciting new director in America today.” *Time Magazine*

which followed immediately, also enjoyed similar critical and public acclaim. *Picture Show* examines the lives of three teenagers confronted with a dilemma. They are young, pure of heart and yet their future seems to have been carved in stone on the day they were born. The film’s black and white photography, a conscious choice on the part of Bogdanovich that went against New Hollywood’s preference for color photography, accentuates the monotony of the characters’ lives. The majestic skies above shine the only ray of light on Anarene’s rigidity. The movie is a 1970s masterpiece reveling in a flawlessly recreated 1950s universe. It not only reconstructs a bygone era, but also reclaims the cinematic conventions of the day, revealing its world in long, drawn-out, motionless shots that are seldom interrupted by rapid cuts. The cinematography is elegantly simple. There are noticeably few stagy close-ups. Instead, the film’s look is set by long shots and the search for the eternal salvation of the heavens, two

3

1 Breaking the mold: The classic Western always ends with a duel. But here the duelists are school friends on the brink of adulthood: Sonny (Timothy Bottoms) and Duane (Jeff Bridges).

2 The last cowboy: To the audience, Sam the Lion (Ben Johnson) is a grand relic of a bygone era. To Sonny and backward Billy (Sam Bottons) he is both father figure and role model.

3 Fighting for a future, trying to wrest something from his surroundings, and struggling to find himself—to Sonny, Anarene is just one big Dead End.

characteristics normally associated with the Western. Bogdanovich glorifies his personal heroes like Howard Hawks, John Ford and Alfred Hitchcock in this work. Each moment in the film is driven by a clear objective, and Bogdanovich leaves nothing to chance. Country and easy-listening tunes by Eddie Arnold, Hank Williams and Tony Bennett plink out of the ubiquitous radio sets, following the characters through the story like the haunting echoes of an off-key lullaby. Equally surreal is how the laws of time don't seem to apply here. We experience the lives of the protagonists in individual days often separated by weeks on end; yet we are made to believe that nothing has taken place in the off-screen downtime.

Of the salient episodes that prove that there is indeed life in this barren wasteland, the most poignant takes place between Sonny and the forlorn wife of his gym teacher, Ruth (Cloris Leachman). Their first romantic encounter is a microcosm of the disturbing social repression that surrounds them. Bogdanovich directs a seduction scene that wins the two actors our sincerest compassion as we watch them grovel in their shame, afraid to risk looking at one another while they proceed to undress. Even once under the sheets, something lingers in the atmosphere that tells us Ruth and Sonny will never be able to block out their inexorable, external world. We are left to endure the squeaking of the bedsprings and thumping of the backboard.

We do, however, see hope afloat in these dismal seas in the character of Sam the Lion (Ben Johnson). He owns the movie house and is the moral role model for the kids, and for Sonny in particular. Sam's values stem from a time when striving to achieve ideals still meant something. The

“This is not merely the best American movie of a rather dreary year; it is the most impressive work by a young American director since *Citizen Kane*.”

Newsweek

4 Without the jukebox in Genevieve's little diner, there'd be nothing to listen to in Anarene—only the tireless wind blowing over the dusty road where the occasional truck thunders by.

5 Too young, too rich, too pretty … Jacy (Cybill Shepherd), the daughter of a wealthy oilman, is looking for a little appreciation—and a man for life.

man is like a cowboy who survived the Old West, and it is no coincidence that former Western star Johnson plays the role. When a heart attack claims the middle-aged Sam's life, it appears that the entire future of Anarene's youth population has died with him. Almost in a stupor, Sonny and Duane head over to the Royal for their last picture show. The popularity of television is causing the place itself to shut down. The movie showing is Hawks' *Red River* (1948), and we watch as cowboys prepare to drive a herd of cattle to Montana, with John Wayne calling them to exuberant action. When the lights come up again, Sonny too, will feel called to action. Reinventing his preordained small-town ending, he will step into the Lion's shoes and take a stand against the insidious black and white complacency of his small-minded world.

SR

GET CARTER

1971 – GREAT BRITAIN – 112 MIN.

GENRE

GANGSTER FILM

DIRECTOR

MIKE HODGES

SCREENPLAY

MIKE HODGES, based on the novel
JACK'S RETURN HOME by TED LEWIS

DIRECTOR OF PHOTOGRAPHY

WOLFGANG SUSCHITZKY

EDITING

JOHN TRUMPER

MUSIC

ROY BUDD

PRODUCTION

MICHAEL KLINGER, MICHAEL CAINE for MGM

STARRING

MICHAEL CAINE (Jack Carter), IAN HENDRY (Eric Paice),
BRITT EKLAND (Anna Fletcher), JOHN OSBORNE (Cyril Kinnear),
TONY BECKLEY (Peter), GEORGE SEWELL (Con McCarty),
GERALDINE MOFFAT (Glenda), DOROTHY WHITE (Margaret),
ROSEMARIE DUNHAM (Edna), PETRA MARKHAM (Doreen)

MICHAEL CAINE
GET CARTER
R RESTRICTED Under 17 requires accompanying Parent or Adult Guardian
A MICHAEL KLINGER PRODUCTION STARRING MICHAEL CAINE in "GET CARTER" Co-Starring IAN HENDRY · JOHN OSBORNE and BRITT EKLAND
Screenplay by MIKE HODGES · Based on the novel "JACK'S RETURN HOME" by TED LEWIS · Produced by MICHAEL KLINGER · Directed by MIKE HODGES · IN METROCOLOR
A METRO-GOLDWYN-MAYER RELEASE

1

"Remember, they are killers... Just like you."

Jack Carter (Michael Caine) is back in town. Against the will of his syndicate, the professional killer leaves London and returns to his home town of Newcastle, where his brother has died in a peculiar road accident. Carter suspects murder, and he wants to find the culprits; but his brother's friends, and girlfriend, are no help at all. Undeterred, and driven by a desire for vengeance, Carter becomes brutal in his persistence; and the king of the local underworld, Kinnear (John Osborne), is standing in his way.

Although many film buffs are fans of his work, the British director Mike Hodges has only made one movie that achieved real popular success: *Flash Gordon* (1980). *Get Carter* is no real exception to this rule. Although it eventually became a cult film in Britain—thanks in no small part to Michael Caine's performance—30 years elapsed before its (re)discovery by the rest of the world, on the occasion of a Hollywood remake starring Sylvester Stallone.

Get Carter was Hodges' cinematic debut. Up till then, he had spent years working in television, making reports and documentaries. In 1969, he directed *Suspect*, his first TV drama, a thriller about a child murder that took a critical look behind the mask of British society. *Get Carter* is a film with equally few illusions. While charting the course of a private mission of revenge, it also depicts a nation grown squalid, amoral and violent. Carter cruises

MICHAEL CAINE Michael Caine once said that he and Harold Lloyd were the only bespectacled actors ever to have made a name for themselves. Indeed, the glasses were not the only disadvantage Caine had to contend with. The son of a cleaner and a fishmonger, Maurice Micklewhite (as he was then known) was born in a working-class area of London on March 14, 1933. From an early age, Caine wanted to become an actor; but although he made his cinematic debut in the mid-50s, his breakthrough as the laconic secret agent Harry Palmer in *The Ipcress File* (1965), directed by Sidney J. Furie, was still ten years away. He was equally successful in the film's two sequels. In *Alfie* (1966), Caine played a working-class Casanova. The film made him world-famous and earned him his first Oscar nomination. Since then, he has been one of the busiest stars in the English-speaking world. Michael Caine's trademarks are his understated acting style and his distinctive Cockney accent. In the course of his long career, he has won two Academy Awards as Best Supporting Actor for his performances in Woody Allen's *Hannah and Her Sisters* (1985) and in Lasse Hallström's *The Cider House Rules* (1999).

"There is nobody to root but the smartly dressed sexual athlete and professional killer (Michael Caine) in this English gangland picture, which is so calculated cool and soulless and nastily erotic that it seems to belong to a new genre of virtuoso vicousness. What makes the movie unusual is the metallic elegance and the single-minded proficiency with which it adheres to its sadism-for-the-connoisseur formula."

Pauline Kael

the city like a detective. Wherever he happens to land, from the elegant apartments and villas of the decadent élite to the bleak pubs and terraced houses of the working class, he encounters cunning, mistrust and naked greed. In Hodges' film, we hear the dying echoes of the Swinging Sixties, and all that remains in their wake is a riotous and unconscionable hedonism. Corruption and brutality rule; one rapid sequence combines fast sex and fast cars, but "liberation" is the last word that comes to mind… As if to demonstrate that he was dealing with reality and not just following the conventions of the genre, Hodges filmed on location in the grim and chilly North of

1 In the flesh: To this day, Caine excels at everything from rugged working class hero to demented doctor.

2 Local boy gone bad: Professional killer Jack Carter (Michael Caine) is back in his hometown to investigate the death of his brother.

3 Sex and Crime: Assassin Carter (Michael Caine) knocks 'em all dead.

4 Wherever Carter goes, violence, corruption and ruin are sure to follow.

England; and he did so with the beady eye of a trained documentary filmmaker. In this, he is heir to the Free Cinema of the late 50s and early 60s, a period he pays tribute to by casting the dramatist John Osborne as the gangster boss Kinnear.

And in fact we may well see Carter as a twisted, latter-day "angry young man"—an armed proletarian criminal fighting the status quo. In a key scene, he discovers that his niece has been abused for a shabby porn film; as he watches the images on screen, he loses his distance

"You know, I'd almost forgotten what your eyes looked like. Still the same. Pissholes in the snow."

Film quote: Jack Carter

5

5 Rolling with the times: Sex is just one more aspect of life that's ruled by greed and brutality.

6 A twisted latter-day *angry young man*: Carter rages against an amoral system that has long since corrupted him too.

"One man against an organization. The courage and naivety of an individual versus the overwhelming power and sophistication of a system—a perennial theme in the oeuvre of that underrated director, Mike Hodges." *Süddeutsche Zeitung*

and his icy façade melts into tears. The professional assassin runs amok, slaughtering men and women alike, driven by hatred and the pain of his own loss of innocence. Even in his rage, Carter kills only the guilty; yet he knows he's no better than his victims. He too is part of the system. The film's inner logic can offer him no new beginning, merely a permanent ending. The final showdown takes place on the beach—one of the mythical places of the cinema. Death takes the form of a precision shot from the rifle of a contract killer. On the marksman's signet ring, we see the letter "J." Like Jack Carter, he's a master of his trade; but unlike Carter, he still has the necessary professional distance from the job he's paid to do.

JH

DELIVERANCE

1972 – USA – 105 MIN.

GENRE

ACTION FILM, THRILLER

DIRECTOR

JOHN BOORMAN

SCREENPLAY

JAMES DICKEY,
based on his novel of the same name

DIRECTOR OF PHOTOGRAPHY

VILMOS ZSIGMOND

EDITING

TOM PRIESTLEY

MUSIC

ERIC WEISSBERG, STEVE MANDEL

PRODUCTION

JOHN BOORMAN for ELMER PRODUCTIONS,
WARNER BROS.

STARRING

JON VOIGHT (Ed Gentry), BURT REYNOLDS (Lewis Medlock),
NED BEATTY (Bobby Trippe), RONNY COX (Drew Ballinger),
ED RAMEY (Old Man), BILLY REDDEN (Lonny), SEAMON GLASS (First Griner),
RANDALL DEAL (Second Griner), BILL MCKINNEY (Mountain Man),
HERBERT “COWBOY” COWARD (Toothless Man), LEWIS CRONE (First Deputy),
JAMES DICKEY (Sheriff Bullard)

What did happen on the Cahulawassee River?

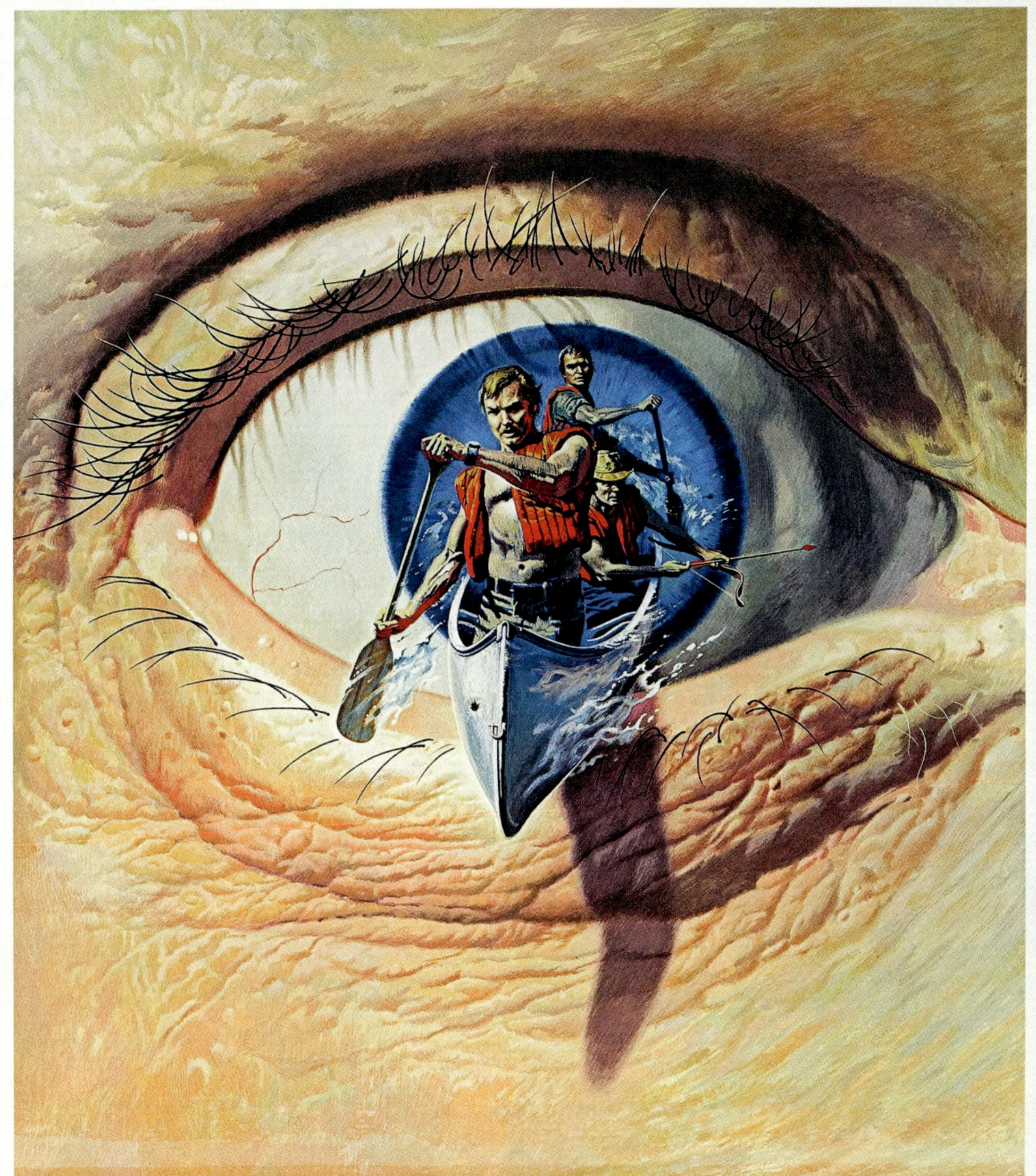

Deliverance

A JOHN BOORMAN FILM Starring **JON VOIGHT · BURT REYNOLDS** in **"DELIVERANCE"**

Co-Starring NED BEATTY · RONNY COX · Screenplay by James Dickey Based on his novel · Produced and Directed by John Boorman · PANAVISION® · TECHNICOLOR®

From Warner Bros., A Warner Communications Company

"That's the game, survival."

A river winds softly through a pristine landscape of craggy cliffs and dense virgin forest. Four men from the city are here to relax while exploring the area by canoe. Lewis (Burt Reynolds), Ed (Jon Voight), Bobby (Ned Beatty) and Drew (Ronny Cox), are paddling downriver in two fragile boats. They've paid some farmers to drive their cars to the final destination, which they expect to reach two days later; but this is an adventure holiday that will turn into pure terror.

The first day is idyllic, a boy-scouts' paradise for four grown men: paddling boats, pitching tents, fishing with bows and arrows, and playing guitar round the campfire. On the second day, the horror begins. Ed and Bobby have gone on ahead in their canoe, and a welcoming-party is waiting for them: two of the farmers, ugly rednecks with very bad teeth. After tying Ed to a tree, they beat, rape and humiliate Bobby. As they turn their attentions to Ed, one of them keels over, pierced by an arrow; Lewis and Drew have caught up with their friends. The other attacker flees, and the four friends bury the corpse. They're sick of adventures and hungry for home, and the canoes are their only means of transport. But down on the river, between the sheer cliffs, they're as open to predators as a hamburger on a plate ...

JOHN BOORMAN Civilized human beings forced to come to terms with barbarism: this is as good a summary of *Deliverance* (1972) as any, and it's also the groundplan for many of John Boorman's films. In the SF movie *Zardoz* (1973/74) Sean Connery struggles against a terroristic slave system; in *The Emerald Forest* (1985), the son of an engineer (Boorman's own son, Charley) falls into the hands of an archaic forest-dwelling tribe. England's John Boorman (born 1933) has made highly idiosyncratic films in a wide range of standard genres. In *Hope and Glory* (1987), he called on his own childhood memories to tell the story of the war from a boy's perspective. The gangster in *The General* (1998) behaves like the gangsters he's seen in the movies. And in *The Tailor of Panama* (2001), Boorman portrays his "hero" (sex symbol and 007 Pierce Brosnan) as a deeply repellent character. Boorman made his cinema debut in 1965 with the Dave Clark Five pop vehicle *Catch Us If You Can (Having a Wild Weekend)*. The big break came in 1967 with his second film, the gangster drama *Point Blank*. Among Boorman's most recent films are *The Tiger's Tail* (2006) and *Queen and Country* (2014). At the 2022 New Year's Honours, Boorman was appointed Commander of the British Empire by Queen Elizabeth II.

2

1 Hell bent over: Ed (Jon Voight) gets a close-up view of prison in the wild.

2 "The voyage down the river echoes the journey of Conrad's demonic Mr. Kurtz to the Congo's heart of darkness." (*The New York Times*)

3 A grassroots movement: Ed hunts his attackers with a bow and arrow.

"A repugnant but fascinating portrait of human beings out of their environment, forced to defend themselves where the laws of civilization no longer apply." *Motion Picture Guide*

With its breathtaking journeys through whitewater rapids and overwhelming images of natural splendor, *Deliverance* is a wonderful action and adventure film. Director John Boorman, his editor Tom Priestley (both of whom received Oscar nominations) and the cameraman Vilmos Zsigmond (who got an Oscar for *Close Encounters of the Third Kind*, 1977) created a visual language of great beauty, combining careful composition with a directness and immediacy that pulls the audience right into the story. The immensity and indifference of the natural world and the threat of sudden attack are almost physically present. Boorman also demonstrates a fine feeling for effective but

"It's the best film I've ever done. It's a picture that just picks you up and sends you crashing against the rocks. You feel everything and just crawl out of the theater." *Burt Reynolds, in: Motion Picture Guide*

4 Bobby (Ned Beatty), Lewis (Burt Reynolds), Drew (Ronny Cox) and Ed are looking forward to some male bonding—two days in virgin nature.

5 The men park their cars in a tiny hamlet—and sacrifice a link to civilization.

6 Sneak attack: Ed resorts to archery.

7 Concealing evidence: Lewis hides the corpse of a redneck he's just neutralized. The men think their nightmare is over, but it's only just begun.

inconspicuous symbolism: In a famous scene, early on in the film, Drew and a retarded farmer's boy begin a tentative musical dialog on guitar and banjo. The game of question-and-answer develops into a regular duet—or duel—in which the city-dweller is eventually defeated by the sheer speed and skill of the hillbilly kid. In beautifully understated manner, this joyful encounter anticipates the deadly power struggle to come.

The film's surface is brilliant, and the depths below it are multi-layered and hard to fathom. With a screenplay by the poet James Dickey, who adapted it from his own novel of the same name (1970), the film resists any easy interpretation. "Man Against Nature" won't do, for the dumb-but-crafty hillbillies can hardly be seen as symbols for a state of unspoilt nature. "Arrogant City-Slickers versus Disadvantaged Rural Population" is an equally unusable model, for neither the canoeists nor their antagonists can be reduced to this kind of cliché. What remains is the story of four men in an alien environment, defending their lives with alien methods; solid citizens far from civilization, struggling to survive with the aid of bows and arrows. Events take their course inexorably, and we are granted no comforting explanations. Lewis, the fittest of the four, is quickly incapacitated by an injury, while the cerebral pipe-smoking Ed is forced to kill in self-defense. When the survivors finally reach safety, they're still far from peace; the Sheriff (author James Dickey in a guest appearance) is a highly skeptical interrogator, and their dreams will long be haunted by memories of their hellish ordeal.

HJK

CABARET

1972 – USA – 124 MIN.

GENRE

LITERARY ADAPTATION, DRAMA, MUSICAL

DIRECTOR

BOB FOSSE

SCREENPLAY

JAY PRESSON ALLEN, based on the Broadway musical of the same name by JOE MASTEROFF, JOHN KANDER and FRED EBB, the drama *I AM A CAMERA* by JOHN VAN DRUTEN, and the collection of short stories *THE BERLIN STORIES* by CHRISTOPHER ISHERWOOD

DIRECTOR OF PHOTOGRAPHY

GEOFFREY UNSWORTH

EDITING

DAVID BRETHERTON

MUSIC

JOHN KANDER, RALPH BURNS

PRODUCTION

CY FEUER for ABC CIRCLE FILMS, AMERICAN BROADCASTING COMPANY

STARRING

LIZA MINNELLI (Sally Bowles), MICHAEL YORK (Brian Roberts), HELMUT GRIEM (Maximilian von Heune), JOEL GREY (Master of Ceremonies), FRITZ WEPPER (Fritz Wendel), MARISA BERENSON (Natalia Landauer), ELISABETH NEUMANN-VIERTEL (Fräulein Schneider), HELEN VITA (Fräulein Kost), SIGRID VON RICHTHOFEN (Fräulein Mayr), GERD VESPERMANN (Bobby)

ACADEMY AWARDS 1973

OSCARS for BEST DIRECTOR (Bob Fosse), BEST ACTRESS (Liza Minnelli), BEST SUPPORTING ACTOR (Joel Grey), BEST CINEMATOGRAPHY (Geoffrey Unsworth), BEST ADAPTED SCORE (Ralph Burns), BEST FILM EDITING (David Bretherton), BEST ART DIRECTION (Rolf Zehetbauer, Hans Jürgen Keibach, Herbert Strabel), and BEST SOUND (Robert Knudson, David Hildyard)

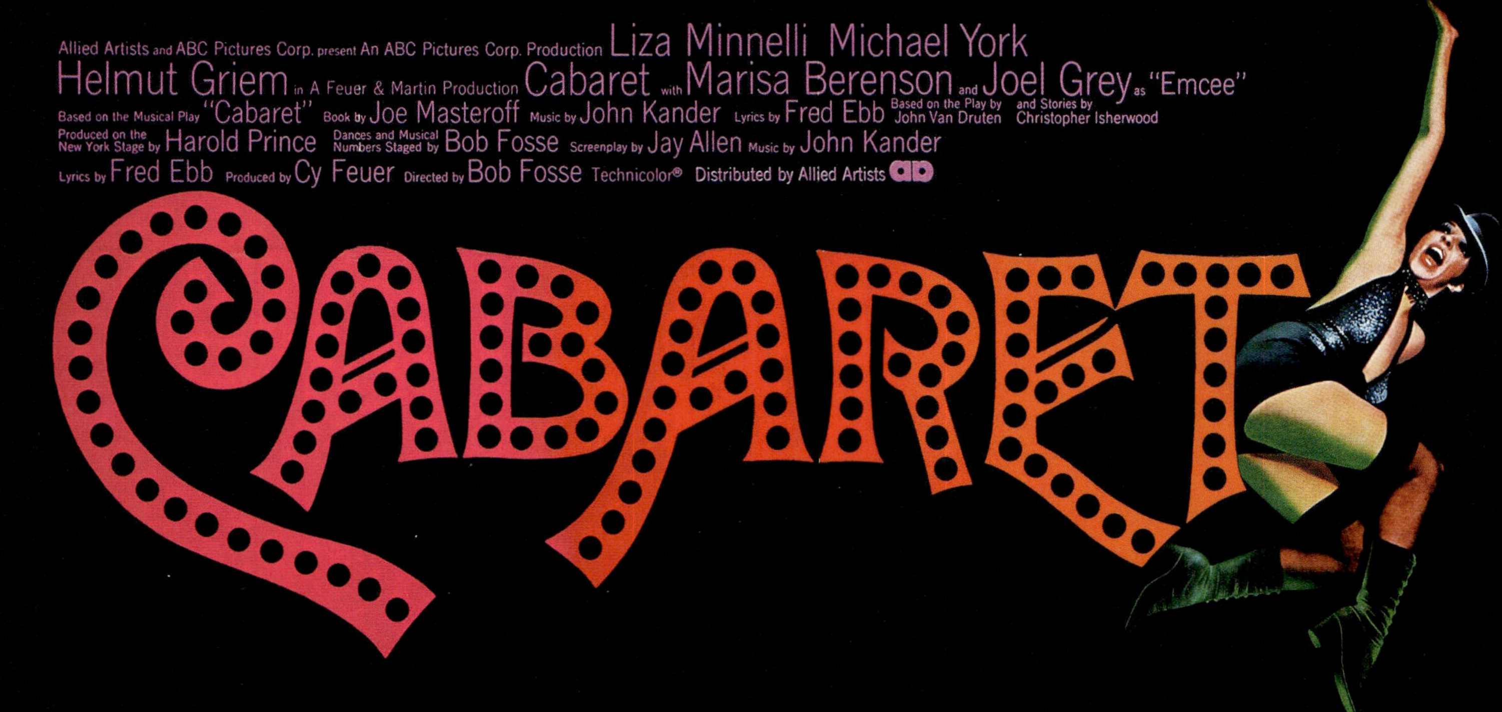
Allied Artists and ABC Pictures Corp. present An ABC Pictures Corp. Production Liza Minnelli Michael York
Helmut Griem in A Feuer & Martin Production Cabaret with Marisa Berenson and Joel Grey as "Emcee"
Based on the Musical Play "Cabaret" Book by Joe Masteroff Music by John Kander Lyrics by Fred Ebb Based on the Play by John Van Druten and Stories by Christopher Isherwood
Produced on the New York Stage by Harold Prince Dances and Musical Numbers Staged by Bob Fosse Screenplay by Jay Allen Music by John Kander
Lyrics by Fred Ebb Produced by Cy Feuer Directed by Bob Fosse Technicolor® Distributed by Allied Artists
CABARET
LIFE IS A

1

"Divine decadence, darling!"

Berlin 1931. Despite a severe economic crisis, the German metropolis is determinedly cosmopolitan and exudes sensuality. Leave your worries at the door and come on into the Kit Kat Club, a dazzling nightclub where evening after evening an enthusiastic emcee greets you in three languages: "Willkommen, Bienvenue, Welcome!" His diabolically painted white face is reflected on the shimmering stage. And like a funhouse mirror, the film presents the cabaret to movie audiences as a caricature of the outside world. "Life is a cabaret!" exclaims Liza Minelli in an unforgettable song that is meant to be taken at face value.

Like so many other foreigners, British student Brian (Michael York) feels drawn to this thriving urban center. Arriving at a boarding house, he quickly makes the acquaintance of American Sally Bowles (Liza Minnelli), who works as a singer at the Kit Kat Club and dreams of making it big one day as a movie star. She's not only willing to capitalize on her charisma to get there, but will readily exploit her body too if need be. Sexually uninhibited with a taste for luxury, Sally is a hedonistic modern whose deep-seated, hidden desire is to find true happiness. Beneath her decadent exterior we are shown more and more of the childish,

LIZA MINNELLI The extent to which her image was shaped by one single film is itself a Hollywood phenomenon. Her belting voice and touching yet extravagant flair breathed so much life into *Cabaret's* (1972) nightclub singer Sally Bowles that from then on world audiences viewed Liza Minnelli as virtually inseparable from the role she had played. The daughter of Hollywood legend Judy Garland and director Vincente Minnelli was literally born into show business in 1946. She made her first appearance in front of a Hollywood camera when she was just two years old. Be it on Broadway, in film, in TV movies or in the music industry, her work has always met with instant success. She received a Tony in 1965 for her performance in the Broadway musical *Flora, the Red Menace*. Her first Oscar nomination came for her portrayal of the eccentric Pookie in *The Sterile Cuckoo* (1969). Another nomination followed in 1970 for Otto Preminger's *Tell Me That You Love Me, Junie Moon*, and in 1973 she won the Best Actress Academy Award for *Cabaret*. She became more popular with audiences than ever before, and in 1972, NBC aired the award-winning television special *Liza with A Z*. Liza Minnelli, who describes herself as both "hopeful and cynical," is a star to this day, even though not all her films are smash hits. She collaborated with her father Vincente Minnelli on *A Matter of Time/Nina* (1976). Images of her superstar mother, who died in 1969, pop up in many of her movies, including Stanley Donen's *Lucky Lady* (1975) and most prominently in Martin Scorsese's musical drama *New York, New York* (1977). She experienced one of her greatest commercial successes in 1981 with *Arthur*. Shortly thereafter, her film career started to dry up. She disappeared completely from the public eye for several years. Alcohol and prescription drug addictions contributed to her personal downfall. In 1984 she sought professional help. She staged a comeback in 1985 in the form of an NBC made-for-TV movie *A Time to Live*, winning the Golden Globe for her performance. She then went on a star-studded tour at the end of the 80s with Frank Sinatra and Sammy Davis Jr. and even recorded a single with the Pet Shop Boys entitled "Losing My Mind" that reached number six in the U.K. charts. In 1997, Liza Minnelli was celebrated on Broadway in Blake Edwards' *Victor/Victoria*, and in 2008 she returned to Broadway with *Liza's at the Palace*.

1 Cigarette, lipstick and a voice that won't quit: The role of Sally Bowles made Liza Minnelli an international superstar.

2 "Life is a cabaret:" The stage as a world of entertainment and politics.

3 A pink-tinted love triangle: Only later does Sally discover that Brian (Michael York) and Maximilian (Helmut Griem) have been playing house.

"*Cabaret* is dance routines and hit songs. It's a murky tale inspired by the novels of Christopher Isherwood. It's the myth of 30s Berlin. And above all, it's Bob Fosse. He has a marvelous grasp of the world of cabaret, its pathos and its poetry: fleeting, illusory, and poignantly authentic." *Le Monde* vulnerable woman she really is. Brian, who at first seems immune to her erotic advances, eventually falls madly in love with her. It is a happy romance until the wealthy, young and rather attractive Baron Max von Heune (Helmut Griem) enters their world. Sally, mesmerized by his charms and riches, becomes more impractically minded with each passing day. Brian is jealous and turned on at the same time. Their love triangle is only spoken of in jest initially, but it soon becomes reality. Both of them have slept with the affluent Baron, and Sally, it turns out, is pregnant. While Sally and Brian are busy tackling their personal catastrophes, the Nazis take to the streets of Berlin in preparation for their rise to power. It seems the couple's lifestyle is doomed, for the epidemic of fascism spreading throughout the nation seeks to extinguish all that is urban and modern. In its place, the Nazi movement prescribes conservative and provincial values for the German people. Brian decides to return to England. Sally, however, stays on in Berlin to try her luck at acting.

Cabaret was one of the last great Hollywood musicals. (Eat your heart out *Chicago* [2002]!) It was awarded an astounding eight Oscars at the Academy Awards. The movie version was based on John Kander and Fred Ebb's Broadway musical, which premiered in 1966. This, likewise, drew heavily from the short stories "The Last of Mr. Morris" and "Goodbye to Berlin" by Christopher Isherwood, which were published in a volume entitled *The Berlin Stories*. Unlike the majority of Hollywood musicals, such as *An American in Paris* (1951) or *Singin' in the Rain* (1952) there is nothing anachronistic about *Cabaret* even today. This is due to its songs, as popular as those of Kurt Weill's *Threepenny Opera* (*Dreigroschenoper*), and to the then 25-year-old Liza Minnelli, whose image is more intrinsically linked to *Cabaret* than almost any other actress's has ever been to a single production. Yet above all else, it is the film's narrative structure that plays the decisive role in its timelessness. Deviating from the traditional Hollywood musical format, *Cabaret* markedly separates its musical numbers from its plot. In other words, none of the characters in the film burst into song for no given reason. Instead, director and choreographer Bob Fosse brilliantly lets the stage acts at the nightclub serve as commentary on both the surrounding political situation and the lives of characters themselves. In particular, the stage appearances of the emcee (Joel Grey), whose character doesn't exist within the framework of the plot outside the

3

nightclub, do a poignant job of this. Plot elements and musical numbers are occasionally brought together through the ironic use of parallel montage. Such is the case when a scene of a staged Bavarian folk dance is cut between rapidly appearing images of Nazis brutally beating up the Kit Kat's manager elsewhere. This sequence feeds violence into the musical number and choreography into the street fight. *Cabaret*, with its strikingly dark palette, is highly reminiscent of the 1920s, as is the music inspired by Kurt Weill and Fosse's stylized dance numbers, which clearly draw from that era's expressionist tradition.

"*Cabaret* may make a star out of Miss Minnelli, but it will be remembered as a chilling mosaic of another era's frightening life-style." *Films in Review*

6

4 Babe in the woods: When Brian comes to Berlin, he's a shy young writer. Sally's attempts to seduce him are initially unsuccessful.

5 Tomorrow belongs to… whom? It remains unclear how fascism will change Sally's wild and extravagant lifestyle.

6 Mirror, mirror on the wall, *Cabaret* was Liza's best picture of all.

Commendably, it does this without trying to ignore the cinematic conventions of the 1970s. The overall impact of the film is born out of its song and dance sequences which, with one exception, all take place on stage. The only time we witness music outside the cabaret setting is when a young blond boy begins to sing what is meant to sound like a traditional German folk song at a beer garden. We just see his face at first, but soon the camera pulls back to show us his swastika armband. One beer garden patron after the next joins in his chant. The rhythm of the piece transforms into a military march and by the end, all have their hands extended in a Hitler salute. It may sound ludicrous, but at the time of the picture's European premiere, this scene was to be cut out for German audiences. Only after a number of critics were up in arms about the decision was the sequence restored.

KK

THE GODFATHER

1972 – USA – 175 MIN.

GENRE

GANGSTER FILM, DRAMA

DIRECTOR

FRANCIS FORD COPPOLA

SCREENPLAY

FRANCIS FORD COPPOLA, MARIO PUZO,
based on his novel of the same name

DIRECTOR OF PHOTOGRAPHY

GORDON WILLIS

EDITING

MARC LAUB, BARBARA MARKS, WILLIAM REYNOLDS,
MURRAY SOLOMON, PETER ZINNER

MUSIC

NINO ROTA

PRODUCTION

ALBERT S. RUDDY for PARAMOUNT PICTURES

STARRING

MARLON BRANDO (Don Vito Corleone), AL PACINO (Michael Corleone),
DIANE KEATON (Kay Adams), ROBERT DUVALL (Tom Hagen),
JAMES CAAN (Santino "Sonny" Corleone), JOHN CAZALE (Frederico "Fredo" Corleone),
RICHARD S. CASTELLANO (Peter Clemenza), STERLING HAYDEN (Captain McCluskey),
TALIA SHIRE (Constanzia "Connie" Corleone-Rizzi), JOHN MARLEY (Jack Woltz),
RICHARD CONTE (Don Emilio Barzini), AL LETTIERI (Virgil Sollozzo), AL MARTINO (Johnny Fantane),
GIANNI RUSSO (Carlo Rizzi), SIMONETTA STEFANELLI (Appollonia Vitelli-Corleone)

ACADEMY AWARDS 1973

OSCARS for BEST PICTURE (Albert S. Ruddy),
BEST ACTOR (Marlon Brando, award declined),
and BEST ADAPTED SCREENPLAY (Mario Puzo, Francis Ford Coppola)

PARAMOUNT PICTURES PRESENTS

The Godfather

AN
Albert S. Ruddy
PRODUCTION

STARRING
Marlon Brando
AND
Al Pacino James Caan Richard Castellano Robert Duvall
Sterling Hayden John Marley Richard Conte Diane Keaton

PRODUCED BY Albert S. Ruddy DIRECTED BY Francis Ford Coppola SCREENPLAY BY Mario Puzo AND Francis Ford Coppola

BASED ON Mario Puzo's NOVEL "The Godfather" MUSIC SCORED BY Nino Rota Color By Technicolor® A Paramount Picture

SOUNDTRACK ALBUM AVAILABLE ON PARAMOUNT RECORDS

1

“I’ll make him an offer he can’t refuse.”

The unmentionable words are never heard. No one dares speak of the “Mafia” or the “Cosa Nostra” in this film, despite the fact that it tells a tale whose roots are at the heart of organized crime. The contents are categorized by another word: family. “It’s a novel about a family, and not about crime,” said its author, Mario Puzo. Francis Ford Coppola initially rejected the offer to direct the film after reading the book over-hastily and dismissing it as just another Mafia vehicle. He eventually changed his mind for a number of reasons, principally because he discovered the family aspect of the story and was fascinated by it.

It is no coincidence that the film begins and ends with traditional family celebrations—a wedding and a baptism. The marriage of Connie Corleone (Talia Shire) and Carlo Rizzi (Gianni Russo) is the occasion for an enchanting celebration. An orchestra plays in the Corleone’s garden, filled with a mass of dancing guests. Feasting and joking, children run wild and glasses are repeatedly raised to toast the bride. During the festivities, FBI agents mill outside the gates of the villa and scrawl down license plate numbers of the guests. The father of the bride, Vito Corleone (Marlon Brando) is one of the five Dons of the Italian community in the New York area and the guest list is accordingly illustrious. According to old Sicilian tradition, the father of the bride cannot refuse any favor on his daughter’s wedding day. Surrounded by his sons and confidants he aristocratically sits in his darkened reception room, glowing in a golden brown light, the perfect expression of

MARLON BRANDO Among the many curiosities surrounding the legendary *The Godfather* (1972) is that its success sprung from a series of coincidences and imponderables. Mario Puzo was unhappy writing the screenplay, Francis Ford Coppola initially didn’t want to direct the film, and the studio had problems with the choice of the male lead. At this time, Marlon Brando (1924–2004) was at a low point in his career, which began in the 1940s in the theaters of New York City. In 1947, his portrayal of Stanley Kowalski in *A Streetcar Named Desire* was a triumph and in 1951 he played the character in Elia Kazan’s film adaptation. Schooled in “method acting,” Brando graduated to Hollywood big-time—four Oscar nominations in a row speak for themselves. Initially he was repeatedly cast as the youthful rebel, but he soon proved his versatility in costume films and musicals. In the 1960s, his notorious moodiness and a string of flops caused him to fall from grace with Hollywood producers. In 1972 he made his comeback with *The Godfather* and *The Last Tango in Paris* (*Ultimo tango a Parigi*/*Le Dernier Tango à Paris*), receiving Oscar nominations for both films. Though he was awarded the Oscar for his role as Vito Corleone in *The Godfather*, he refused to accept it for political reasons.

“Like practically no other Hollywood film of recent years, the tale of the New York Mafia clan Corleone reflects the divisions, the compulsions and the fears afflicting American society. Damaged by Vietnam and shaken by a profound crisis of faith in the nation, America’s hallowed norms of good and evil are looking more beleaguered than ever.” *Kölner Stadt-Anzeiger*

1 A man who won’t take “no” for an answer: Marlon Brando takes life in his stride as Don Corleone.

2 In sickness and in health: Making a deal with Don Corleone is more than a business transaction—it’s a life-long bond.

3 One wedding for fifty funerals: *The Godfather* opens with the Corleone family renewing its vows, whilst Carlo (Gianni Russo) and Connie (Talia Shire) take theirs.

2

dignity and power. He receives the supplicants, listens to their dilemmas, accepts congratulations, and basks in the respect offered from all sides.

Like every scene with Marlon Brando in the role of the Godfather Vito Corleone, these scenes are filled with warmth. The colors fade when his son Michael (Al Pacino) flees to the family's ancestral home in sunny Sicily after committing two murders. Later Michael, who once strived for an honorable life and distanced himself from his family, will become the ringleader of a blood bath: the images change with him, slowly acquiring a cold, bluish tinge.

The cause of the violent clash is Vito Corleone's decision to deny his backing to the plans of Virgil Sollozzo (Al Lettieri) to branch out into the drug-dealing business. Vito's temperamental son Sonny (James Caan) seems to disagree with his father, which inspires Sollozzo to try and topple the patriarch. Five shots bring Corleone down, but the old tiger survives. Michael, who to this point has held himself out of the family business, is shaken. His outsider role makes him seem unsuspicious, and he is therefore sent to the negotiation table. Michael promptly uses the opportunity to murder both Sollozzo and the corrupt police captain McCluskey (Sterling Hayden), and flees to Sicily. His unsuspecting girlfriend Kay (Diane Keaton) remains behind.

In Sicily, Michael's hardening process continues. He falls in love and—with old-fashioned etiquette—asks the bride's father permission for his daughter's hand. But the long arm of vengeance stretches to Italy—his young wife, Appollonia is killed in a car bomb that was meant for Michael. In New York, the war between the families rages on. Michael's brother Sonny is the next victim. The slowly recovering Vito Corleone is devastated, but forgoes his right to vengeance in an attempt to put an end to the killing. Michael returns to the United States. He marries Kay, who has become a teacher. Michael, whose eyes now have a cold, hard expression, knows that the old feud is not over. He plans a large liberating coup. While he is in church at his nephew's baptism, and is solemnly named as the child's godfather, the enemies of the Corleones are killed off one by one. Among them is Connie's husband Carlo, who lured Sonny into a deadly trap.

Connie has become a nervous wreck and Kay begins to ask critical questions. Michael coldly denies responsibility

6

“In scene after scene—the long wedding sequence, John Marley’s bloody discovery in his bed, Pacino nervously smoothing down his hair before a restaurant massacre, the godfather’s collapse in a garden—Coppola crafted an enduring, undisputed masterpiece.”

San Francisco Chronicle

7

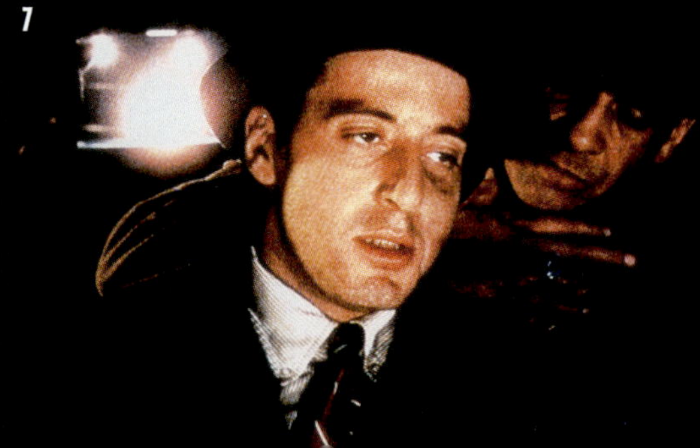

and Kay is forced to experience her utter exclusion from the male circle. Before the doors close in front of her, she sees her husband Michael, the new Don, graciously receive the best wishes of his confidants and associates.

The film stands out for its clever dramatization of the balance of power enjoyed by Vito Corleone and his successor, Michael, as well as its scenes of heavy violence, such as the severed horse’s head in film producer Jack Woltz’s bed, Sonny’s bullet-riddled body, or the gunshot through the lens of casino owner Moe Green’s glasses. The brilliant finale has an Old Testament-like intensity about it

"And all the while, we think we're watching a Mafia crime story; but we're actually watching one of the great American family melodramas." *The Austin Chronicle*

4 European vacation: A hunted man, Michael Corleone (Al Pacino) decides it's time to go back to his roots.

5 After some initial stumbling, Michael learns how to fill his father's shoes.

6 Deadlock: Michael Corleone and bride-to-be Kate (Diane Keaton).

7 The emissary wore black: Michael holds out a Sicilian olive branch to Virgil Sollozzo (Al Lettieri).

8 When in Rome: During his time in Sicily, Michael fares the local cuisine and develops a taste for Appollonia (Simonetta Stefanelli).

8

9 Big brother: When Carlo makes putty of wife Connie, Sonny puts a little love in his heart.

10 Gone with the wind: Sonny Corleone (James Caan) walks into a trap and goes up in smoke.

11 Paying the piper: An attempt to rescue sister Connie from a violent marriage proves more dangerous than Sonny had imagined …

"Cast and designed to perfection, this epic pastiche of 40s and 50s crime movies is as rich in images of idyllic family life as it is in brutal effects." *Der Spiegel*

But these drastic images are mere moments compared to the extensive family scenes. The business activities of the Corleones, which include murder and extortion, invariably take place outside the inner circle—they often follow car rides and trips, literally at a distance from the family core. This distance represents a lack of protection—the attempted hit on Vito Corleone occurs when he spontaneously stops to buy fruit from a street vendor, and hothead Sonny is killed when he leaves the family fortress with too great haste.

In a poignant reversal, Michael Corleone, the initially modern man, is unable to escape the chains of his family. Though he always considered himself an independent individual, he becomes a victim of the family tradition, a marionette whose strings are moved by the hands of fate, a metaphor the image on the book cover and film poster captures with perfection.

HK

11

LE CHARME DISCRET DE LA BOURGEOISIE

THE DISCREET CHARM OF THE BOURGEOISIE

1972 – FRANCE – 102 MIN.

GENRE

SOCIAL GROTESQUE

DIRECTOR

LUIS BUÑUEL

SCREENPLAY

LUIS BUÑUEL, JEAN-CLAUDE CARRIÈRE

DIRECTOR OF PHOTOGRAPHY

EDMOND RICHARD

EDITING

HÉLÈNE PLEMIANNIKOV

MUSIC

GUY VILLETTE

PRODUCTION

SERGE SILBERMAN for GREENWICH FILM PRODUCTIONS

STARRING

FERNANDO REY (Rafaele Costa, Ambassador of Miranda), PAUL FRANKEUR (Monsieur Thévenot), DELPHINE SEYRIG (Madame Thévenot), BULLE OGIER (Florence), STÉPHANE AUDRAN (Madame Sénéchal), JEAN-PIERRE CASSEL (Monsieur Sénéchal), MILENA VUKOTIC (Ines, the Maid), JULIEN BERTHEAU (Bishop Dufour), CLAUDE PIÉPLU (Colonel), MICHEL PICCOLI (Minister)

ACADEMY AWARDS 1973

OSCAR for BEST FOREIGN FILM

SERGE SILBERMAN présente

le charme discret de la bourgeoisie

avec par ordre
d'entrée en scène
FERNANDO REY
PAUL FRANKEUR
DELPHINE SEYRIG
BULLE OGIER
STEPHANE AUDRAN
JEAN-PIERRE CASSEL
JULIEN BERTHEAU
MILENA VUKOTIC
MARIA GABRIELLA MAIONE
CLAUDE PIEPLU
MUNI
FRANÇOIS MAISTRE
PIERRE MAGUELON
MAXENCE MAILFORT

scénario de
LUIS BUNUEL
avec la collaboration de
JEAN-CLAUDE CARRIERE

décors de
PIERRE GUFFROY
Directeur de la Photographie
EDMOND RICHARD
Directeur de la Production
ULLY PICKARD
un film produit par
SERGE SILBERMAN
PANAVISION SPHERIQUE
EASTMANCOLOR
Distribué par 20th Century Fox

UNE PRODUCTION
GREENWICH FILM PRODUCTION
© COPYRIGHT MCMLXXII

Ferracci

UN FILM DE LUIS BUNUEL

1

"There's nothing like a martini, especially when it's dry!"

An anecdote from Oscars Night, 1972, encapsulates the spirit of this film. When Luis Buñuel's movie was officially nominated, the 72-year-old Surrealist and scourge of the bourgeoisie made a statement to Mexican journalists: he was quite sure, he announced, that he would indeed be awarded the Oscar; after all, he insisted, he'd forked out the 25,000 dollars demanded for the prize—and though Americans might have their faults, they could always be relied on to keep their word... The story hit the press, and all hell broke loose in Hollywood. Buñuel's producer, Serge Silbermann, had his work cut out pouring oil on the troubled waters. When *The Discreet Charm of the Bourgeoisie* actually went on to win the Academy Award for the Best Foreign Film, Buñuel smugly told anyone who'd listen: "The Americans may have their faults—but you can always count on them to keep their word."

In his last film but three, the Old Master unleashed the beast of surrealism once more. This time, however, the result was less visually disturbing than the early masterpiece *An Andalusian Dog* (*Un chien andalou*, 1929), made in collaboration with Salvador Dali. After years of struggle and exile, in his hard-boiled but still vital old age, Buñuel

FERNANDO REY He turned up in so many films that almost everyone must have seen him sometime—possibly without even noticing it, for his appearances were sometimes fleeting (though always worthwhile). In the 80s, he appeared in so many movies that one critic dared call him "a prop." His filmography comprises around 200 films.
Yet for all that, the Spaniard Fernando Rey (1917–1994) is best known and best loved for his performances in a handful of films by his friend Luis Buñuel, as well as for his major roles in *The French Connection I* and *II* (1971/1975). In the latter movies, he played a sophisticated French drugs czar who's pursued obsessively by a tough, streetwise New York detective (Gene Hackman). The chase scene in the subway is unforgettable: when Rey, the man with the elegant walking-stick and the perfectly-manicured beard, waves nonchalantly as his train draws away from his frustrated nemesis on the platform, it's surely one of the great moments in movie history. Only Rey could have embodied this figure in all its rich ambiguity: gallant and decadent, cultivated and greedy—a memorably nuanced characterization.
His great career with the exiled Spaniard Buñuel began in Mexico with *Viridiana* (1961). There followed *Tristana* (1969/70), *The Discreet Charm of the Bourgeoisie* (*Le Charme discret de la bourgeoisie*, 1972) and *That Obscure Object of Desire* (*Cet obscur objet du désir*, 1977), Buñuel's last film. Though it may be hard to believe, Buñuel discovered Rey when he was playing the part of a corpse; the director was simply blown away by the actor's "expressive power." An encounter of crucial—indeed vital—importance to both...

2

1 The Mirandan ambassador (Fernando Rey) is a connoisseur of good food. Madame Thévenot (Delphine Seyrig) admires his excellent taste.

2 The more unattainable the goal, the more authoritative the moral law, the more unsuspecting the husband… the more desire grows.

3 Everybody's nightmare: Suddenly on stage without a line in your head.

no longer had any need to prove his credentials as an anarchic, subversive, and unconventional artist. And though one might complain that the film has no plot, that its characters are as lifeless as marionettes, or that they're forced to caper through an all-too-theatrical set, this kind of criticism simply fails to recognize the film's truly revolutionary quality, as a grotesque cinematic carnival of bourgeois ideals, values and clichés.

The story is easily summarized: six *grands bourgeois* are doing their damnedest to meet for an exquisitely cultivated evening meal—but something or other keeps stopping them from doing so. Either they mysteriously get the dates mixed up, or they're inconvenienced by a sudden death in the restaurant. So they try again; and this time, a squad of paratroopers burst into the house in order to carry out a maneuver. The would-be diners persist undeterred; and just as they've all taken their places and lifted their cutlery, they realize they're on a theater stage; the chicken is made of rubber, the audience are booing, and the actors appear to have forgotten their lines…

The title's complacent *grandezza* not only characterizes the bourgeoisie itself, but the visual style of the film, and Buñuel's analytical approach. No other director treats his characters with such distance and apparent passivity (or indifference); and none grants them such unconditional freedom to act according to the milieu or the atmosphere they happen to inhabit—to be new and different in each scene." *DIE ZEIT*

This last scene is not the only one that turns out to have been dreamt by one of the protagonists. Various other nightmares disturb the diners, whose faultlessly polite but utterly trivial activity seems destined to peter out in one dead end after another. On one occasion, a dream within a dream leads to yet another dream. As the film proceeds, it becomes increasingly clear to the audience that they can rely on nothing they are shown. Reality and illusion dissolve and merge into a new actuality, a surreal cinematic universe. Yet however bizarre the events that invade their lives, these six ladies and gentlemen never lose their cool, persevering heroically with their cultivated poses and their gestures of hypocritical friendliness. Quite literally, they never lose face; for when all they have is a succession of masks for every social eventuality, there's no face left to lose.

3

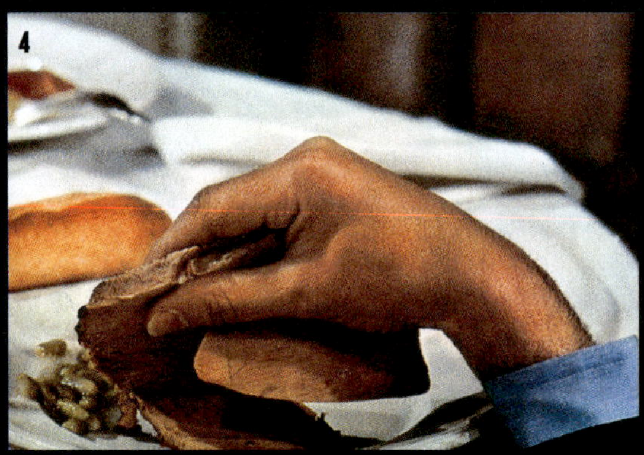

However elegantly the table is set, it's a uniquely hot, dry and spicy meal that Buñuel serves up to his audience, and it's not for tender palates (though he does include an excellent recipe for an extra-dry Martini). In fact, the guests at this dinner table are so wonderfully adroit in their blasé bitchiness that it's hard not to end up liking them a little. The subtle pleasure of *schadenfreude* is something one could quite easily acquire a taste for.

SR

"You may note that I haven't really tried to say what the film is about, what it means. And the reason for that is that I don't know. But, I don't really care, either. A poem should not mean, but be, said someone, and if there was a film poem, this is it." *Guardian Weekly*

4 Opportunity grabs: While the party is hiding from terrorists, the ambassador gets what he can.

5 Topsy-turvy: The dead hold a wake while the living sleep. Buñuel adopted and adapted the principles of Carnival.

6 Absolution: A bishop with a shotgun (Julien Bertheau) executes his father's murderer during Confession.

6

SOLYARIS

SOLARIS

1972 – USSR – 167 MIN.

GENRE

SCIENCE FICTION

DIRECTOR

ANDREI TARKOVSKY

SCREENPLAY

FRIEDRICH GORENSTEIN, ANDREI TARKOVSKY,
based on the novel of the same name by STANISŁAW LEM

DIRECTOR OF PHOTOGRAPHY

VADIM YUSSOV

EDITING

LJUDMILA FEYGINOVA

MUSIC

EDWARD ARTEMYEV, JOHANN SEBASTIAN BACH

PRODUCTION

VIACHESLAV TARASSOV for MOSFILM

STARRING

NATALYA BONDARCHUK (Hari), DONATAS BANIONIS (Kris Kelvin),
NIKOLAI GRINKO (Kris's Father), YURI JÄRVET (Snaut), ANATOLI SOLONITSYN (Sartorius),
VLADISLAV DVORZHETSKI (Berton), SOS SARKISSIAN (Gibarjan),
OLGA BARNET (Kris's Mother), TAMARA OGORODNIKOVA (Aunt Anna),
YULIAN SEMYONOV (Chairman at Scientific Conference)

IFF CANNES 1972

GRAND PRIZE OF THE JURY (Andrei Tarkovsky)

НА XXV КАННСКОМ МЕЖДУНАРОДНОМ КИНОФЕСТИВАЛЕ ФИЛЬМУ ПРИСУЖДЕН
БОЛЬШОЙ СПЕЦИАЛЬНЫЙ ПРИЗ
ХУДОЖЕСТВЕННЫЙ ФИЛЬМ В ДВУХ СЕРИЯХ
СОЛЯРИС
ПО ОДНОИМЕННОМУ РОМАНУ СТАНИСЛАВА ЛЕМА. СЦЕНАРИЙ Ф. ГОРЕНШТЕЙНА И А. ТАРКОВСКОГО
ПОСТАНОВКА АНДРЕЯ ТАРКОВСКОГО
ГЛАВНЫЙ ОПЕРАТОР ВАДИМ ЮСОВ. ГЛАВНЫЙ ХУДОЖНИК М. РОМАДИН. КОМПОЗИТОР Э. АРТЕМЬЕВ
В РОЛЯХ: ДОНАТАС БАНИОНИС, НАТАЛЬЯ БОНДАРЧУК, ЮРИ ЯРВЕТ
АНАТОЛИЙ СОЛОНИЦЫН, НИКОЛАЙ ГРИНЬКО
ПРОИЗВОДСТВО КИНОСТУДИИ «МОСФИЛЬМ»

1

2

"We are dealing with the limits of human understanding."

Based on a novel by Stanisław Lem, this film takes on some very big issues: the nature of self-awareness, knowledge and perception. In an era of space epics that were strong on special effects but weak on content—from *Star Wars* (1977) to *Star Wars: Episode V – The Empire Strikes Back* (1980)—*Solaris* reminds us that the science-fiction genre has its roots in philosophical speculation. And the film begins like a poetic alternative to its high-tech rivals.

Its opening shots are long and slow, idyllic images of the natural world: grass waving softly in the waters of a lake, trees, fog, a solitary horse. In the background, we hear birdsong, frogs croaking, and the soft rustle of flowing water. From beginning to end, *Solaris* maintains this meditative tempo, and it's one of the film's great strengths. With a confidently minimalist use of cinematic means, Tarkovsky presents a maximum of disturbing effects. The world he creates is a kind of utopia; highly idiosyncratic, familiar and yet strange. But Tarkovsky is in any case only marginally interested in doing justice to the conventions of the SF film. Indeed, his almost provocative refusal to serve up the special effects expected of the genre gives him more space to follow the development of the characters as they travel in search of themselves. Their story is told with the greatest of care.

The center of attention is the psychologist Kris Kelvin (Donatas Banionis). His task is to examine the crew of a space station in orbit around the planet Solaris, and to find out the reasons for their strange behavior. Before he departs from Earth, however, he has to order his personal affairs, which means, above all, his relationship with his father (Nikolai Grinko). This is a subject Tarkovsky returns to in each of his films. Kelvin's melancholy farewell is overshadowed by the still-raw memory of his wife Hari, who took her own life.

SCIENCE FICTION Since the 20s, the term has served as a collective name for films and books that speculate on technological developments in fantastic future worlds. The first science-fiction film appeared as early as 1902: Georges Méliès' *Journey to the Moon* (*Le Voyage dans la lune*), based on motifs from Jules Verne and H.G. Wells. While the set design and visual aesthetics of Fritz Lang's *Metropolis* (1926) formed a kind of stylistic prototype still imitated today, science fiction only achieved real popularity in the 50s, with films such as *The Thing From Another World* (1951) and *The War of the Worlds* (1953). The SF film appears to have no difficulty in formulating social and technical utopias, even when these are very far removed from the moviegoers' daily experience. A number of different strategies are available: the *Star Wars* saga (eight episodes between 1977 and 2016) was just one example of an elaborate spectacle driven by special-effects technology; the *Alien* series (1979–2017) showed how horror elements could be integrated; and *Blade Runner* (1982) picked up on the tradition of 40s *Film Noir*. As a rule, all these variants combine a vision of the human future with a scenario of existential threat. The philosophical content varies. In recent times, the genre has experienced a revival, with the satirical *Men in Black* (1997) and *The Matrix* (1999), which owes a lot to comics. The dramatic development of digital animation technology has produced a new "somatic cinema," whose sensuous and physical qualities could barely have been imagined even a few years ago. Films like *Solaris* (*Solyaris*, 1972) however, make it painfully clear that these technical advances have so far only been possible at the expense of real content.

Against this background, the voyage to the space station seems like a welcome departure to a new life. On arriving, Kelvin finds the two astronauts Snaut (Yuri Järvet) and Sartorius (Anatoli Solonitsyn) in a strangely nervous and preoccupied state. Their peculiar behavior appears to have something to do with the ocean of Solaris, whose biostreams are somehow affecting the psychic wellbeing of the crew. It becomes apparent that the planet itself is capable of turning private thoughts and wishes into three-dimensional reality. Kelvin himself is not spared the experience. Soon, he is faced with a materialized copy of his

"The seething planet, turbulent metaphor as much for an imperfect deity as for the psychoanalyst's couch, provides what the men come to recognize as a mirror of themselves, reflecting with inescapable clarity the faults which caused the errors now incarnate before them." *Sight and Sound*

1 In bed with the blues: Color symbolism and religious imagery brighten up the ether of *Solaris*.

2 Scent of a woman: “Humanized” memory Hari (Natalya Bondartschuk) proves little more than a hatful of hollow.

3 Always on my mind: Despite all attempts to stifle the memories of his mistress, Hari lives on.

4 Through the looking glass: Hari realizes that her identity is a sham.

5 Mind scrambler: Snaut (Juri Järvet) and Sartorius have already grasped Hari’s implications for future galactic travelers.

wife Hari (Natalya Bondarchuk). He is drawn into a series of mysterious encounters with this phantom creature—and confronted with the power of his own memories.

Like Bowman, the astronaut in Stanley Kubrick’s *2001: A Space Odyssey* (1968), Kelvin in *Solaris* ultimately attains a new level of consciousness. In many science-fiction movies, outer space is the scene of conquest, of battles for new territory. In *2001* and *Solaris*, by contrast, infinite and apparently empty space provides an opportunity for evolution, for a growth in knowledge and self-awareness. Vast, obscure and barely explored, space is also a metaphor for the human race, a stranger to itself and to its own history, despite all the progress of technology. Thematically, however, *2001* takes a broader view,

Solaris, Tarkovsky is interested primarily in the individual, his unique subjectivity and personal history. The form chosen is a kind of filmic contemplation that forgoes fast cutting in favor of poetic images, long takes, and faces absorbed in thought, thus granting us some deep insights into the characters’ mental states and private spiritual landscapes. What we see is the process of reflection given cinematic form; and, above all, given time to develop. If the methods seem unusual for a science-fiction film, they are more than adequate to the director’s theme. The film is powerfully poetic, and its melancholy atmosphere of loneliness and silence constitutes an invitation to the spectator: to follow Kris Kelvin on his utopian search for the unknown self.

ULTIMO TANGO A PARIGI / LE DERNIER TANGO À PARIS

LAST TANGO IN PARIS

1972 – ITALY / FRANCE – 136 MIN.

GENRE

DRAMA

DIRECTOR

BERNARDO BERTOLUCCI

SCREENPLAY

BERNARDO BERTOLUCCI, FRANCO ARCALLI

DIRECTOR OF PHOTOGRAPHY

VITTORIO STORARO

EDITING

FRANCO ARCALLI, ROBERTO PERPIGNANI

MUSIC

GATO BARBIERI

PRODUCTION

ALBERTO GRIMALDI for LES PRODUCTIONS ARTISTES ASSOCIÉS,
PRODUZIONI EUROPEE ASSOCIATI

STARRING

MARLON BRANDO (Paul), MARIA SCHNEIDER (Jeanne),
JEAN-PIERRE LÉAUD (Tom), MASSIMO GIROTTI (Marcel), VERONICA LAZAR (Rosa),
MARIA MICHI (Rosa's Mother), GIOVANNA GALLETTI (Prostitute),
GITT MAGRINI (Jeanne's Mother), CATHERINE ALLÉGRET (Catherine),
CATHERINE BREILLAT (Mouchette)

PEA
ALBERTO GRIMALDI
PRESENTA

MARLON BRANDO IN
ULTIMO TANGO A PARIGI
UN FILM DI BERNARDO BERTOLUCCI
MARLON BRANDO IN ULTIMO TANGO A PARIGI
CON MARIA SCHNEIDER · MARIA MICHI · GIOVANNA GALLETTI E CON JEAN-PIERRE LEAUD E LA PARTECIPAZIONE DI MASSIMO GIROTTI
PRODOTTO DA ALBERTO GRIMALDI | REGIA DI BERNARDO BERTOLUCCI | FOTOGRAFIA DI VITTORIO STORARO (A.I.C.) | MUSICHE DI GATO BARBIERI
UNA COPRODUZIONE PEA PRODUZIONI EUROPEE ASSOCIATE S.A.S. ROMA · LES PRODUCTIONS ARTISTES ASSOCIÉS S.A. PARIGI | TECHNICOLOR® | DISTRIBUZIONE United Artists Europa Inc.

1

“How do you like your hero? Over easy or sunny side up?”

The camera swoops down on a man, before encircling him with the fast, aggressive movements of a tango dancer. The man (Marlon Brando) is standing under a métro bridge in Paris, and he’s screaming. His name is Paul and his wife has just committed suicide. In the distance, we see the shadowy figure of a young woman (Maria Schneider). She approaches, passes Paul, and turns to look at him once more. These two will meet again. In an empty apartment, their first sexual contact takes place within minutes—no holds barred. The couple are in flight from themselves. Estranged from their lives, enclosed in a barely furnished room and surrounded by diffuse sunlight, they meet to adopt the original male and female roles: Adam and Eve. Neither knows the other’s name nor anything of their life outside the apartment, for what goes on beyond these walls is of no significance. Their relationship can only exist in the hermetic world of the apartment, in which all social links are erased. Paul is a hotelier and a vagabond, whose life has fallen apart since the death of his wife. It’s he who makes the rules, though his bourgeois 20-year-old lover Jeanne adopts them with increasing alacrity. In the end, though, it’s Paul who shatters this artificial unity against Jeanne’s will. He moves out of the flat and announces his desire to marry her; but Jeanne cannot countenance a bourgeois alliance with the man she refers to, disrespectfully, as *maître d’hôtel.* The iron rule remains: no names. As events draw towards the climax, he bursts into her apartment and demands to know her name. She’s

BERNARDO BERTOLUCCI Alongside Godard, Antonioni and Chabrol, the Italian director Bernardo Bertolucci is regarded as one of the last survivors of the European film avant-garde. He alone, however, managed to introduce the aesthetics of the *cinéma des auteurs* into the cinematic mainstream. Indeed, his films were often astonishingly popular, not least the multiple Oscar-winner *The Last Emperor* (1987). Influenced by the theories of Freud and Marx as well as by artists as diverse as Francis Bacon and Giuseppe Verdi, Bertolucci is a great political filmmaker *and* an outstanding visual stylist. His best film is widely agreed to be *The Conformist* (*Il conformista*/*Le Conformiste*, 1970), a tale of guilt and political entanglement in the fascist Italy of the 1930s. The film was adapted from a novel by Alberto Moravia.

Bertolucci (1941–2018) made his directing debut at the age of 21 with *La Commare secca*, based on a short story by Pier Paolo Pasolini. He went on to work with Pasolini as an assistant director on *Accattone* (1961), before achieving international recognition with his own film, *Before the Revolution* (*Prima della rivoluzione*, 1963–64). Other works of the 60s include *Amore e rabbia* (*Love and Anger*, 1969) and *Partner* (1968), a homage to the French *Nouvelle Vague.* The scandal caused by *Last Tango in Paris* (*Ultimo tango a Parigi*/*Le Dernier Tango à Paris*) brought him unheard-of success, but the film was banned in Italy and the country’s authorities even stripped the director of his right to vote.

Bertolucci’s cinematic trademarks include a highly developed epic narrative style and a sophisticated delight in visual imagery. In the 70s, he consolidated his reputation as a director of high-quality films with *1900* (*Novecento*, 1975/76) and *La Luna* (1979). With *Stealing Beauty* (*Io ballo da sola*/*Beauté volée*, 1996), a film set in Tuscany, he made his cinematic return to Italy; but only since *Besieged*/*L’assedio* (1998), the story of an Englishman and an African woman in Rome, has he been fully accepted back in his native land. He made *Paradiso e inferno* in 1999 and *Heaven and Hell* (2001), before his last film *Me and You* (*Io e te*, 2012).

holding a gun in her hand, in self-defense, and as she fulfills his request, the gun goes off. It's impossible to say what killed him—the weapon or the word.

In the early 70s, few films aroused as much attention as Bertolucci's *Last Tango in Paris.* In New York, Pauline Kael celebrated *Last Tango* as a work that had "altered the face of an art form;" in Italy, the movie caused uproar. Bertolucci was only 32 when he made *Last Tango,* and it was already his sixth film. Though he had become world-famous with *1900* (*Novecento*), his epic of the Italian century, *Ultimo tango a Parigi* was eventually banned in his home country. It was the graphic sex scenes that caused all the trouble, for they went far beyond anything ever seen in mainstream cinema and were accused of being pornographic. Yet the censors felt provoked not only by the copulating couple (who are, incidentally, never seen naked) and the spectacular body of Maria Schneider (at that time, a young and unknown actress). They were equally offended by the film's fundamentally nihilistic attitude and its openly stated fantasies of degradation. The movie was a product of its period: without the climate of sexual liberation at the start of the 70s, a film like *Last Tango in Paris* would have been as unthinkable as Liliana Cavani's *The Night Porter* (*Il portiere di notte,* 1974) or Pasolini's *Arabian Nights* (*Il fiore delle mille e una notte,* 1974). Since the 70s, we have grown accustomed to provocation as an artistic principle. It's the film's aesthetic qualities that impress us today. The pictorial composition,

2

1 Alone at last: After his wife's suicide, Paul (Marlon Brando) escapes to the confines of an empty apartment. Jeanne (Maria Schneider) soon follows suit.

2 It takes two to tango… Paul and Jeanne dance to a different tune.

3 If only they knew the real me: The spectator can only see Jeanne through her fiancé's camera.

"This must be the most powerfully erotic movie ever made, and it may turn out to be the most liberating movie ever made, and so it's probably only natural that an audience, anticipating a voluptuous feast from the man who made *The Conformist* and confronted with the unexpected sexuality, and the new realism it requires of the actors, should go into shock. Bertolucci and Brando have altered the face of an art form. Who was prepared for that?" *Pauline Kael*

the light, the camerawork and the editing create a wholly unique atmosphere and provide the actors with the framework they require—especially Marlon Brando. Bertolucci's cameraman Vittorio Storaro had a huge influence on the director's visual style. The artfully lit interiors, the variations in focal depth and the precisely calculated camera movements combine to evoke the atmosphere that made the film so famous: a continual oscillation between sexual tension, power fantasies and sheer hopelessness. This effect is reinforced by Franco Arcalli's montage, with its often bewildering suspension of spatial logic, and the music of Gato Barbieri, till then known only as a composer for B-movies.

With admirable skill, Bertolucci weaves together three narrative threads. There's the story of Paul, mourning his dead wife and hunting for the traces of her

4

"*Tango*'s explosive impact will demonstrate to a wide public what many film buffs already know: that Bertolucci, 31, is Italy's most gifted director in the generation after Fellini and Antonioni, and one of the most gifted younger directors on the world scene." *Time Magazine*

suicide in his strange, labyrinthine hotel. There's the story of Jeanne, whose life we see filtered through the camera of her fiancé Tom (Jean-Pierre Léaud) as material for a TV documentary entitled "The Portrait of a Young Girl." This film-within-the-film is a parody of *cinéma vérité*; while Tom believes he's portraying the real Jeanne, all he can produce is a string of tired clichés. And finally we have the story of Paul *and* Jeanne, another manifestation of the old dream of innocence regained, of a new self beyond economic status, culture or civilization. The scene in which the couple sit naked on the bed has since become famous. Their bodies are bathed in warm, yellow light, and they converse only in sounds, in a series of grunts and chirrups. For language is civilization, words

4 *A Streetcar Named Desire* (revisited): Domestic violence behind closed doors.

5 Empty chairs and empty tables: Vittorio Storaro's camera captures the character's inner isolation.

petrify social relationships, and these are the very things the two deeply different protagonists are seeking to escape in the secret world of the apartment. Yet this Garden of Eden, as a refuge from civilization, is also a place in which the rules of civilized behavior seem to have lost their normative force. Here, violence, raw sex and obscene fantasies can achieve expression, as putative manifestations of a non-social way of being. The film is permeated by an existential despair that evokes the world of Francis Bacon. Not only does the film open with two Bacon paintings; Bertolucci also imitates the colors and compositional techniques of the artist, with shots framed in arches and faces filmed through a sheet of glass, shifting and dissolving their contours.

KK

WHAT'S UP, DOC?

1972 – USA – 94 MIN.

GENRE

SCREWBALL COMEDY

DIRECTOR

PETER BOGDANOVICH

SCREENPLAY

BUCK HENRY, DAVID NEWMAN, ROBERT BENTON, based on a story by PETER BOGDANOVICH

DIRECTOR OF PHOTOGRAPHY

LÁSZLÓ KOVÁCS

EDITING

VERNA FIELDS

MUSIC

ARTIE BUTLER

PRODUCTION

PETER BOGDANOVICH for SATICOY PRODUCTIONS

STARRING

BARBRA STREISAND (Judy Maxwell), RYAN O'NEAL (Professor Howard Bannister), MADELINE KAHN (Eunice Burns), AUSTIN PENDLETON (Frederick Larrabee), MABEL ALBERTSON (Mrs. Van Hoskins), SORRELL BOOKE (Harry the Detective), STEFAN GIERASCH (Fritz), KENNETH MARS (Hugh Simon), PHILIP ROTH (Mr. Jones), LIAM DUNN (Judge Maxwell) a SCREWBALL COMEDY. ★ REMEMBER THEM?

Barbra Streisand ★ Ryan O'Neal

IN

"WHAT'S UP, DOC?"

A PETER BOGDANOVICH PRODUCTION

BARBRA STREISAND • RYAN O'NEAL in "WHAT'S UP, DOC?" A Peter Bogdanovich Production Co-Starring KENNETH MARS • AUSTIN PENDLETON • SORRELL BOOKE • MICHAEL MURPHY
And Introducing MADELINE KAHN • Screenplay by Buck Henry and David Newman & Robert Benton • Story by Peter Bogdanovich • Directed and Produced by Peter Bogdanovich
TECHNICOLOR® From Warner Bros., A Warner Communications Company G ALL AGES ADMITTED General Audiences

1

"Once upon a time, there was a plaid overnight case..."

A delicate hand opens a red leather-bound volume with a Warner Bros. insignia on its cover, and we instantly know what Peter Bogdanovich's second feature film has in store for us. As if fondly glancing into a cherished children's storybook or family photo album, we watch pages containing Barbra Streisand's unmistakable singing. A hand, presumably hers, glides across the parchment, gesturing both lovingly and flippantly to the names of cast and crew that appear on screen. This introduction sequence greets the audience with a wink and a smile. Just like the film's title itself, it is a spoof on the classic animated shorts featuring Bugs Bunny, Tex Avery's fast-talking, carrot-munching "wascally wabbit." The 33-year-old Bogdanovich had already earned himself a reputation for being a well-versed chronicler of international and, even more so, American film history. This project, according to the movie's tagline, was to be his very own nostalgic twist on the screwball comedy. Remember them?

What's Up, Doc? gets (and gives) its kicks by poking fun at the icons of Hollywood entertainment. Bogdanovich proudly pays tribute to greats like Hawks, Hitchcock, the Marx Brothers and Buster Keaton. He steals enough of their material and gags to be tried for grand theft larceny a thousand times over. Not that we mind, for the picture's magic is wrapped up in the hidden and overt references to the Golden Age of Hollywood found in each character and scene, as well as in its flow and choreography. When a very svelte Barbra hangs onto a 33rd-story window ledge for dear life, wearing nothing but a towel, we are reminded of Harold Lloyd's bombastic shot of the New York City skyscraper clock from *Safety Last* (1923), and that's just the tip of the iceberg. We watch as 90 minutes of non-stop nyuk nyuk jokes, complete with pies in the face and off-the-wall physical comedy explode onto the screen. There are even traces of the cinematic avant-garde when Bogdanovich humorously resorts to the

BARBRA STREISAND Her own mother didn't think she'd make it as a singer and actress. What chance did a kooky Brooklyn kid with skinny legs, a crooked nose and slightly crossed eyes stand against all the attractive young women out there who were determined to make it big? And so, the Jewish girl born Barbara Joan Streisand (born 1942 in Brooklyn, New York) started out small. She worked as a cleaning lady at a theater, an usher, a telephone operator—anything to get closer to realizing her dream. She sang, acted and hummed her way to the front of the stage until audiences could not help but notice her. Her Broadway debut came with the 1962 musical *I Can Get It For You Wholesale* in the role of Ms. Marmelstein. Against the wish of those auditioning her, she performed the entire number while seated in a rolling chair. Barbra's tactic won out and audiences couldn't get enough of her. She quickly became the toast of the town, and landed the lead in Jule Styne's Broadway musical sensation *Funny Girl*. Streisand's "Hello Gorgeous!" quickly went from being a New York catchphrase to a national one when she reprised the role of Fanny Brice for the 1968 Hollywood film adaptation of *Funny Girl*, a debut performance that won her the Best Actress Oscar in a vote to vote tie with Katharine Hepburn. Further comedies like *The Owl and the Pussycat* (1970) and *What's Up, Doc?* (1972) quickly followed, as did a Best Original Song Oscar for *A Star is Born* (1976). Yet Barbra, who dropped the original second "a" from her first name at her manager's request, wanted more out of life than just comedy, song, stage and glamour—she wanted to play serious roles and to direct. Both wishes came true with the 1983 film *Yentl* (1983), for which she also served as co-screenwriter and producer. Nonetheless, her "ugly duckling" persona had taken its toll. Barbra Streisand soon became known for her eccentricity, her stage fright and her megalomania. She began to purchase art and her gold records were soon eclipsed by the exclusive Art Deco and Jugendstil pieces that decorated her numerous residences. During the mid 1990s she took to the more minimalist functionality of modern art and auctioned off her painstakingly acquired collection. Many years after her divorce from actor Elliott Gould, the one-of-a-kind entertainer married movie and TV star James Brolin, to whom she is still wed. She continues to appear in movies and release new albums.

1 The look of love? Barbra Streisand as zany Judy Maxwell.

2 High-speed bloopers and practical jokes: The twelve-minute "roller-coaster ride" through the streets of San Francisco took four weeks to film.

3 Twists and turns, thrills and spills: Once a screwball comedy gets into gear anything goes.

"subjective camera" and thrusts his audience into the shoes of a homicidal maniac. Here, an outstretched arm points a pistol at petrified party guests, who stare directly into the camera (and at us) as if down the barrel of a gun.

What's Up, Doc? is a laugh attack compilation of film references and visual aesthetics. There are parodies jumping out at every corner, and the roller-coaster pace supplied by the three screenwriters is enough to make you dizzy. Conversations resemble ping-pong tournaments where the spectators are forced do one double take after another in order to keep score. It's a veritable shell game, and to win the audience must concentrate on all the visuals, from rapid cuts and over-the-top facial expressions, to tiny set-dressing and costume details. Then, of course, there are the "shells" themselves—the four plaid overnight cases sought by a sordid cast of characters for the most diverse of reasons. As luck would have it, these four indistinguishable pieces of baggage "just happen" to land in four hotel rooms all on the same floor of one hotel, separated only by a hallway and a matter of feet. Doors fly open and shut, as those who have the suitcases are chased by those who'll stop at nothing to get them.

Five rooms, four bags, about a dozen eccentric characters and one unassuming elevator at the end of the hall—that is the winning recipe behind *What's Up, Doc?*, the Bogdanovich screwball that just won't quit. A virtual study in relentlessness, its crowning achievement is a hare-brained spin on the classic chase scene *à la* Peter Yates' *Bullitt* (1968), packed with shoots and ladder antics, Buster Keaton-style window panes being transported across moving traffic and Chinese dragons. By the end, there's just nowhere else left for its mayhem to go except maybe smack into the middle of the San Francisco Bay or to a court of law where you never know just who you'll heet… Not to worry, it all ends happily, proving the age-old adage about love healing all wounds—and occasionally even scrapes and bruises. This time, the lovers are irresistible home-wrecker Barbra Streisand and bungling straight man Ryan O'Neal, as Howard Bannister, professor of musicology. The academic bears a striking similarity to anthropologist David Huxley (Cary Grant) from Howard Hawks' *Bringing Up Baby* (1938), a picture that provided the foundation for *What's Up, Doc?*—undoubtedly Bogdanovich's greatest cinematic dissertation.

SR

"Bogdanovich is much too clever just to latch on to his role models. One might say he's trying to match up to them by reviewing the last few years of film history. In other words, his film is really an intelligent parody of recent box-office hits." *Frankfurter Rundschau*

4 Meeting of the minds: For a quiet tête-à-tête during a dinner party, what better place than under the table? But they won't be alone for long…

SUPER FLY

1972 – USA – 91 MIN.

GENRE

DRAMA

DIRECTOR

GORDON PARKS JR.

SCREENPLAY

PHILLIP FENTY

DIRECTOR OF PHOTOGRAPHY

JAMES SIGNORELLI

EDITING

BOB BRADY

PRODUCTION

SIG SHORE

STARRING

RON O'NEAL (Youngblood Priest), CARL LEE (Eddie), JULIUS HARRIS (Scatter), SHEILA FRAZIER (Georgia), CHARLES MCGREGOR (Fat Freddie), THE MAN (Sig Shore), POLLY NILES (Cynthia)

Never a dude like this one!
He's got a plan to stick it to The Man!
THE SIG SHORE PRODUCTION
Super Fly
STARRING
RON O'NEAL
AS PRIEST
See and hear CURTIS MAYFIELD play his Super Fly score!
Original soundtrack available on Curtom Records
The SIG SHORE Production "SUPER FLY" Starring RON O'NEAL · CARL LEE · JULIUS W. HARRIS · SHEILA FRAZIER
CHARLES McGREGOR · Music Composed and Arranged by CURTIS MAYFIELD · Screenplay by PHILLIP FENTY · Produced
by SIG SHORE · Directed by GORDON PARKS, JR. · from Warner Bros., a Warner Communications company
R
COPYRIGHT ©1972 WARNER BROS., INC.
72/319

1
2

"Eddie: I know it's a rotten game, but it's the only one The Man left us to play. That's the stone, cold truth."

In this Blaxploitation crime drama, the drug dealer Youngblood Priest (played by Ron O'Neal) has all a man could wish for, like a swanky apartment, the hippest clothes, and loads of coke and cash stuffed in his pockets. On one arm, he has a loyal girlfriend, on the other, a wealthy white lover, and he drives a '71 Cadillac Eldorado. Even so, neither the blinding façade of material prosperity nor his sexual adventures can disguise the fact that Priest lacks any freedom of his own. He wants out from this lousy business. Paradoxically, to do this he will have to sell a massive amount of coke, his biggest deal ever.

Working alongside his business partner Eddie (Carl Lee), Priest wants to do one last big thing. His plan is quite simple. With the savings of previous years, he wants to buy 30 kilos of cocaine through his former mentor, Scatter (Julius Harris), sell it within four months, and with his portion of the deal's profits of one million dollars, start a brighter future with his girlfriend Georgia (Sheila Frazier). But there

RON O'NEAL Born September 1, 1937, in Utica, New York, Ron O'Neal grew up in a Black working-class neighborhood in Cleveland, Ohio. In his early 20s, he was already a permanent member of the Karamu House Theatre ensemble, although the actor earned his living as a house painter on the side. In 1964 he moved to New York City to take a job as an acting coach at the Harlem Youth Arts Program. His numerous attempts to get engagements in off-Broadway productions failed however, due to his relatively light skin and smooth hair; according to many producers, his appearance deviated too far from the stereotype. The role of Gabe Gabriel in Charles Gordone's drama *No Place to Be Somebody* (1969) marked a turning point in his career. For this, O'Neal received several awards, including the renowned Obie, the Drama Desk Award and the Clarence Derwent Award. Even so, after the Blaxploitation epic *Super Fly*, O'Neal had a hard time finding solid work despite his talent, because from then on he was always associated with his iconic pusherman role. Forever typecast, over the next quarter of a century he appeared in several crime and action films, including *The Master Gunfighter* (1975), *A Force of One* (1979) *and Red Dawn* (1984). He gained a role in *Original Gangstas* (1996), a drama about gang violence in Gary, Indiana, in which all the greatest stars of the Blaxploitation era appeared, like Richard Roundtree and the original Foxy Brown Pam Grier. After O'Neal was diagnosed with pancreatic cancer in the year 2000, he appeared in front of the camera for the last time, working on the movie *On the Edge*, with Ice-T. On January 14, 2004, at the age of 66, he died as a result of the disease in Los Angeles.

1 Youngblood Priest (Ron O'Neal) and his partner Eddie (Carl Lee) have already scored $300,000 in the cocaine business. But they need even more to pull off their exit plan.

2 When Priest cruises down the block in his 1971 Cadillac Fleetwood Eldorado, people on the street can't help but stare.

3 The big boss's henchmen jump Priest when he won't back down, something they will soon regret.

4 Priest would never go into battle unprepared, so takes private karate lessons in advance.

5 Eddie threatens the retired dealer Scatter (Julius Harris) when he won't get them any more coke, and he ends up looking down the wrong end of Scatter's gun.

is one thing that film history has taught us: the final coup is always the riskiest.

When *Super Fly* arrived in cinemas in summer 1972, the story of Priest, the dealer looking to get out, became a sensation. Today, the film, alongside Melvin Van Peebles' independent action thriller *Sweet Sweetback's Baadasssss Song* (1971) and the MGM-produced *Shaft* (1971), numbers among the defining classics of the Blaxploitation genre. With the distribution of the independently produced directors' debut *Super Fly*, Warner Bros. too saw the opportunity in the early 1970s to market Black cinema profitably—and did it successfully. The film generated an enormous $24.8 million in two years. This record box office isn't only a result of the outstanding soundtrack, which was released before the film opened and had already produced several top 10 hits. Like the chorus of a Greek tragedy, Curtis Mayfield underpins the plot of the film with a rousing fusion of soul and funk, delivering powerful songs like "Pusherman" and "Freddie's Dead," a sociocritical commentary on the realities of life for Black America in the major cities of the time.

It wasn't just through its music but also its rapid speed that the film won over viewers. The opening sequence shows a heated chase in which Priest pursues two junkies who have robbed him through the grimy backyards of Harlem. Such shots derive from the documentary style of cinematographer James Signorelli, whose dark realism captures memorable images of the streets and neighborhoods of New York. Some awkward camera positions and cuts like the conspicuous continuity errors in the final showdown, make the cinematic craft of *Super Fly* sometimes seem like something from a trashy B-movie. This might also have been due to the small budget of just under $500,000. Nevertheless, the film offers creative visuals and clever sequences of cuts that directly juxtapose the divergent realities of life. There is a sensational bathtub sex scene between the protagonist and his girlfriend Georgia, where the soundtrack evokes walruses splashing around rather than an erotic love game, which flows abruptly into a street fight and, with the narrative power of the editing, comments

4

"If indeed *Super Fly* does encourage young people, I'm happy. And I doubt that they'll be encouraged to become coke hustlers, because they're too intelligent. I'm hoping that the most inspiration will come from our success as filmmakers." *Ron O'Neal, The New York Times*

5

6 Georgia (Sheila Frazier) would prefer her boyfriend to get out right now, before something really bad happens. She would also be happy with a simple life and little money—if only he could also feel the same.

7 Curtis Mayfield not only delivers the funky soul soundtrack, he also performs his song "Pusherman" in the movie in a scene set in a nightclub.

8 His white lover, Cynthia (Polly Niles), does not yet suspect that Priest is planning to leave his dealer lifestyle—and that he is leaving her behind at the same time.

on Priest's inevitable fate. Broadway actor O'Neal is also captivating from his first sniff in his role as the restlessly dissatisfied gangster, which he plays with a blend of pure coolness and subtle vulnerability. In this way, his almost exaggerated macho attitude at times seems like a necessary protective shield, behind which he tries to hide his conflict-laden inner life.

When one of his dealers, the childish Fat Freddie (Charles McGregor), squeals to the cops during a brutal interrogation about the coke deal, Priest's plan comes to a halt. But instead of picking up the pusherman and his partner, the corrupt law enforcement agents recruit the ambitious dealer gang as new contacts for the high-ranking drug boss known as "The Man" (Sig Shore), aka Deputy Commissioner Reardon. Thanks to their new employer, business runs like clockwork, as evidenced by a sophisticated split-screen sequence of single-still images, timed to the length of a Mayfield song. But while Eddie, blinded by success, feels no ambition to hang up the job, Priest is sure that their career in the white establishment-controlled drug cartel will eventually end badly. He becomes painfully aware of how right he is, when an example is made of the ready-to-quit Scatter, who is sent into early "retirement" with an overdose of heroin. After another betrayal from his own ranks, Priest finally dares the almost impossible and stands up to his oppressor alone. Good thing he can rely on solid karate moves and on his own smarts acquired on the street.

Contrary to the voices of the time claiming that the film glorifies the lifestyle of drug deaalers in an irresponsible way, Gordon Parks Jr.'s *Super Fly* is a sharp criticism of an American society plagued by hypocrisy and corruption. He shows how the drug trade became the most promising future prospect for the Black youth of the big cities, and he would even 20 years later go on to influence directors like John Singleton (*Boyz n the Hood*, 1991) and Ernest R. Dickerson (*Juice*, 1992).

MW

7

"The film's gut pleasures are real, and there are a lot of them. But, they always connect with one another in a world so precisely, cruelly, excitingly balanced that there is no movement without countermovement, no pressure without a greater pressure in return. It is a world of the most limited options—all leading to the question of being in or getting out." *The New York Times*

8

BADLANDS

1973 – USA – 95 MIN.

GENRE

DRAMA

DIRECTOR

TERRENCE MALICK

SCREENPLAY

TERRENCE MALICK

DIRECTOR OF PHOTOGRAPHY

BRIAN PROBYN, TAK FUJIMOTO, STEVAN LARNER

EDITING

ROBERT ESTRIN

MUSIC

GEORGE ALICESON TIPTON, GUNILD KEETMAN, JAMES TAYLOR, CARL ORFF, NAT KING COLE, ERIK SATIE

PRODUCTION

TERRENCE MALICK for PRESSMAN-WILLIAMS, BADLANDS COMPANY

STARRING

MARTIN SHEEN (Kit), SISSY SPACEK (Holly), WARREN OATES (Holly's Father), JOHN CARTER (Rich Man), RAMON BIERI (Cato), ALAN VINT (Deputy), GARY LITTLEJOHN (Sheriff), BRYAN MONTGOMERY (Boy), GAIL THRELKELD (Girl), CHARLES FITZPATRICK (Salesman)

He was 25 years old • He combed his hair like James Dean • He was very fastidious • People who littered bothered him • She was 15 • She took music lessons and could twirl a baton • She wasn't very popular at school • For awhile they lived together in a tree house.

In 1959, she watched while he killed a lot of people.

Badlands

PRESSMAN—WILLIAMS Presents A JILL JAKES PRODUCTION "BADLANDS"
Starring MARTIN SHEEN · SISSY SPACEK
RAMON BIERI and WARREN OATES · Executive Producer EDWARD PRESSMAN
Written, Produced and Directed by TERRENCE MALICK · From Warner Bros. A Warner Communications Company PG PARENTAL GUIDANCE SUGGESTED

COPYRIGHT ©1974 WARNER BROS., INC.

74/94

1

"He wanted to die with me and I dreamed of being lost forever in his arms."

Fifteen-year-old Holly (Sissy Spacek) has grown up without a mother and whiles away the hours playing in her backyard. Kit (Martin Sheen) is 25 and works as a garbage man in Fort Dupree, a middle-of-nowhere town in South Dakota. When the two of them lay eyes on each other, it's love at first sight. Holly's father (Warren Oates) forbids her from associating with Kit, but to no avail. One thing leads to another and Kit ends up shooting Holly's father dead, sending the couple on an outlandish escapade in the great American frontier. They flee to the Montana Badlands, committing three more murders en route. In their isolation, they revert to an archaic hunter-gatherer way of life, until they are finally discovered…

The work of filmmaker Terrence Malick is surrounded by legends. He directed two films in the 70s, *Badlands* and *Days of Heaven* (1978), and then disappeared from the scene until 1998 when he re-emerged behind the camera with the critically acclaimed *The Thin Red Line*. His first feature film, *Badlands*, marked an astounding debut. Malick's story of two star-crossed loners is a stunningly aesthetic ballad. From the sleepy town to the abandoned, virtually endless expanses of land, right through the sanctuary of the wilderness, the scenes unfold in a blanket of golden sunlight. The film is a homage to the landscape of the region, showered in a melange of heat and dust. Malick employed the services of three cinematographers

TRUE CRIME DRAMAS In the late fall of 1888, five prostitutes were slaughtered in London's East End. The case remains unsolved to this day and in 2001, brothers Albert and Allan Hughes speculated whether the killings could have been the handiwork of Jack the Ripper in their film *From Hell*. From Hitchcock's *The Lodger* (1926) to the drama *From Hell*, Jack the Ripper, as well as gangsters like Bonnie and Clyde, Al Capone and Lucky Luciano have served as inspiration for many filmmakers. Real-life criminals and crimes often make for good pictures. The added thrill of an act the spectator cannot dismiss as mere fiction and the sheer intrigue surrounding the perpetrators' motivations and psychology have always appealed to cinema auteurs. Other works of the genre including *M* (*M – Eine Stadt sucht einen Mörder*, 1931) about serial killer Peter Kürten (played by Peter Lorre), *The Sugarland Express* (1974) about jailbird Robert Samuel Dent and his wife as well as *The Deathmaker (Totmacher*, 1995), about the serial killer Fritz Haarmann have enriched the spectrum. Perhaps the most famous example is the 1959 case of a Kansas family killed *In Cold Blood* (1967). Director Richard Brooks brought Truman Capote's best-selling work of the same name to the big screen. With his story, Capote launched what he considered to be a new form of literature he called the non-fiction novel. True crime movies do not necessarily have to be about murders: the financial fraud committed by investor Nick Leeson inspired *Rogue Trader* (1999), yet another film that falls into this category.

1 Say say, oh, playmate: Volatile lovers Holly (Sissy Spacek) and Kit (Martin Sheen) are either a pair of innocents or a pair of fools.

2 Tess of the D'Urbervilles: "Holly is an unformed character, willing to be led in any direction, by anyone who pays attention to her." (*Guide for the Film Fanatic*)

3 Runaway train: He came from the wrong side of the tracks and decided to stay there.

to realize his vision. His imagery is underscored, not by country music, but rather by the simple yet soothing xylophone sounds of Carl Orff's *Musica Poetica*.

As luxuriously as the film exhibits its landscape, so it laconically tells the protagonists' story. *Badlands* is coldly distant in the depiction of its subject matter and avoids the psychological. The film is based on the true story of "Mad Dog Killer" Charles Starkweather, a nineteen-year-old who, alongside his fourteen-year-old girlfriend, Carol Ann Fugate, went on a killing rampage that left Carol's father and several others dead. Charles and Carol, according to the tale, were regular kids and not psychopaths. Malick's central characters, too, are seemingly ordinary people, even when, for the most part, they appear apathetic and caught up in their own world, far from reality.

Holly looks like a little girl when we see her playing in the backyard wearing shorts and a T-shirt. Her one genuine interest is her love for movie magazines. We watch as

"The couple has often been compared with Bonnie and Clyde, but Malick had something else in mind—these young rebels are too undeveloped, too emotionally immature to know how to approach each other sexually." *San Francisco Chronicle*

she plows through one after the other. They infiltrate her language, as we hear in the off-camera narratives in which she tells us of her life with Kit. After her mother's death, her father even views her as the "little stranger he found in his house" and Kit as the kid from "the wrong side of the tracks."

To Holly, Kit is a projection of her own desires, an image come to life right out of her magazines. He is thin, muscular, wears white Ts, blue jeans and smokes. Naturally, she immediately sees him as James Dean. At one point, Kit actually takes on Dean's classic stance from *Giant* (1956), with a rifle mounted square across his shoulders. He and Holly are creatures who know nothing of responsibility. They commit their bloody deeds as if they were a game, absent of emotion or compassion. The dead are no more real to Holly than the people she reads about in her Hollywood journals. She often appears more gruesome in her childlike inability to reflect than Kit, whose attempts at emulating James Dean are at times almost endearing. Simply stated, they are two overgrown children, who—for a while—are free to kill in cold blood. Who knows? Maybe it was the director's intention to paint an ironic portrait of the silver screen serial killer, a trend that took off in Hollywood following this production. HJK

4 Living off the land: Kit and Holly return to primordial life in the Badlands of Montana.

5 End of the line: Taken into custody by the authorities, Kit and Holly learn that all good things must come to an end.

6 Field of dreams: *The Badlands* ballad celebrates the virgin frontier.

"The more I looked at people the more I hated them, because I knowed there wasn't any place for me with the kind of people I knowed."

Motion Picture Guide

5

6

ENTER THE DRAGON

1973 – USA / HONG KONG – 99 MIN.

GENRE

EASTERN, MARTIAL ARTS FILM, ACTION FILM

DIRECTOR

ROBERT CLOUSE

SCREENPLAY

MICHAEL ALLIN

DIRECTOR OF PHOTOGRAPHY

GIL HUBBS

EDITING

KURT HIRSCHLER, GEORGE WATTERS

MUSIC

LALO SCHIFRIN

PRODUCTION

FRED WEINTRAUB, PAUL M. HELLER, LEONARDO HO, BRUCE LEE for WARNER BROS., CONCORDE PRODUCTIONS INC., SEQUOIA PRODUCTIONS

STARRING

BRUCE LEE (Lee), JOHN SAXON (Roper), SHIH KIEN (Han), JIM KELLY (Williams), AHNA CAPRI (Tania), BOB WALL (Oharra), YANG SZE (Bolo), ANGELA MAO YING (Su Lin), BETTY CHUNG (Mei Ling), PETER ARCHER (Parsons)

龍爭虎鬥
李小龍
領銜主演
鄒文懷 監製
高洛斯 導演
茅瑛 客串主演
BRUCE LEE IN
ENTER THE DRAGON
尊薩遜
鍾玲玲
安娜姬貝莉
領銜主演
Starring
BRUCE LEE
JOHN SAXON
BETTY CHUNG
ANNA CAPRI
Guest Star
ANGELA MAO
Director
ROBERT CLOUSE
A Concord Production
GH
Distributed by
Golden Harvest
嘉禾發行
協和出品

1

"You have offended my family, and you have offended a Shaolin temple."

Lee (Bruce Lee) is a Shaolin Monk and a masterful kung fu fighter. A British secret agent comes to him with a mission: Lee is to enter a martial arts tournament held every three years by a man named Han (Shih Kien). Han deals in drugs and girls and lives on an island in the middle of the South China Sea that he has converted into a fortress. Entering the tournament is the only way to gain access to the island, and Lee has to use this opportunity to gather evidence against the gangster. He has a personal interest in the matter—Han's sidekick Oharra (Bob Wall) caused the death of Lee's sister. Cornered by Oharra, she committed suicide to prevent herself from being raped. Lee accepts the mission. Among the men accompanying Lee to the tournament are two Americans: white trash gambler Roper (John Saxon), and a black playboy named Williams (Jim Kelly). Both men are first-rate fighters.

Enter the Dragon was the fourth and final completed film starring Bruce Lee, who died in 1973. It was also the first Hollywood film to feature a protagonist of Chinese origin. Producer Fred Weintraub saw Bruce Lee in Hong Kong and was so impressed he immediately decided to produce a film with Lee in the United States. Bruce Lee was the

BRUCE LEE It could be said that Bruce Lee (born 1940 in San Francisco) inherited his success. Or at least that it was written in his birth certificate: Lee Jun Fan, his Chinese name, means "achieves success abroad." His success story did begin away from America—in Hong Kong. Lee initially appeared in a handful of U. S. television series like *The Green Hornet* (1966–67). The international breakthrough—his ascendancy from martial arts instructor and philosophy student to cult star was only achieved upon his return to Hong Kong. There he took over the lead role in martial arts films like *The Big Boss* (*Tang shan da xiong*, 1971) and *Fist of Fury* (*Jing wu men*, 1972). After differences of opinion with director Lo Wei, Lee began to direct himself. With *Way of the Dragon* (*Meng long guojiang*, 1972) he purposely set his sights on the world market. He switched the setting of the story from Hong Kong to Rome and chose the American martial arts sportsman and future action-film star Chuck Norris as his opponent. Lee's next directorial project was to be *Game of Death*, but the postponed filming of *Enter the Dragon* (1973) caused a conflict, and his sudden death prevented the film from being finished. Four years after Lee's death, a film was made and subsequently released using a body double and the ten minutes of fight footage from *Game of Death* (*Si wang you ju*, 1977). After his death, copycats sought to profit from Lee's success, producing films with such no-names as Bruce Li or Bruce Le, none of whom came anywhere close to the style and flair of the icon they imitated.

The man of Shaolin: A master of mental and physical discipline, Lee (Bruce Lee) is a monk, kung fu fighter and irresistible sex symbol.

2 Hugh Hefner of Hong Kong: With an unlimited supply of drugs and human sex toys, Han lives like a king on his own island paradise.

3 The main event: In his island fortress in the South China Sea, the treacherous Han dreams up a tournament to find the world's best fighter.

"Unlike his rivals, Lee, the actor, exploits his sexuality, stripping off his shirt to reveal his rippling muscles, posing for battle with legs spread." *Guide for the Film Fanatic*

unquestionable star of the film, choreographing the fight sequences and supposedly also revising the script. *Enter the Dragon* is a true Bruce Lee film—a star vehicle for the action virtuoso. The film is full of the ingredients of the American films of its time: cool chick-magnets who drink and gamble, a funky 70s soundtrack by Lalo Schifrin, which sometimes sounds like the title theme of the television series *Mission: Impossible* (1966–73), and a plot that employs all the successful concepts and themes of the

The rudiments of the story are strongly reminiscent of *Dr. No* (1962), the first Bond film, with a megalomaniac gangster who has barricaded himself in a fortress-like island full of underground corridors and laboratories. Like Blofeld, 007's adversary, the villain Han even has a white long-haired cat. But the charm of the film lies less in the story than in the fight sequences. It begins with a battle in Lee's monastery (his sparring partner is the future director and actor Sammo Hung, a companion of Jackie Chan, who

3

4

"During a fight scene, Lee performed a flying kick so fast it couldn't be captured on film at 24 frames a second. The cameraman had to film the sequence in slow motion to get it to look like it wasn't faked."

Motion Picture Guide

fights—with Roper, Williams, and Lee—occur on the island and each fight trumps the previous one for choreographic spectaculars. Adhering to the rules of the genre, the film concludes with the fight between the main adversaries, Lee and Han. The fight to end all fights is made all the more astonishing by Han's prosthetic right hand, fitted with sharp blades in place of fingers. The showdown is a marvel of martial acrobatics and is unrivaled for its visual ingenuity, not least because it is staged in a house of mirrors.

Lee and Han are not only fighting against one another. Both are hard-pressed to actually locate their adversary, and are required to separate the physical opponent from his mirror image, adding a game of perception to the dazzling fight choreography. This final scene and its theme—true and illusory enemies—echoes a scene early on in the film where a priest explains to Lee, "The enemy is only an illusion; the real enemy lies within oneself." Supposedly Bruce Lee wrote this scene himself, but unfortunately it is absent from the international version of the film, and only preserved in the Chinese version. *Enter the Dragon* was released in the summer of 1973 in the United States, and in Hong Kong in October of the same year. Bruce Lee did not live to see the premiere, dying on July 20, 1973 from the effects of a brain edema whose cause to this day remains a mystery.

HJK

4 Last rites: African-American Williams (Jim Kelly) is lynched soon after discovering the villain's secret lair.

5 Get those legs up there! Han (Shih Kien), with a prosthetic right hand, and kung fu legend Lee (right) fight to the death in the final battle.

6 She comes with the room: Upon their arrival, contestants in the Han's island "World's Greatest Fighter Showdown" will receive a complimentary fruit basket and a voucher for a 15-min. warm welcome.

6

LA NUIT AMÉRICAINE

DAY FOR NIGHT

1973 – FRANCE / ITALY – 115 MIN.

GENRE

TRAGICOMEDY, DRAMA

DIRECTOR

FRANÇOIS TRUFFAUT

SCREENPLAY

JEAN-LOUIS RICHARD, SUZANNE SCHIFFMAN, FRANÇOIS TRUFFAUT

DIRECTOR OF PHOTOGRAPHY

PIERRE-WILLIAM GLENN

EDITING

MARTINE BARRAQUÉ, YANN DEDET

MUSIC

GEORGES DELERUE

PRODUCTION

MARCEL BERBERT for LES FILMS DU CARROSSE, PECF, PIC

STARRING

JACQUELINE BISSET (Julie), VALENTINA CORTESE (Severine), DANI (Liliane), ALEXANDRA STEWART (Stacey), JEAN-PIERRE AUMONT (Alexandre), JEAN CHAMPION (Bertrand), JEAN-PIERRE LÉAUD (Alphonse), FRANÇOIS TRUFFAUT (Ferrand), NIKE ARRIGHI (Odile), NATHALIE BAYE (Joelle)

ACADEMY AWARDS 1974

OSCAR for BEST FOREIGN FILM

WARNER BROS A Warner Communications Company présente
UN FILM DE FRANÇOIS TRUFFAUT
LA NUIT AMERICAINE
JACQUELINE BISSET
VALENTINA CORTESE
DANI
ALEXANDRA STEWART
JEAN-PIERRE AUMONT
JEAN CHAMPION
JEAN-PIERRE LEAUD
FRANÇOIS TRUFFAUT
Nike Arrighi • Nathalie Baye
David Markham • Bernard Menez
Scénario original de François Truffaut
Jean-Louis Richard • Suzanne Schiffman
Directeur de la photographie Pierre William Glenn
Musique Georges Delerue
Une co-production Franco-Italienne
EASTMANCOLOR - PANAVISION SPHÉRIQUE
LES FILMS DU CARROSSE / P.E.C.F. Paris / P.I.C. Rome · Distribué par Warner Columbia Film
Celébration du 50ème Anniversaire Warner Bros

"Making a film is like driving a coach and horses through the Wild West; when you set off, you're looking forward to a nice trip, but very soon you're wondering if you'll ever reach your destination."

In the studios in Nice, a French film team starts shooting "Je vous présente Paméla," the melodramatic tale of a young man (Jean-Pierre Léaud), whose wife (Jacqueline Bisset) falls in love with his father (Jean-Pierre Aumont) and runs away with him. The work is frequently hindered by technical difficulties and human problems. When one of the leading actors dies in a car accident, the project seems doomed to failure; but the team rallies round and improvises, enabling the director Ferrand (François Truffaut) to bring the work to a successful close.

"La nuit américaine" is the French expression for the process of filming scenes by daylight through a special filter that makes them look as if they had been filmed by night. A technical term, then: yet it also seems to express

JEAN-PIERRE LÉAUD Jean-Pierre Léaud was born in Paris on May 5, 1944, the son of a screenwriter and an actress. At the age of 15 he became famous when François Truffaut chose him for the autobiographical role of Antoine Doinel in his first feature film, *The Four Hundred Blows* (*Les quatre cents coups*, 1958/59). From then on, Léaud's career was inseparably bound up with Truffaut's films. In the course of the next 30 years, he appeared as the director's melancholy and chaotic alter ego in all five films of the Doinel cycle, as well as in two other Truffaut movies: *Two English Girls* (*Les deux anglaises et le continent*, 1971) and *Day for Night (La Nuit américaine*, 1973). But Léaud also appeared in films by other well-known directors, such as Jean-Luc Godard: *Masculine-Feminine* (*Masculin – féminin*, 1965/66), *Pierrot le fou* (1965), *Made in USA* (1966), *La Chinoise* and *Week-End* (both 1967), *Joyful Wisdom* (*Le gai savoir*, 1968) and *Detective* (*Détective*, 1985). He also appeared in Jacques Rivette's *Out 1 – spectre* (1971) and as the film-crazy friend of Maria Schneider in Bernardo Bertolucci's *Last Tango in Paris* (*Ultimo tango a Parigi/Le Dernier Tango à Paris*, 1972). After Truffaut's death in 1984, Léaud, who had cultivated a highly individual, amateurish and slightly comical style, was to be seen almost only in supporting roles. One exception was Aki Kaurismäki's black comedy *I Hired a Contract Killer* (1990), in which he played a suicidal Frenchman in London. In 1996, he appeared in Olivier Assayas' excellent *Irma Vep* as the depressive director of a silent-film remake, who is replaced in mid-shoot by another director.

2

JULIE BAKER

“*Day for Night*, François Truffaut’s heartfelt homage to the joy and pain of making movies, is just as bracing (yet touching) as it was when it was first released. It inevitably reminds us of the loss movie-lovers suffered when Truffaut died at 52 in 1984.”

Los Angeles Times

delight in the ability to create an artificial cinematic reality, and it sounds like the title of an exciting story. Indeed, it’s a wonderful title for a declaration of love—a cineast’s love of film, filmmaking and life. For François Truffaut, the three are in any case inseparable, and in this film they meet and mix with fascinating ease. *Day for Night* is an intelligent meditation on illusion and reality.

The occasion of this unconditional homage is a pretty banal, old-fashioned studio melodrama. This alone is enough to show that *Day for Night* is certainly not an accurate depiction of Truffaut’s own working methods,

"In *Day for Night*, I show a director who's very happy in his work. But there are also directors who are at least as interesting because their films are difficult and painful births. I know a few colleagues who should really make their own *Day for Night*." *François Truffaut*

1 French flair: In François Truffaut's homage to filmmaking, sideline shenanigans matter as much as the actual movie. Here, script girl (Nathalie Baye) seduces the props master (Bernard Menez).

2 Don't mix business and pleasure: Everything grinds to a halt when the star, Julie Baker, locks herself in her dressing room.

3 Sugar and spice and everything nice: Alphonse (Jean-Pierre Léaud) and Bernard (Bernard Menez) never tire of discussing what little girls are made of.

4 Art imitates life: "Alphonse is similar in every detail to the Léaud of the early 70s." (De Baecque/Toubiana, in: *Truffaut – Biografie.* Cologne, 1999).

4

even if he does take on the role of the director, Ferrand. Rather, Truffaut weaves a complex fiction out of countless disparate elements: self-referential moments, friendly nods to the directors he admires, and general reflections on filmmaking. This is an ensemble film, in which the script girl and the production designer seem just as important as the director or the stars. In this sense, *Day for Night* is also a homage to all the colleagues who never see the limelight but who are indispensable to the realization of a film.

This is why Truffaut called his film "democratic," and it is so in more ways than one: it's a film that appeals as much to a broad public as it does to the critics and intellectuals. Truffaut has collected some of the imponderables that can arise in the course of a film production—from an aging diva's alcohol problem to the chaotic love-life of an unstable star, from the pregnancy of an actress to the death of an actor—and made a charming, highly amusing and sometimes melancholy film-within-a-film.

Although it enjoyed a generally euphoric reception when first released, *Day for Night* was also harshly rejected by some, not least by Truffaut's former companion-in-arms Jean-Luc Godard. It was at this time that Truffaut finally broke with Godard. At the time, especially in France, many intellectuals were demanding a more political cinema, and some accused Truffaut of wasting his affections on the wrong object—the making of a conventional studio

5

5 The many shades of gray: In Truffaut's cinematic cosmos, there's no clear distinction between fiction and reality. The relationship between Alphonse and Julie (Jean-Pierre Léaud and Jacqueline Bisset) is troubled—on-screen and off.

6 Not a publicity stunt: Truffaut casts light on the otherwise obscure aspects of filmmaking.

"*Day for Night* has grace, wit and affection enough to be one of the fondest compliments the movies have ever been paid—a tribute to all dream spinners by one of the best." *Time Magazine*

film. One critic wrote that Truffaut had "allowed himself to be bought by the system," and he presumably felt vindicated when *Day for Night* won the Oscar for Best Foreign Film. Truffaut himself never saw it as *the* definitive film about filmmaking. The personal dimension of *Day for Night* is particularly apparent in the words spoken by Truffaut to Jean-Pierre Léaud, the actor who embodied his alter ego in the Antoine Doinel cycle of films: "You know very well that people like you and I can only be happy when we're working, when we're working for the cinema."

JH

WESTWORLD

1973 – USA – 89 MIN.

GENRE

SCIENCE FICTION

DIRECTOR

MICHAEL CRICHTON

SCREENPLAY

MICHAEL CRICHTON

DIRECTOR OF PHOTOGRAPHY

GENE POLITO

EDITING

DAVID BRETHERTON

MUSIC

FRED KARLIN

PRODUCTION

PAUL LAZARUS III for MGM

STARRING

YUL BRYNNER (Mechanical Gunslinger), RICHARD BENJAMIN (Peter Martin), JAMES BROLIN (John Blane), NORMAN BARTOLD (Medieval Knight), ALAN OPPENHEIMER (Chief Engineer), VICTORIA SHAW (Medieval Queen), DICK VAN PATTEN (Banker), LINDA GAYE SCOTT (Arlette), STEVE FRANKEN (Technician)

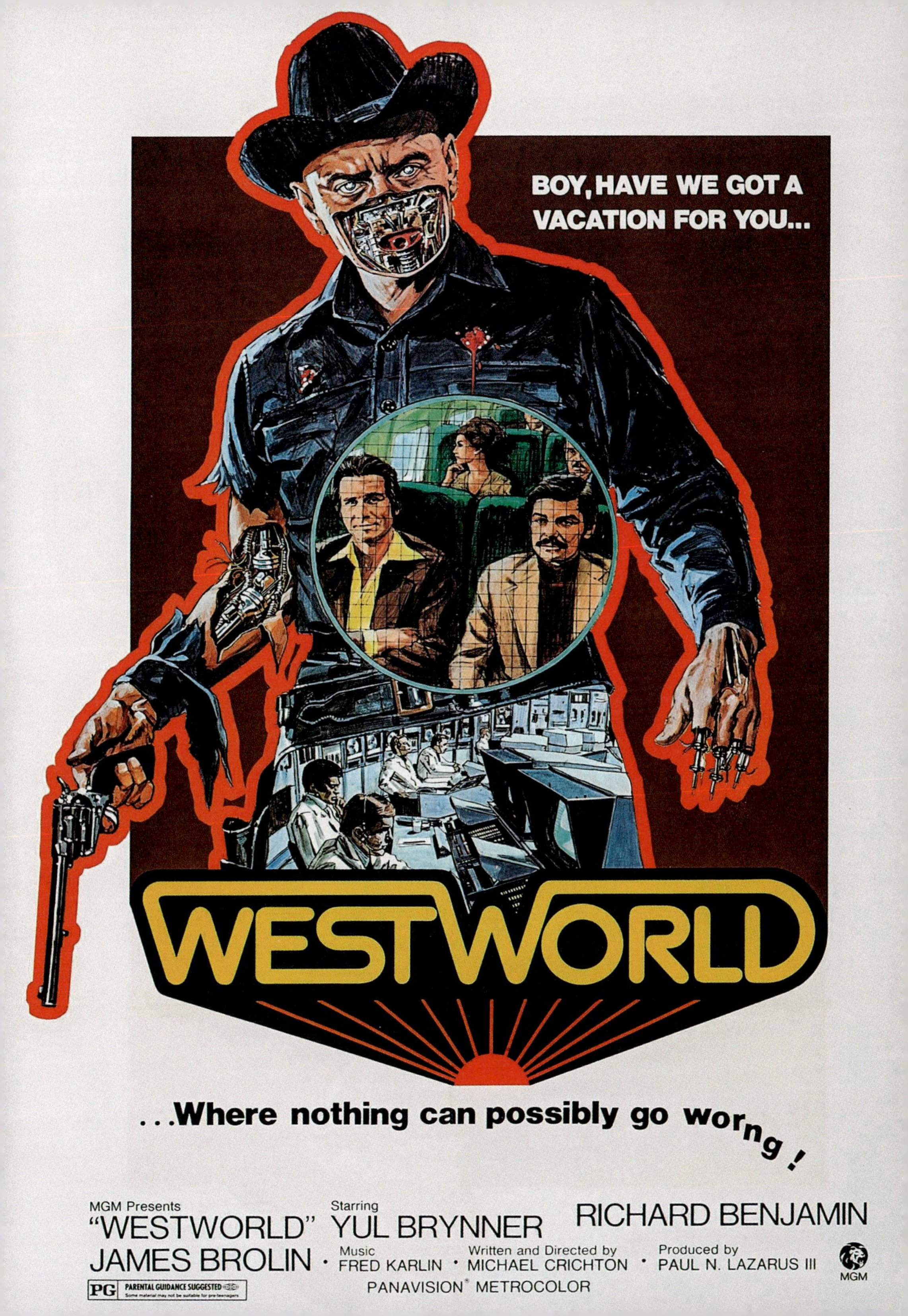

BOY, HAVE WE GOT A VACATION FOR YOU...

WESTWORLD

...Where nothing can possibly go worng!

MGM Presents
"WESTWORLD" Starring YUL BRYNNER RICHARD BENJAMIN
JAMES BROLIN · Music FRED KARLIN · Written and Directed by MICHAEL CRICHTON · Produced by PAUL N. LAZARUS III

PG PARENTAL GUIDANCE SUGGESTED
Some material may not be suitable for pre-teenagers

PANAVISION® METROCOLOR

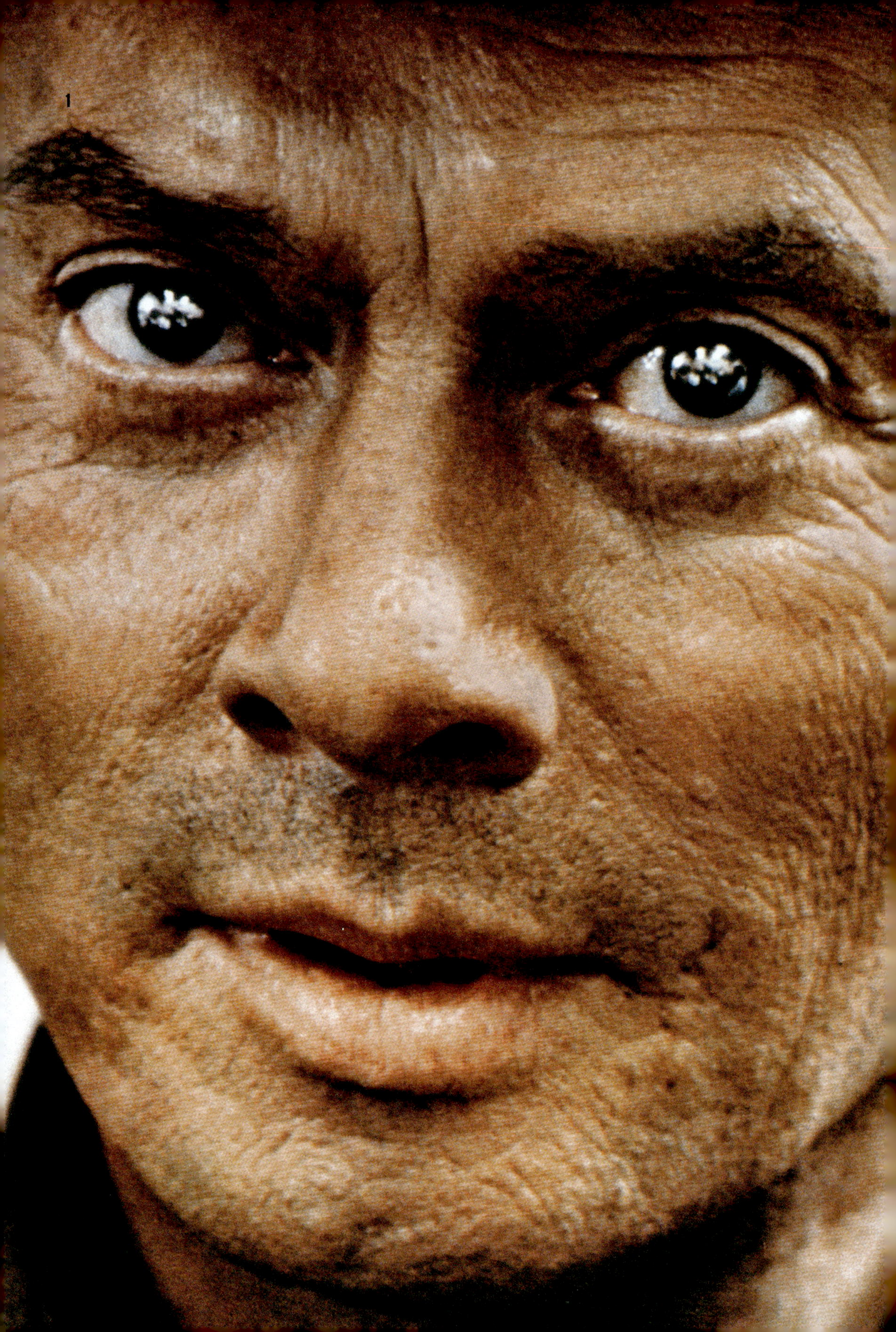

1

“Though casually entertaining, the movie gives the smug, unimaginative feeling of having itself been programmed by a computer.” *The Times*

with one last trace of insecurity, he asks “who can guarantee I won’t kill another guest by accident?” The answer to his question seems simple: there is a safety sensor built into his weapon that prevents objects with human body temperature from getting hit. The boys from Chicago spend the night comfortably in a Western brothel —with female robot companions. They are awakened by the black-clad gunslinger, who—now repaired—once again challenges Peter to an extensive duel. A frantic chase leads through all three worlds of Delos, but now it is the robot that is pursuing Peter. The machine seems to have been wrongly re-programmed and behaves like his creator, refusing to die, returning fire, and killing with live ammunition. The other robots also revolt and incite a bloodbath, slaughtering the visitors. Delos becomes tyrannized by its electronic beings until Peter succeeds in setting fire to the machines. In the end he is the lone survivor in a mass of dead bodies.

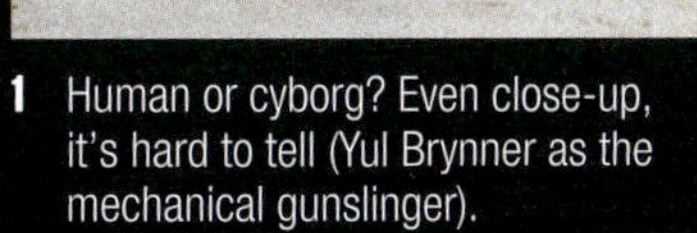

1 Human or cyborg? Even close-up, it's hard to tell (Yul Brynner as the mechanical gunslinger).

2 Entertainment value: For city slickers (James Brolin, right) who've booked the Wild West program, a duel in a saloon is—usually—no sweat…

3 … unless the dueling machine has a very human defect—the thirst for vengeance.

4 Falling to pieces: Artificial life en route to Nirvana.

The first film of the now world-famous Michael Crichton offers yet another variation on the story of artificial humans. It is the tale of parallel humans or the once useful machine that develops into a threat. The superior invasion machines of an external enemy, a favorite storyline of the 1950s, no longer occupy the core of the science-fiction film. Their place in combat is taken by human-parallel machine constructions. The monster is no longer simply a creation cranked up in a secret laboratory, but rather a part of everyday leisure time, an expression of the prevalent greed for pleasure and longing for perfection. Thus *Westworld* marks a new stage in the portrayal of the robot in the history of film—that of subjectivity. We as an audience are supposed to be shaken and punished. In the 70s, the robot becomes a tool of social criticism, an uncontrollable creation that hounds its arrogant creator—a theme Crichton continued and varied in the 1990s for Steven Spielberg's *Jurassic Park* (1993).

Though Yul Brynner's black denim costume is a prop from John Sturges' Western *The Magnificent Seven* (1960)—where he plays the gunman Chris who organizes the liberation of a Mexican village terrorized by bandits—*Westworld* does not criticize film as part of the macabre entertainment industry. On the contrary, the beginning of the film points to television as a temptation and threat to mankind. *Futureworld*, the sequel by Richard T. Heffron was released in 1976. It combines the science-fiction theme of the rebellious human clones with a political conspiracy.

RV

FLESH FOR FRANKENSTEIN / CARNE PER FRANKENSTEIN

ANDY WARHOL'S FRANKENSTEIN

1973 – USA / ITALY / FRANCE – 95 MIN.

GENRE

HORROR FILM

DIRECTOR

PAUL MORRISSEY, ANTONIO MARGHERITI

SCREENPLAY

TONINO GUERRA, PAUL MORRISSEY

DIRECTOR OF PHOTOGRAPHY

LUIGI KUVEILLER

EDITING

JED JOHNSON, FRANCA SILVI

MUSIC

CLAUDIO GIZZI

PRODUCTION

ANDREW BRAUNSBERG, CARLO PONTI,
ANDY WARHOL for BRAUNSBERG PRODUCTIONS,
CARLO PONTI CINEMATOGRAFICA,
RASSAM PRODUCTIONS, YANNE ET RASSAM

STARRING

JOE DALLESANDRO (Nicholas), MONIQUE VAN VOOREN (Baroness Katrin Frankenstein), UDO KIER (Baron Frankenstein), ARNO JUERGING (Otto), DALILA DI LAZZARO (Female Monster), SRDJAN ZELENOVIC (Sasha / Male Monster), NICOLETTA ELMI (Monica), MARCO LIOFREDI (Erik), LIU BOSISIO (Olga), CRISTINA GAIONI (Nicholas' girlfriend)

FRANKENSTEIN

A Film by
Paul Morrissey

ANDY WARHOL'S "FRANKENSTEIN" • A Film by PAUL MORRISSEY • Starring Joe Dallesandro Monique Van Vooren • Udo Kier • Introducing Arno Juerging • Dalila Di Lazzaro • Srdjan Zelenovic A CARLO PONTI – BRAUNSBERG – RASSAM PRODUCTION • COLOR • A BRYANSTON PICTURES RELEASE

1

"Otto, look at this! Finally we find the right head with the perfect nasum! For my male zombie..."

The opening credits to *Andy Warhol's Frankenstein* might have been made by Charles Addams: two children, a boy and a girl, dissect a doll before beheading it with a miniature guillotine.

Baron Frankenstein (Udo Kier with a strong German accent) wants to create not just one human being but a couple, who will conceive and bear the representatives of a new race. In this he is assisted by his henchman Otto (Arno Juerging). Only one body part is lacking, for the male half of the couple: not the brain, as we might expect, but the perfect "Serbian" nose; for the Baron's racist ideology will accept nothing less. In order to secure the propagation of the race, Frankenstein and Otto head off to the village brothel in search of a suitable victim. This turns out to be Sasha (Srdjan Zelenovic), whom they promptly kill not realizing that he is in fact homosexual. His friend Nicholas (Joe Dallesandro), a farm laborer and servant to the Baroness, rushes to Sasha's aid, but too late: Sasha's head already adorns another man's body. In a bloody showdown, almost everyone ends up dead: Sasha murders

ANDY WARHOL'S FACTORY From 1963 onwards, the Pop artist Andy Warhol (1928–1987) produced hundreds of films in his Factory, a meeting place for artists, writers, dancers, transvestites, musicians, exhibition-makers and exhibitionists. These movies were often collective efforts, made in collaboration with avant-garde filmmakers such as Jonas Mekas and Jack Smith. In the initial phase, Warhol was clearly influenced by experimental films of the time: *Empire* (1964), for example, is an eight-hour shot of the Empire State Building, filmed with a static camera and without a single cut. Other works, such as *Chelsea Girls* (1966), were provocative in different ways, featuring endless improvisations, a gritty documentary feel, or pornographic scenes, often explicitly homoerotic. Most of Warhol's actors were amateurs, but he called them "superstars" in line with his credo that in the age of the mass media anyone can be a star. In 1968, he began to produce more commercially oriented films, directed by Paul Morrissey. Although smartened up in appearance by conventional post-production, the imagery, sound and narrative structure of these films are still a very long way from Hollywood. Besides *Andy Warhol's Frankenstein* (*Flesh for Frankenstein/Carne per Frankenstein*, 1973) and *Andy Warhol's Dracula* (*Blood for Dracula/Dracula vuole vivere: cerca sangue di vergine!*, 1973), his best-known films are: *Flesh* (1968), in which Morrissey's protagonist-of-choice Joe Dallesandro played a male prostitute, *Trash* (1970), and *Andy Warhol's Women* (*Women in Revolt*, 1971).

2

both the Baroness and his creator Frankenstein, before killing himself. The only survivors are the Frankenstein children, who have witnessed everything, and who now calmly step up to accept their inheritance—much to the horror of the bound and helpless Nicholas.

Flesh for Frankenstein and the project that followed on its heels, *Andy Warhol's Dracula* (*Blood for Dracula*/*Dracula vuole vivere: cerca sangue di vergine!*, 1973) were low-budget projects, filmed entirely in the Factory in a single seven-week period. Both were produced by Warhol himself. According to the director Paul Morrissey, the actors were given their lines on a daily basis. Viewers of this spectacle are disappointed all along the line, and this is by no means unintentional: if the title misleads anyone into expecting some creepy entertainment or even a faithful adaptation of Mary Wollstonecraft Shelley's novel, what they're given instead is a set of protagonists who are thoroughly bored, blasé or just plain beat. Not that the film isn't pretty much "in your face;" indeed, thanks to the film version's 3-D effects, it's quite often all over your clothes. Lopped limbs and entrails are sometimes close enough to taste.

Flesh for Frankenstein owes much to two genres: splatter and soft porn. Other versions of the story have seen Frankenstein's bodybuilding as a subtle compensation for his repressed sexual needs, and Warhol's Baron is certainly no high-minded Prometheus, no genius of the arts or sciences. He awakens his creatures to life by means of bloody penetration and a variety of necrophiliac activities. While the late 60s had hailed the coming of the sexual revolution, sexuality in this film offers no liberation from the constraints of society. On the contrary, desire is either unfulfilled or can only find expression through exploitation and rape. The plot is dominated by the protagonists' decadence and narcissism; little is to be seen, for example, of the normally obligatory villagers, often portrayed as a revolutionary counterforce to the French aristocracy. Nor is it the holy family of bourgeois mythology that triumphs over the Baron and his monster, revealing the hubris of those who would dare emulate God. Nicholas does manage to expose Frankenstein's doings; but he ends up helpless in the hands of the children—incestuous siblings like their parents before them—who will simply carry on where

***Warhol's Frankenstein* is no biting satire, but a gruesome burlesque. One only hopes that anyone who sees it will have enjoyed a vegetarian meal beforehand."** *Frankfurter Rundschau*

1 Modern day Salomé? Baron Frankenstein (Udo Kier) with his heart's desire—the head of a young man with the perfect nose.

2 Lo and behold! Henchman Otto (Arno Juerging) presents the female prototype (Dalila Di Lazzaro).

3 A new man: Frankenstein's guest Sasha (Srdjan Zelenovic) after his successful head transplant.

3

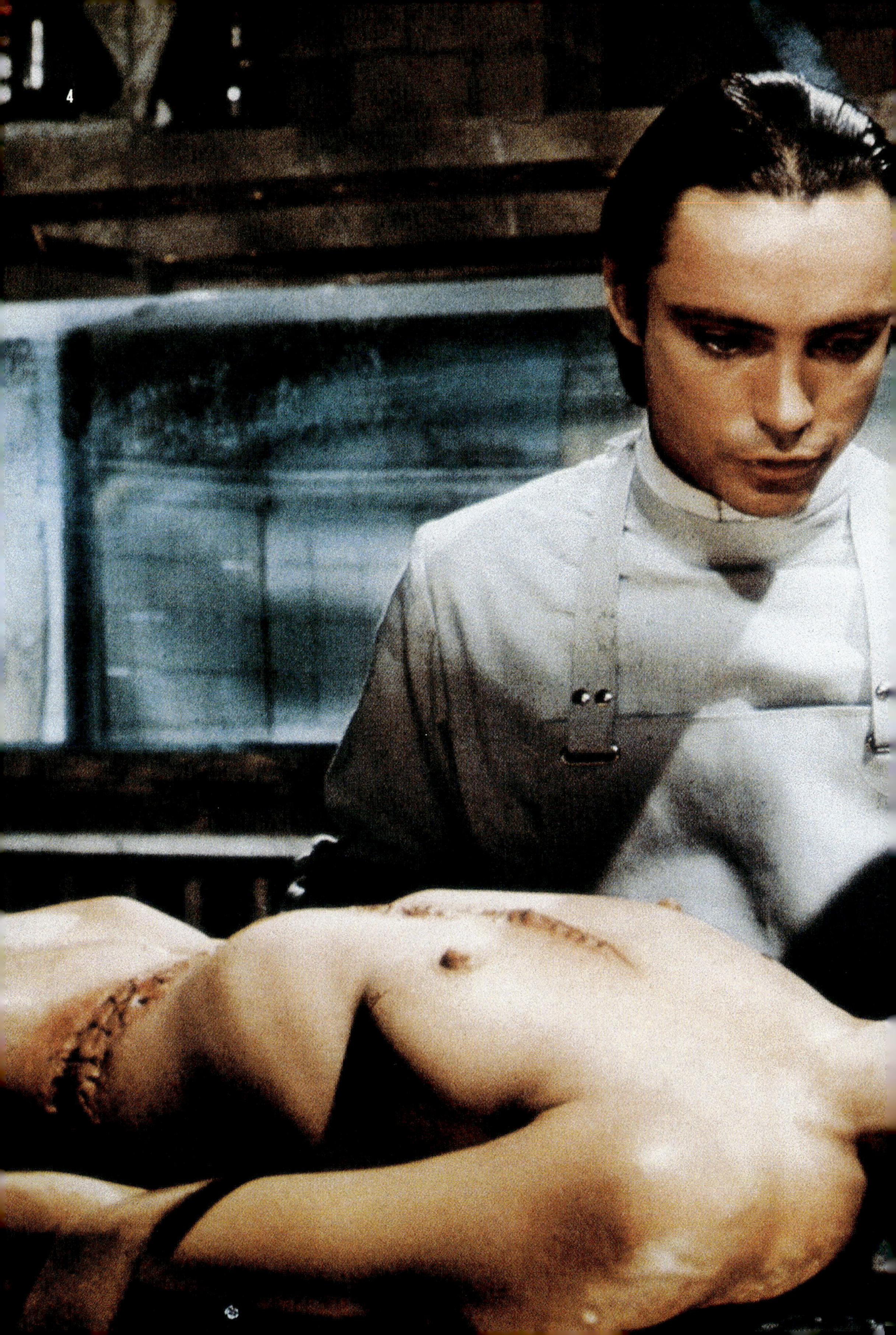
4

5

4 Doctor Frankenstein's anatomy lesson.

5 No cliché too cheap: The insatiable Baroness Katrin Frankenstein (Monique Van Vooren) seduces her willing servants.

6 Bottoms up: Sasha remains indifferent to the charms of the fairer sex.

7 Walking the straight and narrow: Warhol cast Joe Dallesandro, gay underground star, as Nicholas. Here, he takes a trip to the village brothel.

"Each night I'd think of what further absurdity might logically follow from where I began."

Paul Morrissey, in: Maurice Yacowar, The Films of Paul Morrissey

6

the older generation left off. The monstrous Frankenstein family structure remains unscathed, an artificial and hermetically closed system.

Frankenstein is no mere parody: Morrissey dwells exclusively on the negative aspects of the tale, like the misogynistic episodes, Frankenstein's fascist ideas and the children's icy lack of feeling. And faced with this grim lack of alternatives, we soon find the laughter sticking in our throats.

PLB

PAT GARRETT AND BILLY THE KID

1973 – USA – 106 MIN. / 122 MIN. (restored version)

GENRE

WESTERN

DIRECTOR

SAM PECKINPAH

SCREENPLAY

RUDY WURLITZER

DIRECTOR OF PHOTOGRAPHY

JOHN COQUILLON

EDITING

ROGER SPOTTISWOODE, GARTH CRAVEN, ROBERT L. WOLFE, RICHARD HALSEY, DAVID BERLATSKY, TONY DE ZARRAGA

MUSIC

BOB DYLAN

PRODUCTION

GORDON CARROLL for MGM

STARRING

JAMES COBURN (Sheriff Patrick J. Garrett), KRIS KRISTOFFERSON (William H. "Billy the Kid" Bonney), BOB DYLAN (Alias), SLIM PICKENS (Sheriff Baker), KATY JURADO (Mrs. Baker), JASON ROBARDS (Governor Lew Wallace), RICHARD JAECKEL (Sheriff Kip McKinney), CHILL WILLS (Lemuel), JOHN BECK (John W. Poe), RITA COOLIDGE (Maria)

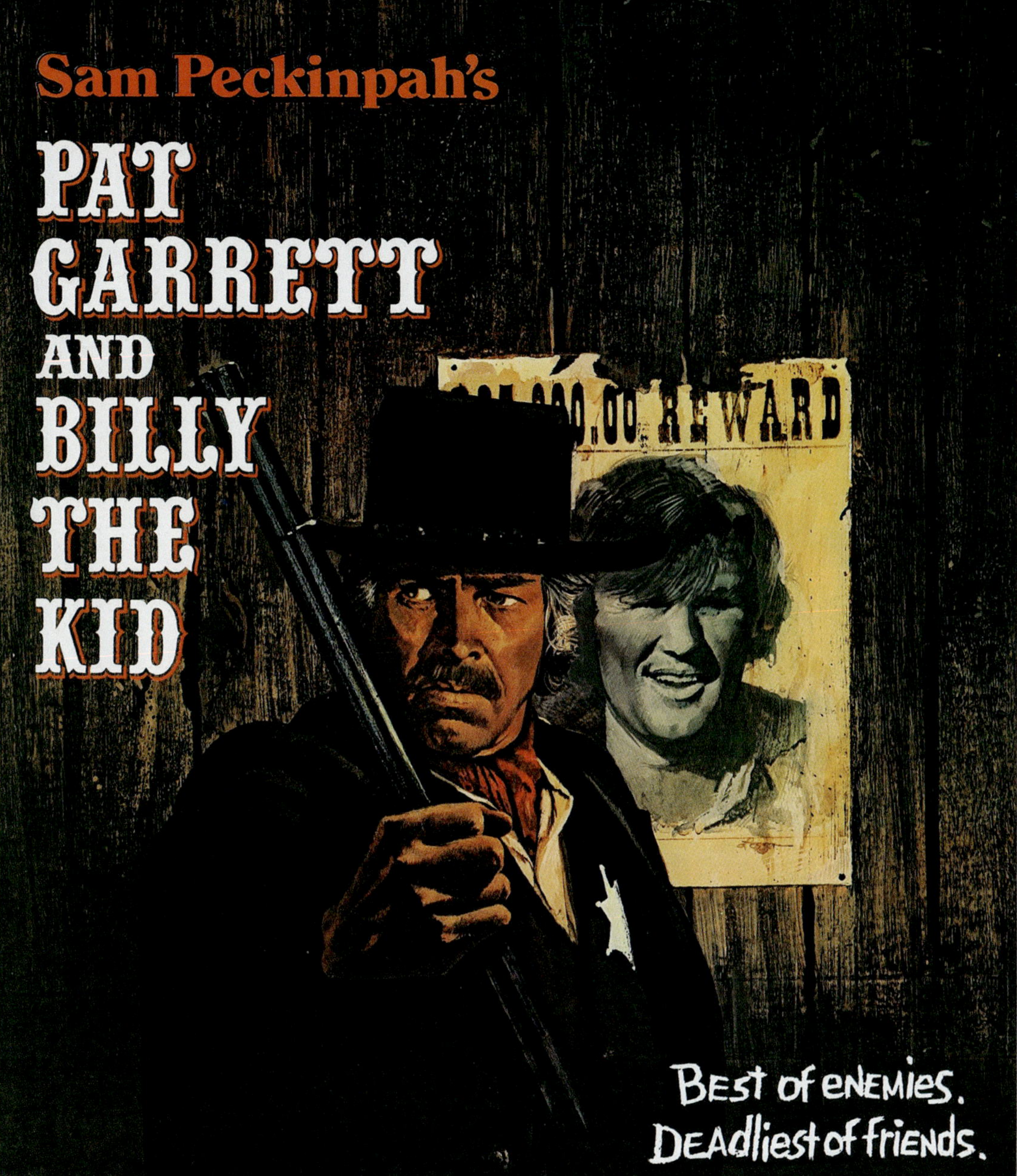

MGM Presents

"PAT GARRETT AND BILLY THE KID"

Starring

JAMES COBURN · KRIS KRISTOFFERSON · BOB DYLAN

And Also Starring JASON ROBARDS · Music by BOB DYLAN · Written by RUDOLPH WURLITZER

Produced by GORDON CARROLL · Directed by SAM PECKINPAH · METROCOLOR · PANAVISION®

R RESTRICTED Under 17 requires accompanying Parent or Adult Guardian

MGM

1

"It feels like times have changed."

New Mexico, 1881. The days of the Wild West are numbered. Although Billy the Kid (Kris Kristofferson) is still living the life of an outlaw, his one-time trusted partner in crime Pat Garrett (James Coburn) has changed sides. He has been elected sheriff of Lincoln County and the cattle barons want Billy out of their hair. Garrett sees no alternative but to advise his compadre to relocate to Mexico. Billy cannot be persuaded. Shortly after their talk, Garrett sets a trap for him. Gunfire breaks out and two of Billy's pals bite the dust. He himself is placed under arrest, but soon spots an opportune moment to fly the coop and Lincoln County while Garrett is away. He fatally wounds two deputies in the process, forcing Garrett to do away with Billy once and for all. And so begins a deadly game of cat and mouse.

Like almost all of Sam Peckinpah's Westerns, *Pat Garrett and Billy the Kid* is about the disappearance of the legendary Wild West. The land has been divvied up, and the settlers have staked their claims. Capital makes its way into the county and the dubious definition of law and

JAMES COBURN James Coburn (born August 31, 1928 in Laurel, Nebraska, died November 18, 2002 in Los Angeles) was among the few American actors who personified the specific brand of raw masculinity dominant in Hollywood Westerns well after their heyday had officially ended. His debut came with Budd Boetticher's Randolph Scott Western *Ride Lonesome* (1958/59), at a time when the genre was still very much alive. His breakthrough came a year later when he played the taciturn sniper in John Sturges' *The Magnificent Seven* (1960). In 1963, he rejoined forces with Sturges for *The Great Escape*, a world-class breakout caper with an all-star cast.

He first collaborated with Sam Peckinpah on the military Western *Major Dundee* (1964/65), and Coburn quickly became the swashbuckling director's favorite son. Wildly popular were Coburn's James Bond spoofs *Our Man Flint* (1965) and *In Like Flint* (1967), in which he starred as the title character and displayed his knack for comedy. Further departures from the world of cowboys and Stetsons followed, including the sex-comedy *Candy/Candy e il suo pazzo mondo* (1968) and the film adaptation of Tennessee Williams' *Last of the Mobile Hot Shots* (1969).

James Coburn will remain eternally etched in our memories as the tough-as-nails man's man, a persona he continued to embody throughout the 1970s in movies like Sergio Leone's *Giù la testa/Duck, You Sucker* (1971) and Peckinpah's *Pat Garrett and Billy the Kid* (1973). After 20 years of very limited appearances due to severe arthritis, Coburn illuminated the screen yet again with a bravado comeback in Paul Schrader's family drama *Affliction* (1997), his only performance to win him an Oscar.

1 Double indemnity: As musician and actor, Bob Dylan chronicles the last days of legendary Western hero, Billy the Kid.

2 A man of principle: While Billy's violence seems inseparable from his passion for freedom, his opponents are often just sneaky and brutal.

3 Laying down the law: For James Coburn, Pat Garrett was the role of a lifetime.

order accompanies it, seeming to provide mainly property owners with a world of opportunity. There is no place left for outlaws. This has become glaringly clear to Garrett and he tries to fit the mold. Billy, on the other hand, has held onto his principles, although the fact is they offer him no chance of survival. Although Peckinpah never tries to brush over the fact that Billy is a killer, he clearly sympathizes with him, a man who's on the "wrong side of the law." For despite all his brutality and self-righteousness, Billy not only embodies qualities like bravery and integrity, but also exhibits free will. All the director's works code these traits as virtues inextricably linked to the great American frontier. The tone of the film is dominated by a sense of mourning for the extinct notion of pioneer country and for the long-forgotten promise of "liberty and justice for all," on which the United States of America was founded. In its ballad-like structure, the film reads like an extended love letter to the West. The melancholy soundtrack by Bob Dylan, who also plays the role of the story's narrator, the young Alias, further emphasizes this. Dylan's songs are a perfect complement to the film's slow rhythm and its softly flowing, dimly lit, broad shots. Here, however, the technique lacks the optimism and sense of excitement about the future that filled the classic imagery of this genre.

Peckinpah's picture does not deal with the expansion or acquisition of the territory, but rather with the violent death of an anachronistic way of life. By taking this

“The changes ordered by the studio are mostly stupid but not disastrous. Even in the maimed state in which it has been released, *Pat Garrett and Billy the Kid* is the richest, most exciting American film so far this year. There are moments and whole sequences here that stand among the best Peckinpah has ever achieved.” *Time Magazine*

4

"The link to contemporary America is clearer than ever before in Peckinpah's Western œuvre, thanks to the relaxed performance of folk-rock star, Kris Kristofferson. His Billy the Kid is a hero that fits none of the genre's jaded clichés. What we have instead is an affable, high-spirited Easy Horserider." *DIE ZEIT*

5

angle, he turns the traditional cinematic perspective of the classic Western on its head and sees the genre through to its inevitable conclusion.

Peckinpah's *Pat Garrett and Billy the Kid* was heavily censored by the film studio, and this recurrent experience led him to direct his next project in Mexico. His original director's cut, which Roger Spottiswoode restored to a great extent in the early 1990s, includes a prolog missing from the studio release. The sequence shows hired guns of the influential ranchers murdering Garrett about thirty years after he killed Billy at their request. It also makes clear that Garrett had purchased land, and was therefore tied up with the cattle barons. These bits of information not only change the nature of his relationship to Billy, but also put a different spin on his character and make Garrett the picture's actual tragic hero. Though he attempts to adapt to the signs of the times, and as he puts it at the top of the film, "grow old with the land," deep down he is a man anchored in days gone by. He goes against his principles, assassinates his best friend and, in the end, never attains his goals. In both the history of the American West and the Hollywood Western, Pat Garrett was a legendary sheriff who enforced the law with all his might. To Peckinpah he is someone who betrayed both himself and the old West. Billy the Kid may be dead by the film's end, but Pat Garrett gave up the ghost even before the curtains open.

JH

4 Free Love in the Old West: Kris Kristofferson's Billy the Kid embodied the ideals of the hippie era.

5 Hang him high: In Peckinpah's post-Western, civilization often looks a world away.

6 Lonesome Doves: For the aging men of the West, even women no longer offer a safe refuge. Time has left them high and dry.

6

THE EXORCIST

1973 – USA – 122 MIN.

GENRE

HORROR FILM

DIRECTOR

WILLIAM FRIEDKIN

SCREENPLAY

WILLIAM PETER BLATTY,
based on his novel of the same name

DIRECTOR OF PHOTOGRAPHY

OWEN ROIZMAN, BILLY WILLIAMS

EDITING

NORMAN GAY, EVAN LOTTMAN, BUD SMITH

MUSIC

JACK NITZSCHE, KRZYSZTOF PENDERECKI

PRODUCTION

WILLIAM PETER BLATTY for WARNER BROS.,
HOYA PRODUCTIONS

STARRING

ELLEN BURSTYN (Chris MacNeil), MAX VON SYDOW (Father Merrin),
LEE J. COBB (Lieutenant Kinderman), LINDA BLAIR (Regan MacNeil),
KITTY WINN (Sharon Spencer), JASON MILLER (Father Damien Karras),
JACK MACGOWRAN (Burke Dennings), REVEREND WILLIAM O'MALLEY (Father Dyer),
BARTON HEYMAN (Dr. Klein), PETER MASTERSON (Barringer)

ACADEMY AWARDS 1974

OSCARS for BEST ADAPTED SCREENPLAY (William Peter Blatty),
and BEST SOUND (Robert Knudson, Christopher Newman)

WILLIAM PETER BLATTY'S

THE EXORCIST

Directed by WILLIAM FRIEDKIN

Something almost beyond comprehension is happening to a girl on this street, in this house ...and a man has been sent for as a last resort. This man is The Exorcist.

ELLEN BURSTYN · MAX VON SYDOW · LEE J. COBB
KITTY WINN · JACK MacGOWRAN JASON MILLER as Father Karras
LINDA BLAIR as Regan · Produced by WILLIAM PETER BLATTY
Executive Producer NOEL MARSHALL · Screenplay by WILLIAM PETER BLATTY based on his novel
From Warner Bros. A Warner Communications Company

1

2

What an excellent day for an exorcism.

Evil neither stems from a dark abyss nor from a cosmic realm. It neither limits its dominion to dark shadows and blind alleys, nor does it attack in the form of a werewolf that can be slain with a silver bullet. When we are struck by the fear that without warning, something horrific could infiltrate our lives and turn our precious little worlds on their heads, perhaps we are tuning into something very real and tangible. Maybe evil has already made a nest for itself, where we'd least expect it. Namely, in our most intimate surroundings.

Although this is the central topic of the story involving American actress Chris MacNeil (Ellen Burstyn), whose twelve-year-old daughter Regan (Linda Blair) is transformed into the Antichrist before her very eyes, *The Exorcist* director William Friedkin opens his film with far-off images of the Middle East. It is on an archaeological dig in Iraq that Father Merrin (Max von Sydow) unearths several ancient artifacts that send him into a state of panic, including decapitated statue heads and a most unnerving amulet.

The ensuing scenes, in which pure evil appears to take possession of Merrin's entire environment, are among the picture's most powerful. The vacant and yet piercing stares of the locals, the hammering of the blacksmiths that Merrin confuses with the sound of his own racing heart, and a clock that stops cold are just a few of the images that contribute to the audience's visceral incorporation of the imminent danger.

When, at the end of this sequence, Merrin sits directly across from a statue of an ominous demon with rabid dogs running rampant at its feet, the essence of the story becomes clear. According to the director, the film is "a Christian parable about the eternal struggle between good and evil."

Cut to "Georgetown." The on-screen caption and the bird's-eye view of the city evoke a deceptive picture of order and distanced safety. Friedkin referred to the fade in technique he often used as the "Means of luring the audience onto the wrong track." Nonetheless, the peac

---

SUBLIMINAL MESSAGES At the speed of 24 frames per second in film and 30 NTSC frames per second in television, subliminal messages are usually only visible for less than the blink of an eye, and certainly not long enough to leave an imprint on the human retina. The term itself comes from the Latin *sub limen*, "below the threshold."

The theory that even an image which people are not capable of consciously perceiving can still impact their minds is an age-old concept. In particular, the advertising industry has tried countless times to make use of scientifically and ethically disputed techniques of visual manipulation. "Invisible advertising" was tested in New Jersey in 1957 during the screening of *Picnic* (1955). The results, which contended that the several spliced-in, split-second-long frames showing popcorn and Coca Cola caused sales to sky rocket, turned out to be falsified. Be that as it may, in the U.S. presidential race in 2000, President George W. Bush ran a smear ad in which the word "rats" appeared in conjunction with a prescription drug proposal put together by his opponent, Al Gore. Strictly speaking, subliminal messages have only had a limited impact on the cinema directly. Filmmakers who experiment with them, like David Lynch, tend to implement montage sequences of image snippets. These, however, can be perceived by the naked eye of an alert viewer. In *The Exorcist: The Version You Haven't Seen Yet* (1973/2000) such a device was used briefly to show Satan's face—yet another attempt on the part of the director to petrify his audience.

of Georgetown's idyllic autumn and the illusion of the stable family unit fall like a house of cards after one of the Jesuit priests from the university, Father Karras (Jason Miller) breaks down and admits that he has "lost faith." With these words, something wicked this way comes.

It comes in the form of an appalling, disfigured little girl spewing out profanities and blaspheming uncontrollably. Wretched displays of gasping, choking and shrieking are let loose on the audio track, accompanied by a visual deluge of regurgitated green mucus. Never before and never since for that matter, has a director been so intent on terrorizing his audience. At the time of its release, screenings often had spectators vomiting in the aisles, fainting and breaking into hysterics. This highly provocative work even made movie critic Roger Ebert question his faith in humanity, asking whether "people (are) so numb that they need movies of this intensity in order to feel anything at all?"

The intoxicating shock value of the gore can make one overlook the masterful web of allusions, contrasts, analogies and sociopolitical arguments Friedkin has woven here. One example of this intricate layering can be witnessed when Regan forms a clay model of a bird with wings that recall those of the demonic statue in the Iraq sequence. Later on, Lieutenant Kinderman (Lee J. Cobb), assigned to investigate the mysterious death of Chris' close friend, finds yet another clay object at the scene of the crime. It is the pagan counterpart to the crucifix, which Chris recently discovered in her daughter's bed.

1 That little devil: Regan (Linda Blair) is about to have a religious experience.

2 Satanic verses: The Prince of Darkness moves in mysterious ways.

3 Who's been sleeping in my bed? Father Damien Karras (Jason Miller) suppresses his doubts and aids Father Merrin (Max von Sydow) in the ancient exorcism.

4 That thing upstairs is not my daughter: Actress Chris MacNeil (Ellen Burstyn) wants to be a good mother to Regan, but Dr. Spock never said anything about spitting up pea soup.

"*The Exorcist* makes no sense, but if you want to be shaken, it will scare the hell out of you."

The New Republic

The way in which the film attempts to diagnose the cause of Regan's possession is also worthy of close examination. The arrogance of the doctors, Chris' outbursts of rage, her friend Burke's alcoholism, the burden of guilt Father Karras feels towards his dead mother are all signs that the source of evil could be human. Karras' work as a psychologist for the university's Jesuit community makes him doubt God's existence, providing the audience with another possible clue to the origin of Regan's infection. Other events, including the Jesuit priest who finds a defiled statue in the chapel, but doesn't acknowledge the Madonna as he enters, also point to lack of faith as a contributory.

All these factors are devices Friedkin uses to vary the film's underlying principle mentioned in the opening paragraph. Namely, that evil lurks in everyday life and even in our very hearts. In this respect, it is not a battle with the devil that Carras ends up winning. It's a battle with his own self.

SH

DON'T LOOK NOW

1973 – GREAT BRITAIN – 109 MIN.

GENRE

HORROR FILM, DRAMA

DIRECTOR

NICOLAS ROEG

SCREENPLAY

CHRIS BRYANT, ALLAN SCOTT,
based on the story of the same name by DAPHNE DU MAURIER

DIRECTOR OF PHOTOGRAPHY

ANTHONY B. RICHMOND, NICOLAS ROEG

EDITING

GRAEME CLIFFORD

MUSIC

PINO DONAGGIO

PRODUCTION

PETER KATZ, FREDERICK MULLER,
STEVE PREVIN for CASEY, ELDORADO FILMS

STARRING

JULIE CHRISTIE (Laura Baxter), DONALD SUTHERLAND (John Baxter),
HILARY MASON (Heather), CLELIA MATANIA (Wendy),
MASSIMO SERATO (Bishop Barbarrigo), RENATO SCARPA (Inspector Longhi),
ANN RYE (Mandy Babbage), NICHOLAS SALTER (Johnny Baxter),
SHARON WILLIAMS (Christine Baxter), BRUNO CATTANEO (Detective Sabbione),
ADELINA POERIO (Dwarf)

Pass the warning.
Paramount Pictures presents
A Peter Katz-Anthony B. Unger Production
JULIE CHRISTIE
DONALD SUTHERLAND
"DON'T LOOK NOW"
A psychic thriller.
Based on a story by DAPHNE DU MAURIER · Produced by PETER KATZ · Directed by NICOLAS ROEG · Screenplay by ALLAN SCOTT and CHRIS BRYANT
R RESTRICTED
Executive Producer ANTHONY B. UNGER · in Color · Prints by Movielab · A Paramount Picture

1

"I have seen her... and she wants you to know that she is happy."

Two children frolic through the autumnal garden of a house in the English countryside. The children's parents, Laura and John Baxter (Julie Christie and Donald Sutherland), sit comfortably inside the house. While John looks over slides, Laura rests on the couch and reads. It is an idyll that is soon brutally shattered. Stirred by a dark premonition, John runs outside. But he is too late. His daughter Christine is already dead—drowned in the garden pond. To gain some distance from the horrible event, the couple travel to Venice, where John begins directing the restoration of a church. But when they meet two odd Scottish sisters (Hilary Mason and Clelia Matania) in a restaurant, their daughter's death catches up with them: one of the two old women is blind and presumably gifted with a supernatural talent. With a friendly laugh, she tells Laura that she has been in contact with Christine. Laura breaks down upon hearing this, but she then gains a new confidence from the stranger's vision and tries to convince John, who considers the entire story absurd, that their daughter is in touch.

JULIE CHRISTIE British actress Julie Christie was born on April 14, 1941 in the Indian province of Chukua, where her father ran a tea plantation. Early on, she traveled to Europe, studied art history in Paris, and collected theater experience before she debuted in the television series *A for Andromeda* in 1961. Without a hitch she made the jump into film and, as the ideal embodiment of the new independent woman of the "swinging sixties," soon became a star. In 1965 she won an Oscar for her depiction of an immoral "Jetset" girl in John Schlesinger's *Darling*. In the same year, she brought tender sensuality to David Lean's sweet and opulent Pasternak adaptation, *Doctor Zhivago*. Despite her distinctive beauty, combining boldness, coolness, and sensitivity, she escaped being typecast and was able to develop as an actress. Truffaut cast her in a double role in *Fahrenheit 451* (1966). Later she portrayed the title character in Richard Lester's *Petulia* (1968) and played alongside Warren Beatty in Altman's *McCabe & Mrs. Miller* (1971), a role that earned her another Oscar nomination. Christie also worked with further directorial stars of the time, such as Joseph Losey in *The Go-Between* (1970), Nicolas Roeg in *Don't Look Now* (1973), and Hal Ashby in *Shampoo* (1974). Toward the end of the 70s things grew quiet around Christie, who, like Jane Fonda, was politically active and apparently lost interest in acting. She enjoyed success in Alan Rudolph's *Afterglow* (1997) and in 2008 was nominated for a Best Actress Oscar for her role in Sarah Polley's *Away From Her* (2006).

"*Don't Look Now* is such a rich, complex and subtle experience that it demands more than one viewing. Roeg's insistence on the power of the image, his reliance on techniques of narrative that are peculiarly cinematic, remind us how undemanding and perfunctory so many movies still are. Roeg's is one of those rare talents that can effect a new way of seeing." *Time Magazine*

Briton Nicolas Roeg began his career toward the end of the 1950s as a cameraman. He quickly became one of the most sought-after men in his field. In the 60s, he worked as director of photography for directorial icons such as Roger Corman, Richard Lester, John Schlesinger, and David Lean, before making his long-overdue directorial debut alongside Donald Cammel with *Performance* (1969), an extravagant gangster film that offered a reflection on the popular culture of the 60s. Roeg worked as director of photography on *Performance*, and again on his second film, *Walkabout* (1971). In *Don't Look Now*, he is also credited alongside Anthony B. Richmond as director of photography, unmistakable evidence that indicates just how important the visual aspect of filmmaking is for Roeg. Accordingly, *Don't Look Now*, which like several Alfred Hitchcock films is based upon a Daphne du Maurier story, is a masterpiece of timeless beauty thanks to its visual qualities.

It's often the case in cinema that an unspecified, implicit threat produces a more lasting scare than any terror explicitly depicted on the screen. This is especially true for movies that convert human fears into a system of symbols, like horror films or thrillers. *Don't Look Now*, which effectively straddles these two genres, is a prime example. Even today, the film derives most of its extraordinarily disturbing effect and subtle horror from the tense atmosphere that Roeg evokes with his powerfully suggestive images, accentuated by a seemingly avant-garde montage technique, which almost anticipates the refined editing of Steven Soderbergh. From the very beginning, the film's time and reality planes are constantly interrupted by unsettlingly stark cuts, abrupt segues and enigmatic associations. A second, hidden meaning seems to lurk behind each image and the constant threat of something

"A modern Hitchcock. His film shows that he has already absorbed and reflected upon the turmoil of the 70s."

Kölner Stadt-Anzeiger

1 The end of innocence: In just minutes, the child in the red raincoat will drown in the garden pond. In Nicolas Roeg's film, each image holds multiple meanings.

2 After the death of his daughter, John Baxter (Donald Sutherland) experiences things in Venice that threaten his rational worldview.

3 Indecent exposure: Tiny red details in gray, wintry Venice recall the drowned girl at the start of the film—Laura's shoulder bag, for example...

3

“... a haunting, beautiful labyrinth that gets inside your bones and stays there. *Don’t Look Now* still has the power to frighten and disorient —to suggest a world that’s perilous, cruel and out of control.”

San Francisco Chronicle

4 ... and her boots.

5 The labyrinthine alleys of Venice reflect John’s inner chaos.

unexpected and inexplicable questions what has just been seen. As with the mosaics John reconstructs in the church, the truth is hidden behind a number of broken pieces in small symbols that seem to defy rational association, for which normal explanations simply do not suffice.

Roeg’s suggestive coloration hugely intensifies the surreal, threatening atmosphere. The color red is given an especially significant meaning. At the beginning, little Christine runs around the garden in a radiant red raincoat. The premonition that the girl is in danger comes to John as he discovers a figure clad in a red hooded jacket on the slide of a Venetian church and a red fluid—it is not clear if it’s John’s blood—subsequently spreads out on the screen. When later in Venice, Laura wears red boots or carries a red bag, it suggests that the Baxters are oppressed by thoughts of their daughter. It seems as if John is even visited by visions, as he repeatedly sees a mysterious small figure in a red raincoat scurrying away. The film appears to slowly but surely take over John’s perspective; in contrast to Laura he is a committed rationalist and fights against his delusional visions, growing more and more bewildered as a result. Far from romantic glamour, wintry gray Venice, with its labyrinthine streets, becomes a mirror image of his inner chaos. In the end, the city exudes an almost gothic horror. It shockingly reveals itself to John as a kingdom of the dead.

The directorial projects of former cameramen are often plagued by a technical brilliance that renders films cold and sterile. The natural interaction between the leading actors, Julie Christie and Donald Sutherland, ensures that is not case here. Their wonderfully long love scene has passed into legend, its discreet sensuality all the more evident today, long after the scent of scandal has faded.

JH

5

THE STING

1973 – USA – 129 MIN.

GENRE

GANGSTER FILM, COMEDY

DIRECTOR

GEORGE ROY HILL

SCREENPLAY

DAVID S. WARD

DIRECTOR OF PHOTOGRAPHY

ROBERT SURTEES

EDITING

WILLIAM REYNOLDS

MUSIC

SCOTT JOPLIN, MARVIN HAMLISCH

PRODUCTION

TONY BILL, JULIA PHILLIPS, MICHAEL PHILLIPS, RICHARD D. ZANUCK for UNIVERSAL PICTURES

STARRING

PAUL NEWMAN (Henry Gondorff), ROBERT REDFORD (Johnny Hooker), ROBERT SHAW (Doyle Lonnegan), CHARLES DURNING (Lieutenant William Snyder), RAY WALSTON (J.J. Singleton), EILEEN BRENNAN (Billie), HAROLD GOULD (Kid Twist), JOHN HEFFERNAN (Eddie Niles), DANA ELCAR (F.B.I. Special Agent Polk), ROBERT EARL JONES (Luther Coleman)

ACADEMY AWARDS 1974

OSCARS for BEST PICTURE (Tony Bill, Julia Phillips, Michael Phillips), BEST DIRECTOR (George Roy Hill), BEST SCREENPLAY (David S. Ward), BEST FILM EDITING (William Reynolds), BEST ADAPTED SCORE (Marvin Hamlisch), BEST ART DIRECTION (Henry Bumstead, James Payne), and BEST COSTUMES (Edith Head)

A BILL / PHILLIPS Production Of a GEORGE ROY HILL Film

"THE STING"

A RICHARD D. ZANUCK / DAVID BROWN PRESENTATION

Written by DAVID S. WARD ▪ Directed by GEORGE ROY HILL

Produced by TONY BILL, MICHAEL and JULIA PHILLIPS

A UNIVERSAL PICTURE • TECHNICOLOR®

Original Soundtrack Album available exclusively on MCA Records & Tapes

PG PARENTAL GUIDANCE SUGGESTED SOME MATERIAL MAY NOT BE SUITABLE FOR PRE-TEENAGERS

1

"What was I supposed to do—call him for cheating better than me?"

Joliet, Illinois, 1936. Con men Hooker (Robert Redford) and Luther (Robert Earl Jones) pull off a lucrative street swindle. But they don't suspect that the money they've stolen belongs to notorious gangster boss Doyle Lonnegan (Robert Shaw), who immediately sets a killer on the trail of the two crooks. After Luther is cold-bloodedly murdered, Hooker flees to Chicago, leaving behind the corrupt cop, Snyder (Charles Durning), who is also after him. He goes into hiding with Gondorff (Paul Newman), an old con man buddy of Luther's whose heyday is long past and who, in an attempt to stay out of trouble with the FBI, has settled down comfortably with brothel owner Billie (Eileen Brennan). But Hooker's determination to avenge Luther's death breathes new life into Gondorff. The two piece together a band of old associates and hatch a refined plan to swindle Lonnegan out of a half a million bucks.

The Sting is a phenomenon. A charmingly lightweight movie about gangsters and swindlers in 1930s Chicago, it was the clear winner at the Oscars and became one of the biggest box office smashes of the decade. Created by an independent production team, the film was a triumph for New Hollywood, though it showed that the methods of old Hollywood could still function provided well-known elements were rearranged. The producers built upon the successful trio from the Western *Butch Cassidy and the Sundance Kid* (1969), casting Robert Redford and Paul Newman in starring roles, and hiring George Roy Hill to direct the project. They also correctly guessed that film audiences of the 1970s would be very receptive to nostalgic films. Accordingly, the squalor of the Depression of the 1930s is hardly noticeable in *The Sting*. From the very beginning when the characters are introduced, it is clear

ROBERT SURTEES Robert Surtees (1906–1985) was one of the most famous of all American cameramen. He came to Hollywood in 1927, at the time of the introduction of the "talkie," and began his career as a camera assistant, initially at Universal and then later at both Warner Brothers and MGM. During these years, Surtees assisted Joseph Ruttenberg and Gregg Toland, the legendary master of focal depth, among others. Surtees graduated to head cameraman in the early 1940s and in subsequent years he developed into one of the most versatile and sought-after technicians in his field, as well as one of the most honored. Over the course of his 50-year career, Surtees was awarded an Academy Award on three separate occasions—for the color photography of *King Solomon's Mines* (1950) and *Ben-Hur* (1959), as well as for the black and white film *The Bad and the Beautiful* (1952). He received 13 further Oscar nominations, in 1967 and 1971 for two films simultaneously. Robert Surtees was one of the few camera virtuosos of the studio system who were also able to collaborate with young directors of New Hollywood, including Peter Bogdanovich in *The Last Picture Show* (1971) and Mike Nichols in *The Graduate* (1967). Surtees' son, Bruce (1937–2012), followed in the footsteps of his father. He is best known as Clint Eastwood's favorite director of photography.

1 Shall I frisk ya? Although *The Sting* itself raked in a slew of Oscars, heartthrob Robert Redford only won the laurels of adoring fans.

2 "Reunited, and it feels so good!" Five years after riding off into the sunset, Butch and Sundance meet up in the Depression Era, striking box-office gold yet again.

3 Pick a card, any card… A tribute to con artistry that examines the tricks of the trade.

"Two of Hollywood's dream men form this genial marriage of criminal minds: Paul Newman, the mature senior partner, is unbeatably dashing; and in Robert Redford, the dream factory's latest young hero, he's found an ideal foil and accomplice." *Stuttgarter Zeitung*

that what lies ahead is pure film fantasy, not an attempt at reconstructing the past. And sure enough, George Roy Hill's film is unadulterated and highly entertaining fiction, in which a perfect mix between historic and historicized set pieces is achieved: Scott Joplin's Ragtime piano, though from the 1920s, brings a sleight of hand and levity to the film that corresponds marvelously with the actions of the actors. Antique segment titles and the use of the fade-out further strengthen the tongue-in-cheek charm of the mischievous swindle. And the pleasant retro-look reminiscent of the color films of the late 1940s, with which camera veteran Robert Surtees impressively refines the studio set, exudes the faded luster of the "good old times," a feeling that was not present in the harsh underworld dramas of the 1930s, the heyday of Warner Brothers' classic gangster films.

3

4

4 Ol' blue eyes: Till his death in 2008, Paul Newman was one of America's most in-demand actors.

5 The way we weren't: Redford makes misery and poverty look stylish and divine.

"How long has it been since you exited from a movie theatre smiling and just plain feeling good?" *Films in Review*

The Sting also mirrors the enthusiasm of filmmaking itself in the playful accentuation of its dramatization. It succeeds in reflecting the love of performance, deception and manipulation that drive the central characters, and around which the entire plot revolves. No one can resist this virus: even the seemingly vice-free Lonnegan is ensnared by Gondorff in a round of poker. Needless to say, the cards are marked. As appropriate vengeance however, Gondorff & Co. find this action far too mundane. Instead, the plan is to get Lonnegan to place and subsequently lose a fortune on a horserace—in a fabricated betting office created just for this purpose. The action is without a doubt a masterpiece of deception and a challenge for true pros. Consequently, as in so many American films, the charm of *The Sting* lies in the pleasure of watching shrewd specialists at work. It is a pleasure that does not limit itself merely to the plot, but expands to the unmistakably brilliant performance of the whole film team—the actors, the cameraman, the art director, the author, and the director. *The Sting* is enthralling thanks to the professionalism of its entire crew. Hill's tour de force is a film by and about people who are clearly in supreme command of their craft—the craft of illusion.

JH

IL MIO NOME È NESSUNO

MY NAME IS NOBODY

1973 – ITALY / FRANCE / FRG – 117 MIN.

GENRE

SPAGHETTI WESTERN, SPOOF

DIRECTOR

TONINO VALERII

SCREENPLAY

SERGIO LEONE, ERNESTO GASTALDI,
FULVIO MORSELLA

DIRECTOR OF PHOTOGRAPHY

ARMANDO NANNUZZI, GIUSEPPE RUZZOLINI

EDITING

NINO BARAGLI

MUSIC

ENNIO MORRICONE

PRODUCTION

FULVIO MORSELLA for RAFRAN CINEMATOGRAFICA,
RIALTO FILM, LES PRODUCTIONS JACQUES LEITIENNE,
LA SOCIETE IMP EX CI, LA SOCIETE ALCINTER

STARRING

TERENCE HILL (Nobody), HENRY FONDA (Jack Beauregard),
JEAN MARTIN (Sullivan), REMUS PEETS (Biggun),
PIERO LULLI (Sceriffo), GEOFFREY LEWIS (Band Leader),
R.G. ARMSTRONG (John), NEIL SUMMERS (Squirrel),
ULRICH MÜLLER (Dirty Joe), LEO GORDON (Red)

Titanus

SERGIO LEONE

PRESENTA

TERENCE HILL HENRY FONDA

IL MIO NOME E' NESSUNO

DIRETTO DA TONINO VALERII

JEAN MARTIN

SOGGETTO FULVIO MORSELLA • ERNESTO GASTALDI SCENEGGIATURA ERNESTO GASTALDI MUSICHE DI ENNIO MORRICONE PRODOTTO DA FULVIO MORSELLA

PRODUTTORE ESECUTIVO CLAUDIO MANCINI

TECHNICOLOR • PANAVISION

Anno di edizione 1973

1

"A hero must die—it has to be so."

Three sinister figures ride into town. Dogs make themselves scarce and the townspeople stay in their houses. The trio make their way to the barber shop. They have no intention of harming the barber. They simply "borrow" his shop and his apron, posing as assistants in the hope of bumping off the next customer, gunslinger Jack Beauregard (Henry Fonda). But he smells a rat, shoves his revolver into an extremely sensitive spot of the fake barber's anatomy and survives the cut-throat razor. At the end of the film, the gunslinger's successor will also sit down in a barber's chair, and he too will know how to protect himself—just like Beauregard, but even more brazenly.

My Name is Nobody tells of a changing of the guard. With this brilliant prelude, an old gunslinger is introduced—a man who trusts his hunches and is quick with his pistol, but who's now tired and ready to hang up his gun. He's waiting for a ship to take him to Europe so he can retire. "Do you know anyone who can draw faster?" asks the barber's son after Beauregard has done away with the three sinister characters. "Nobody," says the father. And Nobody (Terence Hill) soon appears. He is to become *the* new gunslinger. He's just as quick on the draw as Beauregard, and just as cheeky. A fan of the old gunslinger, he can recount all of his "heroic deeds." Nobody wants Beauregard to retire into the history books so he can take his place. He helps matters along, by arranging a showdown between his idol and the so-called "Wild Bunch," a group of 150 men who are "as good as 1,000..."

TERENCE HILL Blond hair and bright blue eyes are the distinguishing characteristics of Terence Hill (born 1939 in Venice). Toward the beginning of his career, however, he had dark hair and appeared under his given name, Mario Girotti. As a twelve-year-old he was discovered by director Dino Risi, and for years played supporting roles in countless films, among them the Karl May adaptation *Winnetou II* (*Vinetu II*, 1964) and Luchino Visconti's masterpiece, *The Leopard* (*Il gattopardo*, 1963). In 1967 he became the blond Terence Hill and appeared for the first time with the colleague at whose side he was to become famous—Bud Spencer (née Carlo Pedersoli). With *Dio perdona... Io no!*, a long collaboration began, which was to make Spencer and Hill famous as the wisecracking pugnacious duo. Many of these films (for example *Lo chiamavano Trinita*, 1970) are parodies of Spaghetti Westerns and were more successful than Leone's serious films. "Leone deserved artistic revenge," commented *Nobody* director Tonino Valerii. "If Terence Hill poked fun at the Spaghetti Western, he should be given an appropriate punishment—he should be the adversary of the most legendary Western actor (Henry Fonda) and he should acknowledge his own nothingness, which is where the title, *My Name is Nobody* (*Il mio nome è Nessuno*, 1973), comes from." Terence Hill remained true to the Western parody later as well—at the beginning of the 1990s he appeared in film adaptations of the comic book cowboy, *Lucky Luke* (1990, 1991, 1992), several of which he also directed. He both directed and appeared in *Doc West* and *Triggerman* (both 2009). In 2018, he fulfilled a long-time wish by starring in his own film *My Name Is Thomas* (*Il mio nome è Thomas*), produced by his son Jess Hill.

The beginning of the film is pure "Leone"—a sweeping paraphrase of Sergio Leone's masterpiece *Once Upon a Time in the West* (*C'era una volta il West*, 1969). Just as in the old Leone Westerns, Ennio Morricone composed the music, and as in *Once Upon a Time in the West*, each character gets a personal melody. Nobody gets the cheerful title song; the "Wild Bunch" get a piece with more than a passing resemblance to Wagner's *Ride of the Valkyrie*. Sergio Leone was both executive producer and co-author, and his one-time assistant Tonino Valerii directed the film. *My Name is Nobody* pays its respects to the Spaghetti Western, and is packed with countless little homages to the Hollywood Western. The "Wild Bunch" is clearly named after Sam Peckinpah's classic, *The Wild Bunch* (1969), and their appearance recalls the troops from Sam Fuller's *Forty Guns* (1957).

"For me, the interesting thing about *My Name is Nobody* was that it confronts a myth with the negation of a myth."
Sergio Leone

1 Nobody knows the trouble I've seen: Rootin' tootin' gunslinger Nobody (Terence Hill) isn't afraid of anything, except maybe gingivitis.

2 See no evil, see no nothin': Nobody has planned out the showdown for his true hero, Jack Beauregard (Henry Fonda, in the distance).

3 Before you can say Jack Robinson: Nobody's West may not be as wild as it once was, but it sure is as dangerous.

2

3

SHOW
THE PLANETARIUM
NATURAL SCENERY

5

4 Basket of goodies: Jack Beauregard may be getting on in years, but he still ain't afraid of no big bad wolf. Is he?

5 Retirement community: Beauregard wants to quit while the going's still good…

6 … but to no avail: As Nobody puts it "A good exit is sometimes trickier than a grand entrance."

The film becomes a parody through the Terence Hill character, Nobody. He has a comedic streak and goes as far as to face his adversary on the fairground. He is silly, perpetually cracks corny jokes, and has none of the tragic honor typical of the classic gunslinger. This aspect makes the film a kind of late Western—the time of the great tragic heroes is over and the new gunslinger is a clown. The film also tells of the ritual of legend building in the West. It depicts the writing of history, so to speak, while it is happening. While Beauregard shoots up the "Wild Bunch," the camera, in a kind of fast forward, continually blends book illustrations into the frame that capture the events and will finally turn the old gunslinger into a Western myth. HJK

"He totes his saddle on his shoulder like a pair of wings, punching and shooting his way through the West right there with the best of 'em."

film-dienst

6

DIE LEGENDE VON PAUL UND PAULA

THE LEGEND OF PAUL AND PAULA

1973 – GDR – 105 MIN.

GENRE

LOVE STORY, DRAMA

DIRECTOR

HEINER CAROW

SCREENPLAY

ULRICH PLENZDORF, HEINER CAROW

DIRECTOR OF PHOTOGRAPHY

JÜRGEN BRAUER

EDITING

EVELYN CAROW

MUSIC

PETER GOTTHARDT

PRODUCTION

ERICH ALBRECHT for DEFA

STARRING

ANGELICA DOMRÖSE (Paula), WINFRIED GLATZEDER (Paul), HEIDEMARIE WENZEL (Paul's Wife), FRED DELMARE (Saft the Tyre Man), ROLF LUDWIG (Professor), DIETMAR RICHTER-REINICK (A Friend), FRANK SCHENK (Schmidt), JÜRGEN FROHRIEP (Blond Martin), PETER GOTTHARDT (A Musician)

Die Legende von PAUL und PAULA

1
Paul
Paul
Paul
Paul
PAUL
Paul

"All or nothing."

In the spring of 1973, there were long queues at the East German movie theaters to see this unusual love story. Paula (Angelica Domröse) is an unmarried mother of two kids, and she works at a supermarket checkout. After an affair with a flute-playing hippie, she meets Paul (Winfried Glatzeder), a not-very-happily married state-employed bureaucrat with one child. Paula is a passionate woman who demands "all or nothing," but at first Paul is reluctant to get too deeply involved. Fearing for his status as an up-and-coming member of the East German elite, he feels compelled to keep up the appearance of a happy marriage, both at home and in the Ministry where he works. Then Paula loses one of her children in an accident and barricades herself in her apartment. Now Paul shows that love rules, even in a socialist society: he throws his career to the winds, stays off work, camps out in the stairwell of Paula's apartment house, and finally takes an axe to the door of her flat—as the neighbors stand round and applaud. East German theater audiences shared their feelings, and the film was an enormous hit. It provoked spontaneous ovations in the cinemas, something unheard of since the state production firm DEFA had commenced operations in 1945. Melodrama was a genre that had previously not been tolerated by the East German cultural bureaucracy, but the public embraced it with open arms. Although Paul knows that another pregnancy could endanger Paula's life, she still wants a child from him… and dies after the child is born, just as a happy ending seems close enough to grasp.

After the Second World War, the German Democratic Republic was a determined attempt to sweep away everything old and discredited and to create a new society, to start again from scratch. This social program is evoked in the very first shot in *Paul and Paula*: a demolition ball tolls the death knell of Berlin's notorious slum tenements, clearing the way for spanking new apartment blocks. The conflict between old and new is one of the film's leitmotifs, and it demonstrates the attitude of the director and screenwriter towards their protagonists' pursuit of happiness: their desire for a better life is formulated, not in

FILM IN THE GDR Unlike any country in the Western world, film production in the GDR (1949–1989) was *state-run*. This had its disadvantages, for both filmmakers and filmgoers. Movies were subject to state control: any scripts—or even completed films—that met with the disapproval of the responsible Party organs were put on ice or went into the archives unseen, and were known as "films for the shelf." The advantage for everyone working in East German film was that they enjoyed a secure existence as steady employees of DEFA or some similar body, even if their work was never shown in the cinema.

DEFA came into existence as a German-Soviet "joint enterprise" even before the GDR was founded. As the company was able to use the former UFA studios in Babelsberg (near Potsdam), it soon developed a reputation for productivity that extended far beyond East German borders. The very first postwar German film was made here: *The Murderers Are Among Us* (*Die Mörder sind unter uns*, 1946). DEFA also produced shorts, children's films, and weekly newsreels (*Der Augenzeuge*, "The Eyewitness"), as well as dubbing foreign films into German.

DEFA's central tasks were to convey the message of anti-fascism by cinematic means, and to show the problems and achievements of a Socialist society in the phase of construction. Genre films were extremely rare, and didn't reach the screens until the mid-60s: a sub-genre of the Western, for example, were the so-called "Indian Films" (Indianer-Filme). More and more, DEFA became a seismograph of everyday life under Socialism; and even today, after the demise of the GDR, it retains its historic importance as the powerhouse of a significant epoch in German film history.

opposition to East German society, but *within* it. Paul is a member of his *Betriebskampfgruppe*—a works militia group, made up of workers under the leadership of the Party—and when he climbs into Paula's blossom-bedecked bed (she's crowned with flowers!), he has to take off his uniform to do so. It's a scene that sent East German audiences wild with joy, and the film had found a perfect image for the tensions of the place and time. On the one hand, we see the strict regulation of everyday life under a communist regime (and the concurrent obligation to maintain a nervous high alertness). On the other, we have a relaxed presentation of the need for physical love, and recognition of the spirit of the age ("Flower Children"). At last it was possible for the East German cinema to deal with love, too, in a "modern" manner.

The Legend of Paul and Paula had a mixed reception in the West: either it was greeted with mild amusement (as a cultural "late-starter"), or it was praised, for

"There's much more to this film than the tabloid love story. The Legend of Paul and Paula is a reflection on love in general, on conformity, on the dialectics of ideal and reality, and—en passant—on the cinema itself." *Der Tagesspiegel*

1 An East German epiphany: An ecstatic trip downriver on a barge (Angelica Domröse and Winfried Gletzeder).

2 Boat and bed are linked by rapid currents and violent storms.

3 Two hippies in the Eastern Bloc: She crowns him with flowers, as in some Polynesian paradise.

3

4

4 Instead of a yellowing family portrait, the oval frame shows the lovers themselves. This film's interest is the present.

5 The New Socialist Woman bids farewell to the old face of womanhood.

6 Facing reality: Dreams of a shared future won't solve the problems of today.

7 Sugar-coated: love is sublime, but it can end in kitsch.

"Sensational! The explosiveness of the subject matter and the frankness with which it's treated is—by East German standards—quite exceptional" *Stuttgarter Zeitung*

ideological reasons, as a breakthrough for individualism in East German society. Yet, as a DEFA film, it has qualities that can only be recognized when we understand the social and political context in which it was made. First, the characters are absolutely typical of the GDR: Paul is an academic for whom an encounter with a shopgirl is something more than a one-night stand. It should also be noted that Paula's "fatherless" children were no moral disgrace in East Germany. Second, (like many other DEFA films), this movie achieved credibility—and managed to capture a critical and skeptical audience—with many precise observations of everyday life. When we see the single mother Paula schlepping coal up to her third-floor apartment, the film's desire to demonstrate its own authenticity is almost palpable. In this sense, East German movies were always documentaries, too: records of how real people really lived, in their particular place and time.

RV

SOYLENT GREEN

1973 – USA – 97 MIN.

GENRE

SCIENCE FICTION, POLITICAL THRILLER

DIRECTOR

RICHARD FLEISCHER

SCREENPLAY

STANLEY R. GREENBERG, based on the novel
MAKE ROOM! MAKE ROOM! by HARRY HARRISON

DIRECTOR OF PHOTOGRAPHY

RICHARD H. KLINE

EDITING

SAMUEL E. BREETLEY

MUSIC

FRED MYROW, EDVARD GRIEG ("PEER GYNT"),
PYOTR ILYCH TCHAIKOVSKY (6TH SYMPHONY),
LUDWIG VAN BEETHOVEN (6TH SYMPHONY – "THE PASTORAL SYMPHONY")

PRODUCTION

WALTER SELTZER, RUSSELL THACHER for MGM

STARRING

CHARLTON HESTON (Detective Robert Thorn), EDWARD G. ROBINSON (Sol Roth), CHUCK CONNORS (Tab Fielding), LEIGH TAYLOR-YOUNG (Shirl), JOSEPH COTTEN (William R. Simonson), BROCK PETERS (Lieutenant "Chief" Hatcher), PAULA KELLY (Martha), STEPHEN YOUNG (Gilbert), LINCOLN KILPATRICK (Priest), ROY JENSON (Donovan), WHIT BISSELL (Governor Santini), LEONARD STONE (Charles)

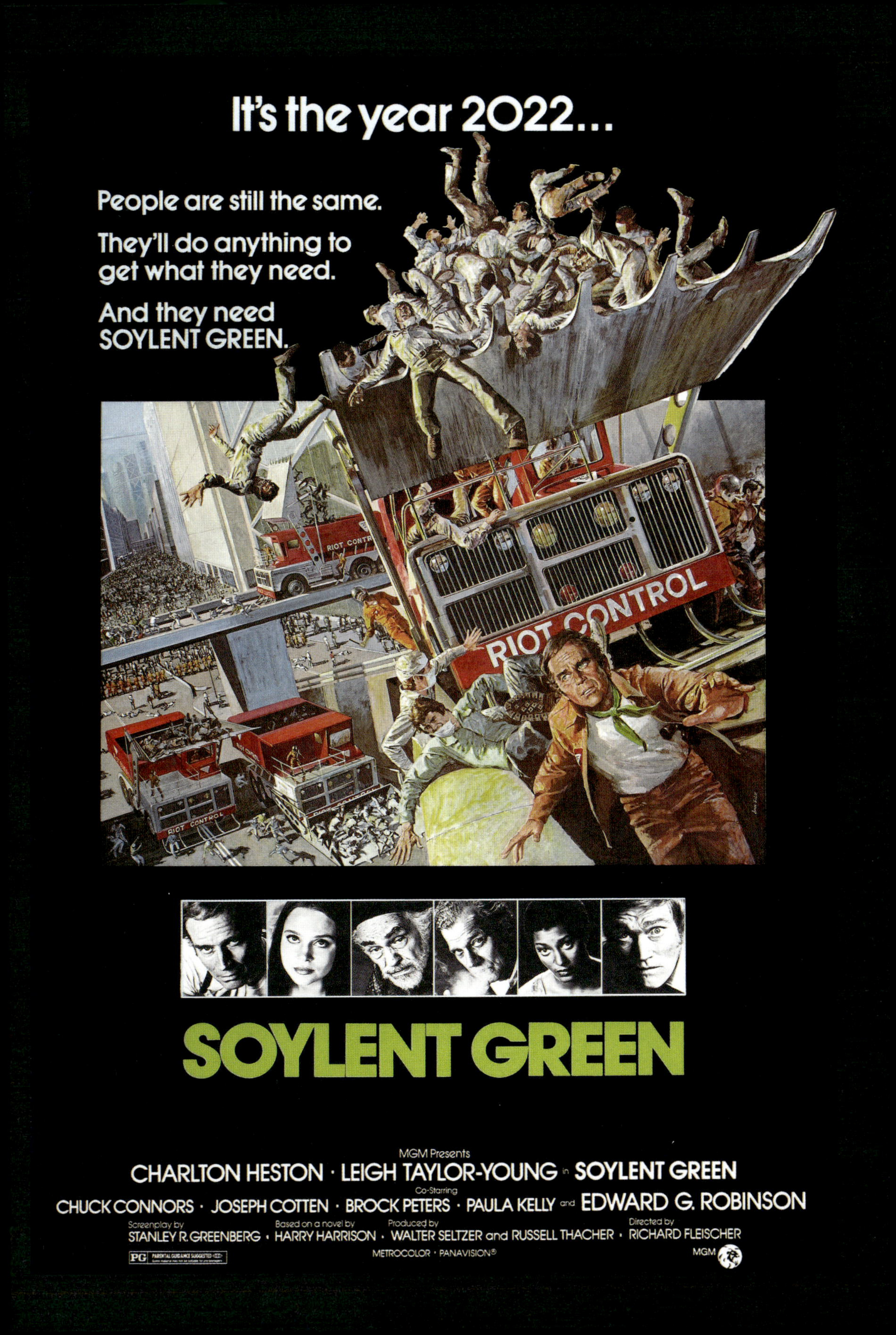

It's the year 2022...

People are still the same.

They'll do anything to get what they need.

And they need SOYLENT GREEN.

SOYLENT GREEN

MGM Presents

CHARLTON HESTON · LEIGH TAYLOR-YOUNG in SOYLENT GREEN

Co-Starring

CHUCK CONNORS · JOSEPH COTTEN · BROCK PETERS · PAULA KELLY and EDWARD G. ROBINSON

Screenplay by STANLEY R. GREENBERG · Based on a novel by HARRY HARRISON · Produced by WALTER SELTZER and RUSSELL THACHER · Directed by RICHARD FLEISCHER

PG PARENTAL GUIDANCE SUGGESTED

METROCOLOR · PANAVISION®

MGM

1

"Ah, people were always lousy. But there was a world, once."

In the year 2022, New York City is a place no one would choose to visit. The city has 40 million inhabitants. Streets and apartment buildings are hopelessly overcrowded. Poverty and food shortages govern the lives of the people. To cap it all, a yellowish-green smog hangs over the city. The ecosystem has collapsed, and green plants are a thing of the past. In the midst of this chaos, there is only one guarantor of order: The New York City Police Department. Robert Thorn (Charlton Heston) is a detective in the homicide division, and he's been given the task of finding the killer of William Simonson (Joseph Cotten), found dead in his luxury apartment and apparently murdered for his money.

Simonson had been CEO of the Soylent Corporation, a powerful organization with a near-monopoly on the production of food. Soylent produce a range of synthetic

RICHARD FLEISCHER Richard Fleischer was born in Brooklyn in 1916. His father was Max Fleischer, the man who invented Betty Boop. In 1942, Richard began his career in the newsreel section of RKO-Pathé in New York, before making his directing debut in RKO's B-movie department in Hollywood. In the early 50s, the new studio boss Howard Hughes discovered Fleischer's *Film Noir* classic *The Narrow Margin* (1952), after the film had spent two years gathering dust in the archives; Hughes was impressed, and promoted Fleischer to the A-list, though he was permitted only to re-shoot parts of the Robert Mitchum film *His Kind of Woman* (1951) and to add a new ending—anonymously. He acquired his reputation as a master of technically complex productions after making *20,000 Leagues Under the Sea* (1954), a classic of its genre. *The Vikings* (1958) brought further confirmation of his powers.
Elaborate widescreen compositions soon became one of his trademarks, as in his black-and-white movie *Compulsion* (1959). This film also demonstrated Fleischer's sure instinct when handling a sensitive theme: it featured Orson Welles as a lawyer who battles to save two young murderers from the electric chair. In Europe, Fleischer adapted a novel by the Swedish Nobel Prize winner Pär Lagerkvist (1951) for Dino De Laurentiis's production company: the biblical epic *Barabbas* (1962). In the 60s, he enjoyed his greatest successes with a series of films for Fox, including the SF spectacle *Fantastic Voyage* (1966), the Rex Harrison musical *Doctor Dolittle* (1967), and his masterpiece *The Boston Strangler* (1968), starring Henry Fonda and Tony Curtis. In 1970, he collaborated with Japanese filmmakers on the Pearl Harbor movie *Tora! Tora! Tora!*, and in the following decade he worked for a range of studios and independent production firms. The 80s again witnessed several collaborations between Fleischer and Dino De Laurentiis, including *Conan the Destroyer* (1984). Whatever the subject, most of Fleischer's films feature the use of documentary techniques in the service of greater realism, and his directing style is always clearly recognizable. His last film was the half-hour feature *Call From Space* (1989), which used the Showscan technique developed by SFX-master Douglas Trumbull. In 1993, Fleischer published his memoirs, entitled *Just Tell Me When to Cry*. Fleischer died in 2006 in Los Angeles.

"Try all of Soylent's delicious flavors: Soylent red, Soylent yellow, and new, delicious, Soylent green. Made from the finest undersea growth." *Film quote: TV commercial*

foodstuffs in handy chocolate-bar formats, distinguishable from each other only by their different colors. "Soylent Green," a natural product made of soy beans and plankton, is the most popular food around, for alternatives such as meat, fruit and vegetables can be afforded only by the upper classes in their protected enclaves. Thorn is supported in his work by a man called Sol (Edward G. Robinson in his last role), a so-called "book," whose task is restricted to researching archives. Together, the two will uncover a shocking scandal, which the murder of Simonson was intended to conceal.

Soylent Green is a detective story, a political thriller, and a dark vision of ecological meltdown. Richard Fleischer's film evokes a world of crass dichotomies: in pursuit of his investigations, Thorn moves to and fro between the luxurious world of the rich and the hopeless squalor of the urban poor. He doesn't hesitate to enjoy the pleasures available in Simonson's stylish loft apartment: running hot water, a house bar, and Shirl (Leigh Taylor-Young), an attractive girl who's just one more of the amenities. The greatest luxury of all, however, is space: the generous dimensions of Simonson's domicile stand in sharp contrast

Director Richard Fleischer has created some shockingly effective scenes." *Die Welt*

1 Close human contact is a scarce commodity in the year 2022.

2 Mass-produced food: Detective Thorn (Charlton Heston) has just found out what's in those little green bars…

3 In 2022, police brutality is a daily occurrence: Thorn is hurt, and his colleagues are still laying into the crowd.

3

4 The law of the jungle: *Soylent Green* offered Charlton Heston another chance to ooze testosterone.

5 Thorn checks the goods after Charles (Leonard Stone, right) has divided them up.

to the crammed housing blocks inhabited by the rest of the citizenry. When night falls, conditions are even more claustrophobic, with massed sleepers stacked in the stairways. As a policeman, Thorn is relatively privileged, but he still belongs to the world of the poor. He shares a tiny room with Sol, covers his nutritional requirements with Soylent Green, and has never eaten anything better. His place of work is no less dismal—the police station is a dilapidated hole, packed with irritable colleagues. Tough and cynical, Thorn shoulders his way through the daily routine of police work.

Critics complained of this SF film's "unrealistically" contemporary look, for the early 70s are everywhere in evidence, from the style of the furniture to the flare in the jeans. These critics were missing the point. Director Richard Fleischer had no intention of emulating the timelessly futuristic ambience of films like *2001: A Space Odyssey* (1968); instead, he wanted to confront the audience of the time with the familiar city of New York grown suddenly nightmarish. The film's imagery is consequently shocking: thus we see the police deploy mechanical excavators to scoop up a group of angry protesters, before tipping them into containers and lugging them off like garbage. The message is clear, and chilling: in a world packed to overflowing, individual lives will lose all significance or value.

In the course of the film, this negative utopia is fleshed out with detail and acquires an almost documentary-like intensity. Fleischer succeeds in combining unpretentious realism with a grim yet spectacular vision of the world that awaits us. In this, *Soylent Green* is reminiscent of his previous film, the police drama *The New Centurions* (1972).

As foreshadowed in the impressively-edited title sequence, pollution is one of the film's main themes. In 1972, the publication of the Club of Rome report had sparked a broad public discussion on environmental protection, and the topic has become no less pressing in the last thirty years. Fleischer's Hollywood film was a timely and vigorous contribution to the debate, and he was clearly interested in taking a realistic stance: He employed Frank R. Bowerman, president of the American Academy for Environmental Protection, as an advisor on the film.

Soylent Green is a robust and uncompromising film, an unlikely, unusual and indubitable classic. Richard Fleischer presents an oppressively gripping scenario in the guise of a conventional thriller, and the film still has the power to disturb. It leaves us, to say the least, with a bitter taste in our mouths.

DG

"It is too likely that such ecological chaos may occur, but there have been so many melodramatic warnings about it in essays and speculative fantasies such as this (Soylent Green) that urgency becomes blunted and worn through repetition." *Time Magazine*

5

PAPILLON

1973 – USA – 150 MIN.

GENRE

PRISON FILM, LITERARY ADAPTATION

DIRECTOR

FRANKLIN J. SCHAFFNER

SCREENPLAY

DALTON TRUMBO, LORENZO SEMPLE JR.,
based on the novel of the same name by HENRI CHARRIÈRE

DIRECTOR OF PHOTOGRAPHY

FRED J. KOENEKAMP

EDITING

ROBERT SWINK

MUSIC

JERRY GOLDSMITH

PRODUCTION

ROBERT DORFMANN, FRANKLIN J. SCHAFFNER
for ALLIED ARTISTS PICTURES CORPORATION,
CORONA-GENERAL, SOLAR PRODUCTIONS

STARRING

STEVE MCQUEEN (Papillon), DUSTIN HOFFMAN (Louis Dega),
DON GORDON (Julot), ANTHONY ZERBE (Toussaint),
ROBERT DEMAN (Maturette), VICTOR JORY (Aboriginal Chief),
WOODROW PARFREY (Clusiot), BILL MUMY (Lariot),
GEORGE COULOURIS (Doktor Chatal), BARBARA MORRISON (Oberin)

THE GREATEST ADVENTURE OF ESCAPE!

ALLIED ARTISTS presents

STEVE McQUEEN DUSTIN HOFFMAN

in a FRANKLIN J. SCHAFFNER film

PAPILLON

Co-starring VICTOR JORY DON GORDON ANTHONY ZERBE Executive Producer TED RICHMOND
Produced by ROBERT DORFMANN and FRANKLIN J. SCHAFFNER Screenplay by DALTON TRUMBO and LORENZO SEMPLE, Jr.
Based on the book by HENRI CHARRIÈRE Music by JERRY GOLDSMITH Directed by FRANKLIN J. SCHAFFNER PANAVISION® TECHNICOLOR®

ORIGINAL SOUND TRACK ON CAPITOL RECORDS An ALLIED ARTISTS Release ab

COPYRIGHT © 1973 ALLIED ARTISTS PICTURES CORP.

1

"If I stay here in this place, I'll die."

Henri Charrière's autobiographical novel *Papillon* appeared in 1968 and became an international bestseller. It describes the experiences of a man who succeeds in escaping from a prison colony in French Guyana. Because of the book's numerous contradictions and inconsistencies, many critics immediately cast doubt on the authenticity of the events it describes. Eyewitnesses confirmed that it gave a truthful representation of the cruel methods used in the colony (which no longer exists), but they criticized the way Charrière had taken the experiences of other prisoners and presented them as his own. Nonetheless, the book's gripping descriptions of desperate escape attempts and sheer density of detail were a goldmine for a Hollywood scriptwriter. The result was a box-office smash, a prison film in an exotic setting with two mega-stars in the leading roles.

Papillon (Steve McQueen), a French safecracker, acquired his nickname thanks to the butterfly tattooed on his chest. In 1931, despite being innocent of the murder he was accused of, he was sentenced to life imprisonment on Devil's Island. Among the others sent down is the weedy accountant and counterfeiter Dega (Dustin Hoffman). During their passage to South America, Dega fears for his life. He has a small fortune in cash concealed in his own back passage, and he has good reason to fear he'll be butchered for the money. Papillon makes a deal with Dega: he'll protect him, and in return Dega will finance his escape. On their arrival in the colony, the two prisoners are assigned to work in the swamps. After Papillon prevents a warder from beating his friend to death, Dega feels deeply indebted to the hard-bitten jailbird. But "Papi's" hasty escape attempt ends in failure: quickly recaptured, he is sentenced

DALTON TRUMBO "France has written you off—so forget France and get your clothes on." In the opening sequence of *Papillon* (1973), these words are spoken by an army commander to a group of naked prisoners lined up before him, shortly before they board the ship for French Guyana. The old officer is played by Dalton Trumbo (1905–1976), co-author of the film. This cameo appearance is a bitterly ironic commentary on the many years spent by Trumbo on Hollywood's notorious blacklist—"written off" by his own country as an alleged Communist. For his refusal to name names before McCarthy's "House Un-American Activities Committee," he had himself spent time in jail.

After his release, Trumbo moved to Mexico, where he wrote scripts for Hollywood under a series of pseudonyms. He had already received an Oscar nomination for *Kitty Foyle* (1940), as well as working with Joseph H. Lewis and others (*Deadly Is the Female / Gun Crazy*, 1949). In 1956, the Oscar for Best Screenplay was awarded to one Robert Rich for *The Brave One.* This led to a scandal, for Mr. Rich was none other than Dalton Trumbo himself. Trumbo endured years as a non-person before his real name finally appeared again in the opening credits to *Exodus* (1960; produced and directed by Otto Preminger). In 1971, Trumbo directed the film version of *Johnny Got His Gun*, his own world-famous, pacifist novel. He died of a heart attack in 1976. Sixteen years later, he received a posthumous Oscar for the screenplay to *Roman Holiday* (1953), a popular romance starring Audrey Hepburn and Gregory Peck. The film won three Oscars in total.

1 Do not pass go: Forger Louis Dega (Dustin Hoffman) has seen better days. The prison camp in French Guayana is hell on earth.

2 Iron will: Even half rations and total isolation can't break his spirit: Papillon (Steve McQueen).

3 Breaking out of solitary: Though known for playing loners and individualists—in *Papillon*, Hoffman's brilliance lies in his on-screen friendship with Steve McQueen.

to two years in solitary confinement. Even in his isolation, however, he still retains tenuous contact to Dega. The latter has bribed his way into a more pleasant job in prison administration, and he provides Papillon with a secret supply of coconuts—an essential supplement to the foul prison rations, which barely ensure survival. When this illegal food bonus is discovered, Papillon's punishment is draconian: he is placed on half-rations and confined for years to a darkened cell. Yet he still holds his tongue and refuses to betray Dega. Years later, the two meet once again in the prison colony; on Papillon's next escape attempt, Dega will accompany him.

Papillon tells the story of an unusual male friendship, marked by kindness and strong fellow feeling. More than once, Dega uses the following words to Papillon: "My thoughts are with you." It's an expression of deeply felt sympathy that sums up their remarkable bond.

Director Franklin J. Schaffner had already enjoyed success with *Planet of the Apes* (1968) and the Oscar-winning *Patton* (1969). In *Papillon*, he accomplishes a delicate balancing act, combining a realistic portrayal of monstrous prison conditions with some very funny moments. When Dega and "Papi" are sent off to retrieve a shot crocodile from the swamp, we witness a slapstick scene, for it turns out that the animal is still far from dead. Even their escape constitutes a kind of comic relief: while the prison orchestra plays marching tunes for the ladies and gents of the French colony, the two jailbirds struggle like Keystone Cops to scale a very high wall. Gallows humor indeed, bitter and funny in equal measure.

The film derives its power from many unforgettable moments that demonstrate the leading character's impressive will to survive. We see him stave off starvation in his darkened cell by catching centipedes and roaches;

"We're something, aren't we? The only animals that shove things up their ass for survival." *Film quote: Papillon*

4 No girls allowed: Homosexuality is another theme examined in this "men's film." *Papillon* features only two small speaking parts for women.

5 Epic grandeur: Director Franklin J. Schaffner demonstrates the same masterful ease with crowd scenes and intimate dialogues alike.

"Papillon inevitably refers us to old movies rather than to reality. Audiences whose expectations do not exceed their grasp will find it a much more comfortable vehicle for escape than any that McQueen & Co. discover on location." *Time Magazine*

taking a draw from the cigar of a leper who could help him escape from the island; and leaping into the sea from the clifftops—a tiny figure against a huge background, an individual victorious against an inhuman, implacable system.

Despite all the sadistic warders and the fugitives wading through swamps, *Papillon* has more to offer than the usual prison-film clichés. Schaffner had always been interested in connecting the history of cinema itself to the historical and political events depicted in his films. In his study of the last Russian royal family, for example (*Nicholas and Alexandra*, 1971), his treatment of the crowd scenes draws on techniques of montage deployed by Sergej M. Eisenstein in *Strike* (*Statschka*, 1924) and *October* (*Oktjabr*, 1927). In *Papillon*, the characterization of the main figure constitutes an equally artful symbiosis between film history and history *per se*. It's no accident, for example, that "Papi," who spends 14 years in jail, bears more than a passing resemblance to another famous cinematic jailbird. In *A Man Escaped* (*Un condamné à mort s'est échappé / Le vent souffle où il veut*, 1956), Robert Bresson depicts the captivity and flight of a resistance fighter in occupied France during WWII. This film was also based on factual reports; and like Papillon, Bresson's protagonist is obsessed with escaping. Both characters are driven by a yearning for freedom that expresses itself in untiring resistance, and each of them is prepared to risk death rather than submit to oppression. Schaffner's composer Jerry Goldsmith reinforced this link by taking his inspiration from the French music of the period. *Papillon's* "French" leitmotif dominates the film's soundscape, and we hear it for the last time after his successful flight: a musical bond between the exiled hero and his distant home country. The despised prisoner of Devil's Island and the heroes of the French resistance share more than their nationality. Thus the music in Schaffner's film is not a merely decorative "quotation;" it adds a dimension beyond Charrière's book and provides an original and illuminating insight into cinematic history.

DG

AMERICAN GRAFFITI

1973 – USA – 110 MIN.

GENRE

COMEDY

DIRECTOR

GEORGE LUCAS

SCREENPLAY

GEORGE LUCAS, GLORIA KATZ, WILLARD HUYCK

DIRECTOR OF PHOTOGRAPHY

RON EVESLAGE, JAN D'ALQUEN

EDITING

VERNA FIELDS, MARCIA LUCAS

MUSIC

BUDDY HOLLY, CHUCK BERRY, BOOKER T. JONES

PRODUCTION

FRANCIS FORD COPPOLA for THE COPPOLA COMPANY, LUCASFILM LTD., UNIVERSAL PICTURES

STARRING

RICHARD DREYFUSS (Curt Henderson), RON HOWARD (Steve Bolander), PAUL LE MAT (John Milner), CHARLES MARTIN SMITH (Terry Fields), CINDY WILLIAMS (Laurie Henderson), CANDY CLARK (Debbie Dunham), MACKENZIE PHILLIPS (Carol), WOLFMAN JACK (XERB Disc Jockey), HARRISON FORD (Bob Falfa), BO HOPKINS (Joe Young)

COPYRIGHT © 1973 BY UNIVERSAL PICTURES COUNTRY OF ORIGIN U.S.A.

73/253

1

"Hey, is this what they call copping a feel?"

Not on your life, sister! The only reason John (Paul Le Mat), the reigning king of the road this side of the Sierra Nevada, presses Carol's (Mackenzie Phillips) face into his lap is out of sheer embarrassment to be seen with a thirteen-year-old while cruising the streets. As far as he's concerned, the kid just got into his roadster by mistake. Be that as it may, young Carol's somewhat naive question pricelessly captures the spirit of 1962, the year in which George Lucas' bittersweet adolescent comedy takes place. *American Graffiti* tells of the last days of teenage innocence, both for the protagonists, who are fresh out of high school and uncertain about what to do next, as well as for the era's way of life in general. For within the coming two years, American president John F. Kennedy will be assassinated and the nation will enter the Vietnam War.

The film tells the story of one night in the life of four adolescents growing up in sleepy Modesto, California. Curt (Richard Dreyfuss) and Steve (Ron Howard) have both won college scholarships and are scheduled to leave in the morning. Steve is starry-eyed and hopeful for the future, while Curt is still contemplating whether he'd be better off spending another year in his comfortable surroundings. Terry (Charles Martin Smith) is younger than the other two. A clutzy dork, he wears a pair of two-inch-thick, horn-rimmed glasses, trying his damnedest to emulate the older guys where women and booze are concerned, but failing miserably. John is a bit older than the rest of the troop and drives around town in a suped-up 1932 Ford Deuce coupe. As far as cars go, John is the undisputed cock of the walk, although the "cool rider" title is beginning to sound a little stale. He eventually admits being jealous of Curt for being able to escape their hometown, a chance he'll never get…

American Graffiti was produced with a budget of 750 thousand dollars and raked in a total of 55 million at the box office. Its enormous appeal then, as now, was its ability to

GEORGE LUCAS George Lucas is among the most commercially successful filmmakers alive today. His personal fortune alone is estimated at 5.5 billion dollars. In the grand scheme of things, Lucas' work as a director accounts for just a small part of his many diverse activities (over the last thirty years he has only actually directed five films himself). Primarily, Lucas has devoted himself to producing, writing and running his personal film "empire," which houses the well-known and phenomenally successful special effects company, Industrial Light and Magic (a part of Lucas Digital). After studying at the University of Southern California Film School and directing a wide range of short films, Lucas made the acquaintance of Francis Ford Coppola in 1967, and worked as his assistant for some time. It was Coppola, in fact, who helped Lucas produce his first full-length feature film, the sci-fi story *THX 1138* (1970). *American Graffiti* (1973), however, proved to be Lucas' first commercial success. He, of course, turned around significantly more profits in 1977 with the first installment of the *Star Wars* saga (1977, 1980, 1983, 1999, 2002). Lucas directed this first picture in the series himself, but then the filmmaker loved and scorned for his perfectionism began to focus exclusively on writing and producing. In the mid 90s, the original *Star Wars* trilogy was re-released in theaters, this time featuring new digital effects. Lucas reclaimed his seat in the director's chair for the long-awaited prequels *Star Wars: Episode I – The Phantom Menace* (1999), *Star Wars: Episode II – Attack of the Clones* (2002), and *Star Wars: Episode III – Revenge of the Sith* (2005). Although all three films were box-office sensations, they won the approval of few critics.

1 Everything is copasetic: Drive-in restaurants and bubbly car hops light up main street.

2 Out of my dreams and into my car: Candy Clark as Debbie Dunham, impressed by an Impala.

3 American Bandstand: Live rock 'n' roll at the high school ball.

4 Speed demon: John Milner (Paul Le Mat) sets off on the open road to nowhere.

reconstruct a beloved era in recent American history. It was a time of carefree better days, of gigantic street intersections, drive-in restaurants with carhops, jacked-up hot rods in illegal drag races, school dances where bands still performed live and radio disc jockey Wolfman Jack's legendary rock 'n' roll broadcast.

Nonetheless, as nostalgic as the story reads, its episodic structure is rooted in the cinematic techniques of the 1970s. Without the use of transitions, director Lucas, who said most of the story was autobiographically inspired, flips back and forth between the separate storylines of the protagonists. Lucas blends comedy and suspense with melodrama, capturing that interplay of boredom and forced excitement that characterized small-town America. Curt frantically searches for a dreamy blonde woman (most likely a prostitute) he saw at a traffic light driving past him in a Thunderbird and gets mixed up with a group of punks known as the "Pharaohs." The gang of ruffians seem to pose a real danger at first, but what starts off threatening has an undeniably humorous outcome. Steve, on the other hand, fights with his girlfriend Laurie (Cindy Williams) the entire evening about his going away. Terry, who was lent Steve's 1958 Impala, picks up cute blonde Debbie (Candy Clark), and takes her on a scenic trip full of ludicrous mishaps. Then there's John, who just can't seem to rid himself of that pesky Carol. Not that he minds as much as he claims. When it comes down to it, he kind of likes the little chatterbox. Intentionally directionless, the plot never reaches a clear climax (even John's drag race against Falfa (Harrison Ford) is just one of many episodes), mirroring the characters' own disorientation. These are, after all, kids who don't really know what they want yet. The film concludes with Curt going away to college and Steve remaining home. Captions, serving as the movie's epilog, inform us of what destiny has in store for these boys later in life. Curt becomes a writer and Steve an insurance salesman. John dies in a car accident at the hands of a drunk driver and Terry is killed in Vietnam. And thus the age of innocence, when everything was copasetic, has come to an irreversible close.

LP

3

"This superb and singular film catches not only the charm and tribal energy of the teenage 1950s but also the listlessness and the resignation that underscored it all, like an incessant bass line in one of the rock 'n' roll songs of the period."

Time Magazine

4

THE GODFATHER – PART II

1974 – USA – 200 MIN.

GENRE

GANGSTER FILM, DRAMA

DIRECTOR

FRANCIS FORD COPPOLA

SCREENPLAY

FRANCIS FORD COPPOLA, MARIO PUZO,
based on his novel *THE GODFATHER*

DIRECTOR OF PHOTOGRAPHY

GORDON WILLIS

EDITING

BARRY MALKIN, RICHARD MARKS, PETER ZINNER

MUSIC

NINO ROTA, CARMINE COPPOLA

PRODUCTION

FRANCIS FORD COPPOLA for THE COPPOLA COMPANY,
PARAMOUNT PICTURES

STARRING

AL PACINO (Michael Corleone), ROBERT DUVALL (Tom Hagen),
ROBERT DE NIRO (Vito Corleone), DIANE KEATON (Kay Adams-Corleone),
JOHN CAZALE (Frederico "Fredo" Corleone),
TALIA SHIRE (Constanzia "Connie" Corleone-Johnson),
LEE STRASBERG (Hyman Roth), MICHAEL V. GAZZO (Frankie Pentangeli),
G. D. SPRADLIN (Senator Pat Geary), RICHARD BRIGHT (Al Neri),
ORESTE BALDINI (Young Vito Corleone), GASTONE MOSHIN (Don Fanucci)

ACADEMY AWARDS 1975

OSCARS for BEST PICTURE (Francis Ford Coppola, Gray Frederickson, Fred Roos),
BEST DIRECTOR (Francis Ford Coppola),
BEST SUPPORTING ACTOR (Robert De Niro),
BEST ADAPTED SCREENPLAY (Francis Ford Coppola, Mario Puzo),
BEST MUSIC (Nino Rota, Carmine Coppola),
and BEST SET DESIGN (Dean Tavoularis, Angelo P. Graham, George R. Nelson)

Al Pacino

AND

Robert Duvall Diane Keaton Robert De Niro

Talia Shire Morgana King John Cazale

Mariana Hill Lee Strasberg

SCREENPLAY BY
Francis Ford Coppola AND Mario Puzo

BASED ON THE NOVEL
"The Godfather" BY Mario Puzo

PRODUCED AND DIRECTED BY
Francis Ford Coppola

CO-PRODUCERS
Gray Frederickson AND Fred Roos

MUSIC SCORED BY
Nino Rota

Color by Technicolor®

SOUNDTRACK AVAILABLE ON ABC RECORDS

A Paramount Picture

Copyright © 1974 by Paramount Pictures Corporation and The Coppola Company. All rights reserved.

1

"There are many things my father taught me here in this room. He taught me: keep your friends close, but your enemies closer."

Francis Ford Coppola's film epic *The Godfather – Part II* forms a narrative frame around its predecessor, *The Godfather* (1972), one of the most successful films of the 1970s. With part two of the story of the rise and fall of a New York Mafia family, Coppola achieved much more than just a continuation of the first film. He made a self-contained masterpiece that was awarded six Oscars and which, according to many critics, even surpassed its predecessor in several ways.

In *The Godfather – Part II*, two narrative strands unfold in parallel. The first strand begins in Sicily at the dawn of the twentieth century: the young Vito Andolini (Oreste Baldini) from the village Corleone is the only member of his family to survive the Mafia's wholesale extinction of his clan. Friends of the family place him on a boat to America—his only chance of survival. Arriving on Ellis Island in New York, Vito, whom the immigration officials have given the surname Corleone, looks at the Statue of Liberty through the barred window in the quarantine station. Shimmering in the sunlight, it embodies the American Dream shared by the immigrants. Years later, when the adult Vito (now played by Robert De Niro) has his own family, he initially tries to make his way with honorable jobs in New York's immigrant quarter, Little Italy. But even

LEE STRASBERG An actor, director, theater director, and drama teacher, Lee Strasberg was born on November 17, 1901 in the Austro-Hungarian town of Budzanow, which is now in the Ukraine. In 1909 he came to New York with his parents. In 1930 he founded the Moscow Artist Theater which influenced the critical Group Theater with Harold Clurman and Clifford Odets. Here he began to realize his idea of theater acting, in which "emotional memory" plays a central role and the actors don't fake emotions, but rather identify with the characters' emotions.

At the beginning of the 40s Strasberg traveled to Hollywood to learn the art of filmmaking. But he was unable to make it as a director, and was convinced by Elia Kazan in 1948 to assume the artistic direction of the Actors Studio in New York, which was founded in 1947. He served as artistic director from 1951 until his death in 1982. He is considered one of the most important acting teachers in the world, and his "method" is still taught at theater schools. The stars he taught include Marlon Brando, James Dean, Steve McQueen, Dustin Hoffman, Robert De Niro, Jack Nicholson, Jane Fonda, Anne Bancroft, Ellen Burstyn, Al Pacino, Harvey Keitel, Marilyn Monroe, and many others.

Strasberg gave acting lessons, but also appeared in film roles. His portrayal of Hyman Roth in Francis Ford Coppola's *The Godfather – Part II* (1974) earned him a 1975 Oscar Nomination as best supporting actor. Lee Strasberg died in February 1982.

2

"I don't feel I have to wipe everybody out, Tom. Just my enemies."

Film quote: Michael Corleone

there, the Mafia has already struck powerful roots. Vito's rise to "Godfather" only begins after he successfully defends himself against the money-hungry Don Fanucci (Gastone Moshin).

The second narrative level picks up the story in 1958, a few years after the end of the first film. Vito Corleone's son Michael (Al Pacino), who has run the family business since his father's death, now lives in Lake Tahoe, Nevada, where he is attempting to legitimize and legalize his activities in Las Vegas. He is also beginning to expand them to Miami and Cuba with the help of the gangster Hyman Roth (Lee Strasberg). Michael has adopted the business principles of his father. One of them is "the family..." Another is "Keep your friends close..."

Family members and business partners assemble at a large celebration that Michael arranges for his son's Communion. While the guests celebrate outside, Michael holds court in his shadowy study and greets the members of "the family." Here it becomes apparent that Michael's enemies really do stand closer than he himself believed.

4

5

1 Put your head on my shoulder: The role of Michael Corleone turned Al Pacino (pictured here with John Cazale) into a Hollywood headliner, who was soon renowned for his bravado performances in the most unconventional of movies.

2 The UN security counsel: Except these guys have the power to make things happen.

3 The actor's studio: Still willing to hit below the belt, legendary acting coach Lee Strasberg (left) appears in *The Godfather – Part II* as gangster Hyman Roth.

4 Let's get one thing straight… Al Pacino doesn't have to beat a brilliant performance out of Robert Duvall.

5 Italian made and tailored: Michael Corleone stylishly epitomized the crassest side of American individuality.

Michael, consummate briber of high-profile politicians and head of a family business that "is more powerful than U.S. Steel," as he will later say, is forced to watch as his attempts to hold the family together do nothing but destroy it.

At the end of the film—his wife, Kay (Diane Keaton) has long since left him—we see Michael Corleone sitting in the garden, alone with his memories and seething with hate. Moments before, during his mother's wake, he gave the order to kill his own brother, Fredo (John Cazale), who like so many others, has betrayed him. The autumn leaves fall from the trees, and through Al Pacino's eyes we stare directly into "the heart of darkness."

Coppola's sequel contrasts the personalities of father and son, weaving a tale of morals, trust, and loyalty, betrayal, and vengeance. Vito is a respectable *paisan* from Sicily whose surroundings force him to adapt to the criminal lifestyle. He becomes powerful by earning the respect and trust of his friends. His son Michael is born into the Mafia and as the Don, must learn how to deal with the responsibility that has been handed down and the power that comes with it. He trusts no one and even makes enemies within the family. But different as the two men are, their stories resemble each other in the fact that both must discover what it means to be a gangster.

The Godfather – Part II is a modern classic. This is predominantly thanks to Francis Ford Coppola, who in continuing the saga accepted a difficult task and rose to the occasion. He was assisted by an eminent ensemble of actors led by Al Pacino and Robert De Niro. De Niro was awarded an Oscar for his performance. Al Pacino shows that the Michael Corleone of *The Godfather* has become an entirely different person—a self-righteous man who harshly and bitterly attempts to achieve his objectives. Robert De Niro on the other hand is a young embodiment of Marlon Brando, in everything from his manner to the coarse, subdued voice. The meandering story, with its multiple tangents, also gives the other characters significant space: John Cazale in his Cain-role as Michael's humiliated brother, Talia Shire as Michael's sister, Connie the black sheep of the family (she was also nominated for an Oscar), and Robert Duvall, who once again plays the loyal family attorney, Tom Hagen.

The historic décor and costumes are meticulously exact, and the camera work of Gordon Willis—who also filmed the first and later the last part of the trilogy—captures the transformation of the family by switching from sepia-colored tones (in the flashbacks) to more sinister hues for the present day. After the success of *The Godfather*, which he assumed as a commissioned work, Coppola was able to secure full control over the second film. And it shows: *The Godfather – Part II* is quieter, more emotional, and more sinister than the first part. It is more authentic. It is Coppola.

APO

This is a bicentennial picture that doesn't insult the intelligence. It's an epic vision of the corruption of America. (...) Within a scene Coppola is controlled and unhurried, yet he has a gift for igniting narrative, and the exploding effects keep accumulating. About midway, I began to feel that the film was expanding in my head like a soft bullet." *The New Yorker*

6 A chicken in every pot and a car in every garage: On occasion, the all-American Corleone family also sports a horse in every bed.

7 Calling the shots: Michael Corleone can tell you firsthand, it doesn't matter how you walk as long as you carry a big stick.

7

THE TEXAS CHAIN SAW MASSACRE

1974 – USA – 84 MIN.

GENRE

HORROR FILM

DIRECTOR

TOBE HOOPER

SCREENPLAY

KIM HENKEL, TOBE HOOPER

DIRECTOR OF PHOTOGRAPHY

DANIEL PEARL

EDITING

LARRY CARROLL, SALLYE RICHARDSON

MUSIC

TOBE HOOPER, WAYNE BELL

PRODUCTION

LOU PERAINO, TOBE HOOPER for VORTEX

STARRING

MARILYN BURNS (Sally Hardesty), ALLEN DANZIGER (Jerry), PAUL A. PARTAIN (Franklin Hardesty), WILLIAM VAIL (Kirk), TERI MCMINN (Pamela), EDWIN NEAL (Hitchhiker), JIM SIEDOW (Old Man), GUNNAR HANSEN (Leatherface), JOHN DUGAN (Grandfather), JOHN HENRY FAULK (Narrator), JOHN LARROQUETTE (Voice of Narrator)

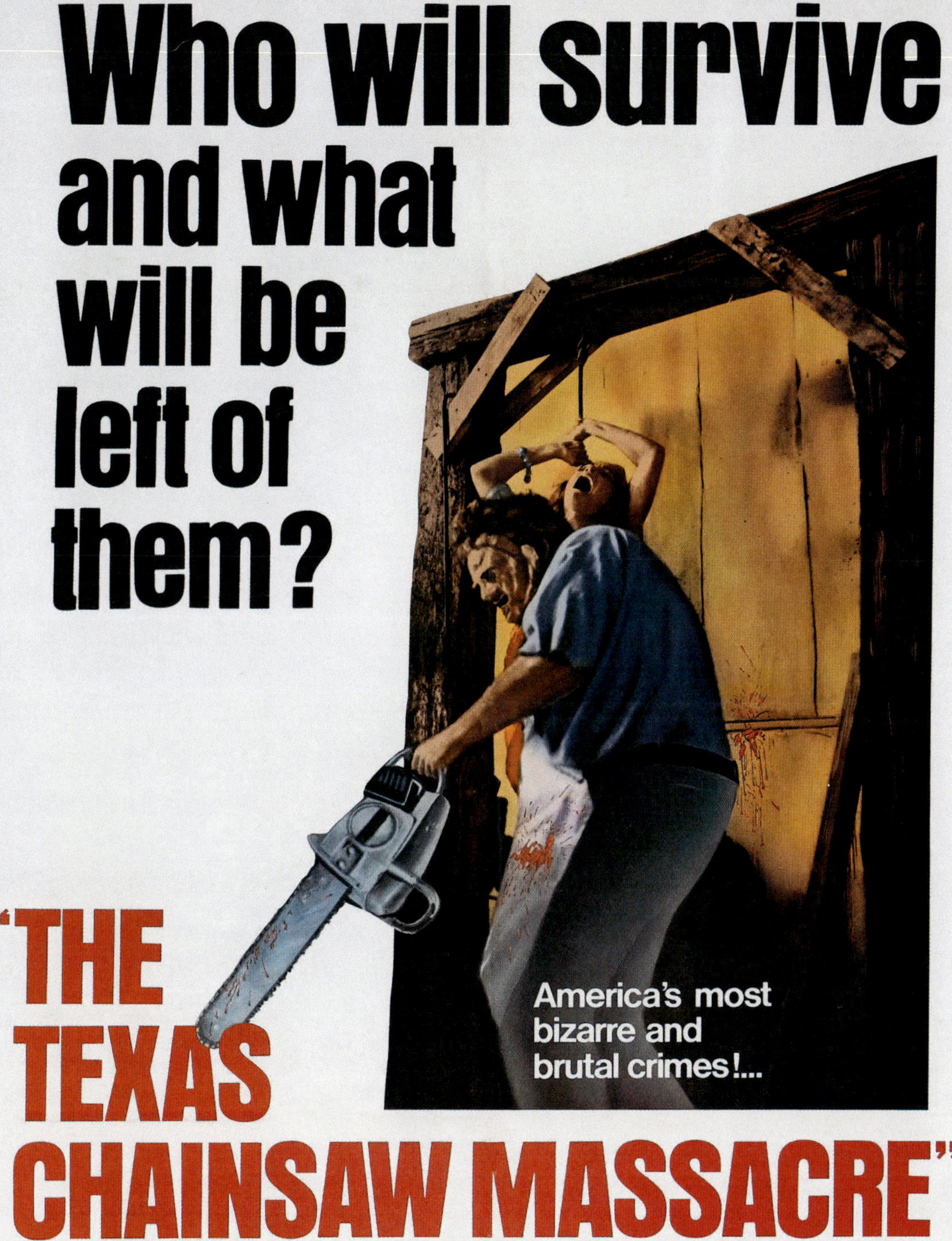
Who will survive and what will be left of them?
America's most bizarre and brutal crimes!...
"THE TEXAS CHAINSAW MASSACRE"
What happened is true. Now the motion picture that's just as real.
THE TEXAS CHAIN SAW MASSACRE · A Film by TOBE HOOPER · Starring MARILYN BURNS, PAUL A. PARTAIN, EDWIN NEAL, JIM SIEDOW and GUNNAR HANSEN as "Leatherface"
Production Manager, RONALD BOZMAN · Music Score by TOBE HOOPER and WAYNE BELL · Music Performed by ARKEY BLUE, ROGER BARTLETT & FRIENDS, TIMBERLINE ROSE,
LOS CYCLONES · Story & Screenplay by KIM HENKEL and TOBE HOOPER · Producer/Director, TOBE HOOPER · COLOR · A BRYANSTON PICTURES RELEASE.
R RESTRICTED

"My old grandpa is the best killer there ever was."

The Texas Chain Saw Massacre begins like a documentary, creating a dense, claustrophobic atmosphere. A blend-in promises the disclosure of one of the most unbelievable crimes in American history and the ensuing sequence leaves no doubt. Darkness, a sinister electronic sound with intermittent hacking and panting sounds, illuminated by flashing images of decaying body parts—followed by a radio report on the desecration of a Texan cemetery. We know that the idyll that follows will end in disaster. Pamela (Teri McMinn), Kirk (William Vail), Sally (Marilyn Burns), and her wheelchair-bound brother Franklin (Paul A. Partain) drive through this area. Short on gas, the friends decide to spend the night in the old house of Sally's grandparents.

But next to the partially dilapidated building live multiple generations of an unemployed butcher family who have developed into cannibals to survive. The youths fall victim to "Leatherface" (Gunnar Hansen) and his chainsaw, and in the end it is only the heroine Sally Hardesty, who in a breathtaking showdown fights for her life and—covered in blood—is ultimately able to escape.

LEATHERFACE—SERIAL KILLERS IN FILM Fritz Lang hunted a serial killer in *M* (1931), but it wasn't until the 70s that this theme gained an immense popularity. One of the most notorious characters is Leatherface in *The Texas Chain Saw Massacre* (1974), who hunts his victims wearing a roughly sewn mask of tanned human skin and a butcher's apron. There are three different masks: the killing mask, an old woman, and a made-up woman, worn when he cooks for the family in his mother role. Whereas in *The Silence of the Lambs* (1991), Jame Gumb also wanted to slip into another skin, patching together a female shell out of the remains of his victims, Leatherface's disguise indicates neither sexual fantasies nor the motive behind his murders. His identity remains a riddle and consequently "the evil" behind this spooky masquerade—as was the case of Michael Myers in *Halloween* (1978)—is not given a true face. Leatherface, who has long since advanced to an international cult figure, is on the one hand a projection surface for subconscious fears and, on the other hand, perfect for identification: in the film, parallels are suggested between the outsider of the group, Franklin, and Leatherface.

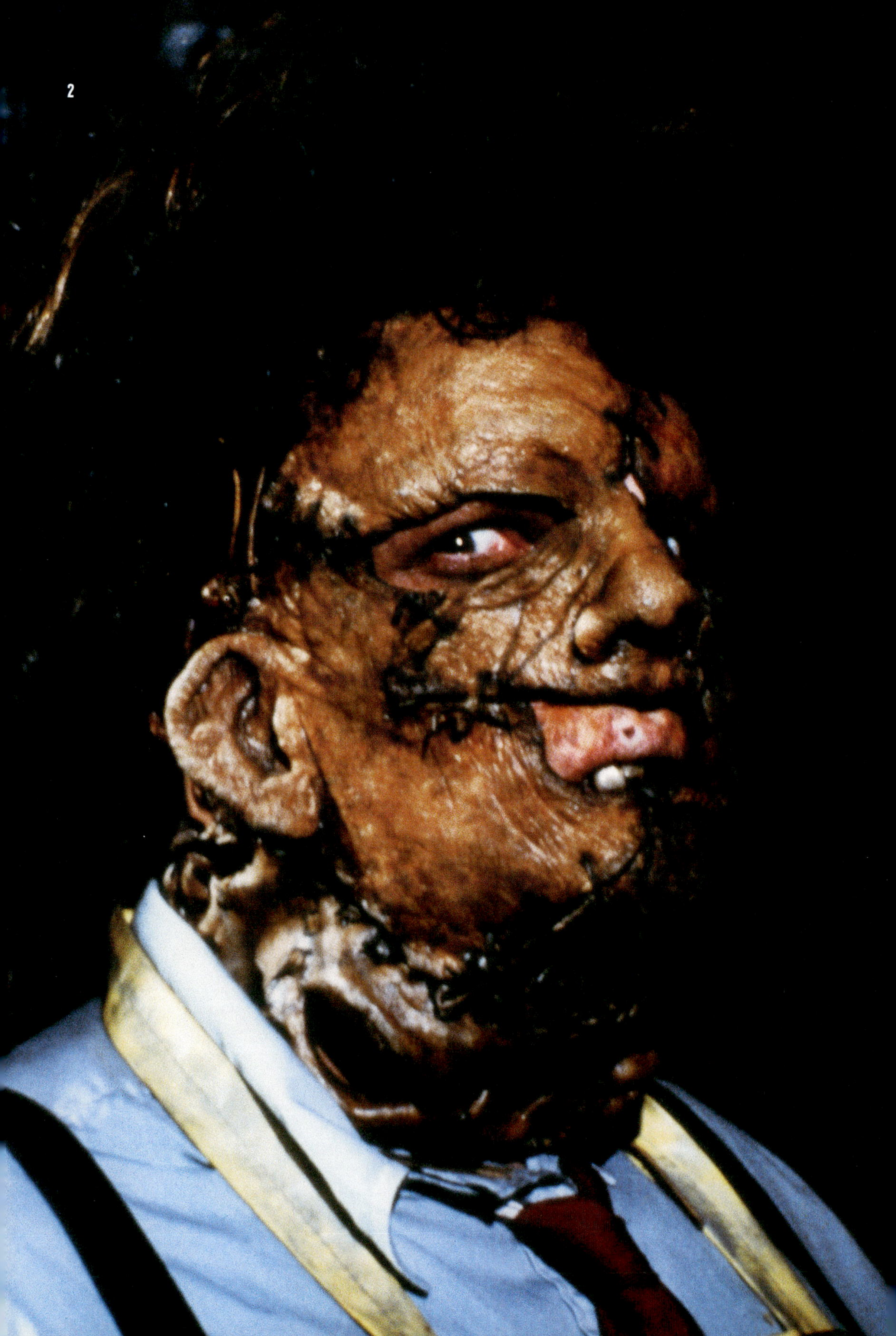

2

1 Cannibals' kitchen: The home as abattoir.

2 Leatherface (Gunnar Hansen) in one of his masks made of human skin.

3 When the chainsaw shrieks… be very afraid.

"The monster is the family, one of the great composite monsters of the American cinema." *Film Comment*

Despite New York's renowned Museum of Modern Art purchase of *The Texas Chain Saw Massacre*, the film still repeatedly falls victim to censors. Watch it for a second time, and it becomes surprisingly apparent that in contrast to other works of the genre, dismembered body parts and organs or mutilations are often not seen directly, but rather disappear behind doors or out of the camera's sight. Nonetheless, Tobe Hooper was still able to depict violence and make it absolutely palpable. There is no psychological or sociological commentary to create distance

4

from what is portrayed or offer an explanation for the overwhelming brutality. The last half hour is particularly stark in its transgression of the boundaries of reason, as the violence is not, as is more usual, diluted with entertaining or aesthetic components. Instead, the audience is increasingly forced to identify with the victim.

When the film was released in America, it was immediately associated with the atrocities of the Vietnam War. Indeed, Tobe Hooper drastically deals with the collective trauma in America—touching on true events like the crimes of the serial killer Ed Gein or the "Manson Family." As in Wes Craven's *Last House on the Left* (1972), it is not monsters or supernatural beings, but rather humans who become cold-blooded murderers. Though Leatherface is surely one of the most famous screen killers, the real monster on a metaphorical level is the American family.

Sally's grandparents' house, and that of their neighbors, is a haunted house with forbidden rooms that are not to be entered. As in a fairy tale, unintentionally breaking a rule results in death or sadistic tortures—tortures that often evoke memories of helplessness or nerve-wracking pranks from childhood or adolescence. Several surreal sequences have the structure of nightmares, for example

5

4 Family values in the American South. **5** Conflict management, country style. **6** Colder than the grave. Take a look in the freezer.

"Rather than choosing violence as its theme, *The Texas Chain Saw Massacre* makes violence tangible. Tobe Hooper doesn't analyze the causes of violence. He shows us what it feels like to run right into it." *Ulrich von Berg*

6

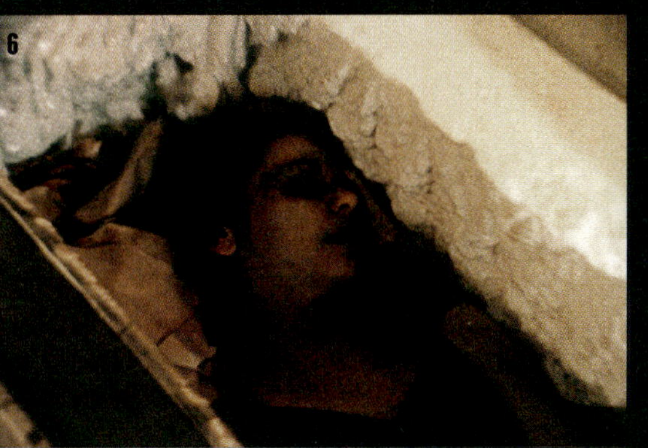

when Sally flees from Leatherface into a large forest and, although she is much faster, she is unable to escape her pursuer. Though the Sally Hardesty character is a female at the mercy of her sadistic tormentor, Hooper's dramatization avoids making her an object of sexual desire. When she tearfully offers to do anything the family ask of her, they respond with sinister cackling. Later, Sally displays an extraordinary strength. Twice she jumps through windowpanes Western-style, and ultimately succeeds in escaping the clutches of this most monstrous of families.

PLB

A WOMAN UNDER THE INFLUENCE

1974 – USA – 155 MIN.

GENRE

DRAMA

DIRECTOR

JOHN CASSAVETES

SCREENPLAY

JOHN CASSAVETES

DIRECTOR OF PHOTOGRAPHY

MITCH BREIT, CALEB DESCHANEL

EDITING

DAVID ARMSTRONG, TOM CORNWELL, ROBERT HEFFERNAN

MUSIC

BO HARWOOD

PRODUCTION

SAM SHAW for FACES

STARRING

PETER FALK (Nick Longhetti), GENA ROWLANDS (Mabel Longhetti), FRED DRAPER (George Mortensen), LADY ROWLANDS (Martha Mortensen), KATHERINE CASSAVETES (Mama Longhetti), MATTHEW LABORTEAUX (Angelo Longhetti), MATTHEW CASSEL (Tony Longhetti), CHRISTINA GRISANTI (Maria Longhetti), O.G. DUNN (Garson Cross), MARIO GALLO (Harold Jensen), EDDIE SHAW (Doctor Zepp)

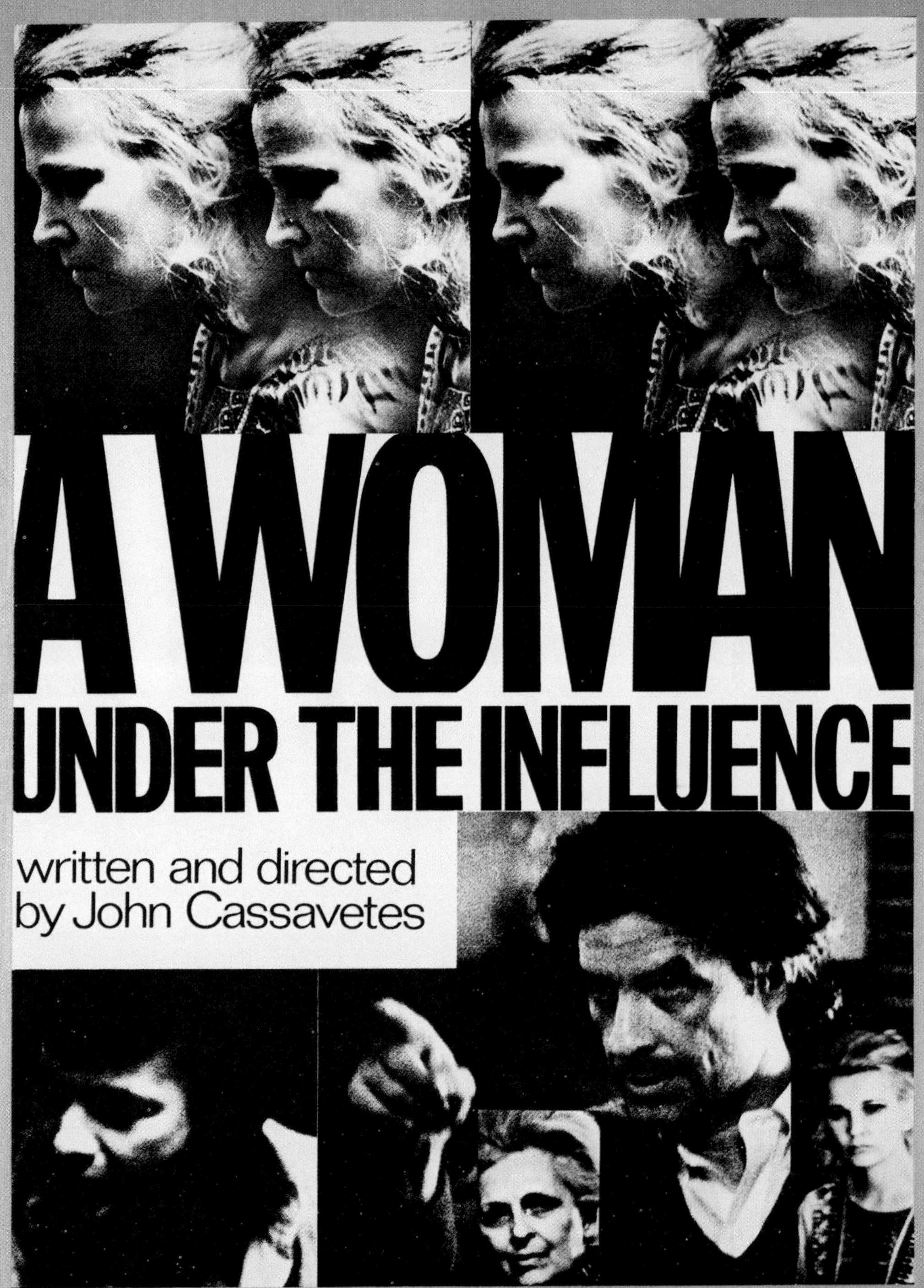

Starts Sunday, November 17! A UNITED ARTISTS THEATRE Columbia I & A UNITED ARTISTS THEATRE Columbia II

2nd Ave.at 64th St. Tel: 832-1670

1

2

"Tell me what you want me to be. How you want me to be. I can be that. I can be anything. Just tell me, Nicky!"

Two adults try to play house and fail miserably. Two actors infuse their roles with every imaginable contour of human dignity and disgrace, taking their audience hostage for two-and-a-half hours as they unleash the demons of Pandora's box on their rocky marriage.

This was the formula that led to one of the greatest cinematic triumphs for independent film-making icon John Cassavetes. In a riveting, powerhouse performance, Gena Rowlands plays a woman on the verge of a mental breakdown. For a long time now, there haven't been words to express what Mabel Longhetti has been feeling, and so she has substituted them with an arsenal of gesticulations and nervous ticks, mimicry and pantomime. She combats the stress of her daily life, which confines her like an iron chastity belt, with deflective hand movements, eye rolls and jerking jaws. These are the mouthed screams of a desperate woman; they pound the audience with an utter devastation that is at times hysterically funny. Peter Falk plays Mabel's husband Nick, a simple blue-collar worker, who has as little control over his words as he does over his own body. He is someone who hollers. His gestures die before completion, often ending in an admonishing pointer finger, or, as on one occasion in the film, in physical abuse. Three children stand in the crossfire as man and wife frantically grasp at straws in the hopes of pinpointing what originally made them fall in love. The couple are certain of their love for one another, yet they have no idea how to go about loving each other.

A Woman Under the Influence was originally conceived for the stage. The idea was scrapped because seasoned theater veteran Gena Rowlands didn't think she was capable of exerting such an extreme amount of emotional force night after night in front of a live audience. And so, with just a dialog script and no true screenplay, an intimate film was shot almost exclusively within the four walls of a small family residence. No shots were predetermined. The camera was free to roam at will, thus partially accounting for the piece's almost documentary feel. Of course, this atmospheric touch is more the result of Cassavetes' unique directing style, chiseled in diehard method acted techniques. This is illuminated in the film by an act of associative thought processes reflected in Mabel's behavior such as when she improvises the "dying swan" from *Swan Lake*. Here, she not only takes on Cassevetes' dual role of actor-director,

JOHN CASSAVETES With his directorial debut, *Shadows* (1959), John Cassavetes (1929–1989) established himself as a permanent fixture in the world of indy-filmmaking. Today's independent director has him to thank for making it possible to shoot a movie without stepping into financial quicksand. Cassavetes was born in New York in 1929 to Greek immigrant parents. He used his acting to raise funds for his directing projects, appearing in front of the camera in such films as *The Killers* (1964), *The Dirty Dozen* (1967) and *Rosemary's Baby* (1968). Friends and family often played a dual role in Cassavetes' works. Despite the little he could pay them, the actor-director received a high degree of commitment and dedication. Thespians like Seymour Cassel, Peter Falk and Ben Gazzara as well as producer Al Ruban were on board for some of his most ambitious undertakings, like *Husbands*, (1970), *Minnie and Moskowitz* (1971), *A Woman Under the Influence* (1974) and *The Killing of a Chinese Bookie* (1976). Gena Rowlands married Cassavetes in 1954 and portrayed the leading roles in many of his pictures, including *Gloria* (1980). Although Cassavetes' pictures cover a wide range of genres, his constant themes remained individuality conveyed through unforgettable characters prone to double standards, the suffocating mechanisms of conventionality and the full expression of a given personality. Cassavetes is the idol of a long list of cutting-edge filmmakers like Larry Clark of *Kids* fame (1995), and *Happiness* director Todd Solondz (1998).

3

1 How much longer will Mabel Longhetti (Gena Rowlands) be able to ward off her nervous breakdown?

2 Loving you is easy 'cos you're beautiful… Mabel's children are her only sanctuary.

3 Was that lonely woman really me? Mabel drinks away her sorrows at a local bar...and falls into the arms of a total stranger.

4 Life of the party: Construction worker, Nick (Peter Falk) loves his wife, but is oblivious to her needs.

5 Big boys don't cry: But they have been known to beat their wives…

"Mabel's not crazy. She's unusual. She's not crazy, so don't say she's crazy!" *Film quote: Nick*

but also that of prima ballerina and choreographer. In another scene, the oblivious Nick surprises her at the door with ten work buddies and she instantly transforms herself into a June Cleaver on amphetamines, whipping up a mess hall portion of spaghetti and doing her best "hostess with the mostest" imitation. Mabel is emotionally electrified when one of the guys breaks into an aria and she implores yet another of the work crew to dance with her. She refuses to take no for an answer, prompting Nick to silence her abruptly. Her spirit and charm have, nonetheless, a miraculous impact on children. Yet upon seeing how the free-spirited Mabel allows the children to run naked through the house, one neighborhood father is convinced that she's off her rocker. Mabel, on the other hand, simply can't understand why he too doesn't just let loose and dance.

Observation of the pictures taken of Cassavetes on the set reveals the actor-director manifesting the same gestures as Mabel, from the ticking Cheshire Cat grin to the chummy yet invasive hooking an arm around someone's shoulder while giving direction. The filmmaker readily

4

encouraged his cast to search for authentic feelings and means of expression that often broke with Hollywood conventions. The product is a family drama and love story, whose tale itself also provides a map of the film's actual genesis.

Be that as it may, the real world is not run according to these rules; it adheres rather to the masculine leadership archetypes seen in Nick. Mabel, as well as all she represents, is too prone to the type of nervous breakdowns that Cassevetes often almost drove his team to. At one point, Nick just stands by and watches as his wife is institutionalized. Completely at a loss as a parent without her, he lets his children sip his beer on one of their family outings. When Mabel is released from the psychiatric hospital six months later, we see how all of his attempts to force his family into neat little roles have failed. Nick packs the house full of family and friends to welcome home his "healthy wife" in a gung-ho effort to "have a party!" Not to be overlooked in this film is that Nick is not one ounce less out of his mind than Mabel. His relentless need to prove his masculinity leads to disaster time after time, and he appears incapable of recognizing this.

Nonetheless, Cassavetes has no intention of pinning the blame on either of them. The film's leitmotif is much more wrapped up in Nick's schizophrenic and seemingly impossible plea to "just be yourself!"—a philosophy that is possibly to blame for the break-up of his marriage. Cassavetes' own take on the matter shed a bit more light on the subject: "I don't believe that Mabel's collapse is a social problem. It is rooted in personal relationships. Someone can love you and still drive you insane."

PB

5

PROFESSIONE: REPORTER / PROFESSION: REPORTER

THE PASSENGER (AKA PROFESSION: REPORTER)

1974 – ITALY / FRANCE / SPAIN / USA – 125 MIN.

GENRE

DRAMA

DIRECTOR

MICHELANGELO ANTONIONI

SCREENPLAY

MARK PEPLOE, PETER WOLLEN, MICHELANGELO ANTONIONI

DIRECTOR OF PHOTOGRAPHY

LUCIANO TOVOLI

EDITING

MICHELANGELO ANTONIONI, FRANCO ARCALLI

MUSIC

IVÁN VÁNDOR

PRODUCTION

CARLO PONTI for CIPI CINEMATOGRAFICA S. A., COMPAGNIA CINEMATOGRAFICA CHAMPION, LES FILMS CONCORDIA, MGM

STARRING

JACK NICHOLSON (David Locke), MARIA SCHNEIDER (The Girl), IAN HENDRY (Martin Knight), JENNY RUNACRE (Rachel Locke), CHUCK MULVEHILL (Robertson), STEVEN BERKOFF (Stephen), AMBROISE BIA (Achebe), JOSÉ MARÍA CAFFAREL (Hotel Owner), ÁNGEL DEL POZO (Police Inspector), MANFRED SPIES (Stranger)

Metro-Goldwyn-Mayer presents

Jack Nicholson

Maria Schneider

A Carlo Ponti Production of

Michelangelo Antonioni's

"I used to be somebody else...but I traded myself in."

Profession: Reporter

Original story by MARK PEPLOE · Screenplay by MARK PEPLOE, PETER WOLLEN and MICHELANGELO ANTONIONI
Directed by MICHELANGELO ANTONIONI · Produced by CARLO PONTI · In METROCOLOR MGM

Copyright © Metro-Goldwyn-Mayer MCMLXXIV. All Rights Reserved.

1

“People disappear every day.”— “Every time they leave the room.”

“No family, no friends—just a couple of obligations and a weak heart.” This is how the arms dealer Robertson (Chuck Mulvehill) sums up his life. British journalist David Locke (Jack Nicholson) encounters his compatriot in a hotel in the middle of the Sahara desert, and a few hours later, he finds him dead in his room.

With hardly a second thought, Locke assumes the dead man's identity—partly for professional reasons, and partly (as the viewer gradually discovers) because he has become as estranged from his own life as from his profession as a war reporter. The ink isn't dry on the famous journalist's obituaries before Locke has arranged to meet with Robertson's contractors—a group of African freedom fighters. Clearly, Robertson had believed in what he was doing; and as conviction is precisely what Locke's life has been lacking, he uses the dead man's calendar to pick up where Robertson had left off.

It seems, at first, that the change of identity has gone off without a hitch. Soon, however, there's a bunch of people pursuing the imposter: Not just Robertson's

MICHELANGELO ANTONIONI Antonioni was born in Ferrara in 1912. He began his career as a writer of short stories and as a contributor to the Italian film journal *Cinema*, the cradle of neorealism. After making several short documentaries, Antonioni retreated from the view that the cinema should serve a political agenda, and his first feature, *Story of a Love Affair* (*Cronaca di un amore*, 1950) broke with conventional narrative techniques. Until the mid-60s, Antonioni's great theme was “the sickness of feelings,” depicted in films such as *The Night* (*La notte*, 1960), *The Eclipse* (*L'eclisse*, 1962) and *Red Desert* (*Il deserto rosso*, 1964). In his later works, *Blow Up* (1966), *Zabriskie Point* (1969) and *The Passenger* (*Professione: reporter/Profession: Reporter*, 1974), he examined the emotional and existential rootlessness of modern humanity. These films also expressed Antonioni's distrust of superficial appearances. To him, the essential nature of a thing was forever hidden beneath its visible surface, and no image or representation could alter this fact. In Antonioni's work, landscapes, buildings, gestures and sounds were the symbols of interior realities; he created what has been termed a “dramaturgy of the fragmentary,” where “the form swallows the content” (Thomas Christen in *du* magazine, 11/1995). At times, his style was almost mannered, perhaps too much in love with effects. Yet his considered use of technical means—like the slow-motion explosion in *Zabriskie Point* or the closing sequence of *The Passenger*—stood in striking contrast to his intuitive working methods, exemplified by his frequent changes to the dialog during filming. Unlike most of his Italian or American counterparts, Antonioni seemed to approach his subjects tentatively, watchfully, as if waiting for an opening, a way into their deeper meaning. As he put it himself: “I know what I have to do. Not what I mean.” Antonioni died in Rome in 2007.

2

1 Lost for words: As gunrunner Robertson, David Locke (Jack Nicholson) loses his grip on reality.

2 Who did you say you were? Despite their unbridled intimacy, Locke and his nameless companion (Maria Schneider) never really get close.

3 One corpse and a fake ID: Locke is surprised how easy it is to become someone else.

4 Ticket to ride: On the road to nowhere, in flight from the unknown.

business partners, but his enemies too; and—last, not least—the "widow" of David Locke... In flight from his own past and another man's future, the journalist is clearly in mortal danger. Locke is joined by a young student (Maria Schneider), who is fascinated by his radical self-erasure and "rebirth." Yet he knows he'll have to come clean eventually, and his attempts to evade his pursuers are half-hearted. The journey ends in a Spanish no-man's-land, a kind of wilderness like the African desert in which it began.

For director Michelangelo Antonioni, the thriller plot of *The Passenger* was a vehicle for reflections on human identity. From the bits and pieces available to him, Locke tries desperately to reconstruct Robertson's life, but the attempt ends in failure. The arms dealer remains a phantom, for Robertson has no reality apart from the complex network of relationships that constituted his unique existence.

Even in his new identity, Locke falls victim to the contradictions inherent in his own profession. Antonioni showed us the journalist as a man doomed to passivity, even in his most active moments. Fragments of interviews from Locke's journalistic past reveal the roots of his crisis. Whether his subject was a magician or a dictator, the actual person, the real significance, always remained hidden. What we see is what we get, but we only ever see what we want to see—or the little we're shown.

In a sense Locke was the director's alter ego, for he too is lumbered with perceivable reality, the only material available to him. As the plot dissolves into a plethora of locations and narrative levels, *The Passenger* emerges as a

"I don't have anything to say but perhaps something to show."

Michelangelo Antonioni, in: The Architecture of Vision. Writings and Interviews on Cinema

3

thesis on the possibility or impossibility of visual representation per se. A recurring metaphor: doors and windows that reveal only a portion of the past or the present. Whatever the image, the camera lingers a little longer than necessary, as if waiting for the magical moment when the visible world will finally yield up its secrets.

The seven-minute final sequence is a final reminder that we wait in vain for revelation. Locke is recumbent on his bed in a hotel room, but the camera-angle makes him invisible to the audience; through the window, we see the village square, and the bullring beyond it; a car drives past; a boy throws rocks at a beggar; and the girl converses with various people. In the midst of these barely decipherable details, the true drama remains hidden, indicated only by the vague sound of a single shot. The camera passes through the barred window, describes a broad curve around the square and comes back round to gaze through the window once more: At the end of his aimless journey, David Locke has arrived at the only inevitable destination.

SH

4

CHINATOWN

1974 – USA – 131 MIN.

GENRE

DETECTIVE FILM, DRAMA

DIRECTOR

ROMAN POLANSKI

SCREENPLAY

ROBERT TOWNE

DIRECTOR OF PHOTOGRAPHY

JOHN A. ALONZO

EDITING

SAM O'STEEN

MUSIC

JERRY GOLDSMITH

PRODUCTION

ROBERT EVANS for LONG ROAD, PENTHOUSE, PARAMOUNT PICTURES

STARRING

JACK NICHOLSON (J.J. "Jake" Gittes), FAYE DUNAWAY (Evelyn Cross Mulwray), JOHN HUSTON (Noah Cross), PERRY LOPEZ (LAPD Lieutenant Lou Escobar), JOHN HILLERMAN (Russ Yelburton), DARRELL ZWERLING (Hollis I. Mulwray), DIANE LADD (Ida Sessions), ROY JENSON (Claude Mulvihill), ROMAN POLANSKI (Man with the knife), RICHARD BAKALYAN (LAPD Detective Loach)

ACADEMY AWARDS 1975

OSCAR for BEST ORIGINAL SCREENPLAY (Robert Towne)

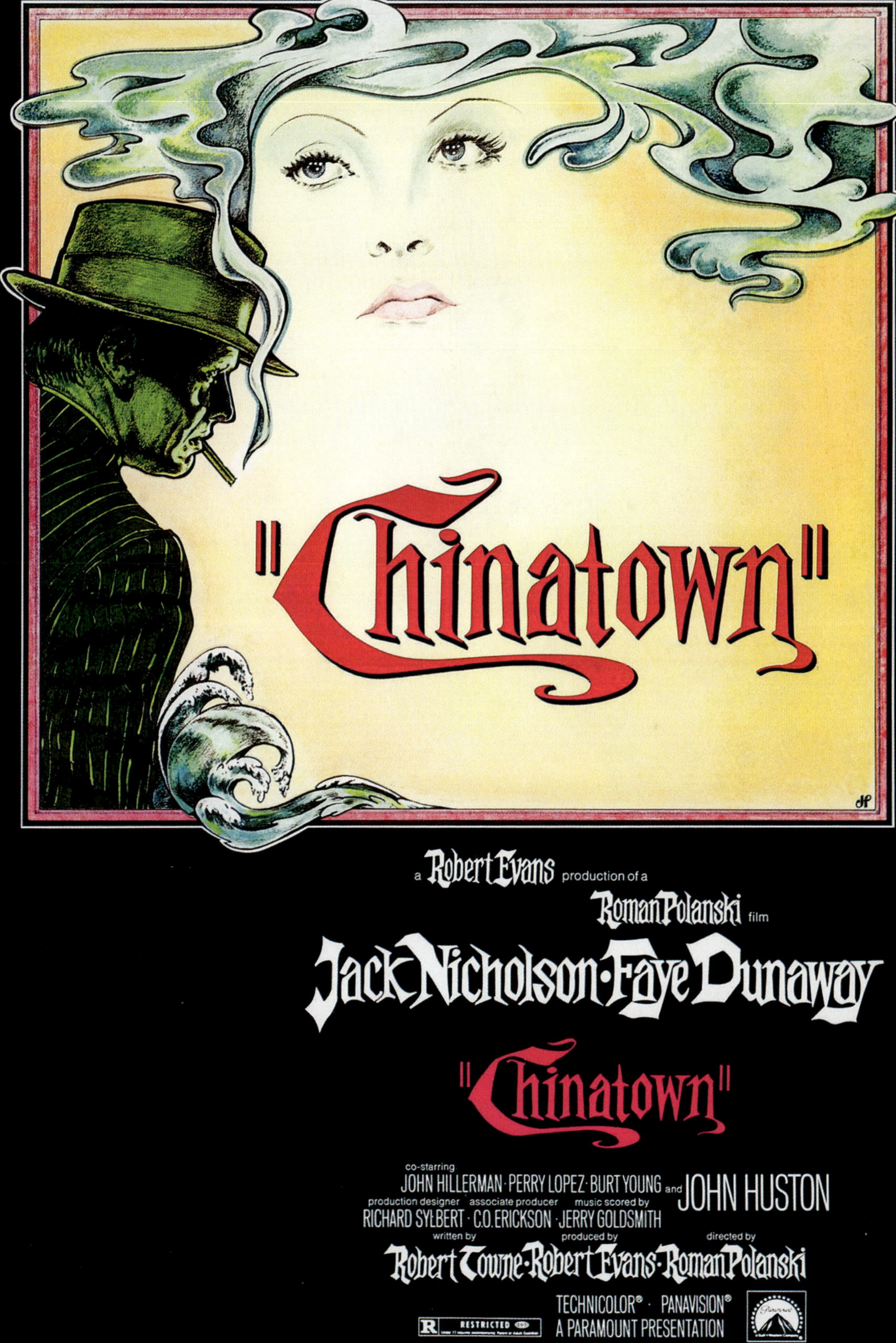

"Chinatown"

a Robert Evans production of a

Roman Polanski film

Jack Nicholson · Faye Dunaway

co-starring

JOHN HILLERMAN · PERRY LOPEZ · BURT YOUNG and JOHN HUSTON

production designer RICHARD SYLBERT · associate producer C.O. ERICKSON · music scored by JERRY GOLDSMITH

written by Robert Towne · produced by Robert Evans · directed by Roman Polanski

TECHNICOLOR® · PANAVISION®

A PARAMOUNT PRESENTATION

1

“I’m just a snoop.”

Los Angeles, 1937. When private detective J. J. Gittes (Jack Nicholson) is hired to keep tabs on an unfaithful husband, he assumes it’s going to be just another routine job. But the investigation takes an unexpected turn. The guy he’s been keeping an eye on, a high-ranking official for the city’s water and power department is bumped off. His attractive widow Evelyn (Faye Dunaway) retains Gittes’ services to find out whodunit. Before he knows it, Gittes stumbles unexpectedly onto a foul-smelling real estate scheme, and soon finds himself entangled in one sordid affair after another. Gittes has several bloody run-ins with thugs determined to put an end to his work on the case, and uncovers clues pointing to the involvement of influential power-players in the sinister dealings. Even Gittes’ alluring employer Evelyn seems to know more about the matter than she’s letting on…

Chinatown is considered by many film critics to be not only one of the greatest films of the 70s, but of all time. How the movie came to be illustrates, like so many other similar moments in Hollywood history, that masterpieces can still be born within the framework of the imperious big studios. *Chinatown* was simply one of those rare instances when the perfect combination of people came together at just the right time. Jack Nicholson who, at the time was not a solid “A list” star, brought prominent “script doctor” Robert Towne on board to write the screenplay. When he got wind of the project, Robert Evans, who was head of production at Paramount, wanted to try his hand at producing a film himself. He finalized an agreement with the writer and actor and secured Roman Polanski, with whom he had collaborated previously on *Rosemary’s Baby* (1968), as the picture’s director. (Understandably,

ROBERT EVANS Robert Evans (1930–2019), was one of New Hollywood’s most illustrious personalities and got his start performing in film at the age of 14. His big break into the business came when actress Norma Shearer, widow of legendary Hollywood tycoon, Irving Thalberg, insisted that Evans play her husband in *Man of a Thousand Faces* (1957). Dissatisfied with the state of his acting career, he began to work as a freelance producer, without ever producing a single picture, and eventually signed a contract with Paramount in 1965. In the blink of an eye, Evans climbed the rungs of the corporate ladder and emerged as the studio’s head of production. He was able to bring the old “mountain” back to its state of former glory as a major studio by taking on a number of blockbuster projects such as *Rosemary’s Baby* (1968), *Love Story* (1970), *The Godfather* (1972), *The Godfather – Part II* (1974) and *Chinatown* (1974).

Chinatown marked the first time Evans was able to realize his long-harbored ambition of producing a film himself, which garnered him an Academy Award nomination for Best Picture. He left Paramount shortly thereafter to produce film independently, working on movies including *Marathon Man* (1976) and *Black Sunday* (1977). These productions were, however, less popular at the box office. In 1984, Evans made headlines for his involvement in *The Cotton Club* (1984), which not only bombed, but also entangled him in disastrous private scandals. As a result, Evans disappeared from the scene completely for several years. He returned to the business in 1990 with *The Two Jakes*, a further instalment of *Chinatown*, also starring Jack Nicholson. Evans published a book entitled *The Kid Stays in the Picture* (1994) about his personal life story, a constant target of media attention since his start in Hollywood. This gripping autobiography was made into a documentary film in 2002 under the same title.

2

1 Portrait of a lady: Femme fatale Evelyn (Faye Dunaway) awakens men's dreams and inspires them to action.

2 In her clutches: The private eye (Jack Nicholson) has lost all professional distance from his seductive client.

3 Masterful execution: Veteran director John Huston plays a brutal patriarch who holds all the cards.

4 Mack the knife: Polanski in a striking cameo as the "nose-slitter."

Polanski had been working in his native Europe following the brutal death of his wife Sharon Tate [1943–1969] in their Los Angeles home.) When Faye Dunaway was cast as the female lead, yet another not quite famous personality was added to the mix. As one might expect, the shoot was not exactly plain sailing. Evans dubbed the verbal fireworks between Towne and Polanski "World War III." The problem probably had something to do with the fact that this was the first project Polanski directed without writing himself. The product was, nonetheless, an international smash. *Chinatown* reeled in a total of eleven Oscar nominations, although Robert Towne was the sole individual who ended up taking a statuette home.

“*Chinatown* was seen as a Neo-Noir when it was released—an update on an old genre. Now years have passed and film history blurs a little, and it seems to settle easily beside the original noirs. That is a compliment.” *Chicago Sun-Times*

Yet what makes *Chinatown* truly fascinating, and the reason it attained its instant status as an uncontested masterpiece, is by and large the film's grace in evoking the Golden Age of 30s–40s Hollywood, without losing itself in the nostalgia of the era or turning the production into just another stiffly stylized homage. Naturally, Polanski's film draws heavily on classic Bogart characters like detective Philip Marlowe from Howard Hawks' *The Big Sleep* (1946) or his more cynical counterpart Sam Spade from *The Maltese Falcon* (1941), directed by Hollywood legend John Huston. Huston himself plays a pivotal role in *Chinatown* as a ruthless and sickeningly sentimental patriarch, who seems to be the key to the entire mystery. Unlike Bogart, Nicholson's character is only capable of being a limited hero. Although J. J. “Jake” Gittes is a likeable, small-time snoop, with a weakness for smutty jokes, the charming sheister fails miserably as a moralist and suffers terribly as a result. The scene featuring Polanski as a gangster who slits open Nicholson's nose is absolutely priceless. The Gittes character also lacks the romantic

4

5

5 Just the facts Ma'am: *Chinatown* evokes classic Hollywood cinema without ever romanticizing it.

6 Still nosing around: J. J. Gittes (Jack Nicholson), bloody but unbowed.

potential of a Bogart hero. Gittes doesn't embody desires, instead he falters on them. Yet his greatest weakness is Chinatown, the place where his career as a cop came to an end and a synonym for all the irresistible, exotic dangers of the urban jungle. This same sweet taboo seems to echo in Faye Dunaway's character. In the end, Chinatown presents Gittes with a double-edged defeat. Although Towne had originally written a happy ending, the film's final sequence, which just screams Polanski, sees Gittes inadvertently aiding the forces of evil and losing the love of his life at the same time.

Another great accomplishment of the piece is Polanski and cinematographer John A. Alonzo's triumph in achieving the impact of a black and white *Film Noir* piece with brilliant color photography. It is uncanny how little the city feels like a movie lot and how convincing the topography looks. Unlike in so many other so-called revisionist noir films, in *Chinatown* L.A. is not a black, smoldering hell's kitchen but rather a vast, often sunny countryside metropolis still in the early stages of development. The imagery lets the viewer sense that the city and its surrounding valleys exist in spite of the imposing desert. We are also made aware of the colossal pipeline supplying the city with water, its artificial lifeblood. Water is, in fact, the major resource being manipulated in the story's diabolical real-estate venture, a scandal with genuine historical roots in the region. Robert Towne based his screenplay on non-fictional accounts dating back to early 20th-century Southern California. It was a time when the foundations for the future riches of the world's movie capital were in construction. The location was chosen primarily on account of the area's year-round sun, ideal for filming, and its affordable purchase price. The boom ushered in a wave of land speculators, corruption and violence. It is a grim bit of Earth that the City of Angels and Hollywood rests upon. A tale that unfolds in *Chinatown*. JH

YOUNG FRANKENSTEIN

1974 – USA – 106 MIN.

GENRE

HORROR FILM, SPOOF

DIRECTOR

MEL BROOKS

SCREENPLAY

GENE WILDER, MEL BROOKS, based on characters appearing in MARY WOLLSTONECRAFT SHELLEY'S novel *FRANKENSTEIN*

DIRECTOR OF PHOTOGRAPHY

GERALD HIRSCHFELD

EDITING

JOHN C. HOWARD

MUSIC

JOHN MORRIS

PRODUCTION

MICHAEL GRUSKOFF for GRUSKOFF / VENTURE FILMS, CROSSBOW PRODUCTIONS, JOUER LIMITED, 20TH CENTURY FOX

STARRING

GENE WILDER (Dr. Frederick Frankenstein), PETER BOYLE (Monster), MARTY FELDMAN (Igor), TERI GARR (Inga), MADELINE KAHN (Elizabeth), CLORIS LEACHMAN (Frau Blücher), KENNETH MARS (Inspector Kemp), RICHARD HAYDN (Herr Falkstein), DANNY GOLDMAN (Medical Student), GENE HACKMAN (Blind Hermit)

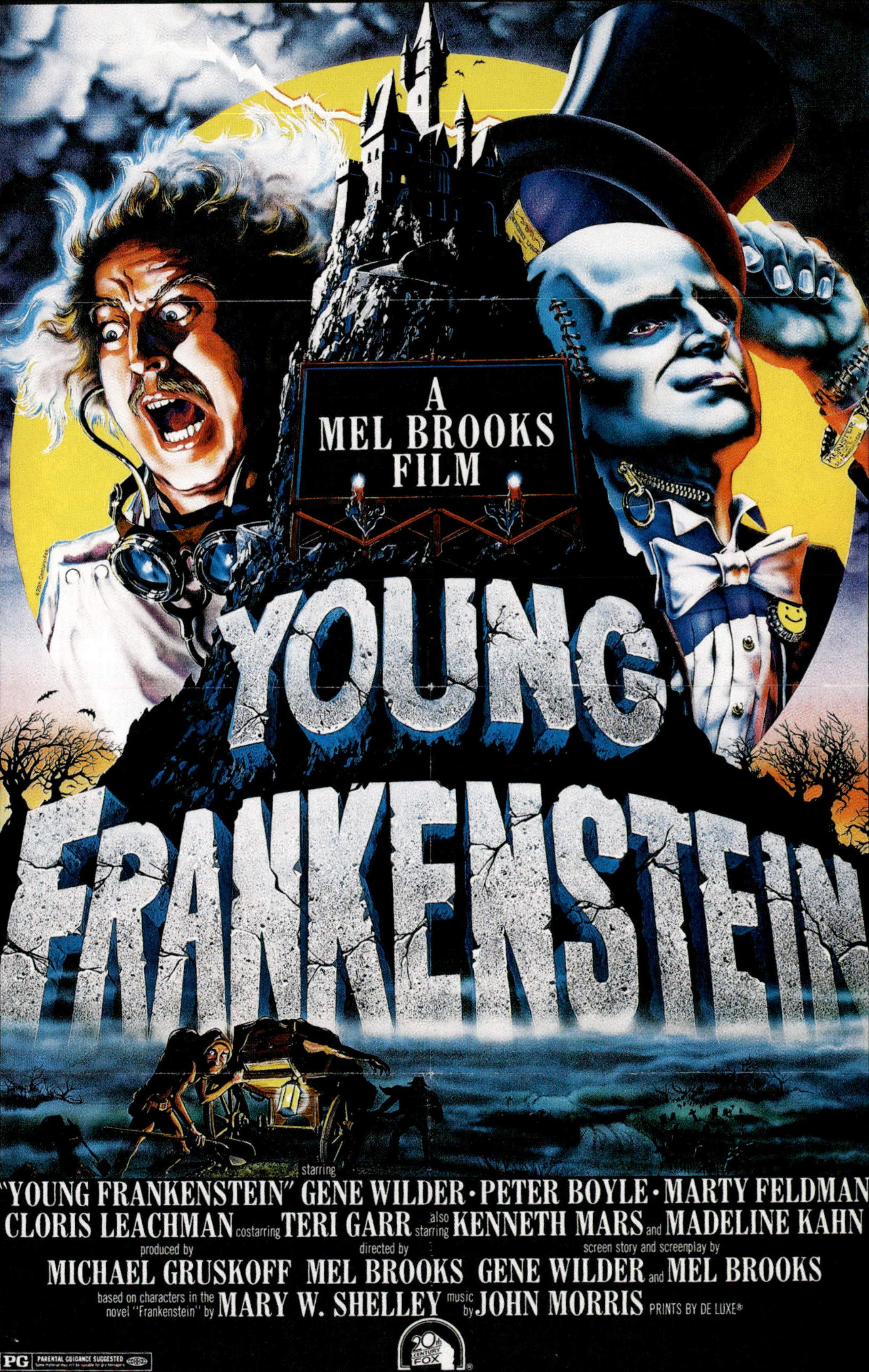

A MEL BROOKS FILM

YOUNG FRANKENSTEIN

starring

"YOUNG FRANKENSTEIN" GENE WILDER · PETER BOYLE · MARTY FELDMAN
CLORIS LEACHMAN costarring TERI GARR also starring KENNETH MARS and MADELINE KAHN

produced by MICHAEL GRUSKOFF directed by MEL BROOKS screen story and screenplay by GENE WILDER and MEL BROOKS

based on characters in the novel "Frankenstein" by MARY W. SHELLEY music by JOHN MORRIS PRINTS BY DE LUXE®

PG PARENTAL GUIDANCE SUGGESTED

1

"It's pronounced Frón-kon-steen."

It's not always easy being the offspring of a celebrity—especially if your famous ancestor made a habit of trying to reanimate bits and pieces of rotting cadavers. With this in mind, it's understandable that neurologist Frederick Frankenstein (Gene Wilder), whose grandfather took part in this peculiar pastime, tries to mask his familial roots by distorting the pronunciation of his surname.

But some origins just won't allow themselves to be brushed aside, and so Dr. "Froderick Fronkonsteen" is unexpectedly compelled to return to the family estate in Transylvania to retrieve the sketches of his grandfather's work. Igor (Marty Feldman), the indispensable family servant and Quasimodo-esque side-kick, alongside the gaunt housekeeper, Frau Blücher (Cloris Leachman), whose name causes wild horses to whinny and rear, succeed in getting the vain scientist to put his newly unearthed monster assembly instruction manual into action. When it comes down to it, all you really need to reanimate a lifeless brain is "the instructions and a clear head."

Nonetheless, before the creature (Peter Boyle) can be let loose on mankind, the audience is going to have to stomach a hearty helping of screwball antics and lewd knee-slappers. Not that the hilarity is going to subside once the monster has been brought to life. After all, it's precisely this brand of humor we fork out good money to experience when we go to see a Mel Brooks movie.

Young Frankenstein thrives on the contrast between the rib-tickling absurdity of its plot and the austere attention to detail with which Brooks and his cinematographer Gerald Hirschfeld based the look of their film on the original horror classics. Primary sources were of course *Frankenstein* (1931) and *Bride of Frankenstein* (1935), both of which

MEL BROOKS Mel Brooks was never what one would describe as the silent type. Born Melvin Kaminsky in Brooklyn on June 28, 1926, he got his start in show business as a drummer with a hotel orchestra. Not surprisingly, his career proved to be anything but linear. After years as a gag writer, working on a Broadway musical, putting out a record and writing the script of *The Critic* (1963), an Oscar-winning animated short in which his voice can also be heard, Brooks directed *The Producers*, his first Hollywood film, in 1968. A satire about show business in which a has-been producer hits it big on Broadway with a wacky musical pageant about Hitler's life at Berchtesgaden, the film garnered Brooks an Oscar for Best Original Screenplay. Nonetheless, despite his success with crowd-pleasers like *Blazing Saddles* (1973) and *Young Frankenstein* (1974) he remains, for the most part, a Hollywood outsider. This could have something to do with his specific brand of irreverence. For instance, in 1983 he turned the Lubitsch classic *To Be or Not to Be* (1942) into a musical comedy without batting an eye. Then again maybe he is shunned as a result of his predilection for smutty wisecracks and tasteless humor. Of course, the reason could be that not all of his colleagues in the entertainment industry can laugh at his merciless parodies like *Spaceballs* (1987) or *Robin Hood: Men in Tights* (1993).

This is, however, not always the case as Burt Reynolds, James Caan, Paul Newman and Liza Minnelli proved in 1976 when this pack of stars appeared in *Silent Movie* and readily made fun of themselves. Even one of the biggest in the business, Alfred Hitchcock, was able to laugh at the Brook's *Vertigo* spoof *High Anxiety* (1977), a film Hitch is reported to have most thoroughly enjoyed. Mel Brooks is one of the few artists to have won an Emmy, a Grammy, an Oscar, and a Tony. In 2023, he also received an honorary Oscar for his lifetime achievement.

were directed by James Whale, starring Boris Karloff as the monster. Brooks also helped himself to a handful of imagery from other legendary movies. The camera work of the opening sequence is an obvious spoof on *Citizen Kane* (1941). With affectionate irony, *Young Frankenstein* resorts to long-antiquated cinematic devices such as lap dissolves to indicate the passing of time.

In order to recreate the cinematic feel of the Frankenstein classics, Mel Brooks' picture was shot on the same site as the first Frankenstein movies, using the original props, set dressing, laboratory and all. Yet when Brooks

"You have to let this Mel Brooks comedy do everything for you, because that's the only way it works. If you accept the silly, zizzy obviousness, it can make you laugh helplessly." *Pauline Kael*

1 "Stay close to the candles:" Loyal assistant Inga (Teri Garr) helps her brilliant employer (Gene Wilder) get to the root of his family tree.

2 A mind for science: Frederick Frankenstein making a professional sacrifice.

3 Choking on Chihuahua: That's precisely what Frankenstein's Elizabeth (Madeline Kahn) will be doing if Inga sees her mitts anywhere near the good doctor.

4 Baby mine, don't you cry: Gene Wilder assures the creature that there's nothing to be frightened of.

toys with genre clichés, he takes them a step beyond, achieving a satiric sort of meta level. A case in point: as their coach approaches the castle in priceless Dracula style (the wolf howl care of the director himself), Igor and Freddy go into an Abbott and Costello style dialog. When the good doctor asks him why he's talking like that, Igor replies, "I thought you wanted to."

Brooks biographer Peter W. Jansen pointed out that his films often raise questions of lineage and father–son relationships. This also holds true for *Young Frankenstein*. How loyally Igor, the grandson of the original doctor's loyal servant, stands at "Fronkonsteen's" side, even if as he says, salaries have since improved. Of course, the father–son theme as it pertains to the Frankenstein story gets a

5

"Hearts and kidneys are tinkertoys! I'm talking about the central nervous system!"

Film quote: Dr. Frederick Frankenstein

Brooks-style twist tacked onto it. To him, the monster is just a reflection of his master. As the doctor throws a temper tantrum despite his highfalutin, intellectual demeanor, the nonsense-babbling mammoth baby shoots us looks that let us know it is fully capable of understanding the absurdity of the situation. And this is how another scene, in which a blind hermit (Gene Hackman) obliviously scorches the monster with hot soup, reaches poetic heights. As we empathize with monster, we key into the grand punchline: he's one of us. SH

5 Brady bunch rejects: Igor (Marty Feldman) still can't get over losing the role to Ann B. Davis.

6 We'll have that Ovaltine after all: Loyal servant, Frau Blücher (Cloris Leachman, right) gets a taste of life when she tunes into Freddy and Inga's romantic interludes.

7 My master told me to pick the very best one…

6

Jesse

THE GREAT GATSBY

1974 – USA – 144 MIN.

GENRE

LITERARY ADAPTATION, DRAMA

DIRECTOR

JACK CLAYTON

SCREENPLAY

FRANCIS FORD COPPOLA, based on the novel of the same name by F. SCOTT FITZGERALD

DIRECTOR OF PHOTOGRAPHY

DOUGLAS SLOCOMBE

EDITING

TOM PRIESTLEY

MUSIC

NELSON RIDDLE

PRODUCTION

DAVID MERRICK for NEWDON PRODUCTIONS, PARAMOUNT PICTURES

STARRING

ROBERT REDFORD (Jay Gatsby), MIA FARROW (Daisy Buchanan), BRUCE DERN (Tom Buchanan), KAREN BLACK (Myrtle Wilson), SCOTT WILSON (George Wilson), SAM WATERSTON (Nick Carraway), LOIS CHILES (Jordan Baker), HOWARD DA SILVA (Wolfsheim), ROBERTS BLOSSOM (Mr. Gatz), EDWARD HERRMANN (Klipspringer)

ACADEMY AWARDS 1975

OSCAR for BEST MUSIC (Nelson Riddle), and BEST COSTUMES (Theoni V. Aldredge)

gone is
the romance
that was
so divine.*

Paramount Pictures presents

DAVID MERRICK'S PRODUCTION OF
A JACK CLAYTON FILM

ROBERT REDFORD and MIA FARROW

co-starring KAREN BLACK SCOTT WILSON SAM WATERSTON
LOIS CHILES and BRUCE DERN as Tom Produced by DAVID MERRICK
Directed by JACK CLAYTON Screenplay by FRANCIS FORD COPPOLA Based on the novel by
F. SCOTT FITZGERALD Associate Producer HANK MOONJEAN

PG PARENTAL GUIDANCE SUGGESTED Some material may not be suitable for pre-teenagers

Music Supervised and Conducted by Nelson Riddle In Color Prints by Movielab A Paramount Picture

*Copyright © 1924 by Irving Berlin. Copyright Renewed 1951

ORIGINAL SOUNDTRACK AVAILABLE ON PARAMOUNT RECORDS AND GRT TAPES.

Paramount

74/89

1

"Rich girls don't marry poor boys."

No one knows for sure who Jay Gatsby really is. Nick Carraway (Sam Waterston), a New York stockbroker, has been hearing the most incredible rumors about the new resident on the island of West Egg. Allegedly, he's earned his money on the black market and someone has even died at his hand. One thing's for sure: Gatsby (Robert Redford) has amassed an insurmountable fortune. He lives in a mansion that eclipses the rest of the affluent city's visible wealth, and has gone so far as to build a fun park on the grounds of his estate. Nick looks on as countless cars pull up for his extravagant parties night after night, where guests dance the Charleston, drink champagne and have a wild time until sunrise. We have arrived in the Roaring Twenties, the Jazz Age, an era wedged between the First World War and the onset of the Great Depression in 1929. British director Jack Clayton, whose previous films *Room at the Top* (1959) and *The Innocents* (1961) had met with success, pulled out all the stops to assure that his big screen interpretation of F. Scott Fitzgerald's 1925 classic novel, *The Great Gatsby*, would perfectly recapture the fashion, atmosphere and intricacies of the age. The pastel gowns are hypnotically elegant, and the classic roadsters a monument to bygone decadence. Riding the wave of 1970s period pieces, *The Great Gatsby* is a full-fledged study in nostalgia. Despite this, a misleading advertising campaign that marketed the piece as a great romance meant that film's reception was disappointing. The screenplay, written by Francis Ford Coppola, who enjoyed a tremendous triumph that same year with *The Godfather – Part II* (1974), can also be cited as somewhat problematic. Although it largely remained true to Fitzgerald's book, it proved impossible to bring his literary devices to life on

MIA FARROW Many consider her to be one of the few great actresses of 1970s New Hollywood. Others see her as a frail crybaby. Perhaps a telling choice of words as actress Mia Farrow's rise to international stardom came with the 1968 picture *Rosemary's Baby*, about a child bride's devastating pregnancy. Farrow was born in 1945 in Los Angeles to actress Maureen O'Sullivan, famous for playing the role of Jane throughout the 1930s in the Tarzan movies, and director John Farrow. She began her acting career in the 1960s on the TV soap opera *Peyton Place* (1964–69). After the success of *Rosemary's Baby* she was offered a large number of promising roles, playing that same year in *Secret Ceremony*. In 1972, she appeared at the side of Jean-Paul Belmondo in *Docteur Popaul*. Other highlights include her 1974 performance opposite Robert Redford in *The Great Gatsby* and a 1978 all-star film adaptation of Agatha Christie's *Death on the Nile*.
A long-standing personal and professional relationship with Woody Allen burgeoned in 1982 when she was cast in his picture, *A Midsummer Night's Sex Comedy*. The once wife of both legendary entertainer Frank Sinatra and composer/conductor André Previn became Allen's favorite leading actress and companion of many years. Over the course of twelve years she performed exclusively in Allen's productions, playing the fragile yet sprightly woman in numerous pieces like *Zelig* (1983), *Broadway Danny Rose* (1983–84), *The Purple Rose of Cairo* (1985), considered by many to be Allen's masterpiece, *Hannah and Her Sisters*, (1985), *September* (1987) and *Alice* (1990). The couple split up in 1992 when it became clear that Allen was having an affair with Farrow's adopted Korean daughter, Soon Yi. After the mudslinging of the public scandal subsided, Farrow began to work again in film and television. In 1994 she stood before the camera in *Widows' Peak* and *Miami Rhapsody*. Mia Farrow is the mother of 13 children, nine of which she adopted. She is also the author of the 1997 autobiography *What Falls Away*. Her most recent appearance was in the miniseries *The Watcher* (2022).

1 Bathtub gin and all that jazz: The film is a loving reconstruction of the fashions and frolics of the Roaring Twenties.

2 One-track mind: Jay Gatsby (Robert Redford) is haunted by the dream of winning back his first love.

3 Roses are red and Jordan is blue: Francis Ford Coppola's script stays true to the novel, but its depth is inevitably lost.

screen. Thus, as with many adaptations of great works of literature, there are moments that take on both a shallow and artificial tone. Previous attempts to turn the book into a movie had met with a similar fate, including a silent version from 1926 and a better-known 1949 movie with Alan Ladd in the title role.

As in the novel, we are soon able to see past the alluring façade that is Jay Gatsby to the broken man beyond. He is someone who has allowed an impossible dream to trap him in the past. Nick quickly discovers that Gatsby throws his parties for the sole purpose of winning the affections of Nick's cousin Daisy (Mia Farrow), who has held his heart for years. She is married to a man named Tom Buchanan (Bruce Dern), and the two of them live with their young daughter in the neighboring town of East Egg. Unlike West Egg, this community represents old money and establishment. It has been eight years since Gatsby last saw Daisy; he was an army officer with no money at the time, and she was a poor little rich girl. His accumulated mountain of status and collateral exists for the sole purpose of sweeping Daisy off her feet and winning her back.

Everything seems to go according to plan. After an arranged rendezvous at Nick's residence, the two lovers get to know each other a bit better. Daisy is bowled over by the opulence of Gatsby's palatial manor, whose neoclassical grandeur seems incomprehensible even for the world of multimillionaires. The plot soon unfolds into a love affair marked by exaggerated romantic conventions and "Vaseline lens" visuals, which prove as grating as Daisy's neurotic behavior. The audience is torn between wondering whether they are watching a farce or simply a world that is "genuinely" as far removed from the realities of ordinary life as is humanly imaginable. It is a dimension that appears even more sensational when compared to the downtrodden, suburban street where impecunious auto-body shop owner George Wilson (Scott Wilson) lives with his wife Myrtle (Karen Black). The ominous eyes of Dr. T. J. Eckleburg on a local billboard watch over this nowhere town and serve as one of the film's most evident symbols. This is a world sucked dry of color, providing a sharp contrast to the rainbow world of the two Eggs. Myrtle is Tom Buchanan's mistress and like Jay Gatsby, hopes to gain access to a new social stratum via her lucrative liaison. Both of these hopefuls are left hung out to dry. Not only does Tom soon find out that Gatsby has indeed, as accused, made a killing in the illegal alcohol trade, but it also becomes clear that Daisy has no intention of leaving her husband. Shortly after this shattering revelation, Myrtle meets an untimely demise when Gatsby unintentionally hits her with his car. In a wild act of desperation, Wilson shoots Gatsby and then himself, leaving the two men dead.

Both the movie and the book equate Gatsby's personal desires with those inherent in the American Dream.

"The aim was to capture the spirit of the book, Fitzgerald's masterly evocation of the lifestyle of the rich and famous in the Roaring Twenties. And indeed, the formula romance + nostalgia + advertising campaign does seem to equal success." *Berliner Morgenpost*

4 Daisy, Daisy give me your answer do… Gatsby has found the love of his life (Mia Farrow) again.

5 Suddenly last summer: Gatsby shortly before his violent death.

6 A race to the finish: Gatsby's car symbolizes wealth and freedom, but in the end it costs him his life.

7 All that glitters is not gold: Mia Farrow and Robert Redford of *Butch Cassidy and the Sundance Kid* fame.

Nevertheless, everything that Daisy represents to this social climber is rooted in the past. Likewise, the American Dream itself is deemed to be a concept that only exists in nostalgic reveries. Several generations separate the time between the mass European exodus to the western shores of the New World and the 1920s, and in *Gatsby*, we bear witness to an opposing trend within the United States. Here, characters from "western" cities like Detroit are returning to the East Coast. For Gatsby, the movement is a harrowing reverse that signals his undoing. KK

7

“The film is faithful to the letter of F. Scott Fitzgerald’s novel but entirely misses its spirit. Much of Fitzgerald’s prose has been preserved, especially in Nick Carraway’s narration, but it only gives the film a stilted, stuffy tone that is reinforced by the dialogue. Fitzgerald wrote dialogue to be read, not said; and the Coppola screenplay (much rejuggled by Director Clayton) treats Fitzgerald’s lines with untoward reverence. When Daisy sighs, ‘We were so close in our month of love,’ she sounds like a kid in creative-writing course reading her first story loud.” *Time Magazine*

YAKUZA

THE YAKUZA

1974 – USA / JAPAN – 112 MIN.

GENRE

GANGSTER FILM, DRAMA

DIRECTOR

SYDNEY POLLACK

SCREENPLAY

LEONARD SCHRADER, PAUL SCHRADER, ROBERT TOWNE

DIRECTOR OF PHOTOGRAPHY

DUKE CALLAGHAN, KOZO OKAZAKI

EDITING

DON GUIDICE, THOMAS STANFORD, FREDRIC STEINKAMP

MUSIC

DAVE GRUSIN

PRODUCTION

SYDNEY POLLACK for TOEI CO. LTD., WARNER BROS

STARRING

ROBERT MITCHUM (Harry Kilmer), KEN TAKAKURA (Ken Tanaka), BRIAN KEITH (George Tanner), HERB EDELMAN (Oliver Wheat), RICHARD JORDAN (Dusty), KEIKO KISHI (Eiko Tanaka), EIJI OKADA (Toshiro Tono), JAMES SHIGETA (Goro), KYOSUKE MASHIDA (Jiro Kato), EIJI GO (Spider)

Separated by blood and centuries-United by a woman-
Now, hurled together against The Yakuza...brotherhood of the East.

ROBERT MITCHUM
TAKAKURA KEN

in a SYDNEY POLLACK Production **"THE YAKUZA"** and **BRIAN KEITH** as "Tanner"
Screenplay by PAUL SCHRADER and ROBERT TOWNE · Story by LEONARD SCHRADER
Produced and Directed by SYDNEY POLLACK · Music by DAVE GRUSIN

PANAVISION® TECHNICOLOR® From Warner Bros. A Warner Communications Company

1

"Paint my eyes on my eyelids, man, and I'll walk through it"

The film opens with the following information: "The Japanese word 'Yakuza' is made up from the characters denoting the numbers 8, 9 and 3. When we add these together, the sum total is 20—a losing number in Japanese gambling. Japan's outsiders have chosen their name with perverse pride. The Yakuza began life in Japan over 350 years ago as gamblers, con men and shady merchants at traveling fairs. They were also said to have protected the poor of the towns and countryside from bands of marauding noblemen. This, they apparently did with matchless skill and courage."

The Yakuza claim to be the descendents of Samurai warriors, and this is already enough to distinguish them from the Mafia. As Japan became increasingly centralized, westernized and militarized in the course of the 19th century, the Samurai were forbidden to carry their traditional longswords in public or to fight duels. Thus the Yakuza ethos is rooted in the choice between the loss of legality and the loss of pride. One of their rules states that an enemy may only be killed by means of the longsword. *The Yakuza*, however, is no costume drama and no mere gangster film, but an examination—from an American perspective—of the rules governing the Japanese world and underworld.

The daughter of a dubious American businessman resident in Japan has been kidnapped. His wheeling and dealing has not been well received in Yakuza circles. By holding his daughter hostage, they hope to force their unwelcome rival to abandon his crooked business practices. Instead of submitting, however, the American calls on the services of an old buddy from the years after WWII when Japan was still occupied by U.S. troops: enter the ex-G. I. and detective Harry Kilmer—played by Robert Mitchum, an actor who's no stranger to the gangster milieu. The man with the heaviest eyelids in Hollywood will surely emerge from this underworld nightmare as luckily intact as a

ROBERT MITCHUM Robert Mitchum (1917–1997) was one of the last great stars of the classic Hollywood cinema. He made his name in the Golden Age of the studio system that dominated the American film industry from the 20s until the late 50s. After the Second World War, a gem of a film brought Mitchum to the attention of a larger public: *Out of the Past* (1947) was originally a B-movie, but it established the archetypal Mitchum character, a man whose past will not leave him in peace. Shortly afterwards, he spent a few weeks in jail for possession of marijuana; but he still developed into one of the most popular actors on screen. Mitchum was the ultimate tough guy. In films such as *River of No Return* (1954), *The Night of the Hunter* (1955), and *Cape Fear* (1962) he embodied loners and outsiders—laconically, with understated charm and a kind of nonchalant slothfulness that only increased with age. The characters he played might all have been created by Raymond Chandler; and in *Farewell, My Lovely* (1975), his dry and unflappable detective was the antithesis of the Humphrey Bogart figure. He fulfilled Raymond Chandler's definition of a hero: "… a complete man and a common man, and yet an unusual man."

Mitchum's legendary indifference to the art of acting is epitomized in his marginal note to the script of *El Dorado* (1967): NAR (= "no acting required"). His last film was Jim Jarmusch's *Dead Man* (1995), in which he performed alongside Johnny Depp.

sleepwalker. But Tokyo is a jungle, an alien metropolis, and unlike most of the figures embodied by Mitchum, Kilmer has no hope of surviving here as a lone wolf. As a soldier during the occupation, he could afford to be indifferent to the moral framework of Japanese society; now, he finds himself obliged to study it. Solidarity is guaranteed by the social glue of the "giri," an ethos of personal obligation or duty that demands unconditional commitment from all who serve it, and especially from members of the Yakuza: anyone who breaks ranks will pay with his life. It's a lot more persuasive than just owing someone a favor…

"At the end, the Yakuza is left contemplating a heap of ruins. He is a victim of the mythology he has subscribed to, a man who vanquished his enemies but lost the moral battle. This paradox embodies Pollack's basic and essential theme: the impossibility of reconciling myth with reality."

Deutsche Volkszeitung

3

1 Eyes wide shut: Robert Mitchum as Harry Kilmer, a stranger in a strange land.

2 Don't make waves: In Japan, male bonding begins and occasionally ends at the pool (Herb Edelman, right).

3 Can I see some I. D.? Ken Tanaka (Ken Takakura) will eliminate the enemy at the drop of a hat.

4 Die by the sword: According to Yakuza, gunfighters ignore sacred rites—and win.

The audience shares Kilmer's feelings as he studies the Japanese rules of conduct: the closer he looks, the stranger they seem. With this, *The Yakuza* leaves the standard formulae of the gangster film far behind. Kilmer has to operate between and across cultures, and he's faced with paradoxical situations. He meets a Japanese family who feel "giri" towards him, for he helped them to survive after the war and they are thus obliged to give him their unconditional support. With their help, he succeeds in forcing a showdown with the Yakuza gangsters and, in the battle between swords and handguns, technological progress carries the day. Kilmer survives, and from now on he "owes one" to his helpers. He cuts off the little finger of his left hand and presents it to them as an IOU-note.

The Yakuza is of more than merely film-historical interest. For one thing, it's a convincing treatment of the conflict between the strict demands of a moral code and the messy ambivalence of everyday life. For another, it combines two very different film traditions: the American gangster movie and the Japanese Yakuza film, a highly popular genre in 60s Japan. Though Yakuza-film screenwriters included authors as serious and important as Yukio Mishima, Western critics and filmmakers never showed any interest in the genre. The only exception was the French director Jean-Pierre Melville: In *The Samurai* (*Le Samouraï*, 1967), the protagonist (Alain Delon) calmly accepts his own death as a simple matter of course, the logical consequence of his strict code of honor. RV

JAWS

1975 – USA – 124 MIN.

GENRE

THRILLER, HORROR FILM

DIRECTOR

STEVEN SPIELBERG

SCREENPLAY

CARL GOTTLIEB, PETER BENCHLEY,
based on his novel of the same name

DIRECTOR OF PHOTOGRAPHY

BILL BUTLER

EDITING

VERNA FIELDS

MUSIC

JOHN WILLIAMS

PRODUCTION

RICHARD D. ZANUCK, DAVID BROWN for
ZANUCK/BROWN PRODUCTIONS, UNIVERSAL PICTURES

STARRING

ROY SCHEIDER (Police Chief Martin Brody), ROBERT SHAW (Quint),
RICHARD DREYFUSS (Matt Hooper), MURRAY HAMILTON (Mayor Larry Vaughn),
LORRAINE GARY (Ellen Brody), CARL GOTTLIEB (Ben Meadows),
JEFFREY KRAMER (Lenny Hendricks), SUSAN BACKLINIE (Chrissie),
CHRIS REBELLO (Mike Brody), JAY MELLO (Sean Brody)

ACADEMY AWARDS 1976

OSCARS for BEST FILM EDITING (Verna Fields),
BEST MUSIC (John Williams),
and BEST SOUND (Robert L. Hoyt, Roger Herman Jr.,
Earl Madery, John R. Carter)

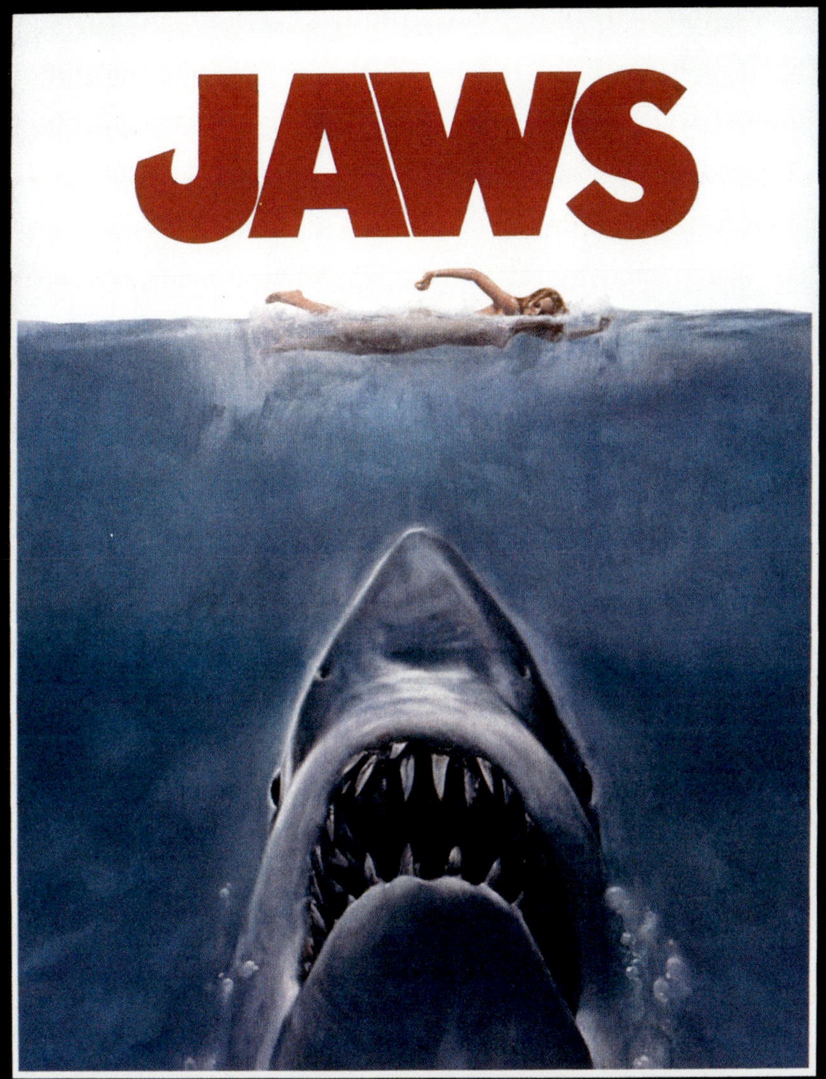

The terrifying motion picture
from the terrifying No. 1 best seller.
JAWS
ROBERT SHAW
ROY SCHEIDER
RICHARD DREYFUSS
JAWS
Co-starring LORRAINE GARY · MURRAY HAMILTON · A ZANUCK/BROWN PRODUCTION
Screenplay by PETER BENCHLEY and CARL GOTTLIEB · Based on the novel by PETER BENCHLEY · Music by JOHN WILLIAMS
Directed by STEVEN SPIELBERG · Produced by RICHARD D. ZANUCK and DAVID BROWN · A UNIVERSAL PICTURE ·
TECHNICOLOR® PANAVISION®
ORIGINAL SOUNDTRACK AVAILABLE ON MCA RECORDS & TAPES

1

"You're gonna need a bigger boat."

A hot summer night, a beach party, a little too much red wine, and some teenage sex is just the stuff Hollywood horror films are made of. While her drunken companion sleeps off his hangover on the beach, young Chrissie (Susan Backlinie) takes a midnight dip in the water and is torn to pieces by a shark. The fact that the monster with the dead eyes cynically emerges in innocent white from the depths of the water makes it all the more threatening. The shark—the fear and guilt in all of us—awakens our prehistoric terror of the incomprehensible, the truly wild. It is evil incarnate.

But in the small American beach town ironically named Amity, nobody wants to hear about the threat to a safe world and free market economy, least of all from the mouth of visiting New York cop Martin Brody (Roy Scheider) who, to cap it all, is afraid of the water.

Accordingly, the authorities, in the form of the mayor Larry Vaughn (Murray Hamilton), and the profit and pleasure-

THE END OF ARTIFICIAL CREATURES "Compressors, tanks, winches, pneumatic hoses, welding torches, blow lamps, rigging, generators, copper, iron, and steel wire, plastic material, electric motors, crammers, hydraulic presses"—just some of the trappings required to make "Bruce," as the film team christened the model of the white shark, come alive. In his book, *The Jaws Log*, co-screenwriter Carl Gottlieb tells of the immense problems encountered trying to simulate real-life shark attacks with a life-sized model (because actually Bruce was made of three different models). Shooting was repeatedly interrupted by technical problems, most memorably when they first put Bruce in the water, only to see him sink like a stone. The hiring of long-retired Hollywood veteran Robert A. Mattey, creator of the special effects for Disney's *Mary Poppins* (1964) and countless other films, makes it clear that the mid-70s marked the end of conventionally created film monsters. "Bruce" was one of the last of his kind and craftsmen like Bob Mattey were increasingly relieved by computer programmers. Spielberg proved his ability to incorporate their work into his projects in 1981 with *Raiders of the Lost Ark*, in which entire sequences were created with the help of computer animation.

“If *Jaws* was a kind of skeleton key to the angst of the 70s, from the puritanical fear of sex to the war in Vietnam, then its heroes were models of America’s wounded masculinity, who meet and join to face a test of character.”

Georg Seeßlen

3

1 Baywatch: Police Chief Martin Brody (Roy Scheider) is fighting nature, the ignorance of those he's trying to protect and his own fears.

2 Beach, blanket, bloodbath: Beautiful Chrissie (Susan Backlinie) is the shark's first victim.

3 Smile for the camera: Three separate models, each seven yards long and weighing over a ton, brought the monster to life. The film crew dubbed the shark "Bruce"—after Steven Spielberg's lawyer.

seeking public win out over Brody, who wants to close the beaches in light of the menacing danger. It comes as no surprise that the town has a new victim the very next day.

A reward of $3,000 for the capture of the shark incites hunting fever in Amity, and the gawking mob on the pier is duly presented with a dead shark. But it is quickly determined that the captured shark can't possibly be the feared killer: upon cutting open its stomach they find a few small fish, a tin can, and a license plate from Louisiana.

It is a motley trio that sets out to capture the beast—a water-shy policeman, a "rich college boy" named Matt Hooper (Richard Dreyfuss), and shark-hunting Vietnam veteran Quint (Robert Shaw), a modern Captain Ahab who unsuccessfully attempts to disguise a wounded psyche

4 Brody's scared of water, but he's about to undergo some shock therapy…

5 Rub a dub dub, three men in a tub: *Jaws* is also a parable about social conflicts in the USA.

6 Shark fin soup: Evil feeds on ignorance and Americans.

with a façade of disgust for everything around him. For each of the three men, the shark hunt also turns into a search for their true selves.

The unmistakably sexual aspect of the story of the unnamed monster—a terrifying mixture of phallus and vagina—which afflicts the home and the family has often been pointed out. But *Jaws* is also a film about human fears and character flaws, the overcoming of which gives birth to heroes. That the story also tells of the capitalistic, self-endangering society, of patriotic America, of mass hysteria, guilt, atonement, and the sacrifice of the individual for the good of the whole is proof of Spielberg's ability to give a simple story plausible readings on multiple levels.

But let's not forget that *Jaws* is one of the most nerve-wracking thrillers of all time. When Spielberg explains that during the filming he felt as if he could direct the audience with an electric cattle prod, it speaks volumes about the cold precision with which, supported by an exceptionally suggestive soundtrack, he was able to

"If Spielberg's favorite location is the suburbs, *Jaws* shows suburbanites on vacation." *Chicago Sun-Times*

raise the tension and lower it again, all in preparation for the next dramatic highlight.

Just one example of Spielberg's virtuoso story-telling technique is the scene in which the men show one another their scars under deck. In the middle of the scene, the audience is told the story of the *ISS Indianapolis*, the boat with which the Hiroshima bomb was transported to the Pacific. Under fire from Japanese submarines, the crew threw themselves into the ocean and the majority of them were eaten by sharks.

During this sequence, which is actually quite humorous, Spielberg and his authors succeed in setting a counterpoint even before the appearance of the shark illustrates the terror of the story. Quint's tale contains a political dimension. Ultimately, this scene also reveals something about story-telling itself—reality catches you up in a flash. Right when Quint and Hooper attempt to stem their apprehension with loud song, Mr. Spielberg is right there with his electric shocker.

SH

6

ONE FLEW OVER THE CUCKOO'S NEST

1975 – USA – 134 MIN.

GENRE

DRAMA, LITERARY ADAPTATION

DIRECTOR

MILOŠ FORMAN

SCREENPLAY

LAWRENCE HAUBEN, BO GOLDMAN,
based on the novel of the same name by KEN KESEY
and a play by DALE WASSERMAN

DIRECTOR OF PHOTOGRAPHY

HASKELL WEXLER, WILLIAM A. FRAKER, BILL BUTLER

EDITING

LYNZEE KLINGMAN, SHELDON KAHN,
RICHARD CHEW (Supervising Editor)

MUSIC

JACK NITZSCHE

PRODUCTION

SAUL ZAENTZ, MICHAEL DOUGLAS for
FANTASY FILMS, N. V. ZVALUW

STARRING

JACK NICHOLSON (Randle Patrick McMurphy),
LOUISE FLETCHER (Nurse Mildred Ratched), WILLIAM REDFIELD (Harding),
BRAD DOURIF (Billy Bibbit), WILL SAMPSON (Chief Bromden),
DANNY DEVITO (Martini), MICHAEL BERRYMAN (Ellis), PETER BROCCO (Colonel Matterson),
DEAN R. BROOKS (Doctor John Spivey), ALONZO BROWN (Miller)

ACADEMY AWARDS 1976

OSCARS for BEST PICTURE (Saul Zaentz, Michael Douglas),
BEST DIRECTOR (Miloš Forman), BEST ACTOR (Jack Nicholson),
BEST ACTRESS (Louise Fletcher),
and BEST ADAPTED SCREENPLAY (Lawrence Hauben, Bo Goldman)

JACK NICHOLSON

ONE FLEW OVER THE CUCKOO'S NEST

Fantasy Films presents

A MILOS FORMAN FILM JACK NICHOLSON in "ONE FLEW OVER THE CUCKOO'S NEST"

Starring LOUISE FLETCHER *and* WILLIAM REDFIELD · *Screenplay* LAWRENCE HAUBEN *and* BO GOLDMAN

Based on the novel by KEN KESEY · *Director of Photography* HASKELL WEXLER · *Music* · JACK NITZSCHE

R RESTRICTED

Produced by SAUL ZAENTZ *and* MICHAEL DOUGLAS · *Directed by* MILOS FORMAN

United Artists

NOW AVAILABLE IN SIGNET PAPERBACK AND VIKING/COMPASS TRADE PAPERBACK

1

"But I tried didn't I? Goddammit, at least I did that!"

The movie's opening shot evokes an image of paradise lost. Rolling hills are reflected in the glistening water by the rising sun, as a peaceful melody drifts through the air. The last shot is equally utopian. Chief Bromden (Will Sampson), a mountain of a man resident at the psychiatric rehabilitation facility tucked away in this picturesque countryside, wrenches a colossal marble bathroom fixture from its anchored position, hurls it through a window and embarks on the road to freedom. What director Miloš Forman manages to pack into the action that takes place between these two points is a mesmerizing parable about both the urge to capitulate and an ideological system that seeks to crush the individual at any cost. The tale is ingeniously coated in a tragicomic drama about life, death and the state of vegetative indifference exhibited by the residents of an insane asylum.

But all that is about the last thing assault and statutory rape convict Randle P. McMurphy (Jack Nicholson) has on his mind when he first arrives at the sterile building with barred windows for clinical observation. To McMurphy, the facility serves as a promising alternative to the hard labor he'd be subjected to at the state penitentiary. This is, of course, precisely why higher authorities suspect him of faking his mental ailments. It soon becomes evident that McMurphy is the sole person at the institution still possessing enough fantasy and initiative to

JACK NICHOLSON Wily, devious and even lecherous at times, Jack Nicholson still possesses all the qualities required to portray characters driven by animal instincts rather than intellect. His caustic mimicry, gestures and trademark sneer vitalize rebels (*One Flew Over the Cuckoo's Nest*, 1975), psychopaths (*The Shining*, 1980), career killers (*Prizzi's Honor*, 1985) and hardboiled P.I.s alike (*Chinatown*, 1974; *The Two Jakes*, 1990). Some might even regard the sinister, eternally grinning "Joker" in Tim Burton's *Batman* (1988) as the culminating fusion of his classic roles. Hard to believe that for many years it seemed the movie star born in Neptune, New Jersey in 1937 was not destined to make it big. In the late 50s, he joined the team of legendary exploitation film director/producer Roger Corman, performing bit roles in his horror flicks and wannabe rockumentaries, as well as writing screenplays. His screenwriting credits include Monte Hellman's Western *Ride in the Whirlwind* (1965) and Corman's LSD exploration entitled *The Trip* (1967). The turning point came with his role as a perpetually inebriated lawyer in *Easy Rider* (1969). Dennis Hopper's drama about the disappearance of the American Dream quickly attained cult status and earned Nicholson his first of many Oscar nods. His rise to superstardom reached its height in the 70s. Among his many credits and honors, Nicholson has been awarded three Oscars, and has directed movies himself. Still very much alive in the business, his later movies often feature him as stubborn, eccentric types, side by side with Diane Keaton in *Something's Gotta Give* (2003), in *About Schmidt* (2003) and as a mob boss in Martin Scorsese's *The Departed* (2006). These parts attest to Nicholson's immense popularity and continuing role as one of Hollywood's all-time favorite actors.

It's your move: Randle P. Murphy (Jack Nicholson) thinks he's in a game—and he thinks he can win.

2 Leading by example: Randle is the hero of the other patients in the psychiatric ward.

3 Shake, rattle and roll: Randle encourages his fellow patients to take control of their lives.

combat the current reign of deadening boredom. His opposition comes in the form of the austere head nurse, Mildred Ratched (Louise Fletcher), who has made it her life mission to suck the marrow out of any bit of excitement within the ward in order to assure her patients' eternal sedation. McMurphy, however, slowly undermines her authority. He begins to question trivialities as well as the inalterable daily schedule by instigating "harmless" acts of defiance, even managing to get the patients to sneak out of the clinic and treating them to a fishing trip. Although McMurphy's actions infuse the sequestered men with newfound self-esteem, Nurse Ratched's festering anger reveals her personal disdain for anything other than the prescribed routine. She, of course, defends the prevailing order by enforcing a strict, borderline totalitarian regime rooted in pseudo-democratic doctrines.

To take the film as a critique of modern psychiatric medicine is to misinterpret it. Director Forman has clearly made an attempt at a more monumental allegory about the power structures at play in modern society. Among the poignant final scenes in *One Flew Over the Cuckoo's Nest* is the moment when we discover that the majority of patients at the clinic are there of their own volition. In other words, they have all willingly acquiesced to the tyranny and perpetual humiliation. The counterpoint to this mentality manifests itself in McMurphy's reticence to resign himself to such blind compliance. One of the few actually incarcerated hospital inhabitants, the unforgettable words he utters following his failed attempt at dislodging a marble bathroom fixture sum up the plea of Forman's picture: "But I tried, didn't I? Goddammit, at least I did that!" Tragically, McMurphy never internalizes the extreme gravity of his own predicament and continues to gamble in a poker game where no one can afford to bluff. At one point he is presented with a *deus ex machina* in the form of an open window offering escape. The camera holds its focus on McMurphy's face for some time before a cunning grin finally unfolds across his lips. He will stay and continue on with the "game."

One Flew over the Cuckoo's Nest is a powerful, smashingly effective movie—not a great movie bt one that will probably stir audiences' emotions and join the ranks of such pop-mythology films as *The Wild One, Rebel without a Cause* and *Easy Rider*." *The New Yorker*

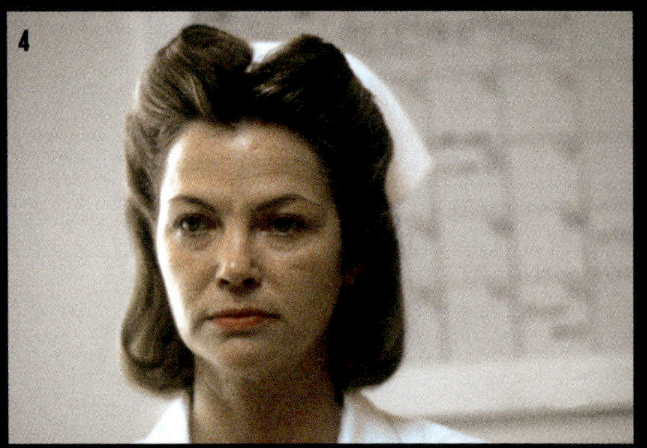

Be that as it may, his tournament is over before he even realizes it. The burgeoning self-confidence and associated mental resilience demonstrated in the wisecracks of the patients cause the hospital staff to implement more drastic physical and psychological measures. The film concludes with a "pacified" McMurphy, who was subjected to a lobotomy, being put out of his misery by his friend, the chief. It is this character who continues what McMurphy has set into motion.

Miloš Forman earned his reputation in Hollywood as the most influential Czech "new wave" import in the 60s

"The 'cuckoo's nest' described by Forman is our very own nest. It's the world we poor lunatics live in, subjected to the bureaucratic rule of one set of oppressors and the economic pressure of another; forever chasing the promise of happiness, which here appears in the guise of liberty—but always obliged to swallow Miss Ratched's bitter little pills."

Le Monde

6

4 First Lady of a mock-democracy: Nurse Ratched (Louise Fletcher) brings the patients to their knees.

5 Born free: "Chief" Bromden carries on the torch when he flies the coop.

6 Sex, drugs and fishing trips: There's nothing Dionysian Randle enjoys catching more than some female tail.

with his sarcastic reflections on everyday life. Although Ken Kesey's novel, on which the screen adaptation is based, is told from the perspective of the mute Native American, McMurphy served as the perfect vehicle for Forman to express his personal cinematic interests and set of reccurring themes. The director transforms the story into a lighter satire, whose socio-political potential takes a slight backseat to the entertainment value, allowing the piece to soar to stunningly beautiful heights. The actual directing in *One Flew Over the Cuckoo's Nest* is primarily evidenced in the world-class acting led by an energized Nicholson, his antithesis, the insidiously pleasant Louise Fletcher, and Will Sampson's gut-wrenching stoicism. Yet, it's not enough to speak of Sampson's Bromden character solely in these terms, for it is he who will undergo the most dramatic metamorphosis. From the ashes of his self-imposed silent retreat and symbolic emasculation arises a true warrior, who lets the eternal flame borne by McMurphy burn on inside him.

LP

DIE VERLORENE EHRE DER KATHARINA BLUM

THE LOST HONOR OF KATHARINA BLUM

1975 – FRG – 106 MIN.

GENRE

LITERARY ADAPTATION, THRILLER

DIRECTOR

VOLKER SCHLÖNDORFF,
MARGARETHE VON TROTTA

SCREENPLAY

VOLKER SCHLÖNDORFF, MARGARETHE VON TROTTA,
based on the novella *DIE VERLORENE EHRE DER KATHARINA BLUM, ODER: WIE GEWALT ENTSTEHEN UND WOHIN SIE FÜHREN KANN* by HEINRICH BÖLL

DIRECTOR OF PHOTOGRAPHY

JOST VACANO

EDITING

PETER PRZYGODDA

MUSIC

HANS WERNER HENZE

PRODUCTION

WILLI BENNINGER for BIOSKOP FILM,
PARAMOUNT-ORION FILMPRODUKTION, WESTDEUTSCHER RUNDFUNK

STARRING

ANGELA WINKLER (Katharina Blum), MARIO ADORF (Commissar Beizmenne), DIETER LASER (Werner Tötges), JÜRGEN PROCHNOW (Ludwig Götten), HEINZ BENNENT (Doctor Blorna), HANNELORE HOGER (Trude Blorna), ROLF BECKER (State Prosecutor Hach), HARALD KUHLMANN (Moeding), HERBERT FUX (Weninger), REGINE LUTZ (Else Woltersheim), WERNER EICHHORN (Konrad Beiters), KARL HEINZ VOSGERAU (Alois Sträubleder)

Angela Winkler
Mario Adorf in
Volker Schlöndorffs
Farbfilm
DIE
VERLORENE
EHRE
DER
KATHARINA
BLUM
mit Heinz Bennent Hannelore Hoger
Rolf Becker Dieter Laser
Jürgen Prochnow
nach der Erzählung
von Heinrich
Boll

1

"The thing is, my little blossom, you're famous now."

"It's dynamite—a German Watergate." These were the words of Volker Schlöndorff just before *The Lost Honor of Katharina Blum* reached the theaters. Expectations were almost unattainably high; but in the hothouse atmosphere of the 70s, with Germany divided by the terrorism debate, the film's impact was massive. It was a huge success at the box office, highly praised by German and foreign critics alike, and showered with awards, including the German Film Prize for 1976. The film is based on a short novel by Heinrich Böll, *The Lost Honor of Katharina Blum, or How Violence Develops and Where It Can Lead.* It is both a gripping thriller and a painful dissection of contemporary German society. Böll himself collaborated on the script, and it was he who suggested casting Angela Winkler in the title role. A German star was born.

Angela Winkler embodies the young housekeeper Katharina Blum, thrown into conflict with the police and the tabloid press as a result of a casual acquaintance. Her performance is powerful and multifaceted, and the film casts a revealing light on the bigoted, divided West Germany of the 1970s. Heinrich Böll's labyrinthine narrative is transformed into a slim, no-nonsense movie. During the Cologne Carnival in 1975, Katharina meets a young man at a party, with whom she falls instantly in love. It's Ludwig Götten (Jürgen Prochnow), a deserter from the West German army who is under police surveillance. The audience doesn't learn much more about Götten: merely that he's on the run, that police spies are following his every move, and that he is indeed eventually arrested. This scant information is enough to evoke some real

TERRORISM IN GERMAN FILM The 70s were a period of political radicalization in Germany. At the heart of this development was the "Red Army Faction" (RAF), also known as the Baader-Meinhof gang. Volker Schlöndorff's *The Lost Honor of Katharina Blum* (*Die verlorene Ehre der Katharina Blum,* 1975) was an early study of the German state's hysterical reaction to the perceived terrorist threat. The confrontation reached its climax in 1977 with the murder of the kidnapped employers' federation chief Hanns Martin Schleyer and the hijacking of the Lufthansa airliner "Landshut." In the same year, eleven German directors—including Rainer Werner Fassbinder, Alexander Kluge and Edgar Reitz—collaborated on a response to these events: the film collage *Germany in Autumn* (*Deutschland im Herbst*, 1977/78). Reinhard Hauff's *Knife in the Head* (*Messer im Kopf,* 1978) is a subtle treatment of the same theme. In 1981, Margarethe von Trotta made *The German Sisters,* aka *Marianne and Juliane* (*Die bleierne Zeit*), a film based on the life of Gudrun Ensslin, who had committed suicide along with Andreas Baader and Jan Carl Raspe in the fall of '77 in Stuttgart's Stammheim prison. In 1985, Reinhard Hauff filmed the story of the Stammheim trial (*Stammheim*). Just over a decade later, Heinrich Breloer made a TV docudrama *Todesspiel – Teil 1 & 2* ("Deadly Game, Parts 1 & 2," 1996–97), a film that was accused of bias for allegedly presenting only the viewpoint of the German state. Since 2000, there has been a new cinematic discourse on the subject of terrorism. It began with Volker Schlöndorff's *The Legends of Rita* (*Die Stille nach dem Schuss*, 1999), a film based on the memoirs of Inge Viett, who went to live in East Germany after leaving the RAF. In 2001, Andreas Veiel produced *Black Box BRD,* a double portrait of the terrorist Wolfgang Grams and the Deutsche Bank's CEO Alfred Herrhausen, murdered by the RAF in 1989. Christopher Roth's *Baader* (2001) depicted the terrorist as a kind of pop star, while Christian Petzold's *The State I Am In,* aka *Internal Security* (*Die innere Sicherheit,* 2000) is one of the best films ever made on the subject; here, the former terrorists are lost souls, who can live neither inside nor outside society. The documentary *Starbuck – Holger Meins* (2002) is a penetrating examination of the process of radicalization in Germany: director Gerd Conradt studied at the German Film and Television Academy in Berlin alongside Holger Meins, who later joined the RAF and died in prison on hunger strike at the age of 33.

1 Carnival confetti: Katharina (Angela Winkler) falls in love with Ludwig (Jürgen Prochnow). He's deserted from the German army, and the police are on his trail.

2 Calling the shots: Author, Heinrich Böll picked Angela Winkler for the role of Katharina Blum.

3 Look on in anger: Dr. Blorna (Heinz Bennent) and his wife (Hannelore Hoger) are appalled at the behavior of the police and the press.

phenomena of the time: the hunt for Andreas Baader and Ulrike Meinhof, and what the foreign press described as "West German anarchist hysteria."

Katharina takes Götten home with her, spends the night with him, and gives him the key to the villa of a university professor called Sträubleder (Karl Heinz Vosgerau). Her motives are completely apolitical; but what she calls love, the police interpret as premeditated political action. The morning after, as Katharina makes coffee in her kitchen, a terrifying masked task force—like something out of Terry Gilliam's *Brazil* (1984)—storms her apartment, armed to the teeth, under the command of Commissar Beizmenne (Mario Adorf). For Katharina, it's the start of a humiliating process. She is arrested and subjected to a series of interrogations, in which it's clear that the police think they know the answers long before they've asked the questions. No one believes she's only just met Götten, nobody wants to know what really happened. It's not just

"Schlöndorff has found a convincing solution to the dramaturgical problem of how to depict the course of events through the eyes of a young woman: allowing the spectator a naive, unmediated view of those events—while managing to keep his distance." *Neue Zürcher Zeitung*

4 Witch hunt: To the cops and the tabloids, Katharina is a "left-wing slut" and has thus been stripped of her rights.

5 Search and seizure: Katharina Blum's arrest results in the shameless debasement of her private life.

the crass and dislikable Beizmenne who rushes to pronounce Blum guilty; the public mood is already aggressively vindictive, and the gutter press is happy to lead the pack. Worst of all is "Die Zeitung," clearly modelled on the *Bild-Zeitung*, Germany's most notorious popular tabloid.

Tötges (Dieter Laser), a slimy, unscrupulous reporter, scavenges around in Katharina's past in search of juicy details to add to the story he's already written. He invents statements from her desperately ill mother, for he knows that "simple people require a little assistance in articulating their thoughts." What follows is a kind of witch hunt: Katharina is portrayed as a whore and a Communist sympathizer, and left to the tender mercies of an enraged public. Day after day, she receives venomous letters and obscene phone calls. Physically and psychically degraded, she can only hold on to her memories of Götten—until one night, she weakens and calls him. The police are listening in, and Götten is arrested.

What happens next seems more a necessity than an act of revenge. Katharina grants Tötges an exclusive interview, and invites him to her apartment. In his cynicism and mendacity, he embodies everyone's worst nightmare of a

"Worth seeing? Definitely. (...) It may not be a masterpiece, but it successfully examines the reality of modern life in West Germany in a way that is accessible to a wide public. That is no small achievement."
Kölner Stadt-Anzeiger

6 Critical condition: Tabloid hack Tötges (Dieter Laser) will do anything to get a quote, even if an elderly woman has to die as a result.

7 Guilty by default: Commissioner Beizmenne (Mario Adorf) never doubts his course of action. "La Blum's" arrest is a pure demonstration of state power.

7

tabloid hack. When he goes so far as to force his sexual attentions on her, Katharina shoots him dead.

The Lost Honor of Katharina Blum showed that the "New German Cinema" of the 70s could also be commercially successful. With its straightforward narrative structure and the intense feelings it depicts and evokes—sadness, pity and rage—the film appealed both to cinephiles and a wider audience. Above all, it makes a powerful appeal to the emotions; this is a melodrama about a woman destroyed by society. Hans Werner Henze's disturbing music underscores the changes Katharina undergoes, from her initial incredulity at the accusations she's faced with to her final fury and despair. The camerawork by Jost Vacano (*Das Boot*, 1981; *The Never Ending Story*, 1984) provides a visual realization of the tale's psychological dimension. As viewers, we share in Katharina's ordeal. Yet the blatant collaboration of the police, the judiciary and the conservative, right-wing press impresses less as a political scandal than as the undeserved nemesis of a woman who's captured the audience's affections. Even at the time, critics accused the film of deploying the very methods it condemns: an undifferentiated black-and-white view of the world, and emotionalism instead of analysis. Yet the film has an undeniable and oppressive logic: those who are humiliated like Katharina Blum can only be expected to defend themselves. Thus the film can be seen above all as a depiction of the way in which state violence begets counter-violence in its turn. KK

SUPERVIXENS

1975 – USA – 106 MIN.

GENRE

SEX FILM

DIRECTOR

RUSS MEYER

SCREENPLAY

RUSS MEYER

DIRECTOR OF PHOTOGRAPHY

RUSS MEYER

EDITING

RUSS MEYER

MUSIC

WILLIAM LOOSE

PRODUCTION

RUSS MEYER for RM FILMS INTERNATIONAL,
SEPTEMBER 19

STARRING

SHARI EUBANK (Super Angel Turner / Super Vixen),
CHARLES PITTS (Clint Ramsey), USCHI DIGARD (Super Soul),
HENRY ROWLAND (Martin Bormann), CHARLES NAPIER (Harry Sledge),
Christy Hartburg (Super Lorna), SHARON KELLY (Super Cherry),
JOHN LAZAR (Cal MacKinney), STUART LANCASTER (Lute),
DEBORAH MCGUIRE (Super Elua)

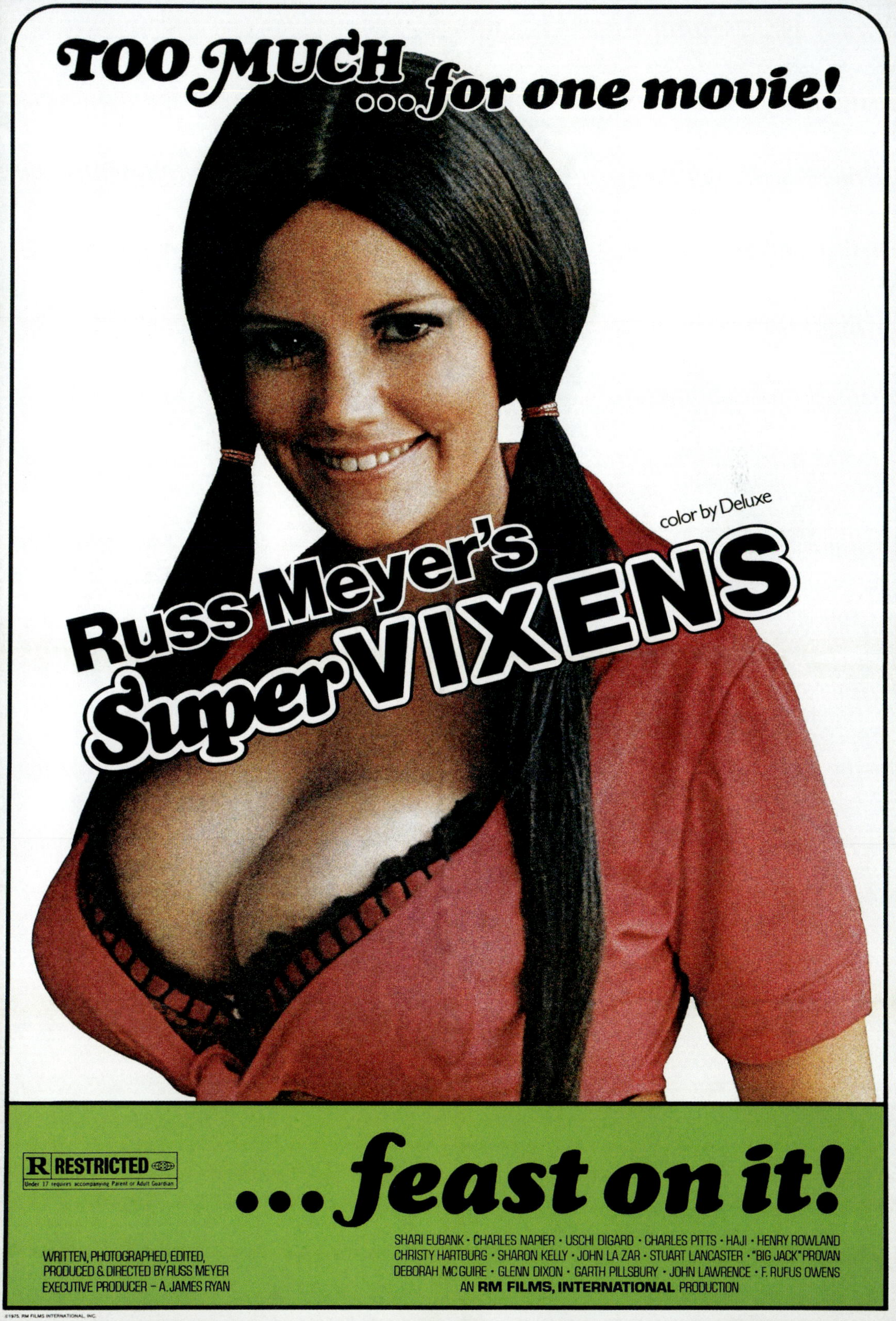
TOO MUCH ...for one movie!
color by Deluxe
Russ Meyer's
SuperVIXENS
R RESTRICTED
Under 17 requires accompanying Parent or Adult Guardian
...feast on it!
WRITTEN, PHOTOGRAPHED, EDITED,
PRODUCED & DIRECTED BY RUSS MEYER
EXECUTIVE PRODUCER – A. JAMES RYAN
SHARI EUBANK · CHARLES NAPIER · USCHI DIGARD · CHARLES PITTS · HAJI · HENRY ROWLAND
CHRISTY HARTBURG · SHARON KELLY · JOHN LA ZAR · STUART LANCASTER · "BIG JACK" PROVAN
DEBORAH MC GUIRE · GLENN DIXON · GARTH PILLSBURY · JOHN LAWRENCE · F. RUFUS OWENS
AN RM FILMS, INTERNATIONAL PRODUCTION
©1975, RM FILMS INTERNATIONAL, INC.

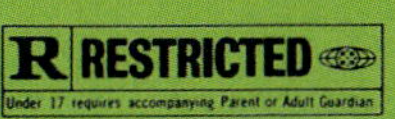

1

"I ask myself if the fucking he has is worth the fucking he gets."

They go by the names of Super Angel, Super Lorna, Super Soul and Super Cherry. The world they live in is a strange and mysterious place tucked away in the Arizona desert. If you saw them there you'd think you were looking at a *Hustler* magazine company picnic at the Duckberg junkyard. These blessed ladies have two striking traits in common. These would, of course, be their blinding set of knock-out melons and a bleeding thirst for good old-fashioned love making. Such a pity that the male element in Meyer's sexual Disneyland is either malevolent, as dumb as they come, or—brace yourselves ladies and gentlemen—cursed with impotence.

The big exception to these atypical archetypal masculine zeroes stomping about Meyer's playground is the

RUSS MEYER In the earlier years of his career, the Oakland, California native born in 1922, worked as a wartime reporter in Europe and a *Playboy* centerfold photographer for the magazine's initial issues. Clearly, these occupations served as preliminary training for the body of work filmmaker Russ Meyer would eventually produce. His directorial debut came in 1959 with his rather mild nudie *The Immoral Mr. Teas.* The picture netted over a million dollars for Meyer and provided him with a foundation for all his subsequent self-financed, self-produced, self-written and self-shot big screen flicks. As a German advertising slogan once put it, "there's always something to see in a Russ Meyer movie." Leading ladies with busts of intergalactic proportion became the calling card of his production company, RM Films International.

For audiences seeking "a more classical Meyer aesthetic," the works of his black and white period including *Lorna* (1964), *Mudhoney*, (1965), *Motor Psycho* (1965) and *Faster, Pussycat! Kill! Kill!* (1966) are highly recommended. *Mudhoney* is by far the picture that the Fellini of the celluloid sex genre endowed with the most artistic merit. After the disproportionate success of *Vixen!* (1968), the bust sizes of his featured females underwent a dramatic inflation, the humor raunched up a notch and the film plots slimmed down significantly. *Megavixens/Cherry, Harry and Raquel!* (1969) was followed by *Beyond the Valley of the Dolls* (1970), *Supervixens* (1975) and his biggest commercial hit *Beneath the Valley of the Ultra-Vixens* (1979). The laurel wreaths won by the hardcore porn industry in the 1980s put an end to his career but he continued to reissue his movies in new formats. The gregarious showman produced both a film autobiography (*The Breast of Russ Meyer*) as well as a written one (*A Clean Breast*). Russ Meyer died in Los Angeles in 2004.

2

1 What beautiful eyes she has… and as long as the men are willing and able, the Supervixens keep smilin'.

2 It's a full moon tonight: Russ Meyer documents a solar eclipse.

3 Climb every mountain! Conquer every peak!

4 Let's get physical! Super Angel (Shari Eubank) puts poor Clint (Charles Pitts) to eternal booty camp.

"Russ Meyer was telling fairytales, in which voyeuristic pleasure was coupled with a cynical take on a seemingly atomized society." *Georg Seeßlen*

"Super Vixen—voluptuous, pure, good, totally giving, self-sacrificing." *Russ Meyer*

simpleminded, honest Joe character that takes the form of Clint Ramsey (Charles Pitts). He's the type of guy who wants nothing more from life than a nice cold beer and a bit of peace and quiet. Clint also happens to possess the skills required to survive this starts with 'f' and rhymes with 'duck' fantasia. The man knows how to repair a car and carries around a monkey wrench you wouldn't want anywhere near your virgin daughters. A guy like this doesn't really need anything more than a gas station, a burger joint and a fine woman like Super Angel (Shari Eubank) to make him happy. She herself could personally while away the livelong day just in bed, getting all revved up for her beau.

However, this missy is a she-devil, who isn't about to let anything, not even a man's career, stand between her and her incessant box-spring mattress acrobatic act. One day, this conflict of interests causes things to get a little out of hand and the ensuing rampage sees a car pulverized to smithereens as well as the intervention of law enforcement officer Harry Sledge (Charles Napier), who steps in and beats some good sense into Clint with his nightstick.

5

Logically, this rough and tough Dirty Harry soon tries to fill the out of commission Clint's place in the sack with the relentless Angel. Harry, nonetheless, makes the mistake of working a double shift that nearly drives him over the edge. Angel reacts to his crude display of neglect by giving the cop a piece of her mind. He snaps and Angel meets with a gruesome demise. The murder is immediately pinned on Clint, who decides to make himself scarce and heads for the endless highway.

What lies ahead are more filling stations, a whole new bunch of wacky characters and countless supervixens waiting to lure the sexually spent hitchhiker from one fiasco to the next. Along his road odyssey, he pulls into "Super Vixen's Oasis" and discovers a pit-stop paradise with a trusty gasoline pump, deluxe cheeseburgers and double-D cups. It would seem that the greater world order has been completely restored as, low and behold, Super Vixen is the spitting image of Super Vixen (Shari Eubank in a double role). Unfortunately, where there are angels, there are sure to be devils close by and that rotten ol' Harry is itching to stick sweet sucker Clint with a few logs of TNT.

5 Old MacDonald had a… Well, let's just say, here we see the benefits of the healthy farming life.

6 What's really behind door No. 3? A "Super Vixens Oasis" or "Bikini Car Wash?" You decide.

7 The Big Bang: Officer Sledge (Charles Napier) and his TNT prosthetic.

"Too much for most men, too much for one movie."

U.S. commercial for the movie

Don't be fooled by the half-baked plotline. Russ Meyer was no storyteller. His tempest of banged-up lead, naked flesh and German military marches were visions of the apocalypse to an American audience. Yet while this Baroque, surreal panorama was the distilled essence of bad taste, the raw worldview it presented was precisely what attested to the filmmaker's great love for his fellow man. Russ Meyer's specialty was his knack for sexually charging every camera shot. Drawing liquid from a tap or even preparing eggs sunny-side-up suddenly became a blatantly obscene act. Perhaps it was therefore only fitting that this "culmination of all wet dreams" read like a children's birthday party for grownups, as did all Meyer's productions.

Frequenters of the "Internet Movie Data Base" will find the most on-target description of the legend that became known as Russ Meyer. "(He) creates his own world in his movies and invites you to visit. And while I may not want to live there, I sure do like to visit!"

SH

6

7

TAXI DRIVER

1975 – USA – 113 MIN.

GENRE

DRAMA

DIRECTOR

MARTIN SCORSESE

SCREENPLAY

PAUL SCHRADER

DIRECTOR OF PHOTOGRAPHY

MICHAEL CHAPMAN

EDITING

TOM ROLF, MELVIN SHAPIRO,
MARCIA LUCAS (Editing Supervisor)

MUSIC

BERNARD HERRMANN

PRODUCTION

JULIA PHILLIPS, MICHAEL PHILLIPS for BILL/PHILLIPS,
COLUMBIA PICTURES CORPORATION

STARRING

ROBERT DE NIRO (Travis Bickle), CYBILL SHEPHERD (Betsy),
JODIE FOSTER (Iris), HARVEY KEITEL (Sport), ALBERT BROOKS (Tom),
PETER BOYLE (Wizard), MARTIN SCORSESE (Passenger),
STEVEN PRINCE (Andy the Gun Dealer),
DIAHNNE ABBOTT (Candy Saleswoman), VICTOR ARGO (Melio)

IFF CANNES 1976

GOLDEN PALM for BEST FILM (Martin Scorsese)

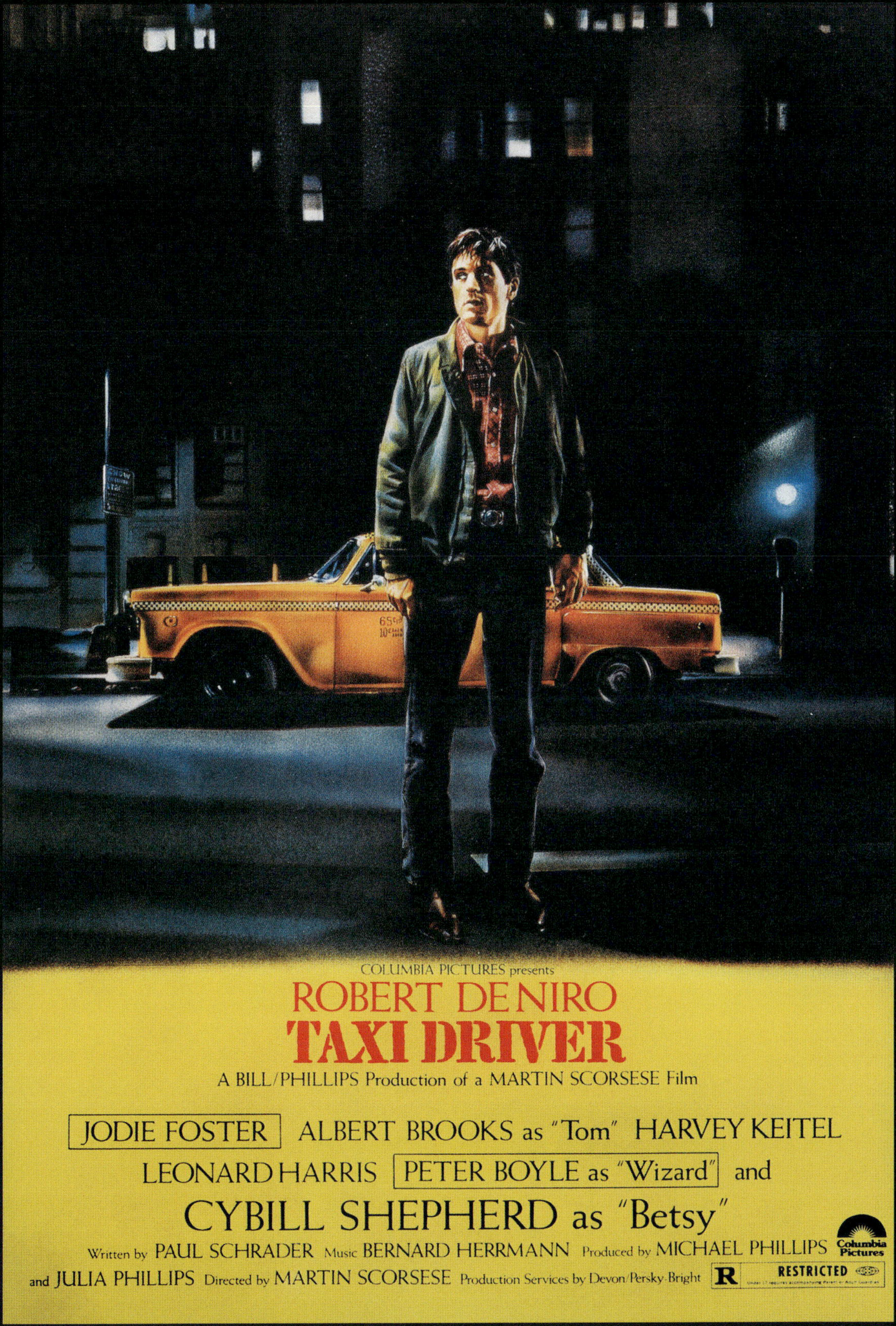

COLUMBIA PICTURES presents

ROBERT DE NIRO

TAXI DRIVER

A BILL/PHILLIPS Production of a MARTIN SCORSESE Film

JODIE FOSTER ALBERT BROOKS as "Tom" HARVEY KEITEL

LEONARD HARRIS PETER BOYLE as "Wizard" and

CYBILL SHEPHERD as "Betsy"

Written by PAUL SCHRADER Music BERNARD HERRMANN Produced by MICHAEL PHILLIPS and JULIA PHILLIPS Directed by MARTIN SCORSESE Production Services by Devon/Persky-Bright

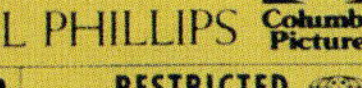

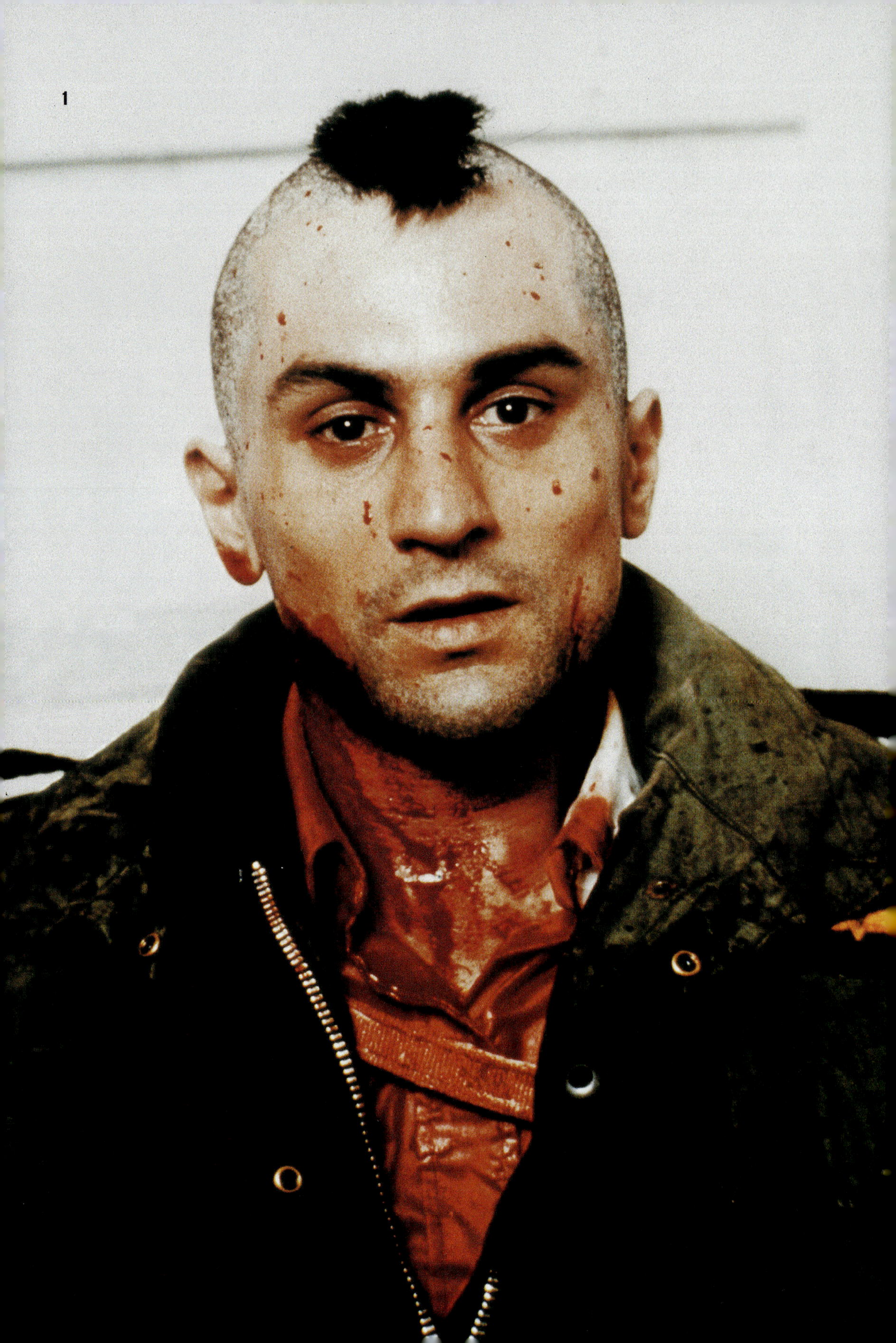

1

The restless, metallic strokes of the musical theme in the opening sequence say it all: this film is a threat. A rising steam cloud hangs over the street and covers the screen in white. As if out of nowhere, a yellow cab penetrates the eerie wall of steam and smoke, gliding through in slow motion. The background music abruptly ends atonally; the ethereal taxi disappears, the cloud closing up behind it. Two dark eyes appear in close-up, accompanied by a gentle jazz theme. In the flickering light of the colorful street lamps they wander from side to side, as if observing the surroundings. They are the eyes of Travis Bickle (Robert De Niro), a New York taxi driver who will become an avenging angel.

Even at the premiere in 1976, *Taxi Driver* split the critics. Some saw the main character as a disturbed soul who revels in his role as savior of a young prostitute, for whom he kills three shady characters in an excessively bloody rampage, an act for which the press fetes him as a hero. Others looked more closely and detected a skillfully stylized film language in the melancholy images and a common urban sociopath behind the figure of the madman Travis Bickle: "On every street, in every city, there's a

BERNARD HERRMANN He made a guest appearance in Hitchcock's *The Man Who Knew Too Much* (1956) as the conductor on the podium of the London Symphony, practically playing himself. He also wrote the music for the film. Born in New York on June 29, 1911, it was Bernard Herrmann who gave a number of film classics the final push towards immortality. He began working for radio, and then moved on to film, collaborating with Alfred Hitchcock, Orson Welles, François Truffaut, Brian De Palma, and Martin Scorsese to name but a few. He gave films like *Vertigo* (1958), *Psycho* (1960), *North by Northwest* (1959), *Citizen Kane* (1941), *The Magnificent Ambersons* (1942), *Fahrenheit 451* (1966), and *Taxi Driver* (1975) an unmistakable musical face, an aura of tonality. No one used the orchestra as eclectically as Herrmann. He could make it sound conservative and classical, or send it into strange tonal regions in which the strings, accompanied by sonorous, dark horns, imitated the sounds of swinging metal wires.
Herrmann was fascinated by the sinister romantic literature of the Brontë sisters and by Melville's *Moby-Dick*. The sea with its elemental force was an inspiration for the scores of his compositions. He could hear and compose the rising and falling of deep waters. Herrmann was not an affable man, perhaps because he was too much of an artist. He was known for his irascible and perverse behavior. He fell out of favor with Hitchcock during work on *Torn Curtain* (1966). He remained an artist through and through while working on his last soundtrack. He finished it on the day before his death on December 24, 1975. It was the music to *Taxi Driver*.

2

nobody who dreams of being somebody," reads one of the film posters.

Travis can't sleep at night. To earn a few cents he becomes a taxi driver. He'll drive anytime and anywhere, he says in his interview. He will even enter the neighborhoods his colleagues avoid at all costs—the districts with either too little or too much light, in which street gangs loiter around and teenage prostitutes wait for punters under bright neon lights. Travis is given the job. He and his taxi become one and the catastrophe takes its course.

"Martin Scorsese's *Taxi Driver* is a homage to home from a homeless man; a New York Western, with a midnight cowboy cruising the canyons in a shabby yellow cab." *Der Spiegel*

1 Robert De Niro in *The Last of the Mohicans?* Call central casting, quick!

2 Soldier of fortune at a buck a mile: Ex-Marine Travis Bickle, at war with New York.

3 Talk to the hand: Travis helps stamp out violent crime.

4 This screen ain't big enough for the two of us: Both pimp (Harvey Keitel) and taxi driver are used to getting their own way.

Like Travis, the audience gazes out of the taxi into the night. Rarely was New York depicted as impressively. The camera style switches between half-documentary and subjective takes. Bernard Herrmann's suggestive music, which accompanies the film, lends it an acoustic structure, creating a unique combination of image and sound. The taxi driving becomes nothing less than a metaphor of film.

Travis' attempt to build a romantic relationship with campaign assistant Betsy (Cybill Shepherd) fails. He can neither express himself, nor his feelings, which is why in the end he turns to the gun. Isolated and aimless, he wanders through the city. Travis' story resembles the yellow taxi cab that sliced through the cloud of smoke in the opening sequence. He too emerges out of nowhere, briefly appears in the night light of the city, and vanishes again into nothingness.

Travis is no hero, even if many applauded the brutal rampage at the premiere. Violence is naturally an important theme of the film, but the violence is not merely physical, but social. Travis embodies a person who has lost himself in the big city. Robert De Niro gave this type a face and an unmistakable body.

5 Jodie Foster as the child prostitute, Iris. Foster's older sister stood in as her body double for the more mature shots.

6 The facts of life: The outside world does not always reflect the inner world.

7 Remember the Alamo: Election campaigner Betsy (Cybill Shepherd) is the object of Travis's desire.

"An utterly strange, disturbing, alarming and fascinating film. Syncretic and glamorous, it is a lurking reptile that changes color like a chameleon; a synthetic amalgam of conflicting influences, tendencies and metaphysical ambitions, raised to the power of a myth: comical, edgy, hysterical." *Frankfurter Rundschau*

Scorsese is known for creating his films on paper. He draws them like sketches in a storyboard, and time and again he shows that images are his true language. The screenplay was the work of Paul Schrader, and marked the first close collaboration between two film-obsessed men. The scene in which Travis stands before the mirror shirtless, clutching his revolver and picks a fight with himself is unforgettable: "You talkin' to me? Well I'm the only one here. Who do you think you're talking to?" The scene has been cited over and over, but the original remains unattainable. It is a modern classic. SR

7

BARRY LYNDON

1975 – GREAT BRITAIN – 184 MIN.

GENRE

LITERARY ADAPTATION, HISTORICAL FILM

DIRECTOR

STANLEY KUBRICK

SCREENPLAY

STANLEY KUBRICK, based on the novel of the same name
by WILLIAM MAKEPEACE THACKERAY

DIRECTOR OF PHOTOGRAPHY

JOHN ALCOTT

EDITING

TONY LAWSON

MUSIC

LEONARD ROSENMAN, JOHANN SEBASTIAN BACH,
WOLFGANG AMADEUS MOZART, FRANZ SCHUBERT,
GEORG FRIEDRICH HÄNDEL, ANTONIO VIVALDI

PRODUCTION

STANLEY KUBRICK for HAWK FILMS, PEREGRINE

STARRING

RYAN O'NEAL (Barry Lyndon/Redmond Barry), MARISA BERENSON (Lady Lyndon),
HARDY KRÜGER (Captain Potzdorf), PATRICK MAGEE (Chevalier de Balibari),
STEVEN BERKOFF (Lord Ludd), GAY HAMILTON (Nora Brady),
MARIE KEAN (Barry's Mother), DIANA KÖRNER (Lieschen),
MURRAY MELVIN (Reverend Runt), FRANK MIDDLEMASS (Sir Charles Reginald Lyndon)

ACADEMY AWARDS 1976

OSCARS for BEST CINEMATOGRAPHY (John Alcott),
BEST ADAPTED SCORE (Leonard Rosenman),
BEST ART DIRECTION (Ken Adam, Roy Walker, Vernon Dixon),
and BEST COSTUMES (Ulla-Britt Söderlund, Milena Canonero)

BARRY LYNDON
a film by
STANLEY KUBRICK
RYAN O'NEAL and
MARISA BERENSON
in BARRY LYNDON
with PATRICK MAGEE · HARDY KRUGER
DIANA KOERNER · GAY HAMILTON
Written for the screen, produced and directed by STANLEY KUBRICK
Based on the novel by WILLIAM MAKEPEACE THACKERAY
Music adapted and conducted by LEONARD ROSENMAN
Executive Producer JAN HARLAN
from Warner Bros. A Warner Communications Company
ORIGINAL SOUNDTRACK AVAILABLE ON WARNER BROS. RECORDS AND TAPES
PG
PARENTAL GUIDANCE SUGGESTED

1

"It was in the reign of George III that the aforesaid personages lived and quarrelled; good or bad, handsome or ugly, rich or poor, they are all equal now."

If Redmond Barry (Ryan O'Neal) hadn't fallen in love with his cousin (Gay Hamilton), his life might have been very different. As it happened, however, he had to fight a duel with an army officer who'd been promised the young lady's hand in marriage. And if Barry hadn't shot the officer, he wouldn't have had to flee his home village in Ireland; which is why he ended up fighting his way across Europe, first in the service of the British army, then for the Prussians. Barry's life is not in his own hands. Yet those who control him also help him, inadvertently, to climb the career ladder to a fairly dizzying height.

He has a talent for being in the right place at the right time. As a reward for saving a high-ranking officer on the battlefield, he is given a position with the Berlin police. Ordered to spy on an Irish aristocrat, he reveals the plot to his compatriot—who repays the compliment by teaching him the tricks of his trade. Barry learns the craft of card playing and becomes a familiar face at the royal courts of Europe. When he has acquired everything but a good name and a wife, he meets Lady Lyndon (Marisa Berenson). The marriage brings him money, land and property, but he squanders it all. At the end of the film, Barry is more or less back where he started: at a gambling table, but now minus his leg, his son, his wife, and his fortune.

We witness the rise and fall of an opportunist, filmed in breathtaking images. *Barry Lyndon* is a visual masterpiece, perhaps the most beautiful movie ever made. To see it in the cinema is like taking a walk through a gallery filled

PAINTING AND FILM The beginnings of film are inseparable from the photography and literature of the 19th century. Yet the medium is most intimately related to painting. Even in the earliest days, filmmakers, like painters, frequently thematized their own work, the processes of creation, and the cinematic medium itself. The very first filmmakers, for example, appeared in front of their own cameras in slyly self-referential slapstick scenes.

Time and again, directors have taken their cue from painting, and not (as one might expect) from the more closely related medium of photography. In *Barry Lyndon* (1975), for example, Stanley Kubrick created scenes that seemed like paintings come alive, like *tableaux vivants*, an aristocratic pastime popular in the 18th century (described, for example, by Goethe in his novel *Elective Affinities*). In *Passion* (1982), Jean-Luc Godard made even more direct use of the Old Masters as an example and inspiration.

In turn, the invention of motion pictures had its effect on painting. First photography, then film robbed the medium of its previous task—or freed it from the burden—of providing a close approximation of external reality. The painters went on to develop new formal languages, such as Cubism and Futurism. Some film directors also paint: David Lynch, Federico Fellini and Akira Kurosawa are examples that come to mind.

2

1 His troops go marching on: Kubrick based his film on the Thackeray novel *The Luck of Barry Lyndon* (1844), but replaced the boastful first-person narrator with an omniscient commentator.

2 Take me, I'm yours: Barry Lyndon (Ryan O'Neil) enlists with the armed forces after losing his horse and his money.

3 Location scout: Kubrick found most of the untouched landscapes he needed in Ireland, but several scenes were shot in Great Britain and the East German city of Potsdam.

4 Going to great lengths: For Kubrick's painstaking reconstruction of the 18th century, the costumes alone took almost a year and a half. Bob Mackie was unfortunately unavailable.

"*Barry Lyndon* is not a warm film—Kubrick's never are—but it is so glorious to look at, so intelligent in its conception and execution, that one comes to respond to it on Kubrick's terms, which severely avoid obvious laughs and sentiment with the exception of two or three scenes."

The New York Times

with works by Gainsborough and Reynolds. Few directors have ever composed a film with such care: each shot resembles an oil painting, and the colors are unparalleled in their intensity. The second half of the 18th century has probably never been resurrected in such detail. *Barry Lyndon* is the ultimate historical epic. In most costume dramas, the characters carry the cloaks and daggers of olden days, but their manners and morals are those of the 20th century. *Barry Lyndon* creates its own world: here, the past is indeed another country, gone for ever yet still alive; and the first half of the film, especially, is notable for its quiet wit.

In creating a film that resembles a series of tableaux, Stanley Kubrick has chosen a form that fits the content: superficiality and the power of the image in an ossified society. One of his main formal techniques is a gradually retreating camera, a kind of reverse zoom effect, as if the viewer were observing a detail of the picture before walking back slowly to gain an impression of the whole. Only a few times does the camera actually move through the pictorial space: namely, whenever the film is dealing not with gestures and rituals, but with the naked struggle for existence. Examples include Barry's boxing match with the strongest man in the unit, or the company's march into the muzzle flash from the muskets of the French army.

In the final shot, the date "1789" appears. Before this time, the ideal of individuality had not yet developed; clothing, for example, was merely an indication of social status, and not an expression of personality. Like a peacock spreading its tail, the army officer puts on his uniform: his rank—and his wallet—is enough to ensure he will win the hand of Barry's cousin. From now on, Barry

5

“Kubrick’s latest is, however, extremely beautiful. It is not only the superb photography that delights the eye. Most remarkable is the atmospheric composition of scene after scene, which reflects the golden glow and subtle moods of a Reynolds canvas. Eighteenth-century Ireland and Germany seem to live again.”

Herald Tribune

5 A discerning eye: Though Kubrick's film might appear cold and forbidding, Scorsese described it as one of the most soulful he had ever seen.

6 We have lift off! Kubrick filmed the interiors without artificial light, using a fast lens specially manufactured for NASA satellite photography. Lady Lyndon's (Marisa Berenson) hairstylist demanded it.

will single-mindedly pursue his goal: riches and reputation. Yet although he will eventually marry the beautiful Lady Lyndon, the off-screen narrator informs us that his wife was of no more importance to him than the carpets and paintings that formed the backdrop to his life.

A duel sends him on his way to wealth and fame, and a duel throws him back out of it again. At the end, Barry is standing in a barn, face-to-face with his own stepson. Kubrick devoted six minutes to this showdown, and it has the sober quality of a ritual. Yet we suddenly realize how terrified the stepson is, as he vomits for fear of his life. It's a moment of naked and public emotion that Barry would never permit himself. But his time has now passed: there's no place left in the world for fellows like him. He probably went back to Ireland, declares the narrator; but it's said he turned up in Europe again—as a gambler. This time, however, without success.

NM

DOG DAY AFTERNOON

1975 – USA – 124 MIN.

GENRE

DRAMA

DIRECTOR

SIDNEY LUMET

SCREENPLAY

FRANK PIERSON, based on a newspaper extract
by P. F. KLUGE and THOMAS MOORE

DIRECTOR OF PHOTOGRAPHY

VICTOR J. KEMPER

EDITING

DEDE ALLEN

PRODUCTION

MARTIN BREGMAN, MARTIN ELFAND
for ARTISTS ENTERTAINMENT COMPLEX

STARRING

AL PACINO (Sonny), PENELOPE ALLEN (Sylvia),
JOHN CAZALE (Sal), SULLY BOYAR (Mulvaney),
BEULAH GARRICK (Margaret), CAROL KANE (Jenny),
CHARLES DURNING (Moretti), LANCE HENRIKSEN (Murphy),
GARY SPRINGER (Stevie), JAMES BRODERICK (Sheldon),
JOHN MARRIOTT (Howard), CHRIS SARANDON (Leon)

ACADEMY AWARDS 1976

OSCAR for BEST SCREENPLAY (Frank Pierson)

AL PACINO

An Artists Entertainment Complex, Inc. Production

DOG DAY AFTERNOON

Also Starring JOHN CAZALE · JAMES BRODERICK and CHARLES DURNING as Moretti

Screenplay by FRANK PIERSON · Produced by MARTIN BREGMAN and MARTIN ELFAND · Directed by SIDNEY LUMET · Film Editor DEDE ALLEN

TECHNICOLOR® From WARNER BROS. A WARNER COMMUNICATIONS COMPANY

BARBER
SHOP
BARBER
SHOP

"The audience is interested in you, Sonny!"—"Yeah! We're hot entertainment, right?"

An unbearably hot afternoon in Brooklyn. Those who don't have to work today are either catching a bit of shuteye at the park or indulging in an excursion to Coney Island. Stray dogs ransack the trash set out on the sidewalk, street laborers battle with heavy machinery in the middle of chaotic traffic, and security guard Howard (John Marriott) is lowering the American flag in front of the First Brooklyn Savings Bank. Soon it will be closing time, and only three more customers manage to squeeze their way through into the branch before its doors are locked up for the evening.

Well, "customers" is perhaps a poor choice of words, for Sonny (Al Pacino), Sal (John Cazale) and Stevie (Gary Springer) are three amateur crooks bent on emptying the bank's coffers. But moments after they set foot inside the building, things begin to go incredibly wrong. Stevie gets weak in the knees and tries to bolt. The tellers are all either making trips to the little girls' room or moaning about the heat. Worst of all, it turns out that the hot tip about the teller desks being full was way off the mark. There isn't more than 1,000 bucks to be found behind non-vaulted walls. Sonny manically attempts to salvage this bust of a predicament. He disables the security camera, scavenges what slim pickings he can and comforts the silently brooding Sal while simultaneously holding the increasingly blasé bank employees in check. Like a whirling dervish, he skates across the bank's slick floor. In just a matter of seconds, the three guys will have successfully carried out the heist. Suddenly, the telephone jumps off the ringer. The call is for Sonny—Detective Moretti (Charles Durning), commanding officer of the special police squadron sent in to "neutralize" the criminals is on the other end of the line. It would appear that the three would-be hoodlums are bang in the middle of a sprung mousetrap.

A show-business veteran, Sidney Lumet got his start in the industry at the tender age of four by acting in a radio show, and rapidly racked up a line of theatrical and live television credits. He opens *Dog Day Afternoon* with a twenty-minute sequence that flips back and forth between two plotlines and physical realms. On the one hand, Lumet shows us the mundane, interior world of the bank, which plays like an intimate theater piece, featuring characters enslaved by spatial and temporal boundaries, which prevent them from dodging the mayhem of the imminent danger. Conversely, we are thrust outside to the sweltering hot streets, where the pressures of the inner world are given free expression, so to speak. Here, we are

BIG SCREEN BANK ROBBERY The bank heist is a stock scenario with endless variations. This film genre lends itself to the most adrenaline-charged tales of cops and robbers, crafty alarm systems and more often even wilier means of trickery. Criminals will risk landing behind bars for a chance at endless riches. Also, because they don't swindle the "little guy," this brand of crook has been popularly deified as the crusader of the common man. *Bonnie and Clyde*, the beloved gangster duo, who financed their romantic escapades with foolhardy robberies, are probably the most oft-cited example. In 1967, Arthur Penn paid cinematic homage to them with his brilliant film of the same name, starring Warren Beatty and Faye Dunaway in the title roles. In the end, however, the bank robber often proves to be no logistical genius. Both Robert De Niro in *Heat* (1995, directed by Michael Mann) and Jeremy Irons in the third *Die Hard* instalment, *Die Hard: With a Vengeance* (1995, directed by John McTiernan) fell victim to this flaw. The four Danish filmmakers Lars von Trier, Thomas Vinterberg, Søren Kragh-Jacobsen and Kristian Levring garnered much media attention for their New Year's Eve of 1999–2000 experiment entitled *D-dag – Instruktørene* (2000), in which four individual stories, broadcast simultaneously on four separate TV stations, wove a tale of bank robbery planned for the last night of the year. The viewer at home could change channels at will, thus enabling each spectator to become an amateur film editor.

2

1 Ready, aim, fire! The police, the FBI and the press have got the robbers surrounded and they'll shoot off their cameras and guns as soon as they get the chance.

2 Kicking and screaming: Moretti (Charles Durning) tries to persuade the gang to leave peacefully.

3 Break the bank: Branch manager Mulvaney (Sully Boyar) had better watch himself because Sonny and Sal (John Cazale) are not about to compromise.

4 Inspiration for Norma Rae: Sylvia has the guts to stand up for her colleagues and tell Sonny to watch his mouth!

exposed to the details of everyday life, which Lumet sketches for us in the documentary-style opening credits. Although the city is still in a deep slumber, within minutes the general public will have transformed itself into a merciless beast fuelled by curiosity. When the police show up on the scene, hundreds of entertainment-hungry spectators get as close to the blocked-off action as they can. Helicopters hover over the street mob and camera crews in search of the perfect shot run around like headless chicken. What started off as a dilettantish, rookie job explodes into a full-fledged media extravaganza.

This twist of fate appears to act initially as a windfall to Sonny. As he conducts negotiations with Moretti on the street in front of the bank about procuring a getaway vehicle, he quickly wins the sympathies of the crowd. To them, he represents the abased common man who stands up to the unjust system. Moretti can do nothing more than watch as Sonny taunts the rooftop snipers, throws wads of cash by the fistful to the cheering fans and inspires them to chant shouts of protest. It seems Sonny has found his calling and he readily takes the insanity to new heights: during a live TV news media interview, for instance, he's the one asking the questions—until the station cuts the coverage, that is. Nonetheless, the tide quickly turns on the apparent inundation of support, when Sonny makes public that he needs the loot to pay for his lover Leon's (Chris Sarandon) sex-change operation. Sonny's thieving bravado makes him a hero, but his sexual practices soon sever him from grace and leave him branded a sodomite.

As it were, there's just no way to tune into the ins and outs of Sonny's antics forever. Agent Sheldon (James Broderick), chief of the FBI, has been following the chaotic chain of events with venomous eyes. When the getaway car that's supposed to transport Sonny, Sal and the hostages safely to the airport finally pulls up, robbers and bank employees alike believe that a happy ending is in store for the Robin Hood-like crusaders. Of course, after the TV crews have stopped rolling tape and the spectators have left the arena, the FBI agents show these clowns what they're really made of. They implement their assault at lightning speed, and Sonny's last glance at the camera lets us know that this is exactly what he'd been reckoning on all along. EP

"Pacino has an utterly pure and unspoiled talent, an absolute feeling for truth. He couldn't act badly if he tried." *steadycam*

THREE DAYS OF THE CONDOR

1975 – USA – 117 MIN.

GENRE

SPY FILM

DIRECTOR

SYDNEY POLLACK

SCREENPLAY

LORENZO SEMPLE JR., DAVID RAYFIEL, based on the novel *SIX DAYS OF THE CONDOR* by JAMES GRADY

DIRECTOR OF PHOTOGRAPHY

OWEN ROIZMAN

EDITING

DON GUIDICE

MUSIC

DAVE GRUSIN

PRODUCTION

STANLEY SCHNEIDER for DINO DE LAURENTIIS CINEMATOGRAFICA, WILDWOOD ENTERPRISES, PARAMOUNT PICTURES

STARRING

ROBERT REDFORD (Joe Turner), FAYE DUNAWAY (Kathy Hale), CLIFF ROBERTSON (Higgins), MAX VON SYDOW (Joubert), JOHN HOUSEMAN (Mr. Wabash), ADDISON POWELL (Atwood), WALTER MCGINN (Sam Barber), TINA CHEN (Janice), MICHAEL KANE (S. W. Wicks), DON MCHENRY (Dr. Lappe)

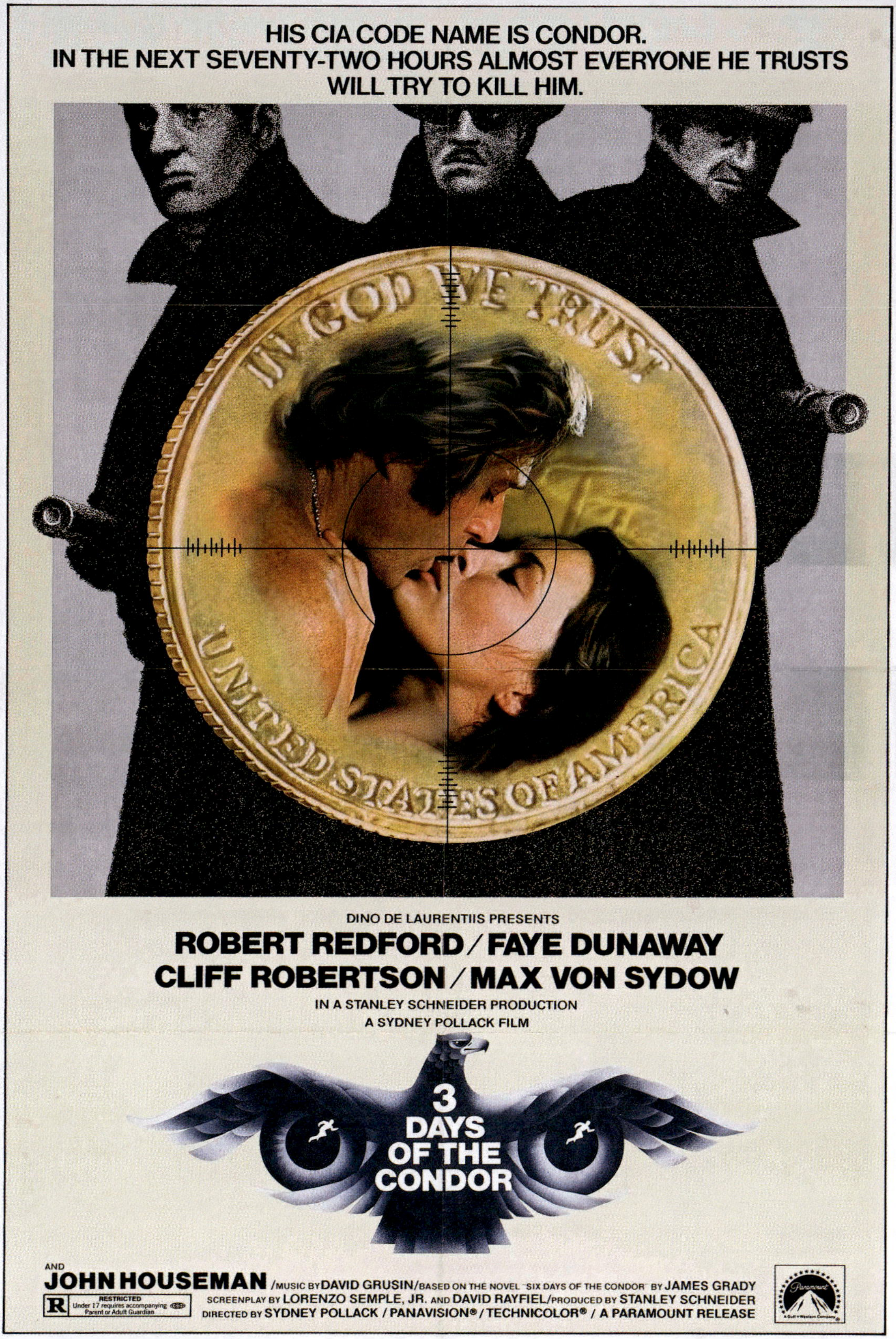

HIS CIA CODE NAME IS CONDOR.
IN THE NEXT SEVENTY-TWO HOURS ALMOST EVERYONE HE TRUSTS
WILL TRY TO KILL HIM.

IN GOD WE TRUST
UNITED STATES OF AMERICA

DINO DE LAURENTIIS PRESENTS
ROBERT REDFORD / FAYE DUNAWAY
CLIFF ROBERTSON / MAX VON SYDOW
IN A STANLEY SCHNEIDER PRODUCTION
A SYDNEY POLLACK FILM

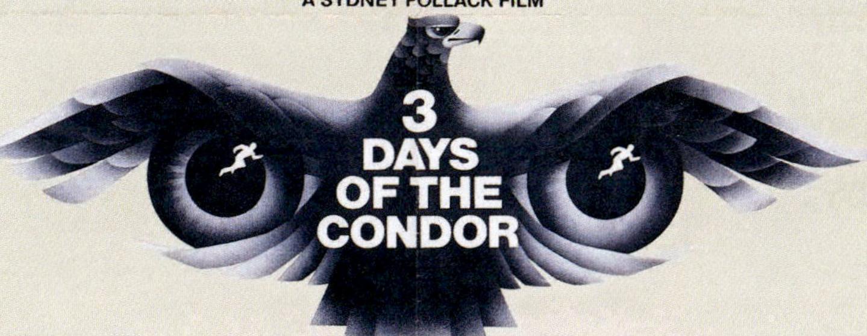

AND
JOHN HOUSEMAN / MUSIC BY DAVID GRUSIN / BASED ON THE NOVEL "SIX DAYS OF THE CONDOR" BY JAMES GRADY
SCREENPLAY BY LORENZO SEMPLE, JR. AND DAVID RAYFIEL / PRODUCED BY STANLEY SCHNEIDER
DIRECTED BY SYDNEY POLLACK / PANAVISION® / TECHNICOLOR® / A PARAMOUNT RELEASE

R RESTRICTED Under 17 requires accompanying Parent or Adult Guardian

1

"You know, you guys are amazing. You think not getting caught in a lie is the same thing as telling the truth!"

The day starts off like any other at the New York "American Literary Historical Society." The small office staff sift through the details of the works they've been studying, run checks on the computers and discuss their findings. It's what you'd describe as a rather relaxed setting. The younger employees are chummy with one another and readily cover for co-worker Joe Turner (Robert Redford) when a supervisor notices that he is running late for the umpteenth time.

A few hours later, a very different atmosphere will dominate this office. All of its staff will be dead, slaughtered by a sort of SWAT team who manage to gain entry into the

FAYE DUNAWAY A starlet beyond good and evil, Florida native Faye Dunaway has breathed life into some of Hollywood's most unforgettable female roles. Whether as the pensive, dissatisfied photographer Kathy Hale, who willingly jeopardizes the course her entire life for the Condor, the hard-as-nails insurance fraud investigator Vicki Anderson in *The Thomas Crown Affair* (1968) or *Film Noir femme fatale* Evelyn Mulwray in Roman Polanski's *Chinatown* (1974), Faye Dunaway has proven time and again that she is indeed worthy of the Best Actress Oscar she won for her role as the no-nonsense TV producer Diana Christensen in *Network* (1976).

Born in 1941, this military officer's daughter had already completed her theater studies and made numerous stage appearances before achieving big screen stardom. Her breakthrough came with her third film, *Bonnie and Clyde* (1967), Arthur Penn's study in glamor and violence about the Barrow gang. The picture earned Dunaway her first chance at an Oscar. Another came in 1974 with Polanski's L.A. mystery *Chinatown.*

It's no secret that Dunaway has a volatile reputation that precedes her. At the time of filming, talk of Dunaway and Polanski's caustic disputes on the set of *Chinatown* was a Hollywood buzz topic.

While the majority of her roles have captured the attention of world audiences, not all of these are rated out-and-out triumphs. Her uncompromising and legendary portrayal of Joan Crawford in the unauthorized biography *Mommie Dearest* (1981) was savaged by the critics. After taking several second string roles in the 1980s, Dunaway won back much prestige with her work in pieces like *Arizona Dream* (1992) and *Don Juan De Marco* (1995). To this day, Faye Dunaway remains an undisputed star. The documentary *Faye*, about her life and career, was released in 2024.

2

facility despite all the hardnosed security measures. For this seemingly ordinary literary society was in fact a secret division of the CIA. Only Joe Turner, codename "Condor," escapes the massacre unscathed. He's out picking up lunch for the entire office and, against regulations, he takes the shortcut through the back entrance and is thereby spared the awful fate of his team mates.

Upon his return, he discovers the gruesome bloodbath. Fearing for his life, the Condor grabs a gun hidden in a desk drawer and takes flight. Submerged in the crowd, he scans each and every face he sees out on the streets of New York, attempting to discern whether there's a psychopath among these pedestrians. At a public telephone booth he contacts CIA headquarters and informs them that his section has been hit. His superiors arrange to meet him at the Ansonia Hotel on Broadway. Turner is apprehensive and only agrees to show up when he is assured that his close friend and school chum, Sam Barber (Walter McGinn), will also be present. His ominous gut instinct is confirmed upon arriving at the spot where Sam is waiting. From out of nowhere, a second unidentified man opens fire on the two friends. Turner shoots back, slightly "damaging" the perpetrator, who has mortally wounded Sam. In an act of blind panic, the Condor kidnaps a random woman and manages to flee. Under duress, she drives him back to her apartment, which he uses as his hideout. Once there, he sees a report on the TV news about the incident at the Ansonia Hotel, but the media depiction distorts the details of the crime. Turner now knows that he can rely on no one other than himself. Nonetheless, over their three days together, his hostage, photographer Kathy Hale (Faye Dunaway), will prove to be an invaluable confidante.

"Espionage drama about the parasite politics of the CIA, which sets spies to catch its own spies." *Sight and Sound*

1 Special delivery: After witnessing Turner (Robert Redford) bump off a postman, Kathy Hale (Faye Dunaway) succumbs to her kidnapper's steely charms.

2 To tell the truth: Joe Turner's tales may be larger than life, but before long Kathy will believe the CIA agent's every word.

3 Executive tricycle: Joe Turner, a man of the people, en route to the office.

4 Too close for comfort? Joe Turner doesn't need a gun to have his way with hostage Kathy.

4

5 A cold-blooded killer: Hitman Joubert (Max von Sydow) leaves his heart at home when he's on the job.

6 Official business: The masterminds of the literary society's massacre are top-ranking U.S. federal officers.

7 The bitter taste of betrayal: Turner realizes who's behind the massacre.

In a 1975 interview with the magazine *Film Comment*, Sydney Pollack described his film *Three Days of the Condor* as an examination of the destructive potential of overblown mistrust. It's undeniably successful. As soon as the light-hearted kidder, Joe Turner (whose name is a tribute to one of John le Carré's novels) falls victim to the wave of paranoia brought on by the atrocities he's survived, the audience is glued to his side in what becomes an utterly suspenseful and action-packed production. Its intrigue lies in the killers' ability to disappear into the world of everyday life. The woman with the stroller, the guy in the elevator or the mailman might all present a deadly menace—and two of them actually do. In a blind sea of millions of people, Joe Turner can't lower his guard. Even trusted work colleagues seem to present a threat to his life.

Cinematographer Owen Roizman depicts Turner's constant frenzy by condensing the cinemascope format for exterior shots with a long focal length lens that deftly plays up the claustrophobia of the skyscrapers and imposing stationary objects. Turner appears to be visually caged in, and the sense of entrapment spills over onto the audience. Though the film's subtext screams "Watergate," the scandal was still to break when the shooting of *Condor* began. According to director Pollack's own words, "we thought it was a really exaggerated idea until we started to read the newspaper headlines while we were in the middle of shooting."

HK

"The director, Sydney Pollack, doesn't have a knack for action pulp; he gets some tension going in this expensive spy thriller, but there's no real fun in it." *The New Yorker*

THE ROCKY HORROR PICTURE SHOW

1975 – USA – 100 MIN.

GENRE

MUSICAL, SPOOF

DIRECTOR

JIM SHARMAN

SCREENPLAY

RICHARD O'BRIEN, JIM SHARMAN, based on the stage play *THE ROCKY HORROR SHOW* by RICHARD O'BRIEN

DIRECTOR OF PHOTOGRAPHY

PETER SUSCHITZKY

EDITING

GRAEME CLIFFORD

MUSIC

RICHARD O'BRIEN, RICHARD HARTLEY

PRODUCTION

MICHAEL WHITE for 20TH CENTURY FOX

STARRING

TIM CURRY (Frank N. Furter), SUSAN SARANDON (Janet Weiss), BARRY BOSTWICK (Brad Majors), RICHARD O'BRIEN (Riff Raff), PATRICIA QUINN (Magenta), NELL CAMPBELL (Columbia), JONATHAN ADAMS (Doctor Everett Von Scott), PETER HINWOOD (Rocky), MEAT LOAF (Eddie), CHARLES GRAY (Criminologist)

He's the hero – that's right, the hero!!

THE ROCKY HORROR PICTURE SHOW

20th Century-Fox Presents
A LOU ADLER - MICHAEL WHITE PRODUCTION
THE ROCKY HORROR PICTURE SHOW
Starring TIM CURRY • SUSAN SARANDON • BARRY BOSTWICK
Original Musical Play, Music and Lyrics by RICHARD O'BRIEN
Screenplay by JIM SHARMAN and RICHARD O'BRIEN • Associate Producer JOHN GOLDSTONE
Executive Producer LOU ADLER • Produced by MICHAEL WHITE
Directed by JIM SHARMAN
Musical Direction and Arrangements by RICHARD HARTLEY
Production Services by RUBY SERVICE COMPANY

R RESTRICTED
Under 17 requires accompanying Parent or Adult Guardian

20th CENTURY FOX

1

"In just seven days, I can make you a man!"

If indeed the *Rocky Horror Picture Show* continues to glow in the minds of world audiences to this day, be assured that film critics of the time had little to do with lighting its eternal flame. Quite the contrary, my pretties. When the movie was beamed down to terrestrial theaters in 1975, the scathing verdict of these professional jurists was unanimous—the celluloid version was nothing more than a sorry adaptation of the London underground stage's surprise hit. According to the reviews, this fine specimen of big screen meningitis belly-flopped between gratuitous displays of histrionics and flawlessly unamusing musical numbers, which managed to completely obscure what little plot its 100 minutes had to offer. The outcome seemed clear. The film was doomed to the depths of oblivion in the vaulted hell of some dark, damp film archiving facility. At most, it would be a poor excuse for a footnote in camp and trash history.

Then something miraculous happened. During *Rocky's* midnight showing at the 8th Street Playhouse in New York, the owner of the movie house began to rant and rave at the screen (allegedly he shouted at Janet, "buy an umbrella, you cheap bitch!"). His words infected the audience and the ball was set rolling, with comments flowing like the downpour of rain. Spectators returned in droves armed with an ample supply of rice and water guns. This time, they were ready to take part in the wedding and the storm, dropping their ironic commentary with increased fanaticism. The enthusiasm climaxed with moviegoers dressing up like their favorite characters, be it Frank N. Furter, Riff Raff or Magenta. The complacent, passive undertaking of watching a film became an interactive black mass. The picture itself was transformed into a blank canvas onto which both the uninhibited and party-crazed could project their most irreverent whims and fancies. Out of the reels of a reproducible mass commodity, indistinguishable in both shape and content, a unique happening was born. No two showings of *The Rocky Horror Picture Show* were fundamentally identical and no action set in stone. The hierarchical fabric of active and passive parties, whether filmmaker and spectator, or producer and consumer had begun to unravel.

THE CULT CLASSIC The more often and more liberally a term is used, the harder it becomes to define. Its semantic essence diminishes with each extension of its meaning. The catchphrase, "cult film" fell victim to the grand mechanisms of movie marketing long ago. How else can one understand the unscrupulous efforts of distributors to deem *American Pie 2* (2001) and dozens of other pictures like it cult classics even prior to their initial release.

Back when it was coined to refer to film, "cult" designated a specific audience reaction, which took the form of an actual "cult following" associated with the film. Whether *Blues Brothers* (1980) inspired costume parties, *Rocky Horror Picture Show* (1975) mayhem, or *Once Upon a Time in the West* (*C'era una volta il West,* 1969) the long duster coat fad, it was the audience's enthusiasm to integrate aspects of these pieces into their pop culture at large that made these pieces attain cult status.

The 1990s were particularly adroit at recognizing the promotional potential of a "cult classic" and proceeded to plant certain contrived elements in actual films and introduce lines of merchandise to accompany theatrical releases. Quentin Tarantino proved he had a remarkable knack for this sort of "cultification" by including some of the most memorable dialog from *Pulp Fiction* (1994) as bonus material on the film's soundtrack album. In no time flat, lines like "I love you, honeybunny, I love you, pumpkin," and "Zed's dead" were being chanted by addicted and adoring fans.

The plot is indeed no more than a light and simple catalyst for the piece's music and spoof aesthetic. Newly engaged lovebirds Brad (Barry Bostwick) and Janet (Susan Sarandon) motor their way to the former's mentor, Dr. Scott (Jonathan Adams). The young killjoy is set on sharing his future plans with the good doctor and getting his blessing. A flat tire and a thunderstorm force the two wholesome (in the biblical sense) Midwesterners to seek help at an old, ominous castle. What awaits them is a colorful cult of creepy-crawlies, who have all gathered to honor the groundbreaking achievements of Dr. Frank N. Furter (Tim Curry), one very "sweet transvestite from transsexual Transylvania." A hunchback butler, a nymphomaniac chambermaid, an inorganically generated He-Man, a frozen solid rock star and even Dr. Scott himself all serve as indicators that this may be an eclectic convention of intergalactic proportion. This proves to be the case when Brad and Janet realize that they have stumbled upon alien life forms who are avidly studying human sexual behavior.

This *Men in Black* style scenario under an altogether different astrological sign never strays from the universe

"Overall most of the jokes that might have seemed jolly fun on stage now appear obvious and even flat. The sparkle's gone." *Variety*

1 Full package and a strand of pearls: Tom Curry as the irreverent Dr. Frank N. Furter.

2 Heart attack: Frank N. Furter catches Rocky (Peter Hinwood) playing doctor with Janet Weiss (Susan Sarandon).

3 Dancing queens …

4 … go cool in the pool.

2

3
4

of cinema and communicates its story through pointedly self-conscious movie references. As the sumptuous, larger-than-life lips vocalize to us during the film's opening number *Science Fiction Double Feature*, the entire picture is little more than one colossal tribute to the horror and sci-fi classics of the 1950s. *Rocky* fills its loins with the innuendoes and themes that once breathed life into the genre, managing to play up their original implications while making them relevant to the context of 1975. The film sends its own decade's sensibilities on a collision course with uptight, Cold War propriety. It thus paints a glaring portrait of revolution that has micromanaged its front to sexual fulfillment.

Taking all this into consideration, the film not only echoes in our hearts as a rich ode to bygone Hollywood, with rock songs that have made history in their own right, but also marks the dawn of a new era in what an audience understands to be its role. Motion pictures ceased to exist solely as entities of passive consumption. The door was now wide open to spectators getting up and playing along, reassessing the on-screen action and introducing elements of the piece into their own lives.

MH

6

7

5 Space oddity: When Metropolis meets King Kong at the film's conclusion, Magenta (Patricia Quinn) and brother Riff Raff try to cut through the standing ovation.

6 Torn curtain: Furter and Brad sail to distant shores.

7 Blame it on the bossa nova: Riff Raff leads the castle guests in a most peculiar space conga line. Richard O'Brien, a writer of the stage version, joins in on the "Time Warp."

"But the greatest 'frisson' that *The Rocky Horror Picture Show* has to offer is that it was shot at Bray Studios, site of the decline and fall of Hammer horrors. It's ironically fitting that this bizarre, ill-conceived hybrid should be dancing on the grave of the real British B-movie tradition."

Monthly Film Bulletin

NOVECENTO
1900

1975/76 – FRANCE / ITALY / FRG – 318 MIN.

GENRE

HISTORICAL FILM, EPIC

DIRECTOR

BERNARDO BERTOLUCCI

SCREENPLAY

FRANCO ARCALLI, BERNARDO BERTOLUCCI, GIUSEPPE BERTOLUCCI

DIRECTOR OF PHOTOGRAPHY

VITTORIO STORARO

EDITING

FRANCO ARCALLI

MUSIC

ENNIO MORRICONE

PRODUCTION

ALBERTO GRIMALDI for ARTÉMIS PRODUCTIONS, PRODUZIONI EUROPEE ASSOCIATI, LES PRODUCTIONS ARTISTES ASSOCIÉS

STARRING

GÉRARD DEPARDIEU (Olmo Dalcò), ROBERT DE NIRO (Alfredo Berlinghieri Jr.), BURT LANCASTER (Alfredo Berlinghieri Sr.), STERLING HAYDEN (Leo Dalcò), DOMINIQUE SANDA (Ada Fiastri Paulhan), DONALD SUTHERLAND (Attila), LAURA BETTI (Regina), WERNER BRUHNS (Ottavio Berlinghieri), STEFANIA CASINI (Neve), ROMOLO VALLI (Giovanni), ANNA HENKEL (Anita)

ALBERTO GRIMALDI présente

UN FILM DE BERNARDO BERTOLUCCI

1900

(NOVECENTO)

DEUXIÈME ACTE

ROBERT DE NIRO GÉRARD DEPARDIEU
DOMINIQUE SANDA

et par ordre alphabétique
FRANCESCA BERTINI • LAURA BETTI • WERNER BRUHNS • STEFANIA CASINI
STERLING HAYDEN • ANNA HENKEL • ELLEN SCHWIERS • ALIDA VALLI • ROMOLO VALLI
et avec STEFANIA SANDRELLI et avec DONALD SUTHERLAND et avec BURT LANCASTER

directeur de la photographie VITTORIO STORARO (A.I.C.) • musique de ENNIO MORRICONE
scénario de FRANCO ARCALLI • GIUSEPPE BERTOLUCCI • BERNARDO BERTOLUCCI / réalisé par BERNARDO BERTOLUCCI

Une Co-production PRODUZIONI EUROPEE ASSOCIATE (ROME) LES PRODUCTIONS ARTISTES ASSOCIÉS (PARIS) ARTEMIS FILM GMBH (BERLIN) distribué par LES ARTISTES ASSOCIÉS TECHNICOLOR

TWEEDE BEDRIJF

IMPRIMÉ EN BELGIQUE

EDICOLOR - Bruxelles - Tél. 343.63.49 - 343.87.43

1

"There are no more masters."

Novecento – Twentieth Century is the actual title of this mammoth project, an opulent epic covering five decades of Italian history, focusing on the lives of three generations whose tales are told in parallel. The year 1900 merely marks the connection to the previous century, which witnessed the emergence of one of the great modern ideas: that life in its totality might be encapsulated in a philosophical system or a work of art. It's an ambition shared by the film itself; and the theory of history as the story of class struggle and social conflict has clearly had a profound influence on Bernardo Bertolucci.

On a country estate in Emilia Romagna at the turn of the century, two baby boys are born on the same day: Alfredo, grandson of the landowner Alfredo Berlinghieri (Burt Lancaster), is heir to the estate; Olmo, the fatherless grandson of the peasant Leo Dalcò (Sterling Hayden), inherits the work. Having shared a childhood, they will grow up to confront one another as class enemies. Yet despite his clear sympathy for the oppressed workers, the artist Bertolucci is no proponent of the primacy of politics. On the contrary: from the faces and landscapes of Northern Italy, he creates a panorama of rural life, assigning each of the four periods depicted—pre-Great War, postwar, fascism and liberation—to a season of the year: Summer, Fall, Winter, and Spring respectively. It's a subtle tribute to the composer Giuseppe Verdi, like Bertolucci a native of the province of Parma, for despite the lamenting of the harlequin in the film's opening scenes, Italy's national composer is far from dead. The film holds only superficially to the facts of recorded history, such as the great land-laborers'

EPIC The first cinematic epic appeared in the early years of the cinema: D.W. Griffith's *The Birth of a Nation* (1915). Yet the historical epic, a mirror of national destinies, is only one variety among many. There are science-fiction epics such as the *Star Wars* films (1977, 1980, 1983, 1999, 2002, 2005, 2015, 2016), and contemporary social epics like *Nashville* (1975). Indeed, the Western, a form that need take no account of historical persons and events, was for a long time the epic form *par excellence.* For the subtext of this super-genre is the mythical, and myths are so infinitely interpretable that a definition of the term "epic" must finally be grounded in subjective perception. Factors such as the length of the film, the number of star actors, or the size of the budget are merely marketing arguments for "big pictures." What count are the high quality of the cinematic realization and the inner logic of the narrative, in which personal, cultural and universally human patterns of behavior are combined in such a way that they mean more than they tell. In this way, the epic acquires a transcendent quality, linking the most important areas of life and history, such as love, family and war.

Epic films depict people forced to contend with difficult, often tragic circumstances. It's interesting to see where the stress lies in different films: thus *Doctor Zhivago* (1965) and *Titanic* (1997) invoke an ideal of romantic love against the backdrop of a significant historical event. The *Godfather* trilogy (1972, 1974, 1990) confronts the American Dream with its relationship to violence and crime, with classical family structures playing an equally important role. Only one other genre can match the popular appeal of the epic, and it stands in almost irreconcilable opposition to this most serious of film forms: comedy.

“This $8 million epic, Bertolucci’s first effort since *Last Tango in Paris*, is a fabulous wreck. Abundantly flawed, maddeningly simple-minded, *1900* nonetheless possesses more brute force than any other film since Coppola’s similarly operatic *Godfather II*. If Bertolucci irritates as much as he dazzles, he never bores: his extravagant failure has greater staying power than most other directors’ triumphs.” *Time Magazine*

1 Animal attraction: The beautiful and unconventional Ada (Dominique Sanda) is married to young Alfredo. But then what's fidelity if you can have Olmo?

2 Gone to the dogs: Padrone Alfredo Berlinghieri (Burt Lancaster) is an Italian landowner of the old school—and now, he's an anachronism.

3 A finger in every pie: The meddlesome schoolteacher Anita (Anna Henkel) becomes Olmo's wife.

4 The Age of Reason: The new master Giovanni Berlinghieri (Romolo Valli) organizes the estate on more economic lines.

"The land needs the people! The soil will rot without them! But who needs the *padrone*?" *Film quote: Voices from the crowd*

strike of 1908: it impresses, above all, as a kind of allegorical opera. Whether red flags are flying or fascist battalions marching through the streets, the choreographed masses have the power of operatic choirs, accompanied by Ennio Morricone's music and Bertolucci's Italian delight in pathos.

From beginning to end, the symbolic imagery of this baroque magnum opus is dominated not only by the colors of the earth and the changing light of the sun, but also by blood, dung, and filth. There is nothing nostalgic in Bertolucci's depiction of the merciless suppression of serfs by their masters. Alfredo Sr. makes a quick departure: the

5

Italian rural aristocracy, so splendidly embodied by Burt Lancaster in Visconti's *The Leopard* (*Il gattopardo*, 1963), expires in a cowstall. The old man's son employs the methods of a bloodsucker to fight the demands of the nascent farmworkers' organization, and ultimately calls on the help of the fascists. Salvation appears in the form of the diabolical estate manager and blackshirt leader Attila (Donald Sutherland). His brutal perversity is not just an expression of Bertolucci's desire to present fascism as an embodiment of evil; he also shows these violent outbursts as a psychological consequence of the conflict between the

"My son will study Law." "My son will steal."

Film quotes: Alfredo Berlinghieri Sr. and Leo Dalcò

5 Over my dead body: A moving manifestation of civil disobedience by peasant women, and just one example of Bertolucci's feminist perspective.

6 Learning by example: Leo Dalcò (Sterling Hayden) is the role model for his grandson Olmo.

7 A little R & R: After preaching *revolution* at the workers' school, Anita *romances* Olmo (Gérard Depardieu).

8 Power trip: After a cocaine orgy at Uncle Ottavio's place, Alfredo has a rude awakening. Ada tells him his father is dead and he is the new padrone.

8

bourgeoisie and the proletariat. The sexual superiority of the working class is manifested in the figure of Olmo (Gérard Depardieu), an eloquent and impassioned agitator. When the new *padrone* Alfredo Jr. (Robert De Niro) can't find his beautiful wife Ada (Dominique Sanda), he looks for her in Olmo's hovel. Not without reason. Even in their childhood years, Olmo had made him painfully aware of his weaknesses, making fun of his immaturity by challenging him to hair-raising tests of bravery. And now, in adulthood, he continues to laugh in his face.

It's hardly possible to say how much irony is intended in this provocative amalgamation of sex and politics. For Bertolucci was himself a middle-class child, and his narrative mannerisms evince a great deal more ambivalence than his depiction of the characters. His mixed feelings are undoubtedly connected to the period in which the film was conceived and created, as is the victorious Olmo's appeal for a "historic compromise." In 1975, the failed alliance between the Christian Democrats and the Communists was *the* political topic in crisis-torn Italy.

A betrayal of the class struggle? Or a transparent misuse of history in the interests of agitation, a pompous marriage between Hollywood and Socialist Realism? At the Cannes festival, Bertolucci's idiosyncratic interpretation of history caused an uproar. But Bertolucci had much more pressing problems ahead. Three U.S. production companies—United Artists, Paramount Pictures and 20th Century Fox—had borne equal shares of the production costs, which totaled six million dollars, and they objected to the "unmarketable" five-and-a-half-hour film delivered by Bertolucci. When the case reached the courts, a judge was forced to watch three versions of the film on three successive days. Besides the original version, there was a 4-hour-40-minute *1900* and a 3-hour-15-minute version cut and pasted by Paramount themselves. As Bertolucci explained later: "The judge was dazed by an overdose of *Novecento,*" but he worked out a "historic" compromise between the filmmaker and the producers. For the American market, Bertolucci assembled a 4-hour version,

"Long live the revolution! Long live the revolutionaries! Long live the General Strike!" *Film quote: Voices from the crowd*

9 The lone white stallion: Ada and Alfredo are soon deeply estranged. Here she rides into the woods, to meet Olmo once again.

10 Brute force: Bailiff Attila builds a concentration camp on the estate. He and his henchmen murder at will. The peasants are powerless to resist.

11 Flags fly for freedom: Spring has come, the war is over, and the revolution is victorious—at least on the Berlinghieri estate.

12

which was prevented from reaching a large audience by the machinations of the studios. Though the director had remarked that this slimmed-down version was the best, he later retracted this statement. Even in its original length, however, the film took a long time to reach Europe. On Bertolucci's own suggestion, the film was divided into two parts, but only years after it was completed did *1900* achieve recognition as an impressive work of art and gain relative popularity as a cult film. The tattered history of the twentieth century had acquired a cinematic memorial.

PB

"The padrone is dead and Alfredo Berlinghieri is living proof of it."

Film quote: Olmo Dalcò

12 Of mice and men: Class-conscious Olmo doesn't have much to say to intellectual Ada. But his sheer masculinity makes Alfredo pale in comparison.

13 Throw me a bone: Attila "the watch-dog," seems devoted to his master. But soon, Alfredo's power-hungry stomach begins to growl…

14 Splendor in the grass: After the Liberation in 1945, Attila is hunted down. Rough justice for the fascist torturer, whose bloody end was anticipated at the beginning of Part 1.

13

"Bertolucci's film is a bucolic opera in the language of cinema, bursting with vitality, orgiastic fecundity and voluptuous urgency. He shows us an Italy without Riviera kitsch or Santa Lucia schmalz, choosing his images from a latifundium in the vast agrarian landscape of the Emilia: its endless wheat fields, its open barns with their brick colonnades, its canal-banks and dykes, its cattle stalls, its threshing floors, and its sparse forests of poplar." *Frankfurter Allgemeine Zeitung*

CARRIE

1976 – USA – 98 MIN.

GENRE

HORROR FILM

DIRECTOR

BRIAN DE PALMA

SCREENPLAY

LAWRENCE D. COHEN, based on the novel of the same name by STEPHEN KING

DIRECTOR OF PHOTOGRAPHY

MARIO TOSI

EDITING

PAUL HIRSCH

MUSIC

PINO DONAGGIO

PRODUCTION

PAUL MONASH, BRIAN DE PALMA for REDBANK FILMS

STARRING

SISSY SPACEK (Carrie White), JOHN TRAVOLTA (Billy Nolan), PIPER LAURIE (Margaret White), AMY IRVING (Sue Snell), WILLIAM KATT (Tommy Ross), NANCY ALLEN (Chris Hargensen), BETTY BUCKLEY (Miss Collins), P. J. SOLES (Norma Watson), PRISCILLA POINTER (Mrs. Snell), SYDNEY LASSICK (Mr. Fromm)

IF YOU'VE GOT
A TASTE FOR TERROR...
TAKE CARRIE TO THE PROM.

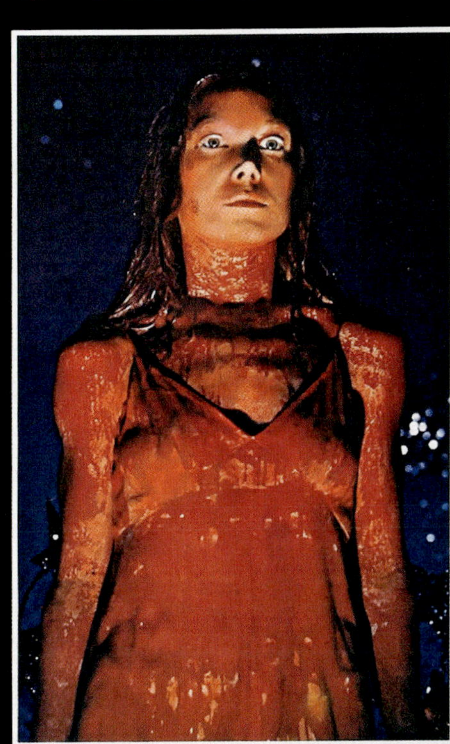

If only they knew she had the power.

A PAUL MONASH Production A BRIAN DePALMA Film "CARRIE"
starring SISSY SPACEK
JOHN TRAVOLTA and PIPER LAURIE · Screenplay by LAWRENCE D. COHEN
Based on the novel by STEPHEN KING · Produced by PAUL MONASH · Directed by BRIAN DePALMA
Production Services by Carrie's Group

United Artists

1

"There're all gonna laugh at you!"

High school can be quite a blood bath. It's a world dominated by vanity, envy and petty fears. For those who don't fit the mold, teasing, sneering and even total ostracism can lie in store. But can't this clichéd view of the growing years be partly attributed to countless soap operas and teen flicks? Maybe so. Nevertheless, real reports of rampant violence repeatedly hit the headlines, a testament to the fact that the social microcosms within schools are no place for kids who journey the path less traveled.

Carrie White (Sissy Spacek) is one such person. She is the daughter of the mentally ill Margaret (Piper Laurie), who became a religious fanatic after Carrie's father left them. In her relentless crusade to protect Carrie from earthly sins, Margaret beats the word of God into her daughter.

While showering in the girls' locker room, the innocent Carrie is horrified when she menstruates for the first time. Only gym teacher Miss Collins (Betty Buckley) extends Carrie her support. Her efforts to discipline the malevolent, traumatizing girls present at the event only add fuel to their sadistic fire. When one of the girls, Chris (Nancy Allen), is banned from attending the prom as a result of the embarrassing incident, she swears revenge on Carrie, which meets with disastrous consequences…

For meanwhile Carrie has discovered that she possesses an extraordinary gift. She is a telepathic medium. When faced with the eternal callousness of her immediate environment, this seemingly mousy homebody turns into a ticking time bomb.

SISSY SPACEK The German newspaper *DIE ZEIT* once described Sissy Spacek (born 1949 in Quitman, Texas) as "the phenomenology of backroads America captured in a single face." Spacek's America is one filled with characters from the nooks and crannies of small towns, like the awkward, intimidated schoolgirl in *Carrie,* and the birdhouse-building handicapped daughter in David Lynch's *The Straight Story* (1999). It is the America associated with romanticized hospitality that Spacek is most familiar with. At one time, she toured the nation's foothills as a country music singer, performing under the name "Rainbow." After completing her acting studies with Lee Strasberg and winning critical acclaim for Terrence Malick's *Badlands* (1973), she cemented her career with her performance in *Carrie* (1976). Shortly thereafter, she was cast as country singer Loretta Lynn in *Coal Miner's Daughter* (1980), a role that must have fit like a glove, and was awarded the Best Actress Academy Award for her outstanding performance. The following year, Spacek received another Oscar nomination for her work opposite Jack Lemmon in *Missing* (1981). Oscar nodded twice more in her direction, for her portrayal of a farmer's wife in *The River* (1984) and her artistry *In the Bedroom* (2001), for which she won a Golden Globe. In 2008, she was nominated for a Best Actress Golden Globe for her role in TV drama *Pictures of Hollis Woods*. To this day, she continues to appear in numerous TV series.

2

3

4
5

1 Baptized in blood: The poster image of Carrie White (Sissy Spacek) remains engrained in the minds of audiences to this very day.

2, 3 Splitting images: De Palma's infernal ending was mannerist to say the least.

4 Just your average, ordinary schoolgirl: Carrie becomes a woman in the girl's locker room.

5 Instilling the fear of God: Margaret White (Piper Laurie) raises a hand to her heretic daughter.

6 Living the dream: For a few blissful minutes, Carrie and Tommy (William Katt) are the dream couple at the prom ball.

7 Coal Miner's Slaughter: The former country singer Sissy Spacek made her breakthrough in the role of poor, monstrous Carrie White.

"Combining Gothic Horror, offhand misogyny and an air of studied triviality, *Carrie* is De Palma's most enjoyable movie in a long while, and also his silliest." *Newsweek*

Even though the image forever engrained in the memories of world audiences is that of the young Sissy Spacek drenched in pig's blood, *Carrie* cannot be deemed a horror film in the classic sense. It is at its most gruesome when it shakes the audience with images of the true-to-life, spiteful machinations of the snide cliques led by John Travolta and De Palma's later wife Nancy Allen. *Carrie* is not, however, a scathing critique of American high schools. Above all else, the film is a heart-pounding thriller that keeps you on the edge of your seat even though the story's ending is clear from the start.

De Palma takes great pleasure in torturing his audience to the bitter end, manipulating its voyeuristic expectations and then tweaking the plot in such a way as to leave everyone hung out to dry. Which, according to Brian De Palma, is giving the audience their just desserts. For when it comes down to it, moviegoers are not that different from the on-screen juvenile brat pack, eager to put a rise in Carrie's sails on prom night. With diabolic precision, he intensifies the audience's basic desire to put an end to the heroine's perpetual ridicule, by pairing it up with the growing anticipation of the most climactic event of every high school girl's life—the prom. The dance's culmination is accompanied by the unleashing of an unstoppable act of apocalyptic wrath.

You could describe the last third of the film as pure mannerism. It's a fireworks display, including the slow-motion camera, split-screen action, extreme close-ups and pointedly dramatic lighting. Though many a director would have shied away from a finale that could be branded as a cavalcade of cheap effects, De Palma implemented it flawlessly and turned its elements into his signature style.

What's more astonishing is that *Carrie* was shot on a spartan budget of just under two million dollars. The financial limitations forced De Palma to abstain from filming the total destruction of the town that takes place in the novel. Nevertheless, *Carrie* proved to be a milestone in the career of the then unknown director. The picture's popularity also contributed to the acclaim of the story's author, Stephen King, who is considered today to be one of the most successful writers of all time.

SH

MARATHON MAN

1976 – USA – 125 MIN.

GENRE

POLITICAL THRILLER

DIRECTOR

JOHN SCHLESINGER

SCREENPLAY

WILLIAM GOLDMAN,
based on his novel of the same name

DIRECTOR OF PHOTOGRAPHY

CONRAD L. HALL

EDITING

JIM CLARK

MUSIC

MICHAEL SMALL

PRODUCTION

ROBERT EVANS, SIDNEY BECKERMAN for
PARAMOUNT PICTURES GELDERSE MAATSCHAPPIJ N. V.

STARRING

DUSTIN HOFFMAN (Babe Levy), LAURENCE OLIVIER (Dr. Szell),
ROY SCHEIDER (Doc Levy), MARTHE KELLER (Elsa Opel),
WILLIAM DEVANE (Janeway), FRITZ WEAVER (Professor Biesenthal),
RICHARD BRIGHT (Karl), MARC LAWRENCE (Erhard),
TITO GOYA (Melendez), BEN DOVA (Klaus Szell, Dr. Szell's Brother)

A thriller

Paramount Pictures presents
a ROBERT EVANS–SIDNEY BECKERMAN production
a JOHN SCHLESINGER film

DUSTIN HOFFMAN
LAURENCE OLIVIER ROY SCHEIDER
WILLIAM DEVANE MARTHE KELLER in

"MARATHON MAN"

screenplay by WILLIAM GOLDMAN from his novel
produced by ROBERT EVANS and SIDNEY BECKERMAN
directed by JOHN SCHLESINGER music scored by MICHAEL SMALL
services by CONNAUGHT PRODUCTIONS in Color a paramount picture
Read the Dell paperback

1

It takes more than physical fitness to run a marathon. Equally important is the will to keep going even when the body is begging to stop. Babe Levy (Dustin Hoffman) is the Marathon Man, a small man with a big heart, and he'll spend most of this film running for his life. Out of the blue, Babe is drawn into a maelstrom of Secret Service machinations, with the elderly German Dr. Szell (Laurence Olivier) at the center of it all. A former concentration camp physician, Szell is now living in hiding in South America, from where he supplies the U.S. with information on the whereabouts of other fugitive top Nazis. In return, the so-called "Division"—a Secret Service unit somewhere between the CIA and the FBI—supplies Szell with the money he needs to survive in Uruguayan exile by paying

POLITICAL THRILLERS In general, the word "thriller" denotes a cinema of fear and existential threat. Thrillers are tense tales of criminal misdeeds. As a rule, the viewer identifies with the heroic protagonists, who often don't know why they're being pursued or how they've suddenly landed in a terrible situation with no apparent way out. The thriller has many faces, depending on its thematic orientation and formal structure: there are psychothrillers, horror thrillers, erotic thrillers and political thrillers. As the name suggests, political thrillers derive their potential from fictional stories that are close enough to real political events to appear credible.

The political thriller tells of political corruption and only rarely refrains from commenting on history. One of the most important directors of political thrillers is the pugnacious Constantin Costa-Gavras. In films such as *Z* (1968) and *State of Siege* (*État de siège*, 1972), he did not merely deal with political themes, but also took up a clear political position. The great political scandals of world history are a particularly fruitful field. The murder of John F. Kennedy, for example, has been the subject of several films, most notably Oliver Stone's controversial *JFK* (1991). Oscars were showered on Alan J. Pakula's *All the President's Men* (1976), which dramatized the exposure of the Watergate scandal surrounding President Richard Nixon.

2

cash for the diamonds he stole from inmates of the camp. Babe's brother Doc (Roy Scheider) is a member of this mysterious Division.

For a piece of Hollywood entertainment, this complex political thriller touches some pretty sensitive nerves. With its close proximity to real events of the recent past, coupled with a style that joins elements of French 60s cinema to classic *Film Noir* conventions, *Marathon Man* is a film with a strong feeling for history and yet is still firmly rooted in its time. Reference is made to the McCarthy-era anti-Communist witch hunts, which drove Babe's father to

"In typical Hollywood fashion, Schlesinger shows us the oil truck first to allow us time to consider the implications of what we are seeing. For this, like the opening sequences of many Bergman and Fellini pictures, is the entire film in nucleo."

Literature / Film Quarterly

1 Run for your life! Dustin Hoffman, one of the biggest names of New Hollywood, stars in the tense thriller *Marathon Man*.

2 An innocent-looking face: But Elsa (Marthe Keller) can't be trusted.

3 All in the family: Babe's brother Doc (Roy Scheider) is a man with a dark secret.

4 Running on empty: Babe Levy (Dustin Hoffman), on a lonely, long-distance race to the truth about his brother's death.

3

suicide. Demonstrations fill the background of many scenes; and the fictitious figure of Dr. Szell cannot fail to evoke the all-too-real Dr. Josef Mengele, who absconded to Argentina after the war and who was never found alive. The film is powerfully effective in its combination of nerve-wracking tension and elements that so closely mirror reality. The politically motivated Secret Service escapades are hardly less disturbing for being strictly fictional, and the film plays suggestively on our most basic and inadmissible fears, intensified by the deadly menace of a hidden and anonymous force. Carefully timed eruptions of violence raise the tension to almost unbearable levels, most dramatically in the sequences in the dentist's chair. Dr. Szell calmly tortures Babe Levy, plucking and poking at nerves laid bare, while repeating the sinister and unanswerable question, "Is it safe?" Here and elsewhere, the film makes quite intentional use of shocking violence as an effective narrative device. The audience is never allowed to forget that the white-haired, bespectacled Szell is no harmless old gent but a monster of cynical cruelty. (After test runs of the film, this torture sequence had to be cut substantially.)

The plot is also quite something. For a long time, the audience is left in the dark as to exactly what's going on. Right at the start, we have a mysterious race between two elderly motorists, trading insults until they crash. Then

there's the enigmatic Elsa Opel (Marthe Keller), who steals the heart of Babe Levy. There's Babe's brother Doc, with his puzzling business in Paris; and we have deadly enemies posing as Babe's friends, like the shady Peter Janeway (William Devane). A long time passes before the various pieces of this complex puzzle can be made to fit together.

The narrative is fragmented, and our feelings are manipulated constantly by shocks, surprises and ironic twists. The audience is as confused and disoriented as the protagonist. Throughout Babe's long flight, we never know more than he does. Near the end of his ordeal, he traps Szell in a reservoir building, where it becomes clear that the Nazi doctor is only interested in one thing: his "life insurance," in the form of the diamonds he stole from his murdered victims. They have financed his retirement very nicely so far, and he wants them to go on doing so. Once again, we see Szell's murderous cynicism at work: he wants these jewels at all costs, and their inhuman price is irrelevant. As Babe forces Szell to eat the diamonds, the story takes one final, unsettling twist: the torturer's victim tortures the torturer. Thus, even at the end of this disturbing thriller-marathon, it's hard to breathe a simple sigh of relief. BR

"While the political implications are pushed further than they are able to go, the film runs into even more trouble when it attempts to work the loosely asserted personal elements deeper into the pattern." *Sight and Sound*

5 Babe turns the tables with a semi-automatic…

6 … and sadistic Nazi war criminal, Dr. Szell (Laurence Olivier), suddenly can't resist his powers of persuasion.

7 Nice work if you can get it: Doc cashes in on the secrets of Szell's merciless past.

THE PINK PANTHER STRIKES AGAIN

1976 – GREAT BRITAIN – 103 MIN.

GENRE

COMEDY

DIRECTOR

BLAKE EDWARDS

SCREENPLAY

FRANK WALDMAN, BLAKE EDWARDS

DIRECTOR OF PHOTOGRAPHY

HARRY WAXMAN

EDITING

ALAN JONES

MUSIC

HENRY MANCINI

PRODUCTION

BLAKE EDWARDS for AMJO PRODUCTIONS

STARRING

PETER SELLERS (Chief Inspector Jacques Clouseau), HERBERT LOM (Ex-Chief Inspector Charles Dreyfus), LESLEY-ANNE DOWN (Olga), BURT KWOUK (Cato), COLIN BLAKELY (Alec Drummond), LEONARD ROSSITER (Inspector Quinlan), RICHARD VERNON (Doctor Fassbender), MICHAEL ROBBINS (Jarvis the Butler), VANDA GODSELL (Mrs. Leverlilly), BRIONY MCROBERTS (Margo Fassbender), OMAR SHARIF (Egyptian Agent)

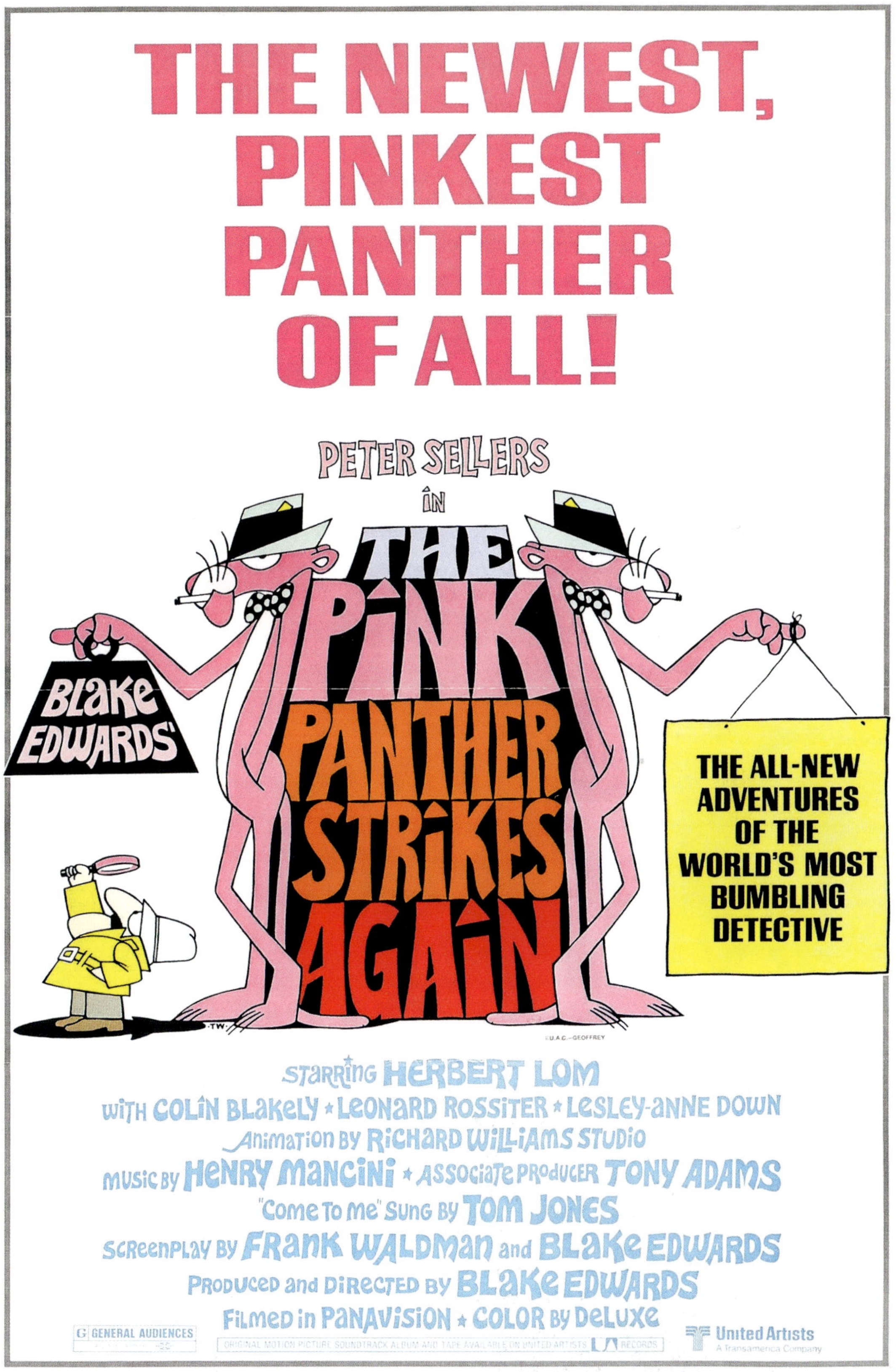

THE NEWEST, PINKEST PANTHER OF ALL!

PETER SELLERS

in

THE PINK PANTHER STRIKES AGAIN

BLAKE EDWARDS'

THE ALL-NEW ADVENTURES OF THE WORLD'S MOST BUMBLING DETECTIVE

TW

©U.A.C.—GEOFFREY

STARRING HERBERT LOM

WITH COLIN BLAKELY ★ LEONARD ROSSITER ★ LESLEY-ANNE DOWN

ANIMATION BY RICHARD WILLIAMS STUDIO

MUSIC BY HENRY MANCINI ★ ASSOCIATE PRODUCER TONY ADAMS

"COME TO ME" SUNG BY TOM JONES

SCREENPLAY BY FRANK WALDMAN AND BLAKE EDWARDS

PRODUCED AND DIRECTED BY BLAKE EDWARDS

FILMED IN PANAVISION ★ COLOR BY DELUXE

G GENERAL AUDIENCES

ORIGINAL MOTION PICTURE SOUNDTRACK ALBUM AND TAPE AVAILABLE ON UNITED ARTISTS UA RECORDS

1

“The mad are the only normal people I have ever met.”

Two flabbergasted nuns watch a hunchback floating in the night sky above Paris. The lump is not a deformity but a cunning disguise, and the airborne Quasimodo is a policeman. His hump is filled with helium, and his inability to control the gas level has just saved his life: seconds before a bomb ripped through his apartment, the overfilled costume had lifted him gently out of the window. Having evaded certain death thanks to his inimitable incompetence, our hero drifts past the Sacre Cœur, letting out the gas to ensure a soft landing in the Seine. It's “Interpol's best man,” Inspector Clouseau (Peter Sellers), as we know and love him.

His latest case begins with a visit to his former boss Charles Dreyfus (Herbert Lom) in a psychiatric clinic. Driven mad by Clouseau's stupidity, the former Chief Inspector is due to meet a commission of doctors who will decide

ISADORE “FRITZ” FRELENG One day in 1963, Isadore Freleng (1905–1995) saw pale red. Between 100 and 150 pink panthers lay before him, sketches for the animated title sequence to Blake Edwards' upcoming project, *The Pink Panther* (1964). In the film, the Panther is an enormous diamond; in the opening titles, Blake Edwards decided, it should be a big cat. Freleng and his cartoonist colleague Hawley Pratt developed a minimalist background world inhabited by a slightly more complex Panther, an elegantly cool cat grooving to the cool jazz sax melody composed by Henry Mancini.

After the success of Saul Bass' closing titles to *Around the World in Eighty Days* (1956), many comedies of the 60s and 70s had featured animated titles sequences. Freleng, however, actually succeeded in emancipating his cartoon creation from its lowly supporting role: in 1964, he was awarded an Oscar for *The Pink Phink,* and the cartoon Panther went on to star in its own TV series.

Freleng, an autodidact, spent 33 years working for Warner Brothers, collaborating with great animators like Chuck Jones and Tex Avery. Three of his films received Oscars: *Speedy Gonzales* (1955), *Birds Anonymous* (1957) and *Knighty Knight Bugs* (1958). His creations included Yosemite Sam and Sylvester, but no other cartoon figure shows his talent for combining animation with music so clearly as the Pink Panther.

2

whether he has recovered sufficiently to be released. In an indescribable slapstick sequence involving Clouseau, a cricket ball, and a park bench, Dreyfus takes a series of involuntary baths in the clinic lake—and succumbs once again to his "insane" hatred of Clouseau.

A short time later, he escapes from the clinic, forms a criminal organization, and kidnaps the physicist Professor Fassbender (Richard Vernon) and his daughter Margo (Briony McRoberts). After bringing them to Castle Mondschein in Bavaria, he forces the scientist to construct a deadly ray-gun. Thus armed, Dreyfus presents an ultimatum to the world: Clouseau must die—or Dreyfus will destroy the human race. The world's secret services don't have to be asked twice, and soon Clouseau is a fugitive. At the Oktoberfest in Munich, the hunt for Inspector Clouseau begins…

For Peter Sellers, Clouseau's imbecility was a blessing, and it made him an international star. Yet he only appeared in the first *Pink Panther* movie after Peter Ustinov had turned down the role at short notice. From then on, no other actor was imaginable as the world's most useless policeman: all attempts to recast the role failed miserably, while the Sellers movies were big box-office hits. This was the third of his five *Pink Panther* films, and many regard it as the best, thanks in no small part to Herbert Lom's excellent portrayal of the diabolical Dreyfus. Resplendent in

3

4

"The series hit its high point with its third film, *The Pink Panther Strikes Again*. The laughs simply don't relent." *At-A-Glance Film Reviews*

1 Confessions of a dangerous mind: Peter Sellers often claimed that "there used to be a real me, but I had it surgically removed." Let's hope Inspector Clouseau can catch the witch doctor who performed the operation.

2 Martial arts: Interpol's best man—a serious match for Hong Kong Phooey.

3 Facial wrap: A serious injury or a cunning disguise?

4 Proof positive: The smoldering sleuth pursues his investigations in a gay bar.

5 Lost in translation: The French answer to Sherlock Holmes is a walking disaster area.

5

6 Riddle me this: “How can an idiot be a policeman?” The series’ comic genius was born out of Clouseau’s deadpan conviction.

7 In a peaceful white room: Clouseau may be off Charles Dreyfus’ (Herbert Lom) payroll, but he’s still the cause of his mental anguish.

a long black cape, he plays the organ in his creepy castle, a kind of latterday silent-film Dracula, but plagued with terrible teeth…

Director Blake Edwards’ successes had included *Breakfast at Tiffany’s* (1961) before he made the *Pink Panther* series. *The Pink Panther Strikes Again* is filled with references to the Hollywood classics, and not only in the Castle Mondschein scenes. Even in the animated titles sequence, the Inspector’s hunt for the Pink Panther is a tour-de-force through movie history, featuring such luminaries of the silver screen as Alfred Hitchcock, King Kong, and Batman. And when Clouseau questions the Professor’s servants after their employer’s abduction, his bizarre interrogation is a parody of the old Agatha Christie adaptations.

The rest of the somewhat loosely constructed plot consists of a series of sketch-like episodes, including the now classic dog-bites-inspector dialog (Clouseau: “I thought you said your dog didn't bite?" Hotelier: "That is not my dog."), and the cacophonous karate duel between Clouseau and his servant Cato (Burt Kwouk). In the end, it's Cato who manages to foul up the Bond-style finale Clouseau fought so hard to achieve—with the help of a striptease. But then it would be strange to see Clouseau ever succeed at anything.

OK

7

"There is a beautiful woman in my bed, and a dead man in my bath." *Film quote: Inspector Clouseau*

8 Kicking the habit: Dreyfus will stop at nothing to free the world from the curse of Clouseau.

9 Eureka! Far from bombing at the box office, the movie raked in 33 million dollars in the U.S. alone. History showed that moviegoers would only accept one actor in the role of Inspector Clouseau.

8

9

ALL THE PRESIDENT'S MEN

1976 – USA – 132 MIN.

GENRE

POLITICAL DRAMA

DIRECTOR

ALAN J. PAKULA

SCREENPLAY

WILLIAM GOLDMAN, based on the factual reports of
CARL BERNSTEIN and BOB WOODWARD

DIRECTOR OF PHOTOGRAPHY

GORDON WILLIS

EDITING

ROBERT L. WOLFE

MUSIC

DAVID SHIRE

PRODUCTION

WALTER COBLENZ for WILDWOOD, WARNER BROS.

STARRING

DUSTIN HOFFMAN (Carl Bernstein), ROBERT REDFORD (Bob Woodward),
JACK WARDEN (Harry Rosenfeld), MARTIN BALSAM (Howard Simons),
HAL HOLBROOK (Deep Throat), JASON ROBARDS (Ben Bradlee),
JANE ALEXANDER (Judy Hoback, Bookkeeper), MEREDITH BAXTER (Debbie Sloan),
NED BEATTY (Dardis), STEPHEN COLLINS (Hugh W. Sloan Jr.)

ACADEMY AWARDS 1977

OSCARS for BEST SUPPORTING ACTOR (Jason Robards),
BEST ADAPTED SCREENPLAY (William Goldman),
BEST ART DIRECTION (George Jenkins, George Gaines),
and BEST SOUND (Arthur Piantadosi, Les Fresholtz, Rick Alexander, James E. Webb)

The most devastating detective story of this century.

REDFORD/HOFFMAN "ALL THE PRESIDENT'S MEN"

ROBERT REDFORD/DUSTIN HOFFMAN "ALL THE PRESIDENT'S MEN"

Starring JACK WARDEN • Special appearance by MARTIN BALSAM, HAL HOLBROOK and JASON ROBARDS as Ben Bradlee

Screenplay by WILLIAM GOLDMAN • Based on the book by CARL BERNSTEIN and BOB WOODWARD • Music by DAVID SHIRE

Produced by WALTER COBLENZ • Directed by ALAN J. PAKULA

A Wildwood Enterprises Production • A Robert Redford - Alan J. Pakula Film

PG PARENTAL GUIDANCE SUGGESTED

TECHNICOLOR® From WARNER BROS A WARNER COMMUNICATIONS COMPANY

1

"Nothing's riding on this except the, uh, first amendment to the Constitution, freedom of the press, and maybe the future of the country."

Extreme close-up of a typewriter. A single date is hammered out onto the page and each keystroke rings out like a gunshot. The date is "June 17, 1972" and right from the first moment of the film one thing becomes vividly clear—the typewriter can be a lethal weapon.

Bob Woodward (Robert Redford) and Carl Bernstein (Dustin Hoffman) are two "hungry" young reporters working at the *Washington Post.* The two end up unmasking the scandal behind what will be forever known as Watergate. They work methodically, soberly and professionally, driven by a journalist's hunter instincts to trap a good story and their own thirst for success. Their goal is to be better, not to mention quicker, than their counterparts at *The New York Times* and they will let nothing stand in their way.

The picture tells the tale of "Woodstein," as the writing team quickly become dubbed by the rest of the reporting staff. We accompany the two on an expedition that will last approximately six months, starting on that ominous night of June 17, with the break in at Democratic headquarters (where the Republican party apparently paid to have bugging equipment planted) up until the day when Nixon is sworn into office for a second term in January

ALAN J. PAKULA Jane Fonda won an Oscar under his direction as call girl Bree Daniels in the detective caper *Klute* (1971), and a decade later he aided Meryl Streep in making a decision that won her the coveted golden statuette for her performance in the Holocaust drama *Sophie's Choice* (1982). Even his screenwriter for *All the President's Men* (1976), William Goldman, was bestowed with the Academy Award. Nonetheless, Alan J. Pakula (1928–1998), director of all these films and a two-time Oscar nominee, always remained the man behind the scenes. This could have to do with the fact that native New Yorker Pakula was never really viewed as a creative force but rather as an actor's director and meticulous craftsman as well as someone who was particularly gifted at helping others achieve their full potential. From 1957 to 1969, at the beginning of his career, he worked as a producer, collaborating on seven films with director Robert Mulligan. In 1969, while he and Liza Minnelli were on the lookout for a "fresh, new director" to take on *The Sterile Cuckoo*, Pakula suggested himself for the project and got his big break at fulfilling his greatest ambition. Much like Mulligan, Pakula had always been interested in political and sociological topics. His thrillers *Klute* (1971), *The Parallax View* (1974) and *All the President's Men*, which have become collectively known as the "paranoia trilogy," are considered exceptionally on-target studies of the political and social tenor of the Nixon era. Pakula further explored the conspiracy theory as a topic in later box-office triumphs like *Presumed Innocent* (1989) and *The Pelican Brief* (1993). In 1998, Pakula lost his life in a freak car accident.

1973. As inauguration day is upon them, it appears that the reporters have failed in their attempts to trace the scandal back to the highest White House officials. Nonetheless, the paper's chief editor Ben Bradlee (Jason Robards) offers them his unwavering support. The film's conclusion comes full circle as a television set placed prominently in the *Washington Post* newsroom shows us Nixon taking his presidential oath as well as the surrounding festivities full of pomp, circumstances and ceremonial gunfire while Bernstein and Woodward plug away at their typewriters. The chattering keys quickly drown out the sound of Nixon's fanfare. The film closes with a relentless news ticker that reports the concessions and sentencing of the case's principle suspects, concluding with President Nixon's resignation in August 1974.

Yet despite the subject matter, it's hard to call *All The President's Men* a political drama as the movie provides no forum for researching the causes of the Watergate affair or

1 Getting to the bottom of things: Reporters Carl Bernstein (Dustin Hoffman) and Bob Woodward (Robert Redford) investigate the Watergate break-in.

2 Out on a limb: Editor Ben Bradlee (Jason Robards Jr.) supports his journalists' detective work.

3 Working 9 to 5: It'll take thousands of phone-calls and hundreds of meetings before Carl Bernstein even has a clue as to what's really going on.

4 Turning cheap theatrics in big pay-offs: The Woodstein team devises a way to get witnesses to spill the beans.

3

an analysis of its aftermath. We do, however, see politicians in actual archived news footage from that year, which is seamlessly integrated into the story's fabric via television sets that appear throughout the film. Because its story unfolds through the eyes of the two investigative journalists, the political scandal seems to read like a detective caper. Although the outcome of the case is far from being a mystery, the path that leads there is what is of real interest. It is a relay race against time that consists of gathering evidence, making phone calls, meeting those involved, making more phone calls and conducting follow-up face to face interviews. We witness as a complex jigsaw puzzle compiled of dozens upon dozens of names, facts, appointments, organizations and secret monetary funds takes shape. This film, whose sights are as ambitious as those of its protagonists, demands our full attention and we gladly acquiesce.

The suspense of *All the President's Men* is born out of the story's authenticity and the impeccable acting. This first aspect is made evident by the film's loyalty to the historical facts and underscored by the Sisyphus-like efforts of the reporters, who screenwriter William Goldman does not even grant private lives. International mega-stars Redford and Hoffman must be credited for their artistic

"By simply sticking to the facts, Pakula and Redford pay tribute to a kind of journalism that has nothing in common with the prevalent clichés, the cheap and deliberate contempt often leveled at this profession."

Der Spiegel

orilliance, which is absolutely electrifying as they cunning-y win over tight-lipped individuals wrapped up in the af-air. Silence suddenly speaks volumes. On one occasion, n a theatrical tour de force, the duo force the truth out of . witness by acting as if that which they only suspect is onfirmed fact. Our eyes are glued to the screen as the vily Bernstein, much the opposite of the cautious, straight-dged Woodward, finesses his way into the home of an in-midated bookkeeper who worked for the "Committee to Re-elect the President," the organization whose coffers unded the break-in at Democratic headquarters. Using

4

"I found it brilliant and gripping. Even though the events and characters are familiar, the film has an understated and realistic quality that gives a completely fresh dramatic intensity to the crisis the United States went through so recently. Despite all the glamor of the actors (...) it is the unglamorous nature of newspaper work, even with such an assignment as trying to break open a government conspiracy that strikes home. The film breaks new ground in taking up a middle position between a documentary and a dramatization." *The Times*

his savvy and charm, he gradually gains the trust of this "sacrificial lamb" and gets her to reveal everything she knows. The scene is parlor room drama at its finest.

The reporter as hero has a long tradition in the American cinema, often appearing as a clichéd "wise guy." Thankfully, director Alan J. Pakula was careful to avoid this stereotype and even spent several weeks observing the goings-on of the actual *Washington Post* newsroom prior to shooting. While Pakula's film does indeed glorify the prevailing legend of an objective, free press that is capable of bringing superpowers to their knees, one can find but little reason to chide him for it. There are, after all, more problematic myths.

LP

5 The first amendment as lethal weapon: The typewriter that brought down a president.

6 A date with Deep Throat: Bob Woodward has to take greater precautions in obtaining information.

6

ROCKY ♛♛♛

1976 – USA – 119 MIN.

GENRE

BOXING FILM

DIRECTOR

JOHN G. AVILDSEN

SCREENPLAY

SYLVESTER STALLONE

DIRECTOR OF PHOTOGRAPHY

JAMES CRABE

EDITING

RICHARD HALSEY, SCOTT CONRAD

MUSIC

BILL CONTI

PRODUCTION

IRWIN WINKLER, ROBERT CHARTOFF for
CHARTOFF-WINKLER PRODUCTIONS

STARRING

SYLVESTER STALLONE (Rocky Balboa), TALIA SHIRE (Adrian),
BURT YOUNG (Paulie), BURGESS MEREDITH (Mickey Goldmill),
CARL WEATHERS (Apollo Creed), THAYER DAVID (Miles Jergens),
JOE SPINELL (Tom Gazzo), JIMMY GAMBINA (Mike),
TONY BURTON (Duke, Apollo's Trainer), JOE FRAZIER (Himself)

ACADEMY AWARDS 1977

OSCARS for BEST PICTURE (Irwin Winkler, Robert Chartoff),
BEST DIRECTOR (John G. Avildsen),
and BEST FILM EDITING (Richard Halsey, Scott Conrad)

His whole life was a million-to-one shot.

ROCKY

A ROBERT CHARTOFF-IRWIN WINKLER PRODUCTION · A JOHN G. AVILDSEN FILM · STARRING SYLVESTER STALLONE IN "ROCKY"

ALSO STARRING TALIA SHIRE · BURT YOUNG · CARL WEATHERS · AND BURGESS MEREDITH AS MICKEY · WRITTEN BY SYLVESTER STALLONE

PRODUCED BY IRWIN WINKLER AND ROBERT CHARTOFF · DIRECTED BY JOHN G. AVILDSEN · EXECUTIVE PRODUCER GENE KIRKWOOD · MUSIC BY BILL CONTI

PG PARENTAL GUIDANCE SUGGESTED
SOME MATERIAL MAY NOT BE SUITABLE FOR PRE-TEENAGERS

ORIGINAL MOTION PICTURE SOUNDTRACK ALBUM AND TAPE AVAILABLE ON UNITED ARTISTS UA RECORDS

A Transamerica Company

COPYRIGHT © UNITED ARTISTS CORPORATION MCMLXXVI ALL RIGHTS RESERVED

77/2

1

Philadelphia, December 1975, shortly after four in the morning. Continental winter and general depression reign. The city sleeps, illuminated by an electric half-light. There's not even a dog to be seen on the streets. It's bitterly cold. A newspaper deliveryman races through the banking district in his station wagon, distributing papers. Rocky appears behind him, a powerfully built man with a broad, somewhat drooping face. He jogs through the city, the white bursts of his breath hanging in the cold air. He wears a baggy jogging suit, a wool cap, and a pair of worn Converse. This is what someone who comes from the bottom looks like. Rocky (Sylvester Stallone) is an unsuccessful boxer from the Italian neighborhood who can't survive on boxing alone and as a result, works as a money collector for a run-of-the-mill Mafioso. His jog leads him to the city art museum, which resembles the Parthenon in Athens, up a wide set of stairs and onto a plateau with a magnificent view over the city. He boxes while he runs, and he runs while he shadowboxes. This is Rocky's first day of training, and it ends with painful cramps. But that doesn't matter—what does matter is taking the first step in conquering one's weaker self. Once that step is taken, one can achieve anything.

Rocky has exactly six weeks to get himself into shape, at which point this third-class "Italian Stallion" is to step into the ring against Apollo Creed (Carl Weathers), a crafty, well-trained heavyweight champion. What Rocky doesn't know is that the bout is a veiled showcase fight for the nation's 200th birthday, an exhibition for the world champion billed as "black boxing champion gives white

SYLVESTER STALLONE Others would have given up ages earlier. Not him. When Sylvester Gardenzio Stallone (born July 6, 1946 in New York City) was born everything was already against him. An accident at birth disfigured his face, leaving it paralyzed on one side, which ironically made Stallone's characteristics in film more interesting. He was teased and called "Sylvie" in school because he was as thin and delicate as a girl. For a long time the son of an Italian hairdresser from a Philadelphia ghetto was nothing more than a marginal American afterthought. He was a pizza baker, a cinema attendant, a small-time actor in third-rate films, and even had a role in a porno.

Then the 30-year-old wrote the frustration from his soul with the script to *Rocky* (1976). At that point he already had a fantastic body he had trained hard to get and that he could display with pride. *Rocky* became his film, his career, and his life. And *Rocky* laid the groundwork for *Rambo* (1982, 1984, 1988, 2008). But those who have success as physical actors have trouble shedding the muscular role. What good is it that Stallone was proven to have an I.Q. of 141, that he collects modern art, and that he paints? "An image is an image is an image…"

He has attempted to break out of this typecasting several times: in the melodramatic *Over the Top* (1986), the ironic *Tango & Cash* (1989), the comic *Stop! Or My Mom Will Shoot* (1991), or the futuristic *Judge Dredd* (1995). For *Get Carter* (2000), he even grew a meticulous goatee. It didn't matter—Stallone remained and remains forever The Italian Stallion. This is how he wanted it—and the public accepted it. He is someone who doesn't give in, who gets knocked down but stands right back up, a man who struggles on because he doesn't have any other choice. He is a true *Cliffhanger* (1993), a cinematic Sisyphus.

1 What doesn't kill you makes you stronger: Rocky, alias Sylvester Stallone, fighting his way to the top of the world.

2 A knock-out sensation: Rocky stands his ground against Apollo (Carl Weathers).

3 "I Want YOU:" Apollo Creed, reigning heavyweight champion, as Uncle Sam.

"Some day, *Rocky* will be seen as a key moment in cinematic history. It's the epitome of the feel-good movie." *Frankfurter Allgemeine Zeitung*

3

4 One man's future is another man's past: Rocky and his mentor Mickey (Burgess Meredith).

5 Down and out in Philadelphia: Paulie (Burt Young) needs a job—but Rocky, the debt collector, wouldn't recommend his own.

6 In this ring, I thee wed: Rocky and Adrian (Talia Shire) are ready to love each other to the bitter end.

Italian-American the chance of a lifetime." The message is simple: in America, the land of infinite possibilities, anyone can make it. What Apollo doesn't know is that Rocky is taking the fight more seriously than he'd ever imagine. Rocky has brains. The fight will last fifteen grueling rounds. And it will take place in a ring, especially in a cinematic ring where every fist, whether poor or rich, black or white, becomes a pounding sledgehammer. Rocky, the guy from next door, who up until this point has never had an even break, who is too good-natured to break the thumbs of the defaulting debtors, and the only man in the neighborhood interested in the shy, barely discernible Adrian (Talia Shire)—this guy shows everyone that you don't have to be a champion to discover yourself. "No revenge," stammers the exhausted Apollo after the fight. Eyes swollen and bloody, Rocky doesn't want a rematch either. He just wants to get to his true love. Like a blinded Samson, he screams her name into the crowd: "Adrian!" She pushes her way through the masses. What happens then is a first in screen history: a woman steps into the ring and passionately kisses the sweaty loser.

Hollywood did not expect *Rocky* to be a success. Quite the reverse in fact—the film was deemed an ideal B-movie and given a $1 million production budget. Only the story's author, Sylvester Stallone, believed in the tale of the small man that makes it big. Rocky's story became Stallone's story, and Stallone's determined assertiveness was mirrored in Rocky's stamina. The Rocky character was tailor-made for Stallone and consequently he didn't want the role handed to Paul Newman or Burt Reynolds. He worked without a salary and negotiated a deal worth 10% of the profits. The film was a box-office hit. After four months, it had earned $28 million and in the end it took home over $140 million. It won three Oscars. Stallone and the young director John G. Avildsen suddenly found themselves at the top of the heap.

"Sometimes reality is crazier than all shit," says a Mafioso in Sergio Leone's *Once Upon a Time in America* (1983), the film about the ultimate American Dream. *Rocky* was a smash hit and Sylvester Stallone showed the world that it was time to believe in the dream of the individual's rise once more. Because the winnings were good for the victor in and out of the boxing spectacle, Rocky would step into the film ring four more times. "The Italian Stallion" from the gutters of Philadelphia had become a cult figure.

SR

5

"*Rocky* batters our emotions like almost no other movie before it. Stallone and his brilliant director John Avildsen play to the gallery so effectively that critical objections seem almost irrelevant." *Der Spiegel*

6

NETWORK 🏆🏆🏆🏆

1976 – USA – 122 MIN.

GENRE

DRAMA

DIRECTOR

SIDNEY LUMET

SCREENPLAY

PADDY CHAYEFSKY

DIRECTOR OF PHOTOGRAPHY

OWEN ROIZMAN

EDITING

ALAN HEIM

MUSIC

ELLIOT LAWRENCE

PRODUCTION

HOWARD GOTTFRIED for MGM, UNITED ARTISTS

STARRING

FAYE DUNAWAY (Diana Christensen), PETER FINCH (Howard Beale), WILLIAM HOLDEN (Max Schumacher), ROBERT DUVALL (Frank Hackett), WESLEY ADDY (Nelson Chaney), NED BEATTY (Arthur Jensen), ARTHUR BURGHARDT (Ahmed Kahn), BILL BURROWS (TV Director), BEATRICE STRAIGHT (Louise Schumacher), KATHY CRONKITE (Mary Ann Gifford), CONCHATA FERRELL (Barbara Schlesinger)

ACADEMY AWARDS 1977

OSCARS for BEST ACTOR (Peter Finch), BEST ACTRESS (Faye Dunaway), BEST SUPPORTING ACTRESS (Beatrice Straight), and BEST ORIGINAL SCREENPLAY (Paddy Chayefsky)

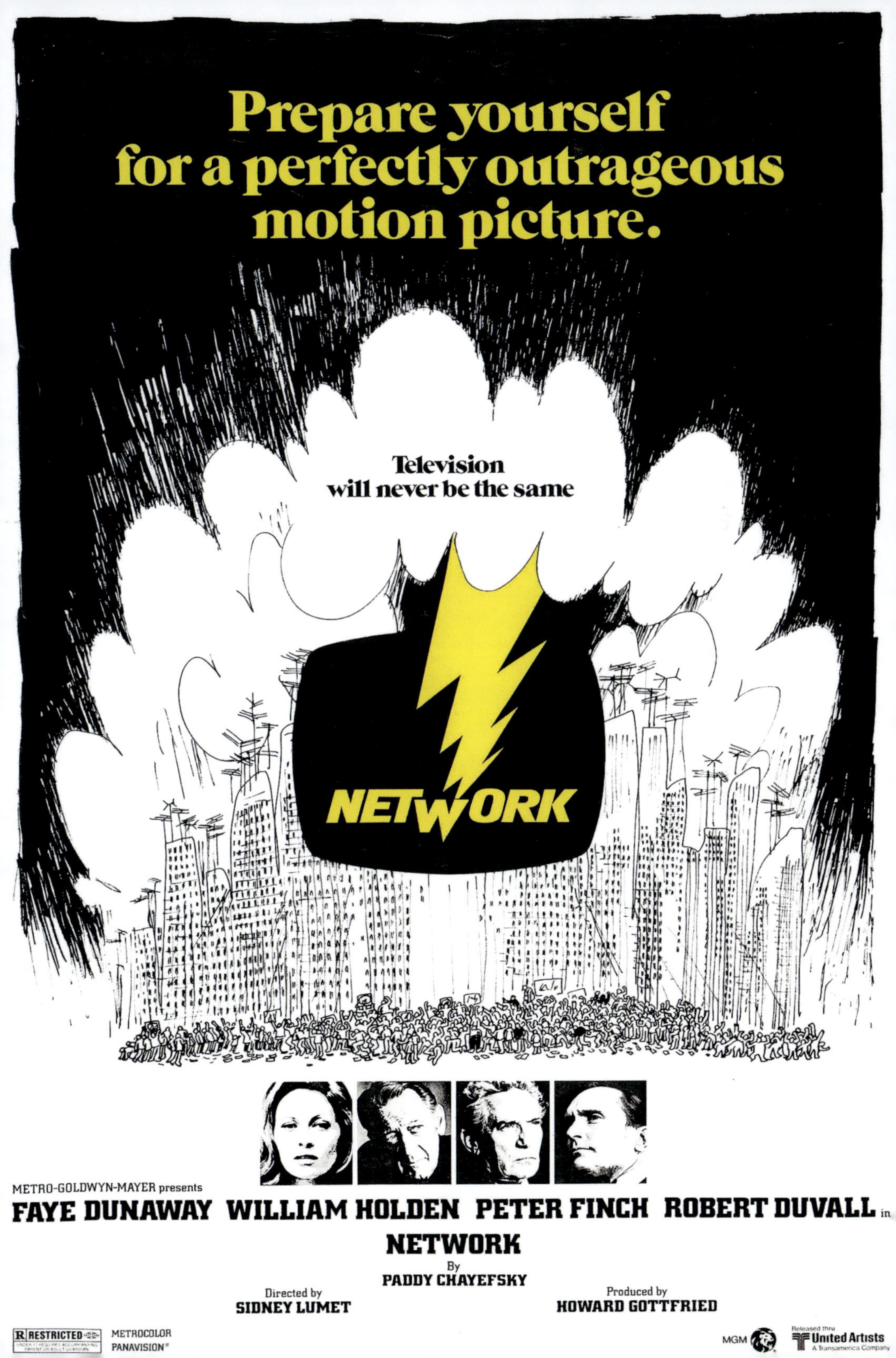

Television
will never be the same

NETWORK

METRO-GOLDWYN-MAYER presents

FAYE DUNAWAY WILLIAM HOLDEN PETER FINCH ROBERT DUVALL in

NETWORK

By
PADDY CHAYEFSKY

Directed by
SIDNEY LUMET

Produced by
HOWARD GOTTFRIED

METROCOLOR
PANAVISION®

MGM

Released thru
United Artists
A Transamerica Company

1

"Who knows what shit will be peddled for truth on this network!?"

The United States felt its impact as early as the 40s. In Europe it hit during the 50s, and before long it had overtaken the world. At the speed of light, television, the "small screen," had claimed its throne as the supreme lord of the mass media, feeding culture and politics into homes worldwide. Between actual sales of sets, station programming and its unparalleled potential as an advertising platform, television quickly became a key factor in national economies. Time and again, the constant headway of the sector's audio-visual capabilities (VHS, DVD) has led to crises within the movie industry. This explains one of the many reasons why television is often presented in film as a medium rooted in competition, as in *The Truman Show* (1998) or *EDtv* (1999). Both of these pictures brand television as nothing more than a boob tube that feigns authenticity as it tries to pull the wool over the eyes of its viewers, which these films construe as uncritical and blind.

THE BOOB TUBE ON THE BIG SCREEN To this day, the prevailing impression of the relationship between film and television is one of rivalry. This feud between the two dominant forms of mass entertainment dates back to the 1950s, when television was still in its infancy. During this decade, the movies tended to write off television as a pesky little upstart, which could boast nothing better than a screen the size of a postage stamp.

Modern cinematic depictions devoted to "the second medium" more readily combine satire with cultural criticism. *The Truman Show* (1998), *EDtv* (1999) and *Pleasantville* (1998), for example, emphasize its artificiality as well as its potential to manipulate and enslave. All three assert that television programming seduces its audience by presenting an alluring candy-coated universe from which there is no need to escape. These films also argue that genuine fulfillment can be attained by those who manage to free themselves of the medium's grasp.

This ongoing dialog between film and TV took off in a whole new direction in the 1990s. New technological advances and forms of marketing made partners of the former arch-enemies. They began to work together in all imaginable types of production, like the manufacture and distribution of videocassettes and DVDs. The so-called "home theater" allowed for big screen blockbusters to be brought into the comfort of one's own home, while TV and film both made a small fortune. Today, television is far from being considered an intrusive medium intent on luring audiences away from the theaters in a ploy to bring the movie industry to its knees. Television and the movies have become trusted cohorts who rely on each other for survival.

"Television has revolutionized the world, but so gradually that we now take for granted what's simply unbelievable. This, for example: every day, millions of people around the world gather to stare at a wood-and-glass box." *Frankfurter Allgemeine Zeitung*

Network can be considered the first movie to open the investigation on television and take us behind the scenes to witness how its programming is created. The three classic arguments, condemning television's potential to manipulate, to encourage conformity and to commercialize at the expense of its audience, are so crassly depicted here that, at times, we believe ourselves to be watching a documentary.

Howard Beale, played by Peter Finch (who died shortly after filming and was awarded the Oscar for Best Actor posthumously), is the first man in television history to die on the air as a means of boosting ratings. This bizarre stunt is induced by the management of an American TV network. The execution, scheduled to take place in front of running cameras as a part of regular programming, riles the spirits of citizens nationwide, who function as a sort of people's liberation army. In truth, it is Beales himself who opts for the dramatic sign off. Yet the network must be held at least partially accountable for inciting the incident.

1 Posthumous accolades: Peter Finch won the Oscar for his performance as TV news anchor Howard Beale.

2 Eye on America: William Holden as Howard's boss, news director Max Schumacher.

3 The clock is ticking: And time is running out for the "mad prophet of the airwaves."

3

Confronted with the alcoholic television commentator's long trend of low ratings, the station executives present Beale with his pink slip. Devastated, he responds to the news by announcing in front of a studio audience that for his upcoming final broadcast he will put a bullet through his head on live television. Beale's fantastic and macabre promise skyrockets his popularity to new heights and prompts young, savvy Diana Christensen (Faye Dunaway), a ratings-hungry programming executive, to win the has-been a second chance.

Beale quickly becomes the voice of a fed-up America, sounding off about the cumulative gripes of the nation into his microphone. Like a wrathful televangelist, he denounces decadence, corruption, egotism and the endless pack of lies facing modern-day society. "I'm mad as hell and I'm not going to take it anymore!" cries America's new favorite son, urging his viewers to run to their windows and scream their frustration at the top of their lungs. From coast to coast, from Maine to Montana, the prophet's chant is echoed by countless U.S. citizens.

This almost utopian dialog between the television medium and its viewers is quickly silenced when Beale announces that the culprit behind the demise of culture and politics is none other than television itself. Soon the TV execs set the ball rolling for his last live presentation…

“With four Golden Globes and ten Oscar nominations, *Network* is one of the most highly-decorated films of the season. And for Hollywood, it’s the perfect revenge on TV.”

Berliner Morgenpost

Network is rooted in the principle that television would go so far as to kill or undermine the foundations of human civilization like morality, social conscience and freedom of speech to attain its goals. As a result, the movie presents us with a much respected and widely spread critical take on pop culture, a thesis which would be revisited ten years later by American author Neil Postman in his provocative bestseller *Amusing Ourselves to Death.* Postman’s exploration of infotainment, show business, and the visually reinforced world outlook prescribed by television is as pertinent today as when it was first published. The same holds true for *Network,* a scathing satire about television’s demented “entertainment value.”

RV

4 Scheduling change: Diana Christensen (Faye Dunaway) makes Beale a national phenomenon.

5 That’s a wrap! Robert Duvall and Faye Dunaway watch the ratings soar and the profits roll in.

6 Broadcast news: “Television is not the truth… We’re in the boredom-killing business.”

"You're beginning to believe the illusions we're spinning here, you're beginning to believe that the tube is reality and your own lives are unreal! You do! Why, whatever the tube tells you: you dress like the tube, you eat like the tube, you raise your children like the tube, you even think like the tube! This is mass madness, you maniacs! In God's name, you people are the real thing. WE are the illusion!" *Film quote: Howard Beale*

AI NO CORRIDA / L'EMPIRE DES SENS

IN THE REALM OF THE SENSES

1976 – JAPAN / FRANCE – 110 MIN.

GENRE

EROTIC FILM

DIRECTOR

NAGISA OSHIMA

SCREENPLAY

NAGISA OSHIMA

DIRECTOR OF PHOTOGRAPHY

HIDEO ITÔ

EDITING

KEIICHI URAOKA

MUSIC

MINORU MIKI

PRODUCTION

ANATOLE DAUMAN for OSHIMA PRODUCTIONS, ARGOS FILMS, SHIBATA ORGANISATION INC

STARRING

TATSUYA FUJI (Kichizo), EIKO MATSUDA (Sada Abe), AOI NAKAJIMA (Toku, Kichizo's Wife), TAIJI TONOYAMA (Beggar), MEIKA SERI (Maid), KANAE KOBAYASHI (the old Geisha Kikuryû), YASUKO MATSUI (Tagawa Inn Manager), KYÔJI KOKONOE (Ômiya), NAOMI SHIRAISHI (Geisha Yaeji), SHINKICHI NODA (Old Man)

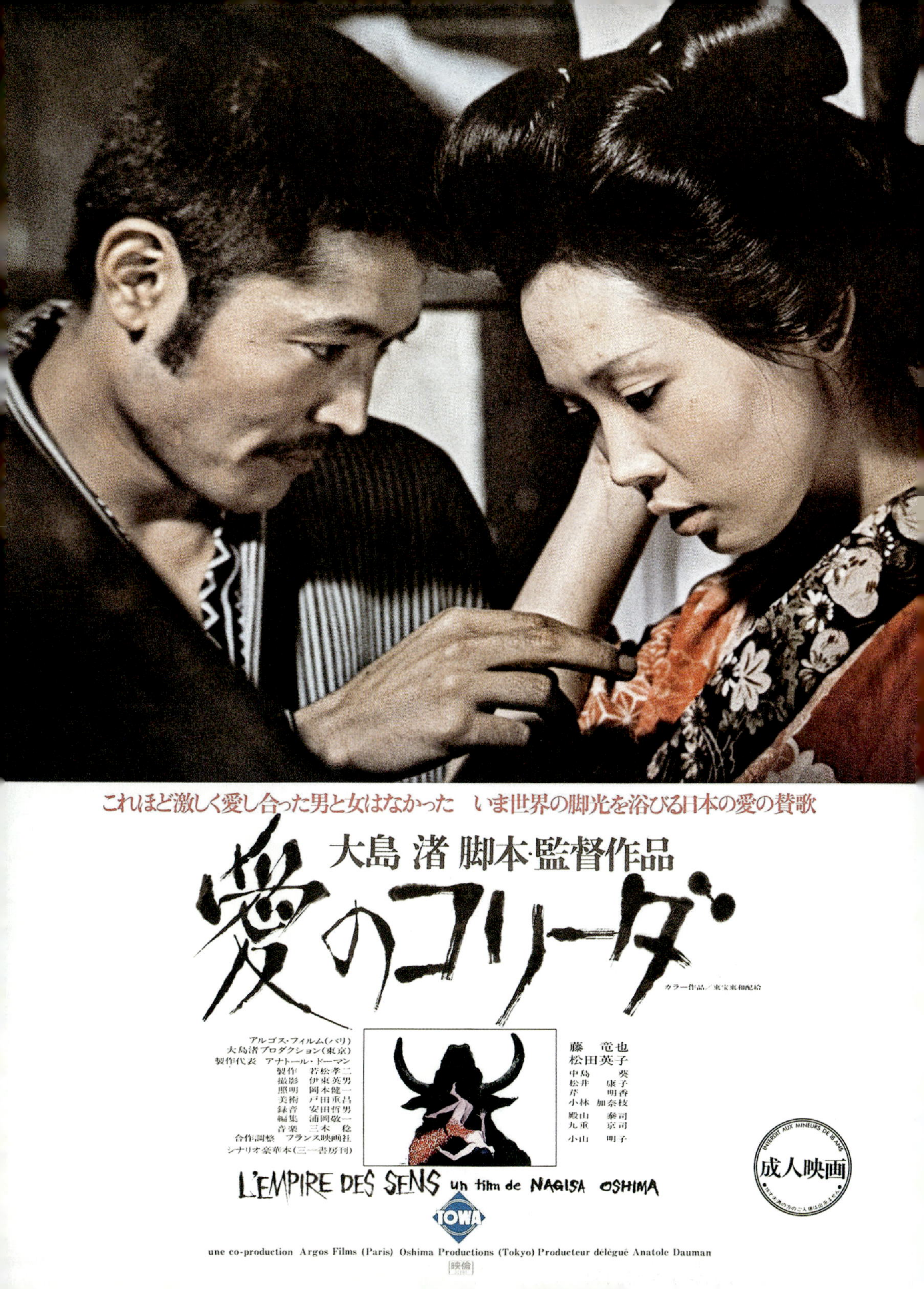

これほど激しく愛し合った男と女はなかった　いま世界の脚光を浴びる日本の愛の賛歌

大島 渚 脚本·監督作品

愛のコリーダ

カラー作品／東宝東和配給

アルゴス·フィルム(パリ)
大島渚プロダクション(東京)
製作代表　アナトール·ドーマン
製作　若松孝二
撮影　伊東英男
照明　岡本健一
美術　戸田重昌
録音　安田哲男
編集　浦岡敬一
音楽　三木 稔
合作調整　フランス映画社
シナリオ豪華本(三一書房刊)

藤 竜也
松田英子
中島 葵
松井 康子
芹 明香
小林 加奈枝
殿山 泰司
九重 京司
小山 明子

L'EMPIRE DES SENS un film de NAGISA OSHIMA

une co-production Argos Films (Paris) Oshima Productions (Tokyo) Producteur délégué Anatole Dauman

映倫

1

"Sada, don't let our pleasure ever end."

It begins like a harmless flirtation and ends in tragedy. In the tea-house managed by his wife (Aoi Nakajima), Kichizo (Tatsuya Fuji) discovers a beautiful new geisha named Sada (Eiko Matsuda). He pursues the young woman, joking, flirting, and generally making his intentions very clear. His wife, thinking this is just one more of his countless affairs, even offers her services as a go-between; and so the affair begins. Kichizo and Sada are soon seeing more and more of each other, and there's something obsessive about their relationship. They do nothing but make love, and they don't mind being watched while they do so. Their love-nest becomes a kind of cage or prison-cell, and the outside world practically ceases to exist for them. They drink to quench their thirst, and they eat nothing. Gradually, Sada becomes increasingly dominant and increasingly demanding. She wants Kichizo to sleep with her incessantly, grows ever more possessive, and insists he should no longer touch his wife. When Sada is forced to go to work again to earn money for herself and Kichizo, she hides his clothes to prevent him leaving while she's meeting her client. And she's the one who introduces ever more extreme practices into their loveplay: slapping, hitting, pinching, and finally choking…

Ai no corrida was a scandal. It showed sex organs in close-up, erect penises and actual intercourse. Previously, such things had been seen only in pornographic films, and never in a work with any claims to artistic legitimacy. The director, Nagisa Oshima, worked under conditions of the utmost secrecy. *Ai no corrida* was the first film made by his newly-formed production company. Filming took around 30 days, with Oshima and his cast and crew working 15 hours a day in a strictly cordoned-off studio. After each day's work, he sent the exposed film material to his producer Anatole Dauman in France. It was the only way to get the film made. Under Japan's strict censorship laws, no laboratory in the country would have developed the film. Oshima also edited the movie in France.

NAGISA OSHIMA The problems involved in the making and showing of *Ai no corrida*/*L'Empire des sens*, (1976) were nothing new for Nagisa Oshima (1932–2013). He was already accustomed to difficulties. In 1960, his second film, *Night and Fog in Japan* (*Nihon no yoru to kiri*, 1960), was withdrawn from circulation by the production company after only four days. The film took an embittered look at the Japanese student movement; and Oshima's entire œuvre is characterized by its focus on the young generation, an interest in the associated topics of violence and sex, and a frequently angry confrontation with the traditional values of Japanese society. He became the central figure in the film renaissance of the 60s, which might be described as a Japanese *Nouvelle Vague*. In *Death by Hanging* (*Koshikei*, 1967/68) for example, he attacks the oppression of the Korean minority in Japan; in *Boy* (*Shonen*, 1969), he portrays greedy parents exploiting their son for their own criminal ends. Oshima's formal language is often brilliant: *The Cruel Story of Youth* (*Seishun zankoku monogatari*, 1960), for instance, tells the wild love story of a gangster couple—in candy colors, with a crazy handheld camera, and in widescreen cinemascope format. After *Ai no corrida*, Oshima achieved international fame one more time with the psychological war drama *Merry Christmas, Mr. Lawrence* (1983), starring David Bowie.

“The story of Sada and Kichizo unfolds like a Catholic Mass, till the final, inevitable, ‘Ite missa est’.” *Cinema*

In 1976, *Ai no corrida* was screened at the festival in Cannes, amidst protests. The organizers of the Berlin Film Festival planned to show it in the same year, but after sensationalized reports appeared in the tabloid press, the film was confiscated by the Public Prosecutor's Department on the suspicion that it breached pornography laws. In Japan, where it is forbidden to show naked sex organs on screen, *Ai no corrida* reached the cinema only in a heavily censored form, with some parts cut and other parts concealed by strategically placed figleafs in the form of black bars. It came to a court case, which Oshima won in 1982.

Yet there's nothing titillating about the anatomical detail in this radical and disturbing film. Oshima tells the story of a sexual obsession, a love that consists entirely of physical desire, shutting out the whole world beyond the lovers' purview. This is a love that demands complete submission to the lover, a love that's indifferent to such epithets as "embarrassing" or "distasteful." With pitiless logic, Oshima takes the romantic idea of "belonging" to the loved one, and follows it through to its deadly conclusion. This love story also acquires an almost subversive undertone when we consider that it's set in 1936, something that only becomes apparent in the few scenes that take place outdoors. This was the year that marked the birth of Japanese fascism. While the nation girds its loins for a megalomaniac imperialist campaign, Kichizo and Sada are interested in nothing but each other.

Ai no corrida was based on a true story. In 1936, a woman cut off her lover's penis and wandered around Tokyo with it for four days. Her obsessive passion aroused a wave of public sympathy, and she was sentenced to only six years in prison.

HJK

1 Love you to death: Thinking it's only another meaningless affair, teahouse proprietress Toku (Aoi Nakajima) aids Kichizo (Tatsuya Fuji) in making geisha Sada's acquaintance.

2 Miss Scarlet with the knife: "The case is still very much alive in the minds of the Japanese. It is thought of with reverence, as an eternal ode to the love sick." (*Frankfurter Allgemeine Zeitung*)

3 Dream weaver: Sada plants one on Kichizo.

3

L'AILE OU LA CUISSE

THE WING OR THE THIGH

1976 – FRANCE – 104 MIN.

GENRE

COMEDY

DIRECTOR

CLAUDE ZIDI

SCREENPLAY

CLAUDE ZIDI, MICHEL FABRE

DIRECTOR OF PHOTOGRAPHY

CLAUDE RENOIR, WLADIMIR IVANOV

EDITING

MONIQUE ISNARDON, ROBERT ISNARDON

MUSIC

VLADIMIR COSMA

PRODUCTION

CHRISTIAN FECHNER for FILMS CHRISTIAN FECHNER

STARRING

LOUIS DE FUNÈS (Charles Duchemin),
COLUCHE (= MICHEL COLUCCI) (Gérard Duchemin),
JULIEN GUIOMAR (Jean Tricatel), ANN ZACHARIAS (Marguerite II.),
CLAUDE GENSAC (Marguerite I.), RAYMOND BUSSIÈRES (Chauffeur Henri),
DANIEL LANGLET (Lambert), MARCEL DALIO (The Tailor),
PHILIPPE BOUVARD (Himself), VITTORIO CAPRIOLI (Vittorio)

LOUIS DE FUNES
COLUCHE

LOUIS DE FUNES
COLUCHE
dans

l'Aile
ou la Cuisse

un film de CLAUDE ZIDI
Scénario et dialogues de CLAUDE ZIDI
avec la collaboration de MICHEL FABRE

Photographie CLAUDE RENOIR
Décors MICHEL DE BROIN
Montage MONIQUE et ROBERT ISNARDON
Directeur de Production ROGER MORAND

Producteur exécutif PIERRE GRUNSTEIN
Producteur Délégué BERNARD ARTIGUES
Musique VLADIMIR COSMA · Éditions Musicales Vogue International

Tourné en PANAVISION® Anamorphique · Distribué par AMLF

1

"A loin of beef—Argentinian, three years old, southern slopes."

The delicate flavor and aroma of fine foods and wines makes life worth living for Duchemin (Louis de Funès), a man whose entire existence revolves around eating. Every day, he visits the best and most expensive restaurants in town with the reverence of a worshipper and the vigilance of a vestal virgin. To him, a prizewinning chef is a high priest of the palate, a privileged guardian of the Grail of good taste. Charles Duchemin is the most respected restaurant critic in France; and today and every day, he expects each cook to do his sacred duty.

He carries out his tests in a series of cunning disguises. One day he's an old lady, the next, he's an American, resplendent in a pink jacket and a Stetson. When he's sure no-one's watching, he checks the temperature of the schnitzel with his trusty thermometer, stores samples of the wine in the tanks in his tailor-made jacket, or tucks anything he can't face eating into a Tupperware box. The laboratory, and his tastebuds, decide how many stars a restaurant will be deemed to deserve. In this way, he and his colleagues banquet and burp their way through the restaurants of the nation, before publishing the verdicts in the *Guide Duchemin*: the gourmets' bible and a signpost to culinary Nirvana.

It's an achievement of national significance, and it's only fitting that Charles should be invited to join the hallowed ranks of the Académie française. But he's failed to reckon with his arch-enemy Jean Tricatel (Julien Guiomar), manufacturer of industrial grub and owner of a chain of junkfood restaurants. The scheming Tricatel, who is every bit as slimy as the food he produces, smuggles a spy into Duchemin's house to steal the names of the distinguished restaurants before the book is published. With the help of this list, he plans to buy up some of the best restaurants in the country and force them to accept his own inferior products. And by this somewhat roundabout route, he hopes to see his zero-quality fodder elevated to the rank of *haute cuisine*.

When Charles gets wind of this plot, he is understandably appalled: "I could give a restaurant two stars and this scoundrel would serve the customers dog food with tinned rice. On a saucer." The fanatical epicure resolves to save French cooking by putting Tricatel in his place: he will challenge his rival to a TV talkshow duel and show the world who's boss. But his culinary crusade ends in a trip to Gourmet Hell, for suddenly he's confronted by an irate gastronome whose business he ruined with a bad review.

LOUIS DE FUNÈS They called him Rumpelstiltskin, the Poison Dwarf, Mr. Hyperactive and Poltergeist: the small man with the big nose, the World Champ of hysterical rage. A typical de Funès character is the uptight *petit bourgeois* who despises his social inferiors, sucks up to his bosses, schemes to get ahead, and ultimately falls flat on his face.
(Carlos) Louis de Funès (De Galarza) was born in Courbevoie in 1914, the son of a Spanish diamond merchant. His trademark was his rubber face, which he could twist into the most incredible grimaces, combined with some truly wild body language. He was apparently able to increase the length of his nose in order to play it like a violin. While performing such esoteric practices, he occasionally lost the ability to speak his native language, resorting to bizarre onomatopoeic sounds said to be reminiscent of Donald Duck, to whom many of his film characters bore a striking resemblance. He learned a series of trades—furrier, decorator, bar pianist—before making his breakthrough at the advanced age of 50, in *Le Gendarme de Saint Tropez* (1964). After 20 years in supporting roles, he was suddenly a popular favorite, capable of making up to five films in a single year. Many of these were highly successful. Examples include the *Gendarme* series, the *Fantomas* films (1964, 1965, 1966) and *Oscar* (1967). His ascent marked the beginning of the comedy boom in France, and he won countless fans worldwide. They referred to him affectionately as "Fufu." De Funès died in 1983.

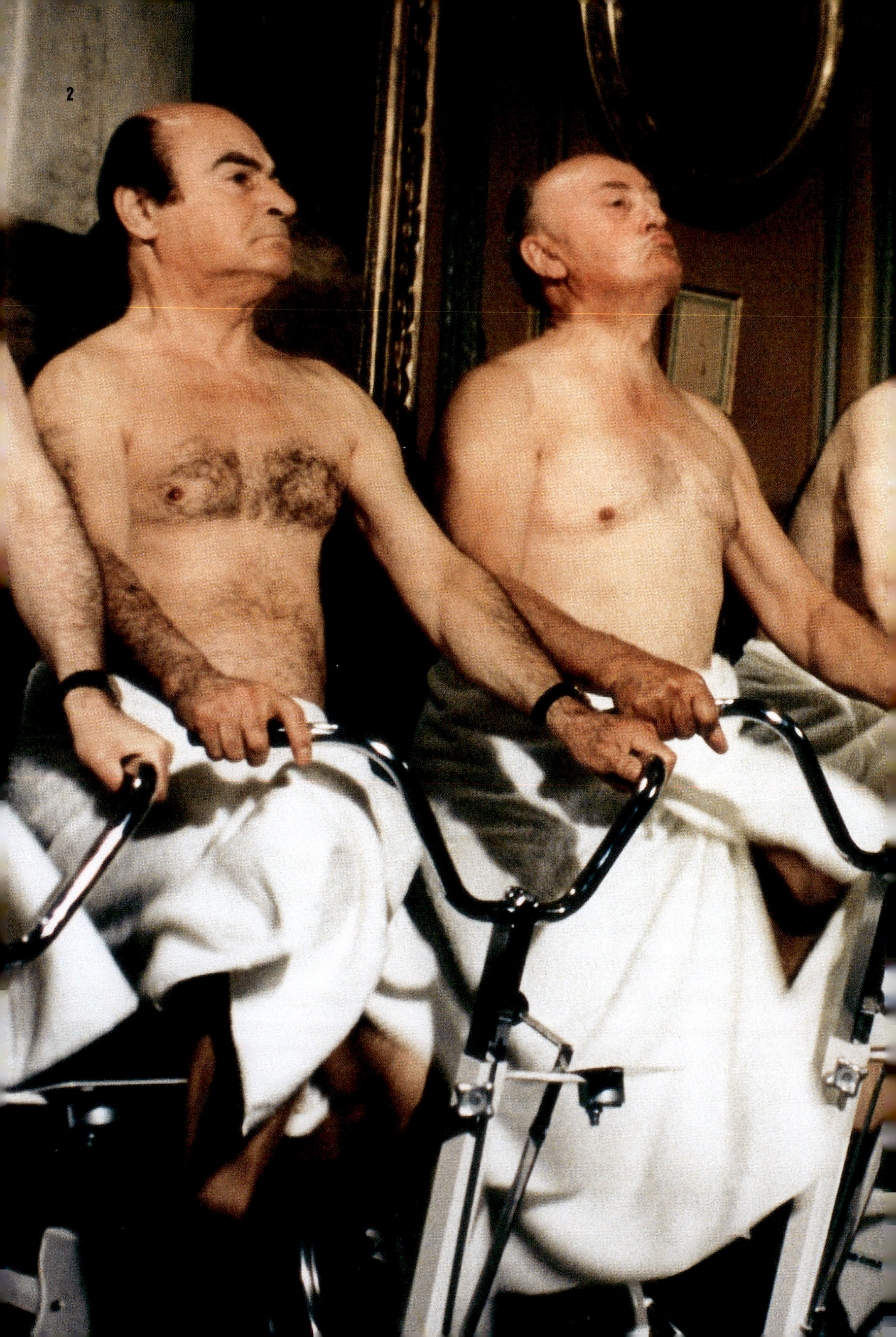

2

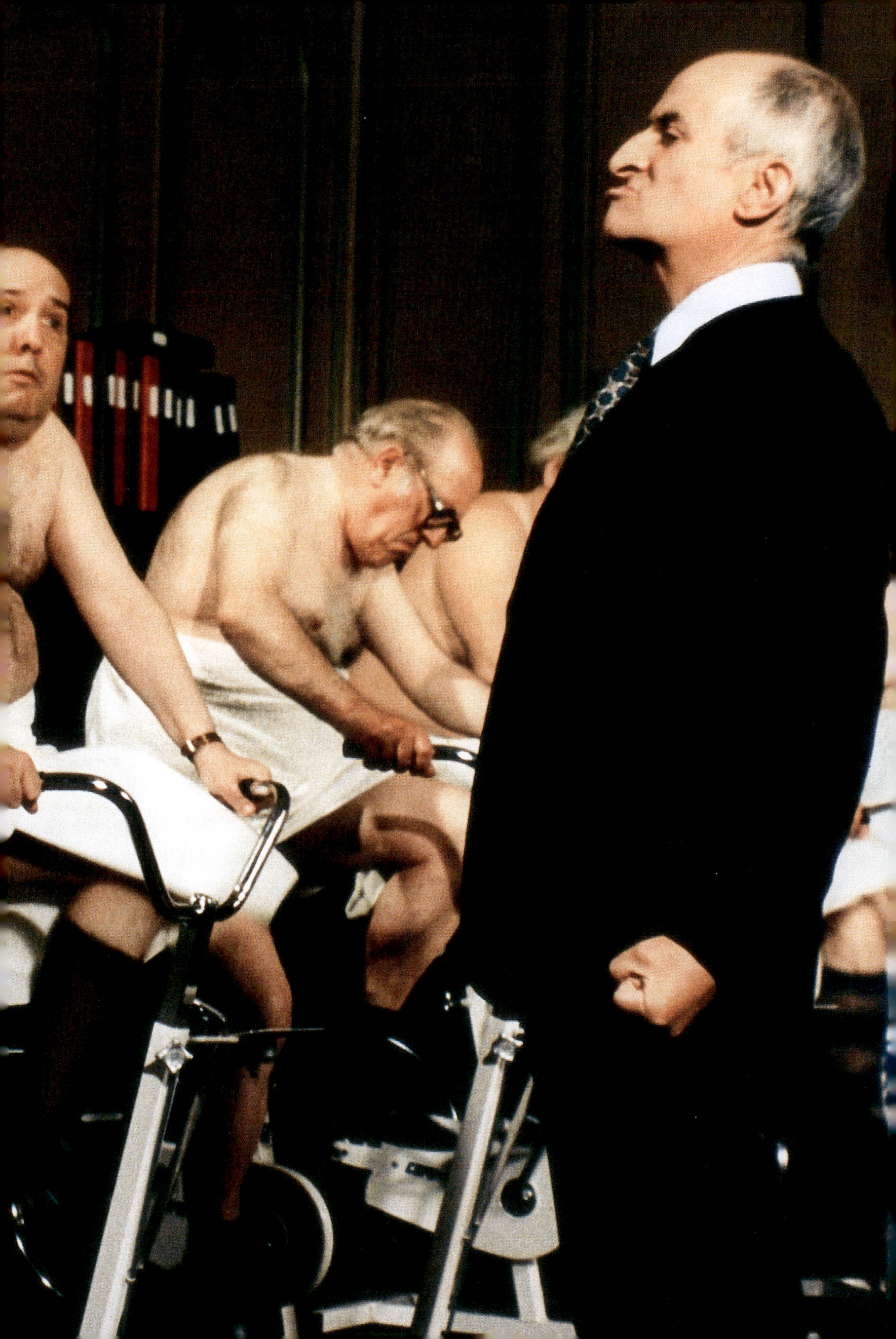

With a shotgun at his head, he's forced by his tormentor to eat a Tricatel menu… The expression on Charles' face as he swallows the snails is one of sheer horror, the elderly oysters bring him out in blotches, and the platter of slimy sauerkraut is more than he can bear.

After this culinary inferno, Charles is far from his normal self; more to the point, he's lost his sense of taste. Just 24 hours before his TV showdown with Tricatel, he can't tell the difference between a green bean and a wad of cotton wool. Rescue is at hand, however, in the shape of his son Gérard, played by De Funès' equally famous compatriot,

1 Frugal gourmet: When Charles Duchemin (Louis De Funès) partakes in France's national pastime, he turns up the heat on farce and tomfoolery.

2 Tour de France: Charles will stop at nothing to get his taste testers into prime physical condition.

3 A night at Benihana's: This learned Teppan performance artist makes a laughing stock of the Cuisinart.

4 Catch of the day: Duchemin and his staff close in on an unsavory intruder.

5 A wolf in she's clothing: One false move and this black widow will spoil the soup with her poisoned pen. Here, food critic Charles moonlights as the happy homemaker.

6 Pigs in a blanket: Keeping in line with his sugary menu, director Claude Zidi's recipe for success also calls for these little weenies to be honey-glazed.

4

5

the comedian Coluche; and soon this very odd couple—the father a French Foghorn Leghorn, the son as meek as a mouse—have entered the lion's den: Tricatel's food factory. In the surreal setting of the production halls, father and son only barely escape ending up as canned meat before uncovering the shameless tricks of Tricatel's trade: Among many other sins, he's been using the blessings of modern technology to pass off green bathing caps as lettuces.

L'Aile ou la cuisse is hardly a subtle comedy, but then it never tries to be. Its strength is in its snappy visual gags: a spell in hospital and the resetting of a broken leg are excuses for an orgy of slapstick. But the film also has its quiet moments. Take the scene in which Charles discovers that his son has been leading a double life as a clown: when the outraged father pours a bucket of foam over his son's head, the comedy is so bittersweet that the laughter sticks in our throats. *L'Aile ou la cuisse* is a choice morsel of a movie, and it's often deliciously funny. OK

"Louis de Funès doesn't quite explode, but he certainly makes sparks fly, and his sheer comic energy is as powerful as ever." *Le Monde*

6

IL CASANOVA DI FEDERICO FELLINI

FELLINI'S CASANOVA

1976 – ITALY – 154 MIN.

GENRE

LITERARY ADAPTATION

DIRECTOR

FEDERICO FELLINI

SCREENPLAY

FEDERICO FELLINI, BERNARDINO ZAPPONI, based on the memoirs *STORIA DELLA MIA VITA* by GIACOMO CASANOVA

DIRECTOR OF PHOTOGRAPHY

GIUSEPPE ROTUNNO

EDITING

RUGGERO MASTROIANNI

MUSIC

NINO ROTA

PRODUCTION

ALBERTO GRIMALDI for PRODUZIONI EUROPEE ASSOCIATI

STARRING

DONALD SUTHERLAND (Giacomo Casanova), TINA AUMONT (Henriette), CICELY BROWNE (Madame D'Urfe), CARMEN SCARPITTA (Madame Charpillon), CLARA ALGRANTI (Marcolina), CHESTY MORGAN (Barberina), MARGARET CLEMENTI (Maria Magdalena), SANDRA ELAINE ALLEN (Angelina the Giantess), CLARISSA MARY ROLL (Anna Maria), ADELE ANGELA LOJODICE (Mechanical Doll), OLIMPIA CARLISI (Isabella).

ACADEMY AWARDS 1977

OSCAR for BEST COSTUMES (Danilo Donati)

Titanus

ALBERTO GRIMALDI presenta

IL CASANOVA DI FEDERICO FELLINI

con

DONALD SUTHERLAND

SCENEGGIATURA DI FEDERICO FELLINI E BERNARDINO ZAPPONI

FOTOGRAFIA DI GIUSEPPE ROTUNNO (A.I.C.) SCENE E COSTUMI DI DANILO DONATI MUSICA DI NINO ROTA

TECHNICOLOR

1

"Peace comes only with death."

With 600 wigs, more than 1,000 costumes, 186 actors—including a giant woman 2.38 meters tall weighing 270 kilos—200 people working behind the scenes and 2,500 extras, this really was a monumental undertaking. No expense was spared in filming these episodes from the life of the Venetian Giacomo Girolamo Casanova (Chevalier de Seingalt, as he ennobled himself, 1725–1798), the epitome of the Rococo Age. Casanova's memoirs, although incomplete, are almost 4,000 pages long, and they remain a fascinating storehouse of detailed descriptions and observations. This uncompromising documentation allows us a close-up view of the century that was ended by the French Revolution.

Those who know these memoirs will barely recognize the figure created by Fellini. No frivolous adventurer, no salon lion here. Instead of the historical Casanova, we have a creature of artifice, a kind of human *objet d'art*; instead of the gallant chevalier who allegedly "possessed" 1,000 women, a melancholy Don Quixote. The Casanova we see here is not the master but the prisoner of his own sexuality. King Sex rules supreme.

Fellini cast the Canadian Donald Sutherland in the leading role, seeing him as an actor "with a vague, dissolved, watery face, reminiscent of Venice." Sutherland's Venice-face had impressed Fellini in Nicholas Roeg's *Don't Look Now* (1973), a quiet horror film that takes place in the canal city. For the role of Casanova, the make-up department provided Sutherland with more than 100 different "faces"—the virtuoso of love as a hero of labor, a downtrodden slave to his own desperate vanity.

FEDERICO FELLINI Federico Fellini was born and brought up in Rimini. In Italy, he became a national institution. When he died in Rome in 1993 at the age of 73, the title pages of the Italian newspapers were printed with black borders, and news and politics made way for the obituaries. Six months previously, the "maestro"—who had never made a film outside Italy—had been given a special Oscar for his life's work. He was the first and—so far—the only Italian to be so honored. Foreign distributors frequently added his name to the films' titles (e.g. *Fellini's Roma / Roma*, 1971; *Fellini's Amarcord / Amarcord*, 1973), and this is also unique in the hundred-year history of the cinema. Fellini began as an assistant to Roberto Rossellini, as he helped the Italian cinema make a new start immediately after the war: *Open City* (*Roma, città aperta*, 1945) and *Paisan* (*Paisà*,1946). In 1954, Fellini attracted international attention as director of *La Strada*, featuring Anthony Quinn as the traveling fairground artiste Zampanò alongside Fellini's wife Giulietta Masina as the naive and passive Gelsomina. *La Strada* also won the Oscar as Best Foreign Film, but the film divided the Italian public into two camps, who carried on their struggle well into the 70s: the Communists, who swore by Visconti (*The Leopard*, *Il gattopardo*, 1963), and the Catholics, who swore by life, suffering and charity. Fellini himself, however, always claimed a third, independent position. His 22 films, half of them world-famous (e.g. *La Dolce Vita*, 1959/60), know neither enemies nor ideologies. Although Fellini's films lack any kind of traditional religious message, they are essentially "touching," for it is necessary to let oneself be touched, and to touch others, when the world is full of people who have to struggle through life and can't help themselves.

"The birth of cinematic art from the spirit of Eros."

Der Spiegel

At regular intervals, we are shown Casanova pursuing his vocation, but any pornographic expectations are sadly disappointed. This is hard labor indeed. When we see the sweat streaming down his distorted face, it's difficult to believe there's any kind of pleasure involved. To help him out, Fellini's Casanova takes an exquisite mechanical bird with him wherever he goes. When wound up, it functions as a kind of metronome, nodding its head and flapping its wings, setting out the rhythm of love (accompanied by Nino Rota's circus-like music) for Casanova to keep time to. And Casanova's lust is no less mechanical than the movements of the metal bird.

1 Come on baby, light my fire! Donald Sutherland as Casanova, with his flames guttering.

2 A real doll: The ideal woman for Fellini's Casanova…

3 … she takes a licking and keeps on kicking.

3

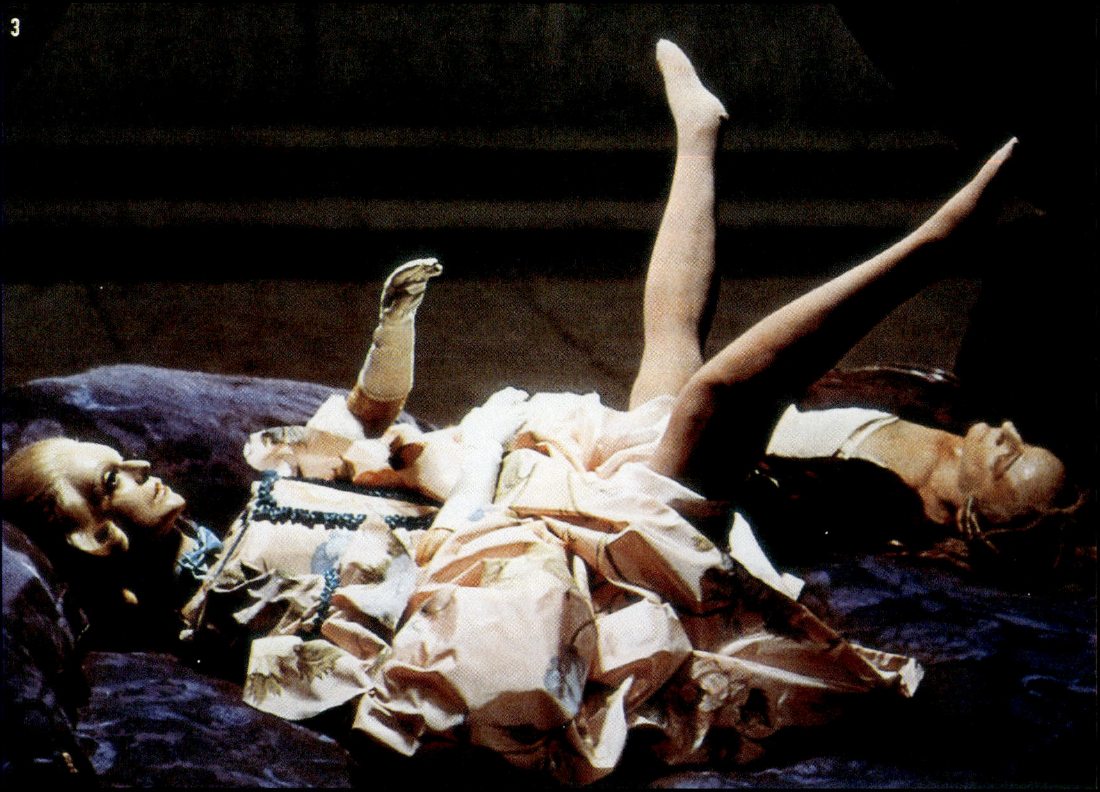

4

"Donald Sutherland commands a stunning array of gestures both precise and revealing. He manages to lend tension to a vacuum; and the final, magnificent close-up of his rheumy old eyes, alive nevertheless with the first faint glimmer of self-realization, is, in the context, unbearably moving."

Sight and Sound

4 Going through the motions: According to Fellini's, the legendary lover is a hollow man, and quite mechanical.

5 Blind sighted: Casanova can't see past his own mask.

6 Delusions of grandeur: As a guest at the royal courts of Europe, Casanova fails to recognize that he is no more than a minor actor in a vast theater, a bit-part player in a cynical power game.

In the opening sequence of the film, Fellini had already shown us a kind of pleasure-machine: the Carnival in Venice, Europe's garden of earthly delights. Having long since lost its military power, Venice is here seen feeding off the remains of its accumulated wealth. The masked revelers come to a halt, the noisy crowd falls silent: the great Masque on the Grand Canal is just about to begin. Slowly, majestically, the head of an enormous woman emerges from the water, as the masked multitude cries in unison: "Blessed Venezia! Venezia is born!" ... and then the ropes snap. The woman/Venice/the Rococo age—all swallowed up by the sea. Thus the main motifs of the film are established early on: machines imitating life, or else the living made weirdly mechanical.

Only once, towards the end of these 10 episodes from the life of Casanova, does the Great Lover show any tenderness. He seems to have found his ideal woman: a life-sized doll, the perfect partner for the machine he has become. In the end, Casanova is all mask, pure artifice. The electrified human marionette with the erotic aura of a piston engine performs its last *danse macabre* on the icy surface of the Canale Grande; a Dance of Death, in which all that's left of desire is the empty shell of mechanical motion.

Fellini's Casanova is the maestro's darkest and most pitiless film, and it's still a memorable settling of accounts with machismo, chauvinism, and the excesses of male ego. In the deliberately artificial settings of this film, windows are either completely lacking or else they are "blind." There are no prospects, no heavens, no horizon. In the 70s, the main reactions to the film were shock, bewilderment and point-blank rejection. Now, however, one might venture an interpretation: while many films show us an artificial paradise, this one takes us to an artificial hell. RV

6

ASSAULT ON PRECINCT 13

1976 – USA – 91 MIN.

GENRE

ACTION FILM

DIRECTOR

JOHN CARPENTER

SCREENPLAY

JOHN CARPENTER

DIRECTOR OF PHOTOGRAPHY

DOUGLAS KNAPP

EDITING

JOHN T. CHANCE (= JOHN CARPENTER)

MUSIC

JOHN CARPENTER

PRODUCTION

J. S. KAPLAN for TURTLE, CKK

STARRING

AUSTIN STOKER (Bishop), DARWIN JOSTON (Napoleon Wilson),
LAURIE ZIMMER (Leigh), TONY BURTON (Wells),
CHARLES CYPHERS (Special Officer Starker), NANCY LOOMIS (Julie),
PETER BRUNI (Ice Cream Man), JOHN J. FOX (Warden),
KIM RICHARDS (Kathy Lawson), MARTIN WEST (Lawson)

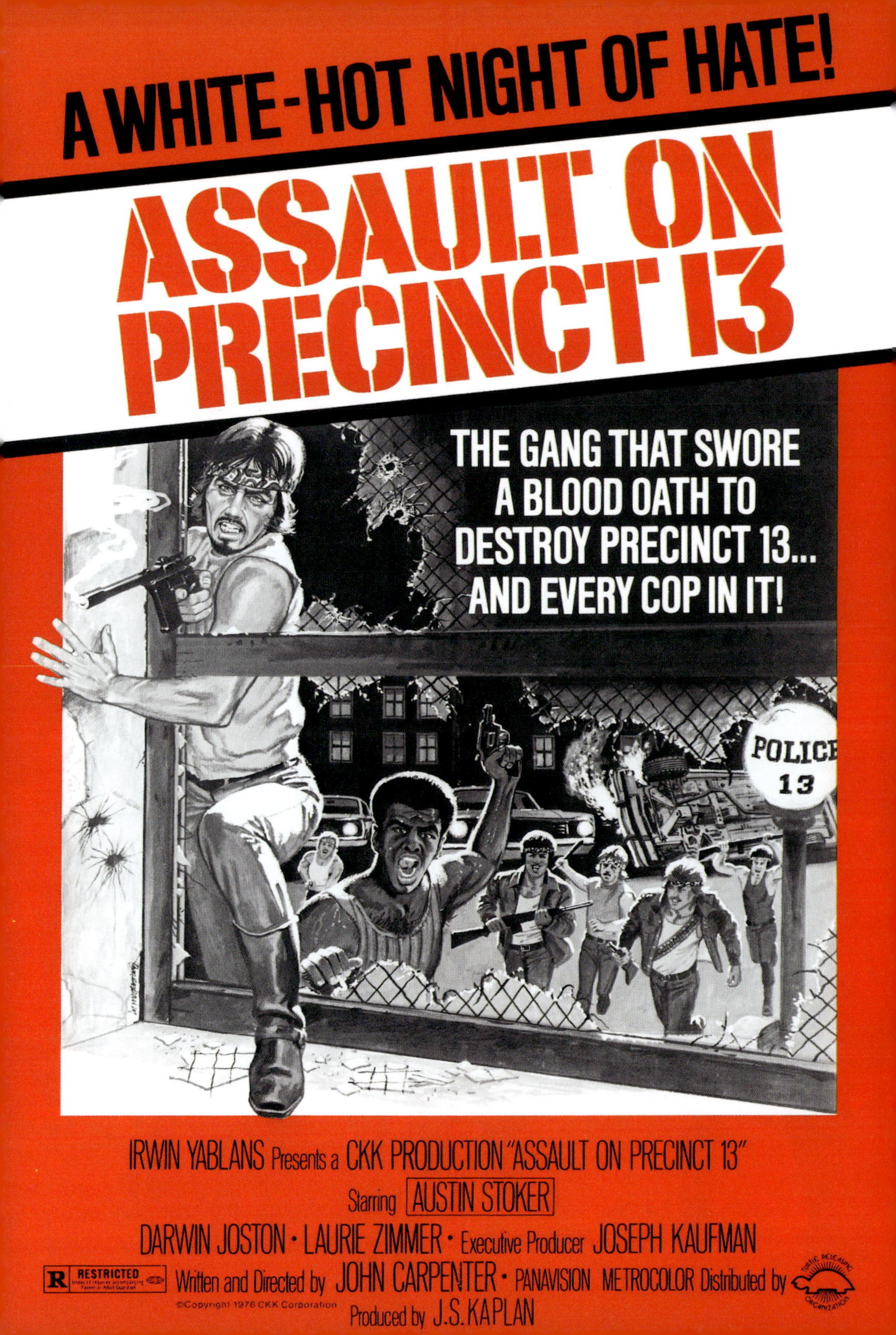

A WHITE-HOT NIGHT OF HATE!

ASSAULT ON PRECINCT 13

THE GANG THAT SWORE
A BLOOD OATH TO
DESTROY PRECINCT 13...
AND EVERY COP IN IT!

POLICE
13

IRWIN YABLANS Presents a CKK PRODUCTION "ASSAULT ON PRECINCT 13"

Starring AUSTIN STOKER

DARWIN JOSTON · LAURIE ZIMMER · Executive Producer JOSEPH KAUFMAN

R RESTRICTED

Written and Directed by JOHN CARPENTER · PANAVISION METROCOLOR Distributed by

©Copyright 1976 CKK Corporation

Produced by J.S. KAPLAN

"It's a god-damn siege."

Dum-da-da-da-dum. A threateningly minimalist synthesizer theme brings terror, as a street gang lays siege to an isolated police precinct. A hail of bullets and countless dead bodies signify the arrival of the Wild West in the midst of the city.

The night had begun so quietly for police lieutenant Bishop (Austin Stoker), whose task it was to watch over an empty precinct during the last evening before its closure. This seemingly boring task takes him back to the district where he grew up: Anderson, a section of Los Angeles on the edge of anarchy. But the night turns out to be anything but boring. A bus full of prisoners stops at the precinct to unload an inmate who has fallen sick, and it just so happens that the members of a street gang have simultaneously come to the precinct to avenge the deaths of six of their comrades shot during a police action the night before. A state of siege ensues—with scores of attackers thirsting for revenge, silencers on their weapons, and an apparently endless supply of ammunition on the outside, and a group of police officers and inmates inside the precinct who are unable to call for help. The electricity and phone lines have been cut, they're running out of ammunition, and they drop like flies until, aside from Bishop, only secretary Leigh (Laurie Zimmer), and two inmates, Napoleon Wilson (Darwin Joston) and Wells (Tony Burton), are left standing.

JOHN CARPENTER John Carpenter (born 1948) gets a chapter all to himself in almost every book about fantastic cinema. As a student, Carpenter worked on the screenplay to the short film *The Resurrection of Bronco Billy* (1970), which won an Oscar. In 1974 he made his full-length film debut with *Dark Star*, a satire of the science fiction classic, *2001: A Space Odyssey* (1968). In 1978 he made the horror classic, *Halloween*, and three years later *Escape from New York* (1981), the prototype for all apocalyptic films. His effective use of cinematic methods (like the subjective camerawork in *Halloween*) and his familiarity with film history distinguish his films. In *Someone's Watching Me!* (1978), he paraphrased Hitchcock's *Rear Window* (1954). *The Thing* (1982) is a remake of the Howard Hawks classic of the same name (1951). In the 80s and 90s Carpenter made several more fantasy films, which were mostly uninteresting, with the exception of *Prince of Darkness* (1987), a kind of horror version of *Assault on Precinct 13* (1976) and the outstanding *In the Mouth of Madness* (1994). In September 2023, it was announced that Carpenter would direct again for the first time in 13 years and be involved in the series Suburban Screams.

3

1 Moving day: Napoleon Wilson (Darwin Joston) and other prisoners are transported to their new holding cells on death row…

2 … but when one of the prisoners falls ill, the inmates are re-routed to a non-operational precinct.

3 You'd best watch your back: The vengeful band of assassins is about to make its next move.

4 The emperor's new clothes: Ringleader Napoleon Wilson has nothing to lose. He's already scheduled for execution.

5 Calling all cars: "Carpenter cited three sources of inspiration: a newspaper clipping, the Western flick *Rio Bravo* and his own fear of random acts of violence." (*Cinema*)

With his cleverly conceived but straightforward film, 28-year-old John Carpenter, who acted as director, author, editor and composer, accomplished a stroke of genius that is still a textbook example of how to create an impressive film with modest means. *Assault on Precinct 13* (production cost $200,000) is both plain and overwhelmingly suggestive in its narration: A few images of the shoot-out during which the gang members are killed and a single radio message suffice to reveal that the city is a powder keg just waiting to explode. Images of gangsters skulking through the neighborhood, views through a telescopic lens, and the horrible shooting of a small girl establish the gang's total lack of scruples. Carpenter brilliantly constructs the siege scenario. Though the precinct is in the city, it is completely cut off from the rest of the world—no electricity, no telephone. The gangsters follow a perfidious strategy, clearing the streets after each attack so that neither corpses nor bullet-ridden cars indicate what has occurred.

A group of attackers surrounding a handful of captives is a scenario familiar from Westerns like Howard Hawks' *Rio Bravo* (1959) or George Romero's horror classic, *Night of the Living Dead* (1968). Carpenter shifts the setting from a lonely farmhouse in the Wild West directly into the heart of civilization—a modern city. The parallels to *Rio Bravo* go even further, as the captives save themselves with explosives, just as John Wayne's sheriff did. Interestingly, Carpenter adopted Wayne's character

“A low-budget and taut update of the classic Howard Hawks western, Rio Bravo.” *Motion Picture Guide*

name, John T. Chance, as a pseudonym for his work as film editor. Carpenter also pays homage to Alfred Hitchcock. The story Bishop tells his secretary toward the beginning of the film—how his father used to send him to the police precinct as a small boy—is an anecdote Hitchcock liked to tell about his own childhood.

Carpenter revealed himself to be a student of film history with *Assault on Precinct 13*, and the film itself became a model for countless others: various gang films and the “Blaxploitation” films of the 80s and 90s suggest his influence, and many action directors were inspired by his no-frills direction. The superb economy of the production is exemplified by Carpenter’s soundtrack, which is comprised of merely two themes—the threatening synthesizer theme and an electrical piano melody that evokes sympathy. Both are entirely enthralling.

HJK

5

DER AMERIKANISCHE FREUND

THE AMERICAN FRIEND

1977 – FRG / FRANCE – 126 MIN.

GENRE

GANGSTER FILM, LITERARY ADAPTATION, DRAMA

DIRECTOR

WIM WENDERS

SCREENPLAY

WIM WENDERS, based on the novel
RIPLEY'S GAME by PATRICIA HIGHSMITH

DIRECTOR OF PHOTOGRAPHY

ROBBY MÜLLER

EDITING

PETER PRZYGODDA,
BARBARA VON WEITERSHAUSEN

MUSIC

JÜRGEN KNIEPER

PRODUCTION

WIM WENDERS for ROAD MOVIES FILMPRODUKTION,
FILMVERLAG DER AUTOREN, MOLI FILMS, LES FILMS DU LOSANGE,
WESTDEUTSCHER RUNDFUNK

STARRING

DENNIS HOPPER (Tom Ripley), BRUNO GANZ (Jonathan Zimmermann),
LISA KREUZER (Marianne Zimmermann), GÉRARD BLAIN (Raoul Minot),
NICHOLAS RAY (Derwatt), SAMUEL FULLER (Gangster),
PETER LILIENTHAL (Marcangelo), DANIEL SCHMID (Igraham),
RUDOLF SCHÜNDLER (Gantner), SANDY WHITELAW (Doctor in Paris)

DENNIS HOPPER BRUNO GANZ

DER AMERIKANISCHE FREUND

LISA KREUZER GERARD BLAIN

Ein Film von
WIM WENDERS

nach »Ripley's Game«
von Patricia Highsmith

mit ANDREAS DEDECKE DAVID BLUE
GERTY MOLZEN HEINZ JOACHIM KLEIN
AXEL SCHIESSLER
STEFAN LENNERT RUDOLF SCHÜNDLER
HEINRICH MARMANN SATYA DE LA MANITOU
ADOLF HANSEN ROSEMARIE HEINIKEL

als Gäste NICHOLAS RAY SAMUEL FULLER PETER LILIENTHAL DANIEL SCHMID JEAN EUSTACHE SANDY WHITELAW und LOU CASTEL
Kamera ROBBY MÜLLER Musik JÜRGEN KNIEPER Schnitt PETER PRZYGODDA Ausstattung HEIDI und TONI LÜDI Originalton MARTIN MÜLLER PETER KAISER
Produktionsleitung MICHAEL WIEDEMANN PIERRE COTTRELL Herstellungsleitung RENEE OTTO-GUNDELACH MARGARET MENEGOZ
Buch und Regie WIM WENDERS

gefilmt mit ARRIFLEX
GEYER

Eine Coproduktion der ROAD MOVIES Filmproduktion GmbH, Berlin mit WIM WENDERS Produktion, München, LES FILMS DU LOSANGE, Paris und dem Westdeutschen Rundfunk, Köln Der Roman »Ripley's Game oder Regel ohne Ausnahme« erschien bei Diogenes

FILMVERLAG DER AUTOREN

1

"I don't know what to do."

In Wim Wenders' melancholy gangster film, based on a novel by Patricia Highsmith, no one really knows what to do any more. The two main characters are wandering in a kind of no-man's-land, bored, existentially desperate and in danger of losing their lives. On the one hand, we have the smart gangster Tom Ripley (Dennis Hopper), who commutes between New York and Hamburg, visiting auctions and buying expensive paintings by the forger Derwatt (Nicholas Ray), while cultivating his links to the underworld. And then we have the meek, unassuming picture-framer Jonathan Zimmermann, played by Bruno Ganz. Deliberately given the false impression that his illness is fatal—Jonathan is a hemophiliac—he is soon a compliant victim of criminal machinations, even becoming a contract killer to ensure the financial survival of his family after his death. Two men, two lives, and the contrasts could hardly be greater: one of them footloose and fancy-free, the other bound to his family and his tiny business—the globetrotting dandy Tom Ripley and the introspective framer in the bleak, depopulated docklands of Hamburg. The political graffiti on the grimly monotonous walls place the film firmly in 1970s Germany.

Ripley encounters Jonathan at an auction and hears about his treacherous illness. Devoid of scruples, Ripley sells the information to the French gangster Raoul Minot, who tempts Jonathan with a suggestion: he will put up the money to treat Jonathan's allegedly fatal hemophilia, if Jonathan carries out a murder for him in return. And—how could it be otherwise?—Jonathan loses his moral integrity. After the first murder, he allows himself to be blackmailed into committing another, this time in a Trans-Europe Express train. Just as things are going badly wrong on this second job, Ripley appears from nowhere and helps Jonathan complete his deadly mission. Having begun by betraying

WIM WENDERS Wim Wenders was born in Düsseldorf in 1945. He took his first steps as a film director when his father gave him a Super-8 camera in 1954. From 1967 to 1970, he studied at the Film and Television Academy in Munich. During this period, he also made short films and wrote critical essays. In 1970, he made his first full-length film, *Summer in the City*. This was followed by a number of successful features, including *Alice in the Cities* (*Alice in den Städten*, 1974), *Kings of the Road* (*Im Lauf der Zeit*, 1975/76), *The American Friend* (*Der amerikanische Freund/L'Ami américain*, 1977), *Paris, Texas* (1984), *Wings of Desire* (*Der Himmel über Berlin/Les Ailes du désir*, 1987), *Faraway, So Close!* (*In weiter Ferne, so nah!*, 1993) and *Buena Vista Social Club* (1998/99). These films made Wim Wenders one of the most internationally renowned German directors. His style is characterized by long, steady shots and careful cutting. We become aware of the camera as an observer, and we also have time to examine the pictures in detail. Wenders' narratives are correspondingly detailed. They focus on rootless characters and tight-lipped heroes incapable of making contact with their fellow human beings. In many of his films, Wenders uses this constellation to examine the influence of American culture on postwar Germany. At the same time, his poetic-philosophical filmmaking stands in sharp contrast to the fast-moving action-packed cinema of Hollywood, with its one-dimensional characters and transparent motivations. Although Wenders has produced fascinating new interpretations of Hollywood myths—especially in his road movies and gangster films—he advances the tradition in his own, specifically "European" way. He received Oscar nominations, among others, for his documentary film *Salt of the Earth* (2014) and *Perfect Days* (2023).

2

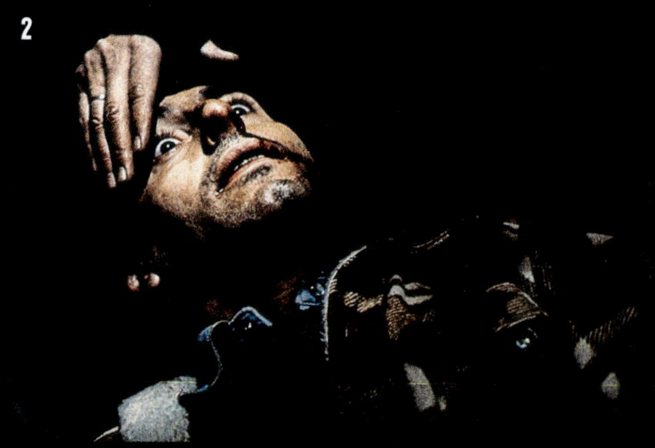

> **"Essentially, the film is about colonization— or more specifically, about the need to resist the American colonization of the unconscious."**
> *Literature / Film Quarterly*

Jonathan, Ripley seems suddenly to have befriended him: he's now Jonathan's dubious "American friend."

And yet they remain strangers. The audience can practically feel their spiritual isolation in the bleak images, half-suppressed movements and distrustful glances, interior monologs and softly-whispered dialogs. A feeling of petrifaction spreads, telling of Jonathan's defenselessness and the ruthlessness of those who exploit him for their own criminal ends. Death for life and life for death: for Jonathan, there seems to be no way out of this vicious circle. Symbolically, he often holds a frame before his face, checking its quality, as if searching for an identity, a suitable frame for his own life.

In *The American Friend,* Wim Wenders created a little gem of a film, minutely detailed and without embellishment. Many critics read his work as a parable on the "colonial" relationship between American and German culture, on the triumph of an aggressive, corrupt and bullying attitude that has no time for doubt or self-criticism. At the same time, Wenders delivered a contemporary reinter-

3

1 Flying paper dragons: Melancholy gangster Tom Ripley (Dennis Hopper) is holding all the strings.

2 Making quota: Monthly casualties keep business in the black.

3 His hands are tied: There's just no freeing himself from a criminal bind for Jonathan (Bruno Ganz).

4 Down and out in the underworld: Buddy Ripley gives Jonathan's morale a jump start.

pretation of the social realism that has dominated gangster films since the earliest days of the genre, with protagonists who struggle to defend themselves even when all the political and economic odds are stacked against them. Wenders is part of this tradition, which he renews and updates. *The American Friend* is an intelligent thriller that easily combines great seriousness with a suspenseful plot. It's a complex film, not easily pigeonholed, in which almost all identities, relationships and motivations remain open. So too the friendship between Jonathan and Ripley. The film ends with a sequence of images almost surreal in their effect: Jonathan and Ripley, on a beach at the mouth of the river Elbe, set fire to an ambulance containing the bodies of two gangsters who had been pursuing them. But this final test of their friendship ends in failure: Jonathan flees with his wife, leaving Ripley behind him—alone. BR

CET OBSCUR OBJET DU DÉSIR / ESE OSCURO OBJETO DEL DESEO

THAT OBSCURE OBJECT OF DESIRE

1977 – FRANCE / SPAIN – 103 MIN.

GENRE

DRAMA

DIRECTOR

LUIS BUÑUEL

SCREENPLAY

JEAN-CLAUDE CARRIÈRE, LUIS BUÑUEL, based on the novel
LA FEMME ET LE PANTIN by PIERRE LOUŸS

DIRECTOR OF PHOTOGRAPHY

EDMOND RICHARD

EDITING

HÉLÈNE PLEMIANNIKOV, LUIS BUÑUEL

MUSIC

RICHARD WAGNER and others

PRODUCTION

SERGE SILBERMAN for GREENWICH FILM PRODUCTIONS,
LES FILMS GALAXIE, IN-CINE COMPAÑÍA INDUSTRIAL
CINEMATOGRÁFICA S. A.

STARRING

FERNANDO REY (Mathieu), CAROLE BOUQUET (Conchita),
ÁNGELA MOLINA (Conchita), JULIEN BERTHEAU (Edouard, the Judge),
ANDRÉ WEBER (Martin), MILENA VUKOTIC (Train Passenger),
BERNARD MUSSON (Police Inspector), MARÍA ASQUERINO (Conchita's Mother),
DAVID ROCHA (El "Morenito"), MUNI (Concierge),
ISABELLE SADOYAN (Gardener)

SERGE SILBERMAN présente

UN FILM DE LUIS BUNUEL

Cet Obscur Objet du Désir

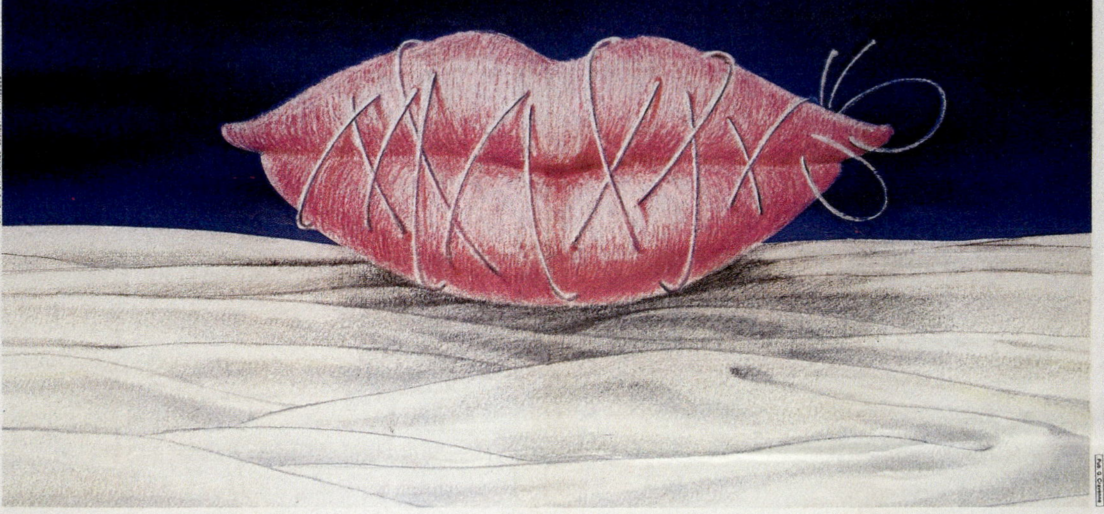

Scénario de LUIS BUNUEL en collaboration avec JEAN-CLAUDE CARRIERE
Inspiré de l'œuvre de PIERRE LOUYS "LA FEMME ET LE PANTIN" · Editions ALBIN MICHEL
avec FERNANDO REY · CAROLE BOUQUET · ANGELA MOLINA · JULIEN BERTHEAU · ANDRE WEBER · MILENA VUKOTIC
Chef Décorateur PIERRE GUFFROY · Directeur de la Photographie EDMOND RICHARD · Directeur de la Production ULLY PICKARD
Un film produit par SERGE SILBERMAN · Une co-production franco-espagnole GREENWICH FILM PRODUCTION · LES FILMS GALAXIE · PARIS / IN CINE · MADRID
Une production GREENWICH FILM PRODUCTION · PARIS · © Copyright PARIS MCMLXXVII Distribué par G.E.F.-C.C.F.C.

1

"You're not my father and you're not my lover!"

The great Luis Buñuel, hero of the Surrealist movement in the 1920s, was already 77 when he took the director's chair one last time to film the tale of the aging *grand bourgeois* Mathieu and his hopeless obsession with a young dancer from the lower orders. After only a few days, Buñuel broke off filming, dissatisfied with the performance of Maria Schneider (who had achieved fame five years previously in *Last Tango in Paris*) as the teasing temptress Conchita. In desperation, he suggested to the producer Serge Silberman that the role be recast—with two actresses. To his surprise, Silberman was delighted by this apparently absurd idea, so that Carole Bouquet, a classically cool French beauty with a Chanel face, shared the honors with Angela Molina, a sultry Spanish Carmen.

Film history will provide numerous examples of double roles—where an actor or actress plays two characters in the same film—but never before had two actresses shared a single role. Interpretations were not slow in coming: it was said that people always have several sides to their characters; or that Mathieu is actually in love with two different women; or that Conchita embodies Woman As Such. Bullshit, said Buñuel, dismissing these philosophical pirouettes: it was simply the only solution he could think of, a decision arising out of sheer desperation. True to the spirit of Surrealism, Buñuel resists the rationalization of unconscious processes, adducing accidents and moments of inspiration whose meaning he himself cannot comprehend because there's simply nothing there to be understood. Surrealism had long tried to overcome the rational mind and its sly and stubborn self-censorship, using a range of techniques from automatic writing to the "exquisite cadaver" parlor game. In *That Obscure Object*

LUIS BUÑUEL Luis Buñuel summed himself up with an immortal aphorism: "I'm still an atheist, thank God." Born in 1900 and educated by the Jesuits, he left Spain for Paris in 1925, accompanied by his extrovert friend Salvador Dalí. In 1929, they collaborated to create *An Andalusian Dog* (*Un chien andalou*), which was followed a year later by *The Golden Age* (*L'Âge d'or*); virulently anticlerical and sexually unabashed, each of the films became a *succès de scandale* for the Surrealist movement. After a variety of projects in the course of the 30s, including the ironic ethnographical film document *Las Hurdes – Tierra sin pan* (1933), Buñuel was forced to emigrate by the Second World War. In New York, he re-edited Leni Riefenstahl's *Triumph of the Will* (*Triumph des Willens*, 1935) for the Latin American market, transforming the Nazi propaganda into an antifascist statement. At the end of the 40s, he moved to Mexico, where he began his second directing career with a series of extravagant melodramas and adventure films.

His return to Spain was worthy of a Surrealist. While making *Viridiana* (1961), he succeeded in misleading Franco's censors as to the nature of the work in progress. Only when the pungently anticlerical film was shown at the Cannes festival (where it received the Golden Palm) did it become painfully clear to the Spaniards that Buñuel had taken perfidious revenge on the detested Franco regime. The Vatican protested to the Spanish government, which had a thoroughly deferential attitude towards the Church of Rome, and the Minister responsible was forced to resign. Buñuel, who had been heavily criticized for his apparent collaboration with the totalitarian regime, must have relished having the last laugh.

In his old age, Buñuel enjoyed the Olympian status of a great European *auteur*, and his films featured stars such as Catherine Deneuve, Franco Nero, Jeanne Moreau and Michel Piccoli. He died in 1983, in his adopted home country, Mexico.

1 Human kindness is overflowing: Conchita relinquishes the key to her heart and falls flat on her face.

2 Rear view vixen: Mirrors confirm that Conchita is indeed "double trouble."

3 Gated: Is it people or his own emotions that Mathieu (Fernando Rey) is blocking out?

4 Another kinky role-play: Carole Bouquet (4, 5) shares the part of Conchita with Angela Molina (1, 2) without reason, without rhyme.

5 Feel your way: Director Luis Buñuel often cast Fernando Rey as an imposing bourgeois trapped by his own class.

of Desire, Buñuel carries this tendency to its limits once again, for here the apparently irrational is presented as if it were the most natural thing in the world.

What's astonishing is how quickly we forget that two actresses are sharing the same role, even though there's not the slightest resemblance between Bouquet and Molina. This merging of two individuals is facilitated by the film's austere and businesslike style. For Buñuel, the Catholic atheist, the iconoclastic lover of images, creates a world in which even bizarre occurrences appear perfectly plausible. During a solemn conference in an elegant office, a mousetrap snaps shut with a loud report; in the background of another scene, a car bomb explodes and the characters seem utterly unfazed. Thus we are not merely presented with an abstract problem—the deadening effects of habit and convention—but are forced to experience our own gradual acceptance of the most absurd phenomena. The unexplained terrorism of the "Revolutionary Army of the Infant Jesus" is as good an example of this as the two faces of Conchita.

The film is based on Pierre Louÿs' novel *La Femme et le pantin*, which had already been filmed twice. In *The Devil Is a Woman* (*Der Teufel ist eine Frau*, 1935), Josef von Sternberg had cast Marlene Dietrich as the seductive Conchita, another of his attempts to define the essence of femininity, manfully supported by the German diva. In Julien Duvivier's *La Femme et le Pantin (1958,* aka *The Female* or *A Woman Like Satan*), Brigitte Bardot had been a demon of sexual aggression under a mask of perfect naturalness. So this erotically charged fable from the turn of the century served three times—in the 30s, the 50s, and the 70s—as an opportunity to get to grips with Woman (that impossible enigma...). In fact, these films supply little support to any theory of the Eternal Feminine; but—like the science-fiction genre—they do tell us a lot about the mentality of their time and about changes in social attitudes—not least towards actresses and the roles they are asked to embody.

MH

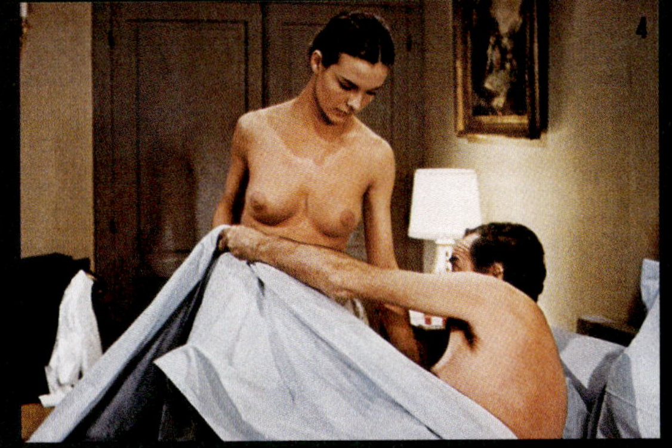

"Different species of terrorism abound in the film, starting with the very evident sexual terrorism practiced by Conchita, and the less evident (except to Conchita who persistently resists being bought) financial terrorism practiced by Mathieu." *Monthly Film Bulletin*

5

STAR WARS

1977 – USA – 121 MIN.

GENRE

SCIENCE FICTION

DIRECTOR

GEORGE LUCAS

SCREENPLAY

GEORGE LUCAS

DIRECTOR OF PHOTOGRAPHY

GILBERT TAYLOR

EDITING

PAUL HIRSCH, MARCIA LUCAS, RICHARD CHEW

MUSIC

JOHN WILLIAMS

PRODUCTION

GARY KURTZ for LUCASFILM LTD.

STARRING

MARK HAMILL (Luke Skywalker), HARRISON FORD (Han Solo), CARRIE FISHER (Princess Leia Organa), ALEC GUINNESS (Ben "Obi-Wan" Kenobi), PETER CUSHING (Tarkin), DAVID PROWSE (Darth Vader), JAMES EARL JONES (Darth Vader's voice), KENNY BAKER (R2-D2), ANTHONY DANIELS (C-3PO), PETER MAYHEW (Chewbacca), PHIL BROWN (Owen Lars), SHELAGH FRASER (Beru Lars)

ACADEMY AWARDS 1978

OSCARS for BEST MUSIC (John Williams), BEST FILM EDITING (Paul Hirsch, Marcia Lucas, Richard Chew), BEST SET DESIGN (John Barry, Norman Reynolds, Leslie Dilley, Roger Christian), BEST COSTUMES (John Mollo), BEST SOUND (Don MacDougall, Ray West, Bob Minkler, Derek Ball), BEST SPECIAL EFFECTS (John Stears, John Dykstra, Richard Edlund, Grant McCune, Robert Blalack), and SPECIAL PRIZE FOR SOUND EFFECTS (voices of the aliens and robots, Ben Burtt)

TWENTIETH CENTURY-FOX Presents A LUCASFILM LTD. PRODUCTION STAR WARS

Starring MARK HAMILL HARRISON FORD CARRIE FISHER

PETER CUSHING

and

ALEC GUINNESS

STAR WARS

Written and Directed by
GEORGE LUCAS

Produced by
GARY KURTZ

Music by
JOHN WILLIAMS

PANAVISION® PRINTS BY DE LUXE® TECHNICOLOR®

Making Films Sound Better
DOLBY SYSTEM®
Noise Reduction · High Fidelity

Original Motion Picture Soundtrack on 20th Century Records and Tapes

© 1977 20TH CENTURY-FOX

PRINTED IN U.S.A.

ONE SHEET STYLE "C"

1

There's something rotten in the state of the galaxy. With the blessings of the Emperor, Grand Moff Tarkin (Peter Cushing) and the sinister Lord Vader (David Prowse/James Earl Jones) have been conquering and subjugating one planet system after the other in the old Republic. Tarkin commands a massive spaceship, whose firepower has the ability to annihilate entire planets. This "Deathstar" is the most dangerous weapon in the universe—perhaps with the exception of "The Force," a mysterious, all-pervading energy. Anyone who learns to master this force through years of ascetic training is possessed with superhuman powers. In the past, the Jedi Knights secured justice and kept the peace with the help of "The Force." But now Darth Vader, a renegade Jedi, is one of the last people with control of its powers, forming with Tarkin an almost invincible alliance of evil in the once peaceful expanses of the universe.

Only a small group of rebels resist the might of the Empire and fight to restore the old order. To achieve their aspirations, the construction plans of the "Deathstar", which the rebels have acquired, could be of great assistance. But the spaceship of Princess Leia (Carrie Fisher) is captured just as she is returning to her home planet with

SERIAL SPACE OPERAS An overture: in the beginning of *Star Wars* (1977), a long block of text rolls up the screen, setting the stage and recounting the background story. What follows is no singular adventure; it is an entire universe. From the very beginning *Star Wars* was created as a multi-episode project. After the first episode came *Star Wars: Episode V – The Empire Strikes Back* (1980) and then *Star Wars: Episode VI – The Return of the Jedi* (1983). The pre-history of the saga was also conceptualized as a trilogy. Even during the first screenplay drafts, Lucas' Star-world was getting bigger and bigger. This is no exception in the fantasy and science-fiction genre. Where new, exotic worlds are created, there will always be questions about how it all began. With the interest in both past and future, the plot possibilities are endless.

Serial science-fiction stories were already prevalent and popular in the 1930s. Space heroes like *Flash Gordon* (1936) and *Buck Rogers* (1939) helped their comic forefathers to big screen success. Each 13-part series told of despotic rulers, beautiful women, and heroic men saving the universe; after 20 minutes the plot stopped at the most exciting moment—to be continued next week in this theater!

The *Star-Trek* universe has been massively popular and has experienced considerable expansion. Since the first episode of the television series about the Starship *Enterprise* was broadcast in 1966, five spin-off series and 13 films have been created, each piece of this long chain of individual stories adding to the colossal inventory of characters, events, time periods, and places that make up this fantastic world.

1 May the Force be with you: With a monk's habit and light sabre, Ben "Obi-Wan" Kenobi (Alec Guinness) links medieval mythology to a hi-tech future.

2 Iron lung of evil: Darth Vader (David Prowse) will stop at nothing to conquer the galaxy.

3 Man's best friend according to Lucas: Princess Leia (Carrie Fisher) confides in R2-D2 (Kenny Baker).

the plans in hand. At the last moment she is able to save the blueprint of the "Death Star" inside the droid R2-D2 (Kenny Baker). If this tiny robot can get the plans to the old Jedi Knight Obi-Wan Kenobi (Alec Guinness) in time, there could still be a remote hope for the rebels' cause.

The journey of R2-D2 and his companion, the dithering and etiquette-conscious communication robot C-3PO (Anthony Daniels), takes them to the planet Tatooine, where they are purchased by farmer Owen Lars (Phil Brown). His nephew, Luke Skywalker (Mark Hamill) longs for a life more exciting than that of an agricultural worker. He would much rather fight with the rebels against the Empire—just as his father, a legendary Jedi whom he has never met, once did…

Skywalker's dreams of adventure begin to become reality when the two droids meet Obi-Wan. Soon the imperial Storm Troopers are at their heels, and the old Jedi Knight is left with no other alternative but to travel with Luke and the droids to Alderaan, Leia's home planet, bringing the plans of the "Death Star" to help plan a counterattack.

They receive assistance from Han Solo (Harrison Ford), an old pro who, with his ship, the *Millennium Falcon*, manages to speed away from the fast-approaching imperial cruisers in the nick of time. Even so, they do not reach their destination: Tarkin and Darth Vader have already destroyed the planet Alderaan.

After our heroes free Princess Leia from the "Death Star," nothing stands in the way of the final battle between the Empire and the rebels in the Javin System. The Achilles heel of the gigantic space station is a small ventilation shaft, and in the end, after several intense battles,

“I wanted to make a film for kids, something that would present them with a kind of elementary morality. Because nowadays nobody bothers to tell those kids, ‘Hey, this is right and this is wrong.’”

George Lucas, interview with David Sheff

3

"A combination of past and future, Western and space odyssey, myth and dream world, *Star Wars* may be the most enduring piece of escapism ever put on film." *Sacramento Bee*

it is Luke who is able to hit the weak spot and destroy the "Death Star" in a powerful explosion. Only Darth Vader escapes the blazing inferno. And while one battle may have been won in this war in the stars, it won't be long before the Empire strikes back…

George Lucas began working on his star-saga just as his teenage drama, *American Graffiti*, was poised to become the surprise hit of 1973—a success from which the director profited much less than the studios that produced the film. For Lucas, this experience was the driving motivation never to give control of one of his projects to anyone else again. *Star Wars* was produced entirely by his own company and the special effects were created by Industrial Light & Magic, also a Lucas company. Rounding out the deal was a clause giving rights to merchandizing (toys, clothing, etc.) and the use of film music to Lucas, initiating a new period in cinema in which the biggest proceeds of a film were no longer made at the box office. The blockbuster movie was born.

Real success always did depend on reaching the largest possible audience. Lucas stressed over and over that he wrote the screenplay with 8- and 9-year-olds in

4 Rebels without a shave: Individualists Chewbacca (Peter Mayhew) and Han Solo (Harrison Ford) battle against the evil Empire.

5 About face: The imperial storm troopers are trained and ruthless killers.

mind. But in the end, the film was able to connect with virtually every age group, primarily because with his "space opera," Lucas was neither attempting to depart from old genres, nor to enthusiastically deconstruct them. In fact, his goal was just the opposite. Like his colleague Steven Spielberg, Lucas pursued a higher path, which led him back to the classical narrative form, meeting the expectations of the public and employing the highest levels of technical mastery.

The subject matter of *Star Wars* is akin to a trip through the annals of cultural and film history. Lucas fused elements from the tales of knights and the myths of heroes with the high-tech world of spaceships, was inspired by German and Soviet military uniforms, based the Jedi religion on the Shaman cults of Central America, and created the Empire in the image of an Orwellian dictatorship. The android C-3PO is unmistakably based on the machine woman from Fritz Lang's *Metropolis* (1926), and the concluding hero-honoring ceremony is an obvious reference to Leni Riefenstahl's Nazi party film, *The Triumph of the Will* (*Triumph des Willens*, 1935). In short, with *Star Wars*, an inter-cultural super-cosmos was created, containing something for every audience member to recognize.

The real highlight, however, was that Lucas' film, despite its complex plot, tells a story easily reduced to the battle of good versus evil. *Star Wars* is not a story of broken heroes. Lucas sends clearly defined characters into battle, and the audience are never left in doubt as

6 Budget getaway: Protocol droid C-3PO (Anthony Daniels) speaks millions of languages; but unlike brave little R2-D2, he's an exasperating penny-pincher.

7 Putting their lives on the line for a pleasant tomorrow: Princess Leia and Luke Skywalker (Mark Hamill).

8 Everyday life in the not-too-distant future: The furniture of the *Star Wars* universe is sometimes credibly and recognizably shabby.

"It's a terrifically entertaining war story, it has memorable characters and it is visually compelling. What more do we want in movies?" *San Francisco Chronicle*

to who will triumph in the end. The result is that the science-fiction opus became an effortlessly digestible mixture of vignettes, whose charm lay not in complicated conceptual worlds, but rather in its fantastic moments and visual spectacles. It was these moments that made the film an ideal springboard for the budding entertainment industry of video and computer games. The space battles were replicated and prolonged on consoles and monitors all over the world, helping to pass the time between episodes ...

EP

ERASERHEAD

1974/77 – USA – 90 MIN.

GENRE

HORROR FILM, PSYCHO DRAMA

DIRECTOR

DAVID LYNCH

SCREENPLAY

DAVID LYNCH

DIRECTOR OF PHOTOGRAPHY

FREDERICK ELMES, HERBERT CARDWELL

EDITING

DAVID LYNCH

MUSIC

DAVID LYNCH, PETER IVERS (Songs),
FATS WALLER

PRODUCTION

DAVID LYNCH for AMERICAN FILM INSTITUTE

STARRING

JACK NANCE (Henry Spencer), CHARLOTTE STEWART (Mary X),
ALLEN JOSEPH (Mr. X), JEANNE BATES (Mrs. X), JACK FISK (Man in Planet),
JUDITH ANNA ROBERTS (Beautiful Girl Across the Hall),
LAUREL NEAR (Lady in the Radiator), JEAN LANGE (Grandmother),
THOMAS COULSON (Boy), DARWIN JOSTON (Paul)

ERASERHEAD

A FILM BY DAVID LYNCH

A Libra Films RELEASE

1

"In heaven everything is fine."

The man in space (Jack Fisk) is dreaming. His pock-marked face stares out the window as he works a lever, and a printer named Henry Spencer (Jack Nance) appears against the backdrop of a sad, hermetic, black-and-white world. We see a factory, pipes, courtyards, and one-room apartments—an industrial microcosm in which both the near and distant whine of machines and the buzz of menacing electric lines behind the wallpaper can be heard everywhere.

Henry hasn't heard from his girlfriend Mary (Charlotte Stewart) for ages. Suddenly, her parents invite him to a bizarre dinner. All the women in turn are

LOW-BUDGET PRODUCTIONS No art is as expensive as filmmaking. While the big Hollywood productions can easily eat up hundreds of millions of dollars, there have always been films that were realized on a financial minimum, so-called low- or no-budget productions. But necessity can become a virtue. The compulsory renunciation of personal and technical expenditure often contributes to a unique demonstration of a director's personal style. And so it can happen that films made without big studios and without huge budgets can recover their production costs and gross much more than they cost to make.

At the beginning of the 70s, a series of directors who now belong to Hollywood's crème de la crème succeeded in making low-budget productions: Dennis Hopper with *Easy Rider* (1969), Sidney Lumet with *Serpico* (1973), or David Lynch with *Eraserhead* (1974/77). If minimal production expenditures are viewed almost as a prerequisite for artistic films—like, for example, the "Dogma" directors surrounding Lars von Trier (*Breaking the Waves*, 1996)—then the relationship to inexpensively produced B-movies illuminate the difference between art and trash, as with Russ Meyer's orgies of sex and violence (*Supervixens*, 1975), the provocative cinema of John Waters (*Pink Flamingos*, 1972) or the in hindsight path-blazing horror masterpieces by George A. Romero (*Night of the Living Dead*, 1968) and Tobe Hooper (*The Texas Chain Saw Massacre*, 1974), whose influence is also evident in artistic productions like *Eraserhead*.

2

1 Seeing is believing: Jack Nance as Henry Spencer in *Eraserhead*. The film's admirers have included directors as diverse as Stanley Kubrick, John Waters and William Friedkin.

2 Headed for greatness: Henry is the eraser factory's diamond in the rough.

3 All good things to those wait: Three years filming, one year in post-production. To save money, the impoverished director David Lynch actually lived on the set of Henry's apartment for a while.

"The imagery of this eerie film is impossible to pin down, the sound is unnerving, the lighting is dreadful, the settings are execrable, and the characters are horrendous."

Cinema

shaken by nervous fits. Mary's father serves mini chickens whose legs twitch when they are cut, while something that looks like bloody bubbles pours out over the plates. Then his girlfriend's lascivious mother tells Henry that he has become a father.

But it remains questionable whether he is truly the progenitor of the tightly bandaged being that looks more like a sheared sheep than a baby. In any case, Mary moves in with him, only to leave during the first night to go back to her parents, irritated by the constant screaming. Henry remains alone. The monstrous "child" gets sick, an affair with the beautiful girl across the hall (Judith Anna Roberts) ends in humiliation, and Henry dreams of an angelic, though horribly disfigured lady in the radiator (Laurel Near) and of a machine that transforms his head into an eraser. He ultimately kills the pitiful, reviled being and when he does so, his world dissolves into nothingness.

Despite the essentially linear plot, the story of *Eraserhead* evades explanation. Just as Henry seems to be merely a vision of the man in space shown at the beginning of the film, who at the end returns to the completely surreal and unbelievable, the narrated story seems to be permanently put into question by the suggestive quality of the images, the menacing drone of the soundtrack, the surreal events of the subplots, the torturously slow

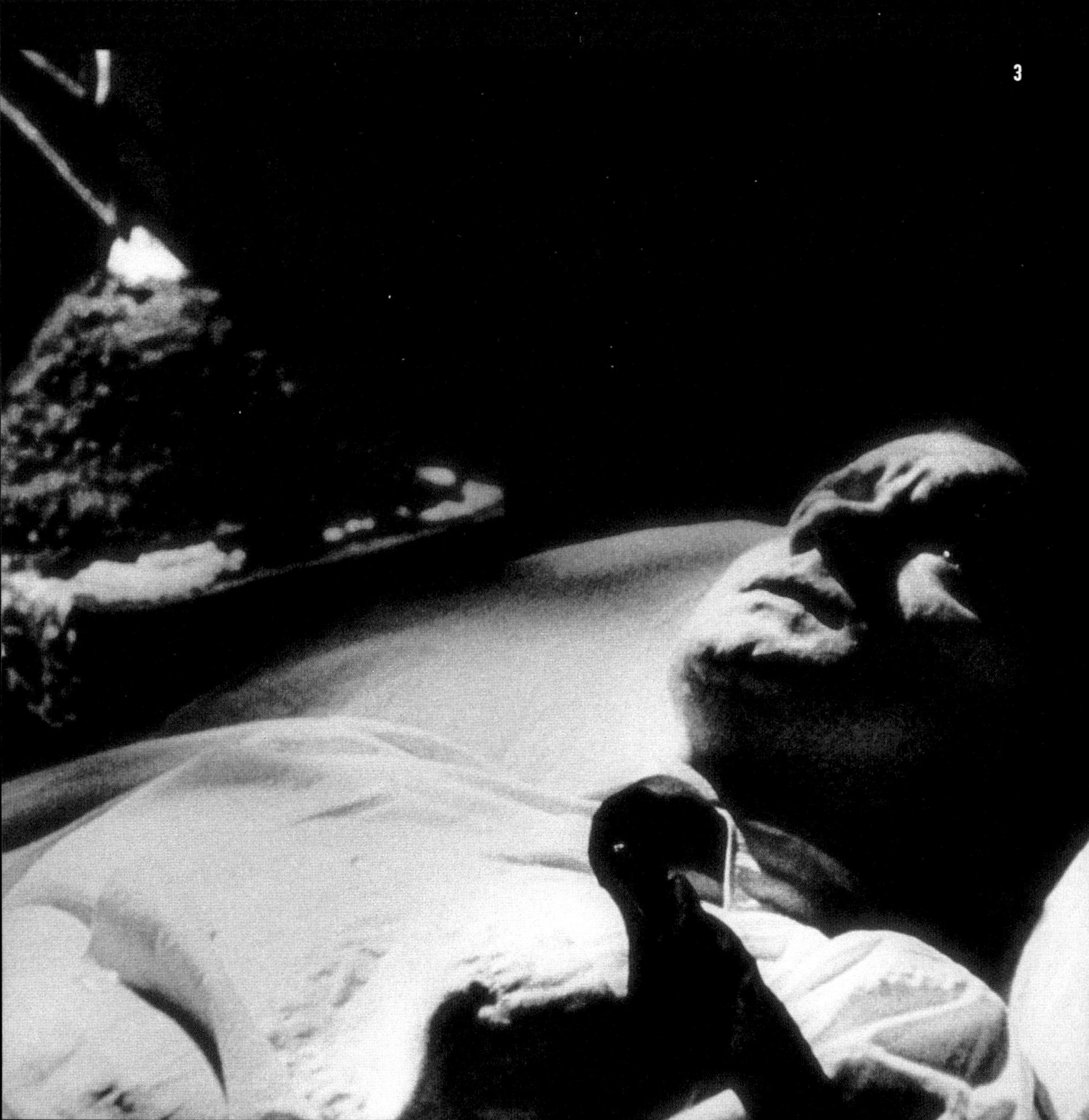
3

“The only artist I ever felt could be my brother was Kafka.”

David Lynch, in: Chris Rodley (ed.), Lynch on Lynch

movements, and the characters' strange speech. In the leaden atmosphere of this world, the half-hearted manifestations of life and helpless gestures of the humans have no permanence.

There are plenty of starting points for interpretation. The episode in which Henry's head—his vertical hair is already highly suggestive—is used to make erasers for pencils can be read as a metaphor for oblivion and speechlessness. Lynch's daughter Jennifer Chambers Lynch saw herself as an infant in the portrayal of Henry's baby—as an unwanted child that prevented the artist from pursuing his actual vocation.

Confronted with such theses, Lynch routinely responded with such lines as “I don't want to talk about that,” or “I can't answer that question.” Lynch's anger regarding those who blurt out the technical and artistic secrets of

4 Mary, mother of God!! Is Henry really the father of Mary's (Charlotte Stewart) monstrous child?

5 A living hell: In Henry's world, reality and nightmare are practically indistinguishable.

film indicates that he views a glimpse behind the scenes, and one-dimensional interpretations in general, as attempts to demystify the cinematic art form, an intrusion into a fragile, opaque system of meanings, references, and associations that must be protected from outside influences. "No matter how weird a story is," said Lynch, "as soon as you set foot inside it, you realize that this world has rules you have to follow."

For over four years, the young director worked with a small team on the film that Stanley Kubrick once called his favorite movie. Often on the brink of financial ruin, Lynch meticulously created each and every scene down to the smallest detail and despite warnings from family members and friends he was unable to put the project down—it was almost as if he could only free himself from Henry's claustrophobic artificial world by completing the film.

"I felt *Eraserhead*, I didn't think it up," explained the director. Similarly, the audience is asked to look, instead of trying to understand at all costs.

SH

SATURDAY NIGHT FEVER

1977 – USA – 118 MIN.

GENRE

DANCE FILM, DRAMA

DIRECTOR

JOHN BADHAM

SCREENPLAY

NORMAN WEXLER, based on the magazine article
"TRIBAL RITES OF THE NEW SATURDAY NIGHT" by NIK COHN

DIRECTOR OF PHOTOGRAPHY

RALF D. BODE

EDITING

DAVID RAWLINS

MUSIC

BARRY GIBB, ROBIN GIBB,
MAURICE GIBB, DAVID SHIRE

PRODUCTION

MILT FELSEN, ROBERT STIGWOOD for
ROBERT STIGWOOD ORGANIZATION, PARAMOUNT PICTURES

STARRING

JOHN TRAVOLTA (Tony Manero), KAREN LYNN GORNEY (Stephanie),
BARRY MILLER (Bobby C.), JOSEPH CALI (Joey), PAUL PAPE (Double J),
DONNA PESCOW (Annette), BRUCE ORNSTEIN (Gus),
JULIE BOVASSO (Flo), MARTIN SHAKAR (Frank), SAM COPPOLA (Fusco)

...Where do you go when the record is over...
SATURDAY NIGHT
FEVER
Copyright © 1977 by Paramount Pictures Corporation. All Rights Reserved.

1

"Nice move. Did you make that up?"

One movie embodies everything that disco stood for in the late 70s, and all that it has continued to stand for in the years since its disappearance from the public eye. To this day, audiences around the world hear mention of John Travolta and his trademark white leisure suit and are instantly transported to the streets of Brooklyn and the world of *Saturday Night Fever!* The picture itself is not only a golden shrine to the nightlife of the era with the glamorous decadence of its disco dance palaces, but also to its prevailing fashions and zeitgeist. *Saturday Night Fever's* uncanny assessment of these trends is attested to by the waves of disco revivals, each of which has inevitably cited this film's semiotics in its act of tribute.

At the time of its 1977 release, Manhattan dance club Studio 54 was the throbbing hub of disco. The audience for what was known as dance music had by then branched out from non-Caucasians and homosexuals to include the white middle class. *Saturday Night Fever* played a decisive role in contributing to the extreme popularity of the disco movement. Overnight, it launched unknown 22-year-old John Travolta to superstardom. More than his fancy threads or even the beat-pumping Bee-Gees tunes, it was Travolta's sexy gyrations that set a precedent in popular music for all time to come. From that day on, Top 40 hits would be judged on the basis of how danceable they were.

DANCE MOVIES Dance is part of a grand Hollywood tradition. One of its earlier highs came in the 30s and continued well into the 40s with great spectacles featuring Fred Astaire and Ginger Rogers such as *Shall We Dance* (1937), as well as with Eleanor Powell in pieces like *Broadway Melody of 1940* (1939–40). These marvels revolutionized the art form and instantly became living legends. Nonetheless, the dance film as we know it today stems from a later cinematic movement that first became widely popular with the unstoppable disco drama *Saturday Night Fever* (1977). The film turned dance into a metaphor for self-realization and a passion for life. For these reasons as well as for its intrinsic connection to current pop music, these films have historically spoken to a primarily younger audience and produced a large number of top 40 hit songs. The 80s took the genre to new heights with Adrian Lyne's *Flashdance* (1982). Arguably the greatest dance movie of all time, *Flashdance* took the crisp visual aesthetics of the 80s music video age and magnified them with theatrical, stylized imagery. The film's title song "Flashdance... What A Feeling!" written by Irene Cara, Keith Forsey and Giorgio Moroder took home the Oscar for Best Original Song and the entire soundtrack has since gone triple-platinum. A supplementary instalment of *Saturday Night Fever* hit theaters at the peak of the boom in 1983. That same year, Herbert Ross' enormously successful *Footloose* made its appearance on the film scene. Similar to the 1978 sensation *Grease*, starring John Travolta and Olivia Newton-John, the nostalgic tribute took viewers back to the 50s when modern pop music and teen culture were still in their infancy. Jennifer Grey and Patrick Swayze took 1987 by storm in *Dirty Dancing* and captured the hearts of countless young audiences with yet another picture whose story was set in this beloved bygone era. After lying more or less dormant for over an entire decade, Randa Haines' 1998 *Dance with Me*, about the Latin music star Chayanne, was received by an enthused audience and contributed to salsa's popularity at the movies. Two years later, *Cinema* magazine deemed Nicholas Hytner's *Center Stage* (2000) a new teen version of *Flashdance*. Other dance flicks that year included Thomas Carter's hybrid of ballet and hip hop *Save the Last Dance* (2000) and *The Dancer* (2000), about yet another girl who dreams of becoming a dance superstar. The latter movie's soundtrack included a star-studded soundtrack featuring The Prodigy, Fat Boy Slim and Neneh Cherry. The genre has expressed renewed interest in tap dancing as evidenced by diverse pieces such as Dein Perry's modern stomp *Bootmen* (2000), which was also an appeal for social reform. Even more successful was Stephen Daldry's *Billy Elliot* (2000), both a great example of the aesthetic trends in British cinema as well as a touching dance drama about a little boy whose family tries to pressure him into becoming a boxer, although his dreams are just of ballet.

“Energetically directed and well acted (...), *Saturday Night Fever* succeeds in capturing the animal drive of disco music and the social rituals of the people who dance to its beat.” *Time Magazine*

The film itself tells the story of a group of twenty-somethings linked by the socio-economic stratum they have inherited, much like the protagonists of Martin Scorsese's *Mean Streets* (1973). Tony Manero (John Travolta) comes from an Italian-American family and still lives with his parents, who treat him more like a kid than a full-grown adult. He works at a mundane job selling paint and finds the recognition denied him at home on the dance floor. Every Saturday night, he and his buddies head over to “2001,” a disco with a rainbow-colored blinking floor and a fast-talking disk jockey who can always get the crowd moving. The sea of people parts when stallion Tony struts his way over to his table. Women worship him and his amassed following goes wild when he takes the stage with his smooth-as-butter choreography. Tony is a tightly packaged macho stud and takes great care with his

1 Bright lights, big city: Tony Manero (John Travolta) with his goods on display in the legendary white leisure suit.

2 Music as the universal equalizer: But the disco ball's magic won't last forever.

3 "If I Can't Have You:" Annette (Donna Pescow) is in love with Tony, but the feeling isn't mutual.

appearance. Each night before going out, he partakes in a meticulous ritual surrounded by posters of his idols Al Pacino and Sylvester Stallone as Rocky. Transfixed by his reflection, Tony slicks his hair, pulls on a dress shirt with flared collar and adorns himself with gold chains. He tops it off with a lascivious upward swing that slides the zipper of his hip-hugging slacks into place. Tony is the man with all the right moves and doesn't he know it? "I like the way you walk," remarks Annette (Donna Pescow) with girlish naivety and undying devotion. Tony, however, is shamelessly hurtful toward this ordinary admirer. He clearly has problems dealing with the female species and drops crude comments to girls who want to go bed with him, asking Annette whether she's "a nice girl or a slut?" She responds that maybe she's both, throwing the already twisted male logic of Tony and his crew into a loop. These guys think that women who engage in casual sex are filthy whores, while they seek out such specimens night after night. Tony's small world revolves around work, family, dancing and ladies. It is a lifestyle that lacks both goals and direction. Stephanie (Karen Lynn Gorney), the girl of his dreams, lives in another universe altogether, although this wasn't always the case. She has made the quantum leap from Brooklyn to Manhattan, working at a swanky agency that affords her the luxury of looking back on her previous life with a degree of arrogance and disdain. To Tony, she comes across as a sexy, hardened woman of the world, whose glamorous career requires her to consort with the rich and famous on a daily basis.

It's no coincidence that *Saturday Night Fever* opens with the image of a bridge. The device is both a physical link between Brooklyn and Manhattan as well as a metaphoric link between a suffocating life of entrenched tradition and the opportunistic, self-determined escapism of modernity. Tony is an expert on everything there is to know about the Brooklyn Bridge, right down to the exact amount of cement

4 Shaking off the past: In the end, however, only Tony will manage to escape.

5 Prophet of the Disco Cult: As his brother, a priest, puts it, "When Tony hits the dance floor, the crowd parts like the Red Sea before Moses."

"John Badham's film is a snapshot of a period. Though born of a passing pop-cultural fashion, it has survived in the collective unconscious right up to the present day." *Frankfurter Allgemeine Zeitung*

and steel contained in the architectural wonder. The bridge serves as a symbol of ultimate desire, which Tony and his clique pay homage to in adolescent initiation rituals and daredevil stunts, like scaling the mammoth structure. To the shy Bobby (Barry Miller), this foolhardy activity proves to be as deadly as the call of the ancient Sirens. His fall into the East River abyss is both a departure from a life that has nothing to offer him other than disco, cruising the streets and casual sex, as well as a convenient exit from dealing with the responsibilities brought on by his girlfriend's pregnancy. Although Tony manages to successfully cross the imposing barriers of the bridge, it remains unclear whether he will choose to live out his newfound adulthood in the Manhattan universe that lies beyond. Making it in the big city has always been a central theme in American film. *Saturday Night Fever* takes an in-depth look at what this entails, subjecting its characters to dire hardships, and its eloquent message resonates to this day. The film triumphs precisely where attempted follow-ups like the sequel *Staying Alive* (1983), fall short. Martin Scorsese's 1968 picture *Who's That Knocking at My Door* told a similar story of an unquenchable thirst for Manhattan life and women trouble among male youth. Yet for all their similarities, *Saturday Night Fever* has the unique distinction of being the disco movie to end all others, forever reminding us that history is made at night! KK

CLOSE ENCOUNTERS OF THE THIRD KIND

1977 – USA – 135 MIN.

GENRE

SCIENCE FICTION

DIRECTOR

STEVEN SPIELBERG

SCREENPLAY

STEVEN SPIELBERG

DIRECTOR OF PHOTOGRAPHY

VILMOS ZSIGMOND

EDITING

MICHAEL KAHN

MUSIC

JOHN WILLIAMS

PRODUCTION

JULIA PHILLIPS, MICHAEL PHILLIPS for COLUMBIA PICTURES CORPORATION

STARRING

RICHARD DREYFUSS (Roy Neary), FRANÇOIS TRUFFAUT (Claude Lacombe), TERI GARR (Ronnie Neary), MELINDA DILLON (Jillian Guiler), BOB BALABAN (David Laughlin), CARY GUFFEY (Barry Guiler), J. PATRICK MCNAMARA (Project Director), WARREN KEMMERLING (Wild Bill), ROBERTS BLOSSOM (Farmer), LANCE HENRIKSEN (Robert)

ACADEMY AWARDS 1978

OSCAR for BEST CINEMATOGRAPHY (Vilmos Zsigmond) and SPECIAL ACHIEVEMENT AWARD for BEST SOUND EFFECTS EDITING (Frank Warner)

CLOSE ENCOUNTER OF THE FIRST KIND:
Sighting
CLOSE ENCOUNTER OF THE SECOND KIND:
Evidence
CLOSE ENCOUNTER OF THE THIRD KIND:
Contact

CLOSE ENCOUNTERS
OF THE THIRD KIND

A COLUMBIA/EMI Presentation CLOSE ENCOUNTERS OF THE THIRD KIND
A PHILLIPS Production A STEVEN SPIELBERG Film Starring RICHARD DREYFUSS with FRANCOIS TRUFFAUT as Lacombe
Music by JOHN WILLIAMS Visual Effects by DOUGLAS TRUMBULL Director of Photography VILMOS ZSIGMOND, A.S.C.
Produced by JULIA PHILLIPS and MICHAEL PHILLIPS Written and Directed by STEVEN SPIELBERG
Read the Dell Book
© Columbia Pictures Industries, Inc. 1977
Making Films Sound Better
DOLBY SYSTEM ®
Noise Reduction · High Fidelity

Columbia Pictures

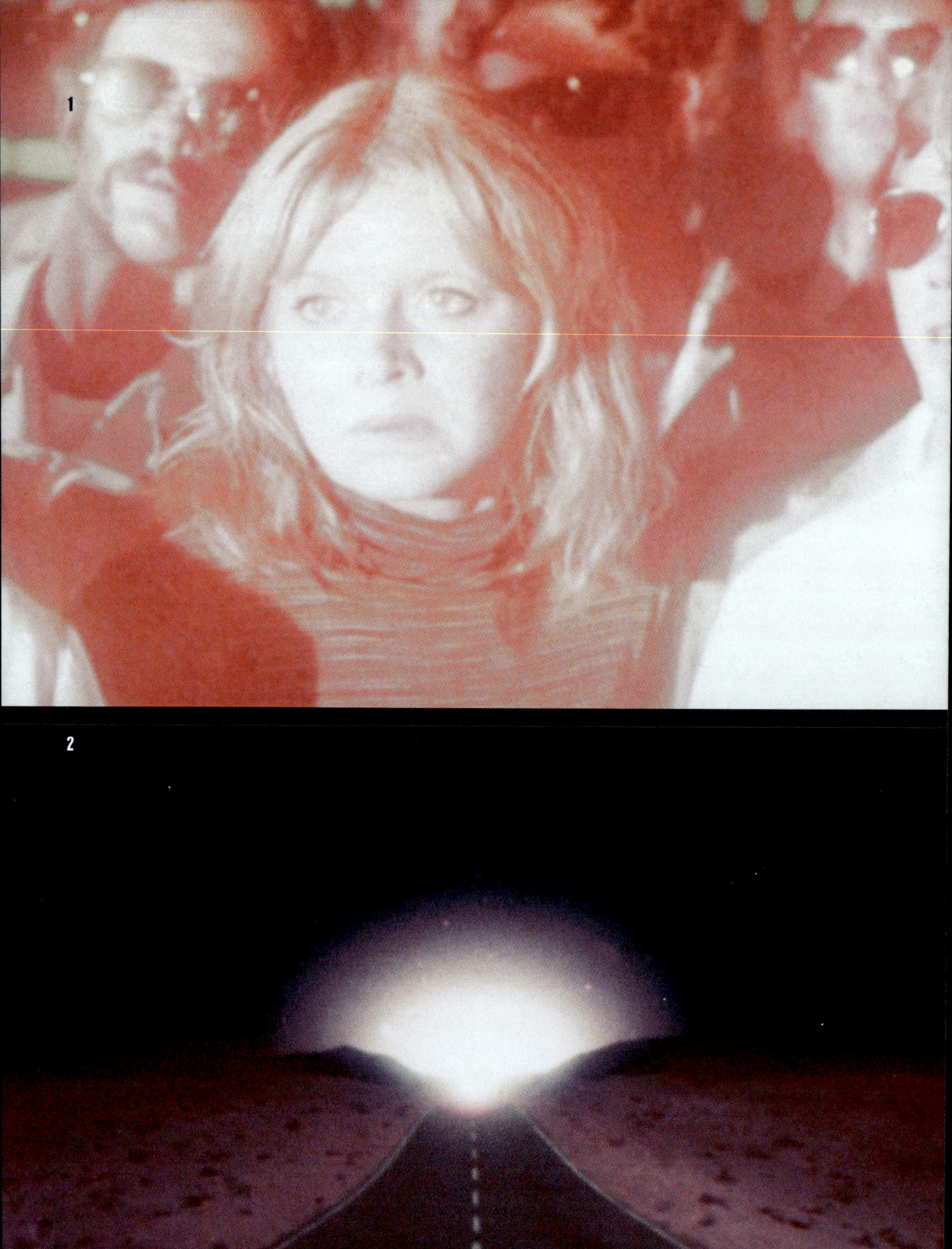
1
2

"It's as big as a house!"

Suddenly, a gleaming light fills the sky. Car engines and radios go on the blink and the night is illuminated with brilliant colors. During a night-time procedure, electrical engineer Roy Neary has a strange experience: he sees aliens. But no one believes him. Consequently, he is fired by his company, continually made fun of, and totally misunderstood by his family. What Roy doesn't know is that his encounter is part of a string of strange phenomena that have been occurring around the world. Fighter bombers reported missing since 1945 suddenly appear in the desert of New Mexico, and the people of North India hear a melody coming from the sky.

Since his experience, Roy has been tortured by visions of an oddly formed mountain. He later sees the mountain again in a television program—apparently it's the "Devil's Tower" in Wyoming. The report tells of an accident during which poisonous gas was released near the mountain. The entire area is being immediately evacuated. It becomes clear to Roy that he must travel to Wyoming. He begins his journey to the mountain with Jillian (Melinda Dillon), a single mother who had an encounter with aliens on the same night. Five years later in *E. T. – The Extra-Terrestrial* (1982), director Steven Spielberg again portrayed a visit from outer space. But the earlier narration is more serious, more complex, and above all, more mature. Parallel to Roy's experiences, Spielberg depicts a worldwide UFO research team, led by Lacombe, a scientist from France (played by French director François Truffaut). The main plot of the

DOUGLAS TRUMBULL Special effects wizard Douglas Trumbull (1942–2022) began his career as a background illustrator for NASA promotional films. Stanley Kubrick saw one of these films and hired Trumbull as "special photographic effects supervisor" for his film, *2001: A Space Odyssey* (1968). Kubrick's masterpiece founded Trumbull's reputation as special effects magician and cleared the way for his directorial debut, the apocalyptic drama *Silent Running* (1971). When, afterwards, he was unable to realize further projects as a director, he started working as a trick specialist once again. He received Oscar nominations for his effects for *Close Encounters of the Third Kind* (1977), *Star Trek – The Motion Picture* (1979), and *Blade Runner* (1982). For many of his films, Trumbull, son of an engineer, invented technical devices, like the so-called Slit-Scan, a machine with which he captured the psychedelic color haze in the final sequence of *2001* (the flight through the star gate), or a zoom-microscope for *The Andromeda Strain* (1971). For his second film as director, *Brainstorm* (1983), he experimented with various film formats. He later developed the "Show-Scan" procedure. The film is projected at 60 frames per second instead of the normal 24, which results in a sharper image. But the format never caught on and was seldom used in the production of feature-length films. Trumbull created the special photographic effects for Terrence Malick's *The Tree of Life* (2011). In 2018, Grégory Wallet dedicated the documentary *Trumbull Land* to him.

3

film—an alien landing on the Earth—is accompanied by two subplots. One shows how Roy (excellently portrayed by Richard Dreyfuss) believes he is going mad and begins to doubt his own reason, ultimately causing his family to break apart. The other plot is a criticism of the media, which is still pertinent a quarter of a century later. The government, military, and media collaborate to spread lies about a poisonous gas disaster that never occurred. Their aim is to evacuate people from the area where they are expecting the alien landing to take place. In so doing, they even anesthetize animals to make their fairy-tale appear more believable.

"I had such a yearning for the stars, such a longing for space travel. I wanted to take off and fly away from our planet. My childhood wasn't particularly happy, which is why I was always looking for ways to escape."

Steven Spielberg, in: Tony Crawley, The Steven Spielberg Story

5

6

1 Mine eyes have seen the glory: Jillian Guiler (Melinda Dillon) has been touched by an angel, if that's what you want to call it.

2 An alien landing looks like that pot of gold at the end of the rainbow.

3 Star light, star bright: "Of all the UFO films ever made this is the most edifying—a wonder of superb special effects." (*Motion Picture Guide*)

4 Group therapy: Roy (Richard Dreyfuss) had begun to question his own sanity until Jill shared her own out-of-this-world experience with him.

5 Spirits in the sky: Master technician Douglas Trumbull composed a forty-minute special effects extravaganza for the film's conclusion that left audiences in awe.

6 Keeping the faith: Electrical engineer Roy Neary is publicly ridiculed for his convictions and abandoned by his family.

The "main story" tells of the alien landing. As in *E. T.*, these aliens come to the Earth with peaceful intentions. The aliens, who appear only at the end of the film, are fragile, child-like figures who spread harmony, and with whom communication is only possible via music. They come to Earth as a kind of savior and their arrival is accompanied by unmistakably religious symbols, including celestial light and the mountain itself, which recalls Mount Sinai, where God gave the Ten Commandments to Moses. The almost forty-minute climax is an overwhelming orgy of special effects, with glowing spaceships of every size and shape, and a brilliant choreography of light in the sky. The effects were the work of Douglas Trumbull.

Close Encounters did not win the Oscar for special effects—the Oscar went to George Lucas' *Star Wars*, also released in 1977—but the film was a huge success at the box office. Both the production company and fans demanded a sequel, but Spielberg produced only a "Special Edition," which was eventually released in 1980. This version is three minutes shorter than the original—Spielberg cut 16 minutes and added 13 new minutes, including newly shot scenes (including a "stranded" ship in the Gobi desert) and initially unused material.

HJK

ANNIE HALL

1977 – USA – 93 MIN.

GENRE

COMEDY

DIRECTOR

WOODY ALLEN

SCREENPLAY

WOODY ALLEN, MARSHALL BRICKMAN

DIRECTOR OF PHOTOGRAPHY

GORDON WILLIS

EDITING

RALPH ROSENBLUM, WENDY GREENE BRICMONT

MUSIC

CARMEN LOMBARDO, ISHAM JONES

PRODUCTION

CHARLES H. JOFFE, JACK ROLLINS for UNITED ARTISTS

STARRING

WOODY ALLEN (Alvy Singer), DIANE KEATON (Annie Hall),
TONY ROBERTS (Rob), CAROL KANE (Allison), PAUL SIMON (Tony Lacey),
COLLEEN DEWHURST (Mother Hall), JANET MARGOLIN (Robin),
SHELLEY DUVALL (Pam), CHRISTOPHER WALKEN (Duane Hall),
SIGOURNEY WEAVER (Alvy's Date), BEVERLY D'ANGELO (TV Actress)

ACADEMY AWARDS 1978

OSCARS for BEST PICTURE (Charles H. Joffe),
BEST DIRECTOR (Woody Allen), BEST ACTRESS (Diane Keaton),
and BEST ORIGINAL SCREENPLAY (Woody Allen, Marshall Brickman)

WOODY
ALLEN

DIANE
KEATON

TONY
ROBERTS

CAROL
KANE

PAUL
SIMON

JANET
MARGOLIN

SHELLEY
DUVALL

CHRISTOPHER
WALKEN

COLLEEN
DEWHURST

"ANNIE HALL"

A nervous romance.

A JACK ROLLINS - CHARLES H. JOFFE PRODUCTION

Written by WOODY ALLEN and MARSHALL BRICKMAN • Directed by WOODY ALLEN

1

"You know, it's one thing about intellectuals, they prove that you can be absolutely brilliant and have no idea what's going on."

"There's an old joke. Two elderly women are at a Catskills mountain resort, and one of them says: 'Boy, the food at this place is really terrible.' The other one says, 'Yeah, I know, and such… small portions.' Well, that's essentially how I feel about life," says *Annie Hall's* actual protagonist, Alvy Singer (Woody Allen) at the top of the film. "(It's) full of loneliness and misery and suffering and unhappiness, and it's all over much too quickly."

Singer is a stand-up comedian, professional cynic and full-time misanthrope. When a big tall blond crew-cutted guy in a record store tells him that Wagner is on sale this week, Jewish Alvy knows exactly how to take it. He also despises Los Angeles for being a city whose only cultural advantage is that you can make a right turn on a red light. What unifies this seemingly unrelated hodge-podge of scenes and sketches pieced together by editor Ralph Rosenblum from a heap of over 50,000 feet of film is Alvy's relationship to the movie's title character, Annie Hall.

We meet the couple after the two of them have called it quits for the very last time, and then take an endearing yet heart-breaking trip with them down memory lane to discover what led to the demise of their year-long romance. Annie (Diane Keaton) is the quintessential pseudo-intellectual, a caricature of the urban woman. Alvy brands her as eternally flawed for being born with original sin—she grew up in rural America. On the other hand Alvy's cynical remarks about everyone and everything (including himself) are just his way of concealing his own unique, neurotic blend of self-loathing, self-pity and self-worship, which not even 15 years of therapy could cure. As he explains in a TV interview he was deemed "four-P" by a personality assessment test: a hostage in the event of war.

Allen biographer Marion Meade rightly stated that *Annie Hall* could have just as easily been entitled *Alvy Singer* or, even better, *Allan Konigsberg*, Woody Allen's given name. The Alvy character is an unmistakable self-portrait of the director, who himself started out as a gag writer for stand-up comics. Up until three weeks before the premiere, Allen insisted that the film be called *Anhedonia* (the debilitating absence of pleasure or the ability to experience it). Arthur Krim, head of United Artists and Allen's

DIANE KEATON In a quirkily perfect performance that won her the Best Actress Oscar, Woody Allen's then flame Diane Keaton reveals Annie Hall's and her own zany yet huggable nature through the character's stumbling, flailing gestures. These are reinforced by self-conscious, shyly banal statements, particularly her self-effacing "La-dee-dah." The similarities between these two women include their over the top and "not quite with it" manner as well as their taste in clothing, which according to Allen, includes an affinity for football jerseys matched to skirts, combat boots and mittens. Given all this, it should come as no surprise that Keaton's original surname supplied the character with hers.

The actress, who was born on January 5, 1946 in Los Angeles, met Allen in 1969 while acting with him in his Broadway play *Play it Again, Sam.* A few years later, she appeared for the first time in an often-overlooked performance at the side of Al Pacino in the role of Michael Corleone's wife in Francis Ford Coppola's *Godfather* trilogy (1972, 1974, 1990).

She worked on numerous Woody Allen films, both before and after their relationship came to an end. In 1981, she collaborated with Warren Beatty, with whom she was also romantically involved for some time, on the film *Reds*. Before long, Keaton proved she had what it took to join the male-dominated world of directing and has been making pictures and TV shows, including an episode of the legendary TV show *Twin Peaks*, since the 1980s. Her 1995 work *Unstrung Heroes* is a little-known masterpiece in filmmaking. Her 1996 acting and comedic bravado in *The First Wives Club* (1996) and dramatic eloquence in *Marvin's Room* (1996) reconfirmed her star appeal. Diane Keaton won a Golden Globe and was nominated for a Best Actress Oscar for her role as Erica Barry in *Something's Gotta Give* (2003).

paternal role model, allegedly threatened to throw himself out the window if he went through with it.

The almost non-existent cinematic structure of the piece allowed Allen to pack the movie full of amusing quips and snide remarks; more concisely, it supplied him with a vehicle for unabated hilarity. Nonetheless, *Annie Hall* remains a particularly significant work for two main reasons. The first is that the director makes a point of tweaking classic modes of cinematic depictions of reality and storytelling. Whereas he filmed his 1969 piece *Take the Money and Run* (1969) in the style of a news exposé, *Annie Hall* is a

“Personal as the story he is telling may be, what separates this film from Allen’s own past work and most other recent comedy is its general believability. His central figures and all who cross their paths are recognizable contemporary types. Most of us have even shared a lot of their fantasies.”

Time Magazine

1 He'd never join a club that would have him as a member: Alvy Singer is Woody Allen's filmic alter ego.

2 A walk on the mild side: Neurotic New Yorkers Annie (Diane Keaton), Alvy and Dick (Dick Cavett) analyze life, art, and above all themselves.

3 New York is full of interesting, undiscovered places to hang out…

4 Uppers and downers: Alvy reveres European cinema—and especially Ingmar Bergman.

veritable cornucopia of narrative conventions and even manages to weave in an animated sequence. Time and again, Alvy directly addresses his audience sitting in the theater. Such is the case in a movie ticket line, when he wishes to one-up and embarrass the wannabe film buff who loudly pontificates, claims to teach a course on TV, Media and Culture at Columbia University and quotes extensively from influential Canadian media theorist Marshall McLuhan. Alvy quickly wins their debate by surreally calling upon McLuhan to personally step in and set matters straight. In another memorable sequence, Allen uses a split-screen to illustrate two incompatible worlds, as Alvy's New York Jewish family is compared in similar, juxtaposed dinner scenes to Annie's family. On the left third of the screen is the brightly lit, affluent, politely gracious, aloof and sober Hall family discussing subjects such as the Christmas play and the 4-H Club. On the right two-thirds of the screen is a darkly lit, sloppy and informal, noisily argumentative, competitively babbling Singer family talking about illness (diabetes, heart disease) and unemployment (illustrating that Alvy's argumentative nature and fear of marriage were inherited from his family). The genius of the episode is born out of the actual conversation of the two families that takes place *across* this divided split-screen. This brand of narrative anarchy was both a liberating artistic breakthrough and a triumph for Allen.

The second significant achievement for Allen that came out of *Annie Hall* was the creation of his alter ego, which finally succeeded in distancing him from his purely comic self. Since this picture, Allen's cosmopolitan neurotic has been a free-floating entity who can be readily integrated into the context of more serious pieces like *Hannah and Her Sisters* (1985) and *Husbands and Wives* (1992), or just observe the action from the sidelines as in his 1978 drama, *Interiors* (1978). SH

PADRE PADRONE

1977 – ITALY – 113 MIN.

GENRE

DRAMA, LITERARY ADAPTATION

DIRECTOR

PAOLO TAVIANI, VITTORIO TAVIANI

SCREENPLAY

PAOLO TAVIANI, VITTORIO TAVIANI,
based on the novel of the same name by GAVINO LEDDA

DIRECTOR OF PHOTOGRAPHY

MARIO MASINI

EDITING

ROBERTO PERPIGNANI

MUSIC

EGISTO MACCHI

PRODUCTION

GIULIANI G. DE NEGRI for CINEMA SRL, RAI

STARRING

OMERO ANTONUTTI (Gavino's Father), SAVERIO MARCONI (Gavino),
MARCELLA MICHELANGELI (Gavino's Mother), FABRIZIO FORTE (Gavino as a child),
NANNI MORETTI (Cesare), GAVINO LEDDA (Himself), MARINO CENNA,
PIERLUIGI ALVAU, PIETRO GIORDO, MARCO UNALI

IFF CANNES 1977

GOLDEN PALM (Paolo and Vittorio Taviani)

R.A.I. - RADIOTELEVISIONE ITALIANA
presenta

PALMA D'ORO DEL
FESTIVAL DI CANNES
•
PREMIO DELLA CRITICA INTERNAZIONALE

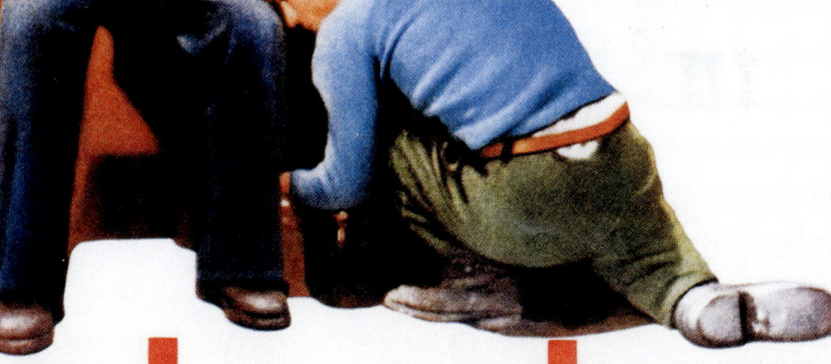

padre padrone

un film di
PAOLO e VITTORIO TAVIANI
liberamente tratto dal libro di GAVINO LEDDA
con OMERO ANTONUTTI · SAVERIO MARCONI MARCELLA MICHELANGELI · FABRIZIO FORTE
STANKO MOLNAR
realizzato da GIULIANI G. DE NEGRI
EASTMANCOLOR

1

"Today it was Gavino that got it— tomorrow it's your turn."

Padre Padrone was originally made for Italian television before being converted to cinema format and shown at the Cannes Film Festival in 1977, where it won the coveted Palme d'Or. Adapted from the autobiography of the Sardinian author Gavino Ledda, "Padre, padrone. L'educazione di un pastore" ("Padre Padrone. The Education of a Shepherd"), the film describes a boy's emancipation from his father (*padre*) and master (*padrone*). Yet it is less a psychogram of one young man in search of himself than the depiction of a cultural revolution. This is no tourist's-eye-view of a simple pre-industrial society fortunate enough to enjoy its own homemade bread, olive oil and cheese. The world inhabited by the shepherds of Sardinia is no pastoral idyll, and the indissoluble family bonds are primarily a guarantee of survival. In a world of unrelenting toil, the father begets his own workforce: serfs in the form of children.

The film begins by certifying its own authenticity: Ledda, the author of the book, assures the audience that this really is the story of his life. He hands the branch of a tree to a man with a face like granite, who carves it into a stick and storms off to the school, where he bursts into the classroom in mid-lesson. The children, no more than six to eight years old, are petrified, because unlike the audience, they know what's coming: "The boy belongs to me!" "Me" meaning the work of the family, and not of the state. Instead of learning to read, write and count, Gavino (Fabrizio Forte) is destined to tend sheep.

Compulsory education, one of the elementary preconditions for the establishment of state control in the 19th century, was not yet enforced on the island of Sardinia. In this wild rural environment, the ancient laws of the clan still apply. The father (Omero Antonutti) brings up his son as if he were training an animal. The boy is sent off into the desolate mountains to tend the sheep. Day and night, these animals will be his only companions. If he leaves his appointed station, he's beaten and sent back. He learns to understand the innumerable languages of the natural world: the sounds of daybreak, the rustling of the oaks in the wind, the river's murmur and the snake's hiss; and he learns the moods of the sheep, who shit in the bucket when he's just finished milking, and who seem to snigger at his rage. He learns; and he forgets. Silenced by loneliness, he loses the habit of speech. While other children suffer as he does, he's forbidden to have anything to do with them. The pastures and the sheep have to be guarded with a terrible patience, and the enemies of the shepherd have been the same for millennia: thieves, wild beasts, and sudden

BIOPIC A biopic is a film that tells the story of a life. It's a highly popular genre. Biopics are inspired by real historical figures, and they drawn on non-fictional sources (biographies and autobiographies) to depict or reconstruct a true-life story.
The biopics of the 30s, 40s, and 50s left their mark on the genre, with portraits of rulers (such as "Sissi," the Austrian Empress immortalized by Romy Schneider, or Kaiser Friedrich II), artists (Mozart or Frida Kahlo), scientists (Pasteur or Madame Curie), and politicians (Lincoln or Bismarck). The shift of attention from members of the elite to popular heroes (such as boxers) is a specific achievement of the movies.
For a long time, it looked as though the genre had disappeared from the cinema, for the focus on a single person seemed a little old-fashioned to contemporary filmmakers. In the early 2000s, though, there have been a number of modern biopics, in which supporting characters play a more prominent role, and which often have an open-ended quality. Examples include *Pollock* (2000) and *A Beautiful Mind* (2001).

2

1 Baa, baa black sheep: Not even his mother's love saves Gavino (Fabrizio Forte) from becoming a shepherd.

2 Picking on the little guy: "My father, the giant; the final instance," said Franz Kafka.

3 Sardinian dialysis: Cut your lips till they bleed.

"Class struggle in the countryside is the battle against the patriarchy." *Vittorio Taviani*

outbreaks of cold weather. In the distance, the mournful tolling of a bell seems to announce a grim fate for a boy whose life has barely begun.

At this point, the narrative leaps forward in time: the boy is now a 20-year-old (Saverio Marconi)—and he's still a shepherd. Once again, it's musical tones that herald his future: two traveling musicians, who seem to have lost their way in the wilderness, come over the mountains playing the accordion. The melody is familiar: the overture waltz from Richard Strauss' *Die Fledermaus*. The young shepherd swaps two lambs for an accordion, and with music as his first foreign language, he seeks and finds a new world. He rebels against his father and labors endlessly to qualify for university, where he studies linguistics. The shepherd's emancipation begins with his recognition that language, too, can be a source of power—and speechlessness a kind of impotence. (That the language of Sardinia is a long way from standard Italian is a detail lost to those who see a dubbed version of the film.)

Padre Padrone combines an almost ethnographic camera with an extremely subjective soundtrack. Shots of a forbidding landscape are accompanied by a soundscape that underlines the feelings and perceptions of the protagonists: The father who has almost beaten his son to death cradles the unconscious boy in his arms and sings a Sardinian "Miserere"—and though only father and son are visible, we hear an overwhelming choral accompaniment. The function of the choir is as old as Greek tragedy: it

4 A smokeless cigarette: Take a drag the wrong way round, and your enemies can't see you in the dark.

5 Emasculated by age: The arm raised in anger by patriarch (Omero Antonutti) is now old and feeble.

6 Tinkle, tinkle little star: Even at school, Gavino is not safe from his father's looming authority.

anchors individual suffering in the collective experience of humanity. Here, however, the heartrending lament seems almost to emerge from the desolate earth itself. Again: a religious procession winds through the valley, and Gavino is among those bearing the statue of Jesus. The men talk of emigrating to Germany, in the hope of escaping their poverty. Suddenly, one of them strikes up with the first line of a German drinking song, "Trink, Brüderlein, trink" ("Drink, brother, drink"), and soon the valley echoes to the sound of the men singing beneath their burden: "Lass doch die Sorgen zuhaus!" ("Leave all your worries at home!") This is the principle that organizes the entire film: again and again, personal suffering is subsumed into collective experience, into shared and universal dreams. RV

COMING HOME

1978 – USA – 126 MIN.

GENRE

DRAMA, VIETNAM FILM

DIRECTOR

HAL ASHBY

SCREENPLAY

NANCY DOWD, ROBERT C. JONES, WALDO SALT

DIRECTOR OF PHOTOGRAPHY

HASKELL WEXLER

EDITING

DON ZIMMERMAN

MUSIC

THE BEATLES, THE ROLLING STONES,
BOB DYLAN, STEPPENWOLF and others

PRODUCTION

JEROME HELLMAN for JAYNE PRODUCTIONS,
JEROME HELLMAN PRODUCTIONS

STARRING

JANE FONDA (Sally Hyde), JON VOIGHT (Luke Martin),
BRUCE DERN (Captain Bob Hyde), PENELOPE MILFORD (Vi Munson),
ROBERT CARRADINE (Bill Munson), ROBERT GINTY (Sergeant Dink Mobley),
MARY GREGORY (Martha Vickery), KATHLEEN MILLER (Kathy Delise),
BEESON CARROLL (Captain Earl Delise), WILLIE TYLER (Virgil)

ACADEMY AWARDS 1979

OSCARS for BEST ACTOR (Jon Voight), BEST ACTRESS (Jane Fonda),
and BEST SCREENPLAY (Nancy Dowd, Robert C. Jones, Waldo Salt)

IFF CANNES 1978

AWARD for BEST ACTOR (Jon Voight)

A MAN WHO BELIEVED IN WAR.
A MAN WHO BELIEVED IN NOTHING.
AND A WOMAN WHO BELIEVED IN BOTH OF THEM.

A Jerome Hellman Production

A Hal Ashby Film

Jane Fonda

Jon Voight Bruce Dern

in

"Coming Home"

Screenplay by Waldo Salt and Robert C. Jones Story by Nancy Dowd

Director of Photography Haskell Wexler Associate Producer Bruce Gilbert

Produced by Jerome Hellman Directed by Hal Ashby

R RESTRICTED UNDER 17 REQUIRES ACCOMPANYING PARENT OR ADULT GUARDIAN

United Artists
A Transamerica Company

1

"In my dreams I ain't sitting in a wheel chair. In my dreams I don't have one. I've got legs."

In 1968, a frenzy sweeps across the United States, dividing the nation. The federal government and the army stick to their guns about the legitimacy and necessity of their involvement in Vietnam. Week after week a number of enthusiastic young men join the service. Blinded by patriotism, they act as ammunition in an ongoing battle that sinks deeper into the quicksands with each passing day. Nevertheless, a vocal and undeniable peace movement has gained momentum. It is an age of hippies, flower power and doves.

In 1968, we meet Sally (Jane Fonda), a naïve, sheltered young woman. Married to Bob (Bruce Dern), an officer with the Marines who is preparing to depart for Vietnam, she lives in the cut-off world of the military base. Cries of dissonance and disgust regarding the atrocities of the battlefield rarely make their way here. Yet, when Bob is called to war, Sally too must abandon the dwelling they share in officers' quarters, and her way of life is about to change dramatically. She buys a convertible, moves into a house on the beach, and befriends the easy-going Vi (Penelope Milford). Suddenly Sally has a new, freer, more self-determined lease of life. She even takes on a new job, volunteering at a veterans' hospital for injured soldiers, where they are rehabilitated in preparation for civilian life.

The pain of the soldiers goes beyond visible injuries. Other wounds lie deeper. Despair resulting from their own suffering or the suffering they inflicted on others dominates many of their lives. Possibly the worst blow the war has dealt is the bitter resignation that now fills their hearts where their patriotic spirit used to be. All the propaganda about becoming a war hero was just that. Vi's brother Bill (Robert Carradine), who eventually cracks as a result of his war experiences and sees no alternative but suicide, illustrates this point perfectly. Another veteran, Luke (Jon Voight), once the captain of the high-school football team and apple of all the girls' eyes, now lives out his days as a vegetating paraplegic confined to a hospital gurney. Full of wrath, the cynical young man makes it his business to raise Cain amongst the stressed-out hospital orderlies—only to be regularly silenced by sedatives and handcuffed to his bed.

JON VOIGHT Jon Voight, born the son of a golf pro in 1938, began his career in show business as a teenager and worked his way up the ranks on the Broadway stage. He first caught the public's eye in John Schlesinger's *Midnight Cowboy* (1969) for his portrayal of a naive young country-bumpkin turned gigolo, who dreams of striking it rich in the Big Apple. The performance also garnered Voight his first Oscar nod. He gained further recognition for his role as one of four city slickers in John Boorman's twisted backwater thriller *Deliverance* (1972); the four buddies embark on a canoe trip and end up fighting for their lives when a pack of inbred river settlers hunt the group down. Voight won international acclaim for *Coming Home* (1978), though he did not respond to his popularity by only accepting roles in prominent productions from then on. Another particularly noteworthy performance came in Andrei Konchalovsky's *Runaway Train* (1985), a pessimistic drama about escape from prison. The hefty number of supporting roles he continues to play show off his wide acting range. Such was the case when he played sports reporter Howard Cosell to a tee opposite Will Smith in Michael Mann's *Ali* (2001), and devised a plan of escape for Robert De Niro in yet another Michael Mann film, *Heat* (1995). This regular chameleon's list of golden cameos also includes assigning Tom Cruise with death-defying tasks in Brian De Palma's *Mission: Impossible* (1996), responding to the Japanese attack as President Roosevelt in Michael Bay's *Pearl Harbor* (2001) and even standing alongside his daughter Angelina Jolie in Simon West's *Lara Croft: Tomb Raider* (2001) as her on-screen dad.

Sally recognizes Luke as an old schoolmate of hers and refuses to be intimidated by his verbal attacks. With a bit of persistence, she is able to break through his caustic exterior and sees him for who he really is—a man with a vulnerable and wounded core. The two become fast friends and eventually lovers. The flame of their romance is doused when Sally's husband Bob comes home from Nam. Yet Sally's infidelity is not the source of Bob's woes. He wanted more than anything to be a war hero, only to end up shooting himself in the leg while taking a shower. Just moments after he is awarded a medal of honor for his bravery, he is overcome with despair and takes his own life. He too becomes a victim of war, and many others will follow…

Hal Ashby's film is a war drama set a million miles away from the grenade-riddled, napalm-scorched jungle battlefields. These are places from which one simply cannot return, for the memories remain. The film's title is also rather misleading. "Home," the bastion of normalcy where one can be revered a hero is proven to be an unattainable illusion. Values like "country," "honor" and "patriotism" have become nothing more than empty words without meaning. This realization usually comes too late, and for many is the true trauma of war. "I need to justify the fact that I'm crippled, that I've killed people. So I tell myself what I did was okay"—is how one of the veterans comes to terms with his past.

Coming Home was filmed at a time when the sociopolitical climate in the U.S. allowed for rawer and more critical cinematic depictions of the Vietnam experience than in the immediately preceding years. *Alice's Restaurant* (1969) directed by Arthur Penn, Michelangelo Antonioni's *Zabriskie Point* (1969) and even George Lucas's *American Graffiti* (1973), presented Vietnam as a far-off topic somewhere on the horizon. But the late 70s could not ignore the nation's blatant wounds. A handful of exceptional films from this period stress the irrationality of war and brand

1 People will say we're in love: The relationship of paraplegic veteran, Luke (Jon Voight) and Sally (Jane Fonda) raises a few eyebrows.

2 Making love, not war: It takes time for Luke and Sally to accept their feelings for each other.

3 Raising Lazarus: Vi (Penelope Milford) and Sally help Luke overcome his bitterness and cynicism.

"An impressionistic meditation on the Vietnam War and the scars it has left on the bodies, minds, and souls of many soldiers and civilians." *Spirituality & Health*

all participants in war as victims. In its distance from direct representations of war, *Coming Home* distinguishes itself from other contemporaries like *The Deer Hunter* (1978, directed by Michael Cimino) and *Apocalypse Now* (1979, directed by Francis Ford Coppola). Both these pieces made fervent pleas against the madness of war, while confronting the viewer with gut-wrenching battlefield images of guerilla warfare.

Its gripping topic aside, *Coming Home* is a great example of world-class acting. Jane Fonda and Jon Voight both received the Oscar for "Best Performance in a Leading Role" (whereas the Oscars for Best Picture and Best Director went to the competing production, *The Deer Hunter*). The highlight of their performances is without a doubt the socially progressive love scene, in which the film went against an age-old taboo and showed a disabled man having sex. It is a cunning slap in the face that far exceeds a flat depiction of the "make love not war" slogan of the era.

The film's soundtrack, comprised of the pop songs of the late 60s, effectively summons the spirit of the time. The plea for a just world put forth by The Rolling Stones, The Beatles, Bob Dylan, Jimi Hendrix, Steppenwolf, Janis Joplin, Richie Havens, Jefferson Airplane, Simon and Garfunkel and many others who were against the military aggression in Vietnam does not fall on deaf ears.

EP

NOSFERATU – PHANTOM DER NACHT

NOSFERATU

1978 – FRG / FRANCE – 107 MIN.

GENRE

HORROR FILM, REMAKE

DIRECTOR

WERNER HERZOG

SCREENPLAY

WERNER HERZOG, based on the novel *DRACULA* by BRAM STOKER, and on motifs from the film *NOSFERATU – EINE SYMPHONIE DES GRAUENS* (1922) by FRIEDRICH WILHELM MURNAU

DIRECTOR OF PHOTOGRAPHY

JÖRG SCHMIDT-REITWEIN

EDITING

BEATE MAINKA-JELLINGHAUS

MUSIC

POPOL VUH, FLORIAN FRICKE

PRODUCTION

WERNER HERZOG, MICHAEL GRUSKOFF for WERNER HERZOG FILMPRODUKTION, GAUMONT

STARRING

KLAUS KINSKI (Count Dracula), ISABELLE ADJANI (Lucy Harker), BRUNO GANZ (Jonathan Harker), JACQUES DUFILHO (Captain), ROLAND TOPOR (Renfield), WALTER LADENGAST (Doctor Van Helsing), JAN GROTH (Harbormaster), CARSTEN BODINUS (Schrader), MARTJE GROHMANN (Mina), RIJK DE GOOYER (Official)

IFF BERLIN 1979

SILVER BEAR for BEST ART DIRECTION (Henning von Gierke)

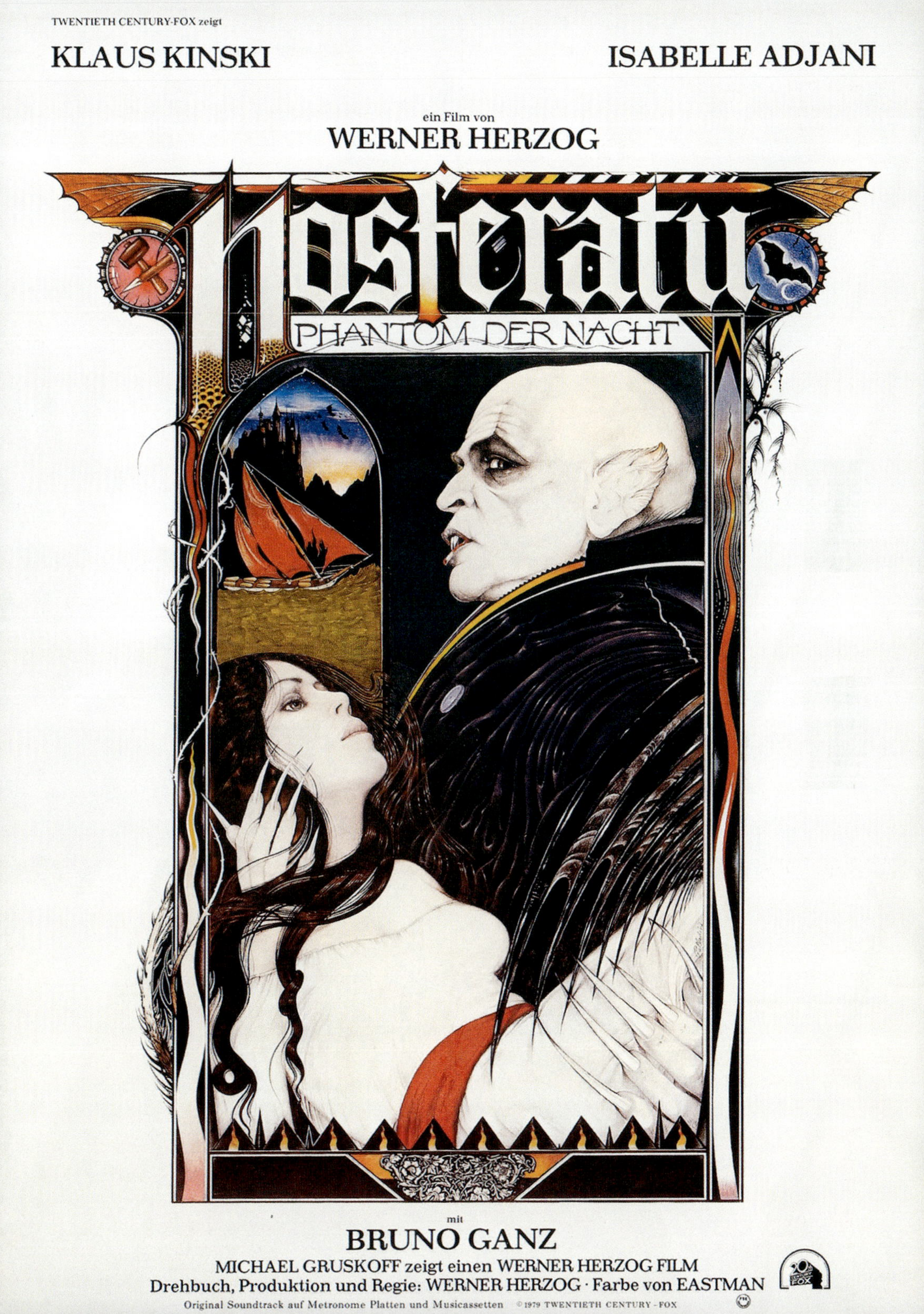

TWENTIETH CENTURY-FOX zeigt

KLAUS KINSKI **ISABELLE ADJANI**

ein Film von

WERNER HERZOG

Nosferatu

PHANTOM DER NACHT

mit

BRUNO GANZ

MICHAEL GRUSKOFF zeigt einen WERNER HERZOG FILM

Drehbuch, Produktion und Regie: WERNER HERZOG · Farbe von EASTMAN

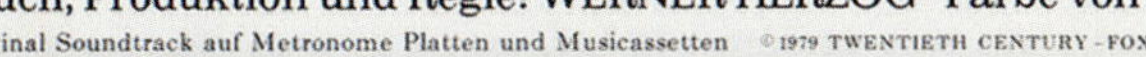

1

"Your wife has a beautiful neck."

The camera crawls past a row of mummified corpses: to judge by their grimacing faces, most of these people died in terror. They look as if they had seen Death itself. Our flesh creeps to the funereal sounds of the German band Popol Vuh. Next image: a bat in slow-motion flight. Cut. A waxen-faced woman awakens with a start and releases a bloodcurdling scream.

Only dreaming…

Thus begins one of the most idiosyncratic vampire films of modern times. *Nosferatu* inhabits a world of dim, constricted spaces; extreme contrasts of light and dark give way to nearly monochrome images; long, static shots contrast with an almost hysterically unbridled handheld camera. The film is a cinematic homage to Murnau's dark and magical *Nosferatu – a Symphony of Terror* (*Nosferatu – Eine Symphonie des Grauens*, 1922), one of the earliest adaptations of Bram Stoker's *Dracula*.

In a dilapidated castle in the Carpathian Mountains, the sinister Count Dracula (Klaus Kinski) exists, or rather vegetates. Only Lucy (Isabelle Adjani), the beautiful wife of Jonathan Harker (Bruno Ganz) can free him from his terrible lethargy. The film begins with Lucy's nightmare, in which Dracula appears as a bat. She has a terrible foreboding that something dreadful is about to take its course,

KLAUS KINSKI Nikolaus Günther Nakszynski was born in 1926 in Zoppot, part of the Free City of Danzig (today Sopot, Poland). Kinski's theater career began after the Second World War, and he soon made a name for himself as a brilliant but "difficult" actor. After his cinema debut in *Morituri* (1948), he appeared in numerous films, in which he usually embodied eccentric villains. These included a large number of Edgar Wallace adaptations. His collaboration with Werner Herzog marked Kinski's breakthrough into "serious" cinema and established his reputation as the *enfant terrible* of European film. Both manically extroverted and a tortured perfectionist, Kinski thrillingly depicted a series of malignant, obsessive and untamable characters, in films such as *Aguirre, Wrath of God* (*Aguirre, der Zorn Gottes*, 1972), *Fitzcarraldo* (1978–81) and *Cobra Verde* (1987). In 1987, Kinski directed for the first and only time: the bizarre film biography *Kinski Paganini*, which he also wrote, and in which he played the main character, the Italian violin virtuoso who was said to be possessed by the devil. Again and again, Kinski produced masterly and shocking performances, combining iron professionalism with the ability to "lose control" unforgettably on screen. Werner Herzog produced a fine memorial to the joys and trials of his working relationship with Kinski, in a documentary whose title speaks volumes: *My Beloved Enemy* (*Mein liebster Feind*, 1999). Klaus Kinski died near San Francisco on November 23, 1991.

2

3

and that there's nothing she can do stop it. Dracula has written to Renfield, a property agent, expressing his interest in an empty house in Wisborg, Lucy's hometown. It's the beginning of an inexorable courtship dance, which will end in the Count's demise.

Nosferatu is more than a skillful reworking of Murnau's film classic and Stoker's novel. Probably only Werner Herzog and his magnificent protagonist Klaus Kinski could have transformed this material into an apocalyptic vision of such unparalleled romantic intensity. Kinski's stylized interpretation of the vampire figure is an unforgettably powerful piece of acting. Take the scene when Dracula receives Jonathan Harker, who has been sent to the castle by Renfield to negotiate the sale of the house in Wisborg. Kinski is the first actor to show the terrifying melancholy at the heart of the Count's murderous obsession. Though the room is gloomy, lit only by candles, Dracula averts his deathly face as if in shame; yet his skinny fingers, with their claw-like nails, seem to reach out for Harker with a terrible life of their own. Jonathan soon falls victim to the undead Count, who can survive only by feeding on the blood of others.

Having placed Harker temporarily out of action, Dracula departs immediately for Wisborg—a pilgrimage to Lucy, from whom he hopes to acquire a new lease of life. He will arrive with an entourage of rats, bringing a plague epidemic to the solid and prosperous German town. In the delirium that follows, we are witness to an apocalyptic drama, a succession of grotesque and chilling scenes: an endless procession of coffins, choreographed like a dance of death; a table set for a feast among the rats, with the human guests vanishing in an instant by means of a simple cut. The horror that engulfs Wisborg could hardly be conveyed more poetically, or with a greater feeling for the sheer sadness of death. In the midst of this calamitous confusion, Lucy is the only person who knows what lies at the root of it all, and her nightmares are the source of her knowledge. But no-one will listen to her, not even Van Helsing, the local doctor, whose medical skills are no match for the mysterious powers he finds himself up against.

The film does a great deal more than simply quoting or imitating its predecessors. Herzog's *Nosferatu* casts an entirely new light on the old story. Aesthetically, the film is groundbreaking: the sparing use of dialog, the ethereal music, the strange images of the natural world and the claustrophobic treatment of space combine to create an

"My head is one big garbage can where everything is jumbled around." *Klaus Kinski*

1 The horrors of a bad manicure: Nosferatu (Klaus Kinski) is ready to scratch the eyes out of anyone who dare compare him to his predecessor, Max Schreck.

2 Bloodlust: Lucy (Isabelle Adjani) is precisely Nosferatu's taste.

3 Your kiss is on my list: Does Lucy have the courage to resist the touch of evil?

4 Struck down by the light of day: The Count cannot survive the sun's caress.

4

5

5 Lucy's premonition: Death is written in the wind.

6 The poetry of death: Nosferatu scuttles through the streets of a plague-ridden city.

7 A man on a mission: Jonathan (Bruno Ganz) rides on to Wisborg.

"With this work, Herzog intended 'to forge a link to one of the great films of the German Expressionist era:' Fritz Murnau's 'symphony of horror,' made in 1921. Indeed, Herzog has laced his film with citations from this classic movie." *Frankfurter Allgemeine Zeitung*

eerie audio-visual *Gesamtkunstwerk*—a total work of art. In content, too, the film opens up new perspectives: unlike Murnau, Herzog depicts Lucy as an autonomous woman, sacrificing herself willingly to free Wisborg from Death's embrace. By pretending to find him attractive, she lures the Count to her bedroom, where she holds him at bay until dawn. The first rays of sunlight are enough to extinguish his life. In the end, however, Lucy's heroism is in vain; for Jonathan Harker, too, has struggled back to Wisborg—and he has become the new Dracula. In a symphony of hypnotic images and sounds, the film shows how the powers of darkness survive, as Jonathan rides towards the darkening horizon with his cloak billowing in the wind — in search of new blood.

6
7

THE DEER HUNTER

1978 – USA – 183 MIN.

GENRE

VIETNAM FILM

DIRECTOR

MICHAEL CIMINO

SCREENPLAY

DERIC WASHBURN, MICHAEL CIMINO,
LOUIS GARFINKLE, QUINN K. REDEKER

DIRECTOR OF PHOTOGRAPHY

VILMOS ZSIGMOND

EDITING

PETER ZINNER

MUSIC

STANLEY MYERS

PRODUCTION

BARRY SPIKINGS, MICHAEL DEELEY, MICHAEL CIMINO,
JOHN PEVERALL for EMI FILMS LTD., UNIVERSAL PICTURES

STARRING

ROBERT DE NIRO (Michael), JOHN CAZALE (Stan), JOHN SAVAGE (Steven),
CHRISTOPHER WALKEN (Nick), MERYL STREEP (Linda),
GEORGE DZUNDZA (John), CHUCK ASPEGREN (Axel),
SHIRLEY STOLER (Steven's Mother), RUTANYA ALDA (Angela),
PIERRE SEGUI (Julien)

ACADEMY AWARDS 1979

OSCARS for BEST PICTURE (Barry Spikings, Michael Deeley,
Michael Cimino, John Peverall), BEST DIRECTOR (Michael Cimino),
BEST SUPPORTING ACTOR (Christopher Walken),
BEST FILM EDITING (Peter Zinner), and BEST SOUND (C. Darin Knight,
Richard Portman, Aaron Rochin, William L. McCaughey)

THE DEER HUNTER

EMI Films present

ROBERT DE NIRO IN A **MICHAEL CIMINO** Film **THE DEER HUNTER**

co-starring

JOHN CAZALE · JOHN SAVAGE · MERYL STREEP · CHRISTOPHER WALKEN

Music composed by STANLEY MYERS · Director of Photography VILMOS ZSIGMOND, A.S.C.

Associate Producers MARION ROSENBERG · JOANN CARELLI · Production Consultant JOANN CARELLI

Story by MICHAEL CIMINO, DERIC WASHBURN and LOUIS GARFINKLE, QUINN K. REDEKER

Screenplay by DERIC WASHBURN · Produced by BARRY SPIKINGS · MICHAEL DEELEY · MICHAEL CIMINO and JOHN PEVERALL

Directed by MICHAEL CIMINO

Technicolor® · Panavision® DOLBY SYSTEM® Stereo Distributed by EMI Films Limited ©1978 by EMI Films, Inc.

There are films that lose all their magic as soon as you know how they end; and there are others that keep their thrill even after several viewings. One of the cinema's undying magic moments is the scene at the end of *The Deer Hunter,* in which Nick (Christopher Walken) walks out of the back room of a Saigon gambling den with a red scarf round his head. His old friend Michael (Robert De Niro) steps towards him—he wants him to come home. But Nick can no longer recognize him; he's spent too long with his temple pressed to the barrel of a revolver with just one bullet in the chamber. He's gambled with his life so often, he can't believe it's still his. He moves towards the crowded gaming table with a bunch of banknotes in his hand. Michael tries in vain to persuade him to leave. And suddenly there's a flicker of recognition in Nick's eyes. He laughs, takes the gun, holds it to his head and pulls the trigger.

It's the end of the 60s. Michael, Nick and Steven (John Savage), three friends from a steel town in Pennsylvania, are sent to Vietnam. By coincidence, they meet again in the midst of war. And by misfortune, they end up in the hands of the Vietcong. The prisoners are forced to play

MICHAEL CIMINO His films were always controversial: *The Deer Hunter* (1978) was showered with Oscars in Hollywood and condemned as a falsification of the Vietnam War in Europe. The epic late Western *Heaven's Gate* (1980) was hailed as a masterpiece in Europe, and decried as a "catastrophe" in the USA. *Year of the Dragon* (1985), in which a sole cop takes on the Chinese mafia in New York, brought accusations of racism. *The Sicilian* (1987), an opulent biography of the Sicilian popular hero Salvatore Giuliano, was dismissed as historical kitsch.

Michael Cimino (1939–2016) came to filmmaking after studying architecture and painting. By the end of the 60s, he was making commercials. In 1973, he joined with John Milius to write the screenplay to *Magnum Force*, starring Clint Eastwood. Cimino's first feature film was *Thunderbolt and Lightfoot* (1974), a tragicomic thriller about a gangster in search of his money, with Eastwood and Jeff Bridges in the leading roles. The debut signaled some of the motifs that would be found throughout Cimino's work: male friendship, detailed milieu studies, and gorgeous landscape panoramas. His expensive obsession with authenticity drove United Artists to bankruptcy, and to this day, *Heaven's Gate* is a synonym for megaflops. Although his last film *The Sunchaser* (1996) was a fairly conventional effort, Michael Cimino is still regarded as one of the most visually brilliant directors in America.

2

1 War on the home front: Linda (Meryl Streep) and Michael (Robert DeNiro) tackle daily life and its many ghosts.

2 Birds of prey: Michael and Nick (Christopher Walken) on a hunting trip in the mountains.

3 Camerawork that is right on target. Cinematographer Vilmos Zsigmond went on to film *Heaven's Gate* (1980) for Cimino.

4 Fun and games in Clairton, Pennsylvania. Cimino shot the Clairton scenes in eight separate locations to breathe life into the fictitious town.

5 Celebrate good times: Steven's (John Savage, fourth from left) wedding marks the last joyous occasion of the boys' lives. Soon they'll be drafted to Vietnam.

Russian Roulette while their captors lay bets on the outcome. Finally, only Michael and Nick are left, face-to-face across the table. Michael demands three bullets instead of one, in order to raise the stakes. His ruse is successful: the two friends overcome the Vietcong guerillas, free Steven from the "tiger cage" (a half-submerged bamboo basket) and flee for their lives. But Michael is the only one who makes it home intact. Steven loses his legs, and Nick gets stuck in Saigon, making money with the game of death.

Only around one-third of this great epic takes place in Vietnam—the middle part. These are among the most impressive images of war ever filmed. The contempt for human life so typical of any war, the hatred, the powerlessness, the fear, and the pride: Michael Cimino brings these together in a single symbolic action—Russian Roulette. Yet Cimino shows the Americans purely as victims of the Vietnam War, and this provoked a lot of protest, especially in Europe. The Americans, it was claimed, were much more guilty than their opponents of torturing POWs. The film was accused of being racist, and the controversy came to a head at the Berlin Film Festival in 1979, as the Soviet Union, followed by the rest of the Eastern Bloc, withdrew all its films in protest.

But Cimino is not even attempting to provide a political commentary to the Vietnam War. Instead, his film tells

3

"Equally at ease in the lyrical and the realistic modes, a virtuoso of the shocking image who never loses sight of the whole, a consummate master of his technique, Michael Cimino is a supremely accomplished filmmaker."

Le Monde

4

5

6 Caught in the crossfire: Robert de Niro called this role "his toughest yet" after shooting was completed.

7 "One of the most frightening, unbearably tense sequences ever filmed—and the most violent excoriation of violence in screen history," wrote *Newsweek*.

8 Secret admirer: Back from the war, decorated soldier Michael visits the true love of his life—Nick's girl, Linda (Meryl Streep).

the story of people uprooted from everything they used to call home, and it shows the destruction of everything that once made friendship possible. The first hour of the film is devoted to the rituals of the two friends, Michael and Nick. We see their last day in the steelmill; we see them drinking with their buddies from the little community of White Russian immigrants; we see their wild celebrations at Steven's wedding reception, after the Russian Orthodox ceremony. One last time before Vietnam, the friends go hunting in the mountains of Pennsylvania, a pristine contrast to the dirty steel town. Michael's hunting ambition, to kill a deer with a single shot, will not survive his experiences in Vietnam. Indeed, when he returns in the third part of the film, he'll have difficulties even finding his home—because someone's missing, and he's made a promise. That's why he leaves once more, to search for Nick in Saigon.

At the end, the little group of mourners in the bar will strike up "God Bless America," but their rendition of the hymn is anything but triumphant. These people are the walking wounded, and each of them has lost something: a friend, physical wholeness, trust in life, or hope for the future. The fault lies with America; and yet America is their home, a part of their very selves. In *The Deer Hunter,* Cimino shows us this painful contradiction, and gives us a subtle, exact and outstandingly photographed portrait of American society after Vietnam.

NM

7

"There can be no quarrel about the acting. De Niro, Walken, John Savage, as another Clairton pal who goes to war, and Meryl Streep, as a woman left behind, are all top actors in extraordinary form."

Time Magazine

8

LA CAGE AUX FOLLES

BIRDS OF A FEATHER

1978 – FRANCE / ITALY – 91 MIN.

GENRE

COMEDY

DIRECTOR

ÉDOUARD MOLINARO

SCREENPLAY

MARCELLO DANON, ÉDOUARD MOLINARO, JEAN POIRET, FRANCIS VEBER, based on the play of the same name by JEAN POIRET

DIRECTOR OF PHOTOGRAPHY

ARMANDO NANNUZZI

EDITING

MONIQUE ISNARDON, ROBERT ISNARDON

MUSIC

ENNIO MORRICONE

PRODUCTION

MARCELLO DANON for DA MA PRODUZIONE, LES PRODUCTIONS ARTISTES ASSOCIÉS

STARRING

UGO TOGNAZZI (Renato Baldi), MICHEL SERRAULT (Albin Mougeotte / Zaza Napoli), CLAIRE MAURIER (Simone), RÉMI LAURENT (Laurent Baldi), CARMEN SCARPITTA (Louise Charrier), BENNY LUKE (Jacob), LUISA MANERI (Andrea Charrier), MICHEL GALABRU (Simon Charrier), VENANTINO VENANTINI (Chauffeur)

MARCELLO DANON présente

UGO TOGNAZZI MICHEL SERRAULT

la Cage aux Folles

d'après la pièce de JEAN POIRET

un film de EDOUARD MOLINARO

scénario et adaptation de FRANCIS VEBER · EDOUARD MOLINARO · MARCELLO DANON et JEAN POIRET
avec CLAIRE MAURIER · REMY LAURENT · BENNY LUKE · CARMEN SCARPITTA · LUISA MANERI

et avec la participation de MICHEL GALABRU · musique de ENNIO MORRICONE

une coproduction franco-italienne les productions ARTISTES ASSOCIÉS - DA MA PRODUZIONE SPA distribué par LES ARTISTES ASSOCIÉS

1

"What I am supposed to do? He's flying the coop."

What happens when an off-the-wall transvestite walks into a bar like a John Wayne impersonator, rolling her shoulders and standing tall? You guessed it, she is immediately ridiculed as a "faggot," forcing her other half to bravely confront the louse who made the remark and defend her honor. Even when the rogue suddenly reveals himself to be two heads taller than the gallant knight, and possibly a close relative of James Bond's nemesis, Jaws (*The Spy Who Loved Me,* 1977; *Moonraker*, 1979), that's no deterrent—honor is honor. Loved ones are not to be profaned with derogatory terms like that, especially when the person is question is not just an artiste but a star!

The drag-queen who has a whirl at playing cowboy is nightclub diva "Zaza Napoli," in a divine performance by Michel Serrault, who is both a "he" on stage and in life, even when his inner "she" bursts out on occasion with glistening mile-long lashes. Her significant other, the mature and dashing Renato Baldi (Ugo Tognazzi), who is forever sporting a white suit and trimmed moustache, is the owner of the "La Cage aux Folles," a club where, night after night, Zaza leads a high-pitched, high-heeled chorus line of silk-stockings and feather boas to victory. Renato and Zaza have been happily "wed" for the last 20 years. Yet married life can have its ups and downs, like the pair of pumps that

MICHEL SERRAULT Aged 50, and after countless supporting roles, Michel Serrault (1928–2007) was finally offered a part that launched him to new heights. With the greatest of ease, the thespian slipped into the skin of *La Cage aux Folles'* Albin, a sensitive, highly-strung transvestite. In addition to his film portrayal, Serrault gave over 2000 stage performances as Albin in the play of the same name. It was on the Paris stage that this gifted artist first flew his comedic colors. At the age of sixteen he received acting instruction from Bernard Blier. His film debut followed in 1954. Serrault was successful in moving on to other projects after the enormous public response to *La Cage aux Folles* and its two sequels (1980, 1985). He received the César for "Albin" and then abruptly switched gears from comedy to character acting. No-one could have played the double role of Biedermann and the arsonist better than Serrault. In both Chabrol's *Les Fantômes du chapelier* (*The Hatter's Ghost*, 1982), and Christian de Chalonge's *Dr. Petiot* (1990), he played perfidious, pathological serial killers masked by a façade of decorum and propriety. Simply clothed as an old man in a black hat with a well-trimmed moustache, he'd just tilt his head, arch his eyebrows and purse his lips and it was instantly clear what sort of sinister intentions were actually harbored in the soul of this upstanding citizen. He played a downtrodden, fatherly private investigator, who combs Europe looking for young murderess Isabelle Adjani in Claude Miller's *Mortelle randonnée* (*Deadly Run*, 1982). He becomes more fixated by her with each passing mile, and is gradually convinced that the modern-day Circe is the embodiment of innocence. "Don't laugh too quickly, and take your time before resorting to tears. The trick is to be sober and then wait." These were the words Serrault used on his 70th birthday to characterize what he considered to be the fundamentals of perfect acting. The last film Serrault acted in was *Have Mercy on Us All* (*Pars vite et reviens tard*, 2007), by French director Régis Wargnier.

are hurled at Renato's head when he bursts into Zaza's flat without first proving his affection. Luckily he's used to such displays of affection and knows exactly when to duck. Just one day in the life of Baldi and Zaza, who goes by the name of Albin Mougeotte during the daylight hours.

This world of fun and games comes to a shuddering halt when Renato's 20-year-old son Laurent (Rémi Laurent) announces his intention to marry Andrea (Luisa Maneri), the young daughter of Simon Charrier (Michel Galabru), deputy general of the Tradition, Family and Morality Party. Unfortunately, Andrea has told her

"Édouard Molinaro's light touch ensures that *La Cage aux Folles* is never embarrassing, and he avoids any *faux pas* in dealing with the topic of love between men. This is a bubbly and highly enjoyable film with an unobtrusive moral." *Karlsruher Filmschau*

1 A little dab will do ya: Michel Serrault is a man—he's just a touch more charming, ostentatious and supple than average.

2 A father's worst nightmare: Not only must Renato (Ugo Tognazzi) embrace his son's heterosexuality; he also has to come to terms with his future daughter-in-law—who happens to be the offspring of Simon Charrier, deputy general of the "Tradition, Family and Morality" party…

3 Charmed, I'm sure: The good-mannered Charrier (Michel Galabru) pays his respects to the supposed woman of the house (Michel Serrault).

4 Birds of a feather: Renato and Albin are storybook soulmates.

4

5

5 They'll never notice: The grand inquisitor of propriety and morality, M. Charrier, makes a graceful exit from the "Cage aux Folles" nightclub in three-inch pumps to dodge the paparazzi waiting at the door.

6 Basking in the limelight: Temperamental diva, Zaza (Michel Serrault), is less than delighted by her new supporting cast.

"Ugo Tognazzi's nonchalant virility constantly threatens to collapse into girlish affectation, and it harmonizes deliciously with the shamelessly exaggerated effeminacy of Michel Serrault."

Neue Zürcher Zeitung

bumptious dad that her father-in-law to be is the Italian consul in Nice. To make matters worse, the putative consul's apartment is full of paraphernalia bound to create an uproar: vases shaped like comely rear-ends, pink frou-frou pillows, a plaster statue of the Greek Adonis and china with lewd kouros motifs. Not forgetting Jacob (Benny Luke), a black manservant who wiggles his way across their deep-pile rugs in a French maid's costume waving a feather duster. None of that would matter, were it not for the fact that the deputy general and his wife announce their imminent visit. The colorful members of this happy family had better put their heads together fast, or they might have one giant catastrophe on their hands...

In *La Cage aux Folles,* virtually every aspect of life is turned on its head. Each paradigm of social normality suddenly indicates its opposite. All that is off-kilter is transformed into the given norm, whereas norms are taboo and leave both the characters and spectators aghast. The film valiantly takes on a barrage of homosexual and effeminate stereotypes, and puts them through the wringer. The depiction of Charrier, the defender of propriety, is also hyperbolized. He and his wife sit twelve feet apart from one another at their grand banquet table, and the interior design of their not-so-humble abode is reminiscent of a medieval torture chamber.

Beyond the over-the-top antics and the hare-brained slapstick lies some genuine depth. This is evidenced in the moments of Albin's fragility, such as when he is driven out of the house because he finds it impossible to act like anyone other than himself. He even makes a concerted effort to play along with the "charade" at one point, entering the living room, here re-decorated in "good taste," in a black suit and tie. Without his makeup and cramped by a heavily starched dress shirt, he attempts to seat himself as masculinely as possible. His posture while lowering himself, not to mention the way in which he places his hand on the arm rest, immediately give him away. Yet it is precisely when Serrault succeeds in showing how Albin fails at getting outside his own skin that *La Cage aux Folles* is at its most brilliant. In the 1980s, two further installments of the saga rode on the coat-tails of the enormous success of this picture. But like the American remake *The Birdcage* (1996), they couldn't hold a candle to the original.

SR

DAYS OF HEAVEN

1978 – USA – 95 MIN.

GENRE

MELODRAMA

DIRECTOR

TERRENCE MALICK

SCREENPLAY

TERRENCE MALICK

DIRECTOR OF PHOTOGRAPHY

NÉSTOR ALMENDROS, HASKELL WEXLER

EDITING

BILLY WEBER

MUSIC

ENNIO MORRICONE, SAINT-SAËNS

PRODUCTION

BERT SCHNEIDER, HAROLD SCHNEIDER
for PARAMOUNT PICTURES

STARRING

RICHARD GERE (Bill), BROOKE ADAMS (Abby), SAM SHEPARD (The Farmer), LINDA MANZ (Linda), ROBERT J. WILKE (Farm Foreman), JACKIE SHULTIS (Linda's Friend), GENE BELL (Dancer), DOUG KERSHAW (Fiddler), RICHARD LIBERTINI (Vaudeville Leader), JOHN WILKINSON (Preacher)

ACADEMY AWARDS 1979

OSCAR for BEST CINEMATOGRAPHY (Néstor Almendros)

IFF CANNES 1979

BEST DIRECTOR (Terrence Malick)

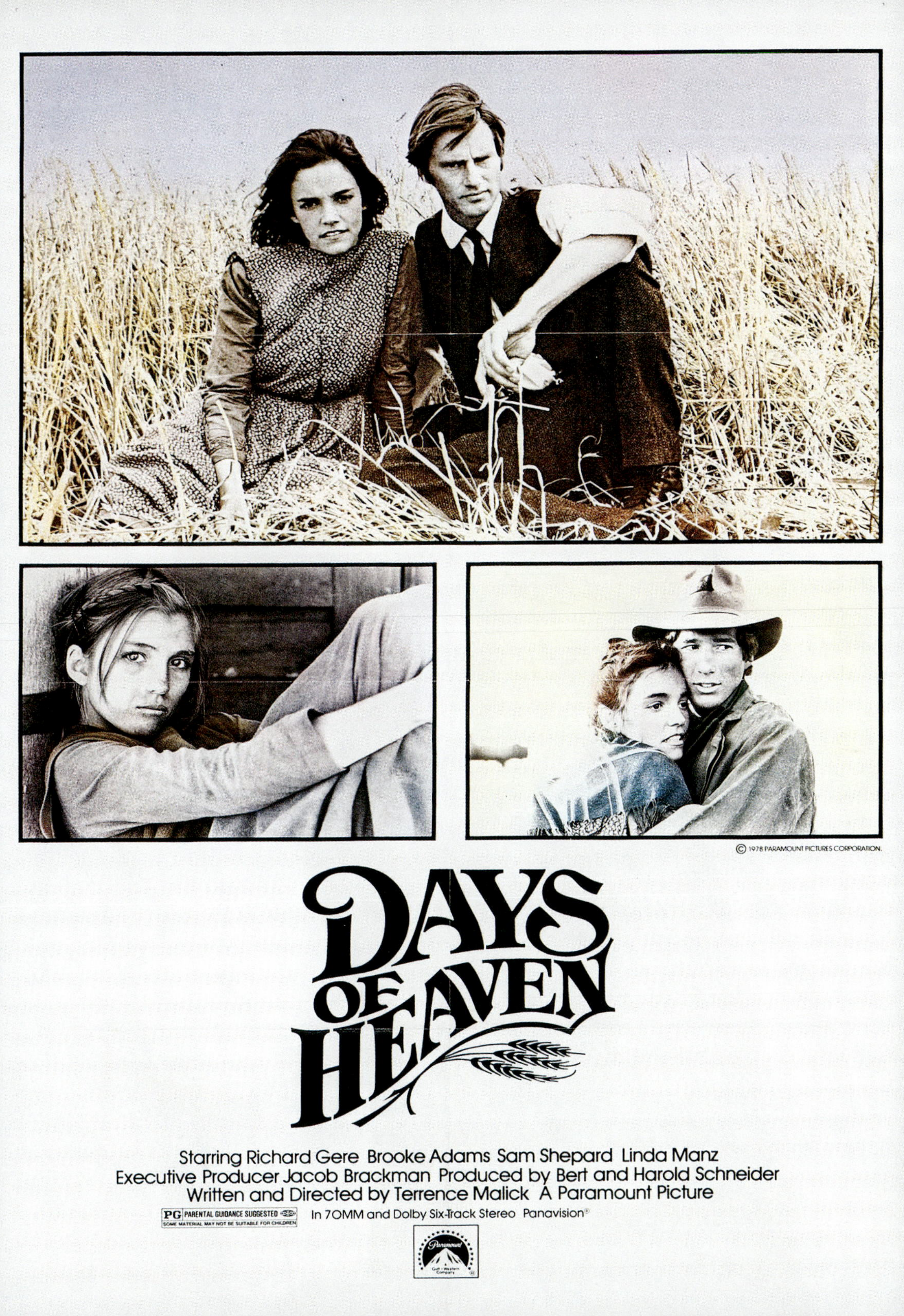

© 1978 PARAMOUNT PICTURES CORPORATION.

Starring Richard Gere Brooke Adams Sam Shepard Linda Manz
Executive Producer Jacob Brackman Produced by Bert and Harold Schneider
Written and Directed by Terrence Malick A Paramount Picture

PG PARENTAL GUIDANCE SUGGESTED
SOME MATERIAL MAY NOT BE SUITABLE FOR CHILDREN

In 70MM and Dolby Six-Track Stereo Panavision®

1

"It just used to be me and my brother. We used to do things together."

The film is a cinematic masterpiece, a veritable cascade of imagery all too seldom experienced on the silver screen. Packed with symbolism, Terrence Malick's drama relates the moving tale of a love triangle set in the social and political upheaval of the industrial revolution. A montage of the work of photographer Lewis Hine (1874–1940) gives us a first taste of this era of radical change. Stark pictures of the day, documenting the lives of the working class, reveal gigantic houses, narrow alleys, filthy inner courtyards and streets. Most striking, however, are the nameless inhabitants we see peering at the camera with mournful stoicism.

These dramatically altered living conditions send young lovers Abby (Brooke Adams) and Bill (Richard Gere) to set sail for new shores. Together with Bill's kid sister Linda (Linda Manz), the vagabonds traipse across the

NÉSTOR ALMENDROS Néstor Almendros was born in Barcelona in 1930. He started his academic studies in philosophy and literature in Havana, continued at the City College of New York and finished at the Centro Sperimentale di Cinematografia in Rome. It was during this time that he got to know avant-garde filmmakers Maya Deren and Jonas Mekas. Following Fidel Castro's rise to power, Almendros shot a considerable number of documentaries in Cuba from 1951–61. After two of his films were banned by censors, he relocated to Paris in the early 60s, where he found work in the media industries of television and short film. Starting in the mid 60s, Almendros became involved in the French *Nouvelle Vague* movement and collaborated with such greats as François Truffaut (*L'Enfant sauvage / The Wild Child,* 1969; *L'Histoire d'Adèle H. / The Story of Adèle H.,* 1975 etc.) and Eric Rohmer (*Le Genou de Claire / Claire's Knee,* 1970; *La Marquise d'O.The Marquise of O.*, 1976). He gained prestige that won him international acclaim as a bright young cinematographer. With a predilection for natural light as well as the stark contrasts of black-and-white photography he played a prominent role in developing the *Nouvelle Vague's* definitive visual style. Upon his arrival in the United States in the late 70s, he successfully transposed his trademark tendencies to color film. This impressive feat can be witnessed in films such as *Days of Heaven* (1978). Almendros wrote on his own professional life and the art of cinematography in many publications. His autobiographical reflection *Un homme à la camera* (*A Man with a Camera*) appeared in print in the 80s. The multifaceted photographer extraordinaire also shot commercial spots for Giorgio Armani and Calvin Klein. In 1992, Néstor Almendros lost his life to AIDS.

“The film, photographed by Néstor Almendros and Haskell Wexler, has a pictorialism, recalling at different moments the works of Corot, Millet, Seurat, Brueghel, Turner, and Murnau’s American films.” *Literature / Film Quarterly*

1 Ouch, gerbils hurt! There’s never a dull moment for Bill (Richard Gere). He rarely enjoys a moment of “inner peace.”

2 A light in the attic: Abby (Brooke Adams) investigates life on the farm.

3 Catcher in the rye: Hard labor reaps golden rewards.

2

3

countryside on the lookout for the next job that will provide them with a meal ticket. After much searching, they find work on a farm as seasonal laborers and help sort the harvest. Not suspecting that Bill and Abby, who pose as brother and sister, are actually romantically involved, the single and gravely ill farmer David (Sam Shepard) falls in love with the radiant Abby. It is the basis for a melancholy love story that ends tragically for both male suitors.

Yet the film is not just a tale of woebegone ties among three individuals. Malick's piece is far more than a patchwork of psychological implications and well-ordered storylines. This is attested to by the non-linear nature of the plot, chronology and various interceding subplots. The piece also benefits tremendously from the poetry of its beautifully composed images, often shot at twilight and dawn. A world apart from simplistic stereotypes, the picture tells of the uprooted nature of its characters, the loss of homeland, the intrusion of technology in the private sphere, and a journey into an uncertain future. The story and the characters do not just deal with individual destinies: they rise up to represent much larger concepts of humanity and cultural history. They are archetypes, symbolizing opposing worldviews locked in mortal combat. Their stories tell of love, jealousy and death, as well as the fundamental challenges and questions that arise when a new way of life replaces an existing one. The principles of modernity are championed by Bill, the hotheaded, aggressive go-getter, whereas tradition and the preservation of a soon-to-be-antiquated way of life are embodied by the reserved farmer, tied to the land.

The visual language of cinematographer Néstor Alméndros reflects the polarized philosophies of this dialog in the juxtaposition of romantic and realistic imagery. The harsh, angular, filthy imagery of industrialization pervading the farming tale is a long way from the gracefully curved and softer lines of the main story, bathed in the magical twilight of the idyllic countryside.

Almendros goes so far as to implement apocalyptic religious symbols like a locust infestation, a torrential blaze, iridescent lanterns, gloom, smoke and screaming in the movie's climactic sequence. But the film takes no sides in the debate it poses. Instead, Malick is interested

4

in the process surrounding cultural and social changes. He explores the mythical nature of life and evolution, while careful not to burden his investigation with rigid observations, leaving the film largely open to interpretation. Seen in this light, *Days of Heaven* presents us with nothing short of a true movie enthusiast's diehard philosophy: Life's truths do not lurk in any story, but are found in the beauty of an image.

BR

"What Malick has done, however, is much more radical than supplying a child's-eye-view of some strange adult drama. His film is split between the much that we see and the little that we know." *Sight and Sound*

4 Needle in a haystack: American Gothic turns Rothko.

5 Oral tradition or just plain gossip: Young Linda (Linda Manz) narrates the tale of Abby and Bill.

6 Love on a pitchfork: Abby has given dying Dave a new lease on life.

DIE EHE DER MARIA BRAUN

THE MARRIAGE OF MARIA BRAUN

1978 – FRG – 120 MIN.

GENRE

DRAMA

DIRECTOR

RAINER WERNER FASSBINDER

SCREENPLAY

PETER MÄRTHESHEIMER, PEA FRÖHLICH

DIRECTOR OF PHOTOGRAPHY

MICHAEL BALLHAUS

EDITING

JULIANE LORENZ

MUSIC

PEER RABEN

PRODUCTION

MICHAEL FENGLER for ALBATROS PRODUKTION, TRIO FILM, FILMVERLAG DER AUTOREN, TANGO FILM, FENGLER FILMS, WESTDEUTSCHER RUNDFUNK

STARRING

HANNA SCHYGULLA (Maria Braun), KLAUS LÖWITSCH (Hermann Braun), IVAN DESNY (Karl Oswald), GOTTFRIED JOHN (Willi Klenze), GISELA UHLEN (Maria's Mother), HARK BOHM (Senkenberg), ELISABETH TRISSENAAR (Betti Klenze), GEORGE BYRD (Bill), CLAUS HOLM (Physician), GÜNTER LAMPRECHT (Hans Wetzel)

IFF BERLIN 1979

SILVER BEAR for BEST ACTRESS (Hanna Schygulla), and BEST TECHNICAL CREW

RAINER WERNER FASSBINDER

DIE EHE DER MARIA BRAUN

...sie währte nur einen halben Tag – und eine ganze Nacht.

mit GOTTFRIED JOHN GÜNTER LAMPRECHT HARK BOHM GEORGE BYRD ELISABETH TRISSENAAR ISOLDE BARTH LISELOTTE EDER Buch PETER MÄRTHESHEIMER und PEA FRÖHLICH
nach einer Idee von RAINER WERNER FASSBINDER Kamera MICHAEL BALLHAUS Schnitt FRANZ WALSCH JULIANE LORENZ Musik PEER RABEN FILMVERLAG DER AUTOREN

1

"I'd rather perform my own miracles than wait for them to happen."

It's 1943. Maria (Hanna Schygulla) and Hermann (Klaus Löwitsch) have been married for half a day and a single night when the war pulls them apart. Hermann is sent to fight on the Eastern Front, while Maria struggles to make a living on the black market. When the war ends, she's informed that her husband is dead. In the postwar period, everything's in short supply; so Maria ensures her material survival by doing something that can get a girl a bad name: she goes to work in a bar for American soldiers. But she soon makes the rules clear to her clientele: "I sell beer, not me." Maria is no man's property, and she takes what she needs: nylons, cigarettes, and above all warmth, which she finds in the arms of Bill (George Byrd), a black G.I. When the husband she had given up for dead appears in the door one day, there's one man too many in her bedroom. In the heat of the moment, Maria kills her naked lover with a blow from a bottle. Cameraman Michael Ballhaus films this scene in such a distanced fashion that Maria's act of murder seems both unspectacular and wholly absurd. In court, Maria insists that while Bill only liked her, her husband

HANNA SCHYGULLA Known as the *femme fatale* of the subculture, Hanna Schygulla was one of the great female icons of the German cinema in the 60s and 70s. It was above all her work with Rainer Werner Fassbinder that made her so instantly recognizable. In no less than 20 productions, she developed a consciously cool, understated style, and an image that made her a kind of anti-star. Born in Kattowitz (now Katowice in Poland) in 1943, she was a young drama student in Munich when she met Fassbinder, who introduced her to his experimental "action-theater" in 1967.

After roles in Danièle Huillet's and Jean-Marie Straub's short film *The Bridegroom, the Comedienne and the Pimp* (*Der Bräutigam, die Komödiantin und der Zuhälter*, 1968) and Peter Fleischmann's *Hunting Scenes from Bavaria* (*Jagdszenen aus Niederbayern*, 1969) she appeared in Fassbinder's *Love is Colder Than Death* (*Liebe ist kälter als der Tod,* 1969). Until 1974, she had roles in all of his subsequent films, including *Katzelmacher* (1969), *The Bitter Tears of Petra von Kant* (*Die bitteren Tränen der Petra von Kant,* 1972) and *The Merchant of Four Seasons* (*Händler der vier Jahreszeiten*, 1972). After *Effi Briest* (1974), there followed a temporary break with the *enfant terrible* of German filmmaking: as Hanna Schygulla explained to the *Berliner Zeitung* in 1994, "There came a time when I no longer wanted to see myself on screen. I felt like a doll, a puppet..." After a four-year pause, the two resumed their collaboration, on a film that achieved international success: *The Marriage of Maria Braun* (*Die Ehe der Maria Braun*, 1978).

In the intervening period, she had worked with other directors, on films including Wim Wenders' *The Wrong Move* aka *The Wrong Movement* or *False Move* (*Falsche Bewegung*, 1974) and Vojtech Jasny's adaptation of a Heinrich Böll story, *The Clown* (*Ansichten eines Clowns*, 1975). Hanna Schygulla cultivated an understated acting style, to such an extent that some of her later films made her look like a caricature of herself; examples include Fassbinder's *Lili Marleen* (1980) and Margarethe von Trotta's *Sheer Madness* (*Heller Wahn / L'Amie*, 1982). The latter film is regarded as a key work of the feminist movement. In *Passion* (1982), Jean-Luc Godard made subtly ironical use of her image: the character she plays is called Hanna, and her performance has a certain self-reflecting quality. During the 80s and early 90s, Hanna Schygulla turned up more frequently in foreign films than in German productions. She appeared in Ettore Scola's *La Nuit de Varennes / Il mondo nuovo* (1982—aka *That Night in Varennes*), in Andrej Wajda's *A Love in Germany* (*Un amour en Allemagne*, 1983), and in Kenneth Branagh's *Dead Again* (1991). In the years since then, she has concentrated on theater and concert appearances, often singing songs by the French film and theater composer Jean-Marie Sénia. Her relationship to Fassbinder is a subject she's struggled to come to terms with, and it continues to find expression in her art. After receiving numerous lifetime achievement awards, she was also honored with the German Film Award in 2024.

1 The dragon lady of new Germany: Hanna Schygulla as radiant opportunist Maria Braun.

2 The price of capitalism: In the ruins of post-war Germany, Maria's man takes the fall for her dirty deeds and her career starts to soar.

3 The truth hurts: Maria is well aware that sexual relationships have both emotional and financial implications.

"With this cool melodrama full of strong emotions, Rainer Werner Fassbinder has created something exceptional: a densely concentrated film, lively, precise and witty. The dramaturgy is coherent, the dialogue tight, and the actors give highly discerning interpretations of their roles—especially Hanna Schygulla, who was crowned Best Actress at the Berlinale." *Kölner Stadt-Anzeiger*

loves her. The judge is uncomprehending, but Hermann understands: he takes the rap for Maria and goes to jail. Maria, meanwhile, goes to work for the textiles manufacturer Karl Oswald (Ivan Desny). In the years that follow, the young woman pursues a brilliant career as a businesswoman and as Oswald's mistress. As she makes clear to the businessman, however, it's not he who's having an affair with her, but she with him. Maria may be calculating, but she's also emotionally honest. She really does like Oswald, but she's saving her money for the house she plans to build for herself and Hermann. By now, Germany is looking tidier: the rubble of wartime has been swept away, and Maria is a wealthy woman, the first member of her family who can afford a house of her own. Suddenly Oswald dies of a heart attack, and shortly thereafter Hermann is released from prison. While the radio transmits the legendary World Cup Final of 1954, the married couple in the big house try to get to know each other all over again. By the time the German soccer team have become World Champions, Maria and Hermann have inherited Oswald's considerable fortune—and they're dead. A gas explosion has destroyed the house and buried the two of them in its ruins.

The Marriage of Maria Braun was Fassbinder's first major international success. Like *The Merchant of Four Seasons* (*Händler der vier Jahreszeiten*, 1972), it paints a depressing and unprettified picture of the German "economic miracle." Maria's story reflects the rise of West Germany from the ruins of the lost war to a society in which money, possessions, and social standing count for more than human relationships. Maria Braun is a woman who takes charge of her own life, single-minded in her determination to build a career and accumulate wealth in order to achieve her dreams of happiness. Only when it's too late does she realize that she's lost the very thing she's been working for, that a shared life with Hermann is no longer possible. The film never makes it entirely clear whether the gas explosion was a tragic accident or an act of suicide.

3

4 Left hanging: Hanna Schygulla was one of the great Fassbinder actresses. But in later years, her inflexible acting style made her little more than a monument to herself.

5 "Who knows Hermann Braun?" Their marriage was only a day and a night old when Hermann departed for the Russian front. When he returns, he'll find life with Maria is not what he bargained for.

"An ambiguous and solidly directed melodrama, *The Marriage of Maria Braun* is undoubtedly the director's best film to date."

Le Monde

Maria begins as an embodiment of the strong women of postwar Germany, who shouldered the reconstruction of the country in the absence of their menfolk. Very soon, however, she's become a typical protagonist of the economic miracle. Hanna Schygulla, one of Fassbinder's favorite actresses, gives a performance of astonishing versatility: the young girl in the American bar is every bit as convincing as the cold and frustrated businesswoman. Yet *The Marriage of Maria Braun* offers no kitchen-sink realism. The narrative is concentrated, attenuated, and

Fassbinder creates a bizarre chronicle of the Adenauer era, in which fragments of superpower politics are strewn casually across the lives of the protagonists. The radio in the living room functions as a link between the private and the public spheres. We hear Adenauer making a speech on the rearmament of the Federal Republic; and a soccer commentary forms a counterpoint to the tragic deaths of Maria and Hermann, as it proclaims the rebirth of the nation in the field of sport. "Germany are World Champions!" indeed; but two of the country's minor players will never

Wer kennt
HERMANN
BRAUN?
Letzte Nachricht aus
dem Raum Smolensk
Fp.Nr. 16310-342
5

HALLOWEEN

1978 – USA – 91 MIN.

GENRE

HORROR FILM

DIRECTOR

JOHN CARPENTER

SCREENPLAY

JOHN CARPENTER, DEBRA HILL

DIRECTOR OF PHOTOGRAPHY

DEAN CUNDEY

EDITING

TOMMY LEE WALLACE, CHARLES BORNSTEIN

MUSIC

JOHN CARPENTER

PRODUCTION

JOHN CARPENTER, DEBRA HILL for
COMPASS INTERNATIONAL PICTURES, FALCON FILMS

STARRING

DONALD PLEASENCE (Doctor Samuel Loomis), JAMIE LEE CURTIS (Laurie Strode),
NANCY LOOMIS (Annie Brackett), P. J. SOLES (Lynda van der Klok),
CHARLES CYPHERS (Sheriff Brackett), KYLE RICHARDS (Lindsey Wallace),
BRIAN ANDREWS (Tommy Doyle), JOHN MICHAEL GRAHAM (Bob Simms),
NANCY STEPHENS (Marion Chambers), TONY MORAN (Michael Myers, 23 years old),
WILL SANDIN (Michael Myers, 6 years old)

HALLOWEEN

MOUSTAPHA AKKAD PRESENTS DONALD PLEASENCE IN JOHN CARPENTER'S "HALLOWEEN"
WITH JAMIE LEE CURTIS, P.J. SOLES, NANCY LOOMIS · WRITTEN BY JOHN CARPENTER AND DEBRA HILL
EXECUTIVE PRODUCER IRWIN YABLANS · DIRECTED BY JOHN CARPENTER · PRODUCED BY DEBRA HILL
PANAVISION® TECHNICOLOR® A COMPASS INTERNATIONAL RELEASE

R RESTRICTED

COPYRIGHT 1978 FALCON INTERNATIONAL PRODUCTIONS

1

"Was that the bogeyman?"— "As a matter of fact—it was!"

His eyes are the eyes of a devil. For 15 years, says psychiatrist Sam Loomis (Donald Pleasence), he has been trying to get a glimpse of what goes on behind those evil eyes, to make sense of what is going on inside that head. But all his efforts have been in vain. The boy seems to be driven by a single instinct: to kill. It was this heinous thirst for blood that propelled him back then, when he brutally stabbed his sister to death at the age of 6. Ever since that fateful day, Michael Myers has been under lock and key in an asylum. But now he's escaped. This dangerous beast is on the loose again and he begins stalking teenagers, returning to Haddonfield, the scene of his last homicidal rampage. And the timing of his escape couldn't be more threatening. It's Halloween, the most terrifying day of the year.

Halloween is a horror classic. Few films have made such a lasting mark on the genre. And this despite the fact that director John Carpenter did nothing to reinvent the art of filmmaking. The critics compared *Halloween* to Hitchcock's *Psycho* (1960), but felt that Hitch composed his murder scenes much more deftly than the young Carpenter. Though they gave him credit for mastering his craft, it was generally agreed that the film was shot far too conventionally.

Nevertheless, *Halloween* became one of the most successful independent films of all time. It cost $325,000 to make and grossed $100 million, perhaps because its strength lies in its supposed weakness: the simplicity of the dramatization. With simple means he made no attempt to camouflage, Carpenter aptly struck the public nerve. The eerie soundtrack hammers away with its few incessantly repetitive notes. The vague images of the subjective camera conjure up an overwhelming insecurity, and excessively protracted tension slowly but surely escalates into naked fear.

This suspense-building quality is palpable when Laurie (Jamie Lee Curtis) ventures across the empty, dark,

SUBJECTIVE CAMERA An arm reaches into the screen—our arm. A hand grabs a knife—our hand. The knife plunges into living flesh—we did it. The beginning of *Halloween* (1978) depicts the young Mike Myers as he butchers his sister. But the boy himself is not shown; we only see his action. The subjective camera assumes his perspective, through which the audience slips into the role of the protagonist and leaves its function as the omniscient and unnoticed observer. The subjective camera is able to create an atmosphere of insecurity or menacing danger because it gives the audience nothing more than the information that the film character also has.

The technique, however, seems to work best if used sparingly. Robert Montgomery failed with his Marlowe thriller *Lady in the Lake* (1947), which he filmed from the protagonist's point of view from beginning to end. Delmer Daves used the subjective camera much more adeptly in *Dark Passage* (1947): the audience only sees Humphrey Bogart's face a half an hour into the film after he undergoes a surgical operation—beforehand the action was filmed entirely from Bogart's perspective. Stanley Kubrick masterfully used the subjective perspective in his horror film *The Shining* (1980), continually leaving the audience in doubt as to whether the images are a part of the plot or just the fantasies of the characters.

"Replete with unobtrusive experiments, simple and clear in conception yet rich in internal links, *Halloween* is one of the finest horror films ever made. It's one of the reasons I'm in love with the cinema—and still go the movies all the time. And it's also one reason why I wanted to make movies myself." *Tom Tykwer, in: steadycam*

small town street to visit her school friends. She lives in a house across the way, and although the course of her path is filmed in standard time, the distance seems endless, because the audience knows something Laurie doesn't: Michael Myers (Tony Moran) is waiting for her on the other side of the street. A few minutes before, he sliced up three of her friends and is now cowering behind the dark window, eagerly sharpening his blade. Every footstep leads Laurie closer to the monster. She jiggles the knob on the front door—to no avail. She timidly makes her way to the back entrance—it is open. She stands in the kitchen, where just a few minutes earlier a knife plunged into the body of a young man. Moving to the stairs she tentatively begins to climb. Once upstairs she finds her friend lying peacefully in bed, but something is horribly wrong—her friend is dead. A second corpse falls from the closet at her feet, and suddenly the masked murderer is towering ominously behind her. Laurie runs. And she screams.

"Scream Queen"—Jamie Lee Curtis was bestowed this title after her first screen role. As Laurie Strode she manages to elude the lethal grasp of Michael Myers, thanks in large part to the psychiatrist Loomis, who empties an entire clip of bullets into the killer. The fact that Laurie is the one to survive, the outsider who prefers to babysit than make-out on the sly, proved ample ground to criticize the film for moral prudery. In self-defense, Carpenter declared that the psychology of the characters in *Halloween* was of little interest to him—he'd rattled off the screenplay in just two weeks with Debra Hill, who also produced his films *The Fog* (1979) and *Escape from New York* (1981).

Carpenter's aim was to deliver terror to the screen —unadulterated shock value and gruesome suspense.

1 A bloody encore: Michael Myers, the Bogeyman (Tony Moran). The mask, bought in a costume shop, was first used in the horror film, *The Devil's Rain* (USA, 1975).

2 You were always on my mind: John Carpenter allegedly named his heroine Laurie Strode (Jamie Lee Curtis) after his first girlfriend.

3 Doctor death: Donald Pleasence was cast as the psychiatrist Samuel Loomis, after Peter Cushing and Christopher Lee turned down the role.

3

Yet a lot of people seem to be convinced that *Halloween* is something special—a classic. Maybe when a horror film is stripped of everything but dumb scariness—when it isn't ashamed to revive the stalest device of the genre (the escaped lunatic)—it satisfies part of the audience in a more basic, childish way than sophisticated horror pictures do." *The New Yorker*

4

5

4 "An audacious hybrid of heterogeneous traditions. Held together by the fluid elegance of its camerawork, it conjures up an atmosphere of subtle terror." (*DIE ZEIT*)

5 Killer instinct: Donald Pleasence (left) also appeared in John Carpenter's *Escape from New York* (1981) and *Prince of Darkness* (1987).

6 Bedtime stories: Laurie tells Tommy that there's no such thing as the bogeyman, and the little boy discovers that adults really don't know everything.

7 The maxims of murder: Perverts will perish.

He hoped to make the true "psychopath film," and he succeeded beyond his wildest dreams. Almost 25 years after his first appearance, Michael Myers continues to slaughter mercilessly on the big screen—he recently appeared in his 10th film. And Jamie Lee Curtis, alias Laurie Strode, is still the most prized victim of the sinister lunatic who seems immune to bullets, knife wounds, and electric shocks. To be continued—you can bet your life on it. NM

6

7

HÖSTSONATEN

AUTUMN SONATA

1978 – FRG / FRANCE / SWEDEN – 93 MIN.

GENRE

DRAMA

DIRECTOR

INGMAR BERGMAN

SCREENPLAY

INGMAR BERGMAN

DIRECTOR OF PHOTOGRAPHY

SVEN NYKVIST

EDITING

SYLVIA INGEMARSSON

MUSIC

JOHANN SEBASTIAN BACH, FRÉDÉRIC CHOPIN,
GEORG FRIEDRICH HÄNDEL, ROBERT SCHUMANN

PRODUCTION

KATINKA FARAGÓ for PERSONAFILM,
FILMÉDIS, SUEDE FILM

STARRING

INGRID BERGMAN (Charlotte), LIV ULLMANN (Eva), LENA NYMAN (Helena),
HALVAR BJÖRK (Viktor), MARIANNE AMINOFF (Charlotte's Private Secretary),
ARNE BANG-HANSEN (Uncle Otto), GEORG LØKKEBERG (Leonardo),
ERLAND JOSEPHSON (Josef), LINN ULLMANN (Eva As A Child),
GUNNAR BJÖRNSTRAND (Paul)

"'Autumn Sonata' has the formal, visual elegance we have come to expect from the great Swedish director. It also contains a performance, Miss Bergman's, that enriches our season and is a high point of her long career."
–VINCENT CANBY, NEW YORK TIMES

"The sense of immediacy and total involvement is wholly extraordinary, as in so many of Ingmar Bergman's films. THIS IS SURELY ONE OF HIS GREAT ONES...In Ingrid Bergman's long, distinguished career it is probable that she has never given a performance the equal of this one."
–ARCHER WINSTEN, NEW YORK POST

"...Ingrid Bergman is the revelation here. Her performance as the mother is a miracle of characterization, making clear that she is not only one of the most beautiful actresses in the world but also one of the most gifted and courageous."
–JOY GOULD BOYUM, WALL STREET JOURNAL

"Ingrid Bergman and Liv Ullmann give bravura performances in one of Ingmar Bergman's most accessible dramas. 'Autumn Sonata' is clear, understandable, passionate and powerful. IT IS A MEMORABLE FILM."
–GENE SHALIT, NBC-TV

"Will rank among his lasting works... Every moment, every single moment is true and forceful...a CLASSIC."
–STANLEY KAUFFMANN, NEW REPUBLIC

"In the twilight of her extraordinary career, Miss Bergman gives what may well stand as her most impressive performance of all, A MASTERPIECE."
–CHARLES CHAMPLIN, LOS ANGELES TIMES

"THE MOST INGENIOUSLY CONCEIVED, BRILLIANTLY ACTED, AND DEEPLY MOVING BERGMAN FILM IN MORE THAN A DECADE."
–DAVID STERRITT, CHRISTIAN SCIENCE MONITOR

"'Autumn Sonata' is the best Bergman film in years. Bergman restores Ingrid Bergman to her proper place as one of the finest of screen actresses, teaming her with the superb Liv Ullmann in a pairing that simply must not be missed."
–JACK KROLL, NEWSWEEK

"BERGMAN DIRECTING BERGMAN JUST HAS TO BE ONE OF THE MOVIE MILESTONES OF THE DECADE."
–REX REED

"Bergman knows more about women than any other filmmaker today. His plunge into the chasms that separate mothers and daughters is jolting, profoundly illuminating and courageous. This is a memorable film."
–MARTINE LATOUR, MADEMOISELLE

"When Ingmar Bergman hones in on a truth as direct as this, and dramatizes it with characters as strong and complex as the ones in 'Autumn Sonata,' THE RESULT IS A STUNNER."
–RICHARD CORLISS, NEW TIMES

Sir LEW GRADE and MARTIN STARGER present

Autumn Sonata

a Film by
INGMAR BERGMAN
with
INGRID BERGMAN
LIV ULLMANN

NEW WORLD PICTURES · INGMAR BERGMAN'S "AUTUMN SONATA"
Also starring LENA NYMAN · HALVAR BJÖRK · Director of Photography SVEN NYKVIST A.S.C.
from SUEDE-FILM, PARIS · FILMEDIS, PARIS
Production Company PERSONAFILM GMBH, MUNICH

PG PARENTAL GUIDANCE SUGGESTED
SOME MATERIAL MAY NOT BE SUITABLE FOR CHILDREN

ITC ENTERTAINMENT

1

"Does one never stop hoping?"

When *Autumn Sonata* was first released, many reviewers spoke of the film as Ingmar Bergman's "homecoming." Though Bergman was at that time still exiled in Germany as the result of a tax dispute (*Autumn Sonata* was a German co-production made in Norway), the film did indeed mark a kind of artistic homecoming. For here—immediately after *The Serpent's Egg* (1977), his "big" movie on the rise of Nazism in 1920s Germany—Bergman returns to the form of the chamber piece, and to his "traditional" subject-matter: the spiritual plight of two individuals trapped in a deadly love-hate relationship.

Autumn Sonata tells of a mother-and-daughter reunion after a separation lasting seven years. Following the death of her companion, Leonardo (Georg Løkkeberg), the celebrated concert pianist Charlotte (Ingrid Bergman) is invited by her daughter Eva (Liv Ullmann) to spend a few weeks with her and her husband Viktor (Halvar Björk). Viktor is a pastor, and he and Eva live in a small parish in a remote region of Norway. There is little in the way of external action, and Bergman constructs the story like a three-act play: Act One: the arrival of the mother in the parsonage; Act Two: a protracted dispute between Eva and Charlotte, staged as a double monolog; Act Three: a kind of cross-cut epilog, depicting the restoration of the women's original relationship: a phony peace based on lies and repression.

The film is a symphony of false notes. Even in the short prolog, in which Viktor talks of his wife and their life together, the pastor is forced to relativize his claim that they're happy and content. For Eva is incapable of love and mistrusts any expression of warmth. This dissonance continues in Eva's letter of invitation to her mother. Though she writes affectionately of her "dearest little mother," they've in fact spent years avoiding each other—and Eva wouldn't even have known of Leonardo's demise if someone else hadn't informed her of the fact. Finally, the lies culminate in an effusively cordial welcome, in which a torrent of words

LIV ULLMANN In 1939, Liv Ullmann was born in Tokyo to Norwegian parents. From the mid-50s, she enjoyed a successful career in the theater, starting work at the National Theater in Oslo in 1960. Her breakthrough as an international film star came in 1966, with the role of the silenced actress Elisabeth Vogler in Ingmar Bergman's classic psychodrama, *Persona*. In the years that followed, she became the Swedish director's favorite actress—and his real-life partner. For him, she created a series of highly complex portraits of modern women. In films such as *Hour of the Wolf* (*Vargtimmen*, 1967), *Shame* (*Skammen*, 1968), *The Passion of Anna* (*En Passion*, 1969), *Cries and Whispers* (*Viskningar och rop*, 1972), *Scenes From A Marriage* (*Scener ur ett äktenskap*, 1973) and *Face to Face* (*Ansikte mot ansikte*, 1976), she combined a disarming naturalness with a broad emotional spectrum. The 70s saw her appear in several Hollywood productions—but mostly without great success. Her most notable roles in non-Bergman films were in collaboration with his fellow-Swede Jan Troell: in *The Emigrants* (*Utvandrarna*, 1971) and *The New Land* (*Nybyggarna*, 1971), she played a farmer's wife who moves to America. Besides her work in the cinema, Ullmann has always continued to pursue her theater career. She also writes books and screenplays. Since 1992, she has directed three movies and a film for TV, all of which were very well received. She won great acclaim and several awards for the role of Åse Evensen in the film *Two Lives* (2012). In 2024 she received an honorary Oscar for her lifetime achievement.

1 Chopsticks: Chopin preludes in a country parsonage. Eva's (Liv Ullmann) uncertainty provokes a harsh reaction from her mother.

2 Music of the heart: Cool, masterly and perfect in every detail, Charlotte's (Ingrid Bergman) Chopin interpretations reflect her dealings with her daughter.

3 Mommie dearest: Eva's ruined childhood is a burden on her marriage to the parson Viktor (Halvar Björk).

and gesticulations merely serves to conceal the fear and desolation at the heart of their relationship.

At first glance, mother and daughter could hardly be more different: Ingrid Bergman plays Charlotte as an elegant star in a stylish trouser-suit; crowned with a hairdo that might be cast in concrete, she chatters airily of concert tours and meetings with the international jet set. Charlotte is always her own favorite topic of conversation, and some of her scenes are not without a certain wicked humor: thus she sashays up to the parsonage dinner-table in a red Yves-St.-Laurent dress, and lies awake in bed worrying where to invest her millions.

During the great nocturnal quarrel between Eva and Charlotte, the façade starts to show its cracks. Bergman and his cameraman Sven Nykvist shot this scene almost entirely in intense close-ups of the women's faces—in stark contrast to the distancing effect of the rigid long shots in the flashbacks to Eva's childhood. When Eva accuses her mother of lovelessness and egotism, Charlotte's sophistication gives way to increasing uncertainty. While she's forced to recognize that she's built her life on the illusion of being a good mother, she's angered that Eva would dare to place her in the wrong.

There's plenty of room for speculation about what motivates Eva, the frumpy parson's wife with the braided hair and the metal-rimmed spectacles. It's probably too much to say she invited her mother as a coolly planned act of revenge. Whenever she meets Charlotte, Eva involuntarily moves and talks like a timid child that yearns for recognition; yet at the same time, she provokes disappointment in order to have her hatred confirmed. In one superb scene, Eva plays some Chopin preludes on the piano—a little clumsily, almost as if she's challenging her mother to criticize her. Finally, Charlotte takes her place at the instrument, puts the music away, and plays to perfection—all the time lecturing her daughter on the difference between feeling and sentimentality.

Eva heaps blame on her mother, and her accusations are undoubtedly monstrous. In her view, Charlotte is responsible for practically everything bad that ever happened to her—or to her sister Helena (Lena Nyman), a handicapped girl who does little more than vegetate. Yet Eva's icy cruelty is ultimately no more than a mirror image of Charlotte's superficiality. Despite the differences, they share many fundamental similarities.

After Charlotte's departure, Eva sends her mother a conciliatory letter. Some critics have seen this as a sign of hope, a crumb of comfort from the director to his audience. Yet the tone of this missive recalls the invitation she had written at the start of the film. And all the while, we see her mother engaged, as ever, in trivial chitchat with her agent. At the very end, Bergman grants each of his protagonists a final close-up: the women's faces are so haggard as to seem almost destroyed. Clearly, nothing has changed.

LP

"The intertwining of love and hate is the key to all intimate human relationships, perhaps most especially—for all sorts of mysterious primal reasons—the relationship between mother and daughter. No artist in any medium today has a greater genius for expressing that deepest human tension than Ingmar Bergman." *Newsweek*

3

DAWN OF THE DEAD / ZOMBIE: DAWN OF THE DEAD

1978 – USA / ITALY – 126 MIN. / 137 MIN. (Director's cut)

GENRE

HORROR FILM

DIRECTOR

GEORGE A. ROMERO

SCREENPLAY

GEORGE A. ROMERO, DARIO ARGENTO

DIRECTOR OF PHOTOGRAPHY

MICHAEL GORNICK

EDITING

GEORGE A. ROMERO

MUSIC

DARIO ARGENTO, THE GOBLINS, AGOSTINO MARANGOLO,
MASSIMO MORANTE, FABIO PIGNATELLI,
GEORGE A. ROMERO (Director's Cut), CLAUDIO SIMONETTI

PRODUCTION

DARIO ARGENTO, RICHARD P. RUBINSTEIN for LAUREL GROUP

STARRING

DAVID EMGE (Stephen Andrews), KEN FOREE (Peter Washington),
SCOTT H. REINIGER (Roger DeMarco), GAYLEN ROSS (Francine Parker),
DAVID CRAWFORD (Doctor Foster), DAVID EARLY (Mr. Berman),
RICHARD FRANCE (Doctor Milliard Rausch), HOWARD SMITH (TV Commentator),
JESSE DEL GRE (Priest), FRED BAKER (Police Commander)

When there's no more room in HELL the dead will walk the EARTH

First there was
'NIGHT OF THE LIVING DEAD'
Now
GEORGE A. ROMERO'S

DAWN OF THE DEAD

HERBERT R. STEINMANN & BILLY BAXTER PRESENT A LAUREL GROUP PRODUCTION in Association with CLAUDIO ARGENTO & ALFREDO CUOMO

Starring: DAVID EMGE KEN FOREE SCOTT H. REINIGER GAYLEN ROSS

Director of Photography: MICHAEL GORNICK Music By: THE GOBLINS with DARIO ARGENTO

Produced By: RICHARD P. RUBINSTEIN Written and Directed by: GEORGE A. ROMERO

READ THE ST. MARTIN'S BOOK TECHNICOLOR® ©DAWN ASSOCIATES MCMLXXVIII Released by UNITED FILM DISTRIBUTION CO.

There is no explicit sex in this picture.
However, there are scenes of violence which may be considered shocking.
No one under 17 will be admitted.

1

"Who the hell cares. Let's go shopping first."

Dawn of the Dead doesn't exactly go easy on its viewers. Terror immediately lunges into the opening shot, dominated by an unsteady camera and distorted voices. It is a portrait of disorientation, clearly indicating that a state of emergency has broken out in the USA. An epidemic that turns humans into the living dead is spreading like wildfire. When police squadrons storm a house in Puerto Rico, annihilating not only zombies but also massacring a large number of healthy humans in cold blood, there is no more denying it: America is at war.

Stephen (David Emge) and his girlfriend Francine (Gaylen Ross), both television station employees, have lost all faith in social cohesion and in the government's ability to uphold law and order. Along with SWAT team sharpshooter Peter (Ken Foree) and his friend Roger (Scott H. Reiniger), they make up their minds to flee the chaos of the city by helicopter, leaving their fellow citizens to fend for themselves. The zombies, however, are everywhere. The four take flight from this perished civilization not to hit ground in undiscovered country, but rather on the roof of a surrounded Pennsylvania shopping center. They quickly barricade themselves inside the mall and even succeed in shutting out the entire contingency of living dead. The plentiful supply of goods within their citadel allows the human crusaders to maintain the illusions of the life they left behind them. That is, until Stephen and Roger fall prey to the undead, making antiheroes of the pregnant Francine and the African American Peter who quickly abort "Consumer Island" and head off in their helicopter towards an uncertain future.

Dawn of the Dead's gratuitous violence, something the critics couldn't stop talking about at the time of the movie's original release, is an unmistakable sign that the Age of Aquarius and its Utopian dreams were suddenly a thing of the past. In its place we find the jarring pessimism of the late 1970s, brought on to a great extent as a response to U.S. involvement in the Vietnam War. Romero's film expands on this American trauma of the last fifteen

GEORGE A. ROMERO American director and screenwriter George A. Romero (1940–2017) studied art, design and theater at Carnegie Mellon University in Pittsburgh. His *Zombie Trilogy* (1968, 1978, 1985) turned him into a household name and sparked an onset of offspring by other filmmakers. Romero's directorial debut, *Night of the Living Dead* (1968), was a radical departure from many of the established conventions of Hollywood movies. In addition to its staunch critique on American politics, the film's underlying tone is one of pessimism and despair. This was also the case for the sequels *Dawn of the Dead/Zombie: Dawn of the Dead* (1978) and *Day of the Dead* (1985). In the 80s, Romero collaborated with Stephen King on two projects: *Creepshow* (1982), a horror movie anthology, and a high-profile production entitled *The Dark Half* (1992/93). George A. Romero worked from time to time as an actor and followed Hitchcock's tradition of making cameo appearances in his own movies. In his zombie trilogy he played a reporter, the C.E.O. of a TV station, and a member of the living dead, respectively. More *Living Dead* films followed: *Land of the Dead* (2005), *Diary of the Dead* (2007) and *Survival of the Dead* (2009). In 2020 his novel *The Living Dead*, was published posthumously. The book was completed by the author Daniel Kraus who used an unfinished manuscript along with additional materials such as notes and letters.

years. Tom Savini, who created the movie's special effects, worked as a battlefield photographer in Vietnam and drew from his endless experience with manifestations of violence. Nonetheless, the actual source of this piece's "horror" is the emotional numbness and egotism of its main characters.

Stephen, Francine, Peter and Roger block out all traces of the apocalypse looming over them and help themselves to the shopping center's commodities. In doing so, they forge a pristine world, a veritable hedonistic wonderland, which they are willing to defend at all costs.

"When the world is falling apart there are no heroes, only the need for self-preservation." *Films in Review*

1 In your head: Stephen (David Emge) and Francine (Gaylen Ross) wonder where the zombies will turn up next…

2 Open for business: It's unclear whether the zombies are hungry for human flesh or mall merchandise.

3 Money-loving humanity arrives at its ultimate destination—the shopping mall.

4 Breeding on a jet plane: Last remnants of humanity, Francine, Stephen and Roger (Scott H. Reiniger) escape on a helicopter in search of the undiscovered country.

5 Nowhere to run: The shopping center does not provide permament protection.

Unlike many other works born out of this genre, the supernatural beings do not manifest themselves as the terrifying pawns of some greater power. Instead, they are intended to function primarily as an out-and-out critique on capitalism. The scenes in which the zombies mindlessly wander about the mall, as if commanded by remote control, hold up a mirror to the face of Middle America. Despite their insatiable hunger, the undead, who nourish themselves exclusively on human flesh, are remarkably passive and often do not appear to pose any physical danger. Additionally, these ungodly creatures represent the army of the impoverished, who have not only been shut off from consumerism, but have also been declared as inhuman so that they may be justifiably eliminated. Even Romero's first zombie movie, *Night of the Living Dead* (1968), voiced strong social criticism against issues like racism in American society. In that earlier picture, Ben, an African American serving as the group's human leader, was the only one to survive the plague of the undead, only to be murdered by the white civilian army. *Dawn of the Dead* expands on this aspect and explores how readily people throw morality to the wind when self-interest is at stake. The film is, therefore, significantly more powerful than its predecessor in the assertion that "we must stop the killing or lose the war."

PLB

MIDNIGHT EXPRESS

1978 – GREAT BRITAIN / USA – 120 MIN.

GENRE

PRISON FILM, DRAMA

DIRECTOR

ALAN PARKER

SCREENPLAY

OLIVER STONE, based on the account of a
personal experience by BILLY HAYES and WILLIAM HOFFER

DIRECTOR OF PHOTOGRAPHY

MICHAEL SERESIN

EDITING

GERRY HAMBLING

MUSIC

GIORGIO MORODER

PRODUCTION

DAVID PUTTNAM, ALAN MARSHALL
for CASABLANCA FILMWORKS

STARRING

BRAD DAVIS (Billy Hayes), JOHN HURT (Max), RANDY QUAID (Jimmy Booth), IRENE MIRACLE (Susan), NORBERT WEISSER (Erich), BO HOPKINS (Tex), PAUL SMITH (Hamidou), PAOLO BONACELLI (Rifki), MIKE KELLIN (Mr. Hayes), FRANCO DIOGENE (Yesil)

ACADEMY AWARDS 1979

OSCARS for BEST ADAPTED SREENPLAY (Oliver Stone), and BEST MUSIC (Giorgio Moroder)

The story of Billy Hayes' unbelievable courage...
It couldn't happen...but it did!

A STORY OF TRIUMPH!

Midnight Express

COLUMBIA PICTURES Presents A CASABLANCA FILMWORKS Production of An ALAN PARKER Film 'MIDNIGHT EXPRESS'
Executive Producer PETER GUBER · Screenplay by OLIVER STONE · Produced by ALAN MARSHALL and DAVID PUTTNAM
Directed by ALAN PARKER · Music created by GIORGIO MORODER · Based on the true story of Billy Hayes from the book Midnight Express
by BILLY HAYES and WILLIAM HOFFER · Original sound track album available from CASABLANCA RECORD AND FILMWORKS

1

It could be the most nerve-wracking panic attack in all of film history: on October 6, 1970, Billy Hayes (Brad Davis), an American student, attempts to leave Turkey with 2.2 kilograms of hash. Hayes is on the verge of a breakdown upon eye contact with the first customs agent, but to his own surprise he is waved along. After the initial relief comes the shock: a dozen soldiers are waiting in front of the airplane. Hayes knows they're there for him and he tries to get rid of the treacherous package taped to his body. But it's too late. He's arrested before his girlfriend's eyes, and so begins a nightmare that is to last for years.

While awaiting trial, Hayes is repeatedly tortured. The devastating sentence is four years and two months in prison. Inside the prison, inhumane conditions are widespread—the violence of the inmates and the excessive

PRISON FILMS According to the Southampton Institute, the Center for Media and Justice, more than 300 prison films have been made since 1910. Nonetheless, the reason why the prison film can hardly be called an independent genre lies primarily in the range of perspectives from which filmmakers have approached the theme. The material has been used to produce dramas, thrillers, comedies, and even musicals. Classification is made more difficult by the fact that a film does not necessarily have to play out in a prison in order to deal with the theme of imprisonment. Again, not all films that use the penal system as a set or as a plot element are automatically prison films. There are classic prison films like *Midnight Express* (1978), John Frankenheimer's *Birdman of Alcatraz* (1962), or Franklin J. Schaffner's *Papillon* (1973), and then pieces such as *The Hoose-Gow* (1929), with Stan Laurel and Oliver Hardy, produced by Hal Roach, or *Jailhouse Rock* (1957) with Elvis Presley, by Richard Thorpe, which stymie usual classification. There is an additional subcategory of films which, like 1932's *I am a Fugitive from a Chain Gang*, primarily deal with escape or flight. A more meaningful definition of prison films could be those that deal with the spatial and temporal conditions of imprisonment, or in a further sense, with the themes of guilt and atonement. Examples of films in this category are Lloyd Bacon's *San Quentin* (1937), Alan Clarke's *Scum* (1979), or Tim Robbins' *Dead Man Walking* (1995).

“Parker magnificently depicts the claustrophobic and irrational world of the prison, increased by the misanthropy and xenophobia of the authorities.”

Edinburgh University Film Society

force of the prison guards are part of the daily routine. But Hayes accepts his situation and befriends his cellmates Jimmy Booth (Randy Quaid) and Max (John Hurt). Max is the man who tells him of the only way out of the living hell—the "Midnight Express:" prison-speak for escape. While the drug-addicted Max has long since resigned himself to his situation, Jimmy Booth clings to the smallest of hopes that he might be able to escape.

Billy Hayes has just 53 days left to serve when the American Ambassador makes a terrible disclosure. At the instigation of the public prosecutor, the case against

"Parker puts the squeeze on us right from the start. It's single-minded in its manipulation of the audience."

Pauline Kael

1 Eyes on the prize: Billy Hayes (Brad Davis) knows that his only chance of freedom is escape.

2 Cry freedom: Billy's pleas for clemency fall on deaf ears.

3 Thick as thieves: Their shared fate makes Billy, Jimmy (Randy Quaid) and Max (John Hurt) inseparable.

4 Caught with his pants down: "There's a perfectly reasonable explanation for this, officer..."

him is to be reopened and this time the authorities are seeking lifelong imprisonment. In a desperate courtroom statement, the accused finally seals his own fate. Ultimately the length of his sentence is set at 30 years. Hayes is now left with no other choice than to try to catch the "Midnight Express."

The film, whose screenplay was written by Oliver Stone and based on an authentic case, was a huge success at the box office. Alan Parker filmed the drama as a vividly image-laden picture, which held audiences spellbound from the very first minute. The actor Brad Davis, who died in 1991, gave a particularly impressive performance. But the film enraged a handful of critics. "Muted squalor with a disco beat in the background," was the harsh criticism of the *New Yorker*.

Indeed, the film leaves behind an inconsistent impression in more ways than one. Accordingly, one may ask whether the extremely aestheticized images of former advertising filmmaker Parker really suit the film's subject matter. Giorgio Moroder's pleasant electro-pop seems almost embarrassing in light of both today's perspective and the film's serious theme. Other critics were offended by the clearly homoerotic motif.

But screenwriter Oliver Stone was the main target of criticism for the racist undertones of the plot. Parker's dramatization was also criticized for its portrayal of Turkey as

5

5 So near and yet so far: Billy's father (Mike Kellin) would do anything to see his son free.

6 The scars of incarceration: Susan (Irene Miracle) hardly recognizes Billy after his prison ordeal.

"Walk into the incredible true experience of Billy Hayes, and bring all the courage you can!" *U.S. commercial for the movie*

a backward, sinister, and threatening country. Stone later admitted his picture of Turkey was too one-dimensional, though he chalked it up to both his youth and Alan Parker's humorless approach: according to Stone, the director left out those elements in the script that aimed to establish some ironic distance.

Midnight Express almost sets a precedent for a film that resorts to manipulation for the sake of better effects. Even today, the film is cited as proof of Western resentment against Turkey. However, the fact remains that according to international human rights organizations like Amnesty International, torture in Turkish prisons and police stations was a routine occurrence.

SH

MANHATTAN

1979 – USA – 96 MIN.

GENRE

COMEDY

DIRECTOR

WOODY ALLEN

SCREENPLAY

WOODY ALLEN, MARSHALL BRICKMAN

DIRECTOR OF PHOTOGRAPHY

GORDON WILLIS

EDITING

SUSAN E. MORSE

MUSIC

GEORGE GERSHWIN

PRODUCTION

CHARLES H. JOFFE for JACK ROLLINS & CHARLES H. JOFFE PRODUCTIONS

STARRING

WOODY ALLEN (Isaac Davis), DIANE KEATON (Mary Wilkie), MICHAEL MURPHY (Yale), MARIEL HEMINGWAY (Tracy), MERYL STREEP (Jill), ANNE BYRNE (Emily), KAREN LUDWIG (Connie), MICHAEL O'DONOGHUE (Dennis), WALLACE SHAWN (Jeremiah), KENNY VANCE (TV Producer)

WOODY ALLEN
DIANE KEATON
MICHAEL MURPHY
MARIEL HEMINGWAY
MERYL STREEP
ANNE BYRNE

MANHATTAN

"MANHATTAN" Music by GEORGE GERSHWIN

A JACK ROLLINS-CHARLES H. JOFFE Production

Written by WOODY ALLEN and MARSHALL BRICKMAN

Directed by WOODY ALLEN

Produced by CHARLES H. JOFFE

Executive Producer ROBERT GREENHUT

Director of Photography GORDON WILLIS

United Artists
A Transamerica Company

R RESTRICTED

Copyright © 1979 United Artists Corporation. All rights reserved

1

"I think people should mate for life, like pigeons or Catholics."

Isaac (Woody Allen) and Tracy (Mariel Hemingway) are a couple. However, since she's only 17 and he's pushing 43, Isaac sees no future prospects for the two of them. "I want you to enjoy me, my wry sense of humor, and astonishing sexual technique, but don't forget you have your whole life in front of you." He dare not term what they have between them as love, instead insisting that it would be better if Tracy regarded him as more of a detour on the highway of her life.

Isaac has enough problems of his own. His second ex-wife, who left him for another woman, is in the process of writing a book about their failed marriage. Even his job as a comedy writer is anything but pleasurable as his true aspiration is to write a novel and establish himself as a serious artist.

Acting on a rash impulse, Isaac resigns from his lucrative job in television, which in turn forces him to give up his apartment and reduce the monthly income he allo-

NEW YORK AS A HOLLYWOOD BACKDROP Be it *Ghostbusters* (1984), *Three Days of the Condor* (1975), *Sleepless in Seattle* (1993), John Carpenter's *Escape from New York* (1981) or Hitchcock's *Rear Window* (1954), the Big Apple plays an integral role in countless Hollywood films but has itself never been awarded the Oscar. The great U.S. metropolis served as the birthplace of the American cinema in 1896 when Thomas Edison unveiled his moving-picture-producing "vitascope" on the corner of 34th St. and 6th Avenue in front of Macy's department store. This new marvel of technology quickly attracted enthusiasts like Edwin S. Porter, who is today deemed to be the inventor of film editing and who shot such film hits as *The Great Train Robbery* (1903) with Edison's equipment. There is, however, no denying the film industry's 1914 mass exodus to California, where more space, better weather, as well as the peace and quiet essential for the talkies that would come were in abundance. Nonetheless, a great deal of the production companies' administrative and executive offices could still be found in New York for years to come.

Ironically, its climb to fame in front of the camera accompanied the filmmakers' departure from the city. Many screenwriters of the day had resided in the East Coast magnet of urban life and began to produce scripts about the place they knew best. The 30s saw Hollywood set designers recreating New York City streets, subway stations, bars and even the megalithic skyline whenever called for. The result gave rise to a larger than life image of the town perfumed by the futuristic allure of concepts like "Gotham" and "Metropolis." New York gradually gained mythical character. By many, it was regarded as a modern-day Sodom and Gomorrah that would just as soon crush a man as crown him.

Following the end of the Second World War, the camera began to return to its actual streets in search of an authenticity inspired by the documentary footage of wartime newsreels and European neorealism. Such was the case when Billy Wilder had Ray Milland walk down the real 3rd Avenue in his *Lost Weekend* (1945) instead of an artificial Hollywood set. This "return to reality" reclaimed a stronghold on the Hudson River and allowed new film studios that lacked true movie lots of their own to appear on the scene. In particular, the New York-based United Artists started to reap some of the sweetest harvests in its company's history. Yet somehow the negative stigma associated with the city lived on at the movies, even in comedies. In the large number of *Superman* and *King Kong* flicks, it continued to represent the bastion of human civilization; in Billy Wilder's classic, *The Apartment* (1960), it embodied isolation and anonymity, whereas *Serpico* (1973) and *Taxi Driver* (1975) branded it the hub of vice and corruption. When one stops to consider the directors who have shown the town's direct impact on their lives through film, the names Sidney Lumet, Martin Scorsese, Spike Lee and Woody Allen immediately come to mind. Of these, Allen stands alone in consistently painting an overwhelmingly positive portrait of the city that has never let go of his heart.

cates his parents. "This is going to kill my father. He's not going to have as good a seat at the synagogue. He'll have to sit at the back, away from God."

One of the few guiding lights that remain in the midst of Isaac's midlife crisis is his friend Yale (Michael Murphy), who surprisingly confides in the writer about his own infidelity. Isaac just can't come to terms with it, and especially not after he happens to run into Yale's mistress, Mary (Diane Keaton), at the Museum of Modern Art. The woman proceeds to praise a cluster of steel cubes to the skies, quite possibly the most revolting exhibition piece Isaac

"A masterpiece that has become a film of the ages by not seeking to become a film of the moment. The only true great film of the 1970s."

Andrew Sarris

1 The May December romance: Sweet young Tracy (Mariel Hemingway) meets old curmudgeon Isaac (Woody Allen).

2 Mixed-up mother goose: Ex-wife Jill (Meryl Streep) is just about ready to break Isaac's crown.

3 Shadow selves: The characters' gestures and attitudes seem out of sync with the small talk.

4 Mary, Mary, quite contrary: Isaac is subject to extreme mood swings. In the midst of all the emotional turbulence, he can't be sure whether he loves or hates Mary (Diane Keaton).

has ever laid eyes on. "To me it was really textural, it was perfectly integrated, and it had a marvelous sort of negative capability. The rest of the stuff downstairs was bullshit." This type of pseudo-intellectual mumbo jumbo is just the kind of crap Isaac can't stand—at least initially.

Anyone who thinks that first impressions are invariably correct clearly never met these two, for little by little romance blossoms between Mary and Isaac. The affair itself is afforded some of the film's most beautiful imagery, including the oft-cited sunrise scene, in which the two Manhattanites are taken aback by the majesty of the 58th St. Bridge and discuss their deep mutual affection for New York on the riverbank. The scene turns cosmic soon thereafter, when Isaac and Mary seek sanctuary from an incoming storm at the Hayden Planetarium; backlighting accompanied by black and white photography transform them to flirting silhouettes and floating celestial shadows, lifting these two loving souls to new levels of sublimity.

After Yale breaks off his affair with Mary, she turns to Isaac for comfort and succumbs to his charms. Before long, he calls it quits with young Tracy and for the blink of an eye appears to have arrived victoriously in the winner's circle. His dreams are crushed before he even he has time to take it all in, as Mary brushes him off to try her luck once more with Yale.

The endearingly neurotic characters, led by Isaac, are like atomic particles buzzing about with their constant quips and puns, randomly encountering one another in restaurants or museums, only to lose each other again for no good reason. Adding some zing to the tune of these often off-beat paramours, director Allen zaps the television and film industry with a few volts of Jewish kvetching

tribute to Ingmar Bergman. By abstaining from the forked-tongue satire and horn-honking yuck-yuck jokes that stole scenes in previous works like *Bananas* (1971) and *Everything You Always Wanted to Know About Sex – But Were Afraid to Ask* (1972), the eternal neurotic and one-time stand-up comic created a subdued yet amusing drama that contemplates the romantic melancholy surrounding 1970s urbanites.

As their appointed knight, Isaac battles the dragons of 60s free love and the ensuing sexual indifference from behind a shield of self-pity and cynicism on his infernally frustrating quest for true love. Yet when the over-the-hill nebbish stands before Tracy like a schoolboy with a crush at the film's conclusion, we are struck by both the vulnerability and the heroic tragedy of his character. It is this heartfelt truthfulness that continues to fill the spectator with joy during each and every subsequent viewing.

APO

and deadpan. "Years ago I wrote a short story about my mother. It was called 'The Castrating Zionist'." Allen once stated in an interview that *Manhattan* was an attempt to blend the comedy of *Annie Hall* (1977) with the seriousness of *Interiors* (1978), his thoroughly unsuccessful

5 The whole kit and caboodle: Sporting a wife and a perfect life, Yale (Michael Murphy) seems to be everything Isaac isn't.

6 All the wrong moves: Feigning seductive nonchalance on a romantic boat trip with Mary, Isaac lets his hand drift casually through the water—and it's soon dripping with something brown and slimy…

7 Showered with affection: From the MOMA to the Planetarium, every inch of Manhattan holds some sentimental value for Woody Allen.

6

"Why is life worth living? It's a very good question. Um... Well, There are certain things I guess that make it worthwhile. Uh... like what... okay... um... For me, uh... ooh... I would say... what, Groucho Marx, to name one thing... uh... um... and Willie Mays... and um... the second movement of the Jupiter Symphony... and um... Louis Armstrong, recording of Potato Head Blues... um... Swedish movies, naturally... A Sentimental Education by Flaubert... uh... Marlon Brando, Frank Sinatra... um... those incredible apples and pears by Cezanne... uh... the crabs at Sam Wo's... uh... Tracy's face..." *Film quote: Isaac*

ALIEN

1979 – GREAT BRITAIN / USA – 117 MIN.

GENRE

HORROR FILM, SCIENCE FICTION

DIRECTOR

RIDLEY SCOTT

SCREENPLAY

DAN O'BANNON, RONALD SHUSETT

DIRECTOR OF PHOTOGRAPHY

DEREK VANLINT

EDITING

TERRY RAWLINGS, PETER WEATHERLEY

MUSIC

JERRY GOLDSMITH

PRODUCTION

GORDON CARROLL, DAVID GILER, WALTER HILL for
20TH CENTURY FOX, BRANDYWINE PRODUCTIONS LTD.

STARRING

TOM SKERRITT (Dallas), SIGOURNEY WEAVER (Ripley),
VERONICA CARTWRIGHT (Lambert), HARRY DEAN STANTON (Brett),
JOHN HURT (Kane), IAN HOLM (Ash), YAPHET KOTTO (Parker),
BOLAJI BEDEJO (Alien)

ACADEMY AWARDS 1980

OSCAR for BEST SPECIAL EFFECTS
(H.R. Giger, Carlo Rambaldi, Brian Johnson, Nick Allder, Denys Ayling)

a word of warning...

TWENTIETH CENTURY-FOX Presents "ALIEN" A BRANDYWINE-RONALD SHUSETT Production

TOM SKERRITT · SIGOURNEY WEAVER · VERONICA CARTWRIGHT

HARRY DEAN STANTON · JOHN HURT · IAN HOLM

and YAPHET KOTTO as "Parker"

Produced by GORDON CARROLL and DAVID GILER

Directed by RIDLEY SCOTT

Screenplay by DAN O'BANNON, WALTER HILL, DAVID GILER

Executive Producer RONALD SHUSETT

Story by DAN O'BANNON and RONALD SHUSETT

PANAVISION® EASTMAN KODAK COLOR®

COMING FROM TWENTIETH CENTURY-FOX

1

The late 70s were overrun by the science-fiction film, a trend that had begun with George Lucas' *Star Wars* (1977). Consequently, when Ridley Scott's *Alien* was released in theaters in 1979, the producers confidently expected the film to attract attention. But audiences were somewhat surprised: the film did not contain impressive space battles, but centered on the almost futile struggle of average, fallible humans against an eerie being, the like of which had never been seen before. *Alien* was pure horror set in outer space—the logical combination of two film genres.

The story takes place somewhere in the near future on the commercial trade space ship *Nostromo*, which is on its way back to Earth filled with cargo. The seven-member crew, among them Captain Dallas (Tom Skerritt), his deputy, Ripley (Sigourney Weaver), and helmswoman Lambert (Veronica Cartwright), routinely go about their daily business. No one wastes a minute thinking about the dangers that might be hidden in outer space. But their routine is interrupted by an emergency signal from a planet previously thought to be uninhabited. There, Dallas, Kane (John Hurt) and Lambert find an empty space ship with a hold full of strange eggs. A ghastly being jumps from one of the eggs and attaches itself to Kane's face, where it remains stuck, as though almost welded to his skin. Back on their ship, the crew determine that the strange being can't be removed from the victim's face. But just a short

H. R. GIGER The Swiss artist Hans Ruedi Giger was born on 5 February 1940 in Chur. He worked for several years as a construction artist and began studying industrial design at the Zurich School of Arts and Crafts in 1962. After graduating in 1966, Geiger worked as a freelance artist, sculptor, and furniture designer for the renowned production company Knoll. In 1967 he met the actress Li Tober, with whom he lived until her suicide in 1975. In 1969 he designed his first "biomechanical" monsters for Fredi M. Murer's thirty-minute film *Swissmade – 2069*. Erotically sinister machine fantasies would soon become his trademark. At the end of 1977 Giger met his future wife, Mia, whom he divorced in 1982. After contacts with director Alejandro Jodorowsky, for whom he later created the world of the Harkonnen in David Lynch's *Dune* (1984), he was brought aboard *Alien,* which won an Oscar for Best Special Effects in 1980. In addition to his work on other films, including David Fincher's *Alien 3* (1992), Roger Donaldson's *Species* (1995), Jean-Pierre Jeunet's *Alien: Resurrection* (1997), and Peter Medak's *Species II* (1998), Giger designed album covers for bands like Blondie, Emerson, Lake & Palmer, and Danzig. From 1992 he ran the Giger-Bar in Zurich, for which he even designed the furniture himself. From 1996, he was with Carmen Maria Scheifele y de Vega, and he lived and worked in Zurich until his death in 2014.

2

1 All systems operational: Second officer Ripley performing a routine maintenance check.

2 Space bait: A member of the *Nostromo* crew investigates the alien distress signal and comes down with a case of indigestion.

3 Shoot the moon: Screenwriter Dan O'Bannon is the veritable bard of futuristic space voyages. In addition to working on *Alien 3 & 4*, he chartered the waters for *Screamers* (Canada/USA, 1995) and John Carpenter's cult classic *Dark Star* (USA, 1974).

"When, as a director, you are offered a project like *Alien*—or any science-fiction film, really—it is an offer to start with and becomes a confrontation afterwards." *Ridley Scott, in: American Cinematographer*

time later it falls off by itself. The danger seems to have been averted. A deadly meal then ensues. As the crew sit down to eat, we initially believe that Kane's hunger is a sign of his recovery, until a disgusting beast pierces its way through his chest and disappears like lightning into the ventilation shafts of the *Nostromo*. Clearly the "Alien" transforms its outer appearance during its development and the crew realize that they are going to have to kill the monster before it gets them. One crew member after the other falls victim to this mysterious being. When Captain Dallas is also killed, Ripley takes command of the ship.

She learns the true reason for their mission from the ship's computer, "Mother." Their corporation on Earth knowingly misled the crew in order to get their hands on one of the aliens.

Sigourney Weaver, who also played the main role in the three sequels (1986, 1992, 1997) is initially an unsympathetic figure in *Alien*. Consequently, the camera depicts her from a slightly low angle during the first half of the film. She acts in a "manly" fashion and refuses to allow herself to be governed by her emotions. She has no sense of humor and follows the rules by the book, while the other crew members behave helpfully and interact harmoniously. When she is left as the lone survivor, she attributes it to her judgment. In what is literally the last minute she finally manages to blow up the *Nostromo* and thereby destroy the alien.

Alien was Ridley Scott's second feature film after *The Duellists* (1977), and its success instantly catapulted him into the first rank of Hollywood filmmakers. Today his film is regarded as a milestone in the history of horror, applauded with numerous imitations and frequent emulation over the following decades. Scott's recipe for success is based on his preference for subtle horror as opposed to roaring action scenes. In *Alien*, one can detect intimations of the dark, cyber-punk vision the director would demonstrate three years later with *Blade Runner* (1982). From the beginning of the film, Jerry Goldsmith's soundtrack, as rousing as it is oppressive, and Derek Vanlint's slow-motion-like camera movements through the spaceship create a sinister and torturous atmosphere, gradually compressing into pure claustrophobic terror in the last third of the film. The monstrous "Alien," created by H.R. Giger, combines the characteristics of a living organism and a machine—the organic and the inorganic. Blood does not flow through its veins, but corrosive acid. It is surely one of the most terrifying monsters in film history.

APO

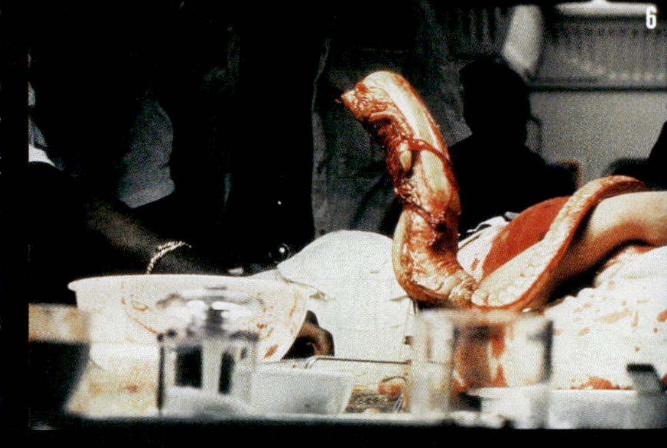

"It's an old-fashioned scare movie about something that is not only implacably evil but prone to jumping at you when (the movie hopes) you least expect it." *The New York Times*

4 Regaining consciousness: An alien distress signal leads Mother to wake up her *Nostromo* crew. Only when it is too late does Ripley realize that the "cry for help" is actually an ominous warning…

5 The A-Team's newest warrior: "Its structural perfection is matched only by its hostility."

6 Raising Cain: The baby alien hatches out of Kane's belly. Unfortunately, the proud mother dies during childbirth.

7 Lip locked: Defying Ripley's orders, Kane is brought back on board the Nostromo along with the alien object hugging his face. Interestingly, Walter Hill was originally signed to direct Alien, but soon passed the baton on to Ridley Scott.

7

DIE BLECHTROMMEL

THE TIN DRUM

1979 – FRG / FRANCE / POLAND / YUGOSLAVIA – 145 MIN.

GENRE

LITERARY ADAPTATION, DRAMA

DIRECTOR

VOLKER SCHLÖNDORFF

SCREENPLAY

JEAN-CLAUDE CARRIÈRE, VOLKER SCHLÖNDORFF, FRANZ SEITZ,
based on the novel of the same name by GÜNTER GRASS

DIRECTOR OF PHOTOGRAPHY

IGOR LUTHER

EDITING

SUZANNE BARON

MUSIC

MAURICE JARRE, FRIEDRICH MEYER

PRODUCTION

FRANZ SEITZ, ANATOLE DAUMAN for BIOSKOP FILM,
ARTÉMIS PRODUCTIONS, ARGOS FILMS, HALLELUJAH FILMS

STARRING

DAVID BENNENT (Oskar Matzerath), ANGELA WINKLER (Agnes Matzerath),
MARIO ADORF (Alfred Matzerath), DANIEL OLBRYCHSKI (Jan Bronski),
KATHARINA THALBACH (Maria), HEINZ BENNENT (Greff),
ANDRÉA FERRÉOL (Lina Greff), CHARLES AZNAVOUR (Sigismund Markus),
MARIELLA OLIVERI (Roswitha), ILSE PAGÉ (Gretchen Scheffler),
OTTO SANDER (The Musician Meyn)

ACADEMY AWARDS 1980

OSCAR for BEST FOREIGN FILM

IFF CANNES 1979

GOLDEN PALM (Volker Schlöndorff)

Der Film
nach dem Roman
von Günther Grass

Die Blechtrommel

Ein Film von
Volker Schlöndorff

Im Verleih UIP

1

The film starts and ends in a field of potatoes. "I begin long before me," says the narrator, and describes the events that led to the conception of his mother. We see policemen pursuing a man, before a country girl grants him refuge under her voluminous skirts, where matters take their course.

The begetting of Oskar, our narrator, is no less strange: his kindly mother Agnes (Angela Winkler) is married to the loudmouthed grocer Alfred Matzerath (Mario Adorf) and in love with the sensitive Pole, Jan Bronski (Daniel Olbrychski). Oskar is conceived "within this trinity." When he's born, his mother promises him a tin drum; on his third birthday he gets it. And on the same day, already disgusted by the drunken, gluttonous, cacophonous world of the adults around him, he makes an important decision: he's going to stay small. He throws himself down the cellar stairs and immediately stops growing. For the next 18 years, he'll go through life in the body of a three-year-old, with a tin drum hanging round his neck. And anyone who tries to take this drum away from him will be subjected to little Oskar's unearthly, glass-shattering scream.

Oskar is no normal child. From the day he's born, he can think and make decisions for himself; and his strangeness sets him apart. *The Tin Drum* is an opulent panorama of German-Polish history, seen through the eyes of an outsider. We are witness to the years between 1899 and 1945, from the peaceful co-existence of Germans and Poles in

VOLKER SCHLÖNDORFF The German weekly *DIE ZEIT* said of Völker Schlöndorff: "Together with Fassbinder, he's undoubtedly the most skilled craftsman in German cinema; but he's not a director whose films can be said to add up to an inimitable style." Yet most of his films can be brought under a single heading: literary adaptations. He learned his trade in the Paris of the Existentialists and the *Nouvelle Vague*. He assisted Jean-Pierre Melville and Louis Malle before making *Young Toerless* (*Der junge Törless*/*Les Désarrois de l'élève Törless*) in 1966—based on a story by Robert Musil. The works of other great writers would follow: Heinrich von Kleist (*Michael Kohlhaas – der Rebell*, 1969), Marcel Proust (*Swann in Love*/*Eine Liebe von Swann*/*Un amour de Swann*, 1983), and Arthur Miller (*Death of a Salesman*, 1985). In the 70s, he turned his attention to the contemporary political scene. Together with his then-wife Margarethe von Trotta, he made *The Lost Honor of Katharina Blum* (*Die verlorene Ehre der Katharina Blum*, 1975), based on a short novel by Heinrich Böll. He then took part in a collective project involving directors such as Alexander Kluge, Rainer Werner Fassbinder and others: *Germany in Autumn* (*Deutschland im Herbst*, 1977/78) described the atmosphere in the country after the abduction of Hanns Martin Schleyer by the Red Army Faction, otherwise known as the Baader-Meinhof Group. Further screen adaptations and films with political themes followed: *Legends of Rita* (*Die Stille nach dem Schuss*, 2000), *The Ninth Day* (*Der neunte Tag*, 2004), *Strike* (*Strajk – Die Heldin von Danzig*, 2006), *Le Mer à l'aube* (2011) and *Return to Montauk* (2017). In 2023, he was awarded the German Film Award (Honorary Award).

1 Toy soldier: On his third birthday, Oskar Matzerath (David Bennent) is given a tin drum...

2 ... and, disgusted at the adult world, he resolves to stop growing immediately.

3 Sins of the fatherland: Oscar's father, grocer Matzerath (Mario Adorf), is a fervent fan of Adolf Hitler.

Danzig, to the German attack on the city, to Oskar's flight westwards as the war draws to a close. In the film's final image, the camera watches from the potato field as he fades into the distance. Tectonic shifts in politics are made visible in tiny details, as when Beethoven's portrait makes way for Hitler's. Oskar takes no sides in all this; he remains an outsider. Once, however, his drumming causes chaos at a Nazi meeting. Oskar carries on drumming till everyone present is swaying happily to the strains of "The Blue Danube." It's reminiscent of the scene in *Casablanca* (1942) in which the "Marseillaise" does battle with "Die Wacht am Rhein." On another occasion, Oskar lets the Nazis draw him in: he meets some kindred spirits at a circus, dwarves employed as clowns and later as "a tonic for the troops." Oskar joins them, and soon he too is wearing a Nazi uniform.

If the story is episodic and discontinuous, the cinematic style is a riot. Adapted from the novel by Nobel Prize-winner Günter Grass, the film is a kind of comical yarn, a burlesque bubbling over with ideas, by turns naturalistic (as in the unforgettable scene in which a horse's head is used to catch eels), grotesque (Oskar's view from the womb) or even slapstick (when Oskar's grandfather is chased across the field in a jumpy, flickering silent-film sequence). These disparate elements are held together by Oskar's precocious and knowing off-screen commentary. The actor who plays Oskar is perhaps the film's most fortunate find. While planning the filming of what the German weekly *DIE ZEIT* called "the most unfilmable novel ever written," Volker Schlöndorff's attention was drawn to the twelve-year-old David Bennent. The son of the well-known German actor Heinz Bennent, he suffers from a growth disorder. He brings

“Schlöndorff deliberately looked for a simpler narrative style. Whole fragments of the book were simply left out. Yet I still feel that he’s succeeded in casting a new light on the whole story.” *Günter Grass, in: Sequenz*

3

4

"A very German fresco: world history seen and experienced from below. Huge, spectacular images, held together by tiny Oskar." *Volker Schlöndorff*

5

6

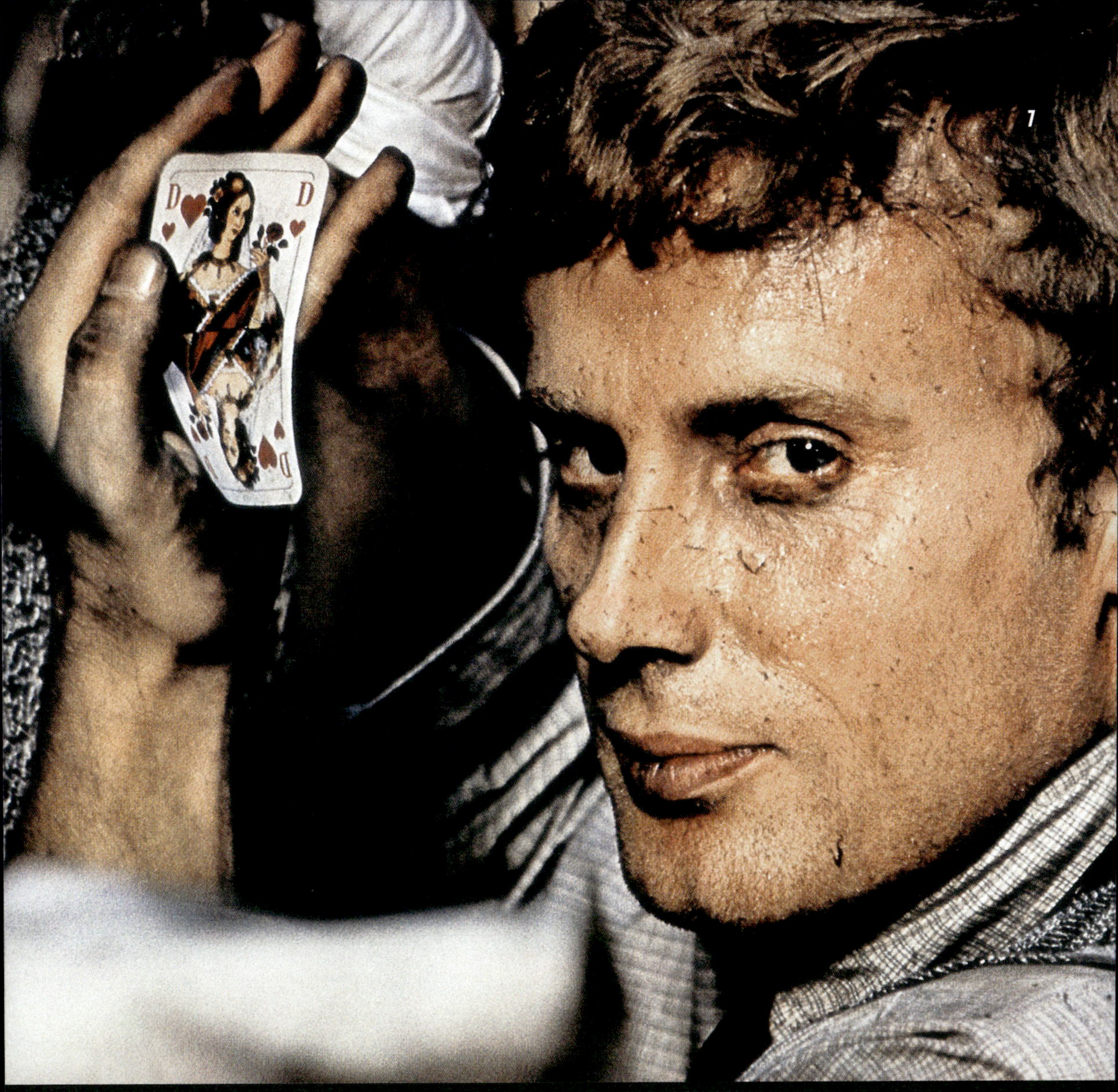

4 Maid to order: A bellybutton full of sherbet marks Oskar's first sexual experience with servant Maria (Katharina Thalbach).

5 Marching band: Oskar's musical interludes disrupt his mother's regular Thursday rendezvous with Jan.

6 An officer and a gentleman: Oskar falls in love with the midget Roswitha (Mariella Oliveri).

7 The joker's wild: Gambler and ladies' man, Jan Bronski (Daniel Olbrychski), is also an anti-fascist.

a wonderful seriousness, depth and presence to the role of Oskar. Schlöndorff was so delighted by David Bennent that he decided not to film the part of the book that takes place after 1945, when Oskar grows up—for he couldn't face replacing Bennent with another actor. In the 80s, Schlöndorff wrote the screenplay for a follow-up, but the film was never made.

In Cannes, *The Tin Drum* shared the Golden Palm with *Apocalypse Now* (1979). Later the same year, it won the Oscar as Best Foreign Film. And in 1997 came a suitably absurd epilogue: a judge in Oklahoma City had videos of *The Tin Drum* confiscated, saying the film was obscene because it showed a person under the age of 18 indulging in sexual intercourse. HJK

KRAMER VS. KRAMER

1979 – USA – 105 MIN.

GENRE

FAMILY DRAMA

DIRECTOR

ROBERT BENTON

SCREENPLAY

ROBERT BENTON, based on the novel
of the same name by AVERY CORMAN

DIRECTOR OF PHOTOGRAPHY

NÉSTOR ALMENDROS

EDITING

GERALD B. GREENBERG

MUSIC

HERB HARRIS, JOHN KANDER,
HENRY PURCELL ("Sonata for Trumpet and Strings"),
ANTONIO VIVALDI ("Concerto in C Major for Mandolin and Strings")

PRODUCTION

STANLEY R. JAFFE for COLUMBIA PICTURES CORPORATION

STARRING

DUSTIN HOFFMAN (Ted Kramer), MERYL STREEP (Joanna Kramer),
JANE ALEXANDER (Margaret Phelps), JUSTIN HENRY (Billy Kramer),
HOWARD DUFF (John Shaunessy), GEORGE COE (Jim O'Connor),
BILL MOOR (Gressen), HOWLAND CHAMBERLAIN (Richter Atkins),
JACK RAMAGE (Spencer), JESS OSUNA (Ackerman)

ACADEMY AWARDS 1980

OSCARS for BEST PICTURE (Stanley R. Jaffe),
BEST DIRECTOR (Robert Benton),
BEST ADAPTED SCREENPLAY (Robert Benton),
BEST ACTOR (Dustin Hoffman),
and BEST SUPPORTING ACTRESS (Meryl Streep)

Kramer vs. Kramer

Columbia Pictures Presents A Stanley Jaffe Production

Dustin Hoffman

in

Kramer vs. Kramer

Meryl Streep   Jane Alexander

Director of Photography Nestor Almendros   Based Upon the Novel by Avery Corman

Produced by Stanley R. Jaffe   Written for the Screen and Directed by Robert Benton

PG PARENTAL GUIDANCE SUGGESTED
SOME MATERIAL MAY NOT BE SUITABLE FOR CHILDREN

Now A Best Selling Signet Paperback.

© 1979 COLUMBIA PICTURES INDUSTRIES, INC.

Columbia Pictures

1

"What law is it that says a woman is a better parent?"

Ted Kramer (Dustin Hoffman), a workaholic absorbed by his job as an advertising executive, is about to have his world ripped out from under him. No sooner does his boss O'Connor (George Coe) put him in charge of a million dollar account, than his wife Joanna (Meryl Streep), awaiting his arrival at home, informs him of her intention to abandon their family unit. As a result, he is left to take care of their five-year-old son, Billy (Justin Henry). Floored, Ted blurts out to friend and neighbor Margaret (Jane Alexander) that this was supposed to be "one of the five best days of (his) whole life." Instead, it turns out to be the first day of his *new life* as a single father! It is an earth-shattering change for both Ted and Billy. It takes a while to make the adjustment, but somewhere down the line life's everyday hurdles like preparing meals, shopping for groceries, as well as taking Billy to school and picking him up, become part of an affectionate daily routine.

Their world is rocked yet again when Joanna turns up at their doorstep 18 months later. She has come with the clear intention of collecting Billy. Ted, however, isn't about to give up his son without a fight and abstain from the father–son relationship that has come to be. He'll even go to court if he has to. The ensuing custody battle is just an additional stress on his already overloaded life, and his private affairs soon cause him to fall out of his boss' good graces. He continually shows up late to critical business meetings, and when he should be dedicating his full concentration to the project he's in charge of he worries too much about what's in his freezer for that night's dinner. It's not long before Ted's out of a job. But he's not down for the count just yet...

Robert Benton, director of *Places in the Heart* (1984), paints a riveting portrait of a burgeoning relationship between a father and son, which is, nonetheless, full of its share of ugly human emotions like rage and despair. Dustin Hoffman, alongside impressive child actor Justin Henry, pulls out all the stops in conveying a tender father–son tie founded on many ecstatic highs and heartbreaking lows. Their bumpy road towards gaining one another's respect is paved with incidents like spilling juice on dad's important business papers, worrying about illness and injury as well as disobeying parental rules. It is precisely moments like these that forge the touching bond between them. All the more reason why Joanna's attorney, Mr. Gressen (Bill

MARITAL MAYHEM The discovery of true love is often the cornerstone of a Hollywood happy ending. Nevertheless, there are also films that paint a more scathing picture of the grand emotion. In 1973, Swedish director Ingmar Bergman's *Scenes from a Marriage* (*Scener ur ett äktenskap*, 1973) took a thorough look at two people who had no idea their wedded life was on the rocks. Produced as a six-part TV miniseries, the three-hour film version accompanies a couple on the long and painful road to separation. One of the most extreme examples of marital malfeasance is Danny DeVito's black comedy *The War of the Roses* (1989), in which a couple literally tear each other's hair out. After 17 years of blissful marriage, husband and wife want to separate, but materialism causes them to turn their shared estate into a battlefield. Each is prepared to send the other to the grave for the finer things in life. The topic of marital instability was handled much more subtly in the 30s and 40s. During the golden age of the screwball comedy, beloved Hollywood couples like Spencer Tracy and Katharine Hepburn in George Cukor's *Adam's Rib* (1949) or Clark Gable and Jean Harlow in Clarence Brown's *Wife vs. Secretary* (1936) mastered the art of verbal fencing. With *Mrs. Doubtfire* (1993), Chris Columbus served up a wild farce on the shattered marriage genre. After losing his kids in a custody battle, Daniel disguises himself as a loveable, middle-aged lady and deceives his ex-wife into hiring him as his own children's nanny so that he can be closer to them.

1 Facing facts: Billy (Justin Henry) can't get used to the idea that Mommy isn't coming home.

2 Three's a crowd: Ted Kramer (Dustin Hoffman) takes Billy to the park…

3 … where mother (Meryl Streep) and son are granted a short afternoon visit.

"What I'm trying to express in *Kramer vs. Kramer* is every man's longing to be a mother."

Dustin Hoffman in: Cinema

3

4

"*Kramer vs. Kramer* is a rare movie that finds its tone, its focus and its poetry in its very first image. The image: a close-up of an anguished woman, her face surrounded by darkness. The shot is so intimate that the audience at first yearns for some relief. But the relief never really comes. *Kramer vs. Kramer* is composed almost entirely of actors' faces, of intense passions and of winter light. Since the actors are Dustin Hoffman and Meryl Streep, and since the suffering is real, the audience quickly finds that it is impossible to turn away. (...) *Kramer vs. Kramer* is the emotional bender of the year." *Time Magazine*

5

4 Growing pains: Ted Kramer and his son Billy.

5 One day at a time: Father and son gradually learn how to set rules and how to live with them.

Moor), pulls the audience's chain with his callous line of questioning and court room theatrics as he tries to prove that Ted is obviously an unfit parent.

Likewise, the trial is no walk in the park for Joanna. It is here in the courtroom, as allegations are lashed out at her, that she relates what an emotional catastrophe the separation was for her as well. With her sensitive portrayal of Joanna Kramer, Meryl Streep secured her position as an "A list" actress. Streep evokes sympathy for her character as she explains how difficult it was for her to break out of what had become a suffocating family life that offered no prospects other than conceding to the role of wife and mother-in-waiting.

Joanna is granted custody at the end of the hearing. The verdict comes as a shock for both Ted and Billy. In a truly unforgettable scene, father and son sit in their kitchen and prepare French toast for the very last time. Billy's impending departure weighs down each hand movement at breakfast. In contrast to the mayhem at beginning of the film, the two of them now sit completely still at the table. The buzzer rings and Joanna lets him know that she is waiting in the lobby. Yet, reminiscent of the film's opening, Joanna surprises Ted once more with her decision. She can't bring herself to tear Billy away again from the parental trust that has shaped his world. She won't take Billy, even with the court's blessing.

With *Kramer vs. Kramer*, Benton creates a collage of emancipation out of the patchwork of a failed marriage. At a time when new modes of living and freedoms were replacing traditional familial roles, the rights and responsibilities of men and women were beginning to change dramatically. By telling the story primarily from the perspective of the single father, Benton provides his drama with an extra provocative punch that, in turn, accentuates the egocentric tendencies in Joanna's own self-realization. It is thus the impeccable acting of the cast that makes us leave the film, not pointing fingers at the characters, but rather full of respect and understanding for the entire Kramer family. EP

MAD MAX

1979 – AUSTRALIA – 93 MIN.

GENRE

ACTION FILM, SCIENCE FICTION

DIRECTOR

GEORGE MILLER

SCREENPLAY

JAMES MCCAUSLAND, GEORGE MILLER

DIRECTOR OF PHOTOGRAPHY

DAVID EGGBY

EDITING

TONY PATERSON, CLIFF HAYES

MUSIC

BRIAN MAY

PRODUCTION

BYRON KENNEDY for MAD MAX FILMS,
KENNEDY MILLER PRODUCTIONS, CROSSROADS

STARRING

MEL GIBSON (Max Rockatansky), JOANNE SAMUEL (Jessie Rockatansky),
HUGH KEAYS-BYRNE (Toecutter), STEVE BISLEY (Jim Goose),
ROGER WARD (Fifi Macaffee), TIM BURNS (Johnny), VINCENT GIL (Nightrider),
GEOFF PARRY (Bubba Zanetti), DAVID BRACKS (Mudguts),
PAUL JOHNSTONE (Cundalini)

THE MAXIMUM FORCE
OF THE FUTURE
POLICE
Mad
Max
SAMUEL Z. ARKOFF Presents "MAD MAX"
Music by BRIAN MAY
Written by JAMES McCAUSLAND and GEORGE MILLER
Produced by BYRON KENNEDY Directed by GEORGE MILLER
with MEL GIBSON Color prints by MOVIELAB
R RESTRICTED
RELEASED BY AMERICAN INTERNATIONAL/A FILMWAYS CO.

1
2

"You've seen it! ... You've heard it! ... and you're still asking questions?"

He's simply trying to make sense of it all, policeman Max Rockatansky (Mel Gibson) explains to his wife Jessie (Joanne Samuel), after one of his colleagues is burned alive by a marauding gang of rockers. But he is unable to unearth any explanation.

Max is not alone in his helplessness. Indeed, Australian director George Miller's low-budget production also gives the audience no explanation for the openly waged "war" between cops and rockers. A blend-in at the beginning of the film succinctly identifies the time and location of the plot: "Somewhere in the near future." A street sign on a dusty highway specifies that "Anarchy Road" stretches from this point on, and another sign displays the number of people who have recently died in the area. Without further ado comes the spectacular car chase between the Nightrider (Vincent Gil), who has declared himself a gas-propelled suicide machine, and the custodians of the law, for whom the murderous race on the desolate country highways is apparently just as much fun as it is for the psychopathic rocker. After several spectacular stunts and half a dozen crashes, he stalls—ultimately there is one obstacle too many on the highway.

Logic plays virtually no role in the story of the worn-down "Interceptor," Max, who turns into a merciless avenger after a band of bikers under the leadership of Toecutter (Hugh Keays-Byrne) murders his wife and child: although the adversaries never seek each other out, they continually meet.

Though the plot of *Mad Max* could have sprung directly from a vengeance Western of the 50s, the scenery

STUNTS A film like *Mad Max* (1979) certainly doesn't belong to those cinematic masterpieces noted for their sleek character portraits or philosophical depths. But even virulent opponents of the film are forced to recognize director George Miller's sovereign command of cinematic forms of expression and the technical brilliance of the stunts coordinated by Grant Page. Presented as a visual attraction, the circus-like perfection of the stunts points to the inception of the cinema—the markets and vaudeville shows where nickelodeons and cinematographs served as entertainment for a wide public. In the early days of the industry (in American films at least), stuntmen were simply extras who realized their chances of employment would increase if they mastered skills not everyone could master. In the labor-divided world of film, a profession quickly developed out of this realization that soon included not only the implementation of actor doubles in dangerous situations, but also the coordination (and dramatization) of action sequences. A special sort of daring was not required, but the opposite: technical perfection and risk minimization are paramount for the stunt coordinator—ultimately a botched take can cost the production not only money, but more importantly, the lives of the stuntmen.

3

1 Officer down: When the highway's a battlefield, there are bound to be some casualties.

2 A light breather: Max (Mel Gibson) will stop at nothing to avenge his murdered family.

3 Remodeling: A rocker practices for the demolition derby.

4 The bad boys of Melbourne: The future's tax collectors.

5 Car on the barbie: *Mad Max* has some grilling action scenes.

and the characters have a comic-like stylization; the protagonists speak in memorable bubbles, and they are motivated by the basic joy of movement.

In a way, *Mad Max* seems like the final stopover in a string of films, including Dennis Hopper's *Easy Rider* (1969) and Richard C. Safarian's *Vanishing Point* (1970), which at the beginning of the decade raised the car and/or motorcycle into the consummate expression of individual freedom. But in *Two-Lane Blacktop* (1971) director Monte Hellman had already identified the motor-madness of his heroes as signifying communication disorders. In *Mad Max*, all that is left for the protagonists is pointless violence.

But we should not label this as social criticism—the film is based on the commercial appeal of action and violence, and accentuates them as cleverly constructed highlights within the plot. Ultimately, it is an exploitative product.

Nonetheless, George Miller only seldom dramatizes the violence against people as the focal point of the images, with plot-related aspects remaining in the foreground (at one point a biker's arm is ripped off). Often the enormously violent and powerful impression of the film is a result of the dynamic montage. The most horrifying details are left to the viewer's imagination. In the scene in which the bikers kill Max's family, Jessie and the child run into the middle of the street while the rockers steadily approach on their bikes from the distance. After the edit, the bikers have already sped past the camera and Jessie's fate is simply suggested by a stray shoe that tumbles to the side of the road. And when Max belatedly arrives on the scene, the camera retains a wide shot—one can see him sinking over the corpses on the highway in the distance.

Mel Gibson was a completely unknown actor when he made his debut in the role of Max, as a star could not and would not have taken the risk of participating in the production. But the film offers its hero an exceptionally interesting entrance: Miller combines takes of Max's boots, gloves, leather gear, and sunglasses to create the mythical image of the cool policeman. And when we finally get to see the cop's face, we're almost surprised to look into Gibson's still boyish features.

LP

4

"*Mad Max* is a Western. It has the same story, but instead of riding horses they are riding motorcycles and cars. People say the Western's dead, but it's not; it's become the car-action film." *Cinema Papers*

5

MONTY PYTHON'S LIFE OF BRIAN

1979 – GREAT BRITAIN – 94 MIN.

GENRE

COMEDY, SPOOF

DIRECTOR

TERRY JONES

SCREENPLAY

GRAHAM CHAPMAN, JOHN CLEESE, TERRY GILLIAM, ERIC IDLE, TERRY JONES, MICHAEL PALIN

DIRECTOR OF PHOTOGRAPHY

PETER BIZIOU

EDITING

JULIAN DOYLE

MUSIC

GEOFFREY BURGON, MICHAEL PALIN ("Brian's Song"), ERIC IDLE ("Always Look on the Bright Side of Life")

PRODUCTION

JOHN GOLDSTONE for HANDMADE FILMS LTD., PYTHON (MONTY) PICTURES LIMITED

STARRING

GRAHAM CHAPMAN (Brian and two other roles), JOHN CLEESE (Reg, Centurion and four other roles), TERRY GILLIAM (Jailor and three other roles), ERIC IDLE (Stan, Loretta and eight other roles), TERRY JONES (Brian's Mother, St. Simon and three other roles), MICHAEL PALIN (Francis, Prophet and six other roles), TERENCE BAYLER (Gregory), CAROL CLEVELAND (Mrs. Gregory), KENNETH COLLEY (Jesus), SUE JONES-DAVIES (Judith)

HANDMADE FILMS Presents MONTY PYTHON'S "LIFE OF BRIAN" Starring and Written by GRAHAM CHAPMAN, JOHN CLEESE, TERRY GILLIAM, ERIC IDLE, TERRY JONES, MICHAEL PALIN Executive Producers GEORGE HARRISON, DENIS O'BRIEN Produced by JOHN GOLDSTONE

Directed by TERRY JONES Animation & Design by TERRY GILLIAM

R RESTRICTED
UNDER 17 REQUIRES ACCOMPANYING PARENT OR ADULT GUARDIAN

ORIGINAL SOUNDTRACK AVAILABLE ON WARNER RECORDS & TAPES.
READ THE PAPERBACK FROM FRED JORDAN BOOKS/GROSSET & DUNLAP.

A WARNER BROS./ORION PICTURES RELEASE
thru WARNER BROS. A Warner Communications Company
© 1979 PYTHON (MONTY) PICTURES LTD. ALL RIGHTS RESERVED.

1

2

"Blessed are the cheese makers?"

The zeal of the righteous knew no limits: this film was banned even in isolated Scottish communities that didn't have a cinema. Yet offense should have been taken only where it was intended: by religious fanatics, who can tolerate opposition as little as they can take a joke. The humor of Monty Python is simply beyond these latter-day scribes and Pharisees. In fact, few of the film's opponents had actually seen the film; and even now, John Cleese and Terry Gilliam insist that their monumental epic has nothing whatsoever to do with the life of Jesus. It can't be denied, though, that the film raises doubts about his uniqueness as a religious founder, telling the tale of a parallel Passion endured by a simple man: Brian of Nazareth, a reluctant Messiah, born on the same day as Jesus and crucified under Pontius Pilate. We should probably count our blessings, for the revolutionary British comedy team had originally planned an alternative biography of the Man from Galilee. The title, proposed by Eric Idle: "Jesus Christ: Lust for Glory"... The real Jesus makes a brief and dignified appearance, but his Sermon on the Mount can barely be heard by most of the people in the massive crowd. ("Blessed are the Greek?")

Brian too, played by Graham Chapman, is sadly misunderstood; indeed, in his clumsiness, he achieves almost tragic stature. His central message, "You're all individuals," (The crowd: "We're all individuals!") brings him into fatal conflict with the merciless yearning for salvation so prevalent at the time. Though he asks his disciples to leave him in peace ("Piss off!"), they refuse to take the hint. A large part of the film's comic effect consists in its impressive attempt to sum up 2,000 years of world history in a very small number of characters; and what's more, they're all played by Pythons. Brian's selfless dedication to the cause of the People's Front of Judea reflects the eternal strug-

CHRIST AT THE MOVIES OR THE NEW TESTAMENT IN FILM Years before *Monty Python's Life of Brian* (1979) and Martin Scorsese's scandalous *The Last Temptation of Christ* (1988), an American-Israeli coproduction delivered the most daring cinematic interpretation of the New Testament. *The Passover Plot* (1976) depicted Jesus as an opportunist who fakes his own resurrection as a clever propaganda trick in the struggle against Roman occupation. The churches' official image of Jesus was more closely approximated in Hollywood's Biblical epics. Cecil B. DeMille's silent classic *The King of Kings* (1927), the 1961 remake by Nicholas Ray (*King of Kings*), and George Stevens' *The Greatest Story Ever Told* (1964) all drew strongly on the visual tradition of Renaissance painting. Such films made no attempt to examine Jesus' personality, presenting him instead as a pious and passive victim of unavoidable events. In movies like *Barabbas* (1962), Biblical sidekicks acquired unexpected promotion, in an effort to accommodate armies of Hollywood stars. In the Stevens blockbuster, John Wayne made a cameo appearance as a Roman centurion at the foot of the Cross. His delivery of the line "Truly this man was the son of God" was indeed unforgettable.

The dilemma was: how could the epic structure of the material be reconciled with a humanized depiction of the central figure? Italian productions indicated a possible answer. Directors such as Franco Zeffirelli and Roberto Rossellini brought a realistic treatment of the historical context to the Bible's message of redemption. It was a self-confessed atheist, however, who came up with the most convincing cinematic solution: austere and evocative in its visual imagery, Pier Paolo Pasolini's *The Gospel According to St. Matthew* (*Il vangelo secondo Matteo,* 1964) places its trust in the poetic power of the Biblical texts. May we be pardoned for remarking that this film had a script made in Heaven.

1 "Larks' tongues! Otters' noses! Ocelot milk!" Brian (Graham Chapman) scrapes a living selling Roman delicacies in the Colosseum. But not for much longer...

2 If only they'd had Dolby Surround: In the Pythons' movie, as in several serious takes on the New Testament, Jesus is relegated to a marginal role.

3 That's all folks! "Always Look on the Bright Side of Life" was the ultimate hymn to optimism.

4 *Au naturel:* The Pythons have never been afraid to look ugly...

5 Cutting room execution: King Otto's suicide squad was axed from the picture before it had a fighting chance.

gle against imperialism and the tortured history of the Holy Land. The movement of resistance against Roman occupation is crippled by internal divisions, and restricted almost entirely to the kind of revolutionary rhetoric to be heard at British universities in the 60s and 70s. Again and again, the film thwarts the audience's expectations of a historical epic, and the results are sometimes astonishing. When Brian scrawls graffiti on the palace walls, he's caught by a Roman centurion (John Cleese); but instead of arresting the culprit, he subjects him to a painful Latin lesson, in which the phrase "Romans go home" is reduced to a grammatical conundrum. This dialectic of form and content is at the root of several successful jokes, involving ex-lepers, proconsuls with speech defects, and women who disguise themselves with false beards in order to take part in a public stoning. The absurdity—the madness—only fully dawns on Brian as he's hanging on the cross, serenaded by Eric Idle and a host of crucified miscreants. Their advice? "Always look on the bright side of life."

Breaking with their usual practice, the sketch specialists worked long and hard on the internal unity of this fulminating late work. The short intermezzo with an alien spacecraft was an affectionate nod to Terry Gilliam's animated fillers, and as such, indispensable. The film owes its visual brilliance to the recycled sets of Franco Zeffirelli's TV mini-series *Jesus of Nazareth/Gesù di Nazareth* (1977)—an elegant solution to the Pythons' permanent problems with money. The Tunisian locations lent further splendor to this parody of bombastic Biblical blockbusters, and additional help was provided by the former Beatle George Harrison, who rescued the project at the last minute by forming Handmade Films. He simply wanted to see one more Python movie. Later, he enabled them to realize projects like *Time Bandits* (1981) and *Monty Python Live at the Hollywood Bowl* (1982). In *The Life of Brian*, he makes a cameo appearance as Mr. Papadopolous, a man trying to sell his olive grove.

PB

4

"Just when you thought that the uproarious English comedy troupe had taken bad taste as far as it could go in *Monty Python and the Holy Grail*, along comes *Monty Python's Life of Brian* to demonstrate that it's possible to go even farther in delirious offensiveness. Bad taste of this order is rare but not yet dead."

The New York Times

5

APOCALYPSE NOW

1979 – USA – 153 MIN.

GENRE

WAR FILM

DIRECTOR

FRANCIS FORD COPPOLA

SCREENPLAY

JOHN MILIUS, FRANCIS FORD COPPOLA, MICHAEL HERR (off-screen commentary), based on motifs from the novella *HEART OF DARKNESS* by JOSEPH CONRAD

DIRECTOR OF PHOTOGRAPHY

VITTORIO STORARO

EDITING

LISA FRUCHTMAN, GERALD B. GREENBERG, RICHARD MARKS, WALTER MURCH

MUSIC

CARMINE COPPOLA, FRANCIS FORD COPPOLA, THE DOORS (Song: "The End")

PRODUCTION

FRANCIS FORD COPPOLA for ZOETROPE CORPORATION, OMNI ZOETROPE

STARRING

MARLON BRANDO (Colonel Walter E. Kurtz), ROBERT DUVALL (Lieutenant Colonel Kilgore), MARTIN SHEEN (Captain Benjamin L. Willard), FREDERIC FORREST ("Chef" Jay Hicks), ALBERT HALL (Chief Quartermaster Phillips), SAM BOTTOMS (Lance B. Johnson), LAURENCE FISHBURNE (Tyrone "Clean" Miller), DENNIS HOPPER (Photo-journalist), G. D. SPRADLIN (General R. Corman), HARRISON FORD (Colonel G. Lucas)

ACADEMY AWARDS 1980

OSCARS for BEST CINEMATOGRAPHY (Vittorio Storaro), and BEST SOUND (Walter Murch, Mark Berger, Richard Beggs, Nathan Boxer)

IFF CANNES 1979

GOLDEN PALM (Francis Ford Coppola)

MARLON BRANDO ROBERT DUVALL MARTIN SHEEN
in APOCALYPSE NOW
FREDERIC FORREST ALBERT HALL SAM BOTTOMS
LARRY FISHBURNE and DENNIS HOPPER
Produced and Directed by FRANCIS COPPOLA
Written by JOHN MILIUS and FRANCIS COPPOLA Narration by MICHAEL HERR
Co-Produced by FRED ROOS, GRAY FREDERICKSON and TOM STERNBERG
Director of Photography VITTORIO STORARO Production Designer DEAN TAVOULARIS
Editor RICHARD MARKS Sound Design by WALTER MURCH
Music by CARMINE COPPOLA and FRANCIS COPPOLA
TECHNICOLOR® AN OMNI ZOETROPE PRODUCTION

Original Soundtrack Album available on Elektra Records and Tapes

DOLBY STEREO™
IN SELECTED THEATRES

Copyright © 1979 Omni Zoetrope. All rights reserved.

1

"I love the smell of napalm in the morning."

Vietnam, 1969. Captain Willard (Martin Sheen) is on a top-secret mission to find Colonel Kurtz (Marlon Brando), a highly decorated U.S. Army officer. And when he's located the man, his next task will be to kill him; for Kurtz has clearly gone mad, is defying the control of his superior officers, and now commands a private army in the jungle beyond the Cambodian border. His soldiers are a mixed bag of indigenous people, South Vietnamese, and rogue G. I.s, who he uses to his own unauthorized and murderous ends. Willard boards a patrol boat and heads upriver through the rainforest in search of Kurtz; and the further he penetrates into the jungle, the more intensely he and his four comrades experience the horror of war.

No other movie of the 70s received so much attention before it was even released. Francis Ford Coppola was the first director to risk making a big-budget film about the Vietnam War, and he did so with almost demonstrative independence. As his own production company American Zoetrope financed the film, *Apocalypse Now* could be made without the usual assistance—and interference—from the Pentagon. (Even today, such help is practically obligatory when a war film is made in the United States.) Coppola said later that he had originally aimed to make a lucrative action movie. Instead, the film became an unparalleled nightmare for the celebrated director of *The Godfather* (1972)—and not just in financial terms.

Coppola was looking for a country with a climate similar to Vietnam's, so he chose to film in the Philippines. As the necessary infrastructure was lacking, conditions were quite hair-raising from the word go. The military equipment, for instance, was the result of a deal with the dictatorial President Marcos, who was fighting a civil war against communist rebels while the film was being made. As a consequence, helicopters were sometimes requisitioned from the set at short notice and sent off by the military to take part in real battles. Conditions as tough as these made it hard to find stars willing to take part. Initially, the role of Willard was taken by Harvey Keitel, but he was replaced by the little-known Martin Sheen after only three weeks' filming, as his expressive acting was not to

FRANCIS FORD COPPOLA Francis Ford Coppola (born April 7, 1939 in Detroit) enjoyed a sheltered middle-class childhood in a suburb of New York. His father Carmine was a composer and musician who would later write the music to some of his son's films. Coppola at first studied theatre at the Hofstra University, then film at UCLA. While still a student, he worked as an assistant director to Roger Corman, who also produced his first feature film, *Dementia 13* (1963). Coppola made his breakthrough at the early age of 31, when his screenplay to *Patton* (1969) was awarded the Oscar.

A short time later, he was also world-famous as a director—and as the Boy Wonder of the New Hollywood: the Mafia saga *The Godfather* (1972) became one of the biggest hits in movie history and won three Oscars, including Best Film. Two years later, he topped even this: *The Godfather – Part II* (1974) scooped six Academy Awards, including Best Director. In the meantime, Coppola had also made an outstanding movie about an alienated surveillance expert: *The Conversation* (1974), which carried off the Golden Palm at the Cannes Festival.

In 1976, Coppola began work on the Vietnam film *Apocalypse Now* (1979), which he produced himself, and which came very close to ruining him. But after four years in production, that film also won the Golden Palm and two Oscars, and even recouped the huge sum that had been spent making it. Only two years later, however, the failure of the love story *One from the Heart* (1981) drove him into such horrendous debt that he was forced to sell his production company, American Zoetrope. Though he has since directed other films, such as *The Cotton Club* (1984) and *The Godfather – Part III* (1990), none have been as successful as his huge hits of the 70s. His most recent film, *Megalopolis* (2024), was Coppola's passion project but a financial flop.

2

1 Tribal titan: Marlon Brando rocked the screen in his role as Colonel Kurtz although he only appeared at the end of the movie.

2 Battle of the Bulge: Captain Willard (Martin Sheen) and the photographer (Dennis Hopper) flesh out the fate of Colonel Kurtz.

3 Duty calls: Filmed on location in the Philippines, *Apocalypse Now's* helicopter was taken off the set and flown into the front lines of battle.

"My film is not a movie. My film is not about Vietnam. It is Vietnam. That's what it was really like. It was crazy." *Francis Ford Coppola, IFF Cannes*

Coppola's taste, and he wanted a more passive protagonist. This was an expensive mistake, but harmless in comparison to the problems the director would later face. There was the deadly typhoon that destroyed the expensive sets; the almost fatal heart attack suffered by Martin Sheen; the difficulty of working with the grossly overweight Brando; and above all, the trouble caused by the director's own constant departures from the script. As a result, work had to stop on several occasions, and the filming period expanded from four to 15 months. Soon, the 16 million dollar budget was exhausted, and Coppola—close to physical and mental collapse—was forced to mortgage his own property in order to raise the same sum all over again. The press could smell a disaster of previously unheard of proportions. But though two more years were taken up by post-production, the film ultimately became a box-office hit—despite mixed reviews, and the fact that other "Vietnam movies" had by then already reached the screen.

The legendary status of *Apocalypse Now* is inseparable from the spectacular circumstances of its making. Many people, including Coppola himself, have drawn an analogy between the Vietnam conflict itself and the ago-

3

nized struggle to complete the film. It's all the more remarkable, then, that Coppola succeeded in freeing himself, gradually but radically, from the superficial realism that tends to typify the war-film genre. The Vietnam War has often been described as a psychedelic experience, but Coppola and his cameraman Vittorio Storaro created images that actually do justice to the description. Willard's trip upriver, inspired by Joseph Conrad's novella *Heart of Darkness*, is a journey into the darkness of his own heart, and so the various stages on his journey acquire an increasingly fantastic, dreamlike quality. At the beginning of his odyssey, Willard encounters the surfing fanatic Lieutenant Colonel Kilgore (Robert Duvall), who sends his squad of choppers in to obliterate a peasant village so that he can enjoy the perfect waves on the neighboring beach. Kilgore's insane euphoria is heightened by the musical accompaniment: Wagner's "Ride of the Valkyrie." At this point, Willard is no more than a passive observer of a monstrous spectacle, which is ironically depicted by Coppola as a kind of hi-tech U.S. Cavalry. It's a grimly satirical scene, in which the director makes masterly use of aesthetic conventions for his own purposes.

Willard's journey terminates in a realm of the dead: Kurtz's bizarre and bloody jungle kingdom, a garishly exotic and obscenely theatrical hell-on-earth. As embodied by Marlon Brando, Kurtz has the quality of a perverted Buddha. When he first receives Willard in his murky temple residence, both men are sunk in the surrounding shadows. At the end

4 The river wild: Civilization on a voyage downstream.

5 The buck stops here: Having made it to the end of his journey, Willard is prepared to kill Colonel Kurtz.

"It is not so much an epic account of a grueling war as an incongruous, extravagant monument to artistic self-defeat."

Time Magazine

of the line, in the heart of darkness, good and evil have grown indistinguishable, and Willard has lost what distance he ever had: Kurtz has become part of his very self. When Willard finally kills him, the act—like an archaic ritual—is at once an exorcism and a manifestation of the darkness at the heart of mankind, a black stain no civilization will ever erase. Ultimately, it's the cause and the irreducible essence of war—whatever the epoch, and whatever the weapons deployed.

In 2001, Coppola brought out *Apocalypse Now Redux*, a director's cut that was 49 minutes longer. It contains some sequences that had fallen victim to the cutter's shears, and the director says it's the closest possible approximation to his original intentions. Yet although the *Redux* version is undoubtedly somewhat more complex than the original, it constitutes neither a radical alteration to, nor a significant improvement on the original.

JH

BEING THERE

1979 – USA – 129 MIN.

GENRE

SOCIAL SATIRE

DIRECTOR

HAL ASHBY

SCREENPLAY

JERZY KOSIŃSKI, based on his novel of the same name

DIRECTOR OF PHOTOGRAPHY

CALEB DESCHANEL

EDITING

DON ZIMMERMAN

MUSIC

JOHNNY MANDEL

PRODUCTION

ANDREW BRAUNSBERG for LORIMAR FILM ENTERTAINMENT,
NORTHSTAR, BSB, ENIGMA

STARRING

PETER SELLERS (Chance, the Gardener), SHIRLEY MACLAINE (Eve Rand),
MELVYN DOUGLAS (Benjamin Rand), JACK WARDEN (The President),
RICHARD A. DYSART (Doctor Robert Allenby),
RICHARD BASEHART (Vladimir Skrapinov), RUTH ATTAWAY (Louise),
DAVID CLENNON (Thomas Franklin), FRAN BRILL (Sally Hayes),
DENISE DUBARRY (Johanna Franklin), OTEIL BURBRIDGE (Lolo)

ACADEMY AWARDS 1980

OSCAR for BEST SUPPORTING ACTOR (Melvyn Douglas)

a story of chance

BEING THERE

"I can't read.
I can't write."
—Chance the gardener
"He can't lose."
—Unanimous

MADE IN U.S.A.

LORIMAR PRESENTS
AN ANDREW BRAUNSBERG PRODUCTION

PETER SELLERS SHIRLEY MacLAINE

IN A HAL ASHBY FILM

"BEING THERE"

ALSO STARRING JACK WARDEN · MELVYN DOUGLAS · RICHARD DYSART · RICHARD BASEHART

SCREENPLAY BY JERZY KOSINSKI • BASED ON THE NOVEL BY JERZY KOSINSKI
MUSIC BY JOHNNY MANDEL • EXECUTIVE PRODUCER JACK SCHWARTZMAN
CINEMATOGRAPHY BY CALEB DESCHANEL • PRODUCED BY ANDREW BRAUNSBERG • DIRECTED BY HAL ASHBY

PG PARENTAL GUIDANCE SUGGESTED
SOME MATERIAL MAY NOT BE SUITABLE FOR CHILDREN

© LORIMAR DISTRIBUTION INTERNATIONAL 1980

FOR DISTRIBUTION BY United Artists

1

"As long as the roots are not severed, all is well. And all will be well in the garden."

The main character, the film's protagonist and leitmotif, appears minutes after the picture has gotten underway. Surrounded by the mayhem of oncoming traffic, Mr. Chance (Peter Sellers) walks down Pennsylvania Avenue's center divider, utterly unperturbed. The spectator is overcome by the uncanny sensation that Chance has literally appeared out of nowhere. As the camera pans up, revealing the hub of the nation's legislature, the Capitol, it quickly becomes clear where destiny will lead him.

As it were, Mr. Chance is a man with no set goals. Since childhood, he has been the ward and faithful gardener of a wealthy eccentric, whose housekeeper saw to his upbringing. Chance has never left home, and the world that he knows is a collage of television images. A kind heart would deem him a pure soul, a more critical one brand him a "simple Simon" or a moron. He walks through life with a wide-eyed grin and, armed with his gardener's grab bag of fortune cookie philosophy, manages to take the world by storm.

When his lifelong employer dies and his estate liquidated, Chance must abandon the only home he has ever known. Utterly clueless, he embarks on new soil, awakening from his chronic lethargy when a video camera in an electronics store window forces him to come face to face with himself. Stunned, he absent-mindedly retreats into the path of a moving stretch limousine, luckily incurring only minor injuries. The vehicle's owner, Eve Rand (Shirley MacLaine) takes him under her wing and brings him home to her millionaire husband. A sound idea, as the terminally ill Mr. Rand has round the clock medical staff tending to him.

Many years Eve's senior, Benjamin Rand (Melvyn Douglas), knows his days are numbered. Impressed by the houseguest's reserved demeanor and the "profound"

HAL ASHBY Born in 1929, Hal Ashby received formal training in film editing at Republic Pictures back in the days of the old Hollywood studio system. Starting in 1953, he began to work as an assistant to editing master Robert Swink. 1965 marked the beginning of his career as head film editor and saw the dawn of a year-long collaboration with director Norman Jewison. Ashby won the Oscar for Best Film Editing for *In the Heat of the Night* (1967). He got his initial shot at directing pictures in 1970. His first film, *The Landlord*, about a hoity-toity white aristocrat who purchases a building in a black populated slum, earned him his reputation as a socially progressive satirist. Ashby remained loyal to the genre in the years that followed, directing films like *Harold and Maude* (1971) as well as *Shampoo* (1974), starring Warren Beatty as hairdresser to Beverly Hills' rich and famous. The film was set in 1968, on the eve of President Nixon's first victory. Further successes came with the film adaptation of the biography of folk music great Woody Guthrie, entitled *Bound for Glory* (1976), as well as for his heartfelt reflection on Vietnam, *Coming Home* (1978). With *Being There* (1979), a satire about a mentally handicapped gardener, whom a twist of fate sends flying into important political circles and possibly into the Oval Office, Ashby struck it big once again—both commercially and artistically. Subsequent projects in the 80s fell short of his previous accomplishments. In 1988, at the age of fifty-nine, Hal Ashby died of cancer.

1 Like a virgin: Mr. Chance (Peter Sellers) is about to leave his familiar surroundings for the very first time.

2 No man's land: Chance wanders aimlessly through an alien world and stumbles upon the nerve center of political power.

3 Green fingers, black prospects: When his master dies, Chance is banished from the garden.

"*Being There*, directed by Hal Ashby, is a rare and subtle bird that finds its tone and stays with it." *Chicago Sun-Times*

natural metaphors he uses to explain the world, the elderly gentleman immediately takes to him. It just so happens that Rand is not only rich but also an influential presidential advisor, and the head of state does, in fact, makes Chance's acquaintance when he comes round the house one day. The man is announced as "Chauncey Gardener," an innocent misunderstanding that Chance doesn't both-

Like the Rands, the president (Jack Warden) is electrified by the gardener's philosophic insight and quotes him during a public address. The window of opportunity immediately opens up for the illiterate Chance, including a silly attempt at seduction on the part of Eve Rand, and he soon emerges as a media sensation. The papers want to interview him. He even appears on a talk show and is offered a book

4 Straight from the bush: With his homespun wisdom, Chance becomes a presidential advisor.

5 An innocent abroad: Eve Rand (Shirley MacLaine) is interested and the childlike Chance is flummoxed.

When the wealthy benefactor passes away, Washington's elite assembles at the burial to pay recognition to their decorated comrade-in-arms. With the coffin still on their shoulders, the political movers and shakers convene to decide upon his successor and agree to appoint Chauncey Gardner to the position. His public appearances have won him the respect of the media and a large following among the people. Chance, however, seeks solitude and, while meandering through a grove, comes upon the bank of a lake, where he proceeds to walk on water without sinking.

Peter Sellers, in the second to last performance of his life, consciously follows in the footsteps of his personal idol Stan Laurel. Much like Laurel's on-screen persona, Chance the gardener has a childlike nature incapable of spite or malice. He is an oblivious soul who tries to rid himself of armed intruders by pointing the remote control at them and changing the channel. He is baffled when nothing happens as this puerile means of self-defense always functioned in the past.

His sophisticated attire—bits and pieces of his former employer's wardrobe—his introverted demeanor and his gardener's maxims all contribute to his astounding success in both social and political arenas. Unfamiliar with challenges, he takes each task asked of him with gratitude, expressing only concern and understanding for his fellow man. Indeed, Chance seems to be some saintly breed of fool.

Contrary to the original screenplay in which the film was supposed to close with a scene of Chance and Eve Rand on a stroll, director Hal Ashby inserted the scene just prior to the film's conclusion that shows Chance walking on water. The underlying message is not, however, that Chance is a saint or modern day messiah. Instead, it is an image rooted in logic: Chance doesn't sink, simply because he doesn't know he's supposed to. HK

Harold and Maude director Hal Ashby has created a wonderful satire full of sly humor. The brilliant Peter Sellers plays Mr. Chance with a stoicism reminiscent of Buster Keaton."

Cinema

THE CHINA SYNDROME

1979 – USA – 122 MIN.

GENRE

POLITICAL THRILLER

DIRECTOR

JAMES BRIDGES

SCREENPLAY

MIKE GRAY, T. S. COOK, JAMES BRIDGES

DIRECTOR OF PHOTOGRAPHY

JAMES CRABE

EDITING

DAVID RAWLINS

MUSIC

STEPHEN BISHOP (Title song "Somewhere In Between")

PRODUCTION

MICHAEL DOUGLAS for IPC FILMS

STARRING

JANE FONDA (Kimberly Wells), JACK LEMMON (Jack Godell), MICHAEL DOUGLAS (Richard Adams), SCOTT BRADY (Herman De Young), JAMES HAMPTON (Bill Gibson), PETER DONAT (Don Jacovich), WILFORD BRIMLEY (Ted Spindler), RICHARD HERD (Evan McCormack), DANIEL VALDEZ (Hector Salas), STAN BOHRMAN (Pete Martin)

IFF CANNES 1979

AWARD for BEST ACTOR (Jack Lemmon)

People who know the meaning of "The China Syndrome" are scared...

Soon *you* will know.

JACK LEMMON

JANE FONDA

MICHAEL DOUGLAS

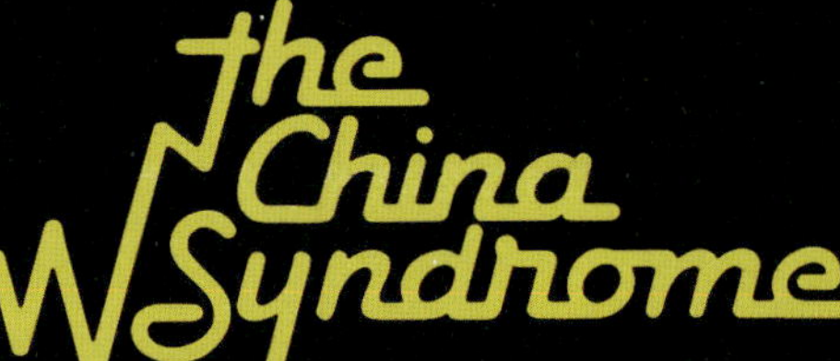

COLUMBIA PICTURES PRESENTS A MICHAEL DOUGLAS / IPC FILMS PRODUCTION A JAMES BRIDGES FILM

JACK LEMMON JANE FONDA MICHAEL DOUGLAS

THE CHINA SYNDROME

Written by MIKE GRAY & T.S. COOK and JAMES BRIDGES · Associate Producer JAMES NELSON
Executive Producer BRUCE GILBERT · Produced by MICHAEL DOUGLAS · Directed by JAMES BRIDGES
"Somewhere In Between" by STEPHEN BISHOP

© 1979 Columbia Pictures Industries, Inc.

1

"Hey! Hey! Is anybody listening to me?"

Perhaps no other science fiction film has ever come as close to reality: on March 28, 1979 a malfunction occurred at the atomic power plant in Harrisburg that was almost identical to the accident depicted in the film *The China Syndrome*, released just twelve days earlier. A realistic docu-drama unexpectedly sprang from a fictitious story that had been harshly criticized by the pro-nuclear faction. One party in particular benefited from this disastrous situation—the stock value of Columbia Pictures experienced a healthy upturn thanks to the masses of people that began streaming into cinemas.

Ironically enough, director and co-author James Bridges initially watered down the critical statement before the film's release: "This is a monster movie and technology is the monster." Leading actress Jane Fonda spoke of a film about "greed," Michael Douglas simply about an "exciting story."

The audience is introduced to the story by a television reporter. Kimberly Wells (Jane Fonda) is the sort of reporter who normally covers events like birthdays at the zoo for a local television station. She would prefer to investigate more serious subjects, but according to the station's bosses, serious journalism and femininity do not mix. One day, however, Wells stumbles upon an explosive, scandalous story by chance. She puts together a report about energy supply in California with cameraman Richard Adams (Michael Douglas) and tours the Ventana atomic plant, where without a hint of criticism she repeats into her microphone exactly what the plant's glib PR manager Bill Gibson (James Hampton) tells her. They are on the visitor's platform to the switchboard area when the plant is shaken by a quiet quaking. An alarm signal rings, warning lights flash, and people become active in the sound and air-proof command center. Though prohibited, Adams surreptitiously continues filming. Gibson's explanation that it is just a standard turbine failure is met with disbelief.

Wells wants to do a report about the unusual event, but her boss Jacovich (Peter Donat) refuses her request. Because it was shot without authorization, they won't use the filmed material. Richard Adams' hotheaded reaction does not improve matters, and he puts Kimberly Wells into an uncomfortable position when he steals the controversial roll of film from the channel's archive and disappears.

While searching for Adams, Wells meets Jack Godell (Jack Lemmon), the head engineer of the atomic plant. He again claims that the situation they observed was not a malfunction. The next day Godell is to give testimony to an

JAMES BRIDGES In the original screenplay of *The China Syndrome* (1979), the leading character was a man. Richard Dreyfuss was briefly a candidate for the role. After the producers won Jane Fonda for the project, the script had to be accordingly revised. Fonda herself collaborated on the changes with James Bridges (born 1936), who had been chosen to direct the film. Bridges had the best qualifications: he was originally an actor himself and played several television roles in the 1950s.

He simultaneously worked on a career as a screenwriter and made a breakthrough in the mid 60s with several genre films. He soon aroused attention with contemporary themes, which also drive his later directorial works. Included in Bridges' directorial projects are the Travolta films *Urban Cowboy* (1980) and *Perfect* (1985), and the film adaptation of Jay McInerney's *Bright Lights, Big City* (1988). His last project was the screenplay for Clint Eastwood's *White Hunter, Black Heart* (1990). Bridges died on June 6, 1993.

2

1 Start spreadin' the news: Jack Godell (Jack Lemmon) is determined to tell the world what he knows.

2 Hazardous to your health: Contaminated material has caused an accident and the possible consequences are being studiously ignored.

3 Won't somebody listen! Desperate to prevent the looming catastrophe, Jack Godell tries to catch the eyes of the reporters.

investigating committee whose findings ultimately exonerate the technicians—the plant's operators breathe a sigh of relief, as they are anxiously awaiting a decision authorizing the construction of a new nuclear reactor. Every delay is a further financial disaster for the already debt-ridden undertaking.

Jack Godell is in fact worried, and he begins inspections of his own. He discovers that to save expenses, the construction firm forged several safety-related documents. His warnings are ignored and the reactor is to be reattached to the network as quickly as possible. In the meantime Kimberly Wells and Richard Adams have received information from independent experts about the true nature of the secretly filmed malfunction. It turns out that it could have come to a melting of the reactor core, which inevitably would have released a large amount of radioactive material. The core could have even wound itself into the Earth's core—all the way to China ("China Syndrome"). They confront Godell with their information. Shaken, he tells of the construction firm's manipulation and promises the journalists hard evidence. The next morning he gives this evidence to a messenger, whose car is forced off the road. The messenger is found seriously injured and the documents have disappeared.

“In the sense that it attacks big business and corporate morality, I suppose it is political; but it’s essentially a gripping thriller which draws its strength from the very real anxiety about the safety of nuclear energy.” *Encore Magazine*

“A precise but appealingly ambivalent performance from Jane Fonda —as a media person who finds both a cause and a career boost in a nuclear energy crisis—centers this melodramatic account of how Harrisburg might have happened.” *Sight and Sound*

Hearing the news, Godell himself sets off. He too is followed, but escapes in the nick of time and reaches the power plant, where he realizes with horror that the reactor is running at full capacity. Again his warnings have not been heeded. In a last moment of desperation he grabs a gun, forces the workers out of the command center and allows Kimberly Wells and Richard Adams to come and do a live report about what has occurred. While the necessary broadcast equipment is being delivered, unbeknownst to the journalists a special unit is attempting to get at Godell. When the cameras finally go live Godell's nervousness overwhelms him and he gets bogged down in technical details. The police force their way in before Godell can reveal his information. Godell is shot and the transmission cables are cut.

Outside, more and more television teams have assembled. Bill Gibson has already prepared a press release, in which he describes Godell as psychologically disturbed. Kimberly Wells interrupts the reading and embarrasses Gibson with pointed questions. At Wells' insistence, Godell's colleague Ted Spindler (Wilford Brimley), who until that point had been strictly loyal to his

4 Hard pressed: Jack Godell finds an ally in TV reporter Kimberly Wells (Jane Fonda)—but her story is rejected.

5 Sabotage? Godell's messenger is badly hurt—and the documents he was carrying have disappeared…

6 Lying on her laurels: Jane Fonda's performance as Kimberly Wells earned her an Oscar nomination.

employer, decides to break his silence. He refutes Gibson's statement and emphasizes that Jack Godell was not psychologically disturbed, but a hero.

The film, accompanied by music only during the title sequence, ends the same way it began: with images of the control center of the television station, where after the dramatic live transmission, the normally programmed entertainment is continued. The malfunction was an exception, a special case, and the medium that was briefly able to show its potential falls back into daily routine.

HK

THE ELEPHANT MAN

1980 – GREAT BRITAIN / USA – 123 MIN.

GENRE

DRAMA

DIRECTOR

DAVID LYNCH

SCREENPLAY

CHRISTOPHER DE VORE, ERIC BERGREN, DAVID LYNCH, based on the memoirs *THE ELEPHANT MAN AND OTHER REMINISCENCES* by SIR FREDERICK TREVES and the book *THE ELEPHANT MAN: A STUDY IN HUMAN DIGNITY* by ASHLEY MONTAGU

DIRECTOR OF PHOTOGRAPHY

FREDDIE FRANCIS

EDITING

ANNE V. COATES

MUSIC

JOHN MORRIS, SAMUEL BARBER ("Adagio for strings")

PRODUCTION

JONATHAN SANGER for BROOKSFILMS LTD.

STARRING

ANTHONY HOPKINS (Dr. Frederick Treves), JOHN HURT (John Merrick), JOHN GIELGUD (Carr Gomm), ANNE BANCROFT (Mrs. Kendal), FREDDIE JONES (Bytes), WENDY HILLER (Mothershead), HANNAH GORDON (Anne Treves), MICHAEL ELPHICK (Night Watchman), JOHN STANDING (Dr. Fox), PHOEBE NICHOLLS (Merrick's Mother)

"I AM NOT AN ANIMAL!
I AM A HUMAN BEING!
I...AM...A MAN!"

THE ELEPHANT MAN

Paramount Pictures Presents A Brooksfilms Production Anthony Hopkins and John Hurt as The Elephant Man Anne Bancroft Sir John Gielgud Wendy Hiller Executive Producer Stuart Cornfeld Screenplay by Christopher DeVore & Eric Bergren & David Lynch Produced by Jonathan Sanger Directed by David Lynch Read the Ballantine Book

PG PARENTAL GUIDANCE SUGGESTED
SOME MATERIAL MAY NOT BE SUITABLE FOR CHILDREN

Based upon the life of John Merrick, the Elephant Man, and not upon the Broadway play or any other fictional account.

© MCMLXXX by Paramount Pictures Corporation. All Rights Reserved. Panavision® A Paramount Picture

1

"I am not an animal! I am a human being! I am a man!"

"Life is full of surprises. Ladies and gentleman, consider the fate of this creature's poor mother. In the fourth month of her maternal condition, she was struck down by a wild elephant. Struck down, if you take my meaning, on an uncharted African island. The result is plain to see, ladies and gentleman... THE TERRIBLE ELEPHANT MAN!" At a freak show in London, a shockingly deformed young man is served up for the delectation of the public. This shy and terrified creature is found, examined and adopted by the surgeon Dr. Frederick Treves (Anthony Hopkins), who discovers a sensitive and intelligent human being behind the monstrous façade. Not only can the "Elephant Man" think and speak; he loves conversation and literature, and creates exquisite paper sculptures with his undamaged left hand.

The Elephant Man is based on the true story of Joseph Carey Merrick, who was born in Leicester in 1862, suffering from multiple neurofibromatosis, a disease that causes spongy growths on the victim's skin and bones. Frederick Treves discovered Merrick at a fairground. In 1923, the physician published his memoirs, *The Elephant Man and Other Reminiscences*. Together with Ashley Montagu's *The Elephant Man: A Study in Human Dignity*, Treves' book formed the basis for the film.

THE CINEMATOGRAPHER FREDDIE FRANCIS *The Elephant Man* has a very particular, "historical" look to it. Despite the extreme contrasts between areas of light and dark, the light is soft, with backgrounds frequently lost in spaces permeated by a diffuse bloom. These images were created by the Director of Photography Freddie Francis (1917–2007), one of England's finest cameramen.

Freddie Francis was born in London. After learning his trade with the British army during the Second World War, he went on to work with some of the greatest directors in British cinema, including Joseph Losey and Karel Reisz. In 1960, he received an Oscar for his work on *Sons and Lovers* (Director: Jack Cardiff)—filmed, like *The Elephant Man*, in black-and-white and in widescreen Cinemascope format. Two years later, Francis took up directing; by 1975, he had made 20 horror films, none of them great works but all finely crafted movies. For *The Elephant Man*, Francis accepted the job of cameraman for the first time since the early 60s, and he remained faithful to the visual style he had developed at that time. In the years that followed, Francis was increasingly active as a cameraman. He continued his collaboration with Lynch on *Dune* (1984) and—15 years later—on *The Straight Story* (1999). In the intervening period, he worked with a variety of directors, among them Martin Scorsese (*Cape Fear*, 1991). For his work on *Glory* (1989), a drama of racial conflict at the time of the American Civil War, Freddie Francis was awarded his second Oscar.

2

1 Sandbagged: A sideshow attraction who proves himself a prince. John Hurt as the piteously deformed Elephant Man.

2 Step right up: Bytes (Freddie Jones) capitalizes on the star of his sidewalk circus.

3 Truncated: Surgeon Dr. Frederick Treves (Anthony Hopkins) "buys" the Elephant Man from Bytes.

"John Hurt gives a magnificent performance, masterfully conveying deep-felt emotions even while hampered by the inability to use his face or even much of his voice."
Motion Picture Guide

Director David Lynch (*Mulholland Drive*, 2001) portrays the deformed man with enormous empathy. In the first half-hour of the film, we see nothing of John Merrick's face, only the reactions of those who do so. By the time he is finally revealed to us, we have already become acquainted with a human being, and our reaction to his appearance is something other than shock. Treves rescues him from the freak show and takes him to hospital, but Merrick's martyrdom is still far from over. To the scientists of the Pathological Society, he is an object of research, a fascinating specimen; in London's better circles, it becomes *chic* to invite the monster to tea; and when Merrick is alone in his hospital bed, the night watchman opens his door to hordes of drunks and streetwalkers hungry for a glimpse of his misery.

Lynch had only made one full-length film before this: the disturbing underground classic *Eraserhead* (1974/77). Though at first glance the two films may seem very different, *Eraserhead* can in fact be seen as a preliminary study to *The Elephant Man*. There are thematic and structural similarities: both movies tell the story of an outsider, and

4

4 Curiosity killed the cat: The clinic's night porter (Michael Elphick) displays the misshapen man to a girl brought in from the street.

5 PhDs at the freak show: Dr. Treves presents the Elephant Man to members of the London Pathological Society.

"The point was to let the audience become familiar with the monster, so that the monster could disappear and the human being come into view."
David Lynch

both are suffused with a nightmarish atmosphere. With its five-million-dollar budget, however, *The Elephant Man* was 250 times more expensive than Lynch's debut. Executive Producer Mel Brooks (whose wife Anne Bancroft appears in the film) had to fight to get Lynch accepted as director. It was worth the struggle; the film is a masterpiece, both brilliantly constructed and deeply moving, and it made Lynch's name worldwide. Apart from the visionary sequences that frame the film, and the nightmare in the middle, the film is thoroughly naturalistic, resurrecting Victorian London in a succession of atmospheric images. The cinematographer Freddie Francis and the costume and production designers achieved something exceptional here, and all were shortlisted for Academy Awards. Indeed, the film was nominated for eight Oscars in total, though, sadly, it received not a single one.

In *The Elephant Man*, Lynch also pays tribute to two great films with related themes: like Quasimodo in *The Hunchback of Notre Dame* (1939), Merrick lives in a bell-tower; and the scene in which he is freed from a cage by his fellow "monsters" is a reference to Tod Browning's classic *Freaks* (1932). HJK

LE DERNIER MÉTRO

THE LAST METRO

1980 – FRANCE / FRG – 131 MIN.

GENRE

DRAMA

DIRECTOR

FRANÇOIS TRUFFAUT

SCREENPLAY

FRANÇOIS TRUFFAUT, SUZANNE SCHIFFMAN, JEAN-CLAUDE GRUMBERG

DIRECTOR OF PHOTOGRAPHY

NÉSTOR ALMENDROS

EDITING

MARTINE BARRAQUÉ

MUSIC

GEORGES DELERUE

PRODUCTION

FRANÇOIS TRUFFAUT for LES FILMS DU CARROSSE, SOCIÉTÉ FRANÇAISE DE PRODUCTION, SÉDIF PRODUCTIONS, TF1 FILMS PRODUCTIONS, MARAN-FILM

STARRING

CATHERINE DENEUVE (Marion Steiner), GÉRARD DEPARDIEU (Bernard Granger), JEAN POIRET (Jean-Loup Cottins), HEINZ BENNENT (Lucas Steiner), ANDRÉA FERRÉOL (Arlette Guillaume), MAURICE RISCH (Raymond Boursier), PAULETTE DUBOST (Germaine Fabre), JEAN-LOUIS RICHARD (Daxiat), SABINE HAUDEPIN (Nadine Marsac), JEAN-PIERRE KLEIN (Christian Leglise)

dans

LE DERNIER METRO

Un film de
FRANÇOIS TRUFFAUT

avec ANDREA FERREOL
PAULETTE DUBOST • SABINE HAUDEPIN
JEAN-LOUIS RICHARD • MAURICE RISCH
et HEINZ BENNENT

Scenario de FRANÇOIS TRUFFAUT et SUZANNE SCHIFFMAN • Directeur de la Photographie NESTOR ALMENDROS • Musique de GEORGES DELERUE
Une production FILMS DU CARROSSE • SEDIF S.A. • TF1 • SOCIETE FRANÇAISE DE PRODUCTION

DISTRIBUTION GAUMONT

1

Paris, 1942. The city is under German occupation. Lucas Steiner (Heinz Bennent), the Jewish director of the Théâtre Montmartre, has gone into hiding; it's rumored he's left France. Since his disappearance, his wife Marion (Catherine Deneuve), the star of the ensemble, has been running the theater. Only she knows that Lucas is actually hiding in the cellar of the building, where a hole in the heating-pipes allows him to listen in on rehearsals. The play: *La Disparue*… Marion's task is made more difficult by the fact that Daxiat (Jean-Louis Richard), a critic who collaborates with the Nazis, is particularly interested in her theater, and she is thus forced to run a very tight ship. The strictness of her regime is also felt by Bernard Granger (Gérard Depardieu), a talented young actor and notorious ladies' man. Though he's rehearsing the male lead at Marion's side, her interest in him seems purely professional.

CATHERINE DENEUVE For more than fifty years, Catherine Deneuve has been one of the biggest stars of European cinema. Born in Paris on October 22, 1943, she was only 19 when she made her breakthrough in Jacques Demy's musical *The Umbrellas of Cherbourg* (*Les Parapluies de Cherbourg*, 1963). After this early success, she proved to be unusually demanding in her selection of roles, and this led to collaborations with some of Europe's most interesting filmmakers. Controversial roles included a woman terrorised by her own aversion to sex in Roman Polanski's *Repulsion* (1965), and a *grande bourgeoise* lady and occasional prostitute in Luis Buñuel's *Belle de jour* (1966). Deneuve's image as an icy, enigmatic blonde beauty was reinforced by her second Buñuel film *Tristana* (1969/70) and by François Truffaut's underrated *Mississippi Mermaid* (*La Sirène du Mississippi*, 1969). Her qualities as an actress were long overlooked, although her popularity was huge. It was only with Truffaut's *The Last Metro* (*Le dernier métro*, 1980) that she finally got the recognition she deserved (she received her first César for this film). Like very few female stars before her, she has been a lasting favorite with moviegoers, critics and directors alike. She also appeared in films such as André Téchiné's *Thieves* (*Les Voleurs*, 1996), Leos Carax' *Pola X* (1999) or François Ozon's *8 Women* (*8 femmes*, 2001). In movies like these, she proved not only that she has the confidence to surprise her fans, but also that she can take a thoroughly ironical view of her status as *grande dame* of the French cinema. Her recent films include *The Beloved* (*Les bien-aimés*, 2011), *On My Way* (*Elle s'en va*, 2013), *The Brand New Testament* (*Le tout nouveau Testament*, 2015) and *Marcello Mio* (2024).

1 Love in the time of Catherine: Deneuve as a woman between two men—her husband (Heinz Bennent) and …

2 … her young beau (Gérard Depardieu).

3 Star-struck: Truffaut's film is also a homage to Catherine Deneuve, the great icon of the French cinema.

"Deneuve, more beautiful than ever, displays a knowing humanity, and a sensuality she rarely shows in film, where she has been used more as icon than actress."
Time Magazine

For many years, François Truffaut had wanted to make a film about his memories of the Occupation. In *The Last Metro*, he combined this with a second ambition: to make a film set in a theater. For the one-time leader of the French *Nouvelle Vague,* it was an unusual project and, above all, a risky one. *The Last Metro* was Truffaut's most expensive film. As he hadn't had a box-office success for years, a flop this time might well have jeopardized his independence. Yet despite the stars in the cast, there was no way of knowing whether the public would like the film. At that time, there had been little serious examination of the period of occupation in France. The few films that broached the topic were either burlesques or heroic epics. But Truffaut wanted to show everyday life in Paris under

German occupation—and the result was a triumph. More than one million people saw the film on its first release in Paris alone. It received ten Césars, was nominated for an Oscar, and the critics were—almost—unanimous in their praise.

The Last Metro is almost classical in appearance. It was shot mainly in the grounds of an old factory, and this gives it a kind of "studio finish" unusual for Truffaut. Nonetheless, the film radiates vitality and authenticity. For one thing, enormous care was expended on getting the smallest details right, on everything from the music of the day to the radio programs of the time. Above all, despite the presence of two big stars, it is a wonderful ensemble film. It's full of utterly believable characters, whose function in the plot arises naturally from their role in the theater, and who give us an impression of the varied reactions of Parisians to everyday life under foreign occupation. Truffaut shows us neither mere normality nor a permanent state of emergency. Instead, he presents a complex and detailed portrait of the time, with all the fine gradations between resistance and collaboration.

The film functions equally well as a dramatic love story set against a background of historical events; but typically, there's nothing stereotyped about Truffaut's use of this well-tried pattern. In his hands, it becomes a free-spirited and intimate study of a painful love triangle.

3

4

“*Le dernier métro* succeeds in making us forget the period and the setting, the symbolism and the morality. Instead, it allows us to share in the real actions of real people, as if we were watching them through a pane of glass.”

Frankfurter Allgemeine Zeitung

5

4 Hats off to Hitler: The German actor Heinz Bennent plays the Jewish theater director Lucas Steiner. A year before, he played a convincing Nazi in Schlöndorff's *The Tin Drum* (*Die Blechtrommel,* 1979).

5 The see-saw of collaboration and resistance: *The Last Metro* is a clear-headed and unglorified portrait of the French during WWII.

6 Air of authenticity: The production designers' endless attention to detail created a convincing image of everyday life in the 40s.

As the film draws to a close, Deneuve, Depardieu and Bennent appear on stage—hand-in-hand. Here, Truffaut is true to himself, and no closer to conventional morality than he was when he made *Jules and Jim* (*Jules et Jim*, 1961). The heart of this film is Catherine Deneuve, a woman torn between two men. This was her second collaboration with Truffaut, after *Mississippi Mermaid* (*La Sirène du Mississippi*, 1969). Now, in 1979, in the play-within-the-film, Truffaut asked her and Depardieu to repeat the wonderful closing dialog from the earlier movie. *The Last Metro*, then, is also a homage to the actress Deneuve, one of the great lovers in cinema history.

JH

DRESSED TO KILL

1980 – USA – 106 MIN.

GENRE

THRILLER

DIRECTOR

BRIAN DE PALMA

SCREENPLAY

BRIAN DE PALMA

DIRECTOR OF PHOTOGRAPHY

RALF D. BODE

EDITING

GERALD B. GREENBERG

MUSIC

PINO DONAGGIO

PRODUCTION

GEORGE LITTO for CINEMA 77 FILMS,
FILMWAYS PICTURES, WARWICK ASSOCIATES

STARRING

ANGIE DICKINSON (Kate Miller), MICHAEL CAINE (Dr. Robert Elliott),
NANCY ALLEN (Liz Blake), KEITH GORDON (Peter Miller),
DENNIS FRANZ (Detective Marino), DAVID MARGULIES (Dr. Levy),
KEN BAKER (Warren Lockman), SUSANNA CLEMM (Betty Luce),
BRANDON MAGGART (Cleveland Sam), AMALIE COLLIER (Cleaning Woman)

BRIAN DE PALMA,
MASTER OF THE MACABRE,
INVITES YOU TO A SHOWING
OF THE LATEST FASHION...

...IN MURDER.

DRESSED TO KILL

A FILMWAYS Picture

SAMUEL Z. ARKOFF Presents A GEORGE LITTO PRODUCTION OF A BRIAN DE PALMA FILM

MICHAEL CAINE • ANGIE DICKINSON • NANCY ALLEN In

"DRESSED TO KILL" WRITTEN BY BRIAN DE PALMA • PRODUCED BY GEORGE LITTO • DIRECTED BY BRIAN DE PALMA

R RESTRICTED UNDER 17 REQUIRES ACCOMPANYING PARENT OR ADULT GUARDIAN

Color by TECHNICOLOR® Prints by MOVIELAB READ THE BANTAM BOOK Cinema 77/Film Group

©1980 Filmways Pictures, Inc.

1

How many psycho-thrillers start like this? A blonde woman gets off in the shower to the sound of violins and the rhythm of the slow-motion camera. Even as early as *Dressed to Kill's* opening sequence, Brian De Palma's imagery operates on multiple levels, making viewers stop to think for a second whether they've accidentally sat down to a soft-porn flick. Though as every versed Hitchcock fan knows, a shower can be a very hazardous location. Just moments into the erotic symphony, a shadowy figure rips Kate Miller (Angie Dickinson) out of her dream and into the waking world. Reality, however, provides no comfort. Kate is fed up with her stale marriage and wants out of her boring little life. Her son Peter (Keith Gordon), an electronic whizz-kid, is eternally engrossed in his high-tech projects, leaving Kate with no one to confide in other than her shrink, Dr. Elliott (Michael Caine).

The scenes that follow take place almost entirely without words. Kate encounters a handsome, dark stranger at the museum and embarks on a romantic adventure. Just before leaving his apartment, she finds a prescription that indicates she may have contracted a venereal disease. Though the wind has been knocked out of her sails, an even more unthinkable doom awaits Kate in the building corridor. Having forgotten her wedding ring at her lover's apartment, she heads back there only to be brutally slashed to death by a razor blade in the elevator.

The only witness to the crime is paid escort Liz Blake (Nancy Allen). She quickly becomes the most interesting

CELLULOID PSYCHOPATHS Psychotic killers have served as stock characters in movies since the advent of the motion picture camera and are among the most reliable audience magnets. We could start with Robert Wiene's *The Cabinet of Dr. Caligari* (*Das Cabinet des Dr. Caligari*, 1919), where a homicidal maniac wreaks havoc on the world, causing a shroud of terror to descend upon society. This classic film illustrates just how suitable the device is to blur the borders between reality and the imagination, by visually externalizing the inner dialog of the protagonists. The condition in which the psychopath finds himself, at least on the big screen, usually involves dealing with a split personality comprised of a dark doppelganger hidden behind an unassuming façade. This lends itself nicely to narrative cinematic devices and allows for plenty of tricks and twists on audience expectations. One could argue that the prototype for the killer who lurks behind the mask of normality is the Norman Bates character (played by Anthony Perkins), from Alfred Hitchcock's *Psycho* (1960). Because all these individuals are dominated by bloodlust as they detach themselves from reality, wild eroticism pairs well with their antisocial behavior. Such was the case in Harold Becker's 1989 picture *Sea of Love*. Lastly, unsavories with eerily voyeuristic tendencies (as in Michael Powell's *Peeping Tom*, 1960) are often found among people who cannot distinguish between reality and fantasy. They might therefore be described as suitable counterparts to cinema spectators.

2

3

person involved in the case to police detective Marino (Dennis Franz), though he is not fully convinced by the call girl's story. Together with Peter Miller, the victim's son, Liz attempts to hunt down the murderess who is also apparently one of Dr. Elliott's patients.

With his deliciously brilliant direction of what can be deemed a fairly cut and dry plot, whose outcome always seems just one step out of reach, De Palma proves himself again to be a master of suspense. De Palma's previous films had established his affinity with the uncontested master of the genre, who died three months prior to the

"My films are very different from Hitchcock's, and I think anyone with a brain can see it." *Brian De Palma*

1 Bored to shreds: A chance affair seals the fate of frustrated housewife Kate Miller (Angie Dickinson).

2 Silk stalkings: With a masked killer, blonde victim and distorted camera angles, De Palma gives Hitchcock's calling card his own personal signature.

3 Blind to the rules of the game: If only Liz Blake (Nancy Allen) woke up to the glaring dangers that await her.

4

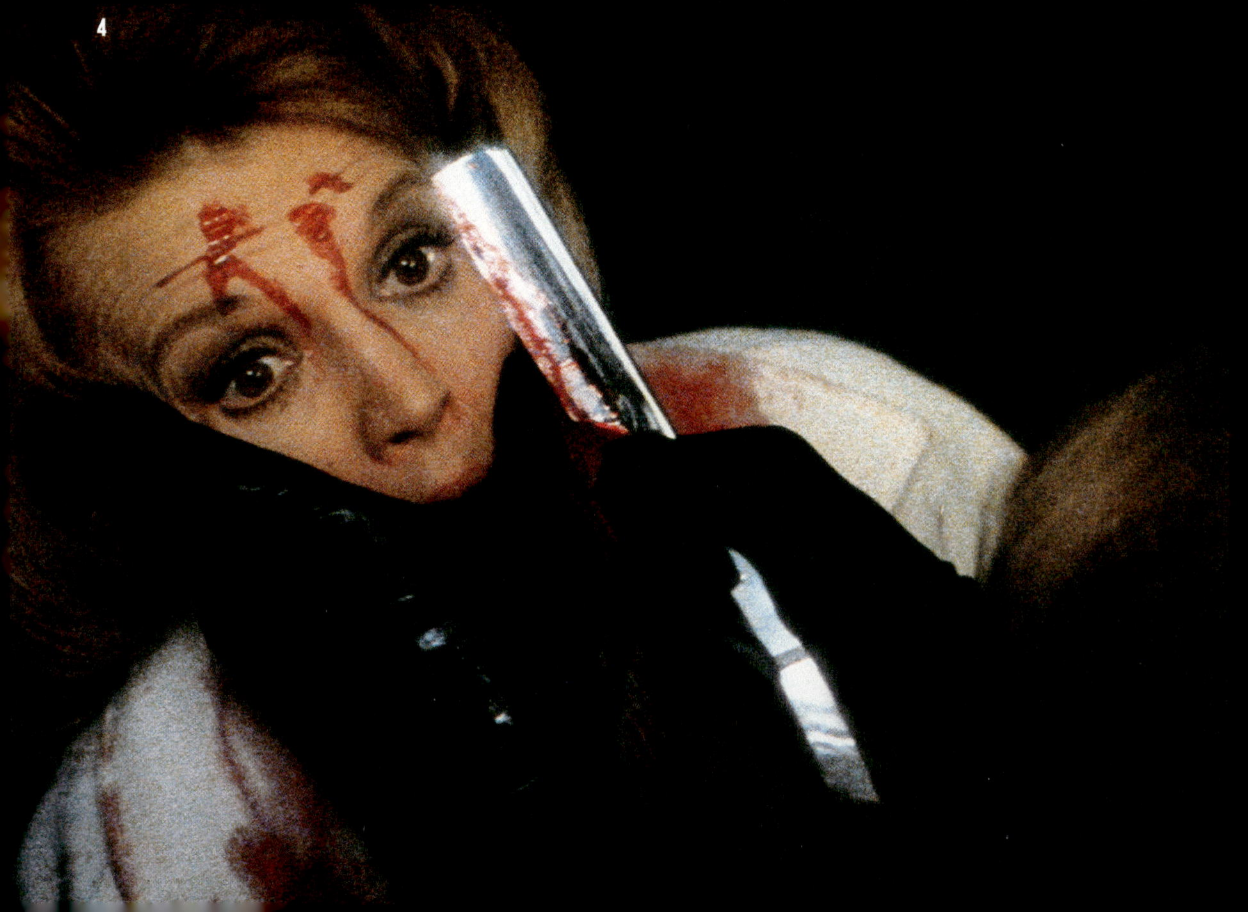

4 Eye opener: According to insiders, director De Palma just can't get enough of a good thing.

5 Doctor patient privileges: Kate confides her innermost secrets to Dr. Elliott (Michael Caine).

picture's release. His tendency to borrow from these works was indeed so conspicuous in *Dressed to Kill* that it caused *Rolling Stone* to pose the following question in the October 16, 1980 issue: "Brian De Palma: the new Hitchcock or just another rip-off?"

Excluding the motifs of transsexuality and disguise, which are an out and out tribute to *Psycho* (1960), there are three major traits characteristic of De Palma's own cinematic roots and objectives as an artist.

First, he has a predilection for stylizing his pieces and allowing visuals to tell his story. Using devices like the split screen to play up the film's mannerism, De Palma significantly surpasses his mentor and proves that he'll implement chancy, avant-garde visual effects even at the risk of appearing trite.

Also in the Hitchcockian vein, De Palma takes an ironically distant stance to his gruesome subject matter, but with a more satirical spin on his work than the British filmmaker. This turns up time and again, whether in the form of the cynical Detective Marino or the deplorable gang of armed hooligans in the New York subway. These flagrant caricatures of modern-day city dwellers read a little like Americanized versions of some of Hitchcock's characters with their flair for subversive British irony.

Finally, De Palma's works are much more upfront and self-assured in their depiction of eroticism, something that the *Dressed to Kill* director was scorned for at the time. Interestingly, the film has its seed in Gerald Walker's novel *Cruising*. William Friedkin's film version of the book *Cruising* (1980), with Al Pacino in the leading role, was released just prior to *Dressed to Kill*. Friedkin had gay rights organizations up in arms over his picture, whereas De Palma, on the other hand, had to ward off feminist groups who saw the film as a "masterpiece of misogyny."

Friedkin's film got thoroughly tangled up in bureaucratic red tape and flopped at the box office. De Palma's *Dressed to Kill* was, at the time of its release, the greatest financial success of his career. SH

GLORIA

1980 – USA – 123 MIN.

GENRE

GANGSTER FILM

DIRECTOR

JOHN CASSAVETES

SCREENPLAY

JOHN CASSAVETES

DIRECTOR OF PHOTOGRAPHY

FRED SCHULER

EDITING

GEORGE C. VILLASEÑOR

MUSIC

BILL CONTI

PRODUCTION

SAM SHAW for COLUMBIA PICTURES CORPORATION

STARRING

GENA ROWLANDS (Gloria Swenson), JULIE CARMEN (Jeri Dawn), JOHN ADAMES (Phil Dawn), BUCK HENRY (Jack Dawn), JESSICA CASTILLO (Joan Dawn), LUPE GARNICA (Margarita Vargas), BASILIO FRANCHINA (Tony Tanzini), TONY KNESICH (Gangster #1), TOM NOONAN (Gangster #2), RONALD MACCONE (Gangster #3)

IFF VENICE 1980

GOLDEN LION

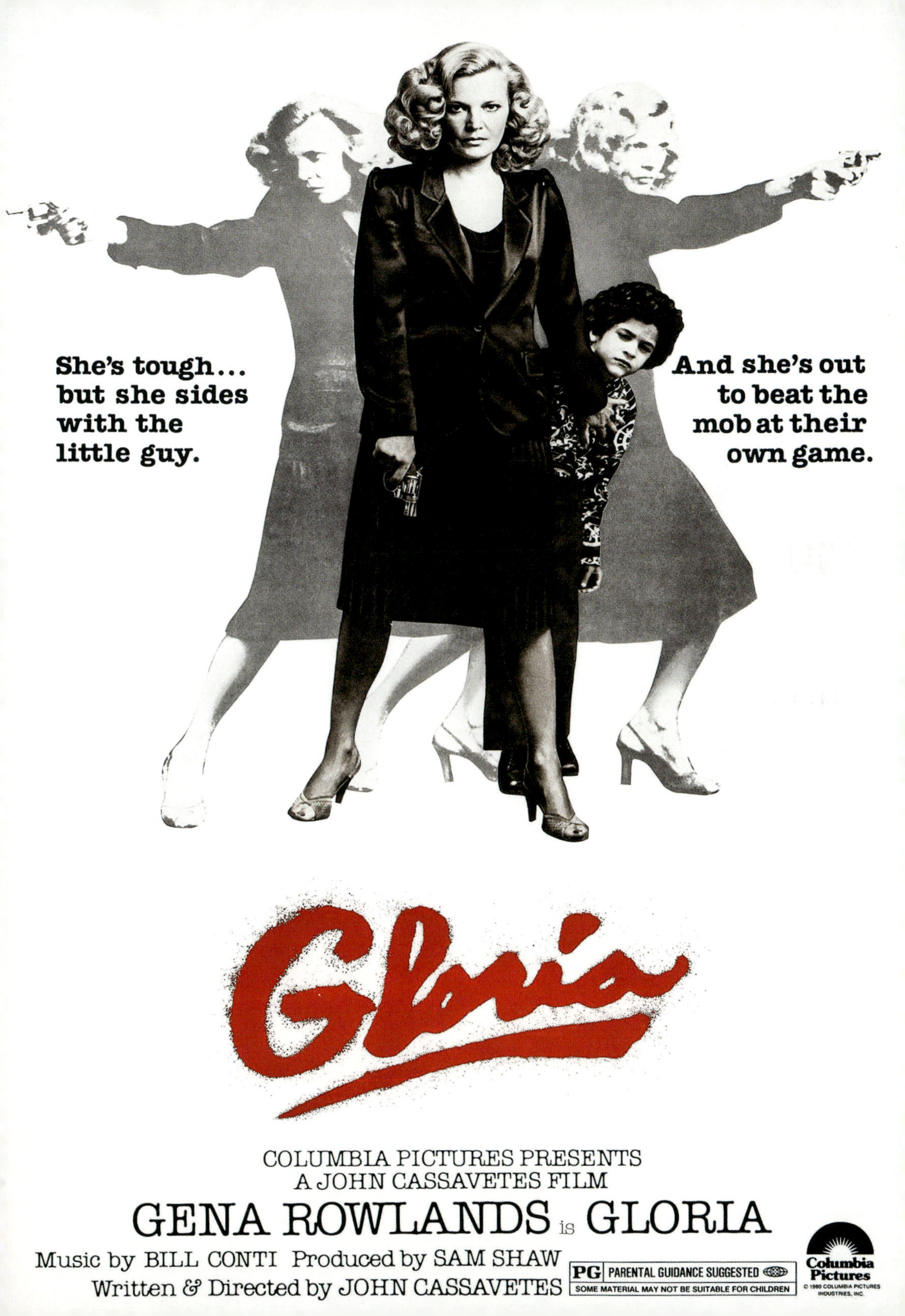

She's tough...
but she sides
with the
little guy.

And she's out
to beat the
mob at their
own game.

COLUMBIA PICTURES PRESENTS
A JOHN CASSAVETES FILM

GENA ROWLANDS is GLORIA

Music by BILL CONTI Produced by SAM SHAW
Written & Directed by JOHN CASSAVETES

1
2

"I'm saving your life, stupid."

Gena Rowlands is Gloria, a tough-talking dame ready to take on the world. A human tornado, she storms through New York by bus, subway, taxi or whatever means of transportation she can find. Her only peace is the occasional pit stop she makes at the odd small hotel to escape the strain. Armed with a shoulder bag containing a large caliber revolver she'll draw at the drop of a hat, this hell-raiser will go to lethal extremes to protect the small boy in her care from a motley bunch of gangsters. Gloria doesn't know why she does it, telling the boy's mother how she can't stand kids, just before his entire family is massacred. "I hate kids. Especially your kids." In this case, it's not exactly a surprise. Seven-year-old Phil (John Adames) is a brat, a pint-sized pain-in-the-ass, who harps on his Hispanic heritage. The audience would fully approve of her putting the kid on the next train to New Jersey with no return ticket. But against her better judgment, Gloria gives him cover and aids his escape. We don't doubt her strength for a second. Right at the beginning of this exercise in urban turmoil, the gangsters confront her openly on the street. Unfazed, she draws her pistol and sends the car-full of her former chums to Kingdom Come without so much as batting an eyelash. Her encore tops the act itself, as with a nonchalant wave of the hand and the magic word "Taxi," she casually hails a yellow limousine.

There is no reason to doubt that Gloria Swenson was indeed once a gangster bride, or "slut," as she puts it. We wouldn't believe her if she claimed the contrary. A living, breathing maelstrom, Gena Rowlands simply sweeps the audience away with the intoxicating presence of a true star. Gloria is swashbuckling, elegant, unpretentious, and capable of anything. In her husband John Cassavetes' other films, Rowlands had always portrayed women on the verge of a nervous breakdown, and these extraordinary performances were a fair suggestion of what might happen were such a fireball ever to get her hands on a gun. An action film like this was most out of character for Cassavetes. The unbridled camera, an expression of the inner unrest of his protagonists, had previously been the trademark of all his projects in the cinema. Yet *Gloria* manages to burst with physical movement just the same. It is not gangster movie conventions, but rather the individual fears of regular people forced into conformity that drive both the narrative and this "hard-boiled momma" to decisive action.

Cassavetes originally wrote the screenplay with the intention of selling it to finance his more "difficult" films. This plan was quickly put to rest, however, when it turned out to be the perfect script for Gena Rowlands and

GENA ROWLANDS "The way she lights a cigarette is a great argument for smoking," remarked actress Winona Ryder after working with Rowlands in Jim Jarmusch's *Night on Earth* (1991). Gena Rowlands' performance as a burnt-out casting agent was her most important role since the death of her husband John Cassavetes. The daughter of a Wisconsin senator, Gena Rowlands (1930–2024) stood at the side of the legendary filmmaker for a total of seven productions. No small feat, but the admiration of many actresses—not to mention directors like Jim Jarmusch and actors like Sean Penn—goes far deeper. Rowlands' sensitive, personal and always modern portrayals of off-the-wall women made her a symbol of female honesty and dignity at a time when the sophistication of Hollywood *grandes dames* like Lauren Bacall and Bette Davis was a thing of the past. She received Oscar nominations for both her hyperactive *tour de force* in *A Woman Under the Influence* (1974) and her extraordinary *Gloria* (1980). For her work in the film *Opening Night* (1977), she was awarded the Best Actress Silver Bear at the International Film Festival in Berlin. Rowlands has worked with Woody Allen, Terence Davies, and Peter Chelsom, and appeared in two films directed by her son, Nick Cassavetes. In 2015 she received an Honorary Academy Award for her life's work.

1 Legendary actress Gena Rowlands plays a chain-smoking, no nonsense momma in a one of a kind picture—Bonnie Parker, eat your heart out.

2 Don't cross Momma! Armed or not, Gloria's mere presence is enough to make mobsters quake with fear.

3 A friend in need: Jeri Dawn (Julie Carmen) turns to Gloria when the lives of her loved ones are at stake.

4 Ratifying the ERA: Gloria blasts the path clear for mini macho Phil (John Adames) and shows those suckers who's boss.

5 Cry baby cavalier: Seven year-old Phil may fancy himself a pint-sized Valentino, but he'd be more convincing if he'd just shut his trap.

6 Do not disturb: Gloria often grabs some shuteye at local hotels to stay fresh for the fight.

"I don't like kids. I hate kids. Especially your kids."

Film quote: Gloria

Columbia Pictures. Here, the great architect of "personal American film" deals with subject matter existing entirely within the context of film and film history. Subtle yet instantaneous, the image of Hollywood diva Gloria Swanson is evoked in the very name of the protagonist. We can see the affection she eventually develops for her protégé Phil coming on from the very start of the picture.

The film's ending also draws from traditional motherly roles, when the dead heroine appears in a fairy tale-like resurrection as loving grandmother. "This is a dream," Gloria repeatedly tells the boy to make the incomprehensible loss bearable. The deceptive realism of the grubby world of tenement shafts and dirty subway tunnels is no exception.

The film developed into a true Cassavetes project in its depiction of the subtle relationship between Gloria and Phil. The reversal of the gender roles is anything but an ironic end in itself. Flouting convention, the two don't play mother and child, but rather husband and wife. Phil is "one of the best guys I've ever slept with," Gloria tells her ex-lover Mafia boss, expertly hitting him where it hurts. She sees through the childish self-inflation in the macho lines the wannabe mobster throws after his veritable Ma Baker. In *Gloria*, the great indy filmmaker suavely unmasks the masculine hubris of the genre and its gangsters, who seldom appear as ridiculous as they do here. He just sets his wife on them. After all, Cassavetes always hated gangsters.

PB

RAGING BULL

1980 – USA – 129 MIN.

GENRE

BOXING FILM, BIOPIC, DRAMA

DIRECTOR

MARTIN SCORSESE

SCREENPLAY

PAUL SCHRADER, MARDIK MARTIN
from the autobiography of JAKE LA MOTTA
together with JOSEPH CARTER and PETER SAVAGE

DIRECTOR OF PHOTOGRAPHY

MICHAEL CHAPMAN

EDITING

THELMA SCHOONMAKER

MUSIC

PIETRO MASCAGNI (*Cavalleria Rusticana*),
diverse songs arranged by ROBBIE ROBERTSON

PRODUCTION

ROBERT CHARTOFF, IRWIN WINKLER for
CHARTOFF-WINKLER PRODUCTIONS, UNITED ARTISTS

STARRING

ROBERT DE NIRO (Jake La Motta),
CATHY MORIARTY (Vickie La Motta),
JOE PESCI (Joey La Motta), FRANK VINCENT (Salvy),
NICHOLAS COLASANTO (Tommy Como),
THERESA SALDANA (Lenore La Motta),
MARIO GALLO (Mario), FRANK ADONIS (Patsy),
JOSEPH BONO (Guido), FRANK TOPHAM (Toppy)

ACADEMY AWARDS 1981

OSCARS for BEST ACTOR (Robert De Niro),
and BEST EDITING (Thelma Schoonmaker)

ROBERT DE NIRO

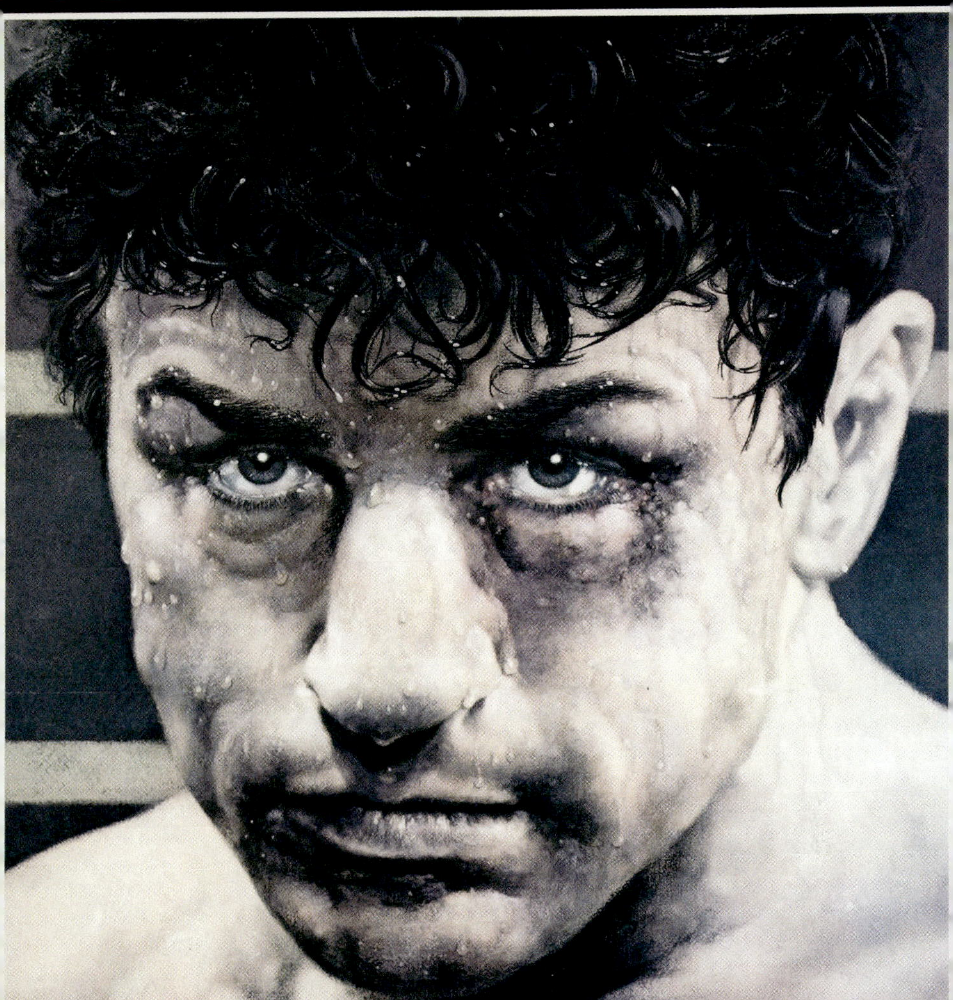

"RAGING BULL"

A ROBERT CHARTOFF-IRWIN WINKLER PRODUCTION
ROBERT DE NIRO
in A MARTIN SCORSESE PICTURE
"RAGING BULL"

Produced in association with PETER SAVAGE Screenplay by PAUL SCHRADER and MARDIK MARTIN
Based on the book by JAKE LA MOTTA with JOSEPH CARTER and PETER SAVAGE
Director of photography MICHAEL CHAPMAN
Produced by IRWIN WINKLER and ROBERT CHARTOFF Directed by MARTIN SCORSESE

R RESTRICTED
UNDER 17 REQUIRES ACCOMPANYING PARENT OR ADULT GUARDIAN

Read the Bantam Book

Copyright © 1980 United Artists Corporation. All rights reserved.

United Artists
A Transamerica Company

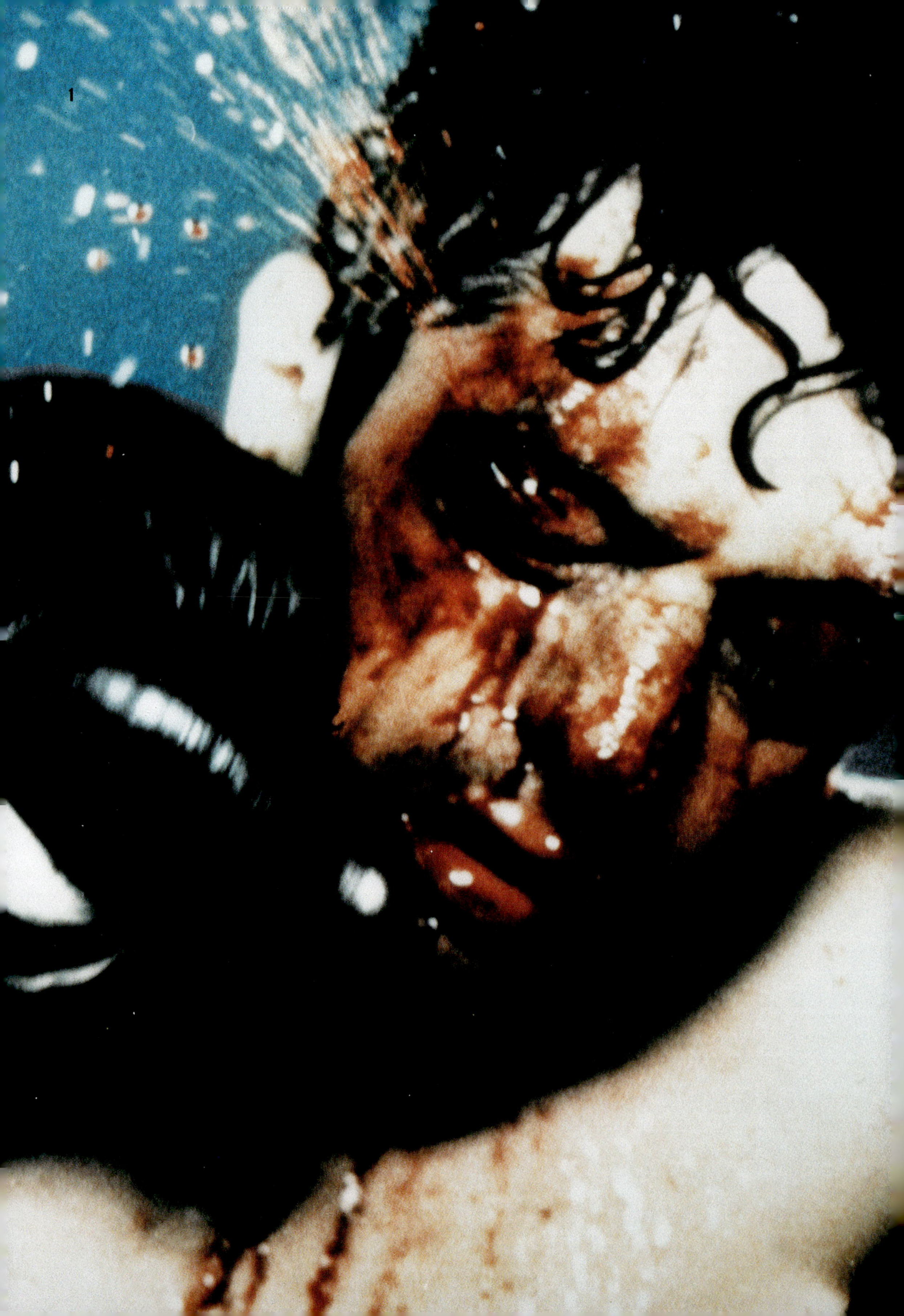

1

It is the beginning of the 40s and Jake La Motta (Robert De Niro) is one of the top middleweight boxers in the world. He's the "Raging Bull," famous for an almost inhuman ability to take a beating and notorious for his unpredictable attacks. He's not a stylist, he's a brutal puncher whose strength comes from a deep-seated aggression he is unable to control—inside or outside of the ring. The brunt of Jake's aggression is leveled at his wife, but his brother and manager Joey (Joe Pesci) are also forced to weather his temper. Even in his interaction with the Mafiosi from Little Italy, Jake is anything but diplomatic. This erratic behavior contributes to his continually being denied a title fight. He soon meets Vickie (Cathy Moriarty), a blonde beauty who is already hanging out with the gangsters of Hell's Kitchen, despite being only 15 years old. Jake gets a divorce and marries her. But he is not calmed down. In fact, his jealous outbursts intensify and he terrorizes everyone around him. When he finally gets the chance to fight for the title in 1949, his predictable demise has been years in the making.

Robert De Niro had long dreamed of acting in a cinematic adaptation of Jake La Motta's autobiography. In the midst of shooting of *Alice Doesn't Live Here Anymore* (1974), he tried to convince Martin Scorsese to direct the project. Though initially unsuccessful, De Niro did not relent. He took another shot at it while Scorsese lay in a hospital bed, psychologically and physically lacerated by the disaster of *New York, New York* (1977). This time around the

MICHAEL CHAPMAN Michael Chapman (1941–2021) became one of the most sought-after American cameramen toward the mid 70s. He began by working as a camera operator for Gordon Willis, whose "classicism" became a major influence. Films he worked on during this period include Alan J. Pakula's thriller *Klute* (1971) and Coppola's *The Godfather* (1972). In 1973, Chapman became director of photography for the first time in Hal Ashby's tragicomedy *The Last Detail*, followed by the Arctic film *The White Dawn* (1974), the first of four collaborations with Philip Kaufman. Chapman worked as operator once again for Spielberg's *Jaws* (1975) before experiencing his real breakthrough with the legendary Scorsese film, *Taxi Driver* (1975), in which he beautifully transmitted the threatening atmosphere of a *Film Noir* into color images. Chapman proved his mastery of black-and-white photography with another Scorsese film, *Raging Bull* (1980), for which he received his first Oscar nomination, and later with Carl Reiner's lovely *Film Noir* homage, *Dead Men Don't Wear Plaid* (1981). In 1993 he received his second Oscar nomination for *The Fugitive*. Chapman repeatedly appeared in small roles as an actor, and had directed films himself since 1983, though without the impact he had as a cameraman. In 2004 he was awarded a Lifetime Achievement Award by the American Society of Cinematographers.

“I put everything I knew and felt into this film, and I thought it would finish my career. I call it ‘kamikaze’, this way of making films: put all of yourself into it, then forget it and start a new life.”

Martin Scorsese, in: Martin Scorsese, David Thompson, Ian Christie (eds.), Scorsese on Scorsese

1 Blood, sweat and tears: *Raging Bull* captures the sheer physicality of the fights in merciless close-up.

2 Method acting and a few black eyes: In order to give a convincing depiction of "The Bronx Bull," Robert De Niro spent months training as a boxer, and even fought some fights as an amateur. He was rewarded for his efforts with an Oscar.

3 Professional scene-stealer: Joe Pesci (left) worked alongside Robert De Niro in the Scorsese masterpieces *Goodfellas* (1989) and *Casino* (1995).

director was fascinated by the subject matter, seizing on La Motta's self-destructive life story as a chance to exorcise his own demons. The film therefore focuses less on the boxer's career—the fight scenes are relatively brief—than the story of a man tortured by his own existence, a man who has only himself to blame for his downfall. The fact that La Motta grew up in the same milieu of Italian immigrants that Scorsese knew well from his own childhood intensified his identification with the subject matter.

Raging Bull was the challenge of a lifetime for De Niro. In the role of Jake La Motta, he radically explored the limits of his craft. The convincing physical presence De Niro lends to the violence La Motta turned on himself and others is as fascinating as it is terrifying. In order to make the fight scenes as believable as possible, he trained —partially under the guidance of La Motta—for months and on several occasions even fought a real bout. Legend has it that De Niro gained over fifty pounds to personify the aging La Motta, who traveled from nightclub to nightclub as a fat has-been entertainer.

The film's technical quality—its skilful sound design and editing—is just as extraordinary as De Niro's Oscar-winning performance, and the rest of the acting. Michael Chapman deserves a special mention for his excellent black-and-white photography, which captures the private life of the boxer with a merciless sobriety that recalls Italian neorealism and the "semi-documentaries" of the 40s. The camera often stands still and focuses on La Motta's violent outbursts. Squeezed into the frame, he resembles an animal caught in a cage, unable to come to

4 Sick with jealousy: Mindless violence soon characterizes Jake's relationship with wife Vicky (Cathy Moriarty).

5 A beached whale: De Niro put on fifty pounds …

6 … to depict Jake La Motta in his decline.

7 That's *amore*: Martin Scorsese, the son of Sicilian immigrants, depicts the Italian milieu in 40s and 50s New York with a documentary filmmaker's attention to detail.

terms with the lack of space and powerless to free himself from its constraints. Jake's torturous frustrations are so painfully depicted in these images that the boxing matches begin to seem like a necessary consequence of his life. The extent of his spiritual barrenness becomes clear during the fights. The camera zooms in on the action in the ring, approaching La Motta's subjective perception. Fists pummel body and face from close range, spraying blood and sweat, the images acoustically underscored by dull blows that sound as if they come from the inside out. The violence exploding in these rapidly edited images have an edge of soothing intimacy. It appears that La Motta is only able to truly express himself within the confines of the ring. He is a lonely man for whom punches are not only a reward, but a means of communication.

JH

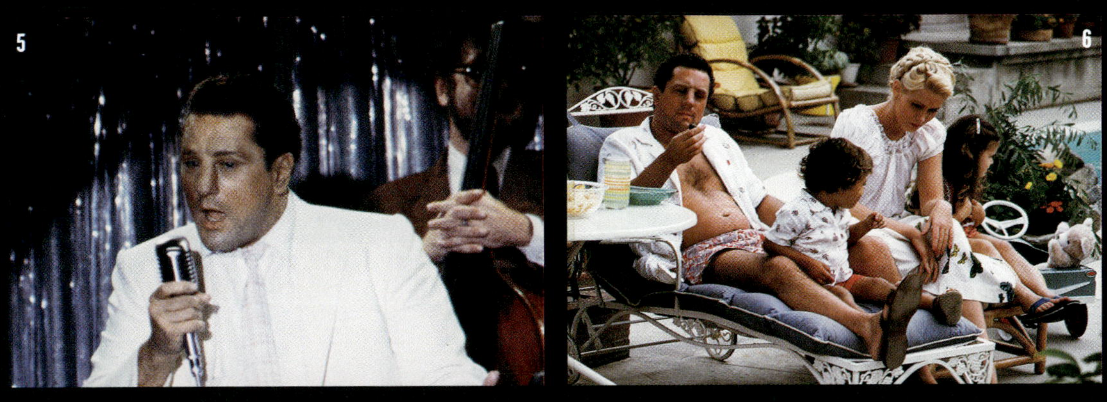

5

6

"An American masterwork, a fusion of Hollywood genre with personal vision couched in images and sounds that are kinetic and visceral, and closer to poetry than pulp." *The Village Voice*

7

THE BLUES BROTHERS

1980 – USA – 133 MIN.

GENRE

MUSIC FILM, COMEDY

DIRECTOR

JOHN LANDIS

SCREENPLAY

DAN AYKROYD, JOHN LANDIS

DIRECTOR OF PHOTOGRAPHY

STEPHEN M. KATZ

EDITING

GEORGE FOLSEY JR.

MUSIC

ELMER BERNSTEIN

PRODUCTION

ROBERT K. WEISS for UNIVERSAL PICTURES

STARRING

JOHN BELUSHI ("Joliet" Jake Blues), DAN AYKROYD (Elwood Blues), KATHLEEN FREEMAN (Sister Mary), CAB CALLOWAY (Curtis), JAMES BROWN (Reverend Cleophus James), RAY CHARLES (Ray), ARETHA FRANKLIN (Mrs. Murphy), CARRIE FISHER (Camille Ztdetelik), JOHN CANDY (Burton Mercer), ALAN RUBIN (Mr. Fabulous), HENRY GIBSON (Nazi-Leader)

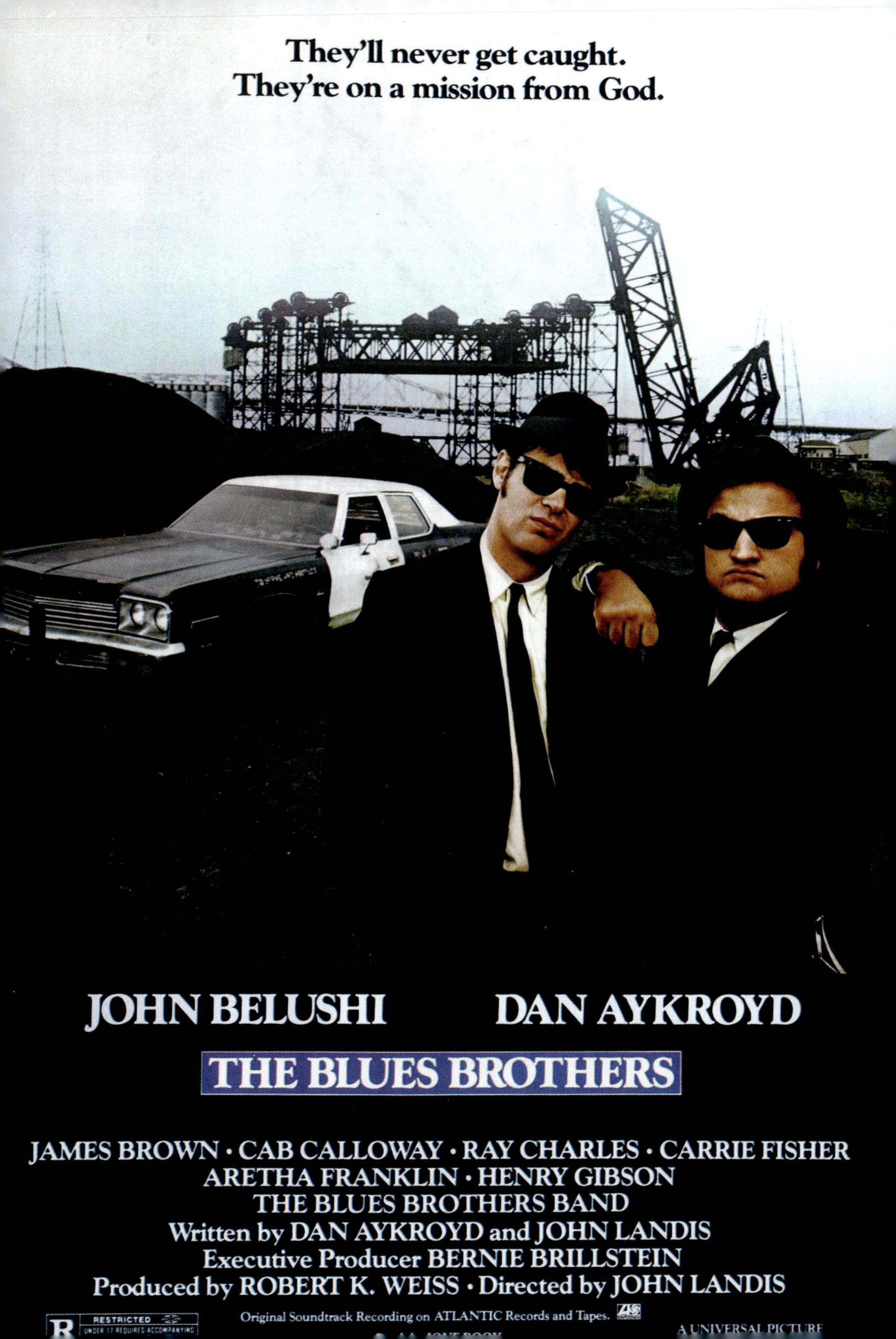
They'll never get caught.
They're on a mission from God.
JOHN BELUSHI
DAN AYKROYD
THE BLUES BROTHERS
JAMES BROWN · CAB CALLOWAY · RAY CHARLES · CARRIE FISHER
ARETHA FRANKLIN · HENRY GIBSON
THE BLUES BROTHERS BAND
Written by DAN AYKROYD and JOHN LANDIS
Executive Producer BERNIE BRILLSTEIN
Produced by ROBERT K. WEISS · Directed by JOHN LANDIS
R RESTRICTED
UNDER 17 REQUIRES ACCOMPANYING
Original Soundtrack Recording on ATLANTIC Records and Tapes.
A UNIVERSAL PICTURE

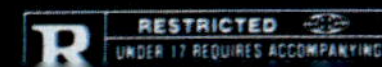

1

"We're on a mission from God!"

Strange that *The Blues Brothers* was initially a flop in the United States. The film has everything an action comedy could possibly require: two television comedy stars, breakneck chase sequences, laconically comic dialogues, and guest appearances by stars including James Brown, Aretha Franklin, John Lee Hooker, Ray Charles, and Cab Calloway. And naturally it has the Blues Brothers themselves, John Belushi and Dan Aykroyd, the most explosive duo since nitro and glycerin (at least that's how the advertising slogan billed them). *The Blues Brothers* first achieved cult status in Europe—and perhaps no other film has shown as often in program cinemas, university theaters, and drive-in theatres.

Why Americans initially gave the film the cold shoulder may also have been due to the abject contempt of the critics: "The massive scale of the production smacks of desperation. Faced with a script devoid of wit or invention, director Landis relies entirely on diversionary tactics—more cars, more extras, more crashes. Has anyone heard of more rewrites?" asked *Newsweek*. Were they looking at the same script? Take the Blues Brothers as they speed through a red light and promptly have a police cruiser hot on their heels:

Elwood Blues: "Shit!"
Jake Blues: "What?"
Elwood Blues: "Rollers."
Jake Blues: "No!"
Elwood Blues: "Yeah."
Jake Blues: "Shit!"

With their black suits, black hats, and dark sunglasses, the Blues Brothers are the essence of cool. Jake (John Belushi), just released from prison, and his brother Elwood (Dan Aykroyd), need to dig up $5,000 to save the Catholic orphanage in which they grew up. During a sermon by Reverend Cleophus James (James Brown), Jake has an epiphany: a tour with their old R&B band! Their first task is to gather together all the musicians. And they do this in their own style. Mr. Fabulous (Alan Rubin), one of

JOHN BELUSHI He was small and fat, but he sure had a temper. Sometimes his energy almost burst out of him at the end of his sketches. John Belushi shot to the top, became a star but then crashed just as quickly as he had arrived. "It's better to burn out than to fade away"—the Neil Young line could have been written for Belushi.

The American comedy show *Saturday Night Live* began in 1975. John Belushi, 26 at the time, was soon to become a star. He appeared as a samurai, a killer bee, as Captain Kirk, and Marlon Brando's Godfather, and often in the company of brother James or Dan Aykroyd, with whom he invented the *Blues Brothers* characters.

In 1978 Belushi left television and took his chances on the big screen. He made his brief debut in Jack Nicholson's Western *Goin' South*. In the same year he played the lead role in *National Lampoon's Animal House* by *The Blues Brothers* director John Landis. He played the dirty, crass, offensive role once again in Steven Spielberg's *1941* (1979), after which came *The Blues Brothers* (1980). Then he tried his luck in Michael Apted's romantic comedy *Continental Divide* (1981). John Belushi died in 1982 from the effects of his excessive drug use. Contributing to his cult status was Bob Woodward's biography, *Wired. The Short Life and Fast Times of John Belushi.*

1 Shake Your Tailfeather: Ray Charles accompanies the Blues Brothers on the electric piano.

2 Hit the road, Jake: In the early summer of 1980, the Blues Brothers Band went on a 22-concert tour. It was one of the many “high” points of Belushi’s (left) career. Right, Dan Aykroyd.

3 Wanted dead or insane: The police have been authorized to “use of unnecessary violence in the apprehension of the Blues Brothers.”

4 Special guest from another star: Carrie Fisher also appeared on the hit TV series *Saturday Night Live*—birthplace of the Blues Brothers.

5 Heil, heil the gang’s all here! Illinois Nazis in hot pursuit of the Blues Brothers. Soundtrack care of Richard Wagner.

Elwood Blues: “It’s 106 miles to Chicago, we’ve got a full tank of gas, half a pack of cigarettes, it’s dark and we’re wearing sunglasses.” _Jake Blues_: “Hit it!” *Film quote: Elwood Blues and “Joliet” Jake Blues*

their band mates, works in a high-class restaurant and has no intention of ever blowing his trumpet again. But a short visit from Jake and Elwood to “Chez Paul” soon puts an end to his hesitation: they burp, slurp champagne, and toss food into each another’s mouths—he is left with no alternative but to capitulate and come along.

The Blues Brothers implement any means necessary to fulfill their mission. The destruction left in their wake is irrelevant. They don’t look back and don’t look forward—they are pure present tense. The film could be viewed as a subversive attack on the state and the white establishment: Jake and Elwood destroy a shopping center with their car, stir up a group of Nazis, and liven up a country bar with their soulful rendition of "Gimme Some Lovin'." When the cowboy hat and plaid-shirt-wearing audience showers them with boos and beer bottles, they placate the enraged mob by singing "Rawhide," the title song of a Western television series starring redneck Clint Eastwood.

Right off the bat, the film caricatures state law and order, such as when Jake is given his worldly possessions with ridiculously exacting bureaucracy—he receives one condom, unused, and one condom, used. The Blues Brothers don't seem to be familiar with traffic rules—Elwood has 116 unpaid parking tickets and 56 additional tickets for other violations. In the end, numerous white police cars chase after the one black "Bluesmobile," and tanks drive into the building in which Jake and Elwood are just able to settle the debts of the orphanage. It seems that the worst enemy does not threaten society from outside, but rather corrodes its values from within. And the state is forced to battle this cancer with the heaviest artillery available.

The joy of destruction, acerbic word play, and infectious music conspire to make *The Blues Brothers* a unique film experience. John Belushi became a legend in the role of Jake Blues. His most memorable scene is the moment when he takes off his sunglasses because an ex-girlfriend of his (Carrie Fisher) is blocking his way with an automatic rifle. Jake falls on his knees before her, begs her to spare his life, and twitches his eyebrows. She can't resist those eyes. She jumps into his arms and he promptly drops her into the mud. After all, Jake and Elwood are on a mission from God. And there are still 106 miles to Chicago—and many, many cars still need to be totaled during the final chase. NM

3

4

5

KAGEMUSHA

1980 – JAPAN – 159 MIN.

GENRE

HISTORICAL FILM, EPIC

DIRECTOR

AKIRA KUROSAWA

SCREENPLAY

AKIRA KUROSAWA, MASATO IDE

DIRECTOR OF PHOTOGRAPHY

TAKAO SAITÔ, MASAHARU UEDA

EDITING

AKIRA KUROSAWA

MUSIC

SHIN'ICHIRÔ IKEBE

PRODUCTION

AKIRA KUROSAWA, MASATO IDE for TOHO

STARRING

TATSUYA NAKADAI (Shingen Takeda / Kagemusha),
TSUTOMU YAMAZAKI (Nobukado Takeda),
KENICHI HAGIWARA (Katsuyori Takeda), DAISUKE RYU (Nobunaga Oda),
MASAYUKI YUI (Ieyasu Tokugawa), KOTA YUI (Takemaru Takeda),
SHUJI OTAKI (Masakage Yamagata), HIDEO MUROTA (Nobufusa Baba),
TAKAYUKI SHIHO (Masatoyo Naito), SHUHEI SUGIMORI (Masanobu Kosaka)

IFF CANNES 1980

GOLDEN PALM (Akira Kurosawa)

さすがは信玄 死してなお三年の間よくぞこの信長をたばかった！
影武者
黒澤明監督作品
武田信玄 その影武者 仲代達矢
武田信廉 山崎努
武田勝頼 萩原健一
山県昌景 大滝秀治
馬場信春 室田日出男
内藤昌豊 志甫隆之
高坂弾正 杉森修平
原昌胤 清水のぼる
跡部大炊助 清水紘治
小山田信茂 山本亘
土屋宗八郎 根津甚八
雨宮善二郎 阿藤海
原甚五郎 島香裕
甘利おくら 金窪英一
友野又市 宮崎雄吾
おゆうの方 倍賞美津子
お津弥の方 桃井かおり
織田信長 隆大介
森蘭丸 山中康仁
徳川家康 油井昌由樹
上杉謙信 清水利比古
田口刑部 志村喬
医師 藤原釜足
海外版エグゼクティブプロデューサー フランシス・コッポラ ジョージ・ルーカス
東宝

1

2

"A shadow is a shadow and must remain a shadow."

Three men, identically dressed, are sitting in a spartanly furnished room: one on a podium; the second on the floor to his right, the third some distance away. The first man is Prince Shingen Takeda, the second is his brother and advisor, the third is a thief under sentence of death (both he and Shingen are played by Tatsuya Nakadai). The thief bears a striking resemblance to his lord and master, and is about to be employed as his double. This six-minute scene precedes the opening titles. Filmed with a static camera, it embodies the formal asceticism of the entire film and announces its essential themes: hierarchy and power, honor and betrayal.

It's 1573, and Japan is being torn apart by a bloody civil war. Shingen Takeda is engaged in a bitter struggle for mastery of the country with his two rivals Nobunaga Oda (Daisuke Ryu) and Ieyasu Tokugawa (Masayuki Yui). Besieging a castle, Shingen is wounded by a marksman and dies. His last will is that the campaign be abandoned and his death kept secret for three years. Accordingly, the thief is installed as his double—or "shadow." Court society is not informed of the deception, nor are the concubines, nor even Shingen's grandson—chosen by Shingen to succeed him on the throne. The only people informed are the most important generals, among them Shingen's illegitimate

JAPAN AS FILM NATION When Akira Kurosawa's *Rashomon* (1950) won the Golden Lion at the Venice Film Festival, Japan suddenly appeared on the map of international cinematography. Although films have been made in Japan since 1899, this was the first time the West had really noticed Japan as a "film nation." Three artists became known above all: Kurosawa (1910–1998) was the all-round genius, who could handle both historical and contemporary material; Yasujirô Ozu (1903–1963) was the master of strict form, who found his great theme in the "family;" and Kenji Mizoguchi (1898–1956) became famous for his long uncut scenes and films that examined the place of women in society. All three made "art films," but there was also plenty of popular cinema—for example, the numerous Godzilla films from 1954 onwards. In the 60s, in parallel to the West, Japan produced its own kind of *Nouvelle Vague*, whose most outstanding representative was Nagisa Oshima (*Night and Fog in Japan/Nihon no yoru to kiri*, 1960). The 80s were dominated by "Young Turks" such as Sôgo Ishii (*Crazy Family/Gyakufunsha kazoku*, 1984), who demonstrated astonishing formal strengths and who often took a highly critical view of Japanese civilization. Katsuhiro Ôtomo's *Akira* (1988) was the first major film adaptation of a Japanese comic (manga) to achieve international success. A highpoint in the popularity of these "animes" was marked by Hayao Miyazaki's *Spirited Away* (*Sen to Chihiro no kamikakushi*, 2001), which won the Golden Bear at the IFF in Berlin in 2002.

son Katsuyori (Kenichi Hagiwara). Almost three years elapse before the trick comes to light. Then Katsuyori seizes power, goes to war, and loses the battle of Nagashino…

Kagemusha is based on real historical events. The film takes place before the Edo period, during the civil war in which several princes fought for control of the country. The Battle of Nagashino was the first to be decided by the use of firearms. In 1603, Ieyasu Tokugawa united the country under his rule. *Kagemusha*'s basic constellation is historically accurate, as are some of the details (such as the use of doubles and the appearance of Jesuit monks in

"The century depicted in *Kagemusha* was distinguished by an aesthetic stance that also influenced the ritual of warfare. I wanted to document this martial aesthetic." *Akira Kurosawa, in: Le Monde*

1 Charge!!! Nobunaga Oda (Daisuke Ryu, second from right) and his compatriots en route to pillage the village.

2 Shingen's illegitimate son Katsuyori advances into the Battle of Nagashino, at which he will suffer a devastating defeat.

3 Ghosts of the past: "I love the 16th century. In Japan, it was an age full of Shakespearean emotions." (Akira Kurosawa)

4 Life insurance: Samurai general Shingen Takeda (Tatsuya Nakadai, center) drafts a policy that will make sure his loved ones are provided for.

5 Looks like a tea ceremony, smells like a coup: Only the most select commanders are privy to the scam involving the dead general's double.

Japan). On this basis, Kurosawa created an overwhelming epic of war and peace, a story told on several different levels. At one level, the film is a psychological drama, showing the ruses and deceptions employed by princes and generals in order to rule and conquer—and showing how the "shadow" Kagemusha comes to terms with his existence as a double. At another level, *Kagemusha* is a splendid battle picture with brilliantly choreographed crowd scenes. Again and again, stylized and very beautiful tableau-like images are inserted, for example the shot in which we see people before a lurid sunset. But however much Kurosawa aestheticizes the war, he never makes it look harmless; one never sees the butchery itself, but the horrible aftermath of corpses and mangled bodies.

As so often, Kurosawa had difficulty getting the film produced. Since his previous work *Dersu Uzala* (1975), he had developed three projects—among them *Kagemusha* —but found a production company for none of them. It was only when American directors Francis Ford Coppola and George Lucas persuaded Twentieth Century Fox to buy the foreign rights to *Kagemusha* for 1.5 million dollars that his regular production firm Toho decided to produce the film. With a budget of 9 million dollars, it was the most expensive Japanese film ever made; but with box-office takings of 10 million dollars, it also became the most successful. It received Oscar nominations for Best Art Direction and Best Foreign Film.

HJK

ATLANTIC CITY

1980 – CANADA / USA / FRANCE – 105 MIN.

GENRE

DRAMA

DIRECTOR

LOUIS MALLE

SCREENPLAY

JOHN GUARE

DIRECTOR OF PHOTOGRAPHY

RICHARD CIUPKA

EDITING

SUZANNE BARON

MUSIC

MICHEL LEGRAND

PRODUCTION

DENIS HÉROUX for CINE-NEIGHBOUR INC., SELTA FILMS, INTERNATIONAL CINEMA CORPORATION, PARAMOUNT PICTURES, MERCHANT FILMS

STARRING

BURT LANCASTER (Lou Paschall), SUSAN SARANDON (Sally Matthews), KATE REID (Grace), ROBERT JOY (Dave Matthews), MICHEL PICCOLI (Joseph), HOLLIS MCLAREN (Chrissie), AL WAXMAN (Alfie), MOSES ZNAIMER (Felix), ANGUS MACINNES (Vinnie), WALLACE SHAWN (Waiter)

IFF VENICE 1980

GOLDEN LION

Where dreamers can be winners.

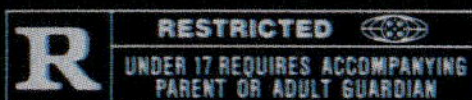

1

2

"The world should be your oyster."

In some films, the true protagonist is the location. The laconic title of this Louis Malle movie certainly suggests it's true in this case. During the 40s, this city on the east coast of the USA was an elegant watering hole. By the 70s, though, Atlantic City had become a mere shadow of its former self: the hotels were crumbling, the promenade was decidedly undercrowded, and the people who lived here formed a panopticon of stranded souls.

There wasn't much life here, but suddenly there was hope: in 1979, gambling was legalized in New Jersey. The city awoke, threw away its crutches, and set out to make its fortune as a second Las Vegas. In Malle's film, which manages to combine a heavy heart with a light touch, this renaissance is marked, tellingly, by the demolition of the decrepit Grand Hotel.

Like the hotel, Lou Paschall (Burt Lancaster) is an embodiment and a leftover of the old days. For him, even the Atlantic is not what it used to be. Once he was a hood with ambitions, running messages for the Godfathers of big-time crime. Now, he's at the beck and call of Grace (Kate Reid), a dilapidated, hypochondriac diva, and her neurotic lapdogs. He's also a small-time bookie on the side, raking in the cents from the little guys who hope Lady Luck might yet come through for them.

While Lou himself has no illusions that better times are just around the corner, Sally (Susan Sarandon) is training in her spare time to become a croupier. She already earns a living in the casino, behind the counter of a seafood buffet; when she gets home, she rubs herself down with fresh lemons to get rid of the stink of fish. Lou lives

CASINOS IN THE MOVIES Las Vegas, Reno and Atlantic City are the biggest casino towns in the USA, and they've also provided the backdrops to a range of very different films. Barry Levinson's *Bugsy* (1991) depicts the last years in the life of Bugsy Siegel, a mobster whose criminal energies played a decisive role in the rise of Vegas. Scorsese's *Casino* (1995) is another movie based on a true story, and it's also set in the Mafia milieu. Glamour, good-time girls and extravagant shows—the racy reputation of these dazzling cities was based on much more than mere gambling. In real-life Las Vegas, the legendary "Rat Pack" painted the town red: in one cinematic version of the gambler's paradise, Frank Sinatra, Dean Martin, Sammy Davis Jr., Peter Lawford, actually robbed a Vegas casino; their criminal caper *Ocean's Eleven* appeared in 1960, while Steven Soderbergh's remake came out in 2001. The latter also boasted an all-star ensemble, featuring George Clooney, Brad Pitt, and Julia Roberts. Casinos are often the locations of human tragedies, as in Karel Reisz's *The Gambler* (1974), starring James Caan, or Paul Thomas Anderson's remarkable feature-film debut *Sydney,* aka *Hard Eight* (1995). In the noir classic *Gilda* (1946), a casino becomes the scene of a murky three-way relationship. The *crème de la crème* of the comedy scene has also discovered the casino as a movie location—see *Dirty Rotten Scoundrels* (1988), or *Vegas Vacation* (1996). Last but not least, a visit to a casino is obligatory for Agent 007. In *Dr. No* (1962), Sean Connery was positioned at a roulette table when he first uttered his most famous line: "My name is Bond… James Bond".

in the apartment opposite, and watches her perform this mysterious erotic ritual every evening.

One day, Sally gets an unexpected visit from a hippie couple: It's her long-lost husband Dave (Robert Joy) and the woman he ran away with—her sister Chrissie (Hollis McLaren). They have stolen a packet of cocaine from the Mafia, and now they need a place to lie low for a while. Lou agrees to help them carry out a drugs deal. A short time later Dave is dead, so Lou carries on alone, quickly making enough money to take on the role of Sally's sugar daddy. Naturally, though, the Mob has already got its beady eye on him—and Lou soon has a real opportunity to prove he's a hero.

In 1981, *Atlantic City* was nominated for five Academy Awards—Best Film, Best Actor, Best Actress, Best Director, and Best Original Screenplay—and won none. Though the film has an American setting, it tells its story with a "European" tempo and rhythm, allowing its brilliant actors enough space to develop their characters. This includes even the supporting players, like Michel Piccoli in the role of Joseph, Sally's teacher and lover. It's one of Malle's greatest strengths that he passes no moral judgment on his characters, a stance reflected in Lou's attitude towards an old friend who now works as a shoeshine boy in a restroom. Lou leaves the man guessing about his own situation, but always treats him with genuine and unpatronising respect.

It's the so-called little guys that interest Malle: those who are filled with the hope of a better life held out by the American Dream, though they can so easily end up as

1 Lucky in love? To hell with it! Sally (Susan Sarandon) and Lou (Burt Lancaster) would rather take their chances with the cards.

2 Crapping out: What happens to guys like Lou when they get mixed up in other people's business?

3 Full speed ahead: For Lou there's just no turning back.

4 Beaten at his own game: After enlisting Lou to deliver drugs, Dave (Robert Joy) soon finds himself on the road to nowhere.

5 Don't talk to strangers: Sally hasn't the foggiest what these people want from her.

6 Game over. Please try again: Sophisticated Joseph (Michel Piccoli) breaks in new dealers and opens up a whole new world to Sally.

3

4

5

"It takes Malle a little while to set up the crisscrossing of the ten or twelve major characters, but once he does, the film operates by its own laws in its own world, and it has a lovely fizziness."

The New Yorker

losers, washed up like driftwood on the edge of society. *Atlantic City* lays bare the divided heart of the United States: a country in which exorbitant wealth exists side-by-side with grim poverty, yet imbued with the naïve belief that anyone can make it if he really believes in himself. Maybe this film could only have been made by an outsider like Malle, so fascinated by America while remaining so thoroughly European as an artist.

SH

6

DIVA

1980 – FRANCE – 117 MIN.

GENRE

THRILLER

DIRECTOR

JEAN-JACQUES BEINEIX

SCREENPLAY

JEAN-JACQUES BEINEIX, JEAN VAN HAMME,
based on the novel of the same name
by DELACORTA (= DANIEL ODIER)

DIRECTOR OF PHOTOGRAPHY

PHILIPPE ROUSSELOT

EDITING

MARIE-JOSÈPHE YOYOTTE, MONIQUE PRIM

MUSIC

VLADIMIR COSMA

PRODUCTION

IRÈNE SILBERMAN for GREENWICH FILM PRODUCTIONS,
FILMS A2, LES FILMS GALAXIE

STARRING

FRÉDÉRIC ANDRÉI (Jules),
WILHELMENIA WIGGINS-FERNANDEZ (Cynthia Hawkins),
RICHARD BOHRINGER (Gorodish), THUY AN LUU (Alba),
JACQUES FABBRI (Jean Saporta), DOMINIQUE PINON (Le curé),
GÉRARD DARMON (L'Antillais), JEAN-JACQUES MOREAU (Krantz),
ANNY ROMAND (Paula), CHANTAL DERUAZ (Nadja, an ex-prostitute)

Ferracci
IRÈNE SILBERMAN
PRÉSENTE
DIVA
UN FILM DE
JEAN-JACQUES BEINEIX
D'APRÈS LE ROMAN DE DELACORTA · ÉDITIONS SEGHERS · ADAPTATION JEAN-JACQUES BEINEIX · JEAN VAN HAMME
DIALOGUES JEAN-JACQUES BEINEIX · AVEC PAR ORDRE ALPHABÉTIQUE FRÉDÉRIC ANDREI · ROLAND BERTIN
RICHARD BOHRINGER · GÉRARD DARMON · JACQUES FABBRI · THUY AN LUU · DOMINIQUE PINON · ANNY ROMAND
AVEC LA PARTICIPATION DE WILHELMENIA WIGGINS FERNANDEZ · DIRECTEUR DE LA PHOTOGRAPHIE PHILIPPE ROUSSELOT
CHEF DÉCORATEUR HILTON Mc CONNICO · MUSIQUE COMPOSÉE ET DIRIGÉE PAR VLADIMIR COSMA · DIRECTEUR DE LA PRODUCTION ULLY PICKARD
CO-PRODUCTION LES FILMS GALAXIE · GREENWICH FILM PRODUCTION · DISTRIBUÉ PAR GEF CCFC
MUSIQUE ÉDITÉE PAR GALAXIE MUSIQUE © COPYRIGHT 1981

1

"There is no such thing as innocent pleasure."

Jules (Frédéric Andréi), a young Parisian postman, loves opera with a passion. He is particularly devoted to the singer Cynthia Hawkins (Wilhelmenia Wiggins-Fernandez), a true Diva who flatly refuses to make records, much to the annoyance of her manager. When she gives a concert in Paris, Jules succeeds in making a top-quality bootleg recording of her performance. His achievement doesn't go unnoticed; from now on, the naive fan will be pursued everywhere he goes by two shady "businessmen" from the Taiwanese pirate-music mafia. As if the situation weren't dangerous enough, Jules is soon the hapless recipient of a second tape, bearing proof that the chief of the Parisian police is also running a drugs-and-prostitution ring. In next to no time, a team of killers are hot on Jules' heels.

Like many a cult film, *Diva* flopped when first released. The French critics were decidedly sniffy about Jean-Jacques Beineix's directing debut, describing it as glossy but hollow, and moviegoers initially also showed little interest. Only after the film received an enthusiastic reception at American festivals did *Diva* begin to attract a mainly young audience in Europe. It gradually became one of the biggest hits of the 80s. *Diva* ran and ran… and what's more, its influence was considerable: it marked the beginning of the French "neon cinema," an anti-intellectual counterblast to

JEAN-JACQUES BEINEIX Jean-Jacques Beineix (1946–2022) originally studied medicine, before beginning his film career as an assistant to directors as famous as René Clément and Claude Berri. He was 34 by the time he came to make his first film, *Diva* (1980), which got off to a poor start in France before being enthusiastically received on the American festival circuit. Word spread back to Europe, and it eventually became one of the most successful films of the 80s, establishing Beineix's reputation as a cult director. The public enjoyed *Diva*'s visual brilliance and its characteristic fairytale atmosphere, qualities that also marked Beineix's later work and had a lasting influence on the "neon cinema" of the 80s. The critics, however, accused him of superficiality, and his subsequent films failed to mollify them. *The Moon in the Gutter* (*La Lune dans le caniveau*, 1983) was a naive love story about a longshoreman and a rich girl; *Betty Blue* (*37°2 le matin*, 1985)—Beineix's second big box-office hit—was a fashionable adaptation of Philippe Dijan's bestseller; and *Roselyne and the Lions* (*Roselyne et les lions*, 1989) was a somewhat unhappy circus film. After *IP5* (*IP5: L'île aux pachydermes*, 1992), noted mainly for the fact that Yves Montand died shortly after the film was completed, Beineix withdrew from the cinema, devoted his time to painting, and made a few documentary films. He attempted a comeback with the surrealistic thriller *Mortal Transfer* (*Mortel transfert*, 2000), but was unable to repeat the success he had enjoyed in the 80s. In 2020, he published the novel *Toboggan*.

2

"A designer fairy tale, in which a decked out pad and Revox stereo are more significant than the protagonist's innermost thoughts." *Süddeutsche Zeitung*

the dominant *cinema des auteurs* of the older generation. Beineix and Luc Besson were to be the leading lights of this brash new movement.

Diva is undeniably a film that likes to be looked at. It's a fairy-tale thriller that focuses entirely on overwhelming visual effects, at the expense of narrative and character development. So while it's fair to say that Beineix's film is superficial, it cannot be denied that it also functions brilliantly at this surface level. For one thing, the film is edited so superbly that sheer tempo makes the holes in the plot seem negligible. Philippe Rousselot's camerawork is particularly outstanding. The artificiality of the film's imagery constitutes an all-but-independent cosmos, a synthetic parallel world consisting entirely of spectacular locations, and intersecting only tangentially with the real city of Paris. The slow-moving camera draws us in, as if we were dreaming Jules' dreams. And these are the daydreams of an overgrown boy who's built a fantastic playpen in his factory flat, complete with clapped-out luxury limousines, sultry Pop Art paintings and a hi-tech beast of

1 Sleek and chic: Diva marked the advent of 1980s French Neon Cinema—a movement that basked in artificiality rather than the realism of the auteurs.

2 Skin-deep: Beineix's characters luxuriate in superficiality, but fail to fathom deeper waters.

3 Prima Wilhelmenia: A set of powerhouse pipes turned Wiggins-Fernandez into a screen icon.

4 Projection room: Lacklustre Jules' (Frédéric Andréi) voyeuristic fixation on the singer win him the hearts of the crowd.

5 Golden opportunity: From the wings of the supporting cast, dashing Bohemian Gorodish (Richard Bohringer) suddenly emerges as the film's true hero.

a sound-system. Safe in this pubertal paradise, Jules can indulge in fantasies of a thrilling existence… until reality intervenes, forcing him to endure a series of perilous adventures before he can win the heart of his opera diva. The lady in question is played by Wilhelmenia Wiggins-Fernandez, and the scenes in which Jean-Jacques Beineix captures her wonderful voice are undoubtedly the highpoints of the film.

Jules, the gawky hero, would hardly have survived without the support of two guardian angels: Gorodish (Richard Bohringer), a master of the art of living, and his Vietnamese companion Alba (Thuy An Luu). At the time, many felt that the eccentric Gorodish was the real hero of the film; not just because he freed Jules from every fine mess he got himself into, and kept his cool while doing so, but because he embodied the essential attitudes of the age. This was a generation that had turned its back on ideological struggle and accepted the fact that the world is corrupt. Thus the 80s witnessed a collective retreat from the public to the private sphere, and lifestyle became indistinguishable from life itself. Gorodish was equally at home in a loft or a lighthouse, and happy behind the wheel of a hoodlum's white Citroën; he could conjure up cars like Felix the Cat, and he smoked fine cigars to the music of the spheres while soaking in a free-standing bathtub. The man was almost heroic in his hedonism, and a perfect paragon of 80s style.

JH

THE SHINING

1980 – USA / GREAT BRITAIN – 144 MIN. / 119 MIN. (Europe and Australia)

GENRE

HORROR FILM, LITERARY ADAPTATION

DIRECTOR

STANLEY KUBRICK

SCREENPLAY

STANLEY KUBRICK, DIANE JOHNSON,
based on the novel of the same name by STEPHEN KING

DIRECTOR OF PHOTOGRAPHY

JOHN ALCOTT

EDITING

RAY LOVEJOY

MUSIC

KRZYSZTOF PENDERECKI, GYÖRGY LIGETI,
BÉLA BARTÓK, WENDY CARLOS

PRODUCTION

STANLEY KUBRICK, ROBERT FRYER, MARY LEA JOHNSON,
MARTIN RICHARDS for HAWK FILMS,
PRODUCERS CIRCLE, PEREGRINE, WARNER BROS.

STARRING

JACK NICHOLSON (Jack Torrance), SHELLEY DUVALL (Wendy Torrance),
DANNY LLOYD (Danny Torrance), BARRY NELSON (Stuart Ullman),
SCATMAN CROTHERS (Dick Hallorann), PHILIP STONE (Delbert Grady),
JOE TURKEL (Lloyd), ANNE JACKSON (Doctor), TONY BURTON (Larry Durkin),
LIA BELDAM (Young Woman In Bathtub)

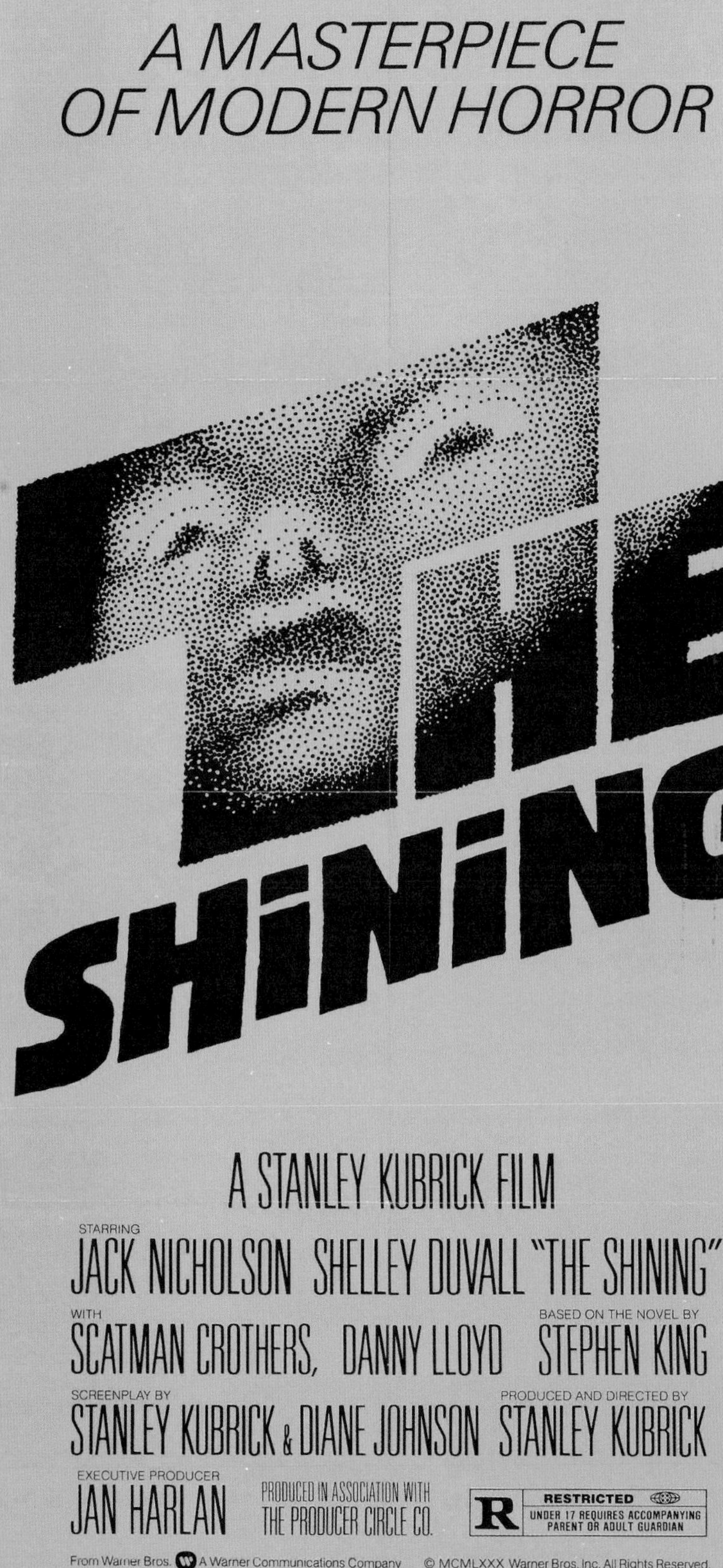

A MASTERPIECE
OF MODERN HORROR
THE SHINING
A STANLEY KUBRICK FILM
STARRING
JACK NICHOLSON SHELLEY DUVALL "THE SHINING"
WITH
SCATMAN CROTHERS, DANNY LLOYD
BASED ON THE NOVEL BY
STEPHEN KING
SCREENPLAY BY
STANLEY KUBRICK & DIANE JOHNSON
PRODUCED AND DIRECTED BY
STANLEY KUBRICK
EXECUTIVE PRODUCER
JAN HARLAN
PRODUCED IN ASSOCIATION WITH
THE PRODUCER CIRCLE CO.
R RESTRICTED
UNDER 17 REQUIRES ACCOMPANYING PARENT OR ADULT GUARDIAN
From Warner Bros. A Warner Communications Company
© MCMLXXX Warner Bros. Inc. All Rights Reserved.

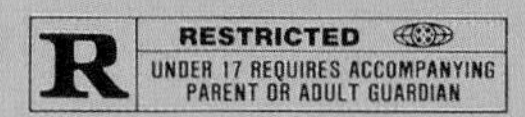

1

"Some places are like people: some shine and some don't."

Wendy (Shelley Duvall) slowly bends over the typewriter. Her jaw drops and her widening eyes move from left to right. "All work and no play makes Jack a dull boy." Wendy scrolls down the leaf of paper. The entire sheet is filled with this identical sentence. She looks next to the typewriter and flicks through the bulky manuscript. Line after line the same words, page after page the same sentence. Wendy immediately realizes that Jack (Jack Nicholson) has lost his mind. But it is too late, because in exactly this moment, her husband is standing behind her, resolved to kill her.

Perhaps the most frightening moment in *The Shining* is when Wendy understands she is at the mercy of a madman and cannot escape. For a month Wendy, Jack, and their son, Danny (Danny Torrance) have been

HORROR FILM Shock, panic, terror—the horror flick feeds on fear and the passion for fear. The basic prerequisite is the audience's suspension of disbelief—the more they identify, the greater their fear for the wellbeing of the protagonists. And as horror movies seem to be a favorite among the younger generation—proved beyond doubt by John Carpenter's *Halloween* (1978)—younger actors generally take the leads in such cinematic enterprises.
The roots of the horror genre lie in German silent film. Friedrich Wilhelm Murnau's *Nosferatu* (1922), *The Golem* (1914/15) by Paul Wegener and Henrik Galeen, as well as Robert Wiene's *The Cabinet of Dr. Caligari* (1919), established the stalwarts of the genre such as vampires, artificial creatures, and madmen. But the greatest terror reigns in the mind: films like Stellan Rye's *Der Student von Prag* (1913), Rouben Mamoulian's *Dr. Jekyll and Mr. Hyde* (1931), or Stanley Kubrick's *The Shining* (1980) beam a searchlight into the murky depths within ourselves.
Light and shadow are the basic ingredients of the genre and Jacques Tourneur most notably and masterfully played with these contrasts, as in his film *Cat People* (1942), a subtly metaphorical exploration of sexuality. It is precisely this reduction to the ABC of filmmaking that creates the best horror movies. Exceptional examples are George A. Romero's sinister social commentary *Night of the Living Dead* (1968) or *The Blair Witch Project* (1999), directed by Daniel Myrick and Eduardo Sánchez.

2

1 It's too late, Baby… By the time Wendy Torrance (Shelley Duvall) acknowledges her marital problems, husband Jack is burning rubber on his hell ride.

2 Writer's block: Jack Torrance (Jack Nicholson) acts out when he can't get his ideas down on paper.

3 Jack the Ripper: "I'm not gonna hurt ya, Wendy. I'm just gonna rip your fuckin' heart out!"

looking after the large, empty Overlook Hotel, which lies secluded somewhere in the mountains. They activate the boiler to avoid frost damage from the long winter and idly pass their time: Danny racing toy cars through the halls, Wendy in the kitchen, and Jack at his desk. He is a novelist and is trying to write a new manuscript. But he sinks into lethargy with the first snowfall. And he encounters people who couldn't possibly be present in the hotel: first a bartender who serves him a long-desired drink, then a naked woman who in his embrace transforms into a zombie-like creature. The ultimate hallucination is when an entire ballroom comes alive with party guests from the 20s and a waiter convinces Jack to call his family to order—with drastic methods.

The Shining is a perfect symphony of horror, composed by Stanley Kubrick, the sublime master of all genres.

Stanley Kubrick doesn't do anything by halves. What this diehard perfectionist has created, during the years of post-production work that went on while tucked away in a British film studio, are exemplary pieces of artistic refinement: *2001, A Space Odyssey* was a masterpiece in science fiction, *Barry Lyndon* set a new standard for historical epics and *The Shining* redefined the meaning of horror altogether."

Der Spiegel

With his obsessive love of detail, he re-shot some scenes as many as 120 times: one example is the scene in which Dick Hallorann (Scatman Crothers), the chef cook of the hotel, receives a telepathic call for help from Danny. Like the old man, the boy possesses a special ability of the "Shining," which allows him to see traces of the past and images of the future. Hallorann makes his way to the snowed-in hotel and becomes Wendy and Danny's last hope.

The terror in *The Shining* does not stem from shocking special effects, but the inexorable straightforwardness that leads to the deadly finale. Jack's path is predestined, steered by the Overlook Hotel. Like a magnet, it attracts the yellow Volkswagen Beetle as Jack drives through the mountains to interview for a job as caretaker. The hotel empowers him when he complains about his wife, and it frees him after Wendy zonks him with a baseball bat and locks him up. It is the location itself that comes alive—to assimilate and engulf the living.

Kubrick placed particular importance on the symmetrical construction of the images to intensify the feeling of imprisonment: the characters stick in the middle of the rooms as if caught in the center of a spider web. In contrast to the film's literary forerunner, Kubrick scrapped the psychoanalysis of the family members, preferring to leave wide room for interpretation. And readings of the films were duly divergent. Some saw *The Shining* as a study of writer's block, while others interpreted the piece as a comment on the oppression of Native Americans by white settlers, because the hotel was constructed on an old Indian burial ground.

Stephen King, the author of the novel, made no secret of his dissatisfaction with the Kubrick version, particularly the finale in the labyrinth next to the hotel. But Kubrick's invention of the hedgerow labyrinth is nothing short of ingenious. To find their way out, they are going to have to lay breadcrumbs, says Wendy when she sees the

4 Victorian Age at the Overlook Hotel: All the interior scenes were shot at a British film studio.

5 Let it shine! Danny Torrance (Danny Lloyd) has a special power, a special friend and runs at the mention of "red rum."

6 All lines are down: Scatman Crothers picks up Danny's distress signal via mental telepathy.

5

Danny: "What about Room 237?"
Hallorann: "Room 237?"
Danny: "You're scared of Room 237, ain't ya?"
Hallorann: "No, I ain't."
Danny: "Mr. Hallorann, what is in Room 237?"
Hallorann: "Nothin'! There ain't nothin' in Room 237. But you ain't got no business goin' in there anyway. So stay out! You understand? Stay out!"

Film quote: Danny Torrance and Dick Hallorann

6

enormous kitchen for the first time. The Overlook Hotel is a labyrinth of endless hallways, forbidden doors, and dead ends like the ballroom. The human brain also resembles a labyrinth. It offers endless possibilities—some paths lead in the wrong direction and one can sometimes get lost. There are ways out, but not everyone is able to find them. Some remain prisoners of their own labyrinth—like Jack.

NM

HEAVEN'S GATE

1980 – USA – 219 MIN.

GENRE

WESTERN, DRAMA

DIRECTOR

MICHAEL CIMINO

SCREENPLAY

MICHAEL CIMINO

DIRECTOR OF PHOTOGRAPHY

VILMOS ZSIGMOND

EDITING

TOM ROLF, WILLIAM REYNOLDS, LISA FRUCHTMAN, GERALD B. GREENBERG

MUSIC

DAVID MANSFIELD

PRODUCTION

JOANN CARELLI for PARTISAN PRODUCTIONS, UNITED ARTISTS

STARRING

KRIS KRISTOFFERSON (Marshal James Averill), CHRISTOPHER WALKEN (Nathan D. Champion), JOHN HURT (Billy Irvine), SAM WATERSTON (Frank Canton), ISABELLE HUPPERT (Ella Watson), JOSEPH COTTEN (Reverend Sutton), ROSEANNE VELA (Pretty Girl), RICHARD MASUR (Cully), JEFF BRIDGES (John L. Bridges), RONNIE HAWKINS (Wolcott), BRAD DOURIF (Mr. Eggleston)

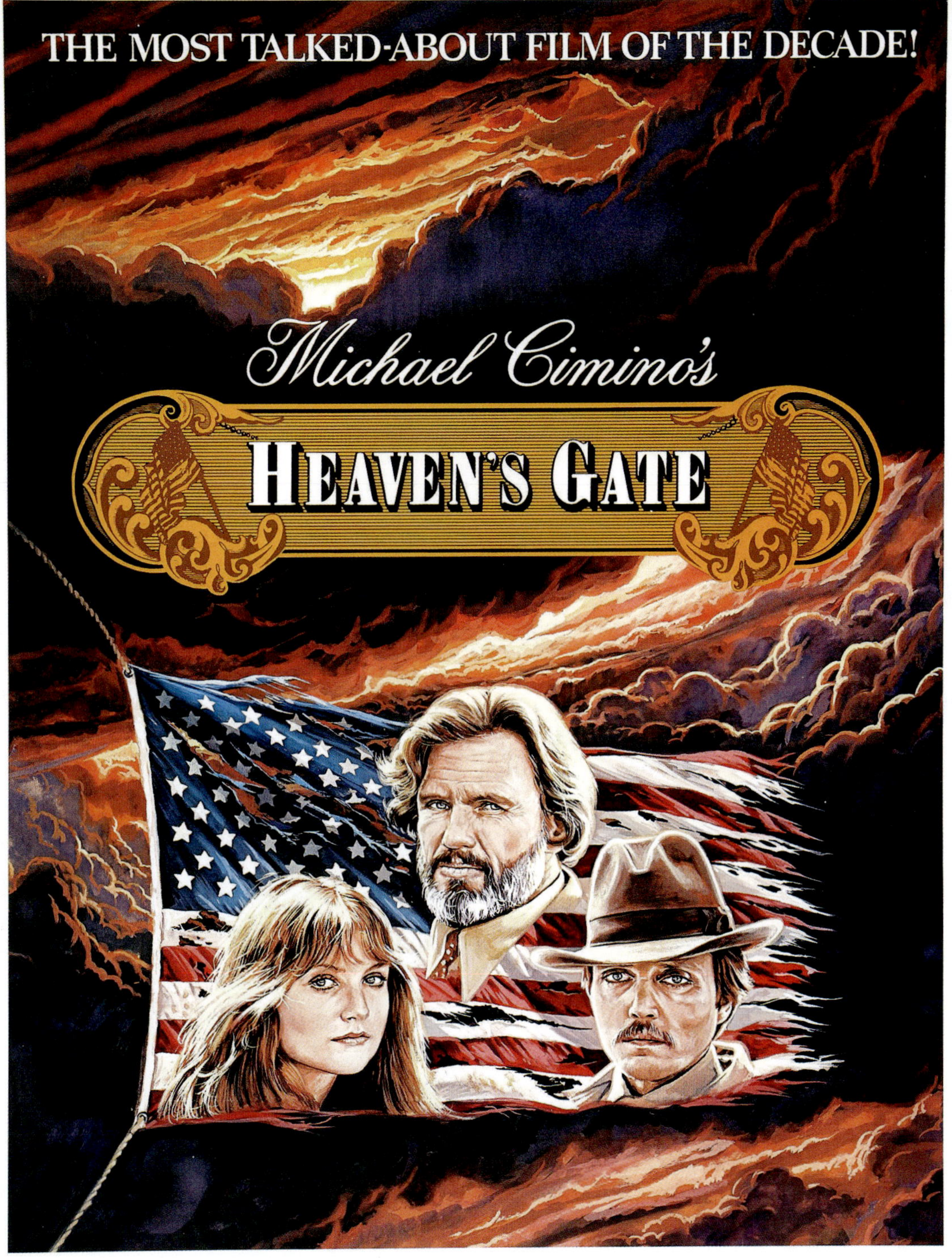

KRIS KRISTOFFERSON IN MICHAEL CIMINO'S HEAVEN'S GATE

CO-STARRING
CHRISTOPHER WALKEN JOHN HURT SAM WATERSTON BRAD DOURIF

ISABELLE HUPPERT AS ELLA JOSEPH COTTEN AS THE REVEREND DOCTOR ALSO STARRING JEFF BRIDGES

MUSIC BY DAVID MANSFIELD DIRECTOR OF PHOTOGRAPHY VILMOS ZSIGMOND, A.S.C. PRODUCED BY JOANN CARELLI WRITTEN AND DIRECTED BY MICHAEL CIMINO

70mm Six-Track DOLBY STEREO™ IN SELECTED THEATRES

ORIGINAL MOTION PICTURE SOUNDTRACK ON LIBERTY RECORDS AND TAPES

Copyright © MCMLXXXI United Artists Corporation. All rights reserved.

TECHNICOLOR®

United Artists
A Transamerica Company

1

"It's getting dangerous to be poor in this country."

Heaven's Gate became notorious as the film that ruined United Artists, a distribution company with a long and proud history. Michael Cimino's late Western was originally budgeted at 7.5 million dollars, but by the time it was completed, the total production costs had risen to more than 40 million. In 1980, this was an unheard-of sum: even if the film had been a major success at the box-office, it wouldn't have put the producers and distributors back in the black. In any case, *Heaven's Gate* was anything but a success: the reviews in the States were unanimously scathing (the film was said to be confused, long-winded, and above all, anti-American), and the distributors withdrew Cimino's three-and-a-half-hour epic from circulation almost before it had reached the theaters. The director was allowed to rework the film, and he eventually produced a version that was only 149 minutes long—but this, too, was a flop. In 1985, a longer version close to the director's original intentions was released in Europe alone—and *Heaven's Gate*, at very long last, was hailed as a masterpiece.

What happened? Cimino had picked up on an episode that had been relegated to the margins of American

KRIS KRISTOFFERSON Kris Kristofferson (1936–2024) was the son of an Air Force General. Before he became known as a country singer-songwriter, he had already seen a fair bit of life as a failed novelist and pop singer in London, and as an Air Force pilot and paratrooper in the States. In 1970, Johnny Cash topped the charts with a Kristofferson song, "Sunday Mornin' Comin' Down," and Janis Joplin's rendition of "Me and Bobby McGee" soon brought him even greater fame. While these successes helped Kristofferson to make his name as an unconventional country musician, the 70s also witnessed his breakthrough as a movie actor. He made his screen debut in Dennis Hopper's *The Last Movie* (1969/71), before Sam Peckinpah cast him as a legendary outlaw in *Pat Garrett and Billy the Kid* (1973). From then on, Kristofferson was destined to embody the virile and vital outsider with a sensitive soul. He played a supporting role in Peckinpah's next film, *Bring Me the Head of Alfredo Garcia* (1974), and the following year he appeared alongside Ellen Burstyn in Martin Scorsese's drama *Alice Doesn't Live Here Anymore* (1974). In the Frank Pierson remake of *A Star Is Born* (1976), he played a self-destructive rock star. His own life may well have fuelled his interpretation of the role, for he too was dependent on alcohol at one time, although he managed to overcome his addiction.

In his third and last Peckinpah film, *Convoy* (1978), Kristofferson played the leader of a truckers' revolt. This was a highpoint in his acting career. After starring in the spectacular box-office disaster of *Heaven's Gate* (1980), Kristofferson was less often seen in the movies, though he remained a presence on TV and as a musician. In the 90s, things changed. Besides giving remarkable performances in John Sayles' present-day Western, *Lone Star* (1996), and James Ivory's *A Soldier's Daughter Never Cries* (1998), Kristofferson also acquired a new generation of younger fans, thanks to his roles in blockbusters such as *Blade* (1998) and *Planet of the Apes* (2001).

2

1 Rich and of a good family: Marshal James Averill (Kris Kristofferson) at an early age.

2 These boots were made for walking: Gunslinger Nate Champion (Christopher Walken) is hoping to step up in society.

3 If you're happy and you know it, clap your hands! These impoverished immigrants sure know how to enjoy themselves.

history: the "Johnson County War" of 1890–92, a conflict between WASP landowners and mainly Eastern European immigrants who had been assigned no land from the government. The clashes between rich and poor grew in frequency and violence, until finally the cattle-barons—with the connivance of the State Governor—hired a gang of killers to liquidate the settlers' leaders. The immigrants defended themselves, until the army intervened, saving the wealthy landowners and their henchmen.

Class struggle in Wyoming: Cimino demystifies both the American Dream and the Western—a genre that had always celebrated the pioneer spirit and the illusion of a big, free country. In *Heaven's Gate*, the immigrants' hope of a better life comes to a sorry end, shattered by a corrupt caste in the name of money. And, as the film makes clear, these newcomers are unwelcome not just because they're poor, but also because they speak a foreign tongue and embody an alien culture.

"I never want people to feel they've been watching something, to feel that they've just seen a movie; I want them to believe they've been somewhere."

Michael Cimino in: Frankfurter Rundschau

4 The sky's the limit! Grandiose sets and inflated costumes added several zeroes to production costs.

5 Riding the golden spike: The settlers end up covering the bill for the march of progress.

7

6 Horsemen of the apocalypse: When the settlers resist the cattle barons' murderous mercenaries, the U.S. Cavalry arrives to restore "order"…

7 Heart of gold or heart of glass: Whorehouse owner Ella (Isabelle Huppert) loves two men. She yearns for a well-ordered family life and two apartments.

8 Dunce cap: John L. Bridges (Jeff Bridges) may be a friend of the Marshal, but that's certainly no invitation to high society.

9 A closed circle: The wealthy and fortunate dance to a trouble-free life.

10 Harvard class of 1870: Their education will last them 200 years.

Heaven's Gate follows the life story of a privileged man. James Averill (Kris Kristofferson), an idealistic young fellow, graduates from Harvard in 1870 and begins the adventure of adult life. Twenty years later, we meet him in Wyoming. Now a Marshal, he is expected to represent a law that has no moral legitimacy. Averill takes the side of the people, while inevitably remaining what he is: a wealthy man who doesn't belong. His antagonist is Nate Champion (Christopher Walken), the gunman hired by the cattle-breeders association. A strange friendship links the two men. For Nate, the Marshal is a kind of role model, embodying the wealth, style and self-assurance to which he has always aspired. At the same time, Averill and Nate are rivals for the love of Ella (Isabelle Huppert), a strong and independent woman who runs a brothel. The fate of these three figures is another clear reflection of the film's moral trajectory. Both Nate and Ella are practically executed by the gang of killers; for the parvenu who stands up to his bosses, and the bourgeois whore who keeps her accounts so assiduously in order, there isn't a hope in hell. Averill, however, is treated a little differently: though he had "betrayed" his class by fighting on the side of the settlers, the landowners still consider him to be one of their own, and his life is spared.

The film meanders, following its characters down roundabout routes, telling of everyday life in the old West, granting even the immigrants faces and stories of their own. Again and again, Cimino shows images of circular movement, mostly dances expressing hope and the joy of living. At the end, however, the last battle is a Dance of Death. The film has a fascinating richness of detail, and the movie's exorbitant cost was due not least to the director's perfectionism: even the least of the extras wears an authentic hat. This material outlay is no mere bombast, but an artistic necessity. For Cimino, it was a way of creating a naturalistic background against which the characters and their story can unfold. LP

8

"*Heaven's Gate* is a magnificent opus. The images, sometimes tinged in sepia tones, have the realistic quality of period photographs. The directing itself is an essay on space, as in certain Anthony Mann Westerns, and on the 'field of history' as seen by Michael Cimino." *Le Monde*

9

10

STAR WARS: EPISODE V – THE EMPIRE STRIKES BACK

1980 – USA – 125 MIN.

GENRE

SCIENCE FICTION

DIRECTOR

IRVIN KERSHNER

SCREENPLAY

LEIGH BRACKETT, LAWRENCE KASDAN

DIRECTOR OF PHOTOGRAPHY

PETER SUSCHITZKY

EDITING

PAUL HIRSCH

MUSIC

JOHN WILLIAMS

PRODUCTION

GARY KURTZ for LUCASFILM LTD

STARRING

MARK HAMILL (Luke Skywalker), HARRISON FORD (Han Solo), CARRIE FISHER (Princess Leia Organa), BILLY DEE WILLIAMS (Lando Calrissian), DAVID PROWSE (Darth Vader), JAMES EARL JONES (Darth Vader's voice), PETER MAYHEW (Chewbacca), ANTHONY DANIELS (C-3PO), KENNY BAKER (R2-D2), FRANK OZ (Yoda), ALEC GUINNESS (Ben "Obi-Wan" Kenobi)

ACADEMY AWARDS 1981

OSCAR for BEST SOUND (Bill Varney, Steve Maslow, Gregg Landaker, Peter Sutton), and SPECIAL PRIZE for VISUAL EFFECTS (Brian Johnson, Richard Edlund, Dennis Muren, Bruce Nicholson)

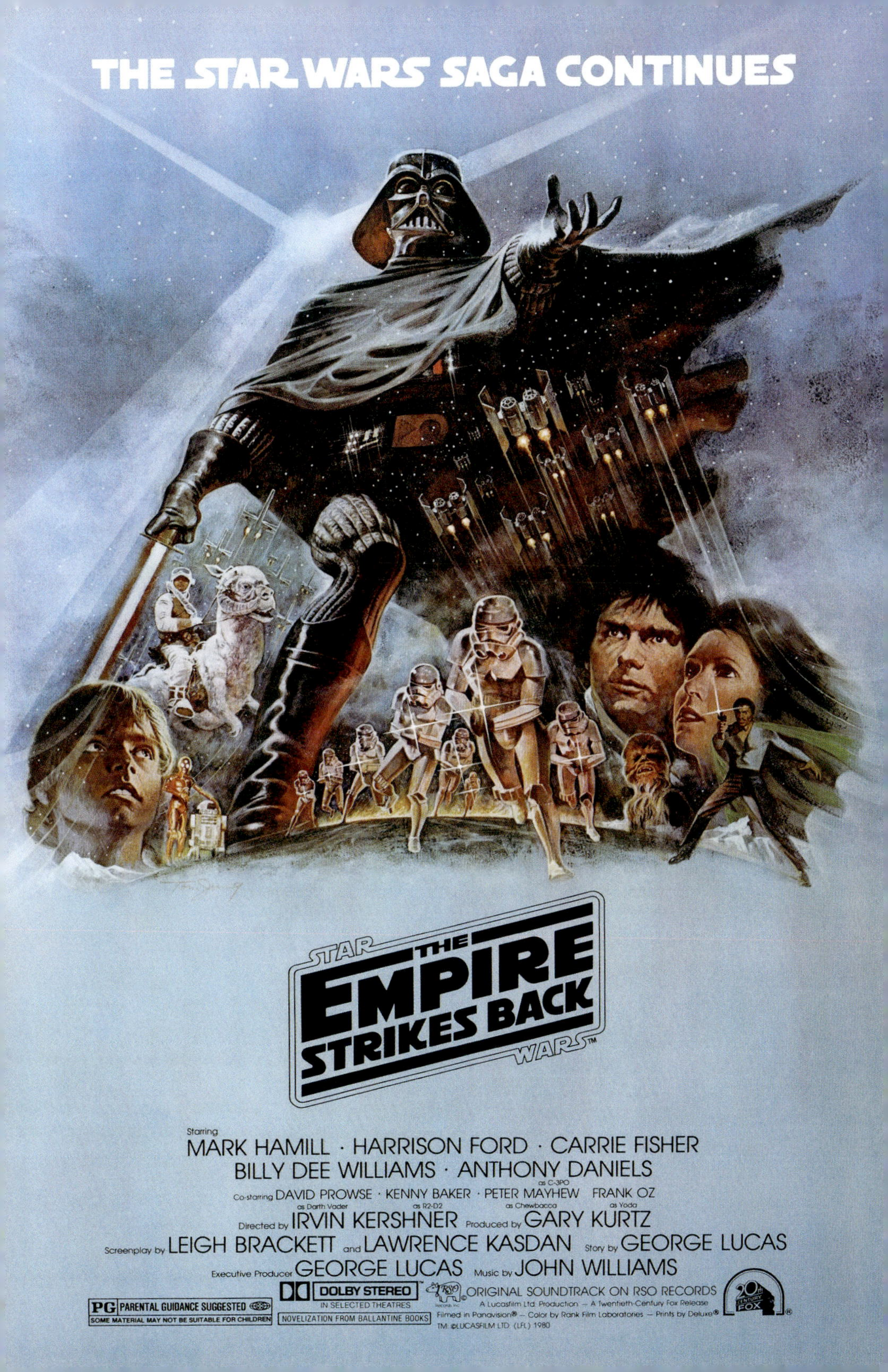

THE STAR WARS SAGA CONTINUES

Starring
MARK HAMILL · HARRISON FORD · CARRIE FISHER
BILLY DEE WILLIAMS · ANTHONY DANIELS as C-3PO

Co-starring DAVID PROWSE as Darth Vader · KENNY BAKER as R2-D2 · PETER MAYHEW as Chewbacca FRANK OZ as Yoda

Directed by IRVIN KERSHNER Produced by GARY KURTZ

Screenplay by LEIGH BRACKETT and LAWRENCE KASDAN Story by GEORGE LUCAS

Executive Producer GEORGE LUCAS Music by JOHN WILLIAMS

PG PARENTAL GUIDANCE SUGGESTED
SOME MATERIAL MAY NOT BE SUITABLE FOR CHILDREN

DOLBY STEREO™
IN SELECTED THEATRES

NOVELIZATION FROM BALLANTINE BOOKS

ORIGINAL SOUNDTRACK ON RSO RECORDS
A Lucasfilm Ltd. Production — A Twentieth-Century Fox Release
Filmed in Panavision® — Color by Rank Film Laboratories — Prints by Deluxe®

TM: ©LUCASFILM LTD. (LFL) 1980

20th CENTURY FOX®

1

"Beware of the dark side."

The Empire Strikes Back is a suspenseful and engaging sequel to the extraordinarily successful first part of the *Star Wars Trilogy*, which has now expanded into a six-part saga. Luke Skywalker (Mark Hamill) and the rebels, who were able to snatch Princess Leia (Carrie Fisher) from the clutches of the evil Empire in the first episode, have been tracked down in their icy hideout on the planet Hoth by Darth Vader, the sinister, intergalactic villain in the service of the Emperor. With the help of their space adventurer friend Han Solo (Harrison Ford) and his companion Chewbacca (Peter Mayhew), they are just able to flee to the cloud city governed by their ally, Lando (Billy Dee Williams). But safety is merely an illusion. Darth Vader and his henchmen have long since located the safe haven and have succeeded in forcing Lando to hand his guests over to the Empire. But the good side of the "Force," which accompanies Luke Skywalker and his friends, will not give up without a fight. In the final showdown between Good and Evil, Darth Vader reveals himself to be Luke Skywalker's father. But his attempt to pull Skywalker over to the dark side to help him triumph over the evil Emperor fails. Skywalker resists the temptations of the dark side of the Force and escapes with Princess Leia.

What this straightforward plot does not immediately divulge is the glut of fairy-tale themes, myths, and figures that come into play. Prime examples are the fairy-tale-like Princess Leia, the chivalrous "space-age Robin Hood," Luke Skywalker, and his loyal sidekicks, Han Solo and Chewbacca. And of course there is the incarnation of Evil himself—Darth Vader, the masked, cloaked villain, as charismatic as he is asthmatic, whose ultimate lightsaber duel with Skywalker is reminiscent of the sword fights of

THE STAR WARS SAGA In the 1970s, no one could have predicted that George Lucas would lay the foundation for an unrivalled career in the film business with his epic fairy tale, *Star Wars* (1977). And to boot, he did so in a time in which science fiction films were decidedly unpopular. His ingenious idea of combining the developing special effects with a serialized blockbuster concept is still unparalleled. But Lucas simply built on the experience of contemporary special effects gurus and previous capital-intensive mega productions. He purchased long-forgotten technical machines, modified them with new electric steering capabilities, and devised a serial marketing concept that foresaw the dual capitalization possibilities provided by merchandizing articles. Lucas' modernization of existent production and marketing strategies proved in hindsight to be exceedingly successful and has often been copied (*Harry Potter and the Sorcerer's Stone*, 2001 or *The Lord of the Rings – The Fellowship of the Ring*, 2001).

The *Star Wars* saga includes nine parts in total. It all began in 1977 with *Star Wars: Episode IV – A New Hope*, then *Star Wars: Episode V – The Empire Strikes Back* in 1980, and *Star Wars: Episode VI – The Return of the Jedi* in 1983. Then came *Star Wars: Episode I – The Phantom Menace* (1999), followed by *Star Wars: Episode II – Attack of the Clones* (2002) and *Star Wars: Episode III – Revenge of the Sith* (2005). It is interesting to note that Lucas produced the last three chapters of the story first, while the first three episodes topped the box office at the end of the 1990s and early 2000s. The digitalization of film productions can be attributed almost solely to the popularity of the *Star Wars* saga. In 2012, Lucas sold his company Lucasfilm, including the rights to Star Wars, to the Walt Disney Company.

The films *Star Wars: The Force Awakens* (2015), *Star Wars: The Last Jedi* (2017), and *Star Wars: The Rise of Skywalker* (2019), followed without his involvement.

"From the first burst of John Williams' powerful score and the receding opening title crawl, we are back in pleasant surroundings and anxious for a good time—like walking through the front gate of Disneyland, where good and evil are never confused and the righteous will always win." *Monthly Film Bulletin*

the classic swashbucklers. But the mythic elements do not end here. The new interpretation of the classic father–son conflict exposes the father as the ruthless perpetrator of the dark side of the force, while the white-clad, youthful Skywalker embodies the liberating, good side. Numerous components of the most disparate genres are simultaneously combined under the roof of science fiction. In addition to the aforementioned elements, pieces of fantasy, war, and action genres have most notably been borrowed. Battle robots that look like outsize, fantastical, mechanical creatures, war scenes with classic battle formations, and risky stunts by the good heroes provide the proof. At the same time, the film affectionately and playfully deals with its own cinematic history: the two robots, R2-D2 and C-3PO wander aimlessly through the scenery like clownish relics of earlier science fiction films and repeatedly provide for laughs.

The Empire Strikes Back marks a further milestone on George Lucas' determined path to create a new, physical cinema of audiovisual effects targeting the audience's perceptive faculties. Computer-steered camera movements and the combination of idyllic calm and dramatic acceleration produced far more intense spatial impressions than any special effects seen before. The underlying scheme of employing extraordinary contrasts is a leitmotif of the film, extending from the basic Good vs. Evil theme through to the explosive war in the icy expanses of the rebel refuge.

Above all, *The Empire Strikes Back* is an inventive children's film for adults, and all age groups can allow themselves to be enchanted by its naïve, cult-like charm. Its secret lies less in the never-ending story of the eternal spiritual conflict between elemental forces, its mix of childish and adult appeal, or the fabulously fantastic and

1 Where there's a will there's a way: Luke Skywalker (Mark Hamill) training with the Jedi Master, Yoda.

2 Pretty as a princess: Carrie Fisher as Leia Organa.

3 Listen to your elders: The ancient Jedi Master wins Luke's undying allegiance in the fight for good.

4 The black death: A shadow fell upon the catacombs of modern day villains with the birth of Darth Vader (David Prowse).

3

the nightmarishly military. With the *Star Wars* saga (1977, 1980, 1983, 1999, 2002, 2005) George Lucas and his special effects team opened our eyes to the idea of a film that stretches far beyond the storyline: they revolutionized our perception of the optical and acoustic potential of the medium itself. *Star Wars* took off our blinkers, widened our horizons and gave us an innocent view into the future of filmmaking. BR

"Ultimately, the success of this genre depends on the special effects. John Dykstra's special effects for Star Wars were some of the best in film history, and those in Empire (by Brian Johnson and Richard Edlund) are equally dazzling and impressive." *Films in Review*

5 Robots, beasts, and dinosaurs...Oh, my! *The Empire Strikes Back* is chock full of fantastic visuals and astounding effects.

6 Worth his weight in gold: Daft but endearing, C-3PO gives a human face to the intergalactic wars.

7 Hi-ho, Silver! *The Star Wars* series deftly reworks motifs from familiar genres.

6

7

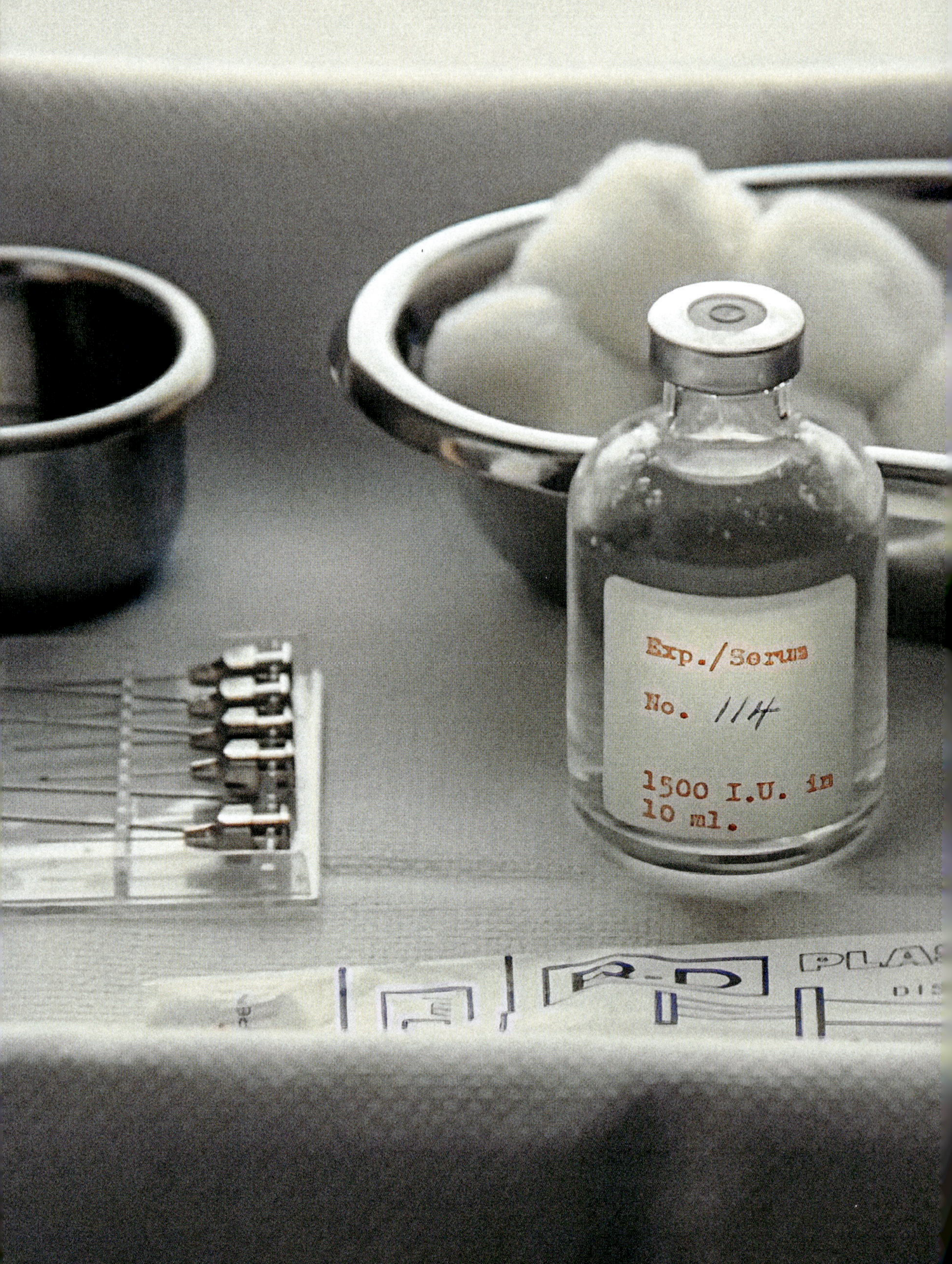
Exp./Serum
No. 114
1500 I.U. in
10 ml.

1972 OSCARS

BEST PICTURE *The French Connection* (Philip D'Antoni)
BEST DIRECTOR William Friedkin for *The French Connection*
BEST LEADING ACTRESS Jane Fonda in *Klute*
BEST LEADING ACTOR Gene Hackman in *The French Connection*
BEST SUPPORTING ACTRESS Cloris Leachman in *The Last Picture Show*
BEST SUPPORTING ACTOR Ben Johnson in *The Last Picture Show*
BEST ORIGINAL SCREENPLAY Paddy Chayefsky for *The Hospital*
BEST ADAPTED SCREENPLAY Ernest Tidyman for *The French Connection*
BEST FOREIGN LANGUAGE FILM *The Garden of the Finzi-Continis* by Vittorio De Sica (Italy)
BEST CINEMATOGRAPHY Oswald Morris for *Fiddler on the Roof*
BEST ART DIRECTION John Box, Ernest Archer, Jack Maxsted, Gil Parrondo, Vernon Dixon for *Nicholas and Alexandra*
BEST FILM EDITING Gerald B. Greenberg for *The French Connection*
BEST MUSIC Michael Legrand for *Summer of '42*
BEST SONG Isaac Hayes for "Theme From Shaft" in *Shaft*
BEST COSTUMES Yvonne Blake, Antonio Castillo for *Nicholas and Alexandra*
BEST VISUAL EFFECTS Alan Maley, Eustace Lycett, Danny Lee for *Bedknobs and Broomsticks*
BEST SOUND Gordon K. McCallum, David Hildyard for *Fiddler on the Roof*
BEST SOUND EFFECTS EDITING Not awarded

1973 OSCARS

BEST PICTURE *The Godfather* (Albert S. Ruddy)
BEST DIRECTOR Bob Fosse for *Cabaret*
BEST LEADING ACTRESS Liza Minnelli in *Cabaret*
BEST LEADING ACTOR Marlon Brando in *The Godfather* (the award was declined)
BEST SUPPORTING ACTRESS Eileen Heckart in *Butterflies Are Free*
BEST SUPPORTING ACTOR Joel Grey in *Cabaret*
BEST ORIGINAL SCREENPLAY Jeremy Larner for *The Candidate*
BEST ADAPTED SCREENPLAY Mario Puzo, Francis Ford Coppola for *The Godfather*
BEST FOREIGN LANGUAGE FILM *The Discreet Charm of the Bourgeoisie* by Luis Buñuel (France)
BEST CINEMATOGRAPHY Geoffrey Unsworth for *Cabaret*
BEST ART DIRECTION Rolf Zehetbauer, Hans Jürgen Kiebach, Herbert Strabel for *Cabaret*
BEST FILM EDITING David Bretherton for *Cabaret*
BEST MUSIC Charles Chaplin, Ray Rasch, Larry Russell for *Limelight*
BEST ADAPTED SCORE Ralph Burns for *Cabaret*
BEST SONG Al Kasha, Joel Hirschhorn for "The Morning After" in *The Poseidon Adventure*
BEST COSTUMES Anthony Powell for *Travels with My Aunt*
BEST VISUAL EFFECTS L.B. Abbott, A.D. Flowers for *The Poseidon Adventure* (Special Achievement Award)
BEST SOUND Robert Knudson, David Hildyard for *Cabaret*
BEST SOUND EFFECTS EDITING Not awarded

1974 OSCARS

BEST PICTURE *The Sting* (Tony Bill, Michael Phillips, Julia Phillips)
BEST DIRECTOR George Roy Hill for *The Sting*
BEST LEADING ACTRESS Glenda Jackson in *A Touch of Class*
BEST LEADING ACTOR Jack Lemmon in *Save the Tiger*
BEST SUPPORTING ACTRESS Tatum O'Neal in *Paper Moon*
BEST SUPPORTING ACTOR John Houseman in *The Paper Chase*
BEST ORIGINAL SCREENPLAY David S. Ward for *The Sting*
BEST ADAPTED SCREENPLAY William Peter Blatty for *The Exorcist*
BEST FOREIGN LANGUAGE FILM *Day for Night* by François Truffaut (France)
BEST CINEMATOGRAPHY Sven Nykvist for *Cries and Whispers*
BEST ART DIRECTION Henry Bumstead, James Payne for *The Sting*
BEST FILM EDITING William Reynolds for *The Sting*
BEST MUSIC Marvin Hamlisch for *The Way We Were*
BEST ADAPTED SCORE Marvin Hamlisch for *The Sting*
BEST SONG Marvin Hamlisch (music), Alan Bergman (text), Marilyn Bergman (text) for "The Way We Were" in *The Way We Were*
BEST COSTUMES Edith Head for *The Sting*
BEST VISUAL EFFECTS Not awarded
BEST SOUND Robert Knudson, Christopher Newman for *The Exorcist*
BEST SOUND EFFECTS EDITING Not awarded

1975 OSCARS

BEST PICTURE *The Godfather – Part II* (Francis Ford Coppola, Gray Frederickson, Fred Roos)
BEST DIRECTOR Francis Ford Coppola for *The Godfather – Part II*
BEST LEADING ACTRESS Ellen Burstyn in *Alice Doesn't Live Here Anymore*
BEST LEADING ACTOR Art Carney in *Harry and Tonto*
BEST SUPPORTING ACTRESS Ingrid Bergman in *Murder on the Orient Express*
BEST SUPPORTING ACTOR Robert De Niro in *The Godfather – Part II*
BEST ORIGINAL SCREENPLAY Robert Towne for *Chinatown*
BEST ADAPTED SCREENPLAY Francis Ford Coppola, Mario Puzo for *The Godfather – Part II*
BEST FOREIGN LANGUAGE FILM *Amarcord by* Federico Fellini (Italy)
BEST CINEMATOGRAPHY Fred J. Koenekamp, Joseph F. Biroc for *The Towering Inferno*
BEST ART DIRECTION Dean Tavoularis, Angelo P. Graham, George R. Nelson for *The Godfather – Part II*
BEST FILM EDITING Harold F. Kress, Carl Kress for *The Towering Inferno*
BEST MUSIC Nino Rota, Carmine Coppola for *The Godfather – Part II*
BEST SONG Al Kasha (text), Joel Hirschhorn (music) for "We May Never Love Like This Again" in *The Towering Inferno*
BEST COSTUMES Theoni V. Aldredge for *The Great Gatsby*
BEST VISUAL EFFECTS Frank Brendel, Glen Robinson, Albert Whitlock for *Earthquake* (Special Achievement Award)
BEST SOUND Ronald Pierce, Melvin M. Metcalfe Sr. for *Earthquake*
BEST SOUND EFFECTS EDITING Not awarded

1976 OSCARS

BEST PICTURE *One Flew Over the Cuckoo's Nest* (Saul Zaentz, Michael Douglas)
BEST DIRECTOR Miloš Forman for *One Flew Over the Cuckoo's Nest*
BEST LEADING ACTRESS Louise Fletcher in *One Flew Over the Cuckoo's Nest*
BEST LEADING ACTOR Jack Nicholson in *One Flew Over the Cuckoo's Nest*
BEST SUPPORTING ACTRESS Lee Grant in *Shampoo*
BEST SUPPORTING ACTOR George Burns in *The Sunshine Boys*
BEST ORIGINAL SCREENPLAY Frank Pierson for *Dog Day Afternoon*
BEST ADAPTED SCREENPLAY Lawrence Hauben, Bo Goldman for *One Flew Over the Cuckoo's Nest*
BEST FOREIGN LANGUAGE FILM *Dersu Uzala* by Akira Kurosawa (USSR)
BEST CINEMATOGRAPHY John Alcott for *Barry Lyndon*
BEST ART DIRECTION Ken Adam, Roy Walker, Vernon Dixon for *Barry Lyndon*
BEST FILM EDITING Verna Fields for *Jaws*
BEST MUSIC John Williams for *Jaws*
BEST ADAPTED SCORE Leonard Rosenman for *Barry Lyndon*
BEST SONG Keith Carradine for "I'm Easy" in *Nashville*
BEST COSTUMES Ulla-Britt Söderlund, Milena Canonero for *Barry Lyndon*
BEST VISUAL EFFECTS Albert Whitlock, Glen Robinson for *The Hindenburg* (Special Achievement Award)
BEST SOUND Robert L. Hoyt, Roger Heman Jr., Earl Mabery, John R. Carter for *Jaws*
BEST SOUND EFFECTS EDITING Peter Berkos for *The Hindenburg* (Special Achievement Award)

1977 OSCARS

BEST PICTURE *Rocky* (Irwin Winkler, Robert Chartoff)
BEST DIRECTOR John G. Avildsen for *Rocky*
BEST LEADING ACTRESS Faye Dunaway in *Network*
BEST LEADING ACTOR Peter Finch in *Network*
BEST SUPPORTING ACTRESS Beatrice Straight in *Network*
BEST SUPPORTING ACTOR Jason Robards in *All the President's Men*
BEST ORIGINAL SCREENPLAY Paddy Chayefsky for *Network*
BEST ADAPTED SCREENPLAY William Goldman for *All the President's Men*
BEST FOREIGN LANGUAGE FILM *Black and White in Color* by Jean-Jacques Annaud (Ivory Coast)
BEST CINEMATOGRAPHY Haskell Wexler for *Bound for Glory*
BEST ART DIRECTION George Jenkins, George Gaines for *All the President's Men*
BEST FILM EDITING Richard Halsey, Scott Conrad for *Rocky*
BEST MUSIC Jerry Goldsmith for *The Omen*
BEST SONG Barbra Streisand (music), Paul Williams (text) for "A World That Never Was" in *A Star Is Born*
BEST COSTUMES Danilo Donati for *Fellini's Casanova*
BEST VISUAL EFFECTS Carlo Rambaldi, Glen Robinson, Frank Van der Veer for *King Kong* (Special Achievement Award); L.B. Abbott, Glen Robinson, Matthew Yuricich for *Logan's Run* (Special Achievement Award)
BEST SOUND Arthur Piantadosi, Les Fresholtz, Rick Alexander, James E. Webb for *All the President's Men*
BEST SOUND EFFECTS EDITING Not awarded

1978 OSCARS

BEST PICTURE *Annie Hall* (Charles H. Joffe)
BEST DIRECTOR Woody Allen for *Annie Hall*
BEST LEADING ACTRESS Diane Keaton in *Annie Hall*
BEST LEADING ACTOR Richard Dreyfuss in *The Goodbye Girl*
BEST SUPPORTING ACTRESS Vanessa Redgrave in *Julia*
BEST SUPPORTING ACTOR Jason Robards in *Julia*
BEST ORIGINAL SCREENPLAY Woody Allen, Marshall Brickman for *Annie Hall*
BEST ADAPTED SCREENPLAY Alvin Sargent for *Julia*
BEST FOREIGN LANGUAGE FILM *Madame Rosa* by Moshé Mizrahi (France)
BEST CINEMATOGRAPHY Vilmos Zsigmond for *Close Encounters of the Third Kind*
BEST ART DIRECTION John Barry, Norman Reynolds, Leslie Dilley, Roger Christian for *Star Wars*
BEST FILM EDITING Paul Hirsch, Marcia Lucas, Richard Chew for *Star Wars*
BEST MUSIC John Williams for *Star Wars*
BEST SONG Joseph Brooks for "You Light Up My Life" in *You Light Up My Life*
BEST COSTUMES John Mollo for *Star Wars*
BEST VISUAL EFFECTS John Stears, John Dykstra, Richard Edlund, Grant McCune, Robert Blalack for *Star Wars*
BEST SOUND Don MacDougall, Ray West, Rob Minkler, Derek Ball for *Star Wars*
BEST SOUND EFFECTS EDITING Frank Warner for *Close Encounters of the Third Kind* (Special Achievement Award); Ben Burtt for *Star Wars* (Special Achievement Award)

1979 OSCARS

BEST PICTURE *The Deer Hunter* (Barry Spikings, Michael Deeley, Michael Cimino, John Peverall)
BEST DIRECTOR Michael Cimino for *The Deer Hunter*
BEST LEADING ACTRESS Jane Fonda in *Coming Home*
BEST LEADING ACTOR Jon Voight in *Coming Home*
BEST SUPPORTING ACTRESS Maggie Smith in *California Suite*
BEST SUPPORTING ACTOR Christopher Walken in *The Deer Hunter*
BEST ORIGINAL SCREENPLAY Nancy Dowd, Waldo Salt, Robert C. Jones for *Coming Home*
BEST ADAPTED SCREENPLAY Oliver Stone for *Midnight Express*
BEST FOREIGN LANGUAGE FILM *Get Out Your Handkerchiefs* by Bertrand Blier (France)
BEST CINEMATOGRAPHY Néstor Almendros for *Days of Heaven*
BEST ART DIRECTION Paul Sylbert, Edwin O'Donavan, George Gaines for *Heaven Can Wait*
BEST FILM EDITING Peter Zinner for *The Deer Hunter*
BEST MUSIC Giorgio Moroder for *Midnight Express*
BEST SONG Paul Jabara for "Last Dance" in *Thank God It's Friday*
BEST COSTUMES Anthony Powell for *Death on the Nile*
BEST VISUAL EFFECTS Les Bowie, Colin Chilvers, Denys N. Coop, Roy Field, Derek Meddings, Zoran Perisic (Special Achievement Award) for *Superman*
BEST SOUND Richard Portman, William L. McCaughey, Aaron Rochin, C. Darin Knight for *The Deer Hunter*
BEST SOUND EFFECTS EDITING Not awarded

1980 OSCARS

BEST PICTURE *Kramer vs. Kramer* (Stanley R. Jaffe)
BEST DIRECTOR Robert Benton for *Kramer vs. Kramer*
BEST LEADING ACTRESS Sally Field in *Norma Rae*
BEST LEADING ACTOR Dustin Hoffman in *Kramer vs. Kramer*
BEST SUPPORTING ACTRESS Meryl Streep in *Kramer vs. Kramer*
BEST SUPPORTING ACTOR Melvyn Douglas in *Being There*
BEST ORIGINAL SCREENPLAY Steve Tesich for *Breaking Away*
BEST ADAPTED SCREENPLAY Robert Benton for *Kramer vs. Kramer*
BEST FOREIGN LANGUAGE FILM *The Tin Drum by* Volker Schlöndorff (FRG)
BEST CINEMATOGRAPHY Vittorio Storaro for *Apocalypse Now*
BEST ART DIRECTION Philip Rosenberg, Tony Walton, Edward Stewart, Gary J. Brink for *All That Jazz*
BEST FILM EDITING Alan Heim for *All That Jazz*
BEST MUSIC Georges Delerue for "Ich liebe dich – I love you – Je t'aime" in *A Little Romance*
BEST SONG David Shire (music), Norman Gimbel (lyrics) for "It Goes Like It Goes" for *Norma Rae*
BEST COSTUMES Albert Wolsky for *All That Jazz*
BEST VISUAL EFFECTS H.R. Giger, Carlo Rambaldi, Brian Johnson, Nick Allder, Denys Ayling for *Alien*
BEST SOUND Walter Murch, Mark Berger, Richard Beggs, Nathan Boxer for *Apocalypse Now*
BEST SOUND EFFECTS EDITING Alan Splet for *The Black Stallion* (Special Achievement Award)

1981 OSCARS

BEST PICTURE *Ordinary People* (Ronald L. Schwary)
BEST DIRECTOR Robert Redford for *Ordinary People*
BEST LEADING ACTRESS Sissy Spacek in *Coal Miner's Daughter*
BEST LEADING ACTOR Robert De Niro in *Raging Bull*
BEST SUPPORTING ACTRESS Mary Steenburgen in *Melvin and Howard*
BEST SUPPORTING ACTOR Timothy Hutton in *Ordinary People*
BEST ORIGINAL SCREENPLAY Bo Goldman for *Melvin and Howard*
BEST ADAPTED SCREENPLAY Alvin Sargent for *Ordinary People*
BEST FOREIGN LANGUAGE FILM *Moscow Does Not Believe in Tears* by Wladimir Menschow (USSR)
BEST CINEMATOGRAPHY Geoffrey Unsworth, Ghislain Cloquet for *Tess*
BEST ART DIRECTION Pierre Guffroy, Jack Stephens for *Tess*
BEST FILM EDITING Thelma Schoonmaker for *Raging Bull*
BEST MUSIC Michael Gore for *Fame*
BEST SONG Michael Gore (music), Dean Pitchford (lyrics) for "Fame" in *Fame*
BEST COSTUMES Anthony Powell for *Tess*
BEST VISUAL EFFECTS Brian Johnson, Richard Edlund, Dennis Muren, Bruce Nicholson for *Star Wars: Episode V – The Empire Strikes Back* (Special Achievement Award)
BEST SOUND Bill Varney, Steve Maslow, Gregg Landaker, Peter Sutton for *Star Wars: Episode V – The Empire Strikes Back*
BEST SOUND EFFECTS EDITING Not awarded

INDEX

1900 418
20th Century Fox
78, 326, 410, 654

A
Abbott, Diahnne 380
ABC Circle Films 124
ABC Pictures Corporation 32
– Action film
116, 188, 502, 678
Adam, Ken 388
Adames, John 738
Adams, Brooke 602
Adams, Jonathan 410
Addy, Wesley 472
Adjani, Isabelle 574
Adonis, Frank 744
Adorf, Mario 364, 662
Albatros Produktion 610
Albertson, Mabel 166
Albrecht, Erich 258
Alcott, John 70, 388, 778
Alda, Rutanya 584
Alexander, Dick 456
Alexander, Jane 456, 670
Allder, Nick 654
Aldredge, Theoni V. 334
Algranti, Clara 494
Alien 654
All the President's Men
456
Allégret, Catherine 158
Allen, Dede 396
Allen, Nancy 432, 730
Allen, Penelope 396
Allen, Sandra Elaine 494
Allen, Woody 556, 646
Allied Artists Pictures Corporation 274
Allin, Michael 188
Almendros, Néstor
602, 605, 670, 722
Alonzo, John A. 94, 318
Alvau, Pierluigi 562
Amerbroco 32
American Broadcasting Company 124
American Film Institute 532
The American Friend 508
American Graffiti 282
Aminoff, Marianne 626
Amjo Productions 448
Andréi, Frédéric 770
Andrews, Brian 618
Andy Warhol's Factory 213
Andy Warhol's Frankenstein 210
Annie Hall 556
Antonioni, Michelangelo
312, 315
Antonutti, Omero 562
Apocalypse Now 690
Arcalli, Franco
158, 312, 418
Archer, Peter 188
Argento, Dario 632
Argo, Victor 380
Argos Films 480, 662
Armstrong, David 306
Armstrong, R. G. 250
Arne, Peter 32
Arnold, Eddie 100
Arnold, Victor 64
Arrighi, Nike 196
Artémis Productions
418, 662
Artemyev, Edward 152
Artists Entertainment Complex 396
Ashby, Hal
94, 568, 698, 701
Aspegren, Chuck 584
Asquerino, María 514
Assault on Precinct 13 502
Atlantic City 764
Attaway, Ruth 478
Audran, Stéphane 144
Aumont, Jean-Pierre 196
Aumont, Tina 494
Autumn Sonata 626
Avildsen, John G. 464
Aykroyd, Dan 752
Ayling, Denys 654
Aznavour, Charles 662

B
Bach, Johann Sebastian
152, 626
Backlinie, Susan 348
Badham, John 540
Badlands 180
Badlands Company 180
Baez, Joan 56
Bakalyan, Richard 318
Baker, Fred 632
Baker, Ken 730
Baker, Kenny 522, 796
Balaban, Bob 548
Baldini, Oreste 288
Ball, Derek 522
Ballhaus, Michael 610
Balsam, Martin 456
Bancroft, Anne 714
Bang-Hansen, Arne 626
Banionis, Donatas 152
Baragli, Nino 250
Barber, Samuel 714
Barbieri, Gato 158
Barnet, Olga 152
Baron, Suzanne 662, 764
Barraqué, Martine 196, 722
Barry Lindon 388
Barry, John 522
Bartók, Béla 778
Bartold, Norman 204
Basehart, Richard 698
Bates, Jeanne 532
Bates, Michael 70
Baxter, Meredith 456
Baye, Nathalie 196
Bayler, Terence 684
BBS Productions 180
The Beatles 568
Beatty, Ned 116, 456, 472
Beck, John 220
Becker, Rolf 364
Beckerman, Sidney 440
Beckley, Tony 108
Bedejo, Bolaji 654
Beethoven, Ludwig van 266
Beggs, Richard 670
Beineix, Jean-Jacques
770, 773
Being There 698
Beldam, Lia 778
Bell, Gene 602
Bell, Wayne 298
Belushi, John 752, 755
Benchley, Peter 348
Benjamin, Richard 204
Bennent, David 662
Bennent, Heinz
364, 662, 722
Bennett, Tony 100
Benninger, Willi 364
Benton, Robert 166
Berbert, Marcel 196
Berenson, Marisa 124, 388
Berger, Mark 670
Bergman, Ingmar 626
Bergren, Eric 714
Berkoff, Steven 312, 388
Berlatsky, David 220
Bernstein, Carl 456
Bernstein, Elmer 752
Berry, Chuck 282
Berryman, Michael 356
Bertheau, Julien 144, 514
Bertolucci, Bernardo
158, 161, 418
Bertolucci, Giuseppe 418
Betti, Laura 418
Bia, Ambroise 312
Bieri, Ramon 180
Big screen bank robbery 399
Bill, Tony 242
Bill/Phillips 380
– Biopic 565, 744
Bioskop Film 364, 662
Birds of a Feather 594
Bisley, Steve 678
Bissell, Whit 266
Bisset, Jacqueline 196
Biziou, Peter 684
Björk, Halvar 626
Björnstrand, Gunnar 626
Black, John D. F. 64
Black, Karen 334
Blain, Gérard 508
Blair, Linda 228
Blakely, Colin 448
Blalack, Robert 522
Blatty, William Peter 228
Blossom, Roberts 334, 548
The Blues Brothers 752
Bochco, Steven 56
Bode, Ralf D. 540, 730
Bodinus, Carsten 574
Bogdanovich, Peter 100, 166
Bohm, Hark 610
Bohringer, Richard 770
Böll, Heinrich 364
Bonacelli, Paolo 638
Bondarchuk, Natalya 152
Bono, Joseph 744
The Boob Tube on the Big Screen 475
Booke, Sorrell 166

Boorman, John 116, 119
Bornstein, Charles 618
Bosisio, Liu 210
Bostwick, Barry 410
Bottoms, Sam 100, 670
Bottoms, Timothy 100
Bouquet, Carole 514
Bouvard, Philippe 486
Bovasso, Julie 540
Boxer, Nathan 670
– Boxing film 464, 744
Boyar, Sully 396
Boyle, Peter 326, 380
Bozzuffi, Marcel 78
Brackett, Leigh 796
Bracks, David 678
Brady, Bob 172
Brando, Marlon
132, 135, 158, 690
Brandywine Productions Ltd.
654
Brauer, Jürgen 258
Braunsberg Productions 210
Braunsberg, Andrew
210, 698
Breetley, Samuel E. 266
Bregman, Martin 396
Breillat, Catherine 158
Breit, Mitch 306
Brennan, Eileen 100, 242
Bretherton, David 124, 204
Brewer, Sherri 64
Brickman, Marshall 556, 646
Bridges, Jeff 100, 103, 786
Bright, Richard 288, 440
Brill, Fran 698
Brocco, Peter 356
Broderick, James 396
Brolin, James 204
Brooks, Albert 380
Brooks, Dean R. 356
Brooks, Mel 326, 329
Brooksfilms Ltd. 714
Brown, Alonzo 356
Brown, David 348
Brown, James 752
Brown, Phil 522
Brown, Steve 56
Browne, Cicely 494
Bruhns, Werner 418
Bruni, Peter 502
Bryant, Chris 234
Brynner, Yul 204
BSB 698
Buckley, Betty 432
Budd, Roy 108
Bumstead, Henry 242
Buñuel, Luis
144, 514, 517
Burbridge, Oteil 698
Burgess, Anthony 70
Burghardt, Arthur 472
Burgon, Geoffrey 684
Burns, Marilyn 298
Burns, Ralph 124
Burns, Tim 678
Burrows, Bill 472
Burstyn, Ellen 100, 228
Burton, Tony 464, 502, 778
Burtt, Ben 522
Bussières, Raymond 486
Butler, Artie 166
Butler, Bill 70, 348, 356
Byrd, George 610
Byrne, Anne 646

C

Caan, James 132
Cabaret 124
Caffarel, José María 312
Caine, Michael 108, 730
Cali, Joseph 540
Callaghan, Duke 342
Calloway, Cab 752
Cambern, Donn 100
Campbell, Nell 410
Candy, John 752
Canonero, Milena 388
Capri, Ahna 188
Caprioli, Vittorio 486
Cardwell, Herbert 532
Carelli, Joann 786
Carlisi, Olimpia 494
Carlo Ponti Cinematografica
210
Carlos, Walter 70
Carlos, Wendy 778
Carmen, Julie 738
Carpenter, John 618
Carow, Evelyn 258
Carow, Heiner 258
Carpenter, John 502, 505
Carradine, Robert 568
Carrie 432
Carrière, Jean-Claude
144, 514, 662
Carroll, Beeson 568
Carroll, Gordon 220, 654
Carroll, Larry 298
Carter, John 180
Carter, John R. 348
Carter, Joseph 744
Cartwright, Veronica 654
Casablanca Filmworks 638
Casanova, Giacomo 494
Casey 234
Casini, Stefania 418
Casinos in the Movies 767
Cassavetes, John
306, 309, 738
Cassavetes, Katherine 306
Cassel, Jean-Pierre 144
Cassel, Matthew 306
Castellano, Richard 132
Castillo, Jessica 738
Cattaneo, Bruno 234
Cazale, John
132, 288, 396, 584
Celluloid psychopaths 733
Cenna, Marino 562
Chamberlain, Howland 670
Champion, Jean 196
Chance, John T.
[= John Carpenter] 502
Chapman, Graham 684
Chapman, Michael
380, 744, 747
Charles, Ray 752
Charrière, Henri 274
Chartoff, Robert 464, 744
Chartoff-Winkler Productions
464, 744
Chayefsky, Paddy 472
Chen, Tina 402
Chew, Richard 356, 522
Chiles, Lois 334
The China Syndrome 706
Chinatown 318
Chopin, Frédéric 626
Christ at the Movies or
The New Testament in Film
687
Christian, Roger 522
Christie, Julie 234, 237
Christmas, Eric 94
Chung, Betty 188
Cimino, Michael
56, 584, 587, 786
Cinema 77 Films 730
Cinema Srl. 562
Cine-Neighbour Inc. 764
Cioffi, Charles 40, 64
CIPI Cinematografica S.A.
312
The City in Film 97
Ciupka, Richard 764
CKK 502
Clark, Candy 282
Clark, Jim 440
Clarke, Warren 70
Clayton, Jack 334
Cleese, John 684
Clementi, Margaret 494
Clemm, Susanna 730
Clennon, David 698
Cleveland, Carol 684
Clifford, Graeme 234, 410
Clive, John 70
A Clockwork Orange 70
**Close Encounters of
the Third Kind** 548
Clouse, Robert 188
Coates, Anne V. 714
Cobb, Lee J. 228
Coblenz, Walter 456
Coburn, James 220, 223
Coe, George 670
Cohen, Lawrence D. 432
Cohn, Nik 540
Colasanto, Nicholas 744
Cole, Nat King 180
Colley, Kenneth 684
Collier, Amalie 730
Collins, Stephen 456
Colucci, Michel 486
Coluche 486
Columbia Pictures Corporation
100, 380, 548, 670, 738
– Comedy 196, 282, 242,
410, 448, 486, 556, 594,
646, 684, 752
Coming Home 568
*Compagnia Cinematografica
Champion* 198
*Compass International
Pictures* 618
Concorde Productions Inc. 188
Connors, Chuck 266

Conrad, Joseph 670
Conrad, Scott 464
Conte, Richard 132
Conti, Bill 464, 738
Coolidge, Rita 220
Coppola, Carmine 288, 670
The Coppola Company 282, 288
Coppola, Francis Ford 132, 282, 288, 334, 690, 693
Coppola, Sam 540
Coquillon, John 32, 220
Corman, Avery 670
Cornwell, Tom 306
Corona-General 274
Corri, Adrienne 70
Cort, Bud 94
Cortese, Valentina 196
Cosma, Vladimir 486, 770
Cotten, Joseph 266, 786
Coulouris, George 274
Coulson, Thomas 532
Coward, Herbert "Cowboy" 116
Cox, Ronny 116
Crabc, James 464
Craven, Garth 220
Crawford, David 632
Crichton, Michael 204, 207
Crone, Lewis 116
Cronkite, Kathy 472
Crossbow Productions 326
Crossroads 678
Crothers, Scatman 778
The Cult Classic 413
Cundey, Dean 618
Curry, Tim 410
Curtis, Jamie Lee 618
Cusack, Cyril 94
Cushing, Peter 522
Cyphers, Charles 502, 618

D
D'Alquen, Jan 282
Dance film 540, 543
D'Angelo, Beverly 556
D'Antoni Productions 78
D'Antoni, Philip 78
Da Ma Produzione 594
Da Silva, Howard 334
Dalio, Marcel 486
Dallesandro, Joe 210
Dani 196
Daniels, Anthony 522, 796
Danny Lloyd 778
Danon, Marcello 594
Danziger, Allen 298
Darmon, Gérard 770
Dauman, Anatole 480, 662
David, Thayer 464
Davies, Paul 32
Davis, Brad 638
Dawn of the Dead 632
Day for Night 196
Days of Heaven 602
De Doses, Pia 86
De Funès, Louis 486, 489
De Negri, Giuliani G. 562
De Niro, Robert 288, 380, 418, 584, 744
De Palma, Brian 432, 730
De Vore, Christopher 714
Deal, Randall 116
Dedet, Yann 196
Deeley, Michael 584
The Deer Hunter 584
DEFA 258
Del Gre, Jesse 632
Delacorta 770
Delerue, Georges 196, 722
Deliverance 116
Delmare, Fred 258
Deman, Robert 274
Deneuve, Catherine 722, 725
Depardieu, Gérard 418, 722
Dern, Bruce 56, 59, 334, 568
Deruaz, Chantal 770
Deschanel, Caleb 306, 698
Desny, Ivan 610
– Detective film 64, 318
Devane, William 440
DeVito, Danny 356
Dewhurst, Colleen 556
Di Lazzaro, Dalila 210
Dickey, James 116
Dickinson, Angie 730
Digard, Uschi 372
Dilley, Leslie 522
Dillon, Melinda 548
Dino De Laurentiis Cinematografica 402
Diogene, Franco 638
Dirty Harry 48
The Discreet Charm of the Bourgeoisie 144
Diva 770
Dixon, Vernon 388
Dog Day Afternoon 396
Domröse, Angelica 258
Donaggio, Pino 234, 432, 730
Donati, Danilo 494
Don't Look Now 234
The Doors 670
Dorfmann, Robert 274
Douglas, Melvyn 698
Douglas, Michael 356
Dourif, Brad 356, 786
Dova, Ben 440
Dowd, Nancy 568
Down, Lesley-Anne 448
Doyle, Julian 684
– Drama 100, 124, 132, 158, 172, 180, 196, 234, 258, 288, 306, 312, 318, 334, 342, 356, 364, 380, 396, 472, 480, 508, 514, 540, 562, 568, 638, 626, 662, 714, 722, 744, 786, 764
Draper, Fred 306
Dressed to Kill 730
Dreyfuss, Richard 282, 348, 548
Druten, John van 124
Du Maurier, Daphne 234
DuBarry, Denise 698
Dubost, Paulette 722
Duering, Carl 70
Duff, Howard 670
Dufilho, Jacques 574
Dugan, John 298
Dunaway, Faye 318, 402, 405, 472
Dunham, Rosemarie 108
Dunn, Liam 166
Dunn, O. G. 306
Durning, Charles 242, 396
Duvall, Robert 132, 288, 472, 690
Duvall, Shelley 556, 778
Dvorzhetski, Vladislav 152
Dykstra, John 522
Dylan, Bob 220, 568
Dysart, Richard A. 698
Dzundza, George 584

E
Early, David 632
Eastern 188
Eastwood, Clint 48
Ebb, Fred 124
Edelman, Herb 342
Edgington, Lyn 48
Edlund, Richard 522, 796
Edwards, Blake 448
Egan, Eddie 78
Eggby, David 678
Eichhorn, Werner 364
Ekland, Britt 108
Elcar, Dana 242
Eldorado Films 234
The Elephant Man 714
Elfand, Martin 396
Ellis, Don 78
Elmer Productions 116
Elmes, Frederick 532
Elmi, Nicoletta 210
Elphick, Michael 714
Emge, David 632
EMI Films Ltd. 584
The End of Artificial Creatures 351
Engles, Judy 94
Enigma 698
Enter the Dragon 188
– Epic 418, 421, 758
Eraserhead 532
– Erotic film 480
Estrin, Robert 180
Eubank, Shari 372
Evans, Robert 318, 321, 440
Eveslage, Ron 282
The Exorcist 228

F
Fabbri, Jacques 770
Fabre, Michel 486
Faces 306
Falcon Films 618
Falk, Peter 306
– Family drama 670
Fantasy Films 356
Faragó, Katinka 626
Farber, Arlene 78
Farrell, Paul 70
Farrrow, Mia 334, 337
Fassbinder, Rainer Werner 610

Faulk, John Henry 298
Fechner, Christian 486
Feldman, Marty 326
Fellini, Federico 86, 494, 497
Fellini's Casanova 494
Fellini's Roma 86
Felsen, Milt 540
Fengler Films 610
Fengler, Michael 610
Fenty, Phillip 172
Ferrell, Conchata 472
Ferréol, Andréa 662, 722
Feuer, Cy 124
Feyginova, Ljudmila 152
Fielding, Jerry 32
Fields, Verna 166, 282, 348
Filmédis 626
Film in the GDR 261
Films A2 770
Films Christian Fechner 486
Films Concordia, Les 312
Films du Carrosse, Les 196, 722
Films du Losange, Les 508
Films Galaxie, Les 514, 770
Filmverlag der Autoren 508, 610
Filmways Pictures 730
Finch, Peter 472
Fink, Harry Julian 48
Fink, Rita M. 48
Fishburne, Laurence 690
Fisher, Carrie 522, 752, 796
Fisk, Jack 532
Fitzgerald, F. Scott 334
Fitzpatrick, Charles 180
Fleischer, Richard 266, 269
Fletcher, Louise 356
Florence, Fiona 86
Folsey Jr., George 752
Fonda, Henry 250
Fonda, Jane 40, 43, 568
Ford, Harrison 282, 522, 690, 796
Foree, Ken 632
Forman, Miloš 356
Forrest, Frederic 690
Forte, Fabrizio 562
Fosse, Bob 124
Foster, Jodie 380
Fox, John J. 502
Fraker, William A. 356
France, Richard 632
Franchina, Basilio 738
Francis, Clive 70
Francis, Freddie 714, 717
Franken, Steve 204
Frankeur, Paul 144
Franklin, Aretha 752
Franz, Dennis 730
Fraser, Shelagh 522
Frazier, Joe 464
Frazier, Sheila 172
Frederickson, Gray 288
Freeman, Joel 64
Freeman, Kathleen 752
Freleng, Isadore Friz 451
The French Connection 78
Fresholtz, Les 456
Fricke, Florian 574
Friedkin, William 78, 228
Friedman, Stephen J. 100
Fröhlich, Pea 610
Frohriep, Jürgen 258
Fruchtman, Lisa 690, 786
Fryer, Robert 778
Fuji, Tatsuya 480
Fujimoto, Tak 180
Fuller, Samuel 508
Furrer, Urs 64
Fux, Herbert 364

G

Gaines, George 456
Gaioni, Cristina 210
Galabru, Michel 594
Galletti, Giovanna 158
Gallo, Mario 306, 744
Gam, Rita 40
Gambina, Jimmy 464
– Gangster film 108, 132, 242, 288, 342, 508, 738
Ganz, Bruno 508, 574
Garfinkle, Louis 584
Garnica, Lupe 738
Garr, Teri 326, 548
Garrick, Beulah 396
Gary, Harold 78
Gary, Lorraine 348
Gastaldi, Ernesto 250
Gaumont 574
Gay, Norman 228
Gaye Scott, Linda 204
Gazzo, Michael V. 288
Geer, Ellen 94
Gelderse Maatschappij N. V. 440
Gensac, Claude 486
George, Nathan 40
George, Susan 32
Gere, Richard 602
Gershwin, George 646
Get Carter 108
Gibb, Barry 540
Gibb, Maurice 540
Gibb, Robin 540
Gibson, Henry 752
Gibson, Mel 678
Gielgud, John 714
Gierasch, Stefan 166
Gierke, Henning von 574
Giger, H. R. 654, 657
Gil, Vincent 678
Giler, David 654
Gilliam, Terry 684
Ginty, Robert 568
Giordo, Pietro 562
Giovannoli, Renato 86
Girotti, Massimo 158
Gizzi, Claudio 210
Glass, Seamon 116
Glatzeder, Winfried 258
Glenn, Pierre-William 196
Gloria 738
Go, Eiji 342
The Goblins 632
The Godfather 132
The Godfather – Part II 288
Godsell, Vanda 448
Goldman, Bo 356
Goldman, Danny 326
Goldman, William 440, 456
Goldsmith, Jerry 274, 318, 654
Goldstone, John 684
Gonzales, Peter 86
Goodman, David Zelag 32
Gooyer, Rijk de 574
Gordon, Don 274
Gordon, Hannah 714
Gordon, Keith 730
Gordon, Leo 250
Gordon, Ruth 94, 97
Gorenstein, Friedrich 152
Gorney, Karen Lynn 540
Gornick, Michael 632
Gottfried, Howard 472
Gotthardt, Peter 258
Gottlieb, Carl 348
Gould, Harold 242
Gover, Michael 70
Goya, Tito 440
Grady, James 402
Graham, Angelo P. 288
Graham, John Michael 618
Grass, Günter 662
Gray, Charles 410
The Great Gatsby 334
Greenberg, Gerald B. 78, 670, 690, 730, 786
Greenberg, Stanley R. 266
Greene Bricmont, Wendy 556
Greenwich Film Productions 144, 514, 770
Gregory, Mary 568
Grey, Joel 124
Grieg, Edvard 266
Griem, Helmut 124
Grimaldi, Alberto 158, 418, 494
Grinko, Nikolai 152
Grisanti, Christina 306
Grohmann, Martje 574
Grosso, Sonny 78
– Grotesque 86
Groth, Jan 574
Grumberg, Jean-Claude 722
Grusin, Dave 342, 402
Gruskoff, Michael 56, 326, 574
Gruskoff/Venture Films 326
Guardino, Harry 48
Guare, John 764
Guerra, Tonino 210
Guffey, Cary 548
Guidice, Don 342, 402
Guinness, Alec 522, 796
Guiomar, Julien 486
Gunn, Moses 64
Gus Productions 40

H

Hackman, Gene 78, 326
Hagiwara, Kenichi 758
Hall, Albert 690
Hall, Conrad L. 440
Hallelujah Films 662

Halloween 618
Halsey, Richard 220, 464
Hambling, Gerry 638
Hamill, Mark 522, 796
Hamilton, Gay 388
Hamilton, Murray 348
Hamlisch, Marvin 242
Händel, Georg Friedrich 388, 626
Handmade Films Ltd. 684
Hansen, Gunnar 298
Harris, Herb 670
Hartburg, Christy 372
Harold and Maude 94
Harris, Julius 172
Harrison, Harry 266
Hartley, Richard 410
Harwood, Bo 306
Hauben, Lawrence 356
Haudepin, Sabine 722
Hawk Films 388
Hawk Films Ltd. 70
Hawkins, Ronnie 786
Hayden, Sterling 132, 418
Haydn, Richard 326
Hayes, Billy 638
Hayes, Cliff 678
Hayes, Isaac 64, 67
Head, Edith 242
Heaven's Gate 786
Heffernan, John 242
Heffernan, Robert 306
Heim, Alan 472
Heller, Paul M. 188
Hellman, Jerome 568
Hemingway, Mariel 646
Hendry, Ian 108, 312
Henkel, Anna 418
Henkel, Kim 298
Henney, Del 32
Henriksen, Lance 396, 548
Henry, Buck 166
Henry, Justin 670
Henze, Hans Werner 364
Herman Jr., Roger 348
Héroux, Denis 764
Herr, Michael 690
Herrmann, Bernard 380, 383
Herrmann, Edward 334
Herzog, Werner 574
Heston, Charlton 266
Heyman, Barton 228
Hickman, Bill 78
Higgins, Colin 94
Highsmith, Patricia 508
Hildyard, David 124
Hill, Debra 618
Hill, George Roy 242
Hill, Terence 250, 253
Hill, Walter 124, 654
Hiller, Wendy 714
Hillerman, John 100, 318
Hinwood, Peter 410
Hirsch, Paul 432, 522, 796
Hirschfeld, Gerald 326
Hirschler, Kurt 188
– Historical film 388, 418, 758
Ho, Leonardo 188
Hodges, Mike 108
Hoffer, William 638
Hoffman, Dustin 32, 274, 440, 456, 670
Hoger, Hannelore 364
Holbrook, Hal 456
Holden, William 472
Holly, Buddy 282
Holm, Claus 610
Holm, Ian 654
Hooper, Tobe 298
Hopkins, Anthony 714
Hopkins, Bo 282, 638
Hopper, Dennis 508, 690
– Horror film 210, 228, 234, 298, 326, 348, 432, 532, 618, 574, 632, 654, 778, 781
Houseman, John 402
Howard, John C. 326
Howard, Ron 282
Hoya Productions 228
Hoyt, Robert L. 348
Hubbs, Gil 188
Huppert, Isabelle 786
Hurt, John 638, 654, 714, 786
Huston, John 318
Hutchison, Ken 32
Huyck, Willard 282

I

Ide, Masato 758
Idle, Eric 684
Ikebe, Shin'ichirô 758
In-Cine Compañía Industrial Cinematográfica S.A. 514
Ingemarsson, Sylvia 626
International Cinema Corporation 764
In the Realm of the Senses 480
Irving, Amy 432
Isherwood, Christopher 124
Isnardon, Monique 486, 594
Isnardon, Robert 486, 594
Itô, Hideo 480
Ivanov, Wladimir 486
Ivers, Peter 532

J

Jack Rollins & Charles H. Joffe Productions 646
Jack's Return Home 108
Jackson, Anne 778
Jaeckel, Richard 220
Jaffe, Stanley R. 670
Japan as Film Nation 761
Jarre, Maurice 662
Järvet, Yuri 152
Jaws 348
Jayne Productions 568
Jenkins, George 456
Jenson, Roy 266, 318
Jerome Hellman Productions 568
Joffe, Charles H. 556, 646
John, Gottfried 610
Johnson, Ben 100
Johnson, Brian 654, 796
Johnson, Diane 778
Johnson, J.J. 64
Johnson, Jed 210
Johnson, Mary Lea 778
Johnstone, Paul 678
Jones, Alan 448
Jones, Booker T. 282
Jones, Freddie 714
Jones, Isham 556
Jones, James Earl 522, 796
Jones, Len 32
Jones, Robert C. 568
Jones, Robert Earl 242
Jones, Terry 684
Jones-Davies, Sue 684
Joplin, Scott 242
Jordan, Richard 342
Jory, Victor 274
Joseph, Allen 532
Josephson, Erland 626
Joston, Darwin 502, 532
Jouer Limited 326
Joy, Robert 764
Juerging, Arno 210
Jurado, Katy 220

K

Kagemusha 758
Kahn, Madeline 166, 326
Kahn, Michael 548
Kahn, Sheldon 356
Kander, John 94, 670
Kane, Carol 396, 556
Kane, Michael 402
Kaplan, J. S. 502
Karlin, Fred 204
Karlin, Miriam 70
Kasdan, Lawrence 796
Katt, William 432
Katz, Gloria 282
Katz, Peter 234
Katz, Stephen M. 752
Kean, Marie 388
Keaton, Diane 132, 288, 556, 559, 646
Keays-Byrne, Hugh 678
Keegan, Robert 32
Keetman, Gunild 180
Keitel, Harvey 380
Keith, Brian 342
Keller, Marthe 440
Kellin, Mike 638
Kelly, Jim 188
Kelly, Paula 266
Kelly, Sharon 372
Kemmerling, Warren 548
Kemper, Victor J. 396
Kennedy Miller Productions 678
Kennedy, Byron 678
Kershaw, Doug 602
Kershner, Irvin 796
Kesey, Ken 356
Kiebach, Hans Jürgen 124
Kien, Shih 188
Kier, Udo 210
Kilpatrick, Lincoln 266
King, Stephen 432

Kinski, Klaus 574, 577
Kishi, Keiko 342
Klein, Jean-Pierre 722
Kline, Richard H. 266
Klinger, Michael 108, 111
Klingman, Lynzee 356
Kluge, P.F. 396
Klute 40
Knapp, Douglas 502
Knesich, Tony 738
Knieper, Jürgen 508
Knight, C. Darin 584
Knudson, Robert 124, 228
Kobayashi, Kanae 480
Koenekamp, Fred J. 274
Kokonoe, Kyôji 480
Körner, Diana 388
Kosiński, Jerzy 698
Kotto, Yaphet 654
Kovács, László 166
Kramer, Jeffrey 348
Kramer vs. Kramer 670
Kreuzer, Lisa 508
Kristofferson, Kris 220, 786, 789
Krüger, Hardy 352
Kubrick, Stanley 70, 388, 778
Kuhlmann, Harald 364
Kurosawa, Akira 758
Kurtz, Gary 522, 796
Kuveiller, Luigi 210
Kwouk, Burt 448

L

La Motta, Jake 744
Laborteaux, Matthew 306
Ladd, Diane 318
Ladengast, Walter 574
Laine, Frankie 100
Lamprecht, Günter 610
Lancaster, Burt 418, 764
Lancaster, Stuart 372
Landaker, Gregg 796
Landis, John 752
Lange, Jean 532
Langlet, Daniel 486
Larch, John 48
Larner, Stevan 180
Larroquette, John 298
Laser, Dieter 364
Lassick, Sydney 432
The Last Metro 722
The Last Picture Show 100
Last Tango in Paris 158
Laub, Marc 132
Laurel Group 632
Laurent, Rémi 594
Laurie, Piper 432
Lawrence, Elliot 472
Lawrence, Marc 440
Lawson, Tony 32, 388
Lazar, John 372
Lazar, Veronica 158
Lazarus III, Paul 204
Le Mat, Paul 282
Leachman, Cloris 100, 326
Leatherface—Serial Killers in Film 301
Léaud, Jean-Pierre 158, 196, 199
Ledda, Gavino 562
Lee, Bruce 188, 191
Lee, Carl 172
The Legend of Paul and Paula 258
Legrand, Michel 764
Lem, Stanislaw 152
Leone, Sergio 250
Lerner, Carl 40
Lettieri, Al 132
Lewis, Andy 40
Lewis, Dave 40
Lewis, Geoffrey 250
Lewis, Mildred 94
Lewis, Ted 108
Libertini, Richard 602
Ligeti, György 778
Lilienthal, Peter 730
Liofredi, Marco 210
– Literary adaptation 32, 70, 78, 124, 274, 334, 356, 364, 388, 494, 508, 562, 662, 778
Littlejohn, Gary 180
Litto, George 730
Lo Bianco, Tony 78
Lojodice, Adele Angela 494
Løkkeberg, Georg 626
Lom, Herbert 448
Lombardo, Carmen 556
Long Road 318
Loomis, Nancy 502, 618
Loose, William 372
Lopez, Perry 318
Lorenz, Juliane 610
Lorimar Film Entertainment 698
Lottman, Evan 228
The Lost Honor of Katharina Blum 364
Louÿs, Pierre 514
Lovejoy, Ray 778
– Love story 258
Low-Budget Productions 535
Löwitsch, Klaus 610
Lucas, George 282, 285, 522
Lucas, Marcia 282, 380, 522
Lucasfilm Ltd. 282, 522, 796
Ludwig, Karen 646
Ludwig, Rolf 258
Luke, Benny 594
Lulli, Piero 250
Lumet, Sidney 396, 472
Luther, Igor 662
Lutz, Regine 364
Luu, Thuy An 770
Lynch, David 532, 714

M

Macchi, Egisto 562
Maccone, Ronald 738
MacDougall, Don 522
MacGowran, Jack 228
MacInnes, Angus 764
MacLaine, Shirley 698
Mad Max 678
Mad Max Films 678
Madery, Earl 348
Magee, Patrick 70, 388
Maggart, Brandon 730
Magnani, Anna 86
Magrini, Gitt 158
Mainardi, Elisa 86
Mainka-Jellinghaus, Beate 574
Maitland, Marne 86
Malick, Terrence 180, 602
Malkin, Barry 288
Malle, Louis 764
The Malpaso Company 48
The Man 172
Mancini, Henry 448
Mandel, Johnny 698
Mandel, Steve 116
Maneri, Luisa 594
Manhattan 646
Mansfield, David 786
Manz, Linda 602
Mao Ying, Angela 188
Maran-Film 722
Marangolo, Agostino 632
Marathon Man 440
Marconi, Saverio 562
Margheriti, Antonio 210
Margolin, Janet 556
Margulies, David 730
Marital mayhem 673
Markham, Petra 108
Marks, Barbara 132
Marks, Richard 288, 690
Marley, John 132
The Marriage of Maria Braun 610
Marriott, John 396
Mars, Kenneth 166, 326
Marshall, Alan 638
Märthesheimer, Peter 610
– Martial arts film 188
Martin, Jean 254
Martin, Mardik 744
Martino, Al 132
Mascagni, Pietro 744
Mashida, Kyosuke 342
Masini, Mario 562
Maslow, Steve 796
Mason, Hilary 234
Masteroff, Joe 124
Masterson, Peter 228
Mastroianni, Ruggero 86, 494
Masur, Richard 786
Matania, Clelia 234
Matsuda, Eiko 480
Matsui, Yasuko 480
Maurier, Claire 594
May, Brian 678
Mayhew, Peter 522, 796
Mayore, Stefano 86
McCaughey, William L. 584
McCausland, James 678
McCune, Grant 522
McDowell, Malcolm 70, 73

McGinn, Walter 402
McGregor, Charles 172
McGuire, Deborah 372
McHenry, Don 402
McKenna, T.P. 32
McKinney, Bill 116
McLaren, Hollis 764
McMinn, Teri 298
McMurtry, Larry 100
McNamara, J. Patrick 548
McRoberts, Briony 448
McQueen, Steve 274
Meat Loaf 410
Mello, Jay 348
Melnick, Daniel 32
– Melodrama 602
Melvin, Murray 388
Menez, Bernard 196
Mercer, Mae 48
Merchant Films 764
Meredith, Burgess 464
Merrick, David 334
Meyer, Friedrich 662
Meyer, Russ 372, 375
MGM 64, 108, 204, 220, 266, 312, 472
Michael Gruskoff Productions 56
Michelangeli, Marcella 562
Michi, Maria 158
Middlemass, Frank 388
Midnight Express 638
Miki, Minoru 480
Milford, Penelope 568
Milius, John 690
Miller, Barry 540
Miller, George 678
Miller, Jason 228
Miller, Kathleen 568
Minkler, Bob 522
Minnelli, Liza 124, 127
Miracle, Irene 638
Mitchell, Gwenn 64
Mitchum, John 48
Moffat, Geraldine 108
Moli Films 730
Molina, Ángela 514
Molinaro, Édouard 594
Mollo, John 522
Monash, Paul 432
Montagu, Ashley 714
Montgomery, Bryan 180
Monty Python's Life of Brian 684
Moor, Bill 670
Moore, Robin 78
Moore, Thomas 396
Moran, Tony 618
Morante, Massimo 632
Moreau, Jean-Jacques 770
Moretti, Nanni 562
Morgan, Chesty 494
Moriarty, Cathy 744
Moroder, Giorgio 638
Morricone, Ennio 250, 418, 594, 602
Morris, John 326, 714
Morrison, Barbara 274
Morrissey, Paul 210
Morse, Susan E. 646
Morsella, Fulvio 250
Mosfilm 152
Moshin, Gastone 288
Mozart, Wolfgang Amadeus 388
Muller, Frederick 234
Müller, Robby 730
Müller, Ulrich 250
Mulvehill, Charles 94
Mulvehill, Chuck 312
Mumy, Bill 274
Muni 514
Murch, Walter 690
Muren, Dennis 796
Murnau, Friedrich Wilhelm 574
Murota, Hideo 758
Murphy, Michael 646
– Musical 124, 410
– Music film 752
Musson, Bernard 514
Myers, Stanley 584
My Name is Nobody 250
Myrow, Fred 266

N

Nakadai, Tatsuya 758
Nakajima, Aoi 480
Nance, Jack 532
Nannuzzi, Armando 250, 594
Napier, Charles 372
Nathan, Vivian 40
Neal, Edwin 298
Near, Laurel 532
Nelson, Barry 778
Nelson, George R. 288
Network 472
Neumann-Viertel, Elisabeth 124
Newdon Productions 334
Newman, Christopher 228
Newman, David 166
Newman, Paul 242
New York as a Hollywood Backdrop 649
Nicholls, Phoebe 714
Nicholson, Bruce 796
Nicholson, Jack 312, 318, 356, 359, 778
Niles, Polly 172
Nitzsche, Jack 228, 356
Noda, Shinkichi 480
Noonan, Tom 738
Northstar 698
Norton, Jim 32
Nosferatu 574
N. V. Zvaluw 356
Nykvist, Sven 626
Nyman, Lena 626

O

O'Bannon, Dan 654
O'Brien, Richard 410
O'Donoghue, Michael 646
O'Malley, Reverend William 228
O'Neal, Ron 172, 175
O'Neal, Ryan 166, 388
O'Steen, Sam 318
Oates, Warren 180
Odier, Daniel 770
Ogier, Bulle 144
Ogorodnikova, Tamara 152
Okada, Eiji 342
Okazaki, Kozo 342
Olbrychski, Daniel 662
Oliveri, Mariella 662
Olivier, Laurence 440
Omni Zoetrope 690
One Flew Over the Cuckoo's Nest 365
Oppenheimer, Alan 204
Orff, Carl 180
Ornstein, Bruce 540
Osborne, John 108
Oshima Productions 480
Oshima, Nagisa 480, 483
Osuna, Jess 670
Otaki, Shuji 758
Oz, Frank 796

P

Pacino, Al 132, 288, 396
Padre Padrone 562
Pagé, Ilse 662
Painting and Film 391
Pakula, Alan J. 40, 456, 459
Palin, Michael 664
Pape, Paul 540
Papillon 274
Paramount Pictures 94, 132, 288, 318, 334, 402, 440, 540, 602, 764
Paramount-Orion Filmproduktion 364
Parfrey, Woordrow 274
Parker, Alan 638
Parks, Gordon 64
Parks Jr., Gordon 172
Parry, Geoff 678
Partain, Paul A. 298
Partisan Productions 786
Pasquale, Frédéric de 78
The Passenger 312
Paterson, Tony 678
Pat Garrett and Billy the Kid 220
Patten, Dick van 204
Payne, James 242
Pearl, Daniel 298
PECF 196
Peckinpah, Sam 32, 35, 220
Peets, Remus 250
Penderecki, Krzysztof 228, 778
Pendleton, Austin 166
Penthouse 318
Peploe, Mark 312
Peraino, Lou 298
Peregrine 388, 778
Perpignani, Roberto 158, 562
Personafilm 626
Persons, Mark 56
Pesci, Joe 744
Pescow, Donna 540

Peters, Brock 266
Peverall, John 584
Phillips, Julia
242, 380, 548
Phillips, Mackenzie 282
Phillips, Michael
242, 380, 548
Piantadosi, Arthur 456
PIC 196
Piccoli, Michel 144, 764
Pickens, Slim 220
Pickles, Vivian 94
Piéplu, Claude 144
Pierson, Frank 396
Pignatelli, Fabio 632
Pingitore, Carl 48
The Pink Panther Strikes Again 448
Pinon, Dominique 770
Pitts, Charles 372
Pleasence, Donald 618
Plemiannikov, Hélène
144, 514
Plenzdorf, Ulrich 258
Poerio, Adelina 234
Pointer, Priscilla 432
Poiret, Jean 594, 722
Polanski, Roman 318
Polaris Productions 70
Polito, Gene 204
– Political drama 440
– Political thriller
266, 440, 443, 456
– Police film 78
Pollack, Sydney 342, 402
Ponti, Carlo 210, 312
Popol Vuh 574
Portman, Richard 584
Potts, Cliff 56
Powell, Addison 402
Pozo, Ángel del 312
Pressman, Lawrence 64
Pressman-Williams 180
Presson Allen, Jay 124
Previn, Steve 234
Priestley, Tom 116, 334
Prim, Monique 770
Prince, Steven 380
– Prison film 274, 638, 641
Probyn, Brian 180
Prochnow, Jürgen 364
Producers Circle 778
Productions Artistes Associés, Les
86, 158, 418, 594
Productions Jacques-Leitienne, Les 250
Produzioni Europee Associati
86, 158, 418, 494
Prowse, David 522, 796
Przygodda, Peter 364, 508
– Psycho drama 532
Purcell, Henry 670
Puttnam, David 638
Puzo, Mario 132, 288
Python (Monty) Pictures-Limited 684

Q

Quaid, Randy 100, 638
Quinn, Patricia 410

R

Raben, Peer 610
Rafran Cinematografica 250
Raging Bull 744
RAI 562
Ramage, Jack 670
Rambaldi, Carlo 654
Ramey, Ed 116
Rassam Productions 210
Rawlings, Terry 654
Rawlins, David 540
Ray, Johnny 100
Ray, Nicholas 508
Rayfiel, David 402
Rebbot, Ann 78
Rebello, Chris 348
Redbank Films 432
Redden, Billy 116
Redeker, Quinn K. 584
Redfield, William 356
Redford, Robert
242, 334, 402, 456
Reid, Kate 764
Reiniger, Scott H. 632
Remake 574
Renoir, Claude 486
Rey, Fernando
78, 144, 147, 514
Reynolds, Burt 116
Reynolds, Norman 522
Reynolds, William
132, 242, 786
Rialto Film 250
Richard, Edmond 144, 514
Richard, Jean-Louis
196, 722
Richards, Kim 502
Richards, Kyle 618
Richards, Martin 778
Richardson, Sallye 298
Richmond, Anthony B. 234
Richter-Reinick, Dietmar 258
Richthofen, Sigrid von 124
Riesner, Dean 48
Riddle, Nelson 334
Rifkin, Ron 56
Risch, Maurice 722
RM Films International 372
Road Movies Filmproduktion 508
Robards, Jason 220, 456
Robbins, Michael 448
Robbins, Rex 64
Robert Stigwood Organization 540
Roberts, Judith Anna 532
Roberts, Tony 556
Robertson, Cliff 402
Robertson, Hugh A. 64
Robertson, Robbie 744
Robinson, Andrew 48
Robinson, Edward G. 266
Rocha, David 514
Rochin, Aaron 584
Rocky 464
The Rocky Horror Picture Show 410
Roeg, Nicolas 234
Roizman, Owen
78, 228, 402, 472
Rolf, Tom 380, 786
Roll, Clarissa Mary 494
The Rolling Stones 568
Rollins, Jack 556
Romand, Anny 770
Romero, George A. 632, 635
Roos, Fred 288
Rosenblum, Ralph 556
Rosenman, Leonard 388
Ross, Gaylen 632
Rossiter, Leonard 448
Rota, Nino
86, 132, 288, 494
Roth, Philip 166
Rotunno, Giuseppe 86, 494
Roundtree, Richard 64
Rousselot, Philippe 770
Rowland, Henry 372
Rowlands, Gena
306, 738, 741
Rowlands, Lady 306
Rubin, Alan 752
Rubinstein, Richard P. 632
Ruddy, Albert S. 132
Runacre, Jenny 312
Running on Empty—
The Big Screen Chase 81
Russo, Gianni 132
Ruzzolini, Giuseppe 250
Rye, Ann 234
Ryu, Daisuke 758

S

Sadoyan, Isabelle 514
Saitô, Takao 758
Saldana, Theresa 744
Salt, Waldo 568
Salter, Nicholas 234
Sampson, Will 356
Samuel, Joanne 678
Sanda, Dominique 418
Sander, Otto 662
Sandin, Will 618
Sanger, Jonathan 714
Santoni, Reni 48
Sarandon, Chris 396
Sarandon, Susan 410, 764
Sarkissian, Sos 152
Saticoy Productions 166
Satie, Erik 180
– Satire 94
Saturday Night Fever 540
Savage, John 584
Savage, Peter 744
Sawyer, William A. 94
Saxon, John 188
Sbarra, Galliano 86
Scarpa, Renato 234
Scarpitta, Carmen 494, 594
Schaer, Cherina 32
Schaffner, Franklin J. 274
Scheider, Roy
40, 78, 348, 440
Schenk, Frank 258
Schickele, Peter 56

Schiffman, Suzanne 196, 722
Schifrin, Lalo 48, 51, 188
Schlesinger, John 440
Schlöndorff, Volker 364, 662, 665
Schmid, Daniel 508
Schmidt-Reitwein, Jörg 574
Schneider, Bert 602
Schneider, Harold 602
Schneider, Maria 158, 312
Schneider, Stanley 402
Schoonmaker, Thelma 744
Schrader, Leonard 342
Schrader, Paul 342, 380, 744
Schubert, Franz 388
Schuler, Fred 738
Schumann, Robert 626
Schündler, Rudolf 508
Schygulla, Hanna 610, 613
Science Fiction 155
– Science Fiction 56, 152, 204, 266, 522, 548, 654, 678, 796
Scorsese, Martin 380, 744
Scott, Allan 234
Scott, Ridley 654
– Screwball comedy 166
Sédif Productions 722
Segui, Pierre 584
Seitz, Franz 662
Sellers, Peter 448, 698
Selta Films 764
Seltzer, Walter 266
Semple Jr., Lorenzo 274, 402
Semyonov, Yulian 152
September 19 372
Sequoia Productions 188
Serato, Massimo 234
Seresin, Michael 638
Serial Space Operas 525
Seri, Meika 480
Serrault, Michel 594, 597
Sewell, George 108
– Sex film 372
Seyrig, Delphine 144
Shaft 64
Shaft Productions Ltd. 64
Shakar, Martin 540
Shapiro, Melvin 380
Sharif, Omar 448
Sharman, Jim 410
Shaw, Eddie 306
Shaw, Robert 242, 348
Shaw, Sam 306, 738
Shaw, Victoria 204
Shawn, Wallace 646, 764
Sheen, Martin 180, 690
Shelley, Mary Wollstonecraft 326
Shepard, Sam 602
Shepherd, Cybill 100, 380
Shibata Organisation Inc. 480
Shigeta, James 342
Shiho, Takayuki 758
The Shining 778
Shiraishi, Naomi 480
Shire, David 456, 540
Shire, Talia 132, 288, 464
Shore, Sig 172
Shultis, Jackie 602
Shusett, Ronald 654
Siedow, Jim 298
Siegel, Don 48
Signorelli, James 172
Silberman, Irène 770
Silberman, Serge 144, 514
Silent Running 56
Silvi, Franca 210
Simon, Paul 556
Simonetti, Claudio 632
Skerritt, Tom 654
Slocombe, Douglas 334
Small, Michael 40, 440
Smith, Bud 228
Smith, Charles Martin 282
Smith, Howard 632
Smith, Paul 638
Snider, Barry 40
– Social grotesque 144
– Social satire 698
Societe Alcinter, La 250
Société Française de Production 722
Societe Imp Ex Cl, La 250
Söderlund, Ulla-Britt 388
Solar Productions 274
Solaris 152
Soles, P.J. 432, 618
Solomon, Murray 132
Solonitsyn, Anatoli 152
Sommer, Josef 48
Soylent Green 266
Spacek, Sissy 180, 432, 435
Spaghetti Western 250
Sparks, Cheryl 56
Spielberg, Steven 348, 548
Spies, Manfred 312
Spikings, Barry 584
Spinell, Joe 464
– Spoof 250, 326, 410, 684
Spottiswoode, Roger 32, 220
Spradlin, G.D. 288, 690
Springer, Gary 396
– Spy film 402
St. John, Christopher 64
Stallone, Sylvester 464, 467
Standing, John 714
Stanford, Thomas 342
Stanton, Harry Dean 654
Starr, Hay 100
Star Wars 522
Star Wars: Episode V – The Empire Strikes Back 796
The Star Wars Saga 799
Stears, John 522
Steinkamp, Frederic 342
Stell, Aaron 56
Stephens, Nancy 618
Steppenwolf 568
Stevens, Cat 94
Stewart, Alexandra 196
Stewart, Charlotte 532
Stigwood, Robert 540
The Sting 242
Stoker, Austin 502
Stoker, Bram 574
Stoler, Shirley 584
Stone, Leonard 266
Stone, Oliver 638
Stone, Philip 778
Storaro, Vittorio 158, 418, 690
Strabel, Herbert 124
Straight, Beatrice 472
Strasberg, Lee 288, 291
Strassberg, Morris 40
Straw Dogs 32
Streep, Meryl 584, 646, 670
Streisand, Barbra 166, 169
Stunts 681
Subjective Camera 621
Subliminal Messages 231
Suede Film 626
Sugimori, Shuhei 758
Summers, Neil 250
Summers, Shari 94
Super Fly 172
Supervixens 372
Surtees, Robert 100, 242, 245
Suschitzky, Peter 410, 796
Suschitzky, Wolfgang 108
Sutherland, Donald 40, 234, 418, 494
Sutton, Peter 796
Swink, Robert 274
Sydow, Max von 228, 402
Sze, Yang 188

T

Takakura, Ken 342
Talent Associates Ltd. 32
Tango Film 610
Tarassov, Viacheslav 152
Tarkovsky, Andrei 152
Taviani, Paolo 562
Taviani, Vittorio 562
Tavoularis, Dean 288
Taxi Driver 380
Taylor, Gilbert 522
Taylor, James 180
Taylor-Young, Leigh 266
Tchaikovsky, Pyotr Ilych 266
Terrorism in German Film 367
The Texas Chain Saw Massacre 298
TF1 Films Productions 722
Thackeray, William Makepeace 388
Thalbach, Katharina 662
Thacher, Russell 266
That Obscure Object of Desire 514
Thomsett, Sally 32
Three Days of the Condor 402
Threlkeld, Gail 180
– Thriller 32, 40, 48, 64, 70, 116, 348, 730, 770

Tidyman, Ernest 64, 78
The Tin Drum 662
Tipton, George Aliceson 180
Tognazzi, Ugo 594
Toho 758
TOIE Co. LTD. 342
Tonoyama, Taiji 480
Topham, Frank 744
Topor, Roland 574
Tosi, Mario 432
Tovoli, Luciano 312
Towne, Robert 318, 342
– Tragicomedy 94, 196
Travolta, John 432, 540
Treves, Sir Frederick 714
Trio Film 610
Trissenaar, Elisabeth 610
Tristan, Dorothy 40
Trotta, Margarethe von 364
True Crime Dramas 183
Truffaut, François 196, 548, 722
Trumbo, Donald 274, 277
Trumbull, Douglas 56, 551
Trumper, John 108
Turkel, Joe 778
Turtle 502
Tyler, Willie 568
Tyner, Charles 94

U

Ueda, Masaharu 758
Uhlen, Gisela 610
Ullmann, Linn 626
Ullmann, Liv 626, 629
Ultra Film 86
Unali, Marco 562
United Artists 472, 556, 744, 786
Universal Pictures 56, 282, 242, 348, 584, 752
Unsworth, Geoffrey 124
Uraoka, Keiichi 480

V

Vacano, Jost 364
Vail, William 298
Valerii, Tonino 250
Valli, Romolo 418
Van Hamme, Jean 770
Vance, Kenny 646
Vándor, Iván 312
Vanlint, Derek 654
Varney, Bill 796
Vasile, Turi 86
Vaughan, Peter 32
Veber, Francis 594
Vela, Roseanne 786
Venantini, Venantino 594
Vernon, John 48
Vernon, Richard 448
Vespermann, Gerd 124
Vidal, Gore 86
– Vietnam film 568, 584, 690
Villaseñor, George C. 738
Villette, Guy 144
Vincent, Frank 744
Vint, Alan 180
Vint, Jesse 56
Vita, Helen 124
Vivaldi, Antonio 388, 670
Voight, Jon 116, 568, 571
Vooren, Monique van 210
Vortex 298
Vosgerau, Karl Heinz 364
Vukotic, Milena 144, 514

W

Wagner, Richard 514
Waldman, Frank 448
Walken, Christopher 556, 584, 786
Walker, Roy 388
Wall, Bob 188
Wallace, Tommy Lee 618
Waller, Fats 532
Walston, Ray 242
Ward, David S. 242
Ward, Roger 678
Warden, Jack 456, 698
– War film 690
Warhol, Andy 210
Warner Bros. 40, 48, 70, 116, 188, 228, 342, 456, 778
Warner, David 32
Warner, Frank 548
Warschilka, Edward 94
Warwick Associates 730
Washburn, Deric 56, 584
Wasserman, Dale 356
Waterston, Sam 334, 786
Watters, George 188
Waxman, Al 764
Waxman, Harry 448
WDR 364, 508, 610
Weatherley, Peter 654
Weathers, Carl 464
Weaver, Fritz 440
Weaver, Sigourney 556, 654
Webb, James E. 456
Weber, André 514
Weber, Billy 602
Webster, Donald 32
Weintraub, Fred 188
Weiss, Robert K. 752
Weissberg, Eric 116
Weisser, Norbert 638
Weitershausen, Barbara von 508
Welland, Colin 32
Wenders, Wim 508, 511
Wenzel, Heidemarie 258
Wepper, Fritz 124
Werner Herzog Filmproduktion 574
West, Ray 522
West, Martin 502
– Western 220, 786
Westworld 204
Wexler, Haskell 356, 568, 602
Wexler, Norman 540
What's Up, Doc? 166
Wheeler, Charles F. 56
White, Dorothy 108
White, Michael 410
Whitelaw, Sandy 508
Wiggins-Fernandez, Wilhelmenia 770
Wilder, Gene 326
Wildwood 456
Wildwood Enterprises 402
Wilke, Robert J. 602
Wilkinson, John 602
Williams, Billy Dee 228, 796
Williams, Cindy 282
Williams, Gordon 32
Williams, Hank 100
Williams, John 348, 522, 548, 796
Williams, Sharon 234
Willis, Gordon 40, 132, 288, 456, 556, 646
Wills, Chill 220
Wilson, Scott 334
The Wing or the Thigh 486
Winkler, Angela 364, 662
Winkler, Irwin 464, 744
Winn, Kitty 228
Wolfe, Robert L. 220, 456
Wolfman Jack 282
Wollen, Peter 312
A Woman Under the Influence 306
Wood, G. 94
Woodward, Bob 456
Wurlitzer, Rudy 220

Y

Yamazaki, Tsutomu 758
Yanne et Rassam 210
Yarbrough, Camille 64
The Yakuza 342
York, Michael 124
Young, Burt 464
Young Frankenstein 326
Young, Stephen 266
Yoyotte, Marie-Josèphe 770
Yui, Kota 758
Yui, Masayuki 758
Yussov, Vadim 152

Z

Zacharias, Ann 486
Zaentz, Saul 356
Zanuck, Richard D. 242, 348
Zanuck/Brown Productions 348
Zapponi, Bernardino 86, 494
Zarraga, Tony de 220
Zehetbauer, Rolf 124
Zelenovic, Srdjan 210
Zerbe, Anthony 274
Zidi, Claude 486
Zimmer, Laurie 502
Zimmerman, Don 568, 698
Zinner, Peter 132, 288, 584
Znaimer, Moses 764
Zoetrope Corporation 670
Zsigmond, Vilmos 116, 548, 584, 786
Zwerling, Darrell 318

ABOUT THE AUTHORS

PHILIPP BÜHLER (PB) studied political science, history, and English studies. He is a film journalist in Berlin, working for various daily newspapers, online media, and educational media publications.

DAVID GAERTNER (DG) studied film and art history. He is the academic head of the media laboratory at the Freie Universität Berlin's Institute for Theater Studies.

MALTE HAGENER (MH) studied literature, media studies and philosophy. He is the author and editor of many publications, and is a professor of media studies at Marburg University, specializing in the history, theory and aesthetics of film.

STEFFEN HAUBNER (SH) studied art history and sociology. He works as a freelance editor, author, and translator for various publications. He lives in Hamburg.

JÖRN HETEBRÜGGE (JH) studied German literature in Hanover. He is an author and journalist and has written many articles on film and art.

HARALD KELLER (HK) is an author, photographer, and media journalist working for national newspapers and writing books and essays on film and television history. He is also a lecturer at the University of Osnabrück.

KATJA KIRSTE (KK) studied literature and film and has worked for multiple broadcasters, production companies, and as a lecturer at the universities of Kiel and Passau and the Media College in Stuttgart. She is currently a freelance writer and communications consultant.

HEINZ-JÜRGEN KÖHLER (HJK) is a film and TV journalist and author of many academic publications and press articles based in Hamburg.

OLIVER KÜCH (OK) studied English and history. He is a media and computer journalist who has written widely on film, television, and IT.

PETRA LANGE-BERNDT (PLB) is a professor in the History of Art Department at the University of Hamburg. Her research spans modern and contemporary art, materiality, art and science, and exhibition history. Writings include a book on animal art and a co-edited book on Sigmar Polke.

NILS MEYER (NM) studied German literature and politics. He has written for print, radio, and television, and works as a public relations officer.

ECKHARD PABST (EP) is a media scholar and film theorist with numerous publications as editor and author. He works at the Institute for Modern German Literature and Media at CAU Kiel and is a freelance lecturer for ZDF.

LARS PENNING (LP), studied journalism, theater studies, and general and comparative literature in Berlin. As a freelance film journalist, he writes for, among others, *tip* and *taz*. He is the author of books on Cameron Díaz and Julia Roberts and has written many critical articles on film history for various publications.

ANNE POHL (APO) has been active as a journalist since 1987. She is the author of numerous academic articles and lives in Berlin.

STEPHAN REISNER (SR) studied literature and philosophy. He has written many articles on film, photography, art, and literature, and lives and works as a freelance writer and photographer in Berlin.

BURKHARD RÖWEKAMP (BR) is a media scholar and lecturer at Philipps University Marburg. His research focuses on film aesthetics, theory and history, media pragmatics, and the militarization of perception in audiovisual media. He has also written on the anti-war film.

RAINER VOWE (RV) was a historian working for the Institute for Film and Television Studies at Ruhr-University Bochum. He wrote many articles on film and television history. Rainer Vowe passed away in 2025.

MAXI WOLLNER (MV) studied art history and Italian philology. She is the Cultural Editor of the *Dresdner Neuesten Nachrichten*, a freelance author, and curator of exhibitions for contemporary art galleries. She has written film historical and analytical contributions for various publications. She lives in Dresden.

CREDITS

CREDITS

The publishers would like to thank the distributors, without whom many of these films would never have reached the big screen.

AFM, APOLLO, ARSENAL, ATLAS, BASIS, CINEMA INTERNATIONAL, COLUMBIA TRI STAR, CONCORDE, CONSTANTIN, FANTASIA, FIFIGE, FILMVERLAG DER AUTOREN UND FUTURA FILM, JUGENDFILM, DIE LUPE, MFA, MGM, NEF, NEUE VISIONEN, P.H.-KNIPP-FILM, PROGRESS, PROKINO, SCOTIA, SILVER CINE, TOBIS STUDIOCANAL, TWENTIETH CENTURY FOX, UIP – UNITED INTERNATIONAL PICTURES, UNITED ARTISTS, WARNER BROS., ZEPHIR, ZORRO, ZUKUNFT.

Academy Award® and Oscar® are the registered trademark and service mark of the Academy of Motion Picture Arts and Sciences.

If, despite our concerted efforts, a distributor has been unintentionally omitted, we apologise and will amend any such errors brought to the attention of the publishers in the next edition.

IMAGE SOURCES

ddp images: pp. 174 top, 179 bottom
ddp images / Courtesy Everett Collection:
pp. 176, 178, 179 top
Entertainment Pictures / Alamy Stock Photo:
pp. 173, 174 bottom, 177 top, 177 bottom
Image courtesy of Heritage Auctions/HA.com:
pp. 33, 41, 49, 57, 65, 79, 95, 101, 109, 117, 153, 159, 167, 181, 189, 197, 205, 211, 221, 229, 235, 243, 251, 267, 275, 283, 289, 299, 307, 313, 327, 335, 343, 365, 373, 389, 397, 403, 411, 419, 433, 441, 449, 457, 465, 473, 481, 495, 503, 509, 515, 533, 541, 549, 569, 575, 603, 611, 619, 627, 633, 639, 647, 655, 671, 685, 699, 707, 715, 723, 731, 739, 745, 753, 759, 765, 771, 779, 787, 797
www.seriebox.com: p. 487
SilverScreen / Alamy Stock Photo: p. 563

ABOUT THE EDITOR

JÜRGEN MÜLLER holds the chair of Early Modern and Modern Art History at the Technical University of Dresden. He studied Art History at the universities of Bochum, Münster, Pisa, Paris, and Amsterdam, and has worked as an art critic and curator of numerous exhibitions. He is also the editor of TASCHEN's movies by decade series.

ABOUT THIS BOOK

The 100 films selected for this book represent a decade of cinema. It goes without saying this involved making a number of difficult choices, some of which may be contested. A note also on the stills from some of the earlier films: It is a regrettable but inevitable fact that the older the film, the more difficult it is to obtain images of the required technical quality.
Each film is presented by an essay, and accompanied by a glossary text devoted to one person or a cinematographic term. To ensure optimal access to all this information, a general index is provided at the end of the book.
As in the preceding volumes, the films are dated according to the year of production, not the year of release

IMPRINT

© 2025 TASCHEN GmbH
Hohenzollernring 53, D–50672 Köln
www.taschen.com

ORIGINAL EDITION
© 2003 TASCHEN GmbH

Printed in Slovakia
ISBN 978–3–8365–8727–3

TEXTS
Philipp Bühler (PB), David Gaertner (DG), Malte Hagener (MH), Steffen Haubner (SH), Jörn Hetebrügge (JH), Harald Keller (HK), Katja Kirste (KK), Heinz-Jürgen Köhler (HJK), Oliver Küch (OK), Petra Lange-Berndt (PLB), Nils Meyer (NM), Eckhard Pabst (EP), Lars Penning (LP), Anne Pohl (APO), Stephan Reisner (SR), Burkhard Röwekamp (BR), Rainer Vowe (RV), Maxi Wollner (MW)

ENGLISH TRANSLATION
Daniel A. Huyssen (texts), Patrick Lanagan (introduction and texts), Shaun Samson (texts and captions) for English Express, Berlin; Isabel Varea-Riley (text: "Super Fly")

EACH AND EVERY TASCHEN BOOK PLANTS A SEED!
Each year, we offset our annual carbon emissions with carbon credits at the Instituto Terra, a reforestation program in Minas Gerais, Brazil, founded by Lélia and Sebastião Salgado.
To find out more about this ecological partnership, please check: www.taschen.com/institutoterra.
INSPIRATION: UNLIMITED.
CARBON FOOTPRINT: (ALMOST) ZERO.

Want to see more? Visit taschen.com to view our current publications, browse our latest magazine, and subscribe to our newsletter.

What do you want?